THE ROYAL MARINES

From Sea Soldiers to a Special Force

Julian Thompson joined the Royal Marines a month after his eighteenth birthday and served for thirty-four years, retiring as a Major General. His service, mainly in the Royal Marine Commandos, took him to seven continents. He commanded the 3rd Commando Brigade, which carried out the initial landings to repossess the Falkland Islands in 1982, and fought most of the subsequent land battles.

He is now Visiting Professor in the Department of War Studies, King's College, London. He has presented a series of short Second World War commemorative films on BBC1. As well as writing books on military strategy, the Commandos and the Parachute Regiment, Julian Thompson also wrote *The Imperial War Museum Book of Victory in Europe*, *The Imperial War Museum Book of War Behind Enemy Lines* and *The Imperial War Museum Book of the War at Sea*.

By the same author

The Imperial War Museum Book of War Behind Enemy Lines

The Imperial War Museum Book of The War at Sea:
The Royal Navy in the Second World War

The Imperial War Museum Book of Victory in Europe:
The North-West European Campaign 1944–45

The Lifeblood of War: Logistics in Armed Conflict

Ready for Anything: The Parachute Regiment at War 1940–82

No Picnic: 3 Commando Brigade in the South Atlantic 1982

Julian Thompson

THE ROYAL MARINES

From Sea Soldiers to a Special Force

PAN BOOKS

First published 2000 by Sidgwick & Jackson

This edition published 2001 by Pan Books
an imprint of Pan Macmillan Ltd
Pan Macmillan, 20 New Wharf Road, London N1 9RR
Basingstoke and Oxford
Associated companies throughout the world
www.panmacmillan.com

ISBN 0 330 37702 7

5 7 9 8 6 4

A CIP catalogue record for this book is available from
the British Library.

Map artwork by ML Design
Typeset by SetSystems Ltd, Saffron Walden, Essex
Printed and bound in Great Britain by
Mackays of Chatham plc, Chatham, Kent

Contents

PART THREE

1920–1943

PART FOUR

1943–1945

REORGANIZATION: A NEW DIRECTION AND PURPOSE

PART FIVE

1945–1999

FIGHTING PEACETIME WARS

APPENDICES

List of Illustrations

First World War and Russia 1919

Second World War

After 1945

Acknowledgements

I wish to express my thanks to William Armstrong of Macmillan, for having thought of the book and suggesting that I should write it, to Nicholas Blake, who edited it with such diligence and expertise, and Wilf Dickie, who designed the book; and to all those in the Imperial War Museum who have been so helpful, as always, to Roderick Suddaby, Nigel Steel, Simon Robbins and Stephen Walton of the Department of Documents; Margaret Brooks, Conrad Wood, Peter Hart and Rosemary Tudge of the Sound Archives; Hilary Roberts and David Parry of the Photographic Archive; and to Chris Newbery the Director of the Royal Marines Museum, and Matthew Little the Librarian and Archivist.

I would like to thank the the following authors, agents and publishers for allowing me to quote from their books: Jeff Beadle from *The Light Blue Lanyard: 50 Years With 40 Commando Royal Marines*; John Murray from Anthony Beevor's *Crete the Battle and the Resistance*; General Sir Peter de la Billière from *Storm Command: A Personal Account of the Gulf War*; Field Marshal the Lord Bramall from *The Chiefs*; the quotations from Winston S. Churchill's *The World Crisis 1911–1918*, volume I, *The Second World War*, volume IV, *The Hinge of Fate*, and *The Second World War*, volume VI, *Triumph and Tragedy*, are reproduced with permission of Curtis Brown Ltd, London, on behalf of the Estate of Sir Winston S. Churchill, Copyright Winston S. Churchill; Leo Cooper from Major General Moulton's *The Royal Marines*; John Day from *A Plain Russet-Coated Captain*; Andrew Gordon from *The Rules of the Game: Jutland and British Naval Command*; Her Majesty's Stationery Office from General Sir Anthony Farrar-Hockley's *The British Part in the Korean War, Vols I & II*; Christopher Hibbert from his *Redcoats and Rebels*; Penguin from C. S. Forester's *The Ship*; Random House for Orlando Figes's *A People's Tragedy: The Russian Revolution* (Pimlico); John Murray from Michael Hickey's *Gallipoli*; André Deutsch Limited, the publishers of General Sir Leslie Hollis's *One Marine's Tale*; Robin Hunter from *True Stories of the SBS*; Bill Jenkins from *Commando Subaltern at War:*

Royal Marine Operations in Yugoslavia and Italy, James Ladd from *The Royal Marines 1919–1980*; the publishers of the late Major General J. L. Moulton's *Haste to the Battle: A Royal Marine Commando at War* (Cassell & Co.), *Battle for Antwerp* (Ian Allan), and *Defence in a Changing World*; The Navy Records Society for *Shipboard Life and Organisation 1731–1815*, and *The Fisher Papers*; Robin Neillands from *A Fighting Retreat: The British Empire 1947–97*; Tom Pocock from *A Thirst for Glory: The Life of Admiral Sir Sydney Smith*, Random House for Martin Gilbert's *Winston S. Churchill*, Vol. III; Nicholas Rodger from *The Wooden World: An Anatomy of the Georgian Navy*; The Director of the Royal United Services Institute for the transcript of the address by Admiral Sir Jock Slater in the December 1998 issue of *The RUSI Journal*; the passage from Hilary St George Saunders' *The Green Beret, The Story of the Commandos: 1940–1945* was reproduced with the permission of Curtis Brown Ltd, London, on behalf of the Estate of Hilary St George Saunders, copyright Hilary St George Saunders; the US Naval Institute granted me permission to quote from *First to Fight: An Inside View of the US Marine Corps* by Lieutenant General Victor H. Krulak USMC (Ret) published by the Naval Institute Press in 1984.

I must thank the Royal Marines Historical Society for permission to quote from their special publications: Derek Oakley's *Behind Japanese Lines*, Peter Thomas's *41 Independent Commando Royal Marines Korea 1950 to 1952*; and from the Society's publication *Sheet Anchor*, Vol. XXI no 2, *Suez* with accounts by Derek Oakley, Bill Billet, and Brian Clark and Tex Cooper, and from the same number, Jon Moffat's *The Plymouth Argylls – Part 1 – The Battle for Singapore*. The Society has also allowed me to quote Peter Thomas's account *Palestine 1948*, from *Sheet Anchor* Vol. XXIII no 1. The Editor of *The Globe & Laurel* has granted me permission to quote from the following issues: March/April 1991, *Royal Marines in the Gulf*, by Captain G. S. Mackenzie-Philps; January/February 1995, *45 RM Commando's Action at Montforterbeek Dyke*, by 'Eddy', and *Burma and the Battle of Kangaw*, by Major General J. I. H. Owen; September/October 1997, *Baptism of Fire: 45 RM Commando at Merville–Franceville – Part 1* by 'Eddy'; and November/ December 1997, *Baptism of Fire: 45 RM Commando at Merville–Franceville – Part 2* by 'Eddy'.

I am grateful to Dr Raffi Gregorian for permission to quote from his extended essay *The Black Cat Strikes Back: Claret Operations during Confron-tation 1964–1966*, written when studying for his Master's degree at the Department of War Studies, King's College London in 1988–9. Bill Jenkins kindly allowed me to reproduce the map of the Comácchio Operation from his book *Commando Subaltern at War*. I must thank Alastair Grant for allowing me to quote from the account by his grandfather, Captain (later Major General) Tom Jameson RMLI, of his detachment's operations in Siberia and Eastern Russia in 1919. Lieutenant Colonel Ewan Southby-Tailyour allowed me to quote from papers relating to his father's experiences in 116th RM Brigade in North-West Europe.

I am deeply indebted to the following who have been most helpful to me, patiently answered many questions, and in all cases read, commented on, and suggested improvements to parts of the draft; and lent me papers, books and other publications; their advice was invaluable: Major Mike Banks, Major Jeff Beadle, Major Mark Bentinck, Mr Budgen, Major Richard Clifford, Mr John Codrington, Lieutenant Colonel Peter 'Pug' Davis, John Day, Mr Dutton, Brigadier Rob Fry, Major General Malcolm Hunt, Bill Jenkins, Major General Pat Kay, Mike McConville, Major David Mitchell, Major General Jeremy Moore, Lieutenant Colonel Andrew Noyes, the late Major General John Owen, Major General David Pennefather, Major General Derek Pounds, Colonel Tom Seccombe, Major 'Ram' Seeger, Major Guy Sheridan, Colonel David Smith, Lieutenant Colonel Ewan Southby-Tailyour, Bill Stoneman, Lieutenant Colonel Peter Thomas, Major General Nick Vaux, Brigadier David Wilson, Major 'Hiram' Wynne-Potts.

Jane Thompson was, as always, an indispensible part of the team, both with research and incisive editorial advice. This book would never have seen the light of day without her support.

Prologue

We have compelled every land and every sea to open a path for our valour, and have everywhere planted eternal memorials of our friendship and of our enmity.

Pericles

As he crawled forward over the bare landscape, Captain Boswell tried to make himself as inconspicuous as possible, conscious that his and his companions' green disruptive-pattern camouflage uniforms stood out on the snow-covered ground. The dark window in the upper floor of the house where an enemy Special Forces patrol was holed up was like an eye watching them as they inched forward. When Boswell judged they were close enough to the house, and also in full view of their own fire group out to a flank supporting them, he ordered, 'Fix bayonets,' and fired a green mini-flare, the signal for the fire group to fire six 66mm light anti-armour rockets at the house. At the first bang, a sentry appeared in the window on the upper floor. Corporal Groves shot him with a sniper rifle. The house burst into flames as the 66mm rockets slammed in. Boswell and his assault group charged forward, halted, fired two more 66s into the house, and charged again. Their quarry ran out of the house into a small stream bed close by, firing as they ran. Sergeant Doyle fell, hit in the shoulder, followed by Corporal Groves, wounded in the chest. Ammunition in the building exploded, the assault group momentarily recoiling in the blast, before running forward, now shielded from their opponents in the stream bed by smoke billowing from the burning building. The enemy commander, trying to make a break for it, was killed by two 40mm projectiles fired from M79 grenade launchers by Corporal Barnacle and Sergeant MacLean. Their adversaries stood up and threw away their weapons. Five enemy dead, and twelve prisoners, including seven wounded, was the score for a morning's work by the

Mountain & Arctic Warfare (M&AW) Cadre, in its wartime role of the Reconnaissance Troop for 3rd Commando Brigade Royal Marines.

The date 31 May 1982, the place East Falkland, the enemy the Argentine invaders. The operation had been part of the preliminaries to 3rd Commando Brigade's move out from the beachhead which they had established at San Carlos ten days earlier. On the day of the landings, cadre Observation Posts (OPs) had been flown forward some thirty to forty miles, to features dominating the route the brigade would follow to the key high ground overlooking Port Stanley, the ultimate objective. The OPs had seen Argentine Special Force patrols move in to Top Malo House, used by shepherds in the summer, but deserted in the southern hemisphere midwinter. A radio message back to Boswell's headquarters sited by the beach, followed by some rapid planning and orders, had seen him and his party of nineteen men inserted by helicopter to a landing zone out of sight of the house. Selecting his approach to make the best use of the terrain, he was in position to assault and eliminate the main body and headquarters of the Argentine Special Force in that locality. Other enemy OPs along the high ground in the vicinity, discouraged by the loss of their commander and so many of their comrades, walked in to surrender to 3rd Commando Brigade units as they marched along the route, now free from unfriendly prying eyes thanks to the cadre's work.

This operation, and others carried out by the cadre in this war, epitomized the professional standards demanded in the latter half of the twentieth century by all members of the corps to which they belonged: the Royal Marines. The cadre was an élite within an élite. A naval padre who spent much of his service with Royal Marines Commandos was only half joking when in the late 1990s he referred to the officers of the Corps as 'Knights Templar'. It was the Second World War which saw the genesis of the Royal Marines as élite troops. Earlier generations of Marines undoubtedly saw their Corps as a thing apart, and there had been many episodes in their history that had encouraged that perception. In reality the place of Marines within the Naval Service, their subservience to it, and hence the tasks they performed, meant that although they may have been regarded with affection and respect by the public, they were not 'crack' troops, as they are rightly regarded today. The events leading up to this transformation, and what came after, is the theme of this book. However, we are all prisoners of our past, and the Royal

Marines are no exception. It is right, therefore, that the first two chapters should be devoted to their first two hundred and fifty years. Thereafter, starting in 1914, their story is told in greater detail, leading up to and beyond the watershed year of 1942. From thence forward, the rate of change was such that by the last quarter of the twentieth century the Corps would have been almost unrecognizable to anyone serving in it during the first quarter.

Marines, in the British service, have always regarded themselves as soldiers who go to sea, not sailors who go ashore. Unlike the French *Fusiliers Marins*, who are sailors employed as soldiers and ship's policemen, the British Marines are not a branch of the Royal Navy, like the aviators, submariners, engineers, and seamen. As the story that follows will show, detachments of soldiers served at sea with the Royal Navy from the time of Charles II. Until 1755 these were provided both by Army regiments raised for the purpose and on occasions other regiments temporarily sent to fight at sea. In action afloat Marines provided a trained and disciplined force stationed on the quarterdeck and poop of their own ship, and in the fighting tops (platforms on the main, fore, and mizzen masts), and able to bring down musket fire on an enemy ship's upper decks. Marines also led boarding parties and repelled enemy boarders. Although seamen also played their part in this sort of fighting, they were usually employed in battle manning the 'great guns' or working the ship, and had to be taken from these tasks to join boarding parties, or assist in repulsing boarders, whereas the Marines were a force under the captain's hand, immediately ready for any eventuality. Marines also took part in landing operations, and capturing enemy ships, usually under the cover of darkness when their quarry was in port or at anchor, known at the time as 'cutting out'. Sometimes, when the occasion demanded it, Marines would land in battalion, or greater, strength for protracted operations ashore. When the Admiralty decided to raise its own Marines as part of the naval service in the mid-eighteenth century, only resorting to embarking Army regiments in extremis, the roles of Marines at sea and ashore remained unchanged, and they played an indispensable part in the wars up to the defeat of Napoleon in 1815. For most of the rest of the nineteenth century, their traditional employment remained unchanged. Although as the nineteenth century drew to its end and technological changes in sea warfare gathered momentum, Marines (Royal since 1802) in ships increasingly became employed on duties that could equally well be done by seamen. By now sailors had for decades been long-service regulars, no longer pressed men, or volunteers taken on only for the duration of a ship's commission. Seamen could be trained as readily as Marines to man guns (boarding parties and cutting-out expeditions became things of the past). Marines as part of the ship's company became an anachronism.

It was well into the twentieth century before this fact was acknowledged. Although several thousand Marines fought ashore with distinction during the First World War, on the Western Front and at Gallipoli, the majority served at sea. Those in the Grand Fleet found that, with the exception of Jutland and one or two other forays, life at sea was tedious indeed. Marines played a leading part in the great Zeebrugge Raid, and in a number of peripheral expeditions. But, as foreseen by Marines pre-war, the most fulfilling employment, bringing the best prospects of promotion and command, was service in battalions and formations alongside the Army. Command of a ship's detachment in a twentieth-century warship was largely an administrative function; the detachment did not fight as one, being spread about the ship at action stations. It did not compare for what we would now call job satisfaction with command of a company, still less of a battalion, or brigade.

Between the two World Wars, attempts to redefine the role of the Royal Marines were, with two exceptions, unsuccessful, and the Corps entered the Second very much as it had the First, with large numbers serving in all the major units of the Fleet, only this time the Royal Navy had a much stiffer fight on its hands, and life at sea was usually eventful and often hazardous. The first of the two exceptions was the raising of a Mobile Naval Base Defence Organisation – eventually there were two of them. Little heed seems to have been paid at the time to the disadvan-tages of investing manpower and effort in these unwieldy, defensive, far from mobile formations which could only lead the Royal Marines into a cul-de-sac as far as gainful employment in action was concerned. They led a mundane existence in the Mediterranean and Indian Ocean theatres, seeing little active service, except in Crete where some units from one of these organizations fought gallantly in the rearguard, many of the officers and men becoming prisoners of war. The second exception was the forming of a Royal Marine brigade, eventually expanding to a division. Neither saw any action, being earmarked for Admiralty oper-ations that never came to pass, but sidelining them in this way allowed the Army to assume the Commando role for the first years of the Second World War, bypassing the Royal Marines to whom this amphibious task rightfully belonged. Eventually, after years of frustration, sense prevailed when the need arose for more commandos and crews for landing craft for the great amphibious operations in the second half of the war. The Royal Marines seized the opportunity, raised nine Commandos and manned large numbers of landing craft, thus taking their rightful place in the forefront of the momentous events from 1943 onwards, fighting with distinction in Sicily, Italy, the Adriatic, France, Holland, Germany, and Burma.

In the half century after the Second World War, hardly a year went by without Royal Marines being on operations somewhere, in Palestine, Malaya, Korea, Egypt, Cyprus, Suez, Aden, Borneo, Northern Ireland, the Falklands (a war which would not have been won without the amphibious expertise of the Corps), the Gulf, and northern Iraq.

This is not a history in the sense that it even attempts to cover all aspects of the Royal Marine story. Rather it seeks to address the key events and defining moments that, for good or ill, shaped the Corps as it is now. The choice of what these are is mine, and mine alone, as is the way I have chosen to portray them; others might select different ones and place the emphasis elsewhere. Someone reviewing another, and more distinguished, author's work, described it as 'history with attitude'; so is this.

PART ONE

THE FIRST 250 YEARS

1664 TO THE OUTBREAK OF THE FIRST WORLD WAR

1

Sea Soldiers

Fall in lads behind the drum,
Colours blazing like the sun

In Whitehall on 28 October 1664, at a meeting of the Privy Council, King Charles II directed:

> That twelve hundred land soldiers be forthwith raised to be distributed into his Majesty's Fleets prepared for sea service. Which said twelve hundred men are to be put into one Regiment, under One Colonel, One Lieutenant Colonel and One Sergeant Major, and to be divided into six companies, each company to consist of two hundred soldiers; and to have One Captain, one Lieutenant, one Ensign, one Drummer, four Sergeants and four Corporals ... The care of all of which is recommended to the Duke of Albemarle his Grace Lord General of his Majesty's Forces.

The regiment was raised as the Duke of York and Albany's Maritime Regiment of Foot. Because James Duke of York was Lord High Admiral, it came also to be known as the Admiral's Regiment, to distinguish it from the Lord General's Regiment, now the Coldstream Guards. For unlike today's Royal Marines, the Admiral's Regiment was part of the Army, under George Monck, the Duke of Albemarle, who, among other appointments, combined in one person the professional and ministerial head of Charles II's army. One of the company colours of this regiment included a sun device in the design.

The regiment first saw action in the Second Dutch War at the sea battles of Lowestoft, the Four Days' Fight, and North Foreland under both Monck and James, Duke of York. For although Monck had learned his soldiering in the Low Countries before the Civil War, and had subsequently risen to major general in the Parliamentary Army, he had also been a successful general-at-sea in Cromwell's navy, and was later created an admiral by Charles II. In the late seventeenth century it was still common for generals to command at sea. The era when all admirals had qualified as sea officers and had 'come up through the system' had yet to come, although it was not far off. Junior officers too saw nothing exceptional in switching from sea to land service, and back again. George Rooke, after commanding a ship in the Third Dutch War, became a lieutenant and subsequently a captain in the Duke's Regiment, as the Admiral's Regiment became after James relinquished the post of Lord High Admiral. Rooke returned to sea service, and is best known for his exploits as an admiral.

The Admiral's Regiment also fought ashore, and near Harwich, at Fort Landguard, repulsed the Dutch in 1667. The regiment was first mentioned as Marines at the start of the Third Dutch War, when de Ruyter surprised the Anglo-British fleet at anchor in Sole Bay. Captain Taylor, Lord Arlington's secretary, wrote: 'Those Marines of whom I so oft have wrote you, behaved themselves stoutly.'

*

The Admiral's Regiment were not the only soldiers to serve at sea. John Churchill, later Duke of Marlborough, distinguished himself at Sole Bay serving with the First Regiment of Foot Guards (today the Grenadier Guards), and was promoted to command a company in the Admiral's Regiment. He took this company to the Low Countries to serve with the Royal English Regiment commanded by the Duke of Monmouth, where they fought at the Battle of Enzheim and the siege of Maastricht under Marshal Turenne.

At the accession of the Duke of York to the throne as King James II in 1685, the colonelcy of the regiment passed to his son-in-law, George Prince of Denmark, and it changed its title to The Prince of Denmark's Regiment, or Prince's. James's tactlessness and intransigence over religious and other matters soon earned him the hatred and distrust of most of the English people, including the Army. When, at the start of the 'Glorious Revolution' of 1688, William of Orange landed at Torbay, the Prince's Regiment remained loyal to James, unlike most others, including John Churchill, and many regiments, who went over to William in the Protestant cause. 'By one spontaneous, tremendous convulsion the English nation repudiated James', wrote Winston Churchill in *The History of the English-Speaking Peoples*. James fled to France, where the verdict of the court of Versailles was: 'You only have to listen to him to realize why he is here.' The Prince's Regiment's loyalty to James was its undoing; it was disbanded in 1689.

A year later James landed in Ireland. Two Marine regiments were raised exclusively for sea service. It was now that the practice of using these sea soldiers as seamen to fill deficiencies in ship's companies began, a habit that was to endure for three hundred years. Owned by the Army, but controlled by the Admiralty, the Marine regiments fell prey to the lax administration and corruption that was a feature of late seventeenth-century bureaucracy. The financial system, for example, could not cope with detachments of Marines distributed round the fleet, and the sea soldiers were owed months and sometimes years of back pay. The Marines fought at Beachy Head in 1690 under Admiral Sir Cloudisley Shovel, and again in 1692 following the Battle of Barfleur, when the Anglo-Dutch fleet defeated the French fleet, and the English ships drove the French into La Hogue. Four days later, two hundred boats manned by seamen and Marines from the English fleet, led by Vice Admiral Sir George Rooke, attacked the ships at anchor. They burned La Hogue and destroyed six French three-deckers. The following day, six more French ships lying under Fort St-Vast were attacked by a force in boats again under Rooke's command, and destroyed. French cavalry who rode into shallow water to assist their fellow countrymen were pulled off their horses by English seamen wielding boathooks. In 1693 an Anglo-Dutch fleet, under Rooke in *Royal Oak* and a Dutch rear admiral, defeated a French fleet off Lagos, destroying or capturing ninety-two vessels. When the war ended in 1697, the Army was reduced to under a quarter of its wartime strength. By now amalgamations and reorganization had resulted in there being four Marine regiments on establishment, taking their names from their colonels as was the custom: Brudenall's, Seymour's, Colt's, and Mordaunt's. Although the Marine regiments were to survive another eighteen months, soon they too were ordered to be disarmed, and turned out into the streets to join 68,000 fellow soldiers who earlier had been treated in the same heedless manner.

The death of Carlos II of Spain in 1701 bought a reprieve for some of the Marines still awaiting disbandment. Carlos died without an heir, and Louis XIV of France claimed the throne for his grandson Philip. The Austrian Emperor did likewise for his son Archduke Charles. Neither England nor the United Provinces, whose economies depended on overseas trade, could countenance France monopolizing the huge Spanish empire in North and South America, and the Pacific. Louis already threatened England and Holland with invasion. England, when threatened by any over-mighty power on the continent of Europe, did what she always attempted, and continued to do for the next two centuries: she formed an alliance with that power's enemies, in this case with Holland and Austria. Among the fifteen regiments authorized by Parliament to increase the size of the Army, six Marine regiments were included. Queen Anne signed the Royal Warrant for the mustering of these six new regiments on 9 April 1702. They were Fox's, Villiers', Shannon's, Mordaunt's, Saunderson's, and Holt's, again taking their names from their colonels who commanded them, rather than princes or royal appointees.

The War of the Spanish Succession was fought in Continental and maritime theatres. The Continental struggle in the Low Countries and along the Rhine was the stage on which that great soldier John Churchill, Duke of Marlborough, played such a dominant role. The maritime theatre encompassed the Atlantic, Mediterranean, and Spain.

The first expedition of the new war, an attempt to seize Cadiz in 1702, included 10,000 Marines and foot commanded by the Duke of Ormonde (in modern parlance the landing force commander), and Sir George Rooke as the commander of the Anglo-Dutch fleet. Thanks to poor planning and execution, the attempt on Cadiz failed. Rooke was able to retrieve his reputation on his return voyage when he discovered a French fleet and Spanish treasure ships lying in Vigo Bay. Marines and foot were landed to silence shore batteries, while all seventeen French warships and seventeen Spanish treasure ships were taken or sunk.

In 1704 a second expedition to Cadiz, again under Rooke, was called off while the force was offshore, at Rooke's insistence. Instead, at the suggestion of Prince George of Hesse-Darmstadt, he sailed for Gibraltar. On 21 July, Prince George, supported by Rooke, landed with 1,900 English and 400 Dutch Marines on the isthmus connecting the 'rock' with mainland Spain. Summoned to surrender, the Spanish Governor refused. Two days later the Anglo-Dutch fleet, having anchored off the waterfront, bombarded the defences, silencing the Spanish guns and breaching the fort on the New Mole. Landing parties from the fleet immediately raced for the shore by boat. Despite a temporary setback when the magazine on the New Mole blew up, killing and wounding at least a hundred men, the landing parties were reinforced and seized all the exits from the town. At this the Spanish Governor agreed to the surrender terms, which allowed him to march out with all the honours of war. With him went most of the inhabitants, leaving Gibraltar as a ghost town to be inhabited by the descendants of people brought in by the victors.

Shortly after the fall of Gibraltar, the French fleet put in an appearance; after an inconclusive battle with them off Malaga, Rooke returned to Gibraltar, landed all his Marines and sixty guns, and stocked the garrison with sufficient supplies for three months, before departing for Lisbon. On 4 October the men who had seized Gibraltar found themselves under siege in their turn. A sizeable Spanish army reinforced by some 3,000 French Marines succeeded in breaching the walls. At the last moment, when the besiegers were about to assault, Vice Admiral Sir John Leake arrived bringing ammunition and rations. The next month he brought 2,000 men of the Guards, Foot, and Dragoons to reinforce the Marines, now reduced to less than 1,000 men fit for duty. The French and Spanish, having failed to overcome the garrison in a major assault on 2 February 1705, abandoned the siege on 20 April, and left. A report of the defence of Gibraltar stated: 'the garrison did more than could humanly be expected, and the English Marines gained an immortal honour'. In one incident, Captain Fisher of the Marines with 17 of his men successfully defended the Round Tower against the continued assaults of 500 French Grenadiers.

There was to be no respite for the garrison after the lifting of the siege. Sir Cloudisley Shovel and the Earl of Peterborough arrived from Lisbon, where they had collected newly raised regiments. Exchanging these for the veteran defenders of Gibraltar, they went on to take Barcelona. The fighting in Spain ebbed and flowed. At one time the Archduke Charles, supported by his English, Portuguese, and Dutch allies, controlled the greater part of the country; by 1711, his fortunes had turned and he controlled little more than a few square miles outside Barcelona. In 1710 political changes in England brought in ministers who were opposed to the war, and who entered into secret talks with the French. Marlborough's last battle, Malplaquet (1709), had been bloody and indecisive. Despite his earlier brilliant victories in the Continental theatre, at Blenheim, Ramillies, and Oudenarde, he was eventually dismissed by Queen Anne, who agreed to peace in 1713. At the Treaty of Utrecht, which set the peace terms, Gibraltar was given to England in perpetuity.

As well as serving at Gibraltar, with Peterborough at Barcelona, and in the subsequent fighting in Catalonia, Marines also took part in the seizure of Sardinia and Minorca. Before the capture of Gibraltar, the Lord High Admiral had assumed control of all the Marine regiments, with the same chaotic administrative outcome as experienced a decade earlier in King William's time. Officers had to find funds out of their own pockets to prevent their men from starving. Captains of ships tried to use Marines as seamen, and restrict the command of ship's Marine detachments to one junior officer. On this occasion the Duke of Marlborough, as Lord General, overrode the Navy.

With peace came orders to disband all Marine regiments. Seymour's, one of King William's Marine Regiments, returned to the Line in 1715, thus surviving this round of defence cuts. Later Fox's, Saunderson's, and Villiers' were also saved by being re-formed as Line regiments (see Appendix 1). The Line in this context meant infantry of the line, as opposed to Guards and, later, Rifle regiments.

For the next twenty-six years there were no Marine regiments, except for companies of 'Invalids'. In 1739, during a series of incidents involving Spanish abuse of British seamen in the Americas, a Spanish coastguard sliced off the ear of one Captain Robert Jenkins, or so the captain claimed. Jenkins was brought before the House of Commons to exhibit his ear in a bottle. As Winston Churchill wrote, 'whether it was in fact his own ear or whether he had lost it in a seaport brawl remains uncertain, but the power of this shrivelled object was immense'.[1] It led to Britain declaring war on Spain. The 'War of Jenkins's Ear' soon became part of a wider conflict, the War of the Austrian Succession, which lasted until 1748, and besides Britain and Spain involved Austria, France and Prussia.

On the outbreak of war, six Marine regiments were raised by transferring men from the Guards and the Line. Another four were raised in the American colonies. When Admiral Anson was preparing his squadron to harry Spanish trade in the Pacific, he asked for Marines. Instead he was sent 500 Chelsea pensioners. Those who could walk deserted at Portsmouth. The remaining 259 bedridden pensioners all died on the voyage. To take the place of the deserters, Anson was given 240 Marines from the new regiments. Few of these survived the circumnavigation of the world which ensued. Only four of Anson's men were lost in action, but 1,300 of his ship's companies, including Marines, died of disease, principally scurvy. However, the difficulties that Anson had experienced in obtaining Marines for his squadron made an impression on him that was to bear fruit a few years later. The War of Jenkins's Ear was the beginning of the most intense period of naval activity in British history, the golden age of the Royal Navy which was at war for fifty of the next seventy-five years. The Marines played a leading role in the dramatic events of an era that saw Britain rise to become what we would now call a superpower.

In 1741 all six Marine regiments were sent with two of Foot to Jamaica to prepare for an expedition against Cartagena in the part of South America which is now Colombia. The Colonel of the 1st Marines, James Wolfe, had intended that his thirteen-year-old son, James, should accompany the expedition. But he became sick and was left in England. Quebec might have remained in French hands if young James Wolfe had gone to the Caribbean with his father. When the force arrived in Jamaica, having left England 9,000 strong, it arrived with 1,500 sick, and 600 having died on the voyage. This was only the beginning.

The attack on Cartagena went well at first. The outer defences fell quickly, but uninspiring leadership by General Wentworth resulted in the assault on the key Fort of St Lazar being repulsed. By now yellow fever, the dreaded 'yellow jack', transmitted by the mosquitoes that infested this region, had begun to spread among the expedition. The troops were re-embarked and instead of putting to sea the ships were anchored in the lagoon off Cartagena for over ten days, enabling the mosquitoes to continue their deadly work among the packed transports. The oppressive heat, the stench of bodies and the black vomit added to the horror in scenes that beggar belief. When the expedition reached Jamaica, only 1,000 men remained fit for service. After sallying forth again, and failing to take Cuba and Porto Bello, the expedition returned once more to Jamaica. At the final count, only one man in ten survived this enterprise.

The War of Jenkins's Ear became part of the wider War of the Austrian Succession. Marines took part in the siege of Louisburg at the entrance to the St Lawrence River. Admiral Boscawen took 800 Marines and 1,200 Foot to India in an attempt to capture the French settlement of Pondicherry.

In 1747, on the prompting of Admiral Anson, it was decided that the
Marine regiments and any additional ones should be under full Admiralty command. A year later peace was signed, and all the Marine
regiments were disbanded. For some years the Marines had been attracting officers who could not afford the cost of a commission in a Line
regiment. Throughout the eighteenth and most of the nineteenth centuries, until the abolition of purchase of commissions in 1871, working
one's way up through the commissioned ranks in the majority of cases,
unless one was fortunate enough to be promoted for distinguished
service in the field, or to have influential acquaintances who had it in
their gift to award commissions by patronage, was a matter of having
sufficient funds, and finding someone who wanted to sell out, when he
no longer wished to serve, or buy up in his turn.[2] A commission was a
valuable investment. In the time of George II, an ensign's commission in
a Line regiment would sell for £400 to £500 and a captain's for around
£1,100, considerable sums at that time (equivalent to over £20,000 and
£40,000 today), and one in the Guards much more. With an ensign's
commission in the Marines at around £250, Marine officers started at a
distinct disadvantage in this market. Furthermore, service at sea as
Marines was unpopular. For example in 1748, the 39th of Foot (later the
1st Battalion Dorsetshire Regiment, and now the Devonshire and Dorset
Regiment), then 'one of the Army's most senior and distinguished
regiments of the line' in the words of Alan Guy,[3] was on the point of
disbandment, or worse (in the view of its officers), conversion to
Marines. Thus a trend was set that was to last for at least two centuries;
the Marines became a poor man's regiment. This continued when new
Marines were raised under the Admiralty in 1755, because in the Navy
neither the securing of an officer's commission nor promotion was by
purchase. Many officers joined the Marines simply because they could
not afford to buy a commission in the Army.

Early in 1755 Parliament approved the establishment of 5,000 Marines
divided into fifty independent companies, to be based in three divisions
at Chatham, Portsmouth, and Plymouth. For almost two hundred years
these divisions were the only permanent units of the Corps. They in no
way equated with the Army fighting formation of the same name, but
were static depots, or pools of manpower, providing Marine detachments
for the fleet, and occasionally ad hoc battalions for service ashore. While
ships-of-the-line might have detachments of a hundred men, smaller

ships might have as few as twenty Marines. So even the independent companies were not a fighting sub-unit which went to sea under its own command structure.

In time the divisions became the focus of the individual Marine's loyalty, and even more so the officers'. Not only was the division 'home', the 'family', occupying almost the same place in a Marine's affections as the regiment in a soldier's, but there were other more tangible considerations. The highest rank to which a Marine officer could aspire at sea was captain, and occasionally major. Ashore in his division he could hope to be appointed commandant with the rank of colonel, and in the late Victorian era brigadier-general. Eventually, divisions were to be presented with colours, yet another focus of 'regimental' loyalty, along with other trappings of the Army way of doing things: officers' mess silver, divisional bugle calls, and sartorial tribalism such as the number of cuff buttons on an officer's blazer proclaiming which division he hailed from. It could be argued that these were the outward manifestations of an inward, and often unacknowledged, yearning by Marines to be soldiers, a thing apart from the mass of the Navy, and not least to share with their fellow redcoats the chance of commanding battalions, brigades, divisions, corps, and armies.

However, all this was in the future when recruiting parties scoured the country for privates to fill up the new independent companies; many officers and non-commissioned officers came from the old Marine regiments, and some from the Line. With little time for training, they were sent to sea. Given the conditions in which they were expected to learn their trade, often a rolling ship in the Bay of Biscay, the comment by the naval historian, Nicholas Rodger, 'they were certainly at least as ill-trained as the average British foot-soldier of the day',[4] is hardly surprising and probably over-optimistic.

It would be mistaken to imagine that these Marines of the mid-eighteenth century, and for many years to come, were recruited, trained, and perceived as an élite crack force such as the Rifle Brigade when it was raised in 1801. On the contrary, Marines were paid less than seamen, and some privates 'left the corps to become able seamen, earning not only higher pay, but a much higher social standing aboard ship'.[5] 'Social standing' had a lot to do with the often delicate division between wardroom and gunroom, and officers like the chaplain, surgeon, purser and even Marine lieutenants, whose pretensions to gentility were insecure, might sleep or mess in one or the other according to luck and circumstances.[6] Marines were a new force and without influential patrons.

Again this is not surprising. The younger sons of impoverished nobility and landed gentry were often sent to join the Navy at a young age. Because commissions in the Navy were not obtainable by purchase, only a small outlay of cash had to be found, although grander and more fashionable captains demanded that midshipmen had an allowance as well. An even greater attraction of a naval career, particularly to those seeking to make their fortune, was prize money. The entire value of a captured enemy vessel and its cargo went to the crews of the captor and any RN or allied vessel of war in sight at the moment of capture (sharing each eighth of the total value of the prize between them – the more people on board, the smaller the share): one eighth divided between the lieutenants, the Marine captain, and the master; one eighth between the Marine lieutenants and warrant officers; one eighth between the petty officers; one quarter between the seamen and Marines; and three-eighths to the captain. When the captor ship was under the command of a flag officer, he took one of the captain's eighths. Great fortunes could be made, if you were lucky. For example, in 1762 the *Active* and the *Favourite* shared the capture of a Spanish ship, the *Hermione*, worth £519,705 after expenses, of which each captain received over £65,000, a huge sum at that time, equivalent to winning the lottery in today's money. These 'wins' were by no means exceptional. One rear admiral made £125,000 in the War of the Austrian Succession.[7] Small wonder that naval officers drank to 'a bloody war and a sickly season'. The first brought the chance of prize money, and both conditions reduced the number of officers to share it, as well as increasing the chance of promotion to fill dead men's boots. The Marine officers' share of any prize money was no doubt welcome, but paltry compared with the largess that captains of ships and admirals might come by. Since these small pickings were all a Marine officer could hope for, it is hardly surprising that few sons of noblemen or the gentry bothered with a commission in the Marines. If they were looking to make their fortune, a career in the Marines was not a means of providing it. If they were already blessed with some wealth, they would purchase a commission in the Guards, the infantry, or the cavalry, all socially smarter than the Marines and not subject to such paralytic promotion and poor prospects.

Less wealthy middle-class boys, provided they had the intellectual ability, were attracted into the artillery and engineers, where they received a rigorous professional training at the Royal Military Academy at Woolwich. Commissions in the artillery and engineers were obtained by nomination, not purchase.

The Army of the East India Company was another military career which attracted middle-class youths. Again, commissions in the Company's Army were not purchased, but granted by the Court of Directors in London, through parents, or friends, with influence. Although parents had to pay for the cadet's training at the Company's military academy at Addiscombe near Croydon (in 1835 this amounted to £65 a term),[8] the burden on the parental purse was small compared with the cost of a commission in the British Army; and the Company's Army did not demand that their officers had a private income as did every Guards, cavalry, and Line regiment in the King's or Queen's Army. Furthermore, company officers were paid more than King's or Queen's officers, and there were additional allowances while on campaign. They could enjoy a far higher standard of living in India than they were accustomed to at home, with servants, shooting, hunting, and other sports all within their means. Company officers were eligible for prize money; small sums when junior, but sizeable for more senior officers. Company officers could aspire to the highest ranks in the three Presidency armies in India: Bombay, Madras, and Bengal. They might in some circumstances transfer to the civil administration, where the financial rewards were even better. With all these other more attractive prospects available, it is fair to say that the Marines were officered by men who could not afford a commission in the Guards, Line, and cavalry, and lacked the aptitude, influence, or inclination to pursue a career as a sea officer, or in the Royal Artillery or Royal Engineers, or in the Army of the East India Company.

The Marines on board ship were not required to go aloft to work the ship, handing or loosing sail, and usually carried out tasks such as heaving round the capstan, pulling on halyards and other running rigging, bracing the yards round, and keeping a part of the ship clean: jobs that required little training in seamanship. In battle they lined the rail on poop, quarterdeck, and forecastle, and manned the tops, to bring down musketry fire on the enemy's decks. They were also in the forefront of boarding parties, and repelling boarders.[9] They fought ashore, landed either from single ships or squadrons, often supported by seaman landing parties. Sometimes a squadron would form its Marine detachments into a battalion under a major or lieutenant colonel sent out for the purpose. Despite the low social standing of the Marines in the naval and civilian pecking order, there was nothing wrong with their fighting spirit, as events would show.

In 1761 a force under Commodore Keppel and Major General Hodgson attacked Belleisle, off the French coast. In addition to Hodgson's nine Army regiments, Keppel landed two Marine battalions: one had come out from England already formed up under Lieutenant Colonel Mackenzie, the other was constituted from detachments in ships sent out to reinforce Keppel. The Marines played a leading part in the capture of Belleisle. When asked which troops had been most active, the French replied, 'les petits grenadiers', alluding to the Marines, who wore grenadier caps, but were not as tall as grenadiers. In the eighteenth century, the grenadier companies of Line regiments, consisting of the tallest and strongest men, frequently led assaults and landings, and dressing all Marines as grenadiers was perhaps a nod in the direction of acknowledging their utility in this role. The laurel wreath in the Corps cap badge is thought to commemorate their achievements at Belleisle. As the war progressed, the strength of the Marines was raised to over 19,000.

With the peace came the inevitable reductions. The Marines were reduced to an official strength of 4,500 within an overall naval strength of 16,000.[10] When the American War of Independence broke out, there was to begin with, and until the French took a hand, no threat at sea, and nothing was done to improve the low state of readiness of ships. The immediate need was for soldiers ashore in the rebellious colonies. A battalion of Marines under Major Pitcairn disembarked in Boston in early 1775. A British column under Colonel Smith, consisting of the light companies based in Boston, was sent to seize rebel arms at Concord. Pitcairn commanded the advance guard. (During the American War of Independence it was a frequent practice to detach the light infantry and grenadier companies of various regiments and form them into one or more light infantry or grenadier battalions for special duties, sometimes for protracted periods.) At Lexington, en route to Concord, Pitcairn encountered the Lexington Militia commanded by Captain Parker. When one of the British officers discharged his pistol in the direction of the

Militia, both Pitcairn and Captain Parker, attempting to defuse the situation, ordered their men not to fire. Suddenly a shot rang out from the Militia, and the order to fire was given to the British troops. They killed eight and wounded ten of the Militia, who ran off. Smith was horrified, and castigated Pitcairn for opening fire. The British column pushed on to Concord. Here they were confronted by the Concord Militia. Again a shot from the Militia drew a British response. This time the Militia did not withdraw, and their return fire wounded four British officers, and killed three soldiers. Unable to drive off the militiamen in Concord, and aware that the countryside swarmed with armed men, Smith ordered a withdrawal to Boston. A running fight with the militiamen ensued. The Americans shot at the British from behind walls, haystacks, and buildings. Many of the British had expended all the thirty-six rounds of ammunition with which they had been issued, and suffered 73 dead and over 200 wounded. In the nick of time help arrived in the shape of a brigade under Colonel Lord Percy consisting of the 4th, 23rd, and 47th Regiments,[11] and Marines, and some cannon, who marched thirty miles to their assistance in under ten hours.

Some of the rebels scalped and cut off the ears of the wounded men who fell into their hands. But Percy reported that they were far from being 'an irregular mob. . . . They have men amongst them who know very well what they are about, having been employed as rangers among the Indians'.[12]

The Marines, having taken part in the somewhat inglorious (from the British point of view) opening skirmish of the American Revolution, participated in the next act, Bunker Hill. By May 1775, the British under Lieutenant General Gage were besieged in Boston by rebels who held most of the high ground overlooking Boston harbour and the town. By now a further 750 Marines had arrived, and with Pitcairn's original battalion formed 1st and 2nd Marine Battalions, with Pitcairn in overall command. When the rebels fortified Bunker Hill and Breed's Hill, on the Charlestown peninsula north of Boston, Gage finally decided that he must eliminate this position before going on to clear the remainder of the rebel positions surrounding the harbour.

On the afternoon of 17 June 1775, the troops marched down to the boats that were to take them to land on the peninsula. Dressed in winter uniforms of thick serge, with rolled blankets and three days' supply of boiled beef in their packs, they were landed without opposition, watched by huge crowds of spectators on the nearby hills, and the rooftops of Boston. The British were drawn up in three lines, including the 1st and 2nd Marines. As they advanced sweating under their heavy packs through long grass, stumbling over rocks and climbing over low stone walls and fences, they came under fire from the houses of Charlestown on their left, until red-hot shot from the British ships in support set the buildings on fire. The Americans had been told to hold their fire, and the effect when they did fire was devastating. Twice the British were beaten back, and each time rallied by Major General Howe. The third time, the 1st Marines and the 47th of Foot advanced and broke through. At the sight of the British advancing steadily with fixed bayonets, shouting and screaming, as they stepped over the bodies of their comrades, the militiamen broke.

The rebels retreated to Bunker Hill, but soon fled. The Americans suffered over 400 killed and wounded, but the British lost nearly forty per cent; 226 killed, including 27 officers, and 828 wounded, including 63 officers. Pitcairn was among the dead. A contemporary report said:

> The reputation of the Marines was never more nobly sustained. Their unshaken steadiness was conspicuous and their valour in closing with the enemy when part of the attacking column wavered gained them not only the admiration of their comrades but the commendation of their distinguished chief.

The British, having decided that Boston was not suitable as a base from which to conduct the campaign, eventually abandoned the town, and withdrew to Halifax, Nova Scotia. Howe moved to attack New York, taking the grenadier companies of 1st and 2nd Marines, who as part of 3rd Battalion of Grenadiers fought in the campaign in New York and Philadelphia (they are not to be confused with The 1st Foot Guards, who were not called The Grenadier Guards until after the Battle of Waterloo). The remainder of 1st and 2nd Marines remained to garrison Halifax.

When General Burgoyne surrendered at Saratoga in 1777, the French, seeing British power in North America faltering, realized there was an opportunity to revenge themselves for the comprehensive defeats they had suffered at British hands in the Seven Years War, including the loss of Canada, and declared war on Britain the following year. The Spanish followed in 1779 and the Dutch in 1780. The Royal Navy was in a parlous state, nothing having been done to bring the ships up to fighting state and man them fully in the intervening four years. Parliament voted, somewhat belatedly, for a Navy of 90,000, including 20,000 Marines, a fivefold increase all round. But it takes time to find men to fill increases of those proportions, and the combined French, Spanish, and Dutch fleets threatened the south coast of England. Large drafts from Army regiments were sent to sea as Marines. The French were defeated off Ushant in 1778 and the Saintes in 1782, the Spanish off Cape St Vincent in 1780, and the Dutch at Dogger Bank in 1781. Marines took part in all these battles, as well as fighting ashore at Savannah and Charleston in North America, in the West Indies, and in India.

With the ending of the American War in 1783, Britain could no longer ship convicts there, and seeking an alternative, chose Australia. In 1786 the 'First Fleet' sailed for Botany Bay carrying 775 convicts. A Marine guard under Major Ross sailed with them, consisting of 21 officers and 192 men, with 40 wives. Although given the nature of the duty it was hardly an event to blazon on one's colours, playing a part in the foundation of Australia was another first for the Marines. When war with France loomed, these Marines were mostly returned to England in 1791.

The French Republic declared war on Britain in 1793. Fortunately the Navy's ships were in a better state than in 1775, but short of men, having again been reduced to 16,000 of whom 4,500 were Marines. Far from Marine battalions being formed to fight ashore, on the outbreak of war, eight Army regiments[13] were sent to serve in ships-of-the-line. Marines served mainly in the smaller ships, frigates and sloops, until, with an increased strength, the Marines replaced all Army detachments at sea.

At the Battle of the Glorious First of June 1794, five of Lord Howe's eighteen ships carried Army detachments. At the Battle of Cape St Vincent three years later, two of Admiral Sir John Jervis's fifteen ships carried detachments of the 29th Foot, and it was a soldier of this regiment who broke open the stern cabin window of the Spanish *San Nicolas* to allow Commodore Nelson to board her from his ship, the *Captain*.

For some years after the outbreak of war there had been discontent in the fleet caused by harsh treatment, low and irregular pay, and possibly rumbles of republicanism from across the Channel, following the French Revolution. The presence of Army detachments on board ships of the

Royal Navy merely served to underline the seamen's grievances. Mutiny broke out in the fleet at Plymouth and at Spithead on 15 April 1797. In 1796 the Army had been awarded a pay rise, but this had not been extended to the Navy, which had not had an increase since 1653, before the Restoration, and the officers had had a rise in 1694 but a pay cut in 1700. Extracts from the petition presented by the Spithead mutineers to Admiral of the Fleet Lord Howe on 18 April 1797 read:

> It is now upwards of two years since your petitioners observed with pleasure the augmentation which had been made to the pay of the Army and militia, and the provision that took place with the respect of their wives and families, of such soldiers serving on board, naturally expecting that they should in their turn experience the same munificence, but alas no notice has been taken of them, nor the smallest provision made for their wives and families except what they themselves sent out of their pay to prevent them being burdensome to the parish. . . . .

Howe dealt sympathetically with the mutineers, and following cabinet agreement to the demands, the mutiny at Spithead and Plymouth ended in mid-May. Just before this, a more violent mutiny broke out at Yarmouth, and at the Nore (the anchorage in the mouth of the Thames Estuary off Sheerness) under the leadership of Richard Parker. By now, as most of the demands had been met, public opinion hardened against the mutineers, and the government refused to negotiate, cutting off supplies to the ships. The mutiny at the Nore ended on 14 June 1797, and the ringleaders, including Parker, were hanged.

It would be pleasing to record that no Marines sided with the mutineers. Unfortunately this would be inaccurate. A sergeant was among those hanged for the Nore mutiny. At Spithead the petitioners claimed to speak for seamen and Marines; the latter were no better paid, and in many cases as badly treated, and sometimes worse. On at least two occasions Marines refused to fire on the mutineers. On the other hand, the Marines prevented Admiral Duncan's flagship, the *Venerable*, falling into the hands of the mutineers, which was to prove absolutely critical. At the Nore the Marines helped bring ships back to duty, and three were commissioned for loyal service at Plymouth, the Nore, and in a single-ship mutiny at Gibraltar.

A detailed ship-by-ship examination of why Marines in some cases helped suppress the mutinies while elsewhere they joined in or gave tacit support by lack of action is impossible for lack of objective evidence, and in any event has no place in this history. It is likely that where Marines were well led by their own officers, and given clear and timely orders, they were effective. Where this was lacking, especially in cases where a ship's captain made no secret of his low opinion of Marines, or was indecisive, it would be unrealistic to expect them to suppress mutiny in their ship. They were still being sent to sea with very little training, and commonly were neither esteemed nor treated as special. As one of the historians of the Royal Marines has written:

> as might be expected, it was those who neglected them, used them merely as a source of unskilled labour, looked down on them as stupid redcoats or lobster-backs, who expected miracles when their neglect of seamen and Marines alike brought about mutiny.[14]

When the discontent spread to the Mediterranean fleet a year later, Admiral Sir John Jervis, now Earl St Vincent, quelled it by firmness and good administration. He took care to see that his Marines were treated in a soldierly manner, being kept free from duties which would split them up among the ship's companies, and ensuring that they were quartered between the seamen and the officers. What is more, his fleet Marine officer was instructed to inspect every ship in the fleet to ensure that the Commander-in-Chief's orders were being carried out, and not being obstructed by captains of ships who thought they knew better. In St Vincent's orders for the Mediterranean Fleet:[15]

22 June 1798
STANDING MEMORANDUM
When at anchor in this position [place], the whole party of marines in the respective ships of the fleet is to be kept constantly at drill or parade under the direction of the commanding officer of marines and not to be diverted therefrom by any of the ordinary duties of the ship. Sighting [sic, probably shifting] the anchors or getting under sail are the only exceptions which occur to the commander in chief.

6 July 1798
Having found it necessary to appoint Lt-Col Flight inspector of the marines serving in His Majesty's fleet under my command, he is to be received as such and be permitted to have marines of the respective ships under arms, to inspect their necessaries, visit the store room, and every other department attached to the marines: and he has my orders to report

any departure from the regulations of the service and the instructions I have thought fit to give.

Both St Vincent and Duncan appreciated what their Marines could do for them if properly treated. Duncan, particularly, had good reason for being grateful to his Marines, for during the Nore mutiny, his flagship, *Venerable*, and the *Adamant*, were the only two line-of-battle ships still operational in his North Sea Squadron. They maintained the blockade of the Dutch fleet by bluff, signalling to *Circe*, his one remaining frigate, who passed on Duncan's messages to an imaginary fleet over the horizon. By the time the Dutch came out, the Nore mutiny was over, and Duncan was able to bring his whole strength to bear and defeat them at the Battle of Camperdown.

In May 1798 Napoleon Bonaparte and his army, with thirteen ships-of-the-line and four frigates, escaped the British blockade of Toulon, and headed for Egypt. Having landed he defeated the Mameluke army at the Battle of the Pyramids. The French fleet anchored in Aboukir Bay. Here, on 1 August, Nelson with a squadron found them. Despite the French being anchored close inshore, and with night imminent, Nelson attacked immediately. He took some of his ships down the landward side of the French line, where they anchored by the stern. With thirteen ships attacking the leading eight ships of the French line, Nelson's squadron battered them into submission, starting at 6.31 p.m. Edward Berry, captain of Nelson's flagship, *Vanguard*, recounted later:

> At about seven o'clock total darkness had come on; but the whole hemisphere was, with intervals, illuminated by the fire of the hostile fleets. . . . . The van ship of the enemy, *Le Guerrier*, was dismasted in less than twelve minutes, and, in ten minutes after, the second ship, *Le Conquérant*, and the third, *Le Spartiate*, very nearly at the same moment were almost dismasted. *L'Aquilon*, and *Le Souverain Peuple*, the fourth and fifth ships of the enemy's line, were taken possession of by the British at half past eight.

Lieutenant Galwey of *Vanguard* with a party of Marines was sent by Berry to take possession of *Le Spartiate*. Galwey remained on board the prize but returned the French captain's sword, which Berry immediately took to Nelson, who was below with a head wound, temporarily blinded by a splinter which had sliced open his forehead and dropped a flap of skin over his eyes. At about ten minutes past nine *L'Orient*, the French flagship, seventh in line, was seen to be badly on fire. Nelson, in spite of his wound, came on deck, and ordered Berry to do all he could to save *L'Orient*'s crew. Berry sent his only surviving boat, as did other British ships, saving about seventy enemy sailors before *L'Orient* blew up with a tremendous explosion. After victory had been secured over the French van, the British ships moved down on the remainder. Four French ships escaped, two of the line (*Guillaume Tell* and *Généreux*) and two frigates (*Diane* and *Justice*).

Napoleon, his fleet destroyed, marched with 10,000 infantry, 800 cavalry, and 1,400 gunners into Syria, from where it was possible that he might threaten Constantinople and Vienna, or, more ambitiously, India. Certainly Napoleon's arrival in Egypt had caused alarm among the British East India Company's officials both in Calcutta and London, including Henry Dundas, who was both President of the Board of Control of the company and Secretary for War in the British government. He, and others, imagined that Napoleon might emulate Alexander the Great and march his army through Persia and Afghanistan to the borders of India. Here, it was believed, he would be welcomed by the anti-British Indian Princes led by Tippu Sultan of Mysore, who was preparing to confront the British. Whether Napoleon's logistic arrangements would have been capable of sustaining such a long march over deserts and mountains is open to question. He certainly never took the same pains with his supply arrangements as Alexander, and once said, 'Qu'on ne me parle pas des vivres' ('Let no one speak to me of provisions').

Having sacked Jaffa, Napoleon moved on Acre. Here Captain Sir Sydney Smith was in command. To reinforce the local Turkish garrison, he landed some 800 Marines and seamen from his two ships-of-the-line, *Theseus* and *Tigre*, together with some ship's guns. After their initial assault had been beaten off, the French settled down to besiege Acre, and mounted a number of assaults, again without success. However, when their siege trenches approached to within half a pistol shot of the walls, it became clear that they were about to sink a mine under one of the main defence posts and destroy it by demolition. It was decided to put in a counterattack by Marines and seamen led by Major Thomas Oldfield, commanding *Theseus*'s Marines, to destroy the mine shaft by counter-demolition. The British charged through heavy fire to the head of the shaft. Oldfield's second-in-command, Lieutenant Wright of the

Tigre, led some pikemen to the end of the mine, and finding that the counter-demolition party had not been able to fight their way through, pulled down the props, caving in the roof. On his way out, he was caught by a French counterattack, and with Oldfield was hit and seen to go down. Sydney Smith's memoirs relate:

> Smith called to one of his men, a gigantic, red-haired Irish Marine, named James Close. Pointing to the mass of carnage that lay sweltering in the ditch below, where the slightly wounded and the actually dying were fast hastening into mutual corruption under the burning sun, Smith said, 'Close, dare you go there and bring us the body of poor Wright?' 'What daren't I do your honour?' was the immediate reply and, exposed to the musketry of the enemy, wading through blood and stumbling over dead bodies and scattered limbs, he unhurt, at length found Wright, not killed but only wounded, and he brought him away from these shambles of death. The French spared him for the sake of the heroism of the act.[16]

Marines searching for Oldfield arrived at the same moment as Frenchmen. Like wild animals over a kill, both pulled and tussled over the body. A Frenchmen dug a halberd into Oldfield's side and hauled him in, breaking the British hold on his neckcloth. He was taken into the French camp, where he was found to be still just alive, and died shortly afterwards. The French buried him with full military honours.

The French assaults continued with unabated fury, but Acre under Smith's inspiring leadership held. Eventually Bonaparte was persuaded by his senior general, Kléber, to retreat, and after a two-month siege the French began their long march south. Napoleon later said of Smith, 'That man made me miss my destiny.'

Napoleon escaped to France, leaving his army in Egypt. On 8 May 1801, Admiral Lord Keith with the Mediterranean Fleet landed a British army under General Sir Ralph Abercromby at Aboukir Bay. Sir Sydney Smith was responsible for the planning and the extensive rehearsals for what turned out to be a model amphibious operation. The Marines in the fleet took no part in the landing, which was made by Army regiments. However, four days later a battalion formed by Marines from the fleet marched to join the Army. The next day it was recalled to attack Aboukir Castle, so missed the main battle outside Alexandria. The Marine battalion subsequently took part in the siege of the city, before being recalled by Lord Keith. The Marines could not be spared from duties with the fleet for protracted periods, a theme that was to recur; it was understandable in the circumstances, but frustrating when operations ashore promised battalion command, fame, and promotion.

There were opportunities for Marines to command at a lower level, as well as the chance of making their names in the numerous cutting-out actions and raids that will be familiar to readers of naval historical novels of the period, of which those by Patrick O'Brian are far and away the best.

The early career of Charles Menzies, who joined the Royal Marines in 1805 just after Trafalgar, illustrates just how such raids were conducted. In 1806 he joined the frigate *Minerva*, and in the twenty-two months he spent as Officer Commanding Royal Marines in that ship he saw plenty of action, including hand-to-hand fighting in numerous cutting-out expeditions and raids. He was awarded a Lloyd's Patriotic Fund sword for 'his intrepidity and zeal when commanding the Marines belonging to the ship, at the storming of Fort Finesterre, and in capturing five Spanish luggers on 22 June 1806'. The raiding party had been sent to cut out the Spanish ships which were lying under the cover of eight 24- and 12-pounder guns of the fort. Led by Menzies, the landing party took the fort by surprise at the point of pike and bayonet. He hauled down the Spanish colours, replacing them with the Union Flag, while his men spiked the guns and threw them over the ramparts into the sea. He did not lose a man, and the five luggers were found to be loaded with wine. A month later he led an attack on the *Buena Dieha*, a Spanish privateer which preyed on shipping sailing to and from Oporto. The approach to the *Buena Dieha* involved a forty-mile row in *Minerva*'s barge. Menzies was wounded in the right arm, and it was amputated. This did not deter him from leading another cutting-out expedition in October, capturing a Spanish ship in Arosa Bay, and subsequently landing to take the enemy commodore prisoner.

Marine detachments in smaller ships were often commanded by sergeants. Casualties also brought opportunities. Sergeant James Dair took over the detachment in the *Leander* (a 50-gun ship), following the death of the Marine lieutenant. After the Battle of the Nile, sailing independently while carrying home Nelson's Nile despatches, *Leander* was intercepted by the *Généreux* (a 74-gun survivor of the battle), and after a fight lasting six and a half hours she was overcome. Dair with a party of Marines on the poop had beaten off repeated attempts to board.

Eventually he was killed along with seven of his men, a further nine being wounded.

By 1801 the Army had ceased providing detachments at sea, but when a battalion-sized force was needed for amphibious operations the shortage of Marines for sea duty meant that the Army was called upon. Nelson's plan for the attack on the heavily fortified port of Copenhagen on 2 April 1801 included an assault on the mighty Trekroner forts. This was assigned to the 49th Foot[17] and one company of the Experimental Corps of Riflemen.[18] The men from these regiments were distributed among the ships detailed for this task, each of whom towed a flatboat alongside which would be used to land the soldiers. The plan was never put to the test, since the assaulting ships were unable to close the forts to land their troops, being beaten off by heavy fire; both regiments were awarded the battle honour 'Copenhagen' despite their somewhat passive part in the action. Also accompanying Nelson's fleet was a troop of Royal Artillery providing the mortar crews in bomb vessels. These small vessels mounted one 13-inch and one 10-inch mortar for coastal bombardment; the mortars fired a spherical bomb packed with powder and its own fuse. Because of its high trajectory, the bomb could be lobbed over fortifications which might be difficult or impossible to engage with direct fire. An expert mortar man could cut the bomb fuse so that it exploded over the target to produce an air-burst effect. The Royal Artillery had been responsible for providing the mortar crews for bomb vessels for many years, although the responsibility would eventually pass to the Marines.

By the time peace was signed with France in March 1802, the Marines were 30,000 strong. They were immediately reduced to 12,119. However, their devoted service since 1755 was recognized on 29 April 1802 when King George III directed that they should be styled the Royal Marines from his birthday, 4 June. This honour had been granted largely thanks to St Vincent, the First Lord of the Admiralty, who said:

> In obtaining for them the distinction of 'Royal', I but inefficiently did my duty. I never knew an appeal to them for honour, courage, or loyalty, that they did not more than realize my highest expectations. If ever the hour of real danger should come to England, they will be found the country's sheet anchor.

In May 1803 Bonaparte's machinations led to the outbreak of war. His intentions from the outset of hostilities were to invade Britain, and for about eighteen months the threat of French occupation hung over the country. The French invasion force concentrated at Boulogne, where about two thousand flat-bottomed boats had been collected.

Although the strength of the Royal Marines rose on the outbreak of war, eventually reaching 31,400, to begin with the Navy was faced by the all too familiar situation of insufficient Marines to man the fleet. Soon new responsibilities were given to the Royal Marines. In March 1804 disputes had arisen in bomb vessels in the Channel and the Mediterranean between the Royal Navy captains and the Royal Artillery mortar detachments. The Royal Artillery officers claimed, rightly as it turned out, that they were not subject to naval discipline. The Admiralty's answer was to form Royal Marine Artillery companies, one to each division, and an Order in Council dated 18 August 1804 authorized their formation.

Ninety-two officers and 2,600 men of the Royal Marines were in Nelson's fleet when he defeated the larger combined French and Spanish fleets at Trafalgar on 21 October 1805. Four officers and 113 men were killed, and 13 officers and 219 men wounded. On the poop deck of Nelson's flagship, *Victory*, where forty Marines were stationed, Captain Adair was killed, and two lieutenants of Marines wounded. Sergeant Secker was the first to Nelson's assistance when he was hit, and helped carry him below.

Marines took part in all the naval actions until the end of the Napoleonic War, including raids and cutting-out expeditions. Landings by Marine battalions also took place, but were often frustrating. For example, a battalion and artillery company was sent to Portugal to assist with holding the flank of the Lines of Torres Vedras, into which Wellington had withdrawn in 1810. When Wellington advanced out of the Lines at the start of his campaign that would eventually take him into France and Paris, he wanted to take the Marine battalion with him. To their disgust they were held at Lisbon for over a year, and eventually shipped to England. In 1812 the battalion with its artillery company embarked in Rear-Admiral Sir Home Popham's Flying Squadron to operate off the northern coast of Spain. Later they were joined by a second battalion. A number of landings were carried out, but on the whole their full potential was not exploited.

The war with the United States of America which began in 1812 saw three Marine battalions employed with considerable success, two of them having been transferred from Spain in 1813, the third from Holland. As in the War of American Independence, the shortage of British troops, with so much of the British Army employed in Spain, led to Marines being employed ashore across the Atlantic. All battalions acquitted themselves well, as did the Royal Marine Artillery companies. Two of the battalions helped repulse the American invasion of Canada. The third battalion raided the shores of Chesapeake Bay and formed part of the force of three brigades under General Ross that defeated the Americans at Bladensburg. United States Marines behaved the most steadfastly of all the American troops during the battle, but even their efforts were insufficient to stop Ross's troops entering Washington and setting fire to government buildings in the city, including the Capitol and the White House. Marines from both sides also took part in the Battle of New Orleans, where General Jackson defeated Major General Sir Edward Pakenham, preventing him from continuing his advance up the Mississippi. The Royal Marines scored the only British success of the battle. With the 85th Foot,[19] and some seamen, they captured a battery on the western bank of the river. Pakenham was mortally wounded. The British lost two other major generals, eight colonels, and seventy-eight other officers, and 2,536 soldiers dead, wounded, or taken prisoner out of a force of 9,000.

Marines fought in the action when USS *Constitution* captured HMS *Guerriere*, and shot Lieutenant Bush of the United States Marine Corps. When the *Shannon* captured the American *Chesapeake* off Boston in less than twenty minutes, Royal and United States Marines fought hand-to-hand.

An early example of the use of tribal levies was provided when Major Nicolls and seventy Marines formed a force from the Creek and Choctaw Indians in eastern Louisiana. His purpose was to draw off American forces from the defence of New Orleans. Nicolls is an interesting character, and his record of service is illustrative of how varied the career of a Royal Marine had become by the late eighteenth and early nineteenth centuries. He was commissioned in 1795; in 1803 he volunteered to command a cutting-out expedition, and with only thirteen men he took the French cutter *Albion*, his second such foray that year. In 1804 he took part in the abortive attack on Curaçoa. In 1807 he led a landing party from the *Standard* during Vice Admiral Sir John Duckworth's passage of the Dardanelles, burning a Turkish frigate, and storming a redoubt and spiking the guns. The landing parties had been put ashore by the rear division of Duckworth's fleet commanded by Rear-Admiral Sir Sydney Smith, that intrepid amphibious sailor. Their success allowed the main force to transit the thirty-eight miles of narrows, at places less than a mile wide; his successor, 108 years later to the day, was not so fortunate. In 1809, Nicolls commanded the landing force that captured the Danish island of Anholt. In all he was in action 107 times, wounded six times, court-martialled twice, but survived to be knighted and, by 1854, promoted full general.

Although the early careers of 'Fighting' Nicolls and Menzies are perhaps among the most colourful in the late-eighteenth- and early-nineteenth-century Royal Marine story, plenty of other officers and men had similar adventures, and what we would now call raiding formed a staple part of the Corps's experience. The wars of the French Revolution and of Napoleon saw the high point of daring operations mounted with such frequency from vessels of the Royal Navy, and the Royal Marines played an honourable and often a leading part in these raids. The ninety-nine years between the end of the Napoleonic War and British involvement in an even greater struggle were to bring many changes, not all beneficial to the Royal Marines.

2

Victoria's Jollies

An' after, I met 'im all over the world, a-doin' all kinds of things,
Like landin' 'isself with a Gatlin' gun to talk to them 'eathen kings;
'E sleeps in a 'ammick instead of a cot, an' 'e drills with the deck on a slew,
An' 'e sweats like a Jolly – 'Er Majesty's Jolly – soldier an' sailor too!
For there isn't a job on top o' the earth the beggar don't know, nor do –

Rudyard Kipling

Kipling's poem 'Soldier and Sailor Too', subtitled the 'Royal Regiment of Marines', written towards the end of Queen Victoria's reign, is flattering but incorrect in one vital fact: the Royal Marines were not then, were never, and are not today, sailors. They were and are soldiers; albeit often misemployed soldiers, increasingly so as the nineteenth century passed. However, it would be churlish to complain too much, for the sentiments expressed in the poem are indicative of how the stock of the Corps had risen in the century and a half since their formation under Admiralty control. Indeed, thanks to devoted service in the latter half of the eighteenth century and the early part of the nineteenth, by the end of the Napoleonic Wars the Royal Marines were well established and spared the disbandment that followed the conclusion of every war before 1755.

This improved status was marked in 1827 when the Duke of Clarence presented new colours to each of the four divisions. King George IV on being asked to choose which of the 106 battle honours to which the Marines were entitled should appear on the colours, decided, according to the Duke of Clarence in his speech at the colour presentation parade, that

the greatness of their number [of battle honours] and the difficulty of selecting amidst so many glorious deeds such a portion as could be inserted in the space determined His Majesty in lieu of the usual badges and mottoes on Colours of the troops of the Line, to direct that the Globe encircled with Laurel should be the distinguishing badge as the most appropriate emblem of the Corps whose duties carried them to all parts of the globe, in every quarter of which they had earned laurels by their valour and good conduct.

The King also directed that his cipher GR IV should be carried in perpetuity in addition to that of the reigning monarch. The colours bore the motto 'Per Mare per Terram' ('By Sea by Land'), and the one battle honour Gibraltar, their first great amphibious operation.

Although George IV was often ridiculed for his fanciful and extravagant ideas, including a penchant for designing flamboyant uniforms and accoutrements, his account of his dilemma when asked to decide which battle honours should appear on the Royal Marines' colours is not hyperbole. At that time the greatest number of battle honours to which a handful of the oldest regiments of the Guards and the Line were each entitled amounted to about twenty, and the majority of regiments considerably less.

This did not mean that the Royal Marines had suddenly become 'smart' in the social sense. Although their status had improved greatly since 1755, and Marine officers had no trouble in passing for gentlemen and messing in the wardroom aboard ship, for reasons explained in the previous chapter the officers were on the whole poor men; often middle-class Irish and Scots, attracted to an honourable profession with low social and financial barriers to entry. In other words, the Royal Marines remained a Corps of low status compared with a regiment of the Line in the King's or Queen's service and of poor prospects compared with the Navy.[1]

Peace made these prospects considerably worse. The size of the Corps fell from 31,000 to around 9,000. Promotion in wartime had been paralytic; it stagnated in peace. This state of affairs can be traced to the formation of the Marines under naval command in the middle of the eighteenth century and dishonesty on the part of the Board of Admiralty. The vexed subject of promotion and prospects had been aired in a letter to the Admiralty at the end of that century by the Commandants of the three Marine Divisions:

In former wars the officers of Marines were established on an equality with those of the line; they had an equal intercourse with them by sale and exchange of commissions.[2] At the reduction in 1748 the half-pay officers of Marines were considered as reduced officers of the Army, and in consequence many of them have since attained the highest rank and command.

Before 1747 the Marine regiments belonged to the Army, although raised for use by the Navy. Those officers put on half-pay from the ten Marine regiments raised in the War of Jenkins's Ear who did not join the 1755 Marine Corps, which was completely under naval control, were often appointed to other regiments, and if lucky, eventually attained general rank. Those who joined the 1755 Marine Corps found they had entered what one historian called a 'cul-de-sac',[3] despite the fact that, as the Divisional Commandants represented to the Admiralty, 'at the first formation of the present body of Marines [1755 Corps], they had the most solemn assurances given them by the Board of Admiralty that they should be put on as advantageous a footing as any other Corps in His Majesty's Services'.

Far from honouring this promise, within four years of making it the Board of Admiralty with calculated dishonesty dealt a blow to the whole fabric of the officer corps of the Marines. At this stage the strength of the Marines, increased because of the Seven Years War, was 18,092 officers, NCOs and privates. The senior officer was Colonel Patterson in London, and there were only one lieutenant-colonel and two majors in each Division. In 1759 the Lords Commissioners of the Admiralty, headed by Anson, wrote to the King to suggest that this was too small a number of senior officers to train and discipline a Corps of such a size; all too true. However, Anson and his fellow Commissioners, instead of taking the logical, and fair, step of increasing the number of senior officers in the Corps, which would have improved promotion prospects, asked that 'Two Flag Officers', be appointed, one as General of Marines at £5 per day, and one as Lieutenant-General of Marines at £4 per day, 'the whole charge thereof being £3,285 a year, will be defrayed out of the four pounds per man per month granted by Parliament for Marines employed on Sea Service'. So funds voted by Parliament to pay for Marines at sea, by skulduggery went into the pockets of lucky naval officers who made no contribution to the training or anything else connected to the Marines. Later a third flag officer was appointed Major-General of Marines, and paid appropriately at £3 a day. Not content

with this, in 1760 another submission was sent to the King, recommend-
ing that the post of Colonel of Marines in London be abolished, and
that he be pensioned off with £750 a year. His place was to be taken by
'Three Sea Captains, whilst waiting promotion to Flag Rank', who would
be made Colonels of Marines at £2 per day. They would each command
one of the divisions, at Chatham, Portsmouth, and Plymouth. This
scheme was duly instituted. As one historian caustically remarked, 'a
splendid way of teaching NCOs and men their military duties while
stationed on shore'.[4]

C. S. Forester has the hero of *Captain Hornblower* appointed Colonel
of Marines after escaping from captivity. Although Forester's writings
generally betray his lack of knowledge, and low opinion, of the Marines,
his account of Hornblower's thoughts on being appointed is credible: 'A
Colonel of Marines received pay to the amount of twelve hundred
pounds a year, and did no duty for it'.[5] On this occasion Forester is
incorrect only insofar as the pay scale; Colonels of Marines received £730
a year. He is right where he says they did no duty for it. These sinecures
lasted until 1837. However, because that is just what they were, the
Commandant in Town, as he was called, remained in post, and Marine
colonels and majors were eventually added to the establishment to do
the work. This hardly improved promotion, and if they could raise the
cash, Marine officers transferred to the Army; like Captain Mackenzie
who bought a majority in the 78th Highland Regiment of Foot in 1794.[6]
He commanded a brigade in Portugal under Wellington, and was killed
in Spain at the Battle of Talavera as a major general in 1809. No Marine
officer of that era could hope for such swift promotion or aspire to field
command of a brigade, or any appointment in the field in the rank of
major general.

Although Britain did not become involved in war in Europe for nearly
one hundred years after Waterloo, the Navy and the Marines were kept
busy with minor scrimmages, and sometimes much more serious affairs.
One of the few occasions when a Royal Marine battalion was supported
by a field battery of Royal Marine Artillery in battle arose during the
Carlist War in Spain. This little-known war broke out in 1833, when
Don Carlos, the brother of the late Ferdinand VII, rebelled against his
widow, the Queen Regent, Maria Cristina. Lacking sufficient troops, the
Spanish government arranged for British, French, and Portuguese legions
to fight on its behalf. The British Legion, around 10,000 strong, consisted

of infantry, cavalry, and artillery. It was recruited in Britain, but was part of and paid by the Spanish forces, and the leading units arrived in Spain in mid-1835. The Royal Marine battalion, which arrived a year later, was composed of detachments landed from the supporting Royal Navy squadron, and a seven-company battalion sent from Britain, combining to make a ten-company battalion. The Royal Marine Artillery manned a battery of six 6-pounders, two 12-pounder howitzers, and a rocket section.

The Royal Marines battalion distinguished itself at the Battle of Oriamendi. The British Legion broke and fled under surprise attack by the Carlists, and only the Royal Marines standing their ground, and covering the rout of their fellow countrymen, prevented the Carlists from cutting the fleeing British to pieces. The Legion did better at Hernani, where again the Royal Marines gave them another example of steadiness by repulsing four times their number. The Legion's commander, Lieutenant General Sir George de Lacy Evans, told his men that the Royal Marines 'afforded you a noble example of the irresistible force of military organization and discipline, which the Lieutenant General feels confident you will be proud to emulate'. Although the British Legion was disbanded in December 1837, the Royal Marines did not leave Spain until 1840.

Throughout Victoria's long reign the Marines saw a good deal of service in many parts of the globe: in the Mediterranean, Egypt, Syria, China, against the Maoris in New Zealand, and in Burma. They first encountered the Argentines when a British and French squadron was sent to save Montevideo from Argentine aggression in 1845. Marines fought against the Russians ashore and at sea in the Crimea and Baltic from 1854 to 1856. The first three Victoria Crosses awarded to the Corps were won by Corporal Prettyjohns RM, Lieutenant Dowell RMA, and Bombardier Wilkinson RMA during the Crimean War.

Detachments of Marines from the *Shannon* and the *Pearl* served in the Indian Mutiny of 1857. A year later in China, battalions, sometimes formed into Marine brigades, formed part of the British forces that seized Canton. Later they entered Peking with the 1st Division. In 1855, the infantry of Royal Marines had been redesignated by Order in Council as The Royal Marines Light Infantry (RMLI), 'this [light infantry] training being considered the best adapted to the nature of the service which the Corps is generally required to perform when employed ashore'. There were now effectively two Corps, the RMA, known as the 'Blue Marines' because, like the Royal Artillery, their uniforms were blue, and the RMLI, the 'Red Marines', who continued to wear the scarlet jackets which they and the infantry of the British Army had worn with such distinction on hundreds of battlefields and in countless minor actions. The RMLI incorporated the light infantry stringed buglehorn into their globe and laurel cap badge. But there is no evidence to suggest that they adopted any other light infantry habits, such as the super-quick step of 140 paces to the minute.

The RMLI and RMA took part in Major General Sir Garnet Wolseley's 1873 Ashanti expedition in West Africa. In 1882, following anti-British unrest in Egypt, the ruler, the Khedive Tewfik, abdicated responsibility, handing over command of the Army to Arabi Pasha. The British fleet bombarded Alexandria, and when Arabi Pasha withdrew landed Marines and seamen to restore order. The British, to protect their investment in the Suez Canal, decided to restore the Khedive as ruler of Egypt. Wolseley with a force of two infantry divisions and a cavalry brigade was sent out from England. On arrival he took under command Marines already in the area, as well as battalions sent out from Malta and elsewhere in the Mediterranean. He decided to advance on Cairo, where Arabi had concentrated his army, from the east, the Suez canal, rather than from Alexandria, the more obvious approach. In the early hours of 20 August, Marines from a naval squadron captured Port Said and Ismailia on the canal, enabling Wolseley's force to start disembarking. The RMLI and RMA battalions arrived the next day, the latter without guns and operating as infantry. Both took part in the battles of Tel-el-Mahuta, Kassassin, and Tel-el-Kebir. On 13 October they marched into Cairo.

The British almost immediately found themselves being sucked into Egyptian politics deeper than the government at home would have liked. In Sudan, then ruled from Egypt, the Mahdi, a religious leader, raised the standards of holy war against the Khedive. A force of Dervishes, the term the British used to describe all the Mahdi's followers regardless of tribe, massacred an Egyptian army in 1883. The following year, one of the Mahdi's subordinate commanders, Osman Digna, inflicted a catastrophic defeat on an Egyptian column near Suakin, on the Red Sea. The British, having been responsible for restoring the Khedive to power, felt obliged to assist him in repressing the uprising. In 1884, Marines seized the port of Suakin in the Sudan, fought the Dervishes, or 'Fuzzy Wuzzies' as they were known to the British soldiers, at El Teb and Tamai, and subsequently remained to garrison the fort at Suakin. For some time General Gordon had been besieged in Khartoum by the Mahdi. After much dithering by Gladstone's government, Wolseley was ordered to relieve him. He decided to advance on two routes: the main force would go up the River Nile, while a Desert Column cut across the great bend of the river between Dongola and Khartoum. The Desert Column included four camel regiments, one of which, the Guards Camel Regiment, had four companies one each of Grenadier, Coldstream, and Scots Guards, and one RMLI. Meanwhile an RMLI battalion formed part of a field force to cover the construction of a railway through the desert to link the Nile with the sea at Suakin.

After an exhausting march of nearly 150 miles, the desert column found the vital wells at Abu Klea, some twenty-four miles from the Nile at Metemmah, defended by the Dervishes. There was no turning back; they had to gain control of the wells, or die of thirst. After a savage battle, in the course of which a British square was broken, the Dervishes were defeated. The battle was later the subject of a poem by Kipling, which includes the gloriously politically incorrect lines:

> So 'ere's to you, Fuzzy-Wuzzy, at your 'ome in the Soudan;
> You're a pore benighted 'eathen but a first class fightin' man;
> An' 'ere's to you, Fuzzy-Wuzzy, with your 'ayrick 'ead of 'air –
> You big black boundin' beggar – for you broke a British square!

Earlier, the RMLI battalion and the Berkshires of the Suakin Field Force had defeated Osman Digna at the Battle of Tamai. Two days later at Tofrik, while the Field Force was building zarebas (protected camps of stone and thorn scrub), Digna's Dervishes came howling over the half-completed walls. The fighting was savage, and at close quarters. At one point the central zareba, occupied by two Indian regiments, was nearly overrun. The Berkshires and RMLI finally drove off the Dervishes, with volley fire, followed up by the bayonet. The battle lasted half an hour, during which time the British had 8 officers and 153 men killed, and a further 5 officers and 117 wounded. The high proportion of dead to wounded is indicative of the savagery of the fighting, and the effectiveness of the Dervishes' huge swords. At this point, Gladstone used the excuse of hostile activity on the North-West Frontier of India, supposedly stirred up by Russia, to order Wolseley to close down the Sudan campaign and withdraw to Egypt.

Few Marines took part in Kitchener's reconquest of the Sudan in 1896–7. Some RMLI officers commanded Egyptian battalions, and Egyptians manning the guns on river gunboats were trained and commanded by RMA NCOs.

In the second Boer War in South Africa, except for officers on detached duty, Marine participation was limited to three companies that formed part of the so-called Naval Brigade (the term given to any sizeable group of sailors landed to fight ashore and not necessarily of brigade strength). Fighting as part of the Naval Brigade at the Battle of Graspan, the Marines lost 9 killed and 82 wounded, which given the poor tactics employed by the Naval Brigade, an advance in close order over open ground against well-concealed Boer marksmen, were surprisingly small losses. The Naval Brigade's tactics, little different from those used by the Army at the time, might have been adequate when pitted against Zulus or Ashanti tribesmen armed mainly with spears. Against opposition both highly proficient in fieldcraft and equipped with magazine rifles, firing high-velocity smokeless ammunition, a great deal more skill was required. One of the outcomes of the frequent landing of naval brigades in the last half of the nineteenth century, especially against second-class enemies, was a perception in many naval officers' minds that soldiering was easy and that little training was required. This mindset was to have repercussions on the Marines well into the next century, as captains of warships were loath to allow their detachments to land for training in skills which on the one hand they considered so simple that little practice was necessary, and on the other hand were irrelevant for a different reason which will become apparent shortly. Soldiering was regarded by many Victorian naval officers as 'fun', and for lack of any opportunities for fleet action in the sixty years between the Crimean War and First World War, fighting ashore was a chance to make one's name, and gain decorations and promotion. The Victorian Navy's propensity to land its bluejackets to join in the soldiering game on all possible occasions survived in the RN Field Gun competition at the Royal Tournament, one of the most exciting of all the events.

The last year of Victoria's reign found the Marines fighting in China once again. This time they were part of an international force defending the European and Japanese legations in Peking against the violently anti-foreign Chinese militants and rebellious soldiers known as the Boxers, who were later joined by Imperial Chinese troops. Marines also formed part of the relief force, which eventually numbered 20,000, and experienced some stiff fighting around Tientsin, before it could march to raise the siege of the legations in Peking.

The decline in the numbers of Marines serving ashore as the Victorian era drew to its close is indicative of the way the Navy was developing in this period. New brooms were beginning to sweep aside the intellectual cobwebs that had gathered in the Navy during the era which one author has called 'the long calm lee of Trafalgar'.[7] Throughout most of Victoria's reign, British naval supremacy was unchallenged. Fleet actions seemed remote. Promotion was dependent on running a smart ship and what we would now call 'bullshit'. Gunnery, which blistered paintwork, often paid for out of the officers' own pockets, was neglected. It was not unknown for ships to throw their annual allocation of practice ammunition overboard, rather then fire it.[8] Now a new generation of admirals, notably Fisher and Beresford, together with bright young captains, commanders, and lieutenants, began to question such attitudes. The reforms, notably under Fisher as First Sea Lord, gained momentum in the early years of the twentieth century. There was little time for any activity which did not contribute to the efficiency of the ship in a major battle at sea, which, following the technological revolution in gunnery, would be fought at increasingly long ranges, and with no prospect of boarding. Cutting-out expeditions, raids, and landing parties were regarded as things of the past, with no place in the Navy of the twentieth century. By the beginning of that century, any operation that involved closing the enemy coast in the face of submarines (at that time thought of primarily as coast-defence craft) and mines was considered to be so daunting that many naval officers viewed the prospect with little enthusiasm. As a consequence nobody thought through how to overcome what was actually a problem that could be solved – as events in the Second World War clearly demonstrated. Most practice landings that were carried out were unconvincing, and bordering on farce.

In these circumstances the Marines were an embarrassment, especially the officers. The NCOs, privates, and gunners of the RMLI and RMA could be used as working hands, or trained to man part of the ship's armament, and on the whole they seem to have been reasonably content with their lot as surrogate sailors. To devote months to training a Marine private as an infantry soldier, in order to employ him mostly scrubbing decks and chipping paintwork, was hardly a cost-effective use of training time: today it would quickly be rumbled on budgetary grounds alone. At sea the Marine officers had very little to do. The better ones found something else to occupy their time. Some managed to obtain appointments with the Army. Others transferred outright. Some joined the Intelligence Division, or even, like Captain Bernard Trench RMLI, became agents or spies. Trench was arrested in Germany in 1910 for taking photographs, making sketches, and preparing reports on the coastal areas in the Frisian Islands, especially in 'restricted zones'. He was sentenced to four years' imprisonment, but released on the orders of the Kaiser after two years. Yet others found fulfilment by specializing in signals, or the newfangled skills of flying. Two of the earliest members of the Royal Naval Air Service (RNAS) were Royal Marines.

Paradoxically, despite the perils of submarine and mine referred to earlier, both Fisher and his successor fostered plans to seize key forts and islands in the Frisian Islands and Baltic in the event of war with Germany. Although the operations Fisher had in mind involved landing Army formations, and not the Marines whom he hated even more than the Army, one suspects that the main purpose of these projected schemes was to upstage the Army, which Fisher loathed as a rival for defence funds. Despite Fisher's formidable ability, his support for these schemes was perhaps a case of ignorance being bliss, for other than ordering some flat-bottomed craft neither Fisher nor his successors did much to progress the art of amphibious operations, or properly staff the vague ideas that had been rotating round in Fisher's head; not least because there was no Naval Staff at that time.

Admiral Sir Arthur Wilson, his successor, presented the Navy's concepts at a meeting of the Committee of Imperial Defence (CID) on 23 August 1911, at which it was intended to decide how and where the British Army should be deployed in the event of war with Germany. Major General Henry Wilson, the Director of Military Operations, was the principal Army spokesman. The Assistant Secretary to the CID, Captain (later Lord) Maurice Hankey RMLI, commented on the Army's well staffed and presented case for deploying in France (as happened in 1914): 'In the morning, Henry Wilson unfolded the General Staff plan with remarkable brilliancy. Nothing had been left to chance; so detailed were the plans that they included "dix minutes pour un tasse de café at

Amiens".'9 In the afternoon, 'Admiral Wilson did little to help the naval case by giving the meeting a pathetically inept presentation of sketchy naval plans for amphibious landings on the German coast aimed at drawing troops away from the Western Front.'10

So simplistic and crude were the plans that one of the outcomes of this meeting, at which Churchill was present as First Lord of the Admiralty, was his order that the Admiralty was to form a proper staff. It was too late to make up for the decades of the Navy's disregard of amphibious operations. The proof of this neglect was to be shown at Gallipoli. In essence the Royal Navy entered the First World War with techniques for amphibious assault that had hardly progressed beyond those used by Abercromby at Aboukir over a century earlier.

Fisher is rightly hailed as the man who dragged the Royal Navy into the twentieth century. For this his countrymen owe him a great deal. The Royal Marines, however, have little reason to regard him with affection, because he did them much harm, reducing their military efficiency and damaging the officer corps. His views on the Royal Marines are absolutely clear from his letters, couched in the dictatorial and partisan Fisher style. He wrote to Lord Selborne on 19 May 1902:

> The only officer we can never educate is the Marine Officer. . . . And if the Marine Officer is to be of any use to us, he is absolutely useless at present (or rather he is worse than useless because he occupies valuable space on board!), we must get rid of his military training or, perhaps better (as so conclusively urged by Sir George Tryon), we ought to get rid of him altogether![11]

Tryon was the brilliantly clever but flawed officer whose ill-thought-out manoeuvre order to his Mediterranean Fleet resulted in the collision in which his flagship HMS *Victoria* was rammed by HMS *Camperdown*, and sank in ten minutes with great loss of life.

Under Selborne's scheme, cadets joining the Navy were offered the option of being commissioned into the Marines as Lieutenants (M), in the same way as engineer officers were commissioned into the engineering branch as Lieutenants (E). From 1907 to 1912, when the system was abandoned, there was no other way of gaining a commission in the Corps from civilian life. Not surprisingly, no one joined under these terms. Despite a surge in numbers starting in 1912, the Corps entered the First World War fifty-eight junior officers short, and with another fifty-nine still under training.

Fisher is at his most venomous when the subject of a Royal Marine Governor and garrison for Gibraltar is mentioned in a letter to Vice Admiral Sir William May, C-in-C Atlantic Fleet, dated 5 October 1905:

> Nothing will ever induce me personally to agree to garrisoning Gibraltar entirely with Marines! or having a Marine General as Governor! The last end would be worse than the first! It must be purely a Naval Government! and solely under the Admiralty! The Marine Officer can't be loyal! Just look at that statue outside the Admiralty in honour of the Marines, recently put up by them! It has its back turned on the Admiralty, and it's looking at the War Office! The Marine Officers (not the Mariners) [Author's note, presumably he means the other ranks] are always hankering after the Army! D..n the Army! Another reason! If we had 3,000 Marines locked up in Gibraltar, we would want another 3,000 Marines at home as their relief, and then the total number of Marines would be so great they would cease to be Marines, as they would have no sea service hardly. Even at present only 30 percent of their whole service is on board ship, and most of that often in a harbour ship![12]

Fisher had formidable powers of persuasion, drive, and ability to get things done, but he was not infallible, as demonstrated by his advocacy of the concept of the battlecruiser, shown to be so flawed at Jutland. Arguably he did the Navy, and his country, a worse disservice by allowing his prejudice to overcome common sense. He failed to use the material he had at hand, the Royal Marines, to ensure that the biggest fleet the world had ever seen had an amphibious capability.

Instead of making supercilious and waspish comments, it would have been better had he asked himself the question, 'What are the Marines for?' His immediate answer would probably have been, 'To man a proportion of the guns of the fleet.' A little more thought might have led him to the view that employing the Marines in the fleet had become obsolescent; and he would have been right. Why? The Marines' original purpose in the seventeenth century had been to make good the deficiencies of the ship's companies and to preserve good order and discipline on board. Taking a leading part in landing operations was soon added to the tasks of boarding parties and musketry teams in naval engagements. By the end of the nineteenth century longer-range engagements effectively eliminated the need for boarding, and even the most

modern rifle is irrelevant in a naval battle. The ever-growing pressure on
accommodation in ships crammed with engines, machinery, and magazines made it impossible to keep anybody on board who did not play a
part in the fighting organization. Every member of the Marine detachment had a place in a gun crew. Without them, part of the ship's
armament became non-operational. They could ill be spared for landing
parties. Yet six months was spent in training a Marine recruit to as high
a standard of infantry skills as any army regiment. Before he joined his
first ship, he would spend another appreciable spell training to be a
naval gunner: Marines were encouraged to specialize in a range of naval
gunnery qualifications, and other shipboard tasks, including joining the
Wireless Telegraphy (WT) department aboard major fleet units. (Until
after the Battle of Jutland in May 1916, a ship's WT department was
kept apart from the signals department, whose business was the flag and
light signals which controlled the fleet's manoeuvres and actions in
battle, and regarded as far more prestigious.)

The long-service regular sailor, no longer a pressed man, could be
trained as readily as the Marine to man the guns, and furthermore, as
one historian remarked, 'once it became apparent that sailors could no
longer have discipline imposed upon them by a separate corps with a
tradition and habit differing from their own, the concept of soldiers as
part of ships' crews became an anachronism.'[13]

Fisher's dislike of the Marines was echoed in the way they were treated
by some of more arrogant ship's captains of the day. The Marines
reciprocated by their attitude towards the Navy. General Sir Leslie Hollis
wrote:

> When I was first commissioned as an officer there was some lack of
> sympathy between marines and bluejackets. The reason for this by no
> means lay on the side of the navy. Before 1914, for example, service at sea
> was not popular with the marines, in part because of a feeling that fleet
> actions were bound to be few, and that service ashore therefore gave more
> scope against the enemy, and better opportunity for individuals to show
> courage, initiative and ability.[14]

Marines who held the opinion expressed above were proved right by the
events of the war that came in 1914.

In 1912, by which time Fisher had retired, the Admiralty considered
that the fleet might need advanced naval bases, and appointed a

committee to consider the organization of a flying column of 3,000 Marines, for securing and holding an advanced base of the fleet, in either British, neutral, or hostile territory. Half of this flying column would consist of active service ranks and the remainder reserves. In 1913 the committee recommended that these tasks be expanded to securing and covering the landing of a large force on a hostile coast and raiding the enemy. Unfortunately no decision was made to implement the committee's recommendation before the outbreak of war in 1914. Nevertheless, as we shall see, when war came the Marines did carry out some of these tasks; but to begin with, without a permanent, properly trained force, some of the results were mixed and others downright amateur. By not putting in train a reform of Marine duties, including dispensing with ship's detachments and using the manpower thus released to create a permanently constituted expert landing force in the early years of the twentieth century, Fisher missed a golden opportunity to give the Corps a new direction. The Royal Marines had to wait for more than thirty years before this day dawned.

One innovation that came about in 1903 was giving the Marines responsibility for providing bands afloat. Until then, each Marine Division had its own band, but bands at sea were found by engaging civilian musicians for the period of a particular ship's commission; only the buglers were Marines. Horace Bethell, the RMLI bugler on board HMS *Inflexible* in 1890/91, remembered that 'the bandsmen were all Italians, who wore blue serge suits with white piping on the edges'. From 1903 until 1950 there were two types of Marine bandsmen: the divisional musicians, who spent their whole service in that band, and never went to sea; and products of the Royal Naval School of Music, actually run by the Royal Marines, who were drafted from ship to ship as required. Senior naval officers became very possessive about their bands, and in later years, whenever the future existence of the Marines as a whole was threatened, more cynical Marine officers would speculate – only half in jest – that only the prospect of the admirals losing their bands would save the day.

At the end of the nineteenth century and leading up to the First World War, the training of Marines, both Blue and Red, was conducted at a fairly leisurely pace; and lacking endurance and assault courses, or long exercises in bad weather over rugged terrain, was, by today's standards, neither physically nor mentally very testing, but with plenty of irksome 'bull', hassle, and ritual. Horace Bethell joined at the age of fourteen and completed eight months' training as a drummer, bugler, and fifer at the RMLI Portsmouth Division at Forton Barracks in Gosport. Later he transferred to 'the ranks' as a private, which the majority of boy drummers did when they reached the age of seventeen, continuing their career in the RMLI or RMA. This practice continued until well after the Second World War, and one could usually pick out the ex-drummers because almost invariably they had the nickname 'Sticks', alluding to their drumsticks. On transfer, Bethell was sent to Deal, the RMLI Recruit Depot, for six months' training with a squad of men who had joined directly from civilian life, and back to his Division for gunnery training, followed, in his case, by a signalling course.

Fred Brookes's father was a Marine who deserted in Australia after eighteen years' service, leaving his wife and three children in England. He was never seen again. Fred Brookes joined as a boy bugler at Stonehouse Barracks near Plymouth, having been in the Marine School in the Barracks since he was seven years old. He remembered:

Stonehouse was mainly a marine town. Because marines who were married had to live within 2 miles of barracks. So Stonehouse was full of marines. The Officer of the day would go round and ask landlords how the tenants were behaving. Buglers used to go round the streets of Stonehouse and sound assembly in an emergency. Also in cold or wet weather they would sound 'great-coats for guard', to give married men time to get their greatcoats off their packs and all their equipment loosened to go on over their greatcoat.

Drummers, privates, and NCOs ate in their barrack-rooms.

Each member of the room except the NCO and the 'old soldier' [trained private, usually addressed as 'trained soldier' up to the late 1950s] took their turn to do 'cooks'. The 'cooks' fetched the meals from the cookhouse and washed up after each meal. They fetched bread and meat from the Quartermaster's store and vegetables from the canteen. Dinners were prepared by the 'old soldier', which included a sweet for afters. When prepared, the room's 'cooks' took the dishes to the cookhouse [where they were cooked].

The mornings were mostly spent on drill. At 1.30 p.m. drummers went to physical drill (physical training – PT), gymnastics, or swimming instruction. This last activity was taken seriously by both Red and Blue

Marines ever since the *Victoria* sank in 1892 and sixty-eight members of her ninety-eight strong Marine detachment drowned, mainly because they could not swim. Brookes:

> Physical drill was carried out either on the parade or in the Drill Shed, and I thoroughly detested it. We drilled with back-boards. These were real instruments of torture especially if the instructor was vicious. The object of the exercise was to straighten the back and throw out the chest. As you ran an agonising pain paralysed the muscles of your arms as the board was jolted down at each step and your shoulder blades forced together at the same time. I have seen tears in many of the boys' eyes while doing this drill.
>
> At 3.15 pm we fell in and marched to school for an hour's schooling to enable us to pass for the necessary educational certificates to carry us through the service. After school a race ensued to get to the room early, as the bread ration left little for tea as far as healthy boys were concerned. Only the first half dozen were lucky to find a slice, the rest having to go without. These latter would scrounge a few coppers and patronise the Refreshment Room.
>
> At 5.0 pm flute [fife] practice was carried out in the rooms until 6.0 pm. After which were allowed out until 8 pm.

Back in barracks after their two hours of freedom,

> Bugles and drums were cleaned ready for the following day. Tin-Gear was also cleaned; all the barrack-room utensils, breadbarges, zinc buckets, tin dishes, knives, spoons and forks, iron fender, coal bunces, stove, fire irons etc. Everyone was responsible for some article and woe betide the boy whose Tin-Gear was not to the old soldier's liking.
>
> The older buglers were allowed out until 10 pm with a midnight pass once a week. These were buglers who had been afloat. Only married men were allowed out all night and were in possession of a reveille pass.
>
> On Wednesdays and Saturdays the boys were allowed out from 2 pm until 10 pm. On these days all our equipment was inspected before we were allowed ashore.[15] Every strap was cleaned and pipe-clayed inside and out, and the brasses polished. Drums were taken to pieces, polished, put together and pulled in, the toggles pipe-clayed. Bugles were polished and the whole laid out on beds for inspection by the Duty Corporal. Any article rejected by him had to be re-cleaned and re-inspected before you were allowed out.
>
> On Saturday forenoons we bathed and shifted clean underclothes. Boys living locally took their washing home. Others took it to the barrack

laundry where women were employed who charged a set price for each article.

On Sundays we had a glorious lay-in until 7 am. By attending Communion at 8 am, we were free for the rest of the day. This did not apply of course to those passed fit for duty [i.e. had passed their drum, bugle, and fife tests], as they were required as members of the drum and fife band to play at Church Parade. Attendance at church was compulsory except for we boys.

Brookes, who also transferred to the ranks when he became seventeen, remembers the 'bull' at Stonehouse when the Commandant inspected his company while he was still a young bugler:

At the Commandant's inspection, one company per week, everything had to be spotless. In the barrack rooms, you would line up, and scrub away. Water had to be fetched in buckets up three flights of stairs from the tap downstairs. I had just left school. It was difficult trying to keep the zinc bucket from rubbing a black mark on the stripe on my trousers. Every drop of water that came up, and every drop mopped up had to be carried up or down the stairs. On the floor would go the sheets from your bed, and on top your blankets, they did not come up until the last minute before inspection. The day of the inspection, 'don't touch this, keep outside'. Everybody was kept out of barracks until 12 noon the time of the inspection. All equipment spotless. The NCOs came round brushing you down all the time. Then you fell in for inspection. By then you didn't care if it was Christmas or Easter.

William Durrant joined in 1902, but as an adult recruit.

I tried to join the Scots Greys because I liked their scarlet tunics, and found the regiment was over-strength. I saw an RM sergeant and he said 'Why not join the Blue Marines?' I passed the doctor, was given a day's pay, and was told to report two day's later. I was sent down to Eastney Barracks by train, and reported to the sergeant on the gate. From here I was taken to the 'receiving room'. There was no dinner [lunch]. For tea I had dried bread and basin of tea. An old gunner showed us around: the gym, dry canteen where you could buy bacon, eggs etc. and then to the [wet] canteen where there were some fine looking gunners. All the time there were bugle calls going which we didn't know. In the morning at reveille, the old gunner showed us where bathrooms and heads [lavatories] were. We were marched to QM's store and kitted out. We started drill on the parade. In those days you could purchase out for £10 [about forty-three weeks' gross pay for a private] for up to [your first] three months [service].

When Horace Bethell joined, 'a private got 4s 8d a week, a corporal got 9s 2d a week, and a sergeant got 16s per week.'

After finishing training at Eastney, William Durrant joined his ship on the China station at Wei Hei Wei, and was made corporal of the gangway as an acting bombardier. After the ship paid off, the detachment was sent back to barracks, the RMA to Eastney, and the RMLI to Forton, Chatham, or Stonehouse. How long a man might have in barracks depended on how many ships were commissioning; on occasions for six months, or longer.

He describes a typical routine on board a warship:

We mixed with Red Marines in mess decks. Blue Marines were carried on battleships and battle-cruisers only. We manned the main armament, the RMLI manned the secondary armament.

The Marine officers inspected us every morning at divisions at 0900. After this we doubled round the ship, followed by PT and both watches for exercise [practising shipboard evolutions or action stations]. Then working parties [painting, chipping paintwork, ship's housework in general]. Dinner was at 1200. Working parties again and at 1600 evening quarters to muster the ship's company. We had one fourth of the armament. I was second captain of the turret, in charge of hydraulic machinery.

Even in 1913, the training of officers was conducted at a leisurely and old-fashioned pace; much of it was irrelevant to the conditions they would face in the battles that lay unseen just round the corner. One of the fifty-nine still under training when the war broke out was Second Lieutenant Arthur Chater:

On 30th September 1913, twenty-one young men of seventeen or eighteen, arrived at the Royal Naval College Greenwich on first appointment as Probationary Second Lieutenants in the Royal Marines. We were all rather pleased with ourselves in our new uniforms, which we wore very badly. To us at that time, wars seemed very far away. Little did we think that within two years four of us would be killed in battle. In the mess one night I drank with Richard Foote to the 'first time we would be under fire'. Within a bare year he had been killed, and I had been wounded.

After nine months at Greenwich, wasted in acquiring knowledge which we never used, we moved to Deal where our military training began.

On the outbreak of the First World War the Blue and Red Marines were more technically advanced, especially in gunnery, than their late Victorian predecessors, but the manner of their employment had changed little. Indeed it could be argued that their prospects in terms of independent action, excitement, and adventure were considerably worse than those experienced by their forebears in the Napoleonic Wars that had ended just under a century before.

The Marines relished the opportunity to fight ashore. In October 1910, George Nettleton was the post corporal in HMS *Newcastle* in Gibraltar, when he noted in his diary that the ship received 'Orders to proceed to Lisbon at once with all possible speed. The cause being revolutionary riots.' Portugal was in the middle of a constitutional crisis that eventually led to the abdication of King Manuel II, and the country becoming a republic. On arrival at Lisbon, HMS *Newcastle*'s captain visited the British Consul, presumably to discuss the evacuation of British nationals. Although George Nettleton's diary does not say why *Newcastle* was in Lisbon, he recorded: 'Everybody ready for immediate landing. Visions of war medals. Several Portuguese warships coming up the river all flying Republican flags. Reports [sound] of rifle firing coming from shore. Great excitement aboard. All want to get ashore.'

Hopes that the ship's company of *Newcastle* might be treated to the sight of fighting between republican ships and those loyal to the King of Portugal were dashed. Eventually *Newcastle* was ordered to return to Gibraltar and onwards to China, her new station.

'No medal', recorded George Nettleton. In four years' time he and many other Royal Marines were to get all the fighting they wanted – although thousands of them would not live to receive their medals.

PART TWO

THE FIRST WORLD WAR

AND ITS IMMEDIATE AFTERMATH

Introduction to Part Two

In the First World War and immediately afterwards the Royal Marines served, as was their wont in previous wars, in dozens of places round the globe, and in a myriad roles. Marines, both Red and Blue, could be found in ships in almost every sea and ocean, and on land from northern China and Siberia to East and West Africa, from Murmansk to the Falklands. Royal Marines flew, they garrisoned advance bases in some of the dreariest spots on earth, they even served in Q-ships. No attempt is made to cover all their activities over a period of five or more years.

The men in Royal Marines units who served on the Western Front, along with those at Gallipoli, spent longer in action, saw far more fighting, and suffered considerably greater casualties than any other members of their Corps in the First World War. Marines in France and Belgium, with their comrades in arms of the British Army, fought the main body of the German Army, one of the best armies the world has ever seen: no light task. Compared with the rest of the Corps engaged, and all too often not engaged, elsewhere, these Marines were a minority, and towards the end a tiny minority. As well as formed units, they included a substantial number of officers who commanded Royal Naval Battalions in the RN Division and Army battalions, and held staff appointments in Army formations. But, out of the whole Corps in the First World War, this minority were the only Marines fighting on what modern soldiers call the main point of effort. The space devoted to Gallipoli and the Western Front reflects the scale of the Corps's contribution in the number of engagements and the price paid.

It is right, considering the number of Marines who served in that Fleet for over four years, that Jutland, the only fleet action fought by the Grand Fleet in the entire war, should also be covered and given a chapter of its own. Due attention is also paid to the great raid on

Zeebrugge, where Marines fought in one of their traditional roles. The
Russian aftermath is included, because Royal Marine involvement in that
country following the revolution is so little known, and there is a moral
to the story.

3

The Outbreak of the
First World War:
The First Months

Commence hostilities against Germany.

Signal from the Admiralty, 4 August 1914

The British fleet, including embarked Royal Marines, was mobilized seven days before Britain declared war on Germany on 4 August 1914. Over the weekend Saturday 25 and Sunday 26 July 1914, the Home Fleet was assembled at Weymouth giving shore leave, following a practice mobilization that had been planned months before. The practice had been used as an opportunity to exercise the recall of seamen and Marine reservists (who had completed seven years' service and had a five-year reserve liability), so the crews of all thirty-two battleships and battle-cruisers, and twenty cruisers and fifty destroyers of the Home Fleet were at war strength. The fleet was due to disperse on Monday, and after landing reservists, reduce to peacetime ship's complements.

Following the assassination of the heir to the Austrian throne by a Serb terrorist a month earlier in Bosnian Sarajevo, the prospect of general war in Europe had increased at an ever accelerating pace. The Austrians, encouraged by the German Kaiser, presented fifteen deliberately humiliating demands to Serbia in an ultimatum which would give them an excuse to invade when, as they hoped, Serbia refused to comply. If invaded, Serbia would be aided by Russia, who in turn would be supported by France. This would give the Germans the longed-for opportunity to smash first the French, followed by the Russians. The unknown factor was Britain, who had no desire to become involved in a war in Europe, much to the irritation of the French, who had allowed themselves to believe that Franco/British staff talks in the years before 1914 automatically guaranteed British assistance in the event of war with Germany. With war looming, and the possibility of a surprise attack by the German fleet, now was not the time to lower the Royal Navy's readiness. So the First Sea Lord, Admiral Prince Louis of Battenburg, without seeking permission from the First Lord of the Admiralty, Winston Churchill (who was out of London), but knowing that he would have approved, sent a signal late on Sunday night cancelling the fleet dispersal and release of reservists.

On Monday 27 July, the German High Seas Fleet was recalled from a cruise in Norwegian waters to its war bases. On Tuesday, the Germans, seeing the opportunity to go to war fading, as the Serbs swallowed their pride and bowed to all but one of the Austrian demands, advised Austria to invade Serbia to present the world with a fait accompli. The British Foreign Secretary implored the Austrians to desist, but the Austrian Ambassador in London told him that to postpone or prevent war with Serbia 'would undoubtedly be a great disappointment in this country [Austria], which has gone wild with joy at the prospect of war'.[1] The following evening, in the hope of deterring the Germans by demonstrating Britain's readiness to fight if need be, Churchill ordered the fleet to its war bases. On Wednesday 29 July the Kaiser, having read for the first time the text of the Austrian ultimatum and Serbian reply, wrote privately to his Foreign Secretary that there was now no cause for Austria to invade and start a war. Too late; an hour later Austria declared war on Serbia. That same day the British fleet headed for the Straits of Dover, and north to its war base at Scapa Flow.

> We may now picture this great fleet, with its flotillas and cruisers, steaming slowly out of Portland Harbour, squadron by squadron, scores of gigantic castles of steel wending their way across the misty, shining sea like giants bowed in anxious thought. We may picture them again as darkness fell, eighteen miles of warships running at high speed and in absolute blackness through the narrow Straits, bearing with them into the broad waters of the North the safeguard of considerable affairs.... The King's ships were at sea.[2]

There were still five days to run before the Germans invaded Belgium, the act that was to propel the British into the war.

Russia, Germany, and France mobilized. Germany declared war on Russia. 'This criminal act of yours', the Russian Foreign minister told the German Ambassador when he handed him the German declaration of war, 'you could have prevented war by one word; you didn't want to.' German patrols entered French territory and declared war on France. Britain stood aside until the Germans announced their intention of invading Belgium, whose neutrality was guaranteed by Britain by treaty. The British demand that Germany respect Belgian neutrality was ignored.

Arthur Chater had just joined the Royal Marines Depot at Deal to start his military training.

> July 1914 was a perfect summer month. The AGRM [Adjutant General Royal Marines][3] carried out his annual inspection of the Depot RM. As the days passed by, excitement in the events in Europe increased. We awoke on Thursday 30th July to be told that many of the trained soldiers were to leave the Depot that day for their mobilization stations. On Saturday [1 August 1914], a cricket match was being played on the South Green when between overs at about 4 pm, an orderly came across the field to give a message to the staff officer who was keeping wicket. This was the order for the Navy to mobilise. Within a few minutes buglers were sounding the 'general assembly' around the town. Many of the staff and senior recruits left Deal that evening.
>
> Church on Sunday morning [2 August 1914] was a moving and for some a very sorrowful service. Immediately after lunch, the twenty-one Second Lieutenants were called to the Commandant's office, and told we were to leave that evening to join our RM Divisions. We were given five minutes in which to choose our Division in order of seniority. I chose Chatham because it was nearest to Germany. Five of us arrived at Chatham that night, and found the whole Division on parade under arms, as though expecting an invasion, although war was not declared until over twenty-four hours later.

When Britain declared war on Germany, on 4 August 1914, the Royal Navy and the British public eagerly awaited a second Trafalgar, one great battle in which the enemy would be swept from the sea, and the war won at a stroke. Some naval officers spoke of this event occurring by the end of August, even quicker than the 'we'll be home by Christmas' to which the soldiers marched off to war.

Approximately 10,000 Marines were at sea in the Grand Fleet and elsewhere, and some were present at the early clashes at sea. On 28 August the light cruiser force based at Harwich 'trailed its coat' in the Heligoland Bight to tempt the Germans out to where Admiral Sir David Beatty waited with his battlecruisers *Lion*, *Queen Mary*, *Princess Royal*, *Invincible*, and *New Zealand*. The ruse was successful, and the German heavy cruisers *Ariadne*, *Köln*, and *Mainz* were sunk. Marines fought in the twelve cruisers as well as in the five battlecruisers at Heligoland.

Nearly 200 Marines were lost at the Battle of Coronel (1 November 1914) when the light cruisers *Good Hope* and *Monmouth* were sunk by Admiral von Spee's more powerful squadron of heavy cruisers. But their comrades in the battlecruisers *Invincible* and *Inflexible*, and cruisers *Bristol*, *Caernarvon*, *Cornwall*, *Kent*, and *Glasgow* (a survivor from Coronel), took part in turning the tables on Spee in the Battle of the Falklands on 8 December 1914. Only the cruiser *Dresden* escaped; *Gneisenau*, *Leipzig*, *Nürnburg*, and *Scharnhorst* went to the bottom, with Spee.

On 10 December 1914, Captain Robert Sinclair RMLI, the second-in-command of the Royal Marines turret in the battlecruiser HMS *Inflexible*, wrote to his cousin Lucy:

Now at last I think the rules of censorship must be relaxed & I can give an account of the action from my point of view. You must remember that my station in action is in the turret superintending the loading of the guns so I am shut in behind armour & unable to see what is going on outside – the only information we inside could get was from the gunlayers at their telescopes & from the Major at his periscope, & they during the action were so busy that they could not tell us much, & indeed they could not see more than the particular ships at which they were firing, & even that was very frequently obscured by the smoke of our own guns & the explosions of our shells. Little did we think in the morning of 8 December that before the night we should have engaged the entire German squadron of 5 ships & have sunk all except one! The forenoon of the 7th saw the arrival at Port William in the Falkland Islands of our squadron. It had been feared that the German squadron would take the Islands & then proceed to the African coast & it was essential that we should get south as soon as possible – as it happened we arrived not a moment too soon. We are apt to imagine that the Germans know all our movements, but on this occasion they were entirely deceived & must have had a tremendous shock when they realised what ships were waiting for them. At 7 in the morning of the 8th we began coaling & were to take in 1,500 tons; soon after 8 it was reported that [indecipherable] had been sighted, and the colliers were shoved off & we began to make ready to leave harbour. While the *Kent* and *Glasgow* who were not coaling went out at once to find out who our visitors were, *Invincible*, *Inflexible*, *Caernarvon*, *Cornwall*, & *Bristol* followed shortly afterwards & it was indeed the German squadron whom we had come all these thousands of miles to meet – we could hardly believe our good fortune! Black as we were [from coaling], we went to action stations, everyone full of enthusiasm.[4] As soon as the *Kent* & *Glasgow* emerged from the harbour, the Germans turned away evidently intending to draw them out for at first they did not know that lurking behind were two large battlecruisers. From the prisoners on board we learned that one officer of the *Gneisenau* reported to his Captain that he saw the tripod masts of 2 battlecruisers & that at first he was not believed, but come the bogey men [sic] & they tried their hardest to escape, but we knew we could catch them & action was inevitable – We were still a long way from them so the hands were piped to clean & after a hurried bath I went on deck and there for the first time I saw the enemy – it was a lovely morning, very calm blue sea & blue sunny sky & far away, funnels & masts showing only, were the 5 ships, *Scharnhorst*, *Gneisenau*, *Nürnburg*, *Dresden*, and *Leipzig*, with volumes of black smoke pouring from their funnels – it was a beautiful picture & a little difficult to realize that shortly we would be doing our utmost to destroy them all! All this time our engine room department were working hard & rising to the occasion magnificently & we soon had our full speed available – The hands went to dinner just before 12, & soon after the Captain informed us that the Admiral intended to engage the enemy at once. This announcement was received with a storm of cheers (contrary to all regulations)! & the men rushed to their stations laughing & joking with their eyes sparkling with joy. I have seldom seen such enthusiasm. We hear that when the *Glasgow* appeared from the harbour the Germans also cheered but then they did not know what was to follow. The action was in two parts. Shortly before 1 pm we fired the first rounds & for some time had no reply, but the *Scharnhorst* and *Gneisenau* knowing that it was impossible to get away gave battle while the German light cruisers made off followed by *Kent*, *Glasgow*, and I think, *Cornwall*. The *Caernarvon* followed us up & only arrived on the scene about an hour before the end. The first part of the action lasted about an hour, resulting in damage to us & none to the enemy so far as we could see, though I daresay that they had been hit. At any rate their speed was not affected, nor were any of their guns out of action.

We had an hour's rest & there was a general search for souvenirs in the shape of fragments of shell.

It was our first occasion under fire & and it might be interesting to know our sensation. Speaking for myself, I felt quite normal & not the least excited, but then I was behind armour and hardly realised that anyone was firing at us. The men in the turret were the same & I think far cooler than at battle practice, when there is usually some little tension & extreme anxiety. Now we were doing the real thing for which we have been practising for so long & the only fault I could find was that the men were inclined to joke & talk – there's enough noise in a turret without that.

After closing up again we renewed the action & engaged the *Scharnhorst*, flag ship of Admiral von Spee. After some time she was seen to have a heavy list to starboard & her guns ceased to fire, upon which we left her and proceeded to engage *Gneisenau* who was already being dealt with by the flag ship. The *Scharnhorst* very shortly afterwards went down with her colours still flying & I am afraid that all hands must have been lost for we could not stop to save life while the *Gneisenau* was still unbeaten. She fought most gallantly against two ships & her sinking was only a matter of time. She took a lot of hammering & had a very terrible time. One by one her guns ceased firing. When it was seen that she could do no more, the cease fire was sounded & we closed her to save life. We all climbed out of the turret & stood on the top & there just ahead of us I saw the ship bows on to us with a heavy list to starboard. She slowly heeled over & finally disappeared leaving many men in the icy cold water hanging on to what they could find floating about. It was a terrible sight & the cries of the men in the water were heart-rending. We threw them over all the wood & life buoys we could find & lowered as many boats as we could. Some men supported by lashed-up hammocks swam towards us & we hauled them up over the side. They were taken below and at once attended to. The men I think are very glad that they will take no further part in the war & I believe they were told they would be shot if they became prisoners. Many of the men speak English & all the officers do.

In January 1915 the Marine detachments in the five battlecruisers and four light cruisers of Beatty's battlecruiser squadron took part in the action off Dogger Bank, in which Beatty intercepted three German battlecruisers, a heavy cruiser, and several light cruisers returning from bombarding Yarmouth, Scarborough, Whitby, and Hartlepool. In the ensuing engagement the German heavy cruiser *Blücher* was sunk. The remaining Germans turned tail and fled at high speed and, thanks to poor signalling and lack of initiative on the part of Beatty's captains, escaped. For the next eighteen months the Grand Fleet, of which Beatty's battlecruiser squadron was a part, saw no more action.

*

On 2 August 1914 the Admiralty ordered the formation of the 'Flying Column' Royal Marines. It will be remembered that plans for this formation had been made in 1912 and 1913, but nothing had been done to implement them. Not surprisingly equipment for what eventually became the Royal Marine (RM) Brigade was not available, and they went on their first operation wearing blue uniform. It is a measure of the half-baked nature of Admiralty plans for amphibious operations that although they had vague concepts of employing the 'Flying Column' in fighting ashore, they failed to take the elementary step of providing khaki uniforms, at the very least.

Initially each division, Plymouth, Portsmouth, Chatham, and, oddly, the RMA, provided a battalion. By a tremendous effort of organization the brigade concentrated at Portsmouth within three days of the order to form. Two weeks later, on 20 August, the Admiralty ordered it to disperse to the divisions, and the brigade staff were disbanded. Suddenly, on 25 August, the brigade was ordered to embark for Ostend that night, occasioned by alarm that the Germans might seize this important Channel port which the Admiralty wanted as a base for the RNAS. After this order and counter-order, it is hardly surprising that considerable disorder ensued, especially as at this stage no mission was given, so that battalions took all their stores 'just in case', and the men were excessively overloaded as a result. Brigadier General Sir George Aston RMA was appointed Brigade Commander. He was one of a small band of Royal Marines officers who had spent much of his service with the Army, away from the lacklustre routines of ship or barracks, including serving for some years as a colonel at the Army Staff College. (He is the only Royal Marine ever to do so, although plenty have served there as lieutenant colonels on the Directing Staff.) On taking over his Brigade, Aston found he had no staff, and quickly make some ad hoc appointments.

Aston's orders, which he brought with him when his brigade had embarked in the 7th Battle Squadron, were to take up a defensive position round Ostend, keeping close to the coast so remaining under the protection of the guns of the fleet. He had no cavalry for reconnaissance, no logistic vehicles or organization, no engineers, and no artillery. Since man-portable radios, or wireless as he would have called it, had not yet been developed, he would have had to rely on heliograph or flag signals to direct the fire of the fleet, which, without land artillery, was his only fire support.

He did however have some aircraft and airships of the RNAS, under Commander Samson RN. These flew over from England, but no one had seen fit to warn the brigade, who almost opened fire on them, providing an early example of the normal reaction of soldiers to the approach of unidentified aircraft in war which can be summed up in a remark made to the author during an air attack nearly seventy years later: 'We'll shoot 'em all down, and sort it out on the ground afterwards.'

Later some armoured cars of the RNAS were landed, and their mobile patrols reported that there was no enemy in the vicinity. The brigade saw no action, although rumours that it was the advance guard of a substantial force alarmed German intelligence, who feared it would pose a threat to the flank of their advance through Belgium and France. The brigade remained for a week, before being withdrawn to England, partly because the 7th Battle Squadron was vulnerable to submarine attacks; the first time in history, but not the last, that fleet dispositions in support of operations ashore would be influenced by such considerations. 'The whole operations [sic] has been carried out in such a way as to be a credit to the Marine Corps', gushed the Admiralty in a signal.

After arriving back in England, the RMA battalion was replaced by RMLI from Deal, which made more sense. Plans to form the RMA battalion into the artillery unit of what was to become the Royal Naval Division came to naught because at that stage of the war there were insufficient 18-pounder guns available, and the RMA was absorbed into Howitzer and Anti-Aircraft Brigades which served with the Army in France, of which more later.

The RM Brigade was now known as the 3rd Brigade of the Royal Naval Division. As the Royal Marines were to give their longest, most continuous service in the First World War, and (at the risk of being contentious) their most valuable contribution to the war effort, in this division, we must briefly digress to see how this remarkable formation was born.

One of the projected tasks for the Royal Marine 'Flying Column', now a brigade, had been to seize and protect any temporary naval bases which might be needed by the fleet either for its own use or in conjunction with the landing and support of the Army in the field. Shortly after the outbreak of war, the Admiralty, concerned about German threats to the RNAS bases on the Belgian coast, decided to add to the RM Brigade two brigades of naval reservists from those surplus to requirement after bringing the fleet up to full strength. In September the likelihood of a German advance to the Belgian coast increased. At the same time the War Office was unable to find any trained formations to operate in this area, and furthermore was pressing the Navy to accept in the Naval Brigades some of the mass of the Kitchener volunteers whom the Army could neither train nor equip. The Admiralty, with the full support of Field Marshal Lord Kitchener, the Secretary of State for War, decided to form the two brigades of naval reservists and the RM Brigade into an infantry division.

The naval brigades were for a time commanded by commodores, although Heaven knows what qualifications they had to command a platoon, let alone a brigade. Some of the naval battalions were commanded by commanders RN, and the others by lieutenant colonels of the Foot Guards; all had majors from the RMLI or Foot Guards as seconds-in-command. The four naval battalions in each brigade were given admirals' names.

The RN Division was lucky in the quality of some of its officers, including the Prime Minister's son Arthur Asquith, who rose to become a highly decorated commanding officer. By far the most distinguished was Bernard Freyberg, a champion swimmer, dental student, and Territorial officer in New Zealand. He was to win a Victoria Cross leading the Hood Battalion later in the War, transfer to the Grenadier Guards after the First World War, and command the New Zealand Division throughout the Second. Many of the junior officers from the Royal Naval Volunteer Reserve (RNVR) were mature men who had already made their way in civilian life before the war, and although their soldiering was perforce learnt on the job were quick to assimilate the necessary skills. Similarly many of the men were individualists. Both combined to give the RN Division a character of its own which it preserved to the

end, despite many vicissitudes, and dilution by thousands of replacements with no naval background as the war took its toll and the needs
of the fleet meant many of the other ranks were replaced by Army
recruits.

At this stage there was no divisional commander. The naval brigades
of the RN Division suffered, as did their fellow New Army formations,
from Britain's unreadiness to fight a major war on the continent of
Europe, and from consequences of the amateur, if enthusiastic, efforts
that ensued when they found themselves in contact with the enemy for
the first time.

Arthur Chater rejoined the Chatham Battalion after a frustrating
period.

> Our early days at Chatham were spent watching elderly Reservists being
> kitted-up, and doing a little spasmodic training. When the RM Brigade
> was formed to go to Ostend, we were first put under orders to go with
> it, and then – to our bitter grief – we were taken out again; but when
> after only a few days the Brigade returned, and was reformed, we were
> appointed to it, and told to provide ourselves with khaki uniform and
> camp kit. I was proud to be in command of No 1 Platoon of A Company.
> I was eighteen. My company Commander a 'dug-out' Major was thirty-
> five years older then me. On 12 September the RM Brigade was concen-
> trated for training in camp near St Margaret's Bay. We had been there
> just a week, and training had barely started, when, on 19 September we
> marched to Dover, and embarked for France.
>
> Landing next morning at Dunkirk, the RM Brigade was first in billets
> and then in camp for some days, during which time the men's blue
> uniform was changed for khaki. The Battalion then moved to Cassel,
> from where we carried out patrolling – in London motor buses.

The RM Brigade would shortly face the most formidable army in the
world. Some of the Marines had completed basic training, but others,
including Chater, had certainly not, and none had done any collective
training to speak of. They were at least spared fighting in blue uniforms
and that military abomination the Brodrick cap.

The RM Brigade was sent to Dunkirk as a result of a request from the
C-in-C British Expeditionary Force (BEF) in France and the French
government. By mid-September, the German advance had been checked
at the Battle of the Marne, and the Allied (French and British) counterattack stopped in its turn on the River Aisne. This had been followed by

the phase known as the 'race to the sea', as both armies moved in a more or less north-westerly direction towards the Belgian coast, in an attempt to find each other's flanks, and renew the offensive. The Germans could not be allowed to win the race and seize the Channel ports through which the BEF was supplied, as well as threatening the Allied left flank.

Winston Churchill, the First Lord of the Admiralty, wrote to Aston on 18 September 1914:

General Aston
1. You will proceed with your Brigade, 2,600 strong or more, but without latest recruits, during 19th September, to Dunkirk. You will there assume command of a mixed force as follows:–
    i) The Marine Brigade.
    ii) Queen's Own Oxfordshire Hussars.
    iii) Commander Samson's aeroplanes and armed motor cars.
    iv) 20 Royal Engineers.
2. You will work in harmony with the Governor of Dunkirk, and establish yourself within his lines, which are strong and extensive.
3. You will give the impression to the enemy that you are the advance guard of a considerable British force acting against the German communications. But in effect your strength only enables you to demonstrate. Minor enterprises to cut railway lines may be launched with armed motor cars where possible; but the main body of your force must make sure of its retreat to Dunkirk if seriously threatened. Germans can undoubtedly bring over-whelming forces, both cavalry and infantry, to bear if they choose. Such a concentration by the enemy would achieve your object.
4. As a guide, subject to circumstances, your mounted forces may in the first instance push forward on a 25 mile radius from Dunkirk to Ypres and Hazebruck with patrols to Lille and perhaps Arras, and your armed motor cars covered by aeroplane reconnaissance till they make contact. After that you must act according to circumstances, reporting daily.
WSC
18.9.

The armed motor cars consisted of a unit which had been formed from 150 officers and men taken from the RM Brigade after the Ostend foray, with the special task of operating with Samson's RNAS aircraft: a classic early example, if not the first, of a combination of motorized units and aircraft. Under the command of the appropriately named Major Risk RMLI, the force was known as the 'Motor Bandits'. Although referred to by some as armoured cars, the majority were not, and Churchill's term is accurate, as all were equipped with Vickers machine-guns. They had several encounters with German cavalry, who usually scattered at high speed. As well as disconcerting the enemy cavalry, the 'Motor Bandits' covered large areas of ground, and brought back valuable information.

Most of the RM Brigade remained at Dunkirk, and had no contact with the enemy. During this time Aston was evacuated sick, and replaced by Brigadier General Archibald Paris RMA. Like Aston, Paris had served for some of his time with the Army, which had given him a taste for something better in the way of career opportunities than the peacetime Royal Marines could offer. In some of his correspondence he talks of his dread of being appointed Second Commandant at Eastney (the RMA Division in Southsea), a humdrum job if ever there was one. Paris's first move was to shift most of his brigade, including his headquarters, to Cassel, where as recorded by Chater earlier they patrolled in buses. The drivers of these buses had been enlisted as Royal Marines at Chatham, and remained in France until the autumn of 1915.

On 30 September the main armies in the 'race for the sea' had reached Lens, and by 3 October some 60,000 German troops were closing on Antwerp. When the Germans broke through the outer line of the Antwerp forts, the Belgians announced their intention to withdraw most of their troops, leaving the defence to the fortress troops alone; the fall of Antwerp was imminent. The British government feared that if Antwerp fell the Germans might overrun Dunkirk, and even Calais, the BEF's port and supply base. Churchill was sent to Antwerp to try and persuade the Belgians to delay the withdrawal of their army, and prolong the defence of the city. The Belgians agreed, on condition the Allies provided assistance. Churchill ordered Paris's brigade into Antwerp.

Chater, with the Chatham Battalion:

> We detrained at Vieux Dieu late that evening, and slept the remainder of the night in billets. Early next morning we started marching along a typical straight Belgian road with tall poplars on either side. [The Lierre road.] Also typical of those days, the men were made to carry more than was humanly possible. Some men threw away the blankets they were

carrying in addition to full marching order with packs. During a halt
when we were fallen out under trees on the right of the road, we saw our
first enemy shell bursts of the war – shrapnel burst high in the air. Just
then we were ordered to fall in facing the road as the First Lord of the
Admiralty was coming to look at us. When Mr Winston Churchill reached
me he asked me how old I was. I had to answer 'Eighteen' in front of my
platoon, and so thought this a tactless question.

Churchill, excited at the prospect of action, which he always found hard
to resist, offered to resign from the Cabinet to take command of the
British forces at Antwerp. In the event he returned to England before
the battle for the city began, but his presence helped restore Belgian
confidence.

The RM Brigade relieved the 21st Belgian Regiment in trenches north
of the Petit Nethe. The trenches were badly dug and sited, being six feet
wide and only three feet deep, with no overhead protection or dugouts.
Chater:

A Company was allotted the main street, the bridge in front of us having
been blown up by the Belgians. We sent a party over the river to demolish
the nearest buildings, which would give cover to the enemy. The town
seemed deserted, but an old woman arrived with a shawl over her head,
carrying her possessions in a basket. The Marines took pity on the poor
old thing, and ferried her across the river and sent her on her way. We
heard later that 'she' was a young German spy, and had been shot by the
Belgians. The officers dined well that night, for their Marine servants
cooked some chickens they found running around, and produced a bottle
of wine from the cellar of a deserted casino.

That night the Germans brought up field guns to the bank of the river
and opened fire so that the advanced posts, of which Chater's company
occupied one, were ordered to withdraw to the main position. Chater:

Towards dawn there were two or three explosions in the road behind us
for which we could not account. We found later that in the dark the
Germans had mounted a gun in the street only some three hundred yards
in front of us, and were firing ranging shots. We stood-to before dawn.
As it was getting lighter, the German gun opened fire. I was looking over
the top of the parapet. A shell burst in front of me and spattered me in
my face. I rolled over and could see nothing, but was able to tell my
platoon sergeant to take over. I was dragged into a house and bandaged

up. Although I could not see, I could walk, and so I was led away to the rear, where I was examined by Dr Louis Greig who sent me to hospital in Antwerp.

Along the RM Brigade front the fighting intensified, and a counterattack by part of the RM Brigade restored positions lost by Belgians on their flanks. The next day the two RN Brigades arrived, and Paris was promoted to acting major general and appointed GOC of the RN Division. His divisional staff consisted of only four officers, two on temporary loan. At the same time Paris decided to withdraw to a position between the Nethe River and the inner forts surrounding Antwerp. All three brigades manned these positions, the sailors of the two Naval Brigades incongruous in their bell-bottom trousers tucked into leather gaiters, and still wearing their round sailors' hats.

A day later, as the Belgian troops on the RN Division's flanks began to crumble, Paris decided to withdraw to the inner line of forts. On 7 October the Germans crossed the River Scheldt between Ghent and Termonde, south-west of Antwerp, threatening to cut the communications between the city and the Channel coast. Paris, discerning that the Belgians were near to giving up the fight, was concerned that his division would be cut off in Antwerp. However, he determined to stay as long as possible, as the defences of the city were formidable and could be held provided they were stoutly defended. On the afternoon of 8 October, having relocated his headquarters alongside that of the Belgian fortress commander, he saw reports coming in of Belgians slipping away. Paris had been ordered by Churchill to exclude his division from any capitulation or surrender (by the Belgians), and as this moment was fast approaching, he ordered his division to withdraw.

A withdrawal, even out of contact with the enemy, is one of the most tricky tactical movements in war. If it is not to degenerate into a shambles, good planning, staff work, and control are essential. In this case, the division was fortunate that the enemy were not following up on their heels. Paris's problem was lack of a skilled staff, and of his three brigades, only one, the RM Brigade, had any training to speak of. His plan was for all brigades to make for a divisional rendezvous in the suburbs west of Antwerp, about fourteen miles from their defensive positions, and march from there to a railway station about seven miles further west in the expectation of continuing the journey to the coast by train: failing that, the division would march to the west towards Bruges and the sea. Unfortunately Paris never received a vital message telling him that Beveren-Waes (now on the N70), where he intended entraining his division, was threatened by the Germans, and that he should use another, St Gillaes-Waes, further to the west.

The order to withdraw, issued at about 1800 hours, was not received by the 1st Naval Brigade because of slipshod staff work by one of the divisional staff officers. This brigade, and the Portsmouth Battalion RMLI, detailed as their rearguard, eventually set off hours after the remainder of the division. At the Divisional RV, Paris was told incorrectly that all three brigades were present, and gave the order to move off again. When the division, less 1st Naval Brigade, arrived at Beveren-Waes, they learned that trains could only get as far as St Gillaes-Waes. Eventually, after an exhausting march through narrow lanes crammed with panicking refugees, they reached the station at 0700, and entrained at 0900.

The 1st Naval Brigade made good progress to the divisional RV, but on finding the remainder of the division had gone halted for two hours. After marching on for some hours, an error in map reading led them to cross the Dutch frontier. The Dutch, being neutral, interned the brigade commander, his headquarters, and the Hawke, Benbow, and Collingwood Battalions for the remainder of the war.

The Portsmouth Battalion RMLI, which had taken a different route, arrived at the RV to find, as Paris had, that the original entraining station could not be used. The Portsmouth Battalion under their commanding officer, Lieutenant Colonel Luard, set off and entrained at a station even further west than the one used by the rest of the division, acting on information from the Belgians that no trains were running from any nearer station. By now Luard's battalion had picked up some 600 stragglers from the 1st Naval Brigade. Luard's train had not gone far when it was partially derailed by a small German detachment. The Marines detrained at once and rallied round their officers. The sailors, stupefied by exhaustion, remained asleep on the train. Most of the Portsmouth Battalion fought their way out of the ambush, and made good their escape by road, but some Marines who had got out on the far side of the train went into the bag with the sailors.

The Antwerp operation was criticized at the time, but by holding out until 10 October the RN Division enabled Lieutenant General Sir Henry

Rawlinson to establish a strong force at Ghent, while the Belgians managed to retreat in reasonably good order, and the BEF to go firm on the line of the River Yser. The enemy were thus barred from taking Calais, Boulogne, and Dunkirk. After the war, the King of the Belgians wrote in a memorandum which was a record of a conversation he had with Paris in 1918:

> You are wrong in considering the Royal Naval Division Expedition as a forlorn hope . . . in the case of Antwerp the delay the Royal Naval Division caused the enemy was of inestimable service to us. Those three days allowed the French and British Armies to move north-west. Otherwise our whole [Belgian] Army might have been captured and the northern French ports secured by the enemy.[5]

Battle casualties to the RN Division were light by First World War standards, 60 dead and 138 wounded; but 37 officers and 1,442 men were interned, and 936 became prisoners of war. Chater was one of the wounded who got away.

> I was lucky to be taken over by the British Field Hospital for the Belgians, who took me by car to Ostend, and thence to London. My eyes were examined, and it was found that I had partially lost the sight of one eye. When my sight had sufficiently recovered, I rejoined the Battalion at Chatham, where training continued.

In September 1914, the Royal Marines had introduced short service engagements for officers and men. Without these willing and versatile volunteers the smooth expansion of the Corps from 17,000 to 55,000 would have been impossible. One of the officers was the twenty-three-year-old Walter Ward, educated at Marlborough and Oxford. He wrote to his parents from Eastney Barracks on 29 September 1914 to describe his first day in the Royal Marines:

> Dear Mother and Daddy
>   This is a most awfully nice place & there are a nice lot of men here.
>   We paraded in a squad this morning at 8.30, & were served out with rifles and equipment. Then we were taken to see the Commandant, & at about 9.30 we started to drill on the cricket field. We went at a terrific rate, in squads of about 6 men under a very efficient sergeant, who always salutes us when he dismisses us. I daresay you have seen that we were gazetted [as Second Lieutenants] today, as from the 20th.

No doubt Ward found life in the palatial officers mess at Eastney more agreeable than living in a barrack room. One of the first privates recruited under the short service scheme was Thomas Baker:

> I saw in an evening paper that men were wanted for the Royal Marines for the duration of War. On 19 September 1914 I enlisted at Whitehall, and got sent to Chatham. I arrived at Barracks, and was met by a Sergeant at the gate, and allocated to companies. I went to A company. We were told there would be no parades until we got uniforms, and we would not be allowed out either. Our bedding consisted of a straw palliasse. Periodically we had to empty them, and re-stuff with straw from the store. There were no washing facilities inside, only cold water in a shed. After four days we were kitted out, then the fun started. We were billeted with old hands and reservists. The old sweats were very good to us. My regimental number was CH 263 S (The S for special or short service). I was the 263rd Chatham special serviceman. Our pay was princely sum of 6s 8d per week.

The barracks accommodation may have been primitive by today's standards, but the training was short and conducted at a leisurely pace. The punishments for misbehaviour could also be surprisingly light in an age when fairly minor misdemeanours in the field could lead to Field Punishment Number One, spending hours lashed to a gun wheel, and the penalty for desertion or cowardice in the face of the enemy was death by firing squad. Baker:

> We paraded at 7 am for physical jerks. Half an hour's PT was followed by breakfast, usually of porridge, and bread and jam. After breakfast we did drill. Having been in the boy scouts it was dead easy to me. We did a great deal of drill. Lunch was about 1 o'clock. From 2 pm to 4 pm we did more training. At 4 pm we ended our day. After a few weeks we looked as good as the regulars. After this we practised extended order attacks but without arms. This was followed by musketry [rifle training] at Gravesend. We spent several weeks on that. I was a crack shot. The Lee Enfield was a good weapon. We concentrated on rapid loading. We did long route marches after we finished our rifle training. We had 200 Notts and Derby chaps transferred to us. They were miners, and very tough and very fine fellows. Beer was 2d a pint. I used to lend them money, 6d would buy 3 pints. They would always pay me back. Doughnuts in the canteen were the size of a cricket ball, and cost 1d. We had plenty of beef and suet puddings with currents in them, plum duff it was called. Plain but

adequate food. Happy days they were. We sometimes got weekend leave. When we applied to the Company Quarter Master Sergeant [Company Sergeant Major] for a week end pass, we had to leave 6d in a saucer on his desk.[6]

Finally we passed out. We were issued with ammunition so we were ready to go anywhere in the country. [Rifles in those days were kept in the barrack room, as they were for years after the Second World War.] One Irishmen, called Peter, got drunk, when he came in he threw himself on his bed, but his mates had fixed his bed so it collapsed dumping him on the deck. He loaded his rifle and fired five rounds through the ceiling. Luckily they did not hit anyone in the room above. They went out through the roof knocked some tiles off and it was raining and soon water came through onto the top floor and down onto us. The guard came running and collected Peter and put him in the cooler. But he only got five days CB [Confinement to Barracks], and got off lightly. We finished our training in December 1914.

Baker joined the Chatham Battalion RMLI, which had returned from Antwerp some weeks before:

We had no training in digging or in trench warfare. After Christmas leave we left Chatham for 'an unknown destination'. We went to Sutton Waldron in Dorset. We stayed until 6 February 1915. I and three others were billeted on a farm labourer's family in a cottage. He earned 12s a week. He fed us very well. He was paid a golden sovereign [£1] for each of us per week.

From contemporary accounts and reports, neither the battalions of the RM Brigade, of which the Chatham Battalion was part, nor the rest of the RN Division, who were all stationed in the vicinity of Blandford at the same time, did any battalion training to speak of. It is the training of all ranks in a battalion (and a brigade and division), in the articulation of the whole, that turns a crowd of individuals and small groups, however well trained, into a fighting unit. The majority of the RN Division were not well trained, even as individuals. The sailors and naval officers in the two naval brigades hardly had any basic military training at all. The RM battalions at least had a leavening of experienced NCOs and older men, including regulars, and all the other men had done some military training.

The Australian Official Historian says, referring to the RMLI battalions he encountered at Gallipoli, 'they looked strangely young and slender':

the author of the Royal Marines History of the period comments, 'this was only too true. These battalions were different from the usual Marine battalions who had served in Egypt and other wars, composed of seasoned long service soldiers.'[7] The majority of trained, regular Marines were afloat, and the battalions had been filled with recruits, both regulars and short service, many of whom had not finished their training, or had undergone a severely attenuated period of instruction in the basics. Many were only seventeen and eighteen years old. The Royal Marines had not imposed an age limit for active service, unlike the Army which had fixed nineteen years as the age for draft overseas, including France. Many of the subalterns were very young, like Chater. Fortunately a fair number of reserve officers recalled for service had only recently retired, and were still young and fit, and there had been some excellent officers promoted from the ranks since the outbreak of war, but most of the platoon commanders had joined in August 1914, or were regulars, like Chater, whose military training stopped almost as soon as it started. The battalions were composed of about 75 per cent recruits, 20 per cent reservists and a mere 5 per cent fully trained regulars. The reservists and NCOs were to form the backbone of the battalions in battle. As far as the proportion of experienced men was concerned, the RM Battalions were probably better off than the Kitchener battalions of the Army, although nothing like the splendid regular Army battalions of the original BEF. However, the RM battalions were denied the opportunity of the year's steady training given to most of the Kitchener battalions, few of whom saw any serious fighting until the Suvla landings at Gallipoli in August 1915. As soon as the RM Battalions were formed they were sent to Ostend. Three weeks after returning, they were sent to Dunkirk, where training was impossible. This was soon followed by the Antwerp operation, where they suffered casualties. On returning to England they received large drafts of recruits to replace casualties and increase battalion strengths from 400 to 1,000 each. The Deal Battalion had an even larger proportion of recruits than the other three. Only three winter months were available to make good shortfalls in individual skills and company and battalion training. After embarking for the Mediterranean, there was little time for further training, and except for a few landings, and a short reorganization period in Egypt, the Chatham and Plymouth Battalions were afloat in their ships for nearly three months. The Portsmouth and Deal Battalions had been originally ordered to take part in an expedition to the Rufigi River in East Africa, and when this was cancelled they were diverted to the Dardanelles, and except for the short period in Egypt, were afloat from 1 March to the end of April.

These deficiencies in training and other matters were still to be revealed to Baker and his comrades, when:

> At 1 am on 6 February we were told we were going to Devonport to embark for an unknown destination. The day before they had issued us with pith helmets. So we thought we were going to a hot country; Egypt we guessed. It poured with rain the whole way on our march to Blandford station where we entrained for Devonport, and we arrived soaked from head to toe. We boarded the *Cawdor Castle* a Union Castle ship.

Although he did not know it when he sailed from Devonport, Baker and his battalion, along with the three other battalions of the RM Brigade, as part of the RN Division, were on their way to the Dardanelles.

4

The Dardanelles:
The Naval Assault

It is no longer possible to force the Dardanelles.... nobody
would expose a modern fleet to such perils.

Churchill, Cabinet Memorandum 1911

In view of this unequivocal assertion, it is astonishing that by early 1915
Churchill should have been such a robust advocate of doing exactly what
he had condemned as impossible less than four years earlier. If anyone
could be said to have driven the Turks into the arms of the Germans, it
was he. When Britain declared war on Germany, he ordered that two
dreadnoughts launched the previous year, and still being fitted out in
British yards, the *Reshadieh* and the *Sultan Osman-i Evvel*, should be
requisitioned for the Royal Navy (they became the *Erin* and *Agincourt*
respectively). There were perfectly good strategic reasons for keeping the
ships out of Turkish hands while they made up their minds on whose
side they would fight, if at all. However the ships had been bought by
public subscription throughout Turkey, and Churchill's action was
greeted with rage. The Germans seized their chance and steamed the
battlecruiser *Goeben* and light cruiser *Breslau* through the Dardanelles
Straits, with Turkish permission, and into Constantinople. The British
Mediterranean Fleet, which had been ordered to shadow and engage
them, was inept, dithered, and allowed them to slip away. In response to
British protests that the Germans were infringing Turkish neutrality, the
German Admiral, Souchon, dressed his men up in fezzes and declared
that the two vessels were now part of the Turkish Navy. The 'in' joke
among the diplomatic community in Constantinople was 'Deutschland
über Allah'.

For nearly three months the British government strove to keep the Turks neutral. But at the end of October 1914 Admiral Souchon took *Goeben* and *Breslau* with a Turkish squadron to bombard the Russian Black Sea ports of Odessa and Novorossik, and the fortress of Sevastopol. On 31 October, following the expiry of a twelve-hour Russian, French, and British ultimatum to Turkey, Churchill ordered the Commander of the Dardanelles Squadron, Vice Admiral Carden, to commence hostilities against Turkey. Carden bombarded the forts at the outer end of the Dardanelles, thus serving the first of a series of notices to the Turks that an attack in this very spot might take place at some time in the future.

The Government body charged with Britain's strategic direction of the war was the War Council. It met at 10 Downing Street, and was chaired by the Prime Minister. Its regular members were the First Lord of the Admiralty, the Secretary of State for War, the First Sea Lord, the Chief of the Imperial General Staff, and the Foreign Secretary, as well as co-opted members brought in for discussion on specific items. The secretary was Lieutenant Colonel Maurice Hankey, RM. The weakness of this council throughout the First World War was the lack of central direction of the defence staffs, or at least a Chiefs of Staff Committee as in the Second World War. Consequently no global strategy was ever formulated. Each member of the War Council fought his own corner, and was prone to the syndrome that affects all badly run committees, that of agreeing with the last speaker, especially if he is a strong character, articulate, and persuasive; and Churchill was all three.

By the end of 1914 there were good reasons for an Anglo-French attack on Turkey. Their Russian allies had suffered a strategic setback at the hands of the German Ninth Army on the northern front in Poland, and were under pressure from the Turks in the Caucasus in the south. Russia's grain fleet was now bottled up in the Black Sea, denying her much-needed foreign currency. Knocking Turkey out of the war, or at least opening up the Dardanelles, would allow troops and supplies to be sent to her assistance against the main enemy, the Germans. At this juncture, the War Council was greatly taken by the idea of mounting a major offensive on Turkey, using some formations of Kitchener's New Armies, still under training and not ready for action in mid-1915, which would allow time for planning and preparation. In early January Kitchener declared his support for a joint Army and Navy attack on Turkey at some time in the future.

Unfortunately the careful planning for such an attack which should have followed this decision was completely torpedoed by a Russian request for an immediate diversionary action, to put pressure on the Turks. Kitchener, with no trained troops to spare, put the idea into Churchill's head that a 'demonstration might have some effect', and the place for it was the Dardanelles. Churchill, ever eager for action, immediately sent Vice Admiral Carden a signal asking him if he thought forcing the Dardanelles by ships alone was a practical proposition. Carden, who was a second-rate nonentity, replied that the straits could not be rushed, but might be forced by 'extended operations with a large number of ships'. In approaching Carden direct, and eventually ordering him to attack, Churchill bypassed the Naval Staff. They might have reminded him that two official reports produced in 1906 had explicitly advised against such an attack.

Sitting in the War Office, just across Whitehall, were comprehensive reports on the Dardanelles defences which had been sent in since 1911 by successive British military attachés from the Embassy at Constantinople, and vice-consuls at Chanak (the town on the Asiatic side overlooking the Narrows in the straits). Lieutenant Colonel Cunliffe-Owen, the military attaché from 1913 to the outbreak of war, had, on his own initiative, undertaken a covert survey of the Dardanelles, including sites of batteries, anti-shipping minefields, and other defensive works. He had passed detailed reports to the War Office. None of this information, which might have given Churchill pause to reflect, was brought to his attention, an indictment of the total lack of joint planning at the time. More slipshod, it was never shown to General Hamilton, or his staff, when the time came for the Army to take a hand in the proceedings. Cunliffe-Owen, on return from Turkey in November 1914, offered his services in the event of operations in the Dardanelles. He was ignored. He eventually fought at Gallipoli, but was not involved in the planning.

Later, defending his decision, Churchill said that he thought that the guns of the British fleet could deal with the Turkish forts lining the shore of the Straits, as the German artillery had smashed the Belgian forts at Namur and Antwerp. He failed to take into account the fact that naval guns, especially at close ranges, have a flat trajectory. Consequently the shells hit the strongest part of a fort, the walls, often protected by earthworks which detonated the shell before it got to the wall, let alone penetrated, whereas the giant German howitzers were able to subject the

Belgian forts to plunging fire, and the massive shells descending from a great height on the roof, weaker than the walls in that era before the heavy bomber, usually penetrated, before exploding with devastating effect.

In mid-January 1915, with the war apparently at stalemate, the War Council having earlier considered a paper by Kitchener proposing a joint operation against the Dardanelles by no less than 150,000 troops, listened to the Commander-in-Chief of the BEF, General French, pressing for more troops to carry out an offensive in France. French's plea was received without enthusiasm, but the War Council eventually agreed to his plan, on the understanding that if he failed the Allies would seek better prospects in another theatre. At the end of a long and somewhat depressing day-long meeting, Churchill, like a conjuror producing a rabbit out of a hat, sprang his idea of a naval attack on the Dardanelles. Hankey, the secretary of the War Council, later wrote:

> The idea caught on at once. The whole atmosphere changed. Fatigue was forgotten. The War Council turned eagerly from the dreary vista of a 'slogging match' on the Western Front to brighter prospects as they seemed in the Mediterranean. The Navy, in whom everyone had implicit confidence and whose opportunities so far had been few and far between, was to come into the front line. . . . . Churchill unfolded his plans with the skill that might be expected of him, lucidly but quietly and without exaggerated optimism.[1]

With minimum discussion, and no thought for how Churchill's scheme would affect the joint plan, the naval-only attack was on; and an all-out push, not just a demonstration. Why was Churchill still so enamoured of the idea? By then the Russians had driven back the Turks in the Caucasus anyway, thus removing the need for urgent action. Perhaps Hankey put his finger on the reason in his reference to the Navy above. As described in the previous chapter, the great naval victory, a second Trafalgar, that the public so confidently expected seemed a long time in coming. The Royal Navy had hardly covered itself with glory in the war so far, and had certainly not come up to expectations, at least for the man in the street. Here was a chance to show what it could do.

It was a pity Churchill was so eloquent. The indications are that the War Council would have approved a properly planned joint attack, which would have very likely succeeded; until February 1915 there was only one Turkish division to defend the 150-mile coastline of the Peninsula.

Fisher, brought back as First Sea Lord by Churchill at nearly seventy-four, was strongly opposed to any operations in the Dardanelles. His eyes were still fixed on amphibious operations in the Baltic. To this end, without consulting Churchill, he ordered the construction of flat-bottomed, shallow-draught ships, each equipped with two big guns in one turret, known as monitors, after John Ericsson's revolutionary design for the USS *Monitor* in the American Civil War. Fisher's monitors were designed to negotiate the sandbanks of the Baltic, and close the coast for bombardment. Fisher, again secretly, ordered a fleet of armoured landing craft with ramps for landing troops and stores. Given his obsession with Baltic operations during his previous tenure as First Sea Lord, one wonders why these invaluable vessels had not been ordered years before.

By early February the notion began to take hold in the Admiralty that some military assistance to the fleet might be necessary, if only to occupy the forts in the Dardanelles once the ships had passed through. At first Kitchener was unwilling to provide troops. He had one trained division left in Britain, the 29th, consisting of eleven regular battalions and one territorial battalion. Everybody who saw this formation has described it as magnificent. The division eventually took part in the Gallipoli campaign, but only after much order followed by counter-order, and, inevitably, disorder. However, on 6 February 1915 it was decided to send two RMLI battalions to the Aegean, to demolish the guns in the Dardanelles forts. On 16 February the War Council decided to send the 29th Division to the Greek island of Lemnos, and that the Australian & New Zealand Army Corps (ANZAC), stationed in Egypt for the defence of the Suez Canal, should be warned for a move to that island. Although the order of battle of the force for any landings following the purely naval operation appeared to be set, Kitchener changed his mind three days later and withdrew 29th Division.

Rear Admiral Wemyss was ordered to Lemnos to set up a base around the huge natural harbour of Mudros. Unfortunately there were no cranes or facilities for unloading ships, no accommodation for troops, and most serious of all, the water supplies were inadequate even for the inhabitants. Thus began the administrative muddle and operational inefficiency that was to characterize the campaign; the most efficient phase was the withdrawal nearly a year later. Troops shipped to Lemnos had to be sent on to Egypt, or in some cases returned there, or remain cooped up on board ship in Mudros harbour. Eventually, thanks to Wemyss, and his successors, the place was converted into a large advanced base with repair ships, a hospital, an air strip, and a sea-plane base, and was used until the end of the war.

The Turkish defences against naval attack were formidable. Between the entrance to the straits up to the entrance to the Sea of Marmara were fourteen large, old, but substantially built forts, mounting large guns, some of 9.4in and others of 14in calibre, with numerous 6in and 4in. Six of these forts dominated the Narrows, less than a mile wide. Although some of the guns were obsolescent, they were capable of inflicting severe damage on ships at the short ranges involved, which once inside the Straits, and depending on the positioning of the ship concerned, were never more than about 5,000 yards. In between the forts were batteries of field howitzers, dug in, but able to be towed to alternative positions. Although the calibre of these howitzers was such that they presented little threat to battleships, they were a major threat to the minesweepers – for the third element in the fixed defences of the Straits was a minefield laid from a point six miles short of the Narrows to the Narrows itself. A military axiom holds that a minefield is not an obstacle unless it is covered by fire, because if it is not, it can be cleared at one's leisure, and with little risk. This minefield was covered by heavy fire. In the Dardanelles, because of the mine threat, the battleships could not close the forts to destroy them, but until they had done so, the minesweepers could not clear the mines. At that time the Royal Navy did not possess any custom-built minesweepers, despite their oft-expressed anxiety about the mine threat in maritime operations generally, dating back for years before the First World War. Fishing trawlers with their civilian crews were requisitioned in lieu of anything better. With sweeps out, steaming against the constant strong current flowing out of the Straits, the trawlers could make three knots if they were lucky. They were sitting targets for the howitzers, and in the event, understandably, their crews' nerve broke under fire, and they turned tail and steamed out. Eventually the civilian crews were replaced by seamen from the fleet.

Carden's plan for penetrating the Dardanelles was divided into several phases: the outer defences would be destroyed by the battleships, and by demolition parties if necessary; the minefields would be swept and the forts commanding the Narrows destroyed; finally the fleet would enter the Sea of Marmara, and steam on to Constantinople.

On 19 February (108 years to the day since Vice Admiral Sir John Duckworth's successful forcing of the Dardanelles), Admiral Carden started his attack with a bombardment of the outer forts of Sedd-el-Bahr and Kum Kale, with the battleships *Inflexible*, *Vengeance*, *Albion*, *Triumph*, *Cornwallis*, and *Irresistible*, the cruiser *Amethyst*, destroyers, and three French battleships. The fire was not effective. The next attack on 25 February was more successful, and that day parties of Marines and seamen from the fleet were landed to spike the surviving guns, before returning to their ships. There was little opposition, but this was soon to change.

It is interesting to speculate what might have happened had all the Marines in the Dardanelles Squadron, a total of some 1,200, been landed to hold these forts then and there. They could have been rapidly reinforced by the leading elements of the RM Brigade, consisting of the Chatham and Plymouth Battalions and Brigade Headquarters (some 2,000 men) who were in their ships off the Dardanelles on 25 February, plus some 5,000 Australians who arrived at Mudros on 4 March. Given the strength of the Turks on the peninsula, and supported by the Navy, they could perhaps have held a bridge-head from which to develop further operations. Carden probably never considered it. Like most naval officers of his generation, major amphibious operations, as opposed to landing parties, were beyond his competence, indeed probably never formed part of his tactical thought-process; and there was no senior army officer with him to propose the idea. Had a Marine suggested it, he would probably have been thought to be getting above himself by Carden and most of the autocratic ships' captains and admirals of the day. They would take it from the Army, but not the Marines, who, in those days, they regarded as only 'tame soldiers, not costing too much, not having any ideas above their station, not quite soldiers'.[2]

The one attempt to land by any part of the RM Brigade in this phase of the campaign was made on 4 March, and then in only company strength. Number 4 Company of the Plymouth Battalion landed at Sedd-el-Bahr, and number 3 at Kum Kale. Both companies were transferred to destroyers from their transport, the SS *Braemar Castle*, before being towed ashore in cutters, five per tow behind a steam pinnace. About 100 yards from the beaches, the tows were slipped and the boats were rowed in.

Number 4 Company's task at Sedd-el-Bahr was to act as a covering force for a demolition party, who were to destroy any guns left service-able by the bombardment and earlier landing parties, and to allow RNAS officers to find a site for an airstrip. The battleships *Triumph* and *Lord Nelson* were in support. The plan was for patrols to precede the company and search the ground including the old fort. When this was reported clear, the demolition party was to move in. Meanwhile the remainder of the company was to deploy inland of the fort to cover the demolition party while it was at work. The company landed unopposed at the foot of the cliff. But when the leading patrol moved along the path into the road between the fort and the village of Sedd-el-Bahr it was subjected to small-arms fire from the village. A platoon attempting to clear the village was driven back. After fire from the supporting ships was brought down on the village, the platoon was able to clear it, finding it occupied by a few dead Turks. By now time was running out, and the demolition party having completed its task the signal to retire was given and the company withdrew to the cutters, under cover of fire from the ships. Lieutenant Charles Lamplough, aged eighteen, a platoon commander in Number 4 Company, and supporting one of the patrols, described the day in his diary.

Well this has been the day of my life. We were called at 5 am. I had breakfast at 6.15 am and we got onto the destroyers at 7 am and sailed off at 18 knots. When we got just off Seddul Bahr [sic] the fleet started bombarding like blazes. It looked very nice and as if we should have no opposition. Well, we got into our cutters and finally got ashore and everything looked in our favour. The patrols got out and went up the cliff. When they got to the top they got it thick – poor old Baldwin (a colour sergeant) was very soon caught. He got one through the head and died a little time after. Then we had a good deal of firing. I finally found we could not get up there as they were in the ruined houses sniping us, so we found where they were and I came down to the beach and signalled which houses we wanted shelling and they (the Fleet) let them have it. Then I took my patrol up and we did not have much opposition. We had quite a nice little scrap and then they [the Turks] sent a lot of shrapnel over, but they did not get us. A sniper killed one man in the picket boat. We found several Turks, some dead and one wounded, and sent for a stretcher party. The old fool flung himself off the stretcher down the cliff – he died on the way back to the *Braemar* [their transport]. We got back about 3.30 pm having had nothing to eat since 6.15 am this morning. I quite enjoyed the day but we were lucky to get out as we did [with] three dead and one wounded.

Number 3 Company, under Major Bewes, was accompanied by the Commanding Officer of the battalion, Lieutenant Colonel Matthews. Their task was more ambitious. Again they were to cover demolition parties, but as soon as the demolitions at Kum Kale were complete, the company was to advance to the village of Yeni-Shehr, about two miles to the south, reconnoitre a site for an airstrip en route, before moving on to cover the demolition party destroying the guns in another fort, known as number eight. In support were the *Cornwallis*, *Irresistible*, *Agamemnon*, *Amethyst*, and *Dublin*. Lieutenant May was to lead a strong patrol to search the Kum Kale fort first, followed by the village, to report if either was occupied. Two machine-guns were to land with the leading platoon, while the remainder of the company, having landed, was to remain in reserve in readiness to move to Yeni-Shehr. When the cutters rowed in to a long pier leading to the beach, it was found to be unsuitable for a landing place, and only about 80 men were landed there, including the machine-guns. The remainder landed on the beach and reached the fort almost unopposed. Despite covering fire from the ships directed on to the fort and the village, there were a few casualties in the boats. The men who had landed on the pier came under fire from two windmills close to the fort, and were ordered to take cover under the fort, leaving the machine-guns on the pier. Sergeant Cook and Private Threlfall volunteered to rescue the guns and ammunition, but Cook was badly wounded in the attempt. Eventually one gun and ammunition was recovered by the men sheltering under the walls of the fort, and the remaining gun and ammunition taken off in a cutter manned by seamen and the RMLI machine-gunners.

May's patrol met stiff opposition, but succeeded in entering the fort and reported all clear. The company then moved on Yeni-Shehr in assault formation. About halfway there they came under heavy small-arms fire, and recognizing that the enemy was in considerable strength, it was decided to withdraw, covered by the remaining machine-gun, which had been sited on Kum Kale fort. The supporting ships bombarded the vicinity of enemy positions, though with what effect it is impossible to say. During the withdrawal an unidentified private was seen carrying a wounded man on his back, under fire from the enemy. He took cover several times, before staggering on, until finally he fell dead. The man he was carrying was later recovered, still unconscious. The company re-embarked and withdrew unopposed from Kum Kale at dusk. The wounded, except for three missing, were evacuated by volunteer boats' crews of seamen and Marines from the *Irresistible*. The two operations cost the Plymouth Battalion twenty-three dead, twenty-five wounded, and three missing, most in number 3 Company. Lieutenant Lamplough:

> It is a sad sight seeing their equipment etc [Number 3 Company's] all bloodstained, being brought on board. They have only brought three bodies back with them and they died on the ships. [They were brought back alive and died of wounds.] We went to sea in the afternoon and buried them. It was by far the most moving thing I have ever witnessed.

Apart from some practical revision in the art of amphibious operations, little of which appears to have been digested in time for the landings on 25 April, these two forays achieved nothing. They merely served to alert the Turks once more to the possibility of landings in support of the fleet. The Turks responded swiftly, and by 25 March the sole division on the Peninsula had been reinforced by five more, to form Fifth Army totalling some 84,000 men, and placed under the command of the German General Liman von Sanders. Notice was also served to the British that the Turks would not run away as predicted, but fight fiercely. This does not seem to have been heeded either.

To return to the narrative of the naval battle, on 26 February, the howitzer batteries were attacked from ships within the Straits, but they were well concealed in the hills, and moved when the fire came too close. On 7 and 8 March the fleet bombarded the defences in the Narrows. But their efforts did little to reduce the howitzer threat, and because the minefield prevented the warships from closing the forts they were forced to engage them at ranges too great to do much damage to the large guns in the forts. At longer ranges there was difficulty observing the fall of shot with sufficient accuracy; overs might fall in dead ground, that is out of sight of ships' spotters. Later generations would solve this problem by using Naval Gunfire Forward Observers (NGFOs) to correct the fall of shot, either from an observation post on land, or in aircraft (latterly in helicopters). Indeed the intrepid Commodore Samson was soon to arrive at Lemnos, with a squadron of the RNAS which it was hoped would assist with spotting for the Navy. But aircraft-to-ship communications were still rudimentary. So for most of the campaign, and throughout the phase when the fleet attempted the passage of the Dardanelles, ships had to engage targets by direct fire, corrected by spotters in the firing ship.

Further attacks on 10 and 13 March saw the minesweepers reach the edge of the main minefield off Kephez Point. On both occasions they were forced to withdraw under heavy fire from the howitzers. By now morale in the fleet was sinking and Carden was under pressure from London to speed up the operation. He planned an all-out attack on the Narrows, but, on the verge of a nervous collapse, he was ordered home by a naval doctor. He was replaced by his second-in-command, Rear Admiral John de Robeck, who made no changes to Carden's plan which involved sixteen battleships, including four French, in three lines, with numerous cruisers and destroyers. Twenty officers, two warrant officers, and 1,118 NCOs, gunners, and privates of the RMA and RMLI were closed up at their action stations in this impressive fleet.

At first all appeared to be going well. Just after midday on the 18th, de Robeck signalled for the French Admiral Guépratte to move his ships forward to engage the Narrows' forts at close range, a task for which Guépratte, in modern parlance a 'press on regardless type', had volunteered. The Turkish fire was fierce and accurate, holing *Gaulois* below the waterline, and damaging the *Inflexible* and *Agamemnon*. The *Gaulois* was hard hit, and was only saved from sinking by being beached on Rabbit Island off Kum Kale. But the damage to the other two was superficial, and less than a dozen men in the whole fleet were casualties.

Corporal Fred Brookes RMLI was in HMS *Triumph* on the Asiatic side.

Our ship was repeatedly hit and 26 times shells penetrated our armour. One howitzer shell went down five decks, but luckily it was too far aft to do any vital damage. Another shell pierced the quarter deck, setting fire to the woodwork in and about the Captain's cabin, but it also burst the water pipes in the bathroom which put out the fire. Another shell penetrated the Royal Marines casemates [secondary armament and not in action then] and killed a midshipman who was there at the time, and wounded the Royal Marines officer. None of the gun's crew was hit, as, being a lull in the firing, they were all behind the gun having a round of cards out of sight of the Marine officer.

The Turks were in far worse condition. Some guns jammed, others were running short of ammunition, some were masked by earth and rubble, in places communications were destroyed; the enemy fire slackened. At about 1400 hours, de Robeck ordered the French to retire, as he wished to move six of his ships forward to cover the move forward of the minesweepers.

The French wheeled out of action, and steamed between the British and the Asiatic shore. Suddenly, the *Bouvet* shook to a vast explosion, then heeled, still steaming fast, and vanished, 'like a saucer slithers down a bath', said one observer. Only 35 out of her crew of 674 were saved. Either a 14in shell had penetrated her magazine or she had struck a mine. The minesweepers were called forward, but soon fled under heavy howitzer fire. Soon afterwards, *Inflexible* struck a mine, and listing badly, limped out of the straits. Five minutes after *Inflexible* was damaged, *Irresistible* struck a mine, and also listed badly. She was close to the Asiatic shore, and the Turkish gunners turned their full attention on to her. De Robeck sent the destroyer *Wear* to her assistance. The *Wear* returned with some 600 of *Irresistible*'s crew, including dead and wounded; the senior officers of *Irresistible* and 10 volunteers remained on board to prepare the ship for towing.

Private Wilcox RMLI in HMS *Ocean* remembers:

We went to try and tow her away. When we got near to her, a 14-inch shell struck the foreturret 12-inch guns of *Irresistible* and they rolled over into the water. A moment or two afterwards our ship, the *Ocean*, struck a mine and our engines were put out of action, so we were stuck there helpless, with shells coming over pretty thick. We got the order abandon ship. Three or four destroyers came alongside and took us all off, except one stoker who was below and could not get out.

I got aboard the destroyer *Chalmer*, when, before we left the side of the *Ocean*, the *Chalmer* was hit with a couple of shells, and started to sink. But she was able to get us alongside the *Lord Nelson* – who managed to keep her afloat and rescued us all. My word were we glad when that battle was over. As we were leaving the *Ocean* she was heeling over, and coming along the deck was a sick berth attendant with two wounded men on each side of him – a brave act, but no notice taken of it.

De Robeck ordered the fleet to withdraw. Fred Brookes in the *Triumph*:

> The action was called off at 5 pm, and we steamed out of the Dardanelles. We had been in action from 9 am and the weight of metal flung on shore must have been enormous. I was in charge of the ammunitioning party supplying the Royal Marine 7.5-inch guns and we passed up 74 rounds – each shell weighed over 200 lbs. The other fourteen 7.5-inch guns must have fired about the same, and added to that were the shells fired by the four 10-inch guns.
>
> When we were outside the Dardanelles and out of range everyone crowded on to the upper deck to get a breath of fresh air. By looking at a man's face you could tell if he had been stationed below as ammunition supply, or engine room or stokehold, or, those who had been at the guns. The latter were full of fight. Whereas those who had been below were white-faced and showed their nerve-wracking experience. They had not the excitement of fighting, or the knowledge of what was going on. From 9 am to 5 pm they had heard nothing but the crash of shells striking our ship and the sound of our own guns firing. Rumour passed from one to another often enlarged on the damage done by enemy fire.

Throughout the day of the great attack, 200 men of the Chatham Battalion had sat in their transport off Rabbit Island standing by to land. Private Thomas Baker was one of them: 'We felt very sad, so many men had died in the ships.'

When Commodore Keyes, de Robeck's gallant and aggressive chief of staff, went that night in the destroyer *Jed* to see if the two battleships *Ocean* and *Irresistible* could be salvaged, he gained a strong impression that the Turks were a beaten foe, and that one more concerted push would do it. On his return to the *Queen Elizabeth*, the flagship, he pressed de Robeck to try again. But de Robeck, rightly, in hindsight, refused. We now know that very little permanent damage had been done to the Turkish forts commanding the Narrows. Of 176 guns in fixed defences, only four had been destroyed, killing no more than 150 defenders. The Fleet had lost almost 700 men, three battleships sunk, and three badly damaged. Only one line of mines had been swept, and the chance of sweeping more with the enemy howitzers still fully in action was nil.

In fact, had the fleet, further battered and reduced in strength, managed by some stroke of good fortune to fight its way through the Dardanelles to Constantinople, and cause panic among the population and government by bombarding the city, it is highly unlikely that any significant strategic results favourable to the Allies would have ensued; quite the reverse. Any damage to the defences of the Straits could have been quickly restored. Mines could have been relaid. The fleet could have refuelled in a Russian Black Sea port, but, short of ammunition, would have been reduced to skulking impotently in the Black Sea, or risking a second passage of the Dardanelles. Even if the Turks had faltered at the sight of the Allied Fleet off the Golden Horn, once they realized that they had bottled up the fleet in the Black Sea their resolve to continue fighting would have been quickly restored.

The failure of the fleet to force a passage on 18 March led to the decision to turn what had been a Navy-only show into a joint operation. By now General Sir Ian Hamilton, appointed as commander of the Army's part in any future land operations in the Dardanelles, had arrived in the theatre of operations. He had witnessed the events of the 18th from the destroyer *Phaeton*, and was deeply affected by the sight of the sunk and damaged ships. Neither he, nor Lieutenant General Sir William Birdwood, the commander of the ANZAC, believed that the Navy could go it alone, and wrote to tell Kitchener so. The scene was now set for the next act.

5

The Dardanelles:
The Landings, 25 April 1915

The Boy Scouts could have handled the operation better.

Private Baker RMLI

Early on 18 March, the day of the great naval assault, General Hamilton, in the destroyer *Phaeton*, collected Major General Paris, commanding the RN Division from Mudros. He was greeted with depressing news. Paris, who had travelled out to the Aegean ahead of his division, had discovered that when the ships transporting the two naval brigades arrived at Mudros they were not, in modern parlance, combat loaded. The stores and sub-units of each of the battalions, and other units, were loaded 'higgledy-piggledy' in several ships, and a complete restow would be required before any landing could take place. The RM Brigade, in contrast, had sailed from England with each battalion embarked as a complete unit with its transport, but 'after some difficulty with the Transport and Stores Department', as the relevant Royal Marines History comments.[1]

Consequently had the fleet succeeded in forcing the Narrows on 18 March, or had Admiral de Robeck opted for another try on 19 March, the only force available to land in support of the Navy would have been the RM Brigade. The units of the 29th Division, which Kitchener had finally agreed to release for operations in the Aegean, had also arrived with their ships not combat loaded. They and the RN Division were packed off to Egypt to sort themselves out. Before the RM Brigade sailed to join the RN Division in Egypt, they were taken in their transports to steam off Gaba Tepe – to what end is uncertain, perhaps in the hope of deluding the Turks into believing that a landing there was imminent. All it probably achieved was to persuade the Turks that this might be one of the areas in which the Allies were interested; and the Turks would have been right. Eventually the intended beaches for the ANZAC were about a mile north of Gaba Tepe. From the outset nearly every rule of amphibious operations was being broken. In this case: do not go openly nosing around off beaches in which you may be interested unless you want to communicate your interest to the enemy. However, to be fair, de Robeck, who presumably ordered this pointless excursion, was not to know that one of the main landing beaches would be near Gaba Tepe, because at that stage there was no plan.

Sixty-five days elapsed between the first naval attack on 19 February and the main landings on 25 April 1915. The Turks made good use of the time. They dug trenches and gun emplacements, wired off beaches, and built or repaired roads to improve the mobility of forces moving to repel landings or reinforce threatened areas. Liman von Sanders deployed his six divisions as follows: two at Besika Bay on the Asiatic Side, two at Bulair, the narrowest part of the Peninsula, one distributed along the tip of the Peninsula coast, and one in reserve at Boghali, more or less in the centre, and able to reinforce in any direction. Sanders' forces were spread thin, and on 25 April the Allies attacked at his weakest point. But his defensive layout, and preparations on and immediately behind the beaches, were sufficient to frustrate the Allies' inept attempts to stake out footholds well inland. Until the naval attack galvanized the Turks into action, no reserves existed on the Peninsula. Had a proper landing been made in force right away, concurrent with the naval attack, it is very likely that the whole Peninsula would have been seized within a few days.

Carden's bombardment of the Dardanelles forts at the end of October 1914 and the subsequent naval actions signalled the Allied intentions to the Turks. Suspicions that a landing was imminent were reinforced by the bustle of activity in Egypt, reported to Constantinople by Turkish and German agents, who were able to operate with very little risk of compromise in the cosmopolitan communities in Cairo and Alexandria.

While most of the troops for the Gallipoli landings, now known as the Mediterranean Expeditionary Force (MEF), concentrated in Egypt, Hamilton's staff planned the operation at Alexandria. The Force consisted of:

— The 29th Division, commanded by Major General Hunter-Weston, of three infantry brigades each of four regular battalions (except for one which had one TA battalion), and a generous allocation of supporting artillery.

— The RN Division, commanded by Major General Paris, of two naval brigades and the RM Brigade, each of three battalions, the Deal Battalion having been lent to 1st Naval Brigade, and meagre artillery support consisting of two 12-pounders, one 6in howitzer, and three 4.7in guns.

— The Australian and New Zealand Army Corps (ANZAC), commanded by Lieutenant General Sir William Birdwood, of two divisions, 1st Australian, which had three brigades each of four battalions and supporting artillery, and the New Zealand & Australian Division, with only two brigades, one of them with only two battalions, and no supporting artillery.

— The French Corps Expéditionnaire d'Orient, commanded by General d'Amade, consisting of two brigades and eight batteries of 75mm quick-firing guns.

Hamilton was bedevilled by problems from the outset, some of his own conception. Most serious was the absence of a joint staff system, and lack of an overall commander in the Aegean theatre of operations. During the planning phase Hamilton's and de Robeck's staffs were physically separated, initially by the width of the Mediterranean, and later, for the rest of the campaign, by several miles, without the benefit of modern communications. Decisions that would impinge on both the Navy and the Army sometimes took days to make and as long to implement. For a few days just before and after the landings, the two commanders were co-located in the battleship *Queen Elizabeth*. On that occasion, Hamilton had his operational staff with him, but his administrative staff were miles away.

Hamilton's administrative staff did not arrive in Alexandria until 1 April 1915. Therefore they were not involved in the planning from the outset, as they should have been. Hamilton compounded the problem by leaving his administrative and medical staffs behind in Alexandria when he moved back to Mudros before the landings, and when they eventually caught up they were still billeted in different ships from the operational staffs. The administrative disaster at Gallipoli was of Hamilton's making.

The ANZAC and RN Division staffs were green. Paris wrote on 10 April 1915:

> Lt Col Hon E Fiennes MP finds it difficult to realise that his duties are restricted – Lt Col Ollivant RA gets brain waves about midnight – I'm afraid he isn't strong enough to last through many days of hard work. Richardson [a bright New Zealander], Sketchley [Major RMLI], and my son [his ADC] are really useful.

Outside Hamilton's control, but adding to the potential for chaos, were such details as the different models of Lee Enfield rifle issued to the 29th and RN Divisions. The Mark VIIs issued to the 29th Division could fire the Mark VI ammunition issued to the RN Division, but the latter's rifles could not fire Mark VII rounds. His formations were of uneven quality. The 29th consisted of pre-war regulars, well officered and superbly trained. The RN Division as we have seen was a patchy formation, the youthful RM Brigade being the best trained. The ANZACs impressed all who saw them by their magnificent bronzed physiques, but were totally inexperienced. The French were very mixed; the Foreign Legion were tough and utterly reliable, unlike the Senegalese Africans, who fulfilled all predictions by running away when they lost their officers.

Hamilton's problems would have been easier to solve had he not been so diffident about asking for help from his master Kitchener in Whitehall, and questioning what he was being asked to do. Looking down on the scene from the high ground of hindsight over eighty years later, it is clear that the expedition carried the seeds of its own destruction to the shores of the Gallipoli Peninsula. Some of those had been planted by the actions of other players, weeks and months before, some were the handiwork of the commander of the MEF and his staff.

Hamilton's concept for the landing had been made following a brief sight of the beaches, and as much of the ground as could be viewed from the bridge of the destroyer *Phaeton*, on 18 March. He had seen the flat plain inland from Suvla, but rejected a landing there because of the hills which surrounded it on three sides. South of Suvla were steep cliffs rising straight from the water's edge. Rocky, broken hills rose to the Sari Bair range from which an observer could overlook the Narrows, the Suvla Plain, and the Aegean. This was what modern soldiers call the vital ground; and Hamilton saw it as such. At the south-western tip of the Peninsula was Cape Helles, dominated by the fort at Sedd-el-Bahr.

Unlike the Turks, who knew exactly how strong the MEF was, Hamilton had no detailed intelligence about his enemy, and estimated his strength as 34,000 in three divisions, instead of over twice that number in six divisions. He correctly assessed that the Turks would hold Bulair in strength, but he thought there was only one division there. He placed the other two divisions at Kilid Bahr overlooking the Narrows, and at Anafarta dominating Suvla Bay and the plain behind. He had seen that the area of Cape Helles had been well fortified, and wired both behind the beaches and underwater on the beach approaches.

His plan was as follows. He aimed to keep the Bulair division fixed with a feint landing by the RN Division in the Gulf of Saros. He would land the Anzacs in the Gaba Tepe area, and the 29th Division at Cape Helles, where he expected the toughest resistance. The French would carry out a diversionary landing at Kum Kale on the Asiatic shore. Having, it was hoped, dealt with any enemy batteries in the vicinity of Kum Kale, they would be transferred to Cape Helles after about forty-eight hours. The RN Division would be landed at Cape Helles following the Bulair diversion.

Following the landings, the Anzacs were to advance in an easterly direction to seize the high ground at Chunuk Bair and Sari Bair overlooking the Narrows. The 29th Division was to advance up the gentle slope of the 700-foot-high Achi Baba, and thence north-eastwards to link up with the Anzacs and dominate the eastern side of the Narrows, at which point the Navy could at last force the Narrows and debouch into the Sea of Marmara. There were five beaches at Cape Helles, clockwise from the south-east: S, V, W, X, and Y.

Hamilton had no purpose-built landing craft. The ones built at Fisher's orders were not made available at this stage, and were still in England. Soldiers would land in cutters and gigs towed by steam pinnaces. Apart from the latter, and one other stratagem, the methods being employed for landing had hardly advanced since Duckworth's passage of the Dardanelles at the beginning of the previous century. The one other stratagem was the conversion of a collier, the *River Clyde*, into an early version of the Landing Ship Infantry of the Second World War. She would be run aground under the walls of Sedd-el-Bahr fort. As she hit the beach, a steam hopper and two lighters would be positioned to form a bridge of boats connecting her bows to the beach, and 2,400 men of the 86th Infantry Brigade would dash out of four doors cut in her side, along sloping gangways that ran to the bows on each side, jump on to the bridge of boats, and run ashore. The Turks' heads would be kept down by machine-gunners in sandbag emplacements in the *River Clyde*'s bows. At least that was the theory.

Apart from the Plymouth Battalion, the RM Brigade, along with the remainder of the RN Division, had no active part to play in the landings on 25 April 1915. The Royal Marines in the fleet were of course extremely busy. So many seamen were required to man boats to land soldiers that only part of one ship's detachment took part in the landings, the remaining Marines being at action stations afloat. Thirty-seven officers, one warrant officer, and 1,908 NCOs and men were present in warships on 25 April 1915.

The Plymouth Battalion, under command of 29th Division, was ordered to land on Y Beach with 1st Battalion King's Own Scottish Borderers (1 KOSB) and one company 2nd Battalion South Wales Borderers (2 SWB). Y Beach consisted of a narrow strip from which steep cliffs, 200 feet high and covered in scrub, rose from the water's edge. A small, steep gully gave access to the top. To the south-west of Y was X Beach where 2nd Battalion the Royal Fusiliers (2 RF) were landing to cover the balance of 87th Infantry Brigade, consisting of 1st Royal Inniskilling Fusiliers (1 R Innis Fus) and 1st Battalion the Border Regiment (1 Border). The aim of the landing on X beach was to attack the Turks in their rear, engage their reserves moving to join the battle at the tip of Cape Helles, and finally, when they were driven back from the landings on the tip of the Cape, to cut them off – ambitious indeed.

When Lieutenant Colonel Matthews, commanding Plymouth Battalion, attended Hunter-Weston's verbal orders, he was told that he had overall command of the force landing on Y Beach because he was senior to Lieutenant Colonel Koe, of 1 KOSB. Hamilton's headquarters were unaware of this decision, and were under the impression that Koe was in command, as was Koe himself, who was sick and did not attend these orders. Hunter-Weston's orders to Matthews were muddled and imprecise. Instead of giving him a mission, he gave him a number of vague and conflicting tasks. Matthews was told by Hunter-Weston to explore inland, destroy or capture a Turkish gun supposed to be in the vicinity, draw in the Turkish reserves to keep them away from the other beaches, and make contact with 2 RF on X Beach. How Matthews was to make contact, whether by sending a message by heliograph, lamp, runner, or physically marrying up was never made clear. He apparently never asked. He was also told to be prepared to join the advance of 29th Division to Krithia, and thence on to the summit of Achi Baba, which was the divisional objective for the first day of the landings. It never occurred to Hunter-Weston to say what the Y Beach force should do if the other Cape Helles landings were stalled, and Matthews did not enquire, for no orders were given to cover such an eventuality. He was never told to exploit inland, and came away from the verbal orders under the impression that his landing was a demonstration, and that he would be on his own, and unsupported for a mere six hours. He was worried about the state of training of his battalion and asked that the far better trained 1 KOSB should land first. The young brother of Commodore Keyes, Lieutenant Commander Adrian Keyes, beach master for Y Beach, wrote some years later that he, Keyes, persuaded Hunter-Weston to reverse the landing order. Why Hunter-Weston should take any notice of a beach master, and naval officer whose experience of soldiering was nil, in deciding the landing order is a mystery; Keyes apparently had not been impressed by the Plymouth Battalion during boat training. Whatever the truth of the matter, Matthews's request was granted. He was given the *Goliath*, *Dublin*, *Amethyst*, and *Sapphire* to support his force.

The first of the main landings on the Gallipoli Peninsula on 25 April 1915 was 2nd Australian Brigade of 1st Australian Division, timed to be in darkness to gain maximum surprise. Unfortunately, thanks to a strong current and poor navigation, compounded by the fact that some of the towing pinnaces were commanded by inexperienced midshipmen aged fifteen, the Australians were landed about a mile north of the intended beach; and late, at dawn. The Turkish defenders saw the approaching boats when they were only about fifty yards off the beach, and immediately opened fire. There were few casualties among the leading wave of Australians. But when they landed, instead of the gentle slope behind the beach they had been led to expect, the troops had to climb cliffs rising almost straight from the waterline, and against an alerted enemy. Space does not permit a detailed account of events on this beach, or any of those where there were no Royal Marines present, but the conduct of the Australians and New Zealanders at Anzac that day saw the start of a legend encapsulated in the words of a British officer, who, speaking of the Australian infantrymen, said, 'The bravest thing on earth God ever made.' At the end of a day of savage fighting, the Anzacs were pinned into a tiny bridgehead. After ten more days of fighting it would never be more than a thousand yards deep at its widest point, and one and a half miles wide. Had it not been for the speed with which Colonel Mustapha Kemal (later Kemal Atatürk) reacted and mounted a counterattack with his 19th Division, the Anzacs might have seized and held the vital ground of Chunuk Bair and the Sari Bair Range. Thanks to him they never did.

The next to land were 1 KOSB and the Plymouth Battalion RMLI. Private John Vickers RMLI Number 1 Company, Plymouth Battalion, described his pre-battle preparations in his diary:

> Prepared our marching order (which is rather weighty). It contains greatcoat, three pairs of socks, canteen and cover, towel and soap, flannel, hard brush, holdall containing knife fork spoon, comb, razor and brush, three days hard rations consisting of 2lb 'bully' beef and 2lb biscuits, a waterproof sheet weighing about 5 lbs. We were to carry 250 rounds of ammunition weighing about 10 lbs, a full waterbottle, rifle and bayonet.

Lieutenant Lamplough reflected in his diary:

> Land about 5.30 am tomorrow morning. I wonder how we shall get on – I should like to see this time next week (May be finished, may be alive – some poor fellows will be finished but I think I shall be alright). I feel quite safe somehow, and with God's help I shall be.

Private Vickers remembered that the moon was shining, as the Plymouth Battalion on the *Braemar Castle* made their final preparations in the early hours of 25 April 1915, while the ships waited until the moon set before closing the coast:

> The ship slowed down and stopped some three miles [five miles] from the Peninsula where the trawlers, which had been detailed to land us came alongside. As we drew near land it grew light quite suddenly and we were able to see the point at which we were to land. It appeared from a distance to be an impossible landing, but as we drew nearer it was not so sheer as at first supposed – although the cliffs were some 200 feet high.

As the trawlers carrying the Plymouth Battalion ran in towards the coast, they could hear the sounds of the naval bombardment on the other

Cape Helles beaches, between two and three miles distant as the crow flies. Vickers:

> The next few minutes were the most exciting I had experienced. The Turks opened fire from all sides and our battleships and battlecruisers [cruisers] and destroyers replied. The intensity of the fire increased and it was plain that the Troops who were landing on the other beaches were having a hot time.

In fact the troops on the other beaches, except on Z Beach, some twenty-three miles to the north-east of Y and better known as Anzac, had not begun landing at this stage. Neither had the Turks at Cape Helles opened fire.

> We got out of the trawlers into small boats holding about 30 men. The boats grounded about 50 yards from the shore, and we jumped into the water and waded ashore – a difficult task as the water was over our waists and we had a decent weight to carry. A few snipers made their presence felt from the top of the cliff but were shelled off before causing any casualties.
>
> As soon as we reached land we took cover under the cliffs and scouts were sent out. The KOSB's scouts [two of them] were killed by a shell from our own ship, who took them for Turks. This mistake happened several times, for a shell from a ship pitched into a section killing and wounding six. We were in an awkward fix, for we were being wiped out by our own men – terrible to think of and very disheartening. The scouts returned and reported all clear. There were no enemy in sight and we climbed up the cliffs, extended [shook out into open formation], and commenced digging in.

Numbers 2 and 3 Companies of the Plymouth Battalion advanced inland, crossing a 100-foot-deep depression they called Gully Ravine, which ran roughly parallel to the beach. The village of Krithia lay just over a mile from Y Beach, and only half a mile from and in full view of the forward positions of the Plymouth Battalion, from where they could plainly hear the incessant roar of firing from the battles raging on the beaches to their south and south-west, where the landings had now begun. The troops on X, their closest neighbouring beach, had landed unopposed. It was a very different story on V and W beaches, and Vickers's earlier comment above about the troops there having a 'hot time' was to prove to be an understatement to say the least.

The naval bombardment on both V and W beaches was directed on targets inland, because it was thought that the high-velocity guns would be ineffective against troops in trenches. As most of the targets were out of sight to the firing ships, and there were no other spotting arrangements, most of this fire was ineffective. Lieutenant Commander Adrian Keyes is clear that the naval gunfire support in most places was highly overrated for much of the early months of the campaign, and especially so on 25 April. Paris echoed this view, writing on 5 May 1915: 'One of the disappointments has been the results of the enormous expenditure of ship ammunition.' Only the captain of the battleship HMS *Implacable*, off X Beach, took his ship inshore and fired at targets over open sights. However, the storm of naval gunfire lashing down, and lack of any sign of life on V and W beaches, deluded some into thinking that the Turks had run away.

As the rowing boats carrying the 1st Battalion Lancashire Fusiliers closed within a few yards of W Beach, the Turks, whose fire discipline had been commendable, unleashed a hail of rifle and machine-gun fire on the packed craft. The Lancashires did the only thing they could: jump over the side. In many places they found themselves out of their depth, the water was sown with mines, and with barbed wire entanglements beneath the surface, the beach and waterline had been made into a death trap by the Turks. Machine-gun positions enfiladed the beach. In an outstanding act of courage and discipline the survivors of the first wave, having paused on the seaward side of the wire above the waterline, broke through onto the high ground above the beach. In a bout of savage hand-to-hand fighting with rifle butt and bayonet they cleared enough elbow room to allow the next wave to land. For this action the battalion was awarded six VCs.

At V Beach, the assault by 1st Battalion Royal Munster Fusiliers and 1st Battalion Royal Dublin Fusiliers was a shambles. Few of the Dublins, landing in boats, made the shoreline. The Munsters landing from the *River Clyde* were mown down as they ran out of the doors in the ship's side, and along the gangways. The lighters connecting the *River Clyde* to the shore were soon piled with bodies. The bravery of the officers and ratings of the Royal Navy at V Beach was beyond praise as they tried to rescue the soldiers, and stood in waist-deep water holding the bridge of boats in place. Commander Samson RNAS, over V Beach in his aircraft, saw with horror that the water was lashed into a foam by bullets, and was red with blood for fifty yards out to sea. Boats drifted offshore packed with dead and dying. A few men huddled under the walls of Sedd-el-Bahr, where they were in dead ground.

The only other Marines to take part in landings on 25 April were from the battleship HMS *Cornwallis* (Captain A. P. Davidson RN), in support of 2 SWB, who had been detailed to take the De Totts Battery at S Beach. The battalion was minus one company, which was assigned to Y Beach. Captain Davidson had been told to give 2 SWB all the assistance he could. He took this to mean more than covering the landing by fire, and lent thirty-six RMLI of his Royal Marine Detachment to replace the company of 2 SWB. He himself, dressed in white uniform armed with pistol and cutlass, accompanied the boats' crews with twenty-five seamen. On approaching the shore, 2 SWB jumped into the water up to their waists, and waded ashore under fire. This very well-trained battalion worked their way up to the top of the battery from two directions and went firm on their objective with the loss of two officers and fourteen other ranks killed, and three officers and fifty-seven wounded. The *Cornwallis* detachment arrived as the right flank of the battalion was about halfway up the cliff, and followed up the advance. The seamen, having beached the boats, seized their rifles and joined in. At this point *Cornwallis* was ordered to V Beach to give support there, leaving her intrepid captain on S Beach. It was some hours before he, his boats' crews, and the Royal Marine Detachment could rejoin. The Turkish opposition on S Beach melted away, and the fighting there died down. The commanding officer of 2 SWB made no effort to follow up, or exploit.

In the early part of that day there was a golden opportunity for Hunter-Weston to reinforce Y, X, and S Beaches, where all was quiet, using the mobility of the Royal Navy. He would then be in a position to mount a pincer attack on the rear of the small force of Turks at V and W Beaches, which consisted of less than a company, and break the stalemate. Hunter-Weston, mesmerized by the disaster at W Beach, and even unaware of conditions at V Beach, did no such thing, even when it was suggested to him by Hamilton at least twice. From the *Queen Elizabeth*, Hamilton had seen the troops strolling about on the cliffs above Y Beach, and realized that for the moment there was little opposition. Unfortunately Hamilton declined to override Hunter-

Weston, as he was to refuse to do with other subordinates throughout the campaign, often with disastrous consequences.

Hamilton was a brilliantly clever, charming, witty, courageous, and highly regarded officer, with a wealth of operational experience. However, much of that experience had been as a staff officer. He had commanded a division in the early stages of the South African War (the Second Boer War), under the eye of his mentor Field Marshal Lord Roberts in conditions very different from that most complicated operation of war, an amphibious landing: an operation of war, moreover, for which by 1915 the Royal Navy and the Army had conspicuously failed to practise, equip, or formulate joint doctrine. So in operational terms Hamilton and de Robeck were stumbling about in the dark with no markers for guidance. Although Hamilton had performed brilliantly as Chief of Staff to Kitchener in the latter part of the South African War, he had been totally dominated by him. This continued to be the case in 1915, and had dire consequences. A staff officer can make a name for himself with all manner of scintillating suggestions and schemes, secure in the knowledge that his master will 'carry the can' if all goes wrong. The chasm between a staff officer, however senior, and the commander of a sizeable formation of all arms, totally responsible for all decisions, and with no senior to turn to for advice, yawns wide indeed, and some of the cleverest staff officers have never been able to cross it. Arguably Hamilton was one of those. He seemed incapable of imposing his will on those he commanded; in a word, he was too 'nice'.

At Y Beach, Matthews walked almost all the way to Krithia with his adjutant. The Turkish garrison had gone to support their comrades at Sedd-el-Bahr, although Matthews could not have known that. Matthews' stroll took him closer to Krithia than any other Allied soldier throughout the campaign, although subsequently thousands would die in attempts to take the village. Meanwhile, Koe, thinking he was in command at Y Beach, flashed a heliograph message to 2 RF at X Beach, asking if he should join them, but received no reply. At about midday, still hearing heavy firing from the direction of V and W Beaches, and believing correctly that the advance was held up, Matthews ordered a withdrawal back over Gully Ravine, and to the cliff top. Soon shells began to fall among the KOSB and Marines, heralding a Turkish counterattack, put in by a battalion of the 25th Regiment between the Gully Ravine and the sea. The first attacks were beaten off with the assistance of naval gunfire, but with the onset of night this was no longer effective. The Turks, now at about regimental strength, pushed home their attacks with great skill and determination, and Matthews was concerned that he would be overrun. He sent a signal to 29th Division, relayed through HMS *Goliath*. Sergeant Meatyard, a pre-war regular, was the Signal Sergeant of the Plymouth Battalion, and had been wounded during the Kum Kale landing on 4 March. He recorded later:

> I had received orders to take no signal lamps whatever when we landed, but when night came on we found that a signal lamp was badly needed there being no other means of communication. By a stroke of luck I thought of the CO's pocket lamp, and with this I was able to send a number of important signals. Some I remember were: 'Send in boats for wounded, spot will be indicated by light', 'Send 30,000 rounds of small arms ammunition, running short', and to the GOC [29th Division] 'Can't hold on without reinforcements of at least one Battalion', 'we are in a serious position', 'We are driven to the beach', 'send boats for us to re-embark'.

The signal asking for reinforcement received no acknowledgement from 29th Division although they received it. The message about ammunition was also received by 29th Division, but ignored. HMS *Goliath*, with commendable initiative, sent in some Mark VII cartridges, but these could not be used in the Marines' Mark VI rifles. Koe lay dying. Matthews sent another message which was received in 29th Division at 6 a.m. on the morning of 26 April. No reply was sent and no action taken. After first light, by which time Koe had died, Matthews suggested to the surviving KOSB officers that the force should try to fight its way out and join 2 RF at X Beach. The KOSB, who had lost most of their officers, and were exhausted and nearly out of ammunition, were less than enthusiastic. The cliffs and beach were crowded with wounded, and rather than leave them to the Turks, about whose behaviour there were doubts, it was decided to stay and continue fighting.

At this point the situation becomes very confused; accounts contradict each other, some of them smacking of wisdom after the event. The rot seemed to have set in when boats were sent in by the ships; according to Matthews, this was without his knowledge, but this runs counter to Meatyard's account. When the boats arrived, according to Matthews again, the KOSB, the SWB, and his own right flank company were ordered to withdraw. Matthews claimed later that when he saw them moving off, he sent his adjutant to find out what was happening, but by the time he arrived, many of the troops had already reached the beach and embarked in the boats. Who gave the withdrawal order is a mystery, and it may be a figment of Matthews's imagination. We shall never know; he was killed later in the war, commanding a brigade.

Keyes was on the beach, and in a rather confused and emotional letter, written three years later, said that he was convinced:

> we could and ought to have held that position, and the reason why we failed was that the majority of the Plymouth Battalion of the RND ran. I made a signal to *Sapphire* or *Goliath*, asking them to collect boats in case we had to re-embark, this was done at the request of Colonel Matthews. I only allowed boats to approach to embark wounded, and as more boats came in they got out of hand, and approached the beach. There were about 400 RMLI on the beach, mostly without officers. These men rushed the boats.[2]

Keyes went up the cliff to find Matthews, but says he could get no sense out of him. At about that time, according to Keyes, the KOSB put in a 'fine counterattack', after which Keyes returned to the beach to find most of the boats had got away full of Marines, but that 'detachments [from whom he does not say] then started to come down under their officers in good order'. He returned back up the cliff, and again claims he could get no sensible reaction from Matthews. According to him he

> begged him [Matthews] to hang on – there were about two companies on the beach in good order – and that I could get the ships' guns [laid] on to the top of the cliff, and we should come over the top and hang on. I closed the ships in and it was a very reassuring sight to see them with their guns covering us. However, he decided to re-embark.[3]

Keyes, who had never seen a land battle before, was understandably wrought up by what he had witnessed, and his letter, written after three years of brooding on the incident, should be treated with caution. For example his description of 400 RMLI on the beach is questionable. If the number of casualties suffered by the Plymouth Battalion is added to the three companies that stood firm, it is inherently unlikely that another 400 spare Marines would have been left over wandering about. In any case, other witnesses say that both KOSB and SWB soldiers were involved in the rush to the boats. Keyes does admit that:

> The two Majors of the Marines, Bewes and Palmer, were both hit [he
> means OC Number 3 Company and the Battalion Second-in-Command].
> Tetley [Captain Tetley RMLI, OC Number 1 Company] brought his
> fellows down to the beach in fine style, at the end.[4]

What is undeniable is that all was not well with the command at Y
Beach. At the subsequent Commission of Inquiry into the Dardanelles,
Matthews accepted full responsibility, giving lack of orders, support, and
reinforcements from his superior headquarters as the reason for the
untimely withdrawal.

At 0830 Matthews, with his Numbers 1 and 4 Companies and a few
KOSB, occupied a position in a trench at the head of a watercourse or
gully running down to the beach. Lamplough picks up the narrative in
what was already a very confused situation, when a 12in shell from one
of the supporting ships burst in the trench, which

> caused the Borderers to retire. In fact it was a stampede and they came
> rushing down the Gully but I was with Captain Andrews and my platoon,
> and we rallied them again and went up the cliff again to make a counter-
> attack. However some shrapnel came over and we had to scatter. Finally I
> got hold of five KOSBs and two of my own men and we were on our own.
> Three of my party got killed so that only five of us arrived and we were
> very lucky. Of course other parties had come up on our right and the
> Colonel was there. After we had captured this trench, we took up a new
> and smaller position round the head of the Gully as we were going to retire.

Patrols were sent out to the front and flanks. The only sign of Turkish
activity was a few snipers. At about 1000 hours the companies retired to
the beach unmolested. Sergeant Meatyard: 'It may be the enemy had had
enough or it was the presence of the warships that checked them.'
Vickers: 'They retired from our front as it grew light for had they stayed
the battleships would have given them their "breakfast".'

Soon after, the order for Number 1 Company of the Plymouth
Battalion to retire was passed down the line, and they pulled back to the
edge of the cliff. Being short of stretchers, they found they had left some
bearers and wounded in their trench. Vickers: 'We made a counterattack
driving back their snipers. On regaining our trenches, we found they had
bayonetted our wounded. Three Scotties near me were in a state of semi-
consciousness through loss of blood. They had all been bayonetted
through the chest.'

Both Meatyard and Vickers were right: the Turks, with the exception of lone riflemen or snipers, had retired inland away from the threat of the big naval guns. Matthews, if he had had enough men left, could have taken Krithia and possibly the summit of Achi Baba. Had Hamilton, watching the withdrawal from the *Queen Elizabeth*, gripped the situation and ordered Hunter-Weston to rapidly reinforce Y Beach, the disasters of the previous day would have been reversed. But such positive action was not in Hamilton's nature, despite the fact that the landing on Y Beach was his idea. Hunter-Weston was still so immersed in the events at V and W Beach that he ignored what was going on on his flanks, despite signals from Matthews. Eventually Hamilton asked d'Amade to land one of his regiments on Y Beach, but it was too late. The British had departed, just as victory was in their grasp.

Why the whole RM Brigade was not used at Y Beach, instead of a mixed force from two different divisions, without a properly constituted headquarters and commander, is a mystery. Both Hamilton and Hunter-Weston were found wanting when put to the test commanding a large formation in an amphibious operation. Muddled orders, a shaky command structure, and lack of drive at the highest level were responsible for the debacle at Y Beach. Matthews did not lack personal courage; reports from his own men speak of him being everywhere during a very trying night, and he was the last man off the beach. Unfortunately he was also indecisive. He was to do better as a brigade commander on the Western Front under a competent divisional commander.

The landing had cost 1 KOSB 296 casualties, including nearly all their officers, and the Plymouth Battalion 14 officers and 317 NCOs and privates. After withdrawing from Y Beach, Vickers, with the remainder of his battalion and the KOSB, embarked on HMS *Goliath*:

> Here many touching scenes took place for we all sought our chums and I felt very relieved to find my chums E. Morris and J. Matthews aboard unscratched. It was very touching to hear men asking for their chums and to be told by others 'I saw him killed'.

6

The Dardanelles:
The Royal Marines at Anzac
and Cape Helles

> The bravest thing I've seen so far was the charge of your two
> battalions up that hill on Bloody Sunday.
>
> Captain Quinn VC to the Staff Captain of the RM Brigade

In the first two days' fighting at Anzac, the Australians and New
Zealanders suffered over 5,000 casualties. By 28 April, despite bitter
fighting and great gallantry, the Anzacs had failed to expand their tiny
bridgehead out to terrain that afforded a naturally defendable position.
Initially their senior commanders were pessimistic about the ability of
the troops to hold on to the bare foothold they had carved out. Paris
commented: 'It was a grievous error landing the Australians [and New
Zealanders] so far away from the 29th [Division]. They are quite out of
touch & can only hold on being besieged all the time. I very much doubt
if they are keeping an equal number of enemy busy.'

The alternative was evacuation, which Hamilton would not countenance, because such a move would release Turkish troops to reinforce
those fighting to contain the Allies at Cape Helles. The Anzacs therefore
set about digging in and constructing a trench system, all the while
under fire, and in the face of continuous attacks. Here they would exist
in a state of siege unless the enemy could be diverted by an Allied
advance from Cape Helles, or the bridgehead enlarged. In the meanwhile
the nature of the first three days' fighting had been such that ANZAC
units were all mixed up with each other, and it was necessary to
reorganize battalions and formations. The troops, desperately tired after

three days and four nights of almost continuous fighting and without sleep, needed some rest. To do this they would have to be pulled out of the line in turn.

Accordingly, it was decided to reinforce the ANZAC bridgehead by the RM Brigade (Brigadier General C. N. Trotman RMLI, Chatham and Portsmouth Battalions), and 1st Naval Brigade (Brigadier General D. Mercer RMLI, Deal and Nelson Battalions). Both brigades consisted of only two battalions because the Plymouth Battalion was still under command of the 29th Division, and the Drake Battalion was already engaged at Cape Helles. The RM Brigade landed at Anzac on 28 April, and were all ashore by 2000 hours. It was a cold evening, with black storms of rain. The men, told that they would be ashore for only forty-eight hours, took few stores, and were dressed in light order. In the event they stayed for fourteen days. The Brigade was placed under Major General Bridges commanding the 1st Australian Division, and ordered to take over from 1st and 3rd Australian Brigades. The historian of the RN Division described the terrain and conditions at Anzac as seen by the two brigades on landing:

> On the beach the crowd and confusion had been astonishing. So great indeed was the admixture of units, and the number of men moving about independently on errands of which they alone knew the nature, that it was extremely difficult to assemble even a platoon and march it off. The difficulty in assembling a battalion, landed in open boats, was correspond-ingly greater ... it was necessary to climb the steep hills leading from the beach to the south of Maclagan's Ridge, and cross the main gully [most of the key terrain at Anzac had very quickly been named by the Australians and New Zealanders]. Here there were no organized lines of reinforcements or supply, no resting places for the reserve formations; but every possible piece of level ground had been appropriated by individuals of different units, many of them resting where they had fallen asleep involuntarily after the exertions of three days' continuous fighting ...
>
> The sides of the gully were rocky, and what, in the wet season, was the bed of a mountain stream, was now the only path which the landscape offered. On the upper slopes, thickly covered with arbutus, dwarf oaks, and other shrubs, the passage of men had, indeed, worn narrow tracks, but these were not serviceable, and merely showed the least dangerous line of approach for individuals to the firing line. This was nothing but a series of hastily dug posts, untraversed [that is without traverses, or zig-zags, to avoid enemy firing down the line of a trench from end to end],

unwired, broken with the wreckage of battle, scarred with the marks of intensive bombardment, just a series of foot-holds on the edge of the plateau, but defending the life-line of the Anzac position. The ground in front of the trenches was covered in thick scrub, broken by small depressions and ravines. Beyond it was another gorge, similar to the gully which formed the centre of the Anzac position. Here were the Turkish reserves, and from here on to and across the plateau there was constant movement of the enemy. Even when the utmost energy and skill had been spent on the fortification of our trenches, the situation at this point remained dangerous, and this key position could only be maintained throughout the campaign by hand-to-hand fighting of a desperate character.[1]

Most Marines were impressed by the Australians and New Zealanders. Private Henry Baker of the Chatham Battalion: 'The Australians and New Zealanders were very brave. They were different to our troops, they called their officers by their first names. They were great fellows, I have a great admiration for them.' The Australians were dismayed when they first saw the Marines and commented on their weedy physique, extreme youth, and bewildered air. But as events would show, appearances can be deceptive, and they could fight.

Arthur Chater, now nineteen years old and still a platoon commander in the Chatham Battalion, described his arrival at Anzac:

Landing in horse boats [barges for transporting horses] on the open beach at dusk, we were led by an Australian guide up the bottom of a steep ravine. This was our first experience of being in enemy country. It was all rather eerie. In the darkness, the guide lost the way, which led to counter-marching, and some confusion. He eventually found the right path, which, as dawn was breaking, brought us to a very steep slope, at the edge of which the Australians were entrenched only a few yards from the edge of the ravine. We took over the trenches, and they withdrew to rest.

For four days the Battalion held this precarious line wholly devoid of depth against attacks, and suffered grievous casualties. The slope behind part of the position was so steep that it could be climbed only with the aid of a rope. Parts of the slope were liable to be sniped. Dashing down on one occasion, I tripped over a field telephone wire, and fell down full length.

Snipers' tactics at Helles, where Paris was commanding a composite division, were similar to those at Anzac:

'sniping' is one of the most trying features. Several of them have been caught inside our lines. They get into holes and hide, with plenty of food and ammunition. It's certainly very brave. We have occasional sniper hunts, & woe betide any unfortunate who appears to be hiding & isn't instantly recognized.

At Anzac, Portsmouth and Chatham Battalions were given so much ground to cover that not all the Australians could be relieved, and parties of the 9th and 12th Australian Battalions remained in the centre of the position. The trenches were shallow scrapings, and at first the Marines only had their entrenching tools with which to improve them, until the next night when picks and shovels were sent forward. One of the Portsmouth Battalion officers described his sector:

In some places there were two lines of shallow trenches with a fair field of fire up to 400 yards; in others no field of fire and only a few feet from the edge of the slope which was too steep to climb without the aid of a rope made from rifle slings. The trenches were quite isolated with 30 or 40 yards of open ground between them, which had to be crossed under accurate and close-range fire. One of the most advanced positions were [sic] held by Lieutenants Empson and Alcock [of C Company Portsmouth Battalion].[2]

The experiences of these two young officers, occupying an isolated position with their two platoons, typified the intensity of the fighting endured by the Marines at Anzac. Empson was wounded on 30 April, and killed the next day. Alcock was finally forced to withdraw after holding for four nights and three days, during which time no food or water could be brought forward to him, and at one time ammunition was down to about fifteen rounds per man.

During the RM Brigade's first day ashore, the enemy only mounted sporadic attacks in small numbers. The next day the 1st Naval Brigade landed, and the Deal Battalion came up into the line with the Chatham and Portsmouth Battalion, while Nelson Battalion remained in reserve. On 30 May the Turks stepped up their attacks, General Mustapha Kemal's third attempt to sweep the defenders of Anzac into the sea. All along the sector occupied by the RMLI Battalions, the front-line companies fought to repel the enemy. The word line gives a false impression of the actual state of the positions, which could be infiltrated by the

Turks, and in places fired on from the flanks, and sometimes almost from the rear. Private Baker:

> The afternoon of our second day ashore the Turks attacked in huge numbers. They came out of the scrub like rabbits. We had a real tough time repelling that. I had two men loading for me because I was a crack shot. They didn't get closer than 50 yards. They were so closely bunched, if you missed one man, you would hit the next. You didn't get much time to aim. Each attack was over after a few minutes. Quite a number of our boys got hit, being a horseshoe position, the attacks came in on several sides. We were short of water, it had to be landed in cans brought all the way from Egypt, and the excitement makes you very dry. One night it rained and we drank water out of the little holes in the rocks. I didn't mind being hungry, but I was very thirsty.

Private Clements was a Maxim machine-gunner with Deal Battalion. The Maxim was the forerunner of the Vickers, which at that stage in the war was only just coming into service in the British Army. The attacks continued into the night. Clements:

> I was swinging the gun back and forward and you couldn't miss, at about 300 yards. It was dark, and you could just see a dark mass. They put in seven attacks in the same place. The number two was feeding the next belt. You couldn't pick out individual people, just a big mass. They got quite close, and then some turned and went, while we continued firing. At one stage we had to use our own water bottle to keep the barrel cool. Other machine guns had problems with splitting barrels from heat. I had no feeling, just wanted to keep the gun going.

In the early hours of the following day the first Royal Marine VC of the First World War was earned, by Lance Corporal Walter Parker RMLI of the Portsmouth Battalion. Since landing, he had been a tower of strength and courage in command of the battalion stretcher bearers. On the night of 30 April/1 May, a message was received at Battalion Headquarters from an isolated trench on Lone Pine Plateau asking for water, ammunition, and medical supplies. A carrying party of NCOs and privates was detailed off, and in response to a call for volunteers to assist Parker came forward. To reach the fire trench involved crossing at least 400 yards of open ground swept by rifle fire, and several men had already been killed in a previous attempt. It was daylight by the time the party emerged from cover, and one man was immediately wounded.

Parker organized a stretcher party to evacuate him before the carrying party moved on. One by one, as all the other ammunition and water carriers were killed or wounded, Parker went on alone and succeeded in reaching the fire trench. Here he gave first aid to the wounded, remaining cool and cheerful. When the trench was finally evacuated, Parker helped carry and tend the casualties, although he was badly wounded himself.

The fighting continued throughout 1 May and the night of 1/2 May. The brunt of the Turks' last assault in Kemal's third attack on Anzac, in moonlight, hit the Deal Battalion. The Marines remained under cover in their trenches until the Turks began to charge, at which orders were given to stand up and fire. Steady rifle fire mowed down the Turks, and only a handful reached the parapet, to be despatched by rifles and revolvers.

On the morning of 2 May the RM Brigade were relieved in their trenches by 1st Australian Brigade, which had rested and reorganized. The Australian Official History records: 'Thus from April 29th, to Saturday, 1st May a considerable portion of the Anzac line was in the hands of the Royal Marines. The Marines bore the brunt of Mustafa Kemal's third attack; though better timed and delivered than the last, it completely failed.'[3]

From then on, there were no more disparaging remarks about the Marines. At least one author, while acknowledging the key part played by the RM Brigade in the defence of Anzac, has commented on their heavy losses largely due, according to him, to their inexperience; by implication in contrast to the Anzacs. In truth the Anzacs, for all their undoubted qualities, were also inexperienced. There were instances on the first day of the landings when their spirit and courage could have been used to better effect, instead of being dissipated in undisciplined and uncoordinated dashes inland by small groups of enthusiasts, Australians especially. In general the New Zealanders yielded nothing to the Australians in spirit and initiative, but were better disciplined. The beach organization at Anzac in particular comes in for criticism from the historian of the RN Division, who compares it unfavourably with that 'which the organizing capacity of the trained staff of the 29th Division had brought about at Cape Helles'.[4]

The promised rest for the RM Brigade did not last long. The night the Marines were withdrawn, the 4th Australian Brigade mounted an attack on Pope's Hill, a vital crest line which commanded much of the

Anzac position, at the head of Monash Valley, a continuation of Shrapnel Gully. In spite of gallant efforts, the attack petered out after capturing two lines of trenches, and the Australians were in places left hanging precariously to the crest, and in others driven back. At 0200 hours on 3 May the RM Brigade was ordered to send two battalions to dig in behind the 4th Australian Brigade and support them at the head of Monash Valley. Arthur Chater, Chatham Battalion:

> As we moved up the ravine, HMS *Bacchante* opened fire on the crest, and began to shell the Australians out of their newly-won trenches. Signalling in those days was slow and uncertain and the message that the position had been taken during the night had not reached the ship.

The Portsmouth Battalion (Lieutenant Colonel Luard) had been ordered to move into the support trenches, behind the front, or firing line. But when the leading company arrived, these trenches were found to be full, and a message was received saying that there was no space in the front line either. So Lieutenant Colonel Luard ordered his battalion to dig in on the right of the support line. As it got light, the front-line troops sent messages saying they were in difficulties. Luard, however, decided to continue entrenching where he was. Suddenly he saw men from the firing line streaming out of their trenches only about fifty yards ahead, and running into the ravine below. Gathering up the only two companies he could see, A and D, Luard shouted, 'Charge!' The cry was taken up by all the officers in the vicinity, and Luard's Marines charged up the slope, taking many of the Australians with them, thus stopping the panic in the ravine below. When the Australians ran back, they had taken some of Portsmouth Battalion with them. But they were rallied by Major Festing RMLI, the Brigade Major, who led them to join the charge. As the Marines topped the crest, they were met by a hail of shrapnel and machine-gun fire, but succeeded in regaining the lost trenches. B Company was pushed out to the left, but their trenches were overlooked by Turkish machine-gunners, so they were withdrawn during the day and following night. Luard was wounded in the knee, and as his second-in-command had already been killed, the senior surviving company commander, Major Clark of D Company, took over the battalion. Portsmouth Battalion was now reduced to 7 officers and 350 other ranks, from an initial strength of some 35 officers and 900 other ranks when they sailed from England.

Chatham Battalion meanwhile attacked Razor Back Hill. Arthur Chater:

> As the Battalion reached the foot of the slope to the crest, A Company was for some reason diverted to the right. From our position near Quinn's Post, we watched the remainder of the Battalion struggling up the steep slope. As the leading waves reached the crest, they were caught by machine gun fire from the flank. Many of the bodies rolled back down the hill they had so laboriously climbed, some lay where they fell, until two days later we went out in darkness and pulled them down.

Not for nothing did the Razor Back acquire the name which it kept to the end of the campaign: Dead Man's Ridge. The desperate charge of the Chatham and Portsmouth Battalions up a near-precipitous cliff against enemy trenches in daylight earned them the accolade from the legendary Australian VC quoted at the start of this chapter.

The charge up to Dead Man's Ridge was led by the Adjutant, Captain Richards. Two lines of trenches were taken, and held for six hours. But without support, and enfiladed from the flank, the Chatham Battalion was eventually driven off the ridge. The gallant Richards was killed. Private Baker, D Company:

> Captain Richards ordered us to open fire at 200 yards. He stood up in full view of the enemy, in front of us. He kept on shouting open fire at 200. Suddenly I saw a huge triangular cut open up on his right shoulder blade. He must have been hit by a dum-dum [more likely a normal exit wound]. He came back and lay down where I was lying, ordering me to move to the left, and he was still shouting open fire at 200, and we lay there shoulder-to-shoulder. There were about 50 of us.
>
> We opened fire as the Turks advanced in a mass. Next to me there was a space, and an Australian came and lay next to me. Men were lying shoulder-to-shoulder. There was no cover. It was like lying on the top of a railway embankment. Suddenly a machine-gun crackled away behind our flank, and higher up, it must have been like mowing grass for him. 'Oh' the Australian said, 'the bastards can't kill me. They've had lots of tries, but they can't kill me'. I looked along at the Machine Gun barking away and it was knocking the sand up hitting every man again. As I saw the bullets coming closer, I thought 'am I going to live?' I heard the bullets thud into the Aussie and he never spoke again. I felt as though I had been kicked by a donkey, and I had a bullet through the right foot. The gun stopped firing. I lay there not knowing what to do.

Chater:

> Monday 3rd May was a black day for the Chatham Battalion. Amongst
> two hundred casualties [three hundred in fact], we had lost Captain
> W. H. P. Richards, the Adjutant, a most able and fearless officer in whom
> all had confidence. This must have been a bitter blow for the elderly
> Commanding Officer [Lieutenant Colonel C. McN. Parsons RMLI], who
> had greatly depended upon him. To my amazement, he sent for me and
> told me to take over the duties of Adjutant.

Private Baker was still in the position when the Chatham Battalion
was forced to withdraw:

> The Turks came along prodding some of the men with their bayonets.
> Fortunately they didn't prod me. I could hear them jabbering away, and
> they moved off. I gave myself a push off and I went bumpety-bump down
> the ravine, over dead men, rifles, bushes and right down to the bottom
> where I was safe except for shrapnel. A New Zealander picked me up and
> dressed my wound. He put me on a donkey on which he was taking the
> wounded to the beach. He was called David Taylor, from South Island.
> The ship's boats collected us. We were towed out to the *Dongola*, which
> they were using for the wounded. It wasn't a hospital ship. It had
> transported some of the Australians. Alongside someone emptied a bucket
> over the side and soaked us. The Middy in charge of our boat, only aged
> about 16, blasted him in the finest language I have ever heard. There were
> only two doctors on this ship and no medical staff of any kind. The crew
> had to act as orderlies.
>
> We were deposited on the bare deck – no beds, and one blanket. All
> the troops had been in hammocks on the way over from Egypt to
> Gallipoli. My officer, Grinling, a regular who went to Haileybury, came
> on board badly wounded but died very soon afterwards. There were over
> 600 wounded. I can not recall there being any RAMC [Royal Army
> Medical Corps]. We were fed and given something to drink. Some men
> were immobile. I could slide along on my backside, and I went up on
> deck and up on to the bridge. For three days after we left Gallipoli we
> had no one to look after us properly. My foot was black with bruising
> and we were nearly at Alexandria before anyone looked at me. On the
> way south, the ship stopped at least three times to push dead over the
> side. Sanitary conditions were very bad. But at least we were not going to
> be shot at. The boy scouts could have handled the operation better.

The Australian History commented:

The attempt to improve the defective position at the head of the Monash Valley had definitely failed, the throwing in of the Marines at daybreak to retrieve a battle already lost resulted only in the slaughter of many brave officers and men, and the disorganisation of these already over-strained battalions.[5]

The battalions cannot have been all that 'disorganized', because Brigadier General Trotman, commanding the RM Brigade, was ordered to command the 3rd Defence Sector of Anzac with Chatham and Portsmouth Battalions, who together totalled some 1,100 all ranks, and, also under his command, 4th Australian Brigade, the freshest formation in the bridgehead. Here, from Pope's Hill on the left, through Quinn's Post in the centre, to Courtney's Post on the right, the RM Brigade held until 12 May during a period of severe and continuous fighting. In the opinion of the Australian Official Historian, 'the Monash sector was the most difficult of the line. Few positions of the nature of Pope's Hill and Quinn's Post were held by any troops during the War.'[6]

Arthur Chater:

The 4th Australian Brigade was commanded by Colonel Monash, who was to become one of Australia's greatest generals. I was sent to confer with Captain Quinn on a plan for reinforcing his vital post. Whilst we were talking, General Godley the Divisional Commander arrived, and I of course, withdrew a short distance. While Godley and Quinn were talking, the Turks attacked, and all but overran the post. The tall general waved his helmet and shouted 'Australia forever!', then spotting me – the only man there wearing a helmet – he shouted 'Come on that officer in a helmet, I want to see you lead a counterattack'. Having no weapon, I picked up the nearest rifle, and disappeared as fast as I could down a trench in the direction of the enemy. The attack was repulsed, but not through any act of mine.

On the afternoon of 12th May, the RM Brigade was relieved at Anzac by the Australian Light Horse, who had been dismounted and left their horses in Egypt. In the dark, the Chatham Battalion re-embarked in the *Cawdor Castle*. The old Captain was shocked when told the numbers of our casualties, and the names of officers killed. In two weeks, the Battalion had lost eleven officers and over three hundred other ranks.

The RM Brigade as a whole had lost 1,153 killed, wounded, and missing.

*

The Plymouth Battalion, after its withdrawal from Y Beach, was brigaded with the Drake Battalion. Together with the 2nd Australian Brigade and the New Zealand Brigade, shipped round from Anzac, they formed a Composite Division under General Paris, while most of his own formations were engaged elsewhere. The Composite Division, with the 29th Division, and the French reinforced by 2nd Naval Brigade, took part in the Second Battle of Krithia, which like the first was an attempt to break out of the Helles bridgehead and advance to the first day's objective, Achi Baba. After three days' fighting, with over a third casualties, the Allies reached a line some three and a half miles from Cape Helles, still short of Y Beach, and well over a mile from Krithia. Troops were thrown in with inadequate artillery support, in daylight, over open ground, against well dug-in Turks, and mown down.

Here in Gallipoli, as on the Western Front and elsewhere in the First World War, problems of command and control were to bedevil operations. As one author remarks, referring to the Second Battle of Krithia, 'On this battlefield, the passage of orders was no faster than it might have been in the eighteenth century.'[7] The methods of passing orders and information, once a battle was mobile, had failed to keep pace with the technology of killing. The missing ingredient was battlefield radios. Once battalions were committed to an advance, field telephones that relied on cable were useless. The lack of radio communications meant that from the outset the brigade, divisional, and higher commanders had no influence on events, and as the battle developed, even battalion commanders could control only those men in their immediate vicinity. Because messages could be passed back and forth only by runner, pigeon, or heliograph, commanders up the chain of command usually had little idea how their troops were, or were not, progressing. Signalling by heliograph was usually impossible in the conditions of a full-blooded battle, even if the sun was shining. When information was received at formation headquarters, it was often completely out of date. So when, hours later, orders to forward units had arrived, based on the situation as perceived at headquarters, their contents were often totally irrelevant to the actual circumstances. Even if, as was the case in the Second Battle of Krithia, the commander was able to site his command post so he could view the battlefield, he would not get the full operational picture for lack of communications, and would still be unable to draw together the threads of the battle. Furthermore he would be unlikely to be able to see all the ground, and would be too far off to 'read' the battle, as Hamilton found on this occasion. He asked why the attacking troops had gone to ground and were not advancing; they were all dead or wounded.

When the Chatham and Portsmouth Battalions, together with the Deal Battalion and the 1st Naval Brigade, arrived in the Helles sector on 13 May from Anzac, General Paris had the whole of the RN Division together under his command for the first time in the Gallipoli campaign. Officer volunteers were called for from the fleet to replace casualties in the RM Brigade, but only five could be spared. Paris again commented on naval gunfire support: 'One of the great disappointments has been the effect of naval gunfire – very erratic and seldom much use.'

The morale of the troops ashore was not improved when HMS *Triumph* was torpedoed off Anzac, on 25 May. Corporal Fred Brookes:

The U-boat poked her periscope up which caused a commotion. We depended on our own torpedo nets [to protect the ship from torpedoes]. No man was allowed below decks unless needed below. I was in charge of two 14-pounders on the starboard side. At one bell [1230 hours], we had just served out the rum, when this sub poked up again. I already had the range and was loaded, and off went my shells. They went over, and before I could fire again, a torpedo was on its way. One of my guns depressed and tried to hit the torpedo. It went straight through the nets, hit the ship. She heeled. Water shot up to the masthead and poured down on to the gun deck. My assistant, a private, was washed over the side. I was talking to myself, I said, 'along the fore and aft bridge, down on the shelter deck, down on the quarter deck, along the after torpedo boom, drop in the ditch'. As I was saying it, I was doing it. On the way, the Chinese messman was hanging on the ladder [the iron ladder down to the torpedo net shelf]. I said, 'drop in the ditch'. He said, 'no can swim'. I couldn't wait for him. She turned turtle in 12 minutes. A lot of our people caught in our nets. One destroyer made an attempt to come to our stern and got quite a lot of people off. The engineer commander sacrificed his life. He went below to start the engines and prevent the engines blowing up. One officer jumped over the side just as the propellers started revolving and was killed. I stayed clear until picked up by a trawler – lots of them appeared. Most of us had thrown off our clothes. The sergeant-major was as undressed as were most of us, but still had his list, and was calling the roll. We were taken and put on a French ship, and [eventually] the Marines were fitted out in Khaki and put ashore on the guns on the entrance of Mudros harbour, protecting the nets.

The immediate reaction by de Robeck was to order all the larger warships to Imbros. The soldiers watched incredulously as the Navy left the scene. The following day, de Robeck, aware that their precipitate departure can hardly have improved the Navy's image, ordered the *Majestic* to Helles. She was torpedoed the following morning, sinking in less than thirty minutes, but with few losses. The cruisers and destroyers increased their support, and later the monitors made up for the absence of the battleships, but for a while the Army felt abandoned.

Paris expressed amazement that *Majestic* had remained at anchor: 'Even naval officers expected she would be sunk & one Captain RN told an officer on board that he better get up early and come ashore.'

The RM Brigade was in reserve for the Third Battle of Krithia on 4 June, which advanced the Allied line by a few hundred yards. They were under orders to advance and occupy Krithia, but were not required because the attack failed. On 6 June, the Chatham Battalion was ordered to move forward to support 127th Infantry Brigade of 42nd Division. Arthur Chater:

> The route lay up the bed of a shallow nullah, which gave little protection from shell fire. We suffered about thirty casualties including three officers. When we reached the forward troops we found they had advanced only a few yards and were still a long way from Krithia. During our three days with the 42nd Division, the Battalion suffered 120 casualties.

After the Third Battle of Krithia, the RM Brigade was not involved in major operations for over a month, although fighting patrols and local attacks were frequent, and took their toll, as did disease. Chater:

> By now the weather was getting hot. Apart from our completely unnecessary helmets, we had no tropical clothes, and were still wearing our thick serge tunics, breeches and puttees. The seams of our shirts were alive with lice. I had one sea bathe in Morto Bay, but the shelling from Asia detracted from the pleasure of that. The flies were indescribable – it was difficult to put food into one's mouth without putting in flies at the same time. The result was universal 'tummy trouble' with the consequent weakening effect. Tins of bully beef were more than plentiful; some trenches were revetted with them. Except in the dug-out of the Divisional Supply Officer, all jam was plum and apple. The supply of fresh water

was very limited, and as time went on, it became dangerously contaminated.

Even in rest areas, the enemy artillery could search one out.

> About this time, whilst we were in 'rest', a shrapnel round burst high above us. I had only time to bend down, and a ball hit me in the middle of the back. I was completely winded, and as I lay gasping for breath, not knowing I was not really injured, I heard the CO shouting for the doctor. Dallas Brooks was not so lucky. A shrapnel ball entered his back near his spine, and has never been removed. We had a number of casualties, some fatal, while in 'rest'.

Meanwhile Paris was having trouble with Commodore Backhouse, commanding 2nd Naval Brigade. During a rest and retraining period at Imbros, he reported that reinforcements to his brigade would not mix with veterans:

> and [Backhouse] recommended breaking up the brigade and that he should go to sea! My reply was simple – 'return here at once', and then I had a heart-to-heart talk with the officers – explained the difference between peace and war. My friends seemed a little astonished when I explained there was no such thing as resignation & their only way of leaving the Peninsula was on a stretcher or as a prisoner! Backhouse put in for sick leave which I sent on – a few hours later he sent me a letter withdrawing it.

Backhouse left for good two months later.

The last attempt to advance to Achi Baba took place in mid-July, by VII Corps, commanded by Hunter-Weston, promoted to Corps Commander the previous month. His corps for the attack consisted of 52nd (Lowland) Division and the RN Division. The 1st and 2nd French Divisions were to attack on his right. The RM Brigade was in Corps Reserve. On 12 July the 52nd Division, with great gallantry and heavy loss, reached and occupied a part of the enemy line, and all three RMLI battalions were ordered up in support. Chater takes up the tale:

> As we approached the 52nd Division Headquarters, which was in the position normally used by our own Brigade Headquarters when we were in the line, the CO said, 'I do not want to have to halt the Battalion here, so run on and find out where they want us to go'. I reached the headquarters dug-out, saluted, and asked for orders. A voice from the

depths said, 'Don't stand up there my lad, you may get shot. Come down here and sit down.' To my surprise I found myself being addressed by the Divisional General. He next remark was, 'I have been up since four this morning and feel so tired'. I suppose that for years past, the old man had an afternoon nap. Without it he was defeated. He was quite unfit to command in battle.

Despite this somewhat condescending portrait of the fifty-six-year-old Major General Egerton by the nineteen-year-old Chater, 52nd Division had carried out a heroic attack with very heavy losses, under very difficult circumstances, following a very sketchy briefing by Hunter-Weston's staff. By nightfall the division found itself in totally unfamiliar terrain, with few surviving officers. The Plymouth Battalion, which had come forward in support of 6th Battalion Highland Light Infantry, suffered a number of casualties during the night, including Matthews, the CO, who was wounded.

The next morning there was considerable confusion, caused partly by doubts as to exactly where the 52nd Division was. A reconnaissance by Major Sketchley, one of Paris's staff officers, and Jerram, the Brigade Major of the RM Brigade, established that part of the 157th Brigade of the 52nd Division was in the process of withdrawing, so that Plymouth Battalion found itself in sole occupation of the brigade position, and drove off a Turkish attempt to follow up 157th Brigade. Major Sketchley, who turned up at this moment, stopped the 52nd Division's withdrawal, leading the men back with the aid of some Marines of Plymouth Battalion. Carrying only a fly whisk, he reoccupied the trenches that had been lost.

During the night of 12/13 July, the Nelson and Drake Battalions had arrived to reinforce the RM Brigade. Nelson was sent to support the Plymouth Battalion. By now, Hunter-Weston, completely out of the picture, had lost control of the battle. He ordered the RN Division to pass through the 52nd Division and to take the remaining enemy trenches, including those that had been lost after a Turkish counter-attack. The briefing given to the staff of the RN Division by VII Corps staff was totally inadequate, at very little notice, and consequently no information of any value percolated down to brigade and battalions. The task was given to Brigadier General Trotman, with Chatham, Portsmouth, and Nelson Battalions. Chater:

At 3.30 pm our Brigade Commander came up to the support line and
dictated orders to the COs of the Chatham and Portsmouth Battalions to
assault and occupy the enemy position to our front at 4 pm. The assault
was to be preceded by a so-called bombardment lasting a few minutes. In
the congested trenches, and time available, it was quite impossible to get
orders issued, and to prepare the Battalion for an assault; so when the
little bombardment took place, no one was ready. About half an hour
later I heard a lot of enemy gun and rifle fire, and looking over the top,
saw, through a cloud of dust and smoke, the Portsmouth Battalion
assaulting on its own, unsupported by artillery fire. The gallant Battalion
Commander took himself and many of his Battalion to death. The
Chatham Battalion did not assault. For a long time I felt very ashamed of
how our Battalion had failed that evening; but our CO at the time was no
leader, and in any case, he could have led us only to death, with no hope
of achieving our objective.

In fact both Nelson and Portsmouth reached their objectives; the former
was out of sight of Chater. The CO of Nelson Battalion, Lieutenant
Colonel Evelegh RMLI, was killed, as was Luard of Portsmouth Battalion,
back in command after his wound at Anzac. Many of Portsmouth
Battalion advanced beyond their objective, the Turkish third line; it was
unrecognizable, being a scrape only eighteen inches deep. Most of them
were killed. The remnants fell back and dug in on the third line. The
Portsmouth Battalion suffered grievous losses of 11 officers, and 226
other ranks, killed, wounded, and missing.

General Paris recommended to Corps Headquarters that his division
should relieve the 52nd Division in all their positions, and he should
consolidate on the line both divisions held. The 52nd and RN Divisions
had achieved a notable success, and had Hunter-Weston and his staff
handled the battle better, keeping a strong reserve in hand, it is possible
that Achi Baba might yet have been taken, providing he had followed up
the gains made by 52nd Division immediately with a properly coordinated attack with the whole of RN Division, fighting as a division. The
Turks were worn out, and in no state to resist a strong attack, but not
for long; soon Turkish Second Army arrived to reinforce the Krithia
sector. Achi Baba, the objective for 25 April, would remain out of the
Allies' grasp for ever.

Battle casualties in the RM Brigade in the battles of June and July
totalled 20 officers and 533 other ranks. To this must be added as many,

if not more, sick with dysentery and jaundice, both endemic at Gallipoli. There was also a daily trickle of casualties whether battalions were in or out of the line, from snipers, artillery, trench raids, and patrolling. Chater:

> by now my strength was giving out. Not only was my eye wound [from Antwerp] giving trouble as a result of the glare and the dust, but I had jaundice, and was generally debilitated. When I left the peninsula on 29 July, I was the only original officer of the Chatham Battalion which had landed on 28 April. I was taken to England, where I was in hospital first at Plymouth and then at Chatham. It then transpired that I had never been passed fit after my Antwerp wound, but owing to the haste with which the Battalion had left for Gallipoli, this had fortunately been overlooked.

Although some reinforcements had been received, there was no prospect of making battalions up to full strength. Therefore it was decided to amalgamate Chatham and Deal Battalions to form 1st RMLI, while Portsmouth and Plymouth formed 2nd RMLI. They retained these titles until the end of the war. The Naval Brigades were similarly short of men, so the RN Division was reduced to two Brigades: 1st Brigade under Brigadier General Mercer RMLI (Drake, Hawke, Nelson, and Hood Battalions), and 2nd Brigade under Brigadier General Trotman (1st and 2nd RMLI, Howe, and Anson Battalions).

The RN Division played no part in the Suvla landings on 6 August, and spent the remainder of the campaign in trenches in the Helles sector. Private Henry Baker, who had been wounded at Anzac and evacuated to England, remembered:

> I was passed fit and told I was in a draft going back to Gallipoli. I asked for leave. I said goodbye to my people thinking I would never see them again. The draft of fifty left on 2 August 1915, Bank Holiday Saturday [sic: 2 August was actually Monday]. I didn't want to go back to Gallipoli. I thought my luck couldn't hold out. We went to Waterloo, and down to Devonport to embark. I stood for as long as I could with one foot on the gangplank and one on the quay, thinking 'I shall never come back here again'. I was the only one of our draft who had ever been in action. The ship was full of drafts from all sorts of regiments, about 1600 men in all.

Baker also kept a diary and recorded his impressions on the first morning after his arrival, when everybody seemed to disappear like moles at dawn:

Friday 20th August 1915
At 5.30 am the sun rose from behind Achi Baba and the land from Cape Helles to the firing line resembled a huge field being drained. Even the horses and carts are placed in dug-outs. The shells from our guns were screaming over as soon as it got light. Asiatic Annie [a large Turkish gun on the Asiatic shore] fired huge shells over.

Saturday 21st August 1915
We received the order to go up to the trenches. Trench order is: rifle & equipment, firewood & rations, entrenching tool, waterproof sheet, blanket, iron rations, helmet & cap, 2 respirators, ammunition, sun helmet, 2 sandbags, bandoleer. At 2 pm we marched up to the trenches through a winding communication trench about 6 feet deep. We arrived in the reserve trench about 4 pm. There was rather a bad smell, as about 700 Worcesters and Hampshires were lying dead in front of our trenches & could not be buried. The Turks' trenches were about 450 yards away.

Baker was eventually evacuated with enteric fever in mid-October, but not before he had experienced the daily round of trench life:

After [evening] stand-to men had to go and lie out between the trench lines. You took out a piece of string connected to a sentry in the trench, to pull if there was any sign of movement. You were unarmed except for a knife. You lay out there for one hour, before being relieved. Men were posted at about 80 yard intervals, alone. One night I lay there (I had cut my trousers down to shorts), I felt something on the back of my right thigh. At that moment a verey light lit up the whole area. I looked round and there was a big mouse sitting there, which I was very glad to see instead of a Turk. I did this duty about three times in my time. I never saw one Turk when I was out in front. Where I stepped out of the trench there was a splintered skull to give you a send off. We had concertina barbed wire about six feet in front of our trench, and another line about 20 yards out. You had to find the gap.

Used to be shelled on average every two days, it was not usually very intensive. Occasionally it went on for several hours. You crouched as low as you could. Not many shells fell into the trench. The ground used to rock, and splinters whined off like cats mewing. Nobody seemed to show signs of having the 'wind up'.

We had been having some some trouble from a sniper. Because I was a known shot, I was told to deal with him. At stand-to, I stuck my head over the parapet and lined up and fired on a Turks head just showing above their trench, and I felt a bullet whistle past my ear. I reckon we must have fired together.

After stand-down in the morning, just a few sentries would man the firestep and watch through periscopes. It was very boring, there was very little to do. You could sleep then though. At night the sentries used to look over the top. Dysentery was a bigger menace than the Turks.

*

Following the failure of the Suvla landings, but not until after much high-level discussion, acrimony, and a visit from Kitchener, it was decided to evacuate the Peninsula. By now Hamilton had been sacked, and eventually replaced by General Birdwood as Commander Dardanelles Army. Hunter-Weston had been invalided after the failure of the July battles at Cape Helles. There were forecasts of huge casualties during the evacuation. Some imaginations worked overtime with gloomy predictions of mass slaughter on the beaches as troops struggled to embark in boats, bayoneted and mown down by screaming Turks following up the panicking Allies. Thanks to brilliant planning, organization, discipline, and ingenuity, the withdrawal, while still in contact with the enemy, and the evacuation were by far the best conducted phases of the campaign. Suvla and Anzac were evacuated first, in the night of 18/19 December 1915, and without the enemy realizing what was happening until it was too late.

The night of 8/9 January 1916 was set for the last troops to be away from Cape Helles. Lieutenant Colonel Hutchinson commanding 2 RMLI was responsible for covering V Beach, and manning a final defensive position a few hundred yards inland from Sedd-el-Bahr. After the remaining troops on the Peninsula had passed through 2 RMLI, the battalion was thinned out, leaving a platoon of C Company commanded by Lieutenant Andrews as the final troops to leave, on the orders of the General Commanding the Evacuation. One of them recorded:

By half past three in the morning we were all through and hence our task was done, so with mingled feelings we turned our back on Achi Baba. With complete silence we marched to the beach and boarded the waiting tug, which got underway immediately for Imbros. We had not proceeded

far before we noticed that all the stores, which could not be got off, were
a mass of flames. Still the Turks were sending up their customary signals,
and holding an imaginary enemy; and now thoroughly awakened, but too
late, the Turks shelled the beach heavily.[8]

When, eventually, the Turks poured into the abandoned positions they
encountered a mass of booby traps left as a welcoming present.

The Plymouth Battalion had made the first landing on 4 March 1915,
and as part of the 2nd RMLI were the last to leave. Of the original 118
Royal Marines officers in the RM Brigade of a headquarters and four
battalions that landed at Gallipoli on 25 and 28 April 1915, only 15 were
present at the evacuation nine months later. The other 103 were dead,
or evacuated with wounds or sickness. (Some of the fifteen originals had
been wounded, and returned to the brigade before the evacuation.)

The 2nd (RM) Brigade remained in the Aegean until early May 1916,
when, with the remainder of the RN Division, it embarked for France.

7

The Battle of Jutland

There seems to be something wrong with our bloody ships today.

Vice Admiral Sir David Beatty to his Flag Captain at Jutland

For eighteen months after the Battle of Dogger Bank in January 1915, the ships of Admiral Sir John Jellicoe's Grand Fleet saw no action. There had been frequent 'sweeps' of the North Sea, and several false alarms. The sole relief for the tedium of countless exercises at sea, gun drill, and occasional training ashore for the Marines was afforded by shore leave. The lucky ones, in the ships of Vice Admiral Sir David Beatty's Battle-cruiser Fleet (BCF) based at Rosyth, could spend their off-duty time ashore in Rosyth, or for the more fortunate, usually the officers, on a half-day trip to Edinburgh. Beatty's trips to that city were usually for the purpose of sharing a bed in the North British Hotel with Eugénie Godfrey-Fausset, the wife of a friend, a brother officer and equerry to the King. The amenities ashore for the main body of the Grand Fleet, the Battle Fleet, based at Scapa in the Orkneys, were so sparse as to be practically non-existent: a wet canteen consisting of barrels of beer and a few tables and chairs, or a bracing walk over the peaty hills. As a result some men went for months without going ashore. One battle squadron from Scapa, with some cruisers and destroyers, took it in turns to base at Invergordon, as a change of scene from Scapa.

General Sir Leslie Hollis, then the Lieutenant of Marines in the heavy cruiser *Duke of Edinburgh*, relates the outcome of a day's recreation ashore at Invergordon, which also reveals what he calls 'the lack of cordiality between the Royal Navy and the Marines' described in Chapter 2.

It was decided to relieve the monotony of our wartime regime by a day ashore for the ship's company, with sports and other pastimes. Much beer was produced and a good few of the wilder elements, mainly stokers, partook freely. When the time came to return the weather had worsened, and instead of embarking from the beach where we landed, we had to make a long march down the coast road to Cromarty. The majority of the men duly went on board without incident, but those who were drunk were left behind in charge of a lieutenant named Lundholm, with an escort of Royal Marines under my command. The drunken sailors did not take kindly to the long march, and fighting soon broke out. Lundholm, who was my senior in rank, ordered me to restore order. I pointed out the ringleaders to my sergeant-major, and almost immediately the blue-jackets found themselves immersed in the sea in no uncertain fashion by the enthusiastic Marines. This led to further disorder. A fight followed which went on almost as far as Cromarty itself. But on the heights above this small town was a battery – the South Sutor battery – which was manned by reservists of the Royal Marine Artillery. They had noticed what was going on and decided to take a hand. Their senior NCO accordingly assembled a small party which charged down the hill in khaki service dress and with fixed bayonets. This was too much for the drunkards. Resistance caved in.[1]

The BCF regarded themselves as the cream of the Grand Fleet. Needless to say, the battle squadrons did not share this view, and regarded them as spoilt prima donnas. This was partly jealousy, because the battlecruisers were the only major units of the Grand Fleet that had seen any action at sea so far. Battlecruisers were one of Fisher's brainchildren: lightly armoured, heavily gunned ships, and very fast (for their time – twenty-five knots, equivalent to a light cruiser). Their task by 1914 was to scout ahead of the battle fleet, brush aside, or crush, the enemy scouting cruisers, locate the enemy battle fleet, and use their five-knot speed advantage to keep out of range, while enticing it into the fire of their own battle fleet. All this was well and good, until the Germans built battlecruisers of their own, which were just as fast, but better armoured than their British equivalents. Furthermore the British gunnery control system installed in all but one of the battlecruisers, *Invincible* (and in all the battleships), took far too long to obtain hits at longer ranges when both firing ship and target were manoeuvring at high speed in conditions of poor visibility caused by funnel and gun smoke, mist, spray, and shell splashes towering over twice the height of the largest ship.

Despite rivalry between the parts of the Grand Fleet, the abiding obsession from admirals down to the youngest boy seaman, and constant source of speculation, was, 'When will they come out?' – 'they' being Vice Admiral Reinhard Scheer's German High Seas Fleet, based at Wilhelmshaven in the Jade Estuary.

The British had been reading German naval wireless traffic since the outbreak of war, when a German signals book and later a cipher book came into the possession of the Royal Navy. On the morning of 30 May 1916 the Admiralty intercepted a German signal ordering a sortie by the High Seas Fleet the following day up the Jutland coast of Denmark, and into the North Sea. Scheer's aim was to draw Beatty's battlecruisers out ahead of the rest of the Grand Fleet, and destroy or inflict maximum damage on them, before the main body of Jellicoe's fleet could come to their assistance. He therefore planned that Rear Admiral Franz von Hipper's 1st Scouting Group of battlecruisers and cruisers should steam well ahead, and out of sight, of the battleships of the High Seas Fleet. If all went to plan, when Beatty (who invariably preceded the Battle Fleet by some miles) saw Hipper's ships, he would engage them. Hipper would then turn, as if to flee, drawing the dashing Beatty on to the main body of the High Seas Fleet. The details of the plan, including the destination of the fleet, were not included in the signal intercepted by the Admiralty, because they had been thrashed out face-to-face by the two German admirals.

The warning of Scheer's sortie was passed to Jellicoe, who ordered all parts of his Fleet to sea after dark that evening. He chose to sail in darkness, to make it more difficult for U-boats to intercept him. He guessed, correctly, they were waiting in ambush at the exits of the Grand Fleet anchorages and moorings at Scapa, the Firth of Forth, and Cromarty Firth.

Between 2200 and 2300 hours, Beatty's BCF slid under the Forth Bridge: six battlecruisers, *Lion* (Beatty's flagship), *Princess Royal*, *Tiger*, *Queen Mary*, *New Zealand*, and *Indefatigable*; four battleships (the 5th Battle Squadron), *Barham* (flag), *Warspite*, *Malaya*, and *Valiant*; and fourteen light cruisers, twenty-seven destroyers, and one seaplane carrier. Jellicoe's twenty-four battleships and four battlecruisers, along with heavy and light cruisers, and their attendant destroyers slipped and proceeded to sea at about the same time. Thanks to good intelligence, the Grand Fleet sailed four and a half hours before the High Seas Fleet had even left harbour. The Grand Fleet consisted of sixty-seven battle-ships, battlecruisers, and cruisers, every one of which carried a Royal Marine Detachment, and eighty destroyers. The RMLI and RMA detachments in the Grand Fleet totalled 93 Royal Marines officers, 39 warrant officers, and 5,700 NCOs, gunners, and privates.

By early afternoon on 31 May, as a result of an unhelpful and incorrect signal from the Admiralty to the effect that the Germans might not be coming out after all, Beatty was about to order the BCF to reverse course and rendezvous with the Battle Fleet. Hopes that action was imminent began to fade, and many in his BCF went to tea. At 1425 on 31 May, just after Beatty had ordered the BCF to turn, *Galatea*, one of Beatty's scouting force consisting of 1st, 2nd, and 3rd Light Cruiser Squadrons (LCS), went to investigate a neutral merchantman being boarded by two German destroyers. Beyond the German destroyers, she sighted two enemy cruisers. She hoisted the flag signal 'enemy in sight', and fired her forward 6in gun to draw attention to it. Beatty at once turned and increased speed, to try to get between the enemy and his base. The 5th Battle Squadron could not read Beatty's flag hoist, and continued on a northwards course at twenty knots, away from Beatty, for several minutes, until *Lion* signalled with a searchlight. Why Rear Admiral Hugh Evan-Thomas did not follow Beatty's turn is a mystery. But Evan-Thomas, an over-promoted officer, was short on initiative, and pedestrian to the point of being thick. This obtuseness on his part was to have a serious effect on the forthcoming battle. The 5th Battle Squadron consisted of the fastest and most powerful battleships in the world, armed with massive 15in guns (two of which can be seen in front of the Imperial War Museum). This battle squadron had been specifically attached to Beatty to give him the 'muscle' to smash the enemy battlecruisers, and to hold off the German battle fleet should he encounter it when he was detached from the main body of the Grand Fleet, giving him time to escape. Exactly his situation now; which he and Jellicoe had foreseen. Now his heavyweights were going to be late.

Bugler Charles Smith RMLI in the light cruiser *Inconstant*, in 1st LCS:

> The *Galatea* and *Phaeton* being within range [of the enemy light cruisers], opened fire on a large three-funnelled enemy vessel. It replied with heavy guns and seemed to concentrate its fire on *Phaeton*, which was not touched. Our battlecruisers were now coming up with the 3rd Light

Cruiser Squadron. They engaged the enemy as soon as they were within effective range. Soon five enemy battlecruisers were made out and were immediately taken on by our battlecruisers.

The German battlecruisers *Lützow*, *Derfflinger*, *Seydlitz*, *Moltke* (flag), and *Von der Tann* were steaming at high speed to join in the light cruiser engagement when Hipper sighted Beatty's battlecruisers. He turned back towards the High Seas Fleet, which had just emerged from the Horns Reef Channel, the northern route from the Jade Estuary which avoided the British minefields off the coasts of Frisia and Schleswig-Holstein. He was pursued by Beatty. Both sides opened fire at 18,500 yards (10½ miles).

The Germans fired faster and better, hitting fifteen times in the first twelve minutes, and being hit only four times. *Queen Mary* hit *Seydlitz* twice, damaging her badly. Princess *Royal*, *Tiger*, and *Lion* were hit.

One German 12in shell exploded in *Lion*'s Q turret blowing off most of the roof, killing or mortally wounding everybody in the gun-house (turret) and control position. Major Francis Harvey RMLI, who was dying with both legs blown off, was heard giving the order to flood the magazine. The magazine party opened the valves controlling the flooding system, and sea water poured in. Lieutenant Jones RMLI, with the crews of the two after 4in gun batteries, hearing that Q turret was out of action, went to see what they could do. The water pressure was too low to work the fire hoses, so they passed fire buckets in a chain to extinguish the fires in the turret. Thinking that they had succeeded they returned to their action station. A few minutes later there was a further explosion, and a great sheet of flame passed right through the turret and down the main trunk (the big tube up which shells and charges passed up into the turret from the magazine and shellroom). It killed all the men in the loading chamber, and the magazine and shell-room parties who had mustered at the foot of the trunk. It is possible that a smouldering fragment had dropped onto a charge in the cage by the gun, which exploded and in turn ignited a charge in the hoist in the main trunk.

Of all ships in the BCF, it was very bad luck that such a chain reaction should have occurred in *Lion*. Anti-flash curtains and doors were fitted at key points in the route from shellroom and magazine to turret in every ship. But in order to speed up the rate of fire, the other battlecruisers had adopted a very dangerous practice, encouraged by no less a person than Chatfield, *Lion*'s captain and Beatty's flag captain. Because these curtains and doors impeded the rapid flow of shell and charge to the turret, the majority of crews either clipped them back, or removed them entirely. In addition, it was common practice to stock the gun-house with charges, so the turret in effect became a mini-magazine, contravening the laid-down drill which stipulated that the next charge should not be in the loading cage in the turret until the previous one had been fired. Furthermore, in some ships, charges were also piled at the foot of the hoist and in passageways, again to speed up loading. These potentially lethal shortcuts were connived at by everybody in the ships concerned; except in *Lion*, where the Chief Gunner, Warrant Officer Grant, successfully defied Chatfield and refused to allow these highly dangerous drills.

Despite this, it is likely that only Harvey's dying order to flood the magazine saved Beatty's flagship from the fate of two of his other battlecruisers. Harvey was awarded the VC posthumously. Six minutes later, the *Indefatigable* blew up. Two sailors stationed in her foretop survived. The remainder of her entire crew of 1,019, including all 91 of her Royal Marine Detachment, went to the bottom with her. Twenty-four minutes passed, and *Queen Mary* was hit abreast of Q turret. After two enormous explosions she vanished in a huge column of smoke, with the loss of over 1,250 of her ship's company, and all 117 of her Royal Marine Detachment. There were 14 survivors. Bombardier Albert Saunders RMA was in the *Princess Royal*'s Royal Marines turret, and although he would have been unable to see anything, recorded his feelings after the battle:

> The first shots we fired, it was like letting off steam. All the bottled-up anxiety of the past months was let loose then. Everyone was ready and eager for what was to come. As the time passed, so news of the fight came trickling through. We heard of the loss of *Queen Mary*, our chummy ship, and many a heart beat a little faster when they thought of chums gone for good.

At last, the 5th Battle Squadron, by cutting a corner, came within range of Hipper's ships, and started hitting hard with shells twice the weight of those fired by the Germans. At this stage, the huge fast battleships of 5th Battle Squadron had taken only one hit. But the

Germans were causing more damage to Beatty's ships than he was inflicting on them.

When Hipper signalled that he had encountered the British cruisers, Scheer was fifty miles away with the main body of the High Seas Fleet, consisting of twenty-two battleships. As Beatty and Scheer increased speed, they approached each other at a combined speed of forty-two knots (48 mph). Beatty was overhauling Hipper, who was not pushing along at full speed, and looked to be about to get between him and home, when Commodore Goodenough in the light cruiser HMS *Southampton* saw on the horizon dense clouds of funnel smoke from the coal-burning German battleships. At Goodenough's report that he had encountered the High Seas Fleet, Beatty ordered an about turn, at 1640 hours, just in time, as the 12in shells of the leading German Battle Squadron (*König*, *Großer Kurfürst*, *Kronprinz Wilhelm*, and *Markgraf*) splashed all around the rear of the four surviving battlecruisers of his BCF, but without hitting. For some reason, probably Evan-Thomas being slow on the uptake again, 5th Battle Squadron delayed its turn and *Barham*, *Malaya*, and *Warspite* were hit hard, *Warspite* a number of times with shells of several calibres. In *Malaya*, the last ship in the line, a German shell burst in the starboard battery and caused 102 casualties, including eight dead, nine who died of wounds, and nine wounded among the Royal Marines. Both 5th Battle Squadron and Beatty's battlecruisers kept up fire on Hipper, as they all, including Scheer, pelted to the north.

It was now Beatty's job to deliver the High Seas Fleet into the hands of his Commander-in-Chief, Jellicoe, who was steaming hard at twenty knots in a south-westerly direction thirty miles to the north of him, his battleships deployed in columns of divisions thus:

1st Division	2nd Division	3rd Division	4th Division	5th Division	6th Division
King George V	Orion	Iron Duke	Benbow	Colossus	Marlborough
Ajax	Monarch	Royal Oak	Bellerophon	Collingwood	Revenge
Centurion	Conqueror	Superb	Temeraire	Neptune	Hercules
Erin	Thunderer	Canada	Vanguard	St Vincent	Agincourt

Jellicoe had sent Rear Admiral Hood's 3rd Battlecruiser Squadron on ahead to join Beatty with his three twenty-five-knot battlecruisers, *Invincible* (flag), *Inflexible*, and *Indomitable*, and the light cruisers *Chester* and *Canterbury*. The course Hood steered would have taken him well to the north of Beatty, but at about 1730 hours, Captain Lawson in *Chester*, hearing gunfire, turned south-west to investigate. Lawson ran into three enemy light cruisers and some destroyers. *Chester* came under hot and accurate fire, putting a number of her guns out of action. Captain Edward Bamford RMLI was in the after control when it was hit by a shell. He was slightly wounded in one leg, but immediately went to work one gun with a scratch crew, controlled another gun, and extinguished a dangerous fire. For his coolness in action he was awarded the DSO. Of the twenty RMLI who manned a gun on each side of the ship, eight were killed and ten wounded, but the guns were kept in action. Of twenty-eight Royal Marines commended for good service in the *London Gazette* for the battle, five belonged to this small cruiser, whose detachment totalled a mere forty all ranks. Boy Cornwell RN who was awarded the VC posthumously was also in this ship.

Hood steered towards *Chester*, hammered the German light cruisers engaging her, and soon had them running for cover back to their own battlecruisers; except for the *Wiesbaden*, which was badly damaged and remained in the area. At 1755 hours, Beatty's approaching battlecruisers were sighted by the Grand Fleet. Captain Evan Hughes RMLI, in the Marines turret of HMS *Revenge*:

> Somewhere about 5.30 pm the sound of guns could be heard, and shortly afterwards small 'flickers' of light could be seen away on the starboard bow. Orders now arrived to load and stand by, so we closed up quickly and reported. The banging was now coming nearer and nearer, when suddenly the battlecruisers streamed past our bows, firing hard. The *Lion* was followed by the *Tiger*. The latter looked a fine sight, with flame and smoke pouring from large rents in her funnels and large columns of water springing up on each side of her. Some of the overs fired at her came well down to us.

At 1816 hours, Jellicoe ordered his fleet to deploy into line of battle, by forming single line ahead on the port wing column, with *King George V* leading, the course being set south-east by east (125° in modern terminology). Hughes in *Revenge* could tell what the ship was doing under him, because his turret was under director control. As the ship's gunnery officer in the director, high up in the ship, trained round to follow the target, a pointer on a dial in each turret moved accordingly. The turret trainer, turning a handle to keep a second pointer over the director pointer, trained the massive turret round. The guns could also be fired centrally by the gunnery officer in the director. The officer of the turret in the control position at the back of the turret had duplicate dials, and could see out through an armoured periscope in case he had to switch to local control, independent of the director, should communications break down, or the director be damaged.

> The squadrons of the Battle Fleet now altered course to port, so round the turret went, following the director on the starboard foremost bearing. No sooner were we 'on' by director than bang went the first salvo, followed by a cheer from within the turret. X Turret's blast screens sailed away like seagulls, the starboard water-tight door screen turned a circle, the starboard ladder disappeared and the salvo fell well short. The left guns then joined in, but were also short. Our target was one of the *Koenig* class.

The next fifteen minutes as the Grand Fleet was deploying were hectic. While Beatty was closing the Grand Fleet, Rear Admiral Sir Robert Arbuthnot decided to take up his allotted station with his 1st Cruiser Squadron, the four obsolescent armoured cruisers *Defence* (flag), *Warrior*, *Black Prince*, and *Duke of Edinburgh*, by going down the enemy side of the BCF. Arbuthnot was a hotheaded none too bright fitness fanatic, whose daughters were customarily detailed off to entertain after-dinner guests with gymnastic displays. On the way to his new station he elected to finish off the *Wiesbaden*, limping to rejoin her light cruiser sisters after their hammering at Hood's hands. In doing so he nearly collided with *Lion*, and put himself in one of the most dangerous places in the battle, right between the two fleets. *Warrior* and *Defence* were engaging *Wiesbaden*, when, as Hollis in *Duke of Edinburgh* recalls,

> British and German battlecruisers hotly engaged came out of the mist. Arbuthnot's flagship, the *Defence*, was hit by two great salvoes in quick succession, and at about twenty past six the Admiral and his flagship disappeared in a sheet of flame. The *Warrior* which was next in line, also came under the concentrated fire of German capital ships at medium range, but was saved for the moment by the chance that the battleship *Warspite*'s helm jammed, causing her to circle between *Warrior* and the enemy and draw their fire. Later the seaplane carrier *Engadine* tried to tow the *Warrior* home, but the following morning she had to be abandoned and eventually sank.[2]

Defence was blown apart and lost with all hands, including all her 84 Royal Marines. *Warrior* had 100 killed, including 78 out of her 83 strong Royal Marine Detachment. Fortunately for Hollis and his shipmates, the *Duke of Edinburgh*, lagging astern, was misplaced to join in this fiasco. *Black Prince* was also too far away, and may subsequently have been damaged in some other part of the fight. We will never know, since she was lost with all hands during the night.

Warspite's rudder had jammed when the steering engine seized during violent manoeuvring at full speed to avoid a collision with *Valiant*. She went round in a circle twice, the second time round the *Warrior*, while the engine room staff frantically disengaged the faulty steering engine and engaged the back-up motor. Her guns were switched to local control, and fired when they could. Although hit repeatedly during this performance, she managed to pull out of range.

Hood with his 3rd Battlecruiser Squadron was now well placed to join Beatty, once the latter had raced across the front of the still deploying Battle Fleet to take up his position on their port bow. As he turned to position himself ahead of Beatty, he saw Hipper's battlecruisers emerge from the mist only 9,000 yards away, and engaged them. At first Hipper's ships could not make out where the fire was coming from, and *Lützow* and *Derfflinger* were hit hard. *Invincible*'s gunnery was deadly – she was the one ship in the Grand Fleet with a really efficient gunnery control system. Then the wreaths of mist parted, and Hipper's ships struck back. A shell burst in *Invincible*'s Q turret, and as in *Lion*, the flash must have gone down the tube. *Invincible* was known to have followed the practice of removing flash curtains. But in this case the magazine was not flooded, and she blew into two halves, her bow and stern sticking out of the water. Six men survived, one of them the only Royal Marine out of the 109 strong detachment, Private Gasson RMLI, who was blown out of the top of his turret.

Captain Robert Sinclair RMLI in *Inflexible* wrote to his cousin Lucy after the battle:

> We passed the remains [of *Invincible*], which I saw, though at the time I had no idea it was all that was left of her. I thought it was a German. We now led the line for some time, and were under a heavy fire from the big German ships opposite us but we were fortunate enough not to be hit at all the whole time. In my turret I couldn't see much except the ship we were firing at, and I was glad to see we got some hits on her.

Captain Chandos Hill RMLI was on the bridge of HMS *Colossus*, in the Battle Fleet:

> By this time [1838 hours] we had deployed into line, and the Fleet presented a beautiful sight. Miles of ships with their guns pointing to where we knew the invisible enemy were. Every ship was flying three or four huge White Ensigns.

Soon afterwards Scheer, thoroughly alarmed at being trapped himself, turned away into the mist, but the Grand Fleet was still between him and home. A little later, he turned back, perhaps thinking he might slip past the tail of the Grand Fleet.

Captain Hill:

> Suddenly out of the mist, only 10,000 yards away emerged a battlecruiser of the *Lutzow* class [probably *Seydlitz*]. Here was worthy game at last. We let her have five salvoes, there was no time for more as she was passing us. The last two salvoes hit her well and we saw flames bursting from her decks. She also disappeared into the mist turning directly away from us. But before she got away, she put two 12-inch shells into our superstructure. Both missed the mast by a few inches, indeed both passed between the main and side struts of the mast. One burst, wrecking the lower part of the superstructure, and setting fire to the cordite for the 4-inch guns. This produced a tremendous blaze, but it was soon over and the smouldering remains were quickly put out before even the fire parties arrived on the scene.
>
> One or two shots from the same salvo burst short and spattered the whole forepart of the ship with splinters. Nearly all the cabins in line with the burst had holes in them. The Captain's office was wrecked, and the damage was increased by a water pipe being shot away, flooding everything. One piece wrecked a searchlight immediately under where I was standing. We all on the bridge had very narrow escapes as bits of steel were flying like hail. It was here our only bad casualty took place. The rangefinder operator who was on his platform immediately behind me had his right arm nearly shot off. It was a ghastly sight. I put on a tourniquet improvised out of a handkerchief and a bit of stick and had the satisfaction of seeing the blood flow stop.

As a result of Scheer's attempt to evade the Grand Fleet, *Lützow*, *Seydlitz*, and *Derfflinger* were hit hard again, and six others hit at least once or twice. The only British ship hit was *Colossus*, and her damage was minor, her casualties light, and no one was killed. Hughes' description bears all the hallmarks of a first-timer in battle, for his brother officers in the RM Brigade would have thought the incident barely worth a mention. Scheer fled back into the mist, not to return again in daylight. The Grand Fleet was still between him and home.

The light began to fade, and Jellicoe redeployed his fleet into a night steaming formation hoping to complete the destruction of the High Seas Fleet in the morning. He based his plans on the Germans returning home by the southern route to the Jade, and headed in that direction. Unfortunately Scheer chose the northern route. This would not have mattered if the units of the Grand Fleet had shown more resourcefulness during the night. Scheer made several attempts to skirt round the tail of the Grand Fleet, and bumped into the 1st and 5th Battle Squadrons. Scheer pulled back on each occasion. But the British battle squadrons did nothing, steaming serenely on; not even reporting the contact. The British destroyers on the other hand put in some gallant attacks, suffering five of their own ships sunk, and several damaged. They sank a battleship, three light cruisers, and possibly a destroyer. During the night, the German destroyers put in some ineffective torpedo attacks, hitting no one. The noise and flashes of these engagements astern of him, which should have provided a clue to what the Germans were trying, were ignored by Jellicoe and his other admirals. Not one of them had the initiative to order his division to turn back and do what Nelson would have done: engage the enemy more closely. The rigid command methods embedded in the Royal Navy, so well described by Andrew Gordon in *The Rules of the Game*, saw to that.

Meanwhile in the British Battle Fleet and BCF, the ship's companies drew breath and took stock, many of them seeing battle casualties for the first time. The ghastly flash burns, the crushing effects of blast, and the horrific butchery caused by large chunks of flying metal all made for a gruesome sight. Bombardier Albert Saunders RMA in *Princess Royal* of Beatty's BCF:

> At 11 pm we fell out from our day action stations to close up at our night defence stations. Some managed to get something to eat and drink. Below decks the sight was awful – just gaping holes, decks flooded with water, dead and wounded everywhere and an awful smell where shells had burst. It was a never to be forgotten sight and one that one never wishes to see again. As you walked round you heard of familiar names who had paid the supreme penalty. You looked down at a burnt, battered mess of what

was a few hours previously a splendid specimen of British manhood, and now you could only tell who it was by a label tied on his coat. The burns of some were awful.

A rush was made after everything was over for pieces of shell as mementos. In their eagerness to obtain a bit they forgot the fact that they were hungry. The gruesomeness of the thing did not strike them. They did not give it a thought that probably that particular piece had laid low someone in the prime of life. It was not from lack of reverence, but rather a feeling of perfect sang-froid. Our total casualties were exactly 100 viz. Killed 19, wounded 81, of these three died during the next two or three days, 73 being sent to hospital, and five cases kept on board [7 Royal Marines killed, and 13 wounded].

At daybreak the High Seas Fleet had gone, its track taking it well astern of the Grand Fleet, whose course had taken it out of Scheer's path home. The Germans claimed this action as a victory because they sank more ships than they lost. The High Seas Fleet ventured out only three more times in the war, twice in 1916, and once in 1918. On both occasions in 1916 it fled when it realized that the Grand Fleet was at sea. On the third occasion, in November 1918, it came out to surrender to Beatty, now Commander-in-Chief of the Grand Fleet. Those are not the actions of a victorious fleet.

Hollis remembered the return of HMS *Duke of Edinburgh* to Scapa:

> By the time we arrived it was common knowledge that three of the four ships of our squadron had gone down, and it was therefore thought that we too had probably suffered losses. We were accordingly requested to signal our casualties. Our reply was 'one case of rubella' – ie German Measles. Compared with our consorts we got off very lightly.[3]

The Royal Marines lost a total of 8 officers, 4 warrant officers, and 526 NCOs, privates, and gunners. A further 51 all ranks were wounded. Total casualties were about one in ten. As the Royal Marines history comments, the list of honours to the Corps was long and in marked contrast to that of Trafalgar, when only one brevet majority was awarded, to Captain Timmins, the senior Royal Marines officer. The harking back to Trafalgar is interesting. The Trafalgar of the First World War never happened. There were no Nelsons in the Grand Fleet. Furthermore, Jutland was the last fleet action of such magnitude in history. Never again would fleets of battleships and battlecruisers in the quantity of those engaged at Jutland fight it out with big guns alone.

8

The Royal Marines on the Western Front, 1915–1917

THE HOWITZER BRIGADE ROYAL MARINE ARTILLERY

The first Royal Marines to serve in France in appreciable numbers were the Royal Marine Artillery. After the RMA Battalion was withdrawn from the RM Brigade following its return from Ostend in 1914, there was some uncertainty as to how it should be used. At first it was proposed that the RMA should form the divisional artillery for the RN Division, which made sense, but unfortunately, as we saw earlier, this idea was rejected. Next the Admiralty and the War Office agreed that the RMA should man three batteries of 6in naval guns on field carriages towed by tractors. The equipment was delivered, and training started. However, the guns were withdrawn and issued to the Royal Garrison Artillery, which used them at the First Battle of Ypres in November 1914. Finally the RMA was ordered to provide a howitzer brigade and an anti-aircraft brigade, a brigade of artillery in the British Army in those days being the term used to describe a unit of three or more batteries, in what today we would call an artillery regiment.

When reports came in of the devastation caused by the huge German howitzers on the forts in Belgium it was decided to build similar weapons. Rear Admiral Bacon (retired), who was the manager of an ordnance factory in Coventry, designed a 15in howitzer for field use which could fire the naval shell of this calibre recently introduced for the *Queen Elizabeth* class battleships. The shell when fired from a short-barrelled howitzer had a maximum range of 10,800 yards. On seeing a prototype, the First Lord, Winston Churchill, ordered twelve. Bacon extracted a promise from Churchill that he would be allowed to take them into action in France, and was commissioned as a colonel in the

RMA. He did not remain long, being appointed Admiral of the Dover Patrol, handing over the Howitzer Brigade to Major F. W. Lumsden RMA on 19 April 1915. Lumsden, of whom more later, commanded for two months, before going on to more challenging tasks.

The first two guns of the Howitzer Brigade, each one constituting a battery on its own, arrived in France in time to take part in the Battle of Neuve Chapelle in March 1915. Eventually ten guns were deployed, each a battery, the other two being kept in England for training and tests. The Howitzer Brigade remained on the Western Front until the end of the war, and the list of its engagements reads like a roll-call of the battles of the BEF on the Western Front. Space does not allow more than a brief description of its activities; one bombardment as seen from the gun position or observation post (OP) is very much like another. Although intended for use against concrete forts, like the Belgian ones at Liège, in the event it were never used for this role, engaging instead pin-point targets such as enemy observation posts in church towers and villages, and in counter-battery shoots.

Second Lieutenant Walter Ward RMA enthusiastically wrote to his parents:

> *Belgium, 8.3.15:*
> Yesterday was our first shoot, & the target was a church tower. Our shooting was extremely accurate, & everyone was very pleased with it. We were all personally congratulated by General French yesterday, & General Smith-Dorrien today, not to mention the Prince of Wales, & a French & a Belgian General.

Later in the same letter he described his activities in the OP spotting with a x 21 magnification telescope:

> It is very thrilling up there. You hear the order to 'stand by'. The next thing you get the report on the telephone, 'Gun fired', about 6 secs later you hear the report, & almost at the same moment you hear the shell shrieking through the air like a train over your head. You watch & think it must have fallen without your noticing it, but just as you are giving up, about 30 secs after firing, you suddenly see a great flash & then a mixture of black & white smoke & dust bursting up for about 50 yards in every direction. The accuracy of the gun has surprised even those people who have had a lot to do with it, & is such that they are going to put us [to

fire] on to some trenches only 170 yards in front of our own. After that we shall be switched on to tackle hostile batteries.

The huge area affected by blast and splinters of each shell meant that these howitzers were not suitable for close support of infantry in the open, and lifted on to other targets in the rear when the infantry moved forward. In May 1915, Ward's battery took part in the preliminary bombardment in the battle for Aubers Ridge. He was in the OP.

Everything in the trenches was quite quiet, & you could see the German fires going for breakfast. It was desperately exciting, as we knew that there were about 30,000 men less than a mile behind us, spread over a front of only about a mile. At 5 o'clock our gun & gun 2 fired & that was the signal for every single gun in the line to start. It was a most magnificent sight, hundreds of shells bursting every minute over the trenches, shrapnel & HE, while every now & then there would be a terrific black burst, hiding everything from view – of a 9.2-inch or 15-inch howitzer. All these were bursting within 300 yards of us, & of course the noise was so great that you couldn't hear each other speak.

Despite the artillery support, as Ward said in the same letter, the big show was a failure in his sector. 'The next day I counted over 50 bodies in front of the hedge within 200 yards of me.'

Some days later he was on the receiving end in his OP:

I am not at all sorry not to have to go up there again, as the last time I was there they gave it a horrid shelling, two batteries firing at it [the OP] for 6 hours about 4 rounds every two minutes. Most of the rounds fell in the village behind us, but we had one right into the house, which knocked us all down & smashed one of our telephones though it only blew out part of the back wall & didn't hurt anyone. It is a horrid feeling to hear it coming nearer & not to stop some distance away, but to come right on, until the sort of whizzing sound changes to a rushing noise. We cleared out to our dug-out in the garden after that, & listened to the rest of it quite comfortably. The effect of the bombardment was to make me feel fearfully sleepy.

In July 1915 the Howitzer Brigade was placed firmly under army control. Ward recorded:

We have been completely taken over by the Army at last, & are not under the Marine Office for anything now. It has its advantages, as the Army supplies us with all our stores now, whereas between the Army & the Admiralty, we could get nothing.

In a letter describing the battle of Loos in September 1915, he mentioned watching repeated attempts by the infantry to take the Hohenzollern Redoubt:

> . . . every time we have attacked it I have seen our infantry crossing the open under a most terrific shell fire. In a line of them perhaps 400 yards long I have seen shells bursting at a rate of 6 a second. It seems wonderful that they are not all wiped out in 10 secs or so, but sometimes a shell seems to burst right on top of them & you still see them going on; other times you will see a shell got right into them & clear a great gap & the people on either side blown over. Sometimes it has been so bad that I have felt I could not look any longer.

By July 1916, now more cynical and hardened, he was spotting for his battery at the Battle of Albert, part of the Somme battle:

> Up here I have had my eye glued to a telescope for about 14 hours a day, & it is very interesting now that the German trenches have been badly smashed, as you see heaps of Bosches. My telescope is very powerful & I can see if a man has a moustache & the shape of his face at 2 miles. There are some RFA (Royal Field Artillery) next door to me, & I go along & let them know if I see anything, & they usually fire on it. One day the Bosche was shelling very heavily & I think preparing for a counter-attack, & I saw a bit of trench about 200 yards long packed with bosches, so I told the RFA & they put four batteries on to it, firing as hard as they could & wiped the whole lot out. It's almost like a cinema. The other day, after we had taken a bit of trench, I saw 4 bosches coming in to surrender. They were only about 2000 yards away so I could see them quite clearly. They were all very young & pale, with their clothes torn; they were holding up their hands & cringing & coming on a bit & then stopping. I have never seen anyone in a more ghastly state of terror, & not without reason, as our people were much too busy to take prisoners & shot them all.

The original commander of Walter Ward's battery, and for a short time of the Howitzer Brigade, was Major Lumsden, certainly the most distinguished RMA officer in its history, and arguably the most renowned in the Royal Marines in the First World War, although Ward clearly found him rather trying on occasions. After handing over command of the Howitzer Brigade at the end of 1915, he earned three DSOs when on the staff of 32nd Division, for reconnaissance work under fire. In April 1917 he was appointed, while still a major, to command 17th Battalion The Highland Light Infantry (HLI), but was only in command for six days, before being sent to take over the 14th Infantry Brigade. During his brief period in command of 17th HLI he was recommended for, and subsequently received, the Victoria Cross. Part of his citation read:

> Six enemy field guns had been captured, but as the enemy kept them under heavy fire, it was necessary to leave them in dug-in positions 300 yards in advance of the line held by our troops. Major Lumsden then undertook to bring these guns back into the British lines. To do this, he personally led four artillery teams and a party of infantry through the hostile barrage. As one of the teams sustained casualties, he left the remaining team in a covered position, and under a very heavy rifle, machine gun and shrapnel fire he led the infantry to the guns. By force of example, and inspiring energy he succeeded in sending back two teams with guns, going through the barrage with the team of the third gun. He then returned to the remaining guns to await further teams, and these he succeeded in attaching to two of the remaining three guns, despite rifle fire, which had become intense at short range, and removed the guns to safety. By this time, the enemy in considerable strength had driven through the infantry covering posts, and blown up the breech of the remaining gun. Major Lumsden then returned and drove off the enemy, attached a team to the gun and got it away.

Ward wrote to his parents:

> Did you see that our Major Lumsden has just got the VC. Isn't it splendid; in addition to getting two bars to his DSO about 3 weeks ago. Of course he has left us now. I used to see him pretty often when I was with V Corps Heavy Artillery, & he had the reputation then of always being ready to volunteer for any job. I always knew that he was out here with the intention of making a big splash, that's why he left the RMA.

Ward was possibly right, certainly Lumsden was one of that rare band who relish action, and looked for something more exciting than command of a heavy howitzer battery. He commanded his brigade with skill, gallantry, and daring. When his brigade took part in a raid on the enemy lines, he first of all supervised them assembling in the front trenches, and advanced with them to each successive objective. At the final objective the exhausted men hesitated because of heavy machine-gun and rifle fire. Lumsden led the assault group to capture no less than seven pillboxes, before continuing on to carry out a reconnaissance of a further enemy position. He took charge of the withdrawal, and as part of the covering party was the last to leave the enemy position. For this action he was awarded the third bar to his DSO.

He was awarded the CB in June 1918, but did not live to know of the decoration. On the night of 3 June 1918 he was killed by a sniper when going to investigate for himself the report of an attack on his brigade position. One officer in 32nd Division said, 'His Brigade became the finest in the Division solely due to his fine influence and example.'

THE ROYAL MARINES LIGHT INFANTRY BATTALIONS ARRIVE IN FRANCE

After the withdrawal of the RN Division from Gallipoli, there was some altercation between the Army and the Navy about where it should be employed next – if at all. Eventually it was decided that the division should go to France under command of the BEF. Major General Paris, on a leisurely trip on his way home from the Aegean, thought that 'the poor old RND was to be broken up and all arrangements to this end had been made'. On arrival in Paris he found 'an urgent wire 5 days old! So finish joyride and come along to be greeted with the news that the WO (War Office) have taken over the RND which is to be completed to a full division, reorganize and train in France at once.'

The formation was redesignated the 63rd (RN) Division, and its brigades reorganized. The two RMLI battalions with the Howe and Anson Battalions made up the 188th Infantry Brigade, and the Hood, Drake, Hawke, and Nelson Battalions formed the 189th Infantry Brigade. Both these brigades were placed under army brigadier generals; all but two of the naval battalions were commanded by RMLI officers, as were some of the sub-units within all these battalions. Brigadier General Trotman RMLI, who had commanded the RM Brigade, and subsequently the 1st Brigade in the old RN Division, took over the third brigade, the newly formed 190th Infantry Brigade, consisting of 7th Battalion Royal Fusiliers, 4th Battalion Bedfordshire and Hertfordshire Regiment,[1] 1st Battalion the Honourable Artillery Company (HAC),[2] and 10th Battalion The Royal Dublin Fusiliers. For the first time in its existence the division was brought up to a proper establishment. The Royal Field Artillery provided three brigades, each of three 18-pounder batteries. The Royal Marines produced the manpower for engineers, a divisional train (transport), field ambulances, and divisional signals.

All did not go smoothly in the provision of manpower. About a month after his division had arrived in France, Paris wrote:

> I wonder if the time will come when this Division will run on ball bearings. We were to have had volunteers from the Army as the Admiralty wouldn't enlist any more. The only hitch is that there are no volunteers! Then the Admiralty have stolen men by the hundred. All who go on leave never return, & some thousands are hidden in ships. It doesn't make it easy. Here the Army say we are fighting the Navy as well as the Hun. The last kick by our AG (Nicholls) – 'no more proper Marine officers or men are to be allowed to drain away to the Army'. What is an improper Marine?

The first unit of the new 63rd Division to land in Marseilles was 1 RMLI, at a strength of 25 officers and 1,021 NCOs and privates. The division had to learn to use some new weapons. The medium machine-guns, now the Vickers, were all centralized into companies, one per brigade. The battalions were issued with the Lewis light machine-gun, eventually one per platoon. The new-fangled Stokes trench mortar had also to be mastered. The division was introduced to the theatre in a careful and structured way, a far cry from the scrappy training it had received before its baptism of fire at Antwerp. In quiet sectors behind the lines battalions underwent platoon, company, battalion, and brigade training, as well as being attached to another division for tours in the line. These tours were far from peaceful; raids and local attacks brought a steady stream of casualties. They had to learn the new conditions of warfare as practised on the Western Front after nearly two years of fighting.

Beginning in 1916, and certainly by 1917, a battalion's front was held by a line of lightly held posts, sometimes not even connected by a lateral trench. The soldiers manning these posts were connected to battalion headquarters by telephone and usually by a rearward communication trench. Their job was to give warning of an attack. Behind them, on the second line, the delaying action would be fought and delayed, or a local attack contained. The third line was the main line of resistance against a serious attack. Here deep dug-outs, trench mortars, and Vickers machine-guns were sited. Behind front-line battalions there would be more positions, sometimes extending back for several miles, connected by literally miles of communications trenches. The main defence in every sector was, however, provided by the artillery. Contrary to public perception that persists to this day of the machine-gun as the chief killer on the Western Front, by far the greatest number of casualties in this war, as in all subsequent ones, was caused by artillery and mortars. Defence in depth was the key to success, and practised by the enemy just as assiduously, if not more so. Herein lay the problem for the attacker, and 63rd Division was to do plenty of attacking as well as defending over the next two and a half years.

Sergeant George Nettleton RMLI, now in 190th Brigade's Machine-gun Company, described his first experience of trench warfare on the Western Front:

> *Sunday 10.9.16*
> Fell in at 9.20 am for first experience of trenches. 1015 arrived at position. Range to enemy 325 yards in front and 300 on left flank. Trench can be enfiladed from left flank, but [Vickers machine] gun position very secure. Only excitement being trench mortar warfare and sniping. Whizz bangs, sausages and minenwherfers fairly frequent. Night very quiet only occasional shots from Fritz's snipers. At night bombing attack by our men on right flank.

> *Wednesday 13/9/16*
> Expected to leave for billets 9 am, but orders came we are not being relieved until tomorrow. Thursday. Relief arrives about 10 am and we proceed to HQ, expecting to return to billets, but find out that we are being shifted from left of sector to right until Sunday. About 100 yards from us is a large battered building between this building and the enemy is our MG emplacement. Inside the building is a T[rench] M[ortar] battery, and enemy trying to shift these TMs with sausages etc makes things rather unpleasant for us. One 2nd Lieut thought he would look over a ridge about 15 yards from our emplacement for observation, falling down not two minutes after wounded in the left leg by a sniper.

THE SOMME: THE BATTLE OF THE ANCRE

The division did not participate in any major operations until the time came in mid-November 1916 for it to take part in the Battle of the Somme, in progress since 1 July. General Paris had been seriously wounded by a shell while visiting 190th Brigade, losing a leg. This was a grievous loss to the division which he had commanded since Antwerp, and was now about to face one of its sternest tests. His GSO 2, Major Sketchley, was killed by the same shell, which fell in between them. Paris was succeeded by Major General Shute from the Army. He did not understand the ways of the 63rd Division, and although efficient, was disliked intensely, being referred to by many in his formation as 'that shit Shute'. He left the division in 1917 on promotion to corps commander, and was replaced first by Major General Lawrie, and subsequently Major General Blacklock, both from the Army.

The battle in which the division was about to participate was the last act in the five-month-long Somme offensive, before rain and mud made continuation of the fighting impossible. It was known as the Battle of the Ancre, after a tributary of the River Somme that ran through the north-west corner of the Somme battlefield. The objectives for the attack on 13 November, by twelve divisions, included two villages, Beaucourt and Beaumont Hamel. They were villages in name only. The buildings had been almost completely smashed flat. The whole area was a sea of mud, water-filled shell holes, wire and fortified positions. Beaumont Hamel had been one of the objectives for the opening day of the Somme battle four and a half months earlier.

Beaucourt was assigned to 63rd Division. The first objective, the German front-line trench complex of three lines, was called the Dotted Green Line. Beyond this lay the second objective, the Green Line, a fortified ridge along which ran the road to Beaucourt station. Beyond this again, the third objective, the Yellow Line, was a trench running parallel to the British front and across the south-west edge of the remains of Beaucourt. The Red Line, beyond Beaucourt, was the final objective, and here the division was to consolidate. The battalions were to leapfrog through each other as each line was taken. The Dotted Green Line and Yellow Line were to be taken by 1 RMLI, Howe, Hawke, and Hood; the Green Line and Red Line by 2 RMLI, Anson, Nelson, and Drake. The 190th Brigade was the divisional reserve.

On 12 November the battalions moved up to trenches just behind their jumping-off positions. Because set-piece attacks usually led to heavy casualties, it was now a rule that the battalion second-in-command, with some officers, two company sergeant majors, and a proportion of NCOs and privates remained behind in the transport lines – to use the official phrase, 'left out of battle' (LOOB). They could be called forward to replace casualties, and also provided the nucleus around which to reorganize the battalion when it came out.

Sergeant Will Meatyard had been Signal Sergeant in the Plymouth Battalion on Y Beach, and was now in the same job in 2 RMLI.

Hearing we were about to move, I handed money and a letter to the safe custody of a Corporal who was staying behind. At 2 pm we moved. It was heavy going in deep mud – arrived at the trenches at 4.30 pm after a struggle. We had not proceeded very far up the trenches before we came to a stop. The trenches were packed with troops, so we had to sit down in the mud and wait until there was a move ahead. The Huns seemed to get the wind up about something, and sent over quite a number of heavy shells. These smashed in the trenches, causing many casualties. I passed a spot where many were buried [by collapsing trenches]. It was dark when we arrived at the dugout told off for headquarters, which was packed. Although we knew it was life or death for some of us the next morning, we spent a very cheerful night, chiefly due to the successful efforts of Jerry Dunn our cook sergeant. Each man was to be served out with a tot of rum before going over in the morning. The Colonel, Adjutant, Doctor, orderlies and other details were in this dugout. Jerry called me over, and he suggested that as he was making cocoa for the morning, I might get permission from the Adjutant to serve out 'the bubbly' right away.[3] The Adjutant consented and I gave Jerry the job, as he had a *very* steady hand [emphasis in original]. Some did not drink the rum so Jerry returned it to the jar, which was taken in the morning.

At about 0300 hours nominated platoons of 1 RMLI moved out into no man's land, and crawled up to the German wire to wait for zero hour. These tactics had proved very successful during earlier offensives on the Somme. The risk of being hit by their own artillery dropping short was offset by not having to cross open ground when the barrage lifted. Following close behind the beaten zone of the artillery bombardment was known as 'leaning on the barrage'. The morning was very dark with a thick mist. Will Meatyard:

> At 5.45 am we were ready and waiting, the morning light was just beginning to show itself. All watches had been synchronised. At five minutes to six the CO announced five minutes to go. What a time it seemed going. There was not a sound to be heard. The question was, was Fritz in the know – as it was nothing new for him to get wind of an attack and the time it was coming off – but this time he was apparently taken by surprise. Each morning at dawn for the last few days our guns had been giving him pepper, and no infantry attacks took place. I expect he got fed up with these false alarms.

The German artillery and machine-gunners reacted swiftly. The enemy artillery barrage fell mostly on 1 RMLI and 2 RMLI as they moved forward. About fifty per cent of casualties occurred in no man's land before reaching and crossing the German first line, including every company commander in 1 RMLI killed. The ground was very muddy, making movement difficult. German machine-guns raked the slopes leading down to Station Road. The enemy trenches were nearly obliterated by British artillery fire, making it difficult to establish one's position.

The Hood Battalion, commanded by Lieutenant Colonel Bernard Freyberg, was luckier than most, passing through the first three lines of German trenches in its attack sector, the Dotted Green Line, with comparative ease. Captain the Hon. Lionel Montagu RMLI commanded D Company. In a letter to his mother he wrote:

> It was weird sight seeing the dim figures of the men advancing in waves through the mist with little bursts of flame coming among them and lighting up the fixed bayonets. I speedily found myself with about 60 men and about two platoons of the Drake Bn too far ahead, having gone over the [enemy] three lines without seeing them, though we bombed a few dugouts. We were right in our own barrage and suffered a few casualties from it. I felt rather lost, but fortunately recognized the station and the station road, which I had previously made a note of. This stood us in good stead now. I knew that I had got too far ahead, but did not like to bring the men back [too far] as nothing was more demoralising.
>
> I brought them back two moves of 20 yards to get more behind our barrage. My servant [batman] Royds, was hit in the leg by our own

artillery, just by me. I wrote [a message] to my CO saying where I was and I would wait until he came up. I saw him soon afterwards on the line of the station road and it began at last to grow lighter. After this all was plain sailing as he immediately took charge of every body and ran the whole show.

Freyberg had not waited for Drake Battalion to pass through him on the Dotted Green line as planned. Seeing that the Drake was held up, he used his initiative, pushed on, and took the Green Line. Here he gathered up the remnants of the Drake, which had taken heavy casualties, including among the killed the CO, Lieutenant Colonel Tetley RMLI, one of the originals in Plymouth Battalion in the Dardanelles.

The Hawke, Howe, and Nelson Battalions suffered huge casualties from a redoubt in the enemy defence system on the Dotted Green Line. The CO of the Hawke, Lieutenant Colonel Wilson RMLI, was seriously wounded, and most of the Nelson Battalion fell here, including their CO, Lieutenant Colonel Burge RMLI. Part of the Howe managed to fight through the German first and second lines, and go firm on the third line. Parties of the Anson passed through them as planned, and unbeknown to Divisional Headquarters and Freyberg's Hood Battalion gained the Green Line. Their CO, Lieutenant Colonel Saunders RMLI, who had also served at Gallipoli, was among the many dead of the Anson Battalion.

In spite of heavy losses, 1 RMLI reorganized in the first and second German lines, but only small parties reached the third line. 2 RMLI had hard hand-to-hand fighting getting through the third line, but part of the battalion reached the Green Line, and made contact with 51st Highland Division on their left. The advance to the Yellow Line was due to begin at 0730 hours, and on cue the barrage began. Hood and remnants of Drake followed up immediately and seized the trench in front of Beaucourt, as did the Anson, with parts of 1st and 2nd RMLI.

Montagu, D Company, Hood Battalion:

We captured German mail and a dump of German rations. We opened their parcels and smoked their cigars. We found lots of good things to eat, including sausages and cakes, as well as socks etc. From the letters we discovered it was the 2nd Guards Reserve Regiment against us.

Here Freyberg told us to dig two lines of trenches. Picks and shovels were scarce but the men dug splendidly with their entrenching tools. Our doctor joined us here, having dressed and evacuated nearly all our wounded. We got news here also that one of our clearing parties had captured a major, five other officers and about 600 men.

The time came to run up a telephone cable forward from Battalion Headquarters, 2 RMLI. Sergeant Will Meatyard:

Receiving a certain codeword the CO, Adjutant and our Headquarters Staff went over amidst not many shells but plenty of spitting bullets, and arrived at a German trench. Under previous arrangements this was now the advanced telephone station. From here I received orders to lay a wire to a certain position ahead and with Pte Peach, or 'Pippy' Peach as he was called, proceeded to lay wire forward. We unreeled it as we went along. Almost everything had been hit by shells, and it was one continual mass of debris and mud pools. Some were half filled with water and many badly wounded men lying helpless in them – a ghastly sight. First aid had been rendered to them in most cases. Eventually reaching the position, I connected up and got through to headquarters. Many around me were getting sniped. As the CO came along I gave him the necessary tip to keep very low, which he did. The Adjutant, Captain Farquaharson, was wounded here, and while getting back was shot again. Captain Muntz, Adjutant of the 1st Bn RMLI, was also sniped here. He was shot in the head and died.

Freyberg, now firmly established on the Yellow Line, wanted to maintain the momentum and advance to the Red Line, but General Shute, concerned that if he allowed Freyberg to advance further he would be out on a limb, decided to bring up more troops on his left first. The 188th Brigade was ordered to advance. Both RMLI Battalions moved out. Will Meatyard:

The CO waving his cap above his head, said, 'Come on Royal Marines' and over they went to the next trench. Leaving a signaller of the RFA with his telephone, I joined on another reel of wire. Having passed a stick through the centre hole of the reel and slung my own telephone, I ran forward and the reel unwound as I went along. I apparently drew the attention of machine gunners at the strongpoint and also some snipers who were lurking in that direction. At about every 15 yards I dropped into a shell hole and took a breather. Then I got my legs free from the mud and made the wire ready to unreel easily. I made another dash, and so on. As I did so each time the machine guns opened up, but each time

I dropped I think it deceived them as they did not know whether I was hit or not. By this means I got to the point I was aiming at.

Having arrived at the new trench, I connected up again and found that communication was still good. I told one of my men at the intermediate stations to bring on [up] the aeroplane shutter [signal lamp]. It was getting dark now and I knew in the morning the 'Communication [Contact] Plane' would be over to find out our exact position, and we would want to communicate with it.

The two RMLI battalions continued to fight their way forward during the night, led by their COs, Hutchison and Cartwright. Throughout the night the cable was often cut by shellfire, but Meatyard and his signallers went out and repaired it time after time. In the morning the contact plane came over, and fired red flares as arranged. 2 RMLI put out their recognition signal panels and signalled with the shutter lamp, the only battalion in the division able so to do. Thanks to the courage and devotion to duty of Sergeant Will Meatyard, his battalion had managed to stay in contact with Brigade Headquarters almost constantly through-out the battle, a rare occurrence during an advance in this war.

He was wounded that morning, bringing in the battalion recognition signals. He was awarded a richly deserved MM. After being hit, he wrote:

When I woke up I found myself in a dugout, head and arm bound up. Hadn't the slightest idea how I got there. One of the stretcher bearers of the Howe Battalion had bound me up. After a while I thought I could walk, and with the assistance of one of the staff, I was taken to the rear. With two other walking wounded we toddled off all together. As we passed a battery of artillery, one of the crew came up with a basin of hot cocoa. It was a Godsend, and showed the kindness one can get at the hands of a soldier.

Meatyard's wounds were dressed in the Field Dressing Station, and on being told he would get home more quickly as walking wounded, he stood in the ambulance all the way to the Casualty Clearing Station. Here he was put on an ambulance train, and 'after 14 hours of agony reached the 1st Canadian Hospital at Etaples. Here I underwent an operation by a very clever doctor. I think it was due to him being such an expert that I kept my arm.'

That morning, 14 November, two tanks came forward, and with their help the strongpoint that had caused so much trouble the day before was finally taken. By this time there were only two officers, including the CO, left in 1 RMLI, and in 2 RMLI the CO and two other unwounded officers. Meanwhile Freyberg had spent the night of 13/14 November planning to take Beaucourt with his battalion, part of the HAC, and remnants of the Drake. The Hood Battalion had nine officers left, including the CO, and the Drake had four. Captain Montagu RMLI, OC D Company, Hood Battalion:

Freyberg soon had things organised. I was to lead the second wave in support of him from the second trench. The prospect seemed to me to be very doubtful. The snipers and machine guns were so active that it was dangerous to show your head, even for an instant, and we were to attack at 7.45 am. By this time the trench of which I was in command had become packed with people jumping in and taking cover. I had always heard that it was impossible to advance against hostile machine guns unless our artillery had first knocked them out. These and the snipers were quite unaffected by our barrage, which seemed feeble. Such were my doubts that I sent a message to Freyberg at 7.15 am to ask him if he intended to attack, by means of one of my runners. He never got the message as the runner was killed, but he told me he had exactly the same doubts and nearly called it off. At 7.45 am our barrage became a little more intense but nothing like enough to stop the snipers and machine guns. I saw Freyberg jump out of the trench and wave the men on. Three men followed from my trench and I got out with my runner, with bullets racing past us (one through my sleeve). The first wave stopped three times. Freyberg was knocked clean over by a bullet which hit his helmet, but he got up again. I and my runner dived into a shell hole and waited about half a minute. I said I would go back and get more men out of the trench and crawled back about 10 yards to do so. About a dozen men came out and I got up and waved the rest on. They all followed. We soon got into Beaucourt (of course absolute ruins) and found the Germans could not face our men and were surrendering in hundreds. It was an amazing sight – they came out of their holes, tearing off their equipment. I myself rounded up at least 50, waving my revolver at them and shouting 'Schnell'.

Freyberg, who had been hit again, joined Montagu, a well-known horse breeder before the war, in his company headquarters:

We had a long talk here. How splendidly the Battalion had done in attacking and carrying three objectives including the strong village of

Beaucourt, and taking over 1,000 prisoners. I told him that if I got out of it all right, I would call a racehorse 'Beaucourt'. Suddenly it started, such heavy shelling as I'd never experienced. Not in ones and twos but in dozens and all big 5.9 [inch] howitzers. The house, telephone, SOS rockets etc were blown to pieces. Freyberg said 'They are ranging on this house', and he and I took cover in the shallow trench where the HAC were. Here we lay for about half an hour. I don't want to exaggerate but I am sure that 30 of these big shells fell within 20 yds of us. During the shelling we discussed the situation and agreed that it probably meant that the 'Boche' were about to attack. I now expected them on top of us at any moment. We passed the word to the HAC to look to their rifles. I remember Freyberg commenting on the fact that a few of the shells were dud. We feared gas shells and took out our gas helmets. Two or three times we were half buried by bits of house, earth and stones. One in particular hit the bricks and smothered us in pink dust. One shell fell a bit closer than the others. I felt something hit me in the small of the back, but it did not seem to hurt at all. I heard Freyberg say 'Goodbye Montagu', and then 'Steady Hood', and I saw he was hit and going a very bad colour. He asked me if I had any morphia. He produced a tube and asked me to give him some. I gave him a quarter grain and labelled him to say I had done so. I dressed his wound with my field dressing (he had none). There was a hole in his neck which was bleeding rather profusely. He lay there for about ten minutes and I thought he was going to die.

Freyberg made an astonishing recovery, and was able to walk back to the Dressing Station with Montagu's help. Montagu took command of the battalion, and led them out when they were relieved the next morning. Freyberg was awarded the VC for his inspiring leadership and gallantry. He was a shining example of what could be done when a weak spot in the line is found and exploited by initiative, determined leadership, and good soldiering. Montagu was given a well-deserved DSO. He survived the war, and named one of his racehorses Beaucourt.

Among the many wounded in the division was Sergeant Nettleton. For the assault on 13 November, each battalion was accompanied by a sub-section of Vickers machine-guns from the machine-gun companies. He wrote up his diary afterwards:

Monday 13th November 1916
Attack started 5.45 am. Our bombardment terrific. 1,000 guns from 18 pdrs to 15-inch howitzers on 1,200 yard front firing as fast as possible. By

6.30 am five of my crew knocked out. By 6.45 another two gone. With only two men and myself left I take the gun. Soon after I received a bullet in left thigh. Gave orders to the other two to get the gun back to HQ. I then got into a shell hole and awaited dark. Enemy 15 yards away. About noon our artillery shelled enemy with shrapnel. Expected every moment to receive present intended for Fritz. Excitement and loss of blood causes me to faint or lose consciousness which was a blessing. Dusk and I awake. Feel very weak but determined to try and crawl to dressing station. Stretcher bearers can not come out because Fritz is firing at them. Reached out trenches safely and rolled in. Assisted to my feet. I tried to make my way to the dressing station which is about 25 yards away as crow flies, but about 150 by trench. Good leg gets stuck in mud. Couldn't put the other leg down to assist. Remain a few minutes and then seen by fellow who I asked to tell stretcher bearers. They arrive in trench too narrow for use of stretcher so they assist me to dressing station where I arrived at 4 am Tuesday 14 Nov.

The 63rd Division remained in position until relieved by 37th Division on 15 November. The Battle of the Somme officially ended on 19 November. 1 RMLI went into action with 400 NCOs and privates, and despite having received reinforcements during the battle from the LOOB party, came out with 138, having suffered 47 killed, 210 wounded, and 85 missing. Of the 23 officers, 6 were killed, 12 wounded, and 3 missing. All the missing, officers and men, were actually dead, although this was not established until much later.

Although the Somme battle had ended, the 63rd Division was to spend from mid-January to mid-March 1917 on the Ancre. The weather was bitter, in this the coldest winter of the war. The two RMLI battalions took part in patrols, local attacks, and trench raids which resulted in a steady stream of casualties. On 7 February a patrol found the German trenches deserted and it became clear that the enemy had gone in that sector. The German withdrawal to what was known as the Hindenburg Line had begun, although exactly what this entailed was as yet unrevealed. The Germans had prepared a formidable position from Arras in the north to River Aisne in the south, shortening their front by twenty-five miles, and releasing thirteen divisions into their reserve. They prepared a host of booby traps and demolitions in their wake as they withdrew, and fought some hard delaying actions in blocking positions as they went. One such was at Miraumont on 17 and 18 February 1917.

The 1st and 2nd RMLI as part of 188th Brigade were ordered to complete the capture of a spur in front of Miraumont. The objective was a sunken road including two strong points, one known as the 'Pimple'. After a bad start caused by navigational problems in the night approach march, all objectives were taken, some after very hard fighting: D Company 1 RMLI eventually captured the 'Pimple' when Sergeant Scott took a party and attacked from the rear, throwing grenades into the entrance. He was awarded the DCM. Subsequent German counter-attacks were beaten off by artillery fire. The Commander-in-Chief, Field Marshal Sir Douglas Haig, sent a congratulatory message direct to the commander of 188th Brigade, which was almost unheard of. As an indication of how tough a little battle it had been, one hardly mentioned in the history books, of the 16 officers and 500 men of 1 RMLI who went into action on 17 February, only 3 officers and 100 men were fit for duty when they marched out on the 22nd.

ARRAS

In April 1917 the 63rd Division was moved up to take part in the Second Battle of the Scarpe (after the river of that name), one of the phases in the Battle of Arras. The 189th and 190th Brigades captured the Gavrelle spur, and it then fell to 188th Brigade to capture the Gavrelle Windmill and trenches in its vicinity. 1 RMLI found that the artillery had failed to cut the wire that lay across the front of its objective. In one place about thirty men did manage to force their way through, but were cut off and taken prisoner. The remainder of the battalion stalled on the forward slope, and took heavy casualties, including the CO and three company commanders killed or dying of wounds. 2 RMLI, having captured the first line of German positions in the vicinity of Gavrelle Windmill, found the wire in front of the second line was cut only in one place. A, C, and D Companies streamed through to reach their objective, but were cut off and suffered very heavy losses. Meanwhile Lieutenant Newling with his platoon of B Company had succeeded in capturing the Windmill, taking about 100 prisoners. He held the Windmill against determined

counterattacks for the rest of the day. The remainder of B Company
spent the day pinned down by machine-gun fire, and finally succeeded
in joining Newling's gallant little band after dark. At one stage the
German counterattacks on 2 RMLI were only beaten off when the CO,
Lieutenant Colonel Hutchison, gathered his headquarters signallers,
cooks, and bottlewashers and joined in the fray. The Windmill was held.
Among the many decorations awarded to Royal Marines for the Gavrelle
battle were three DCMs, including one to Private Glyndywr Davies for
advancing alone to a strong point, and taking 50 prisoners single-handed.
Among those wounded and taken prisoner was Company Sergeant Major
Chapman. He had been an original member of the RM Brigade, joining
as a bugler. He served throughout the Gallipoli campaign, rising to
company sergeant major in France, having like many fine NCOs of the
time started in the drums. He died of his wounds in a prisoner of war
camp in Germany. As the *History of the RN Division* comments tartly,
'the results of this operation were not wholly satisfactory'.[4] The enemy
strengths were greatly underestimated, and the RMLI battalions suffered
huge losses. Including their CO, Lieutenant Colonel F. G. W. Cartwright
DSO, who was mortally wounded, the 1st RMLI had 6 officers killed out
of a total of 500 casualties. The 2nd RMLI lost 10 officers and more than
200 NCOs and privates killed out of nearly 600 casualties.

The two RMLI Battalions spent until mid-August 1917 in the Gavrelle
Windmill sector, relieving each other turn and turn about. As always
there was a steady trickle of casualties when battalions were in the line.
The Royal Marines were fortunate in that their reinforcements were
almost always Marines, until the latter part of the war when the Corps
was short of men.[5] This may strike some readers as logical and obvious,
but in most infantry battalions there was no guarantee that the men they
received from the reinforcement depots would be from the regiment
concerned. It was by no means unusual for men from the English home
counties to be issued with kilts and drafted to Highland battalions, and
for Glaswegians to find themselves serving in Welsh battalions. Men who
had recovered after being evacuated to the base area with wounds or
sickness, and returned to base camps in France, would often be sent to
serve with totally strange units. Most found this extremely unsettling,
and it was the cause of unrest at the reinforcement depots. Men would
often refuse to report sick for fear that they would never get back to
their mates if sent to hospital. Men would sometimes go absent from the

base depots, and move up the line to find their own battalion. On the whole only the Guards and Royal Marines could demand that they had their own people back.

YPRES AND PASSCHENDAELE

In June 1917 most of the Howitzer Brigade RMA was moved up to the Ypres sector to support General Plumer's highly successful Messines offensive. Walter Ward, back from his tour on V Corps Heavy Artillery staff, and an acting major commanding Number 12 Battery, was gassed. He wrote home:

> The main ingredient seems to have been mustard water, though they are not quite certain, as it was a new gas shell. Consequently we are being kept under observation for other symptoms, but we have been five days now so I don't think any thing else will develop. It is a painful and humiliating mixture, which gets you in three ways, internally making you very sick, externally raising large blisters, & worst of all in the eyes, making you absolutely blind for the time being.
>
> My old battery took rather a knock all round, about 50 cases of gas, & six wounded, & two killed. Four officers gassed, & one slightly wounded.
>
> We have most of our men in the same hospital as ourselves, & they are getting on very well.

Happy to relate, he recovered, and returned to the battery.

In early October the 63rd Division was transferred to the Ypres sector in time to take part in the Second Battle of Passchendaele, the village whose name has come to be associated with the whole of what was the Third Battle of Ypres, but was actually one of a series of battles that constituted the three-and-a-half-month-long agony of the British offensive at Ypres. The German front lines were no longer lines of dug-in posts, but consisted of a series of mutually supporting concrete pillboxes (the name for this kind of defensive work derives from this period of the war). Pillboxes were very hard to capture, and could survive a prolonged artillery bombardment. Although a well-executed artillery programme would keep the occupants crouched inside and disinclined to fire their weapons, only a direct hit from the heaviest howitzer shell would have any chance of actually knocking out one of these formidable constructions. Otherwise each pillbox had to be cleared by teams of riflemen and Lewis gunners posting grenades in through the firing slit or the back door. The attackers had to work their way forward from one muddy shell hole to the next, while Lewis gunners fired bursts at the firing slits to keep the enemies' heads down. The conditions made it difficult for attackers to keep pace with the artillery barrage. The Historian of the RN Division has this to say:

> It is safe to say that the Division was never confronted with a task which, on the lines laid down for them, was more impossible of fulfilment. Flanders mud had become proverbial, and even under ordinary conditions exposed the troops in the front system to exceptional hardships. Front lines and communications trenches were non-existent. The forward system consisted of posts isolated from each other by a sea of mud, and the support line of another line of posts, the elements of a trench, or, more probably, of a ruined farmhouse and outbuildings, where a company or so could be concentrated. . . . The enemy posts lay often between our own, and every ration and water party had to be prepared to fight its way forward. . . .
>
> Communications with the reserve positions was equally dangerous, if less difficult. All supplies and reinforcements had to be brought up on duckboard tracks, which with every advance stretched further and further forward. Off these tracks, progress was impossible, yet reliance on them was an evil necessity; they marked to the enemy, as to ourselves, our line of supply, and although used only at night, were a perilous substitute for the old communications trench. From an accurate bombardment of these tracks no party using them could escape. To turn aside by so much as one yard was to plunge waist-deep in a sea of mud where the bodies of the dead were rotting unburied in the primeval slime.[6]

These were the conditions when a battalion was merely holding the line, not attacking. As battalions moved up to their forming-up positions for an attack, their rifles and Lewis guns would become clogged with mud. Efficient divisions, such as the 63rd, would have armourers with cleaning rods posted in the forming-up positions. Without portable radios there was no means of asking for the fire plan to be delayed, or repeat some of the serials, and meanwhile the barrage moved inexorably away from the infantry floundering through the morass. Objectives were usually smashed beyond recognition. A village would just be a smear of red brick dust in the mud. Once an attack was launched, control even of a company became almost impossible, and everything devolved on to the platoon commanders and NCOs.

The ground assigned to the division was a mass of shell holes, flooded to a depth of several feet. The attack sector allocated to the 188th Brigade had a muddy stream called the Paddebeek running right across it, which, added to the rain of the previous two nights and days, made the going very hard indeed. At midnight the rain began again. Each of the RMLI battalions was below strength at about 16 officers and 590 other ranks. The battalions were in the forming-up position by 0200 hours on 26 October, where they lay or crouched for nearly four hours. At 0545 hours, still in heavy rain, 1 RMLI crossed the tapes marking what in this war was called the 'jumping off position, or line', and in later wars would be called the 'start line'. The enemy was alerted to the attack by the machine-gun barrage. The battalion, like all the others, advanced preceded by two thin lines of skirmishers, and behind these the main body moved in small columns of sections and platoons. Two complete rifle platoons (60–80 men) in every battalion were employed as stretcher bearers, the regulation number of these being found insufficient.

By 0720 hours the 1st RMLI had advanced some 700 yards, and gained their objectives, including a ruined farm building called Banff House, but suffered heavy casualties. 2 RMLI then passed through the 1st Battalion, but were only able to make headway on the flanks. Lieutenant (acting Captain) Ligertwood and his A Company managed to get across the Paddebeek, the only company to do so. He was wounded three times, refusing to go to the rear until hit a fourth time, and he subsequently died of wounds. He was one of a number of first-class experienced and battlewise NCOs who had been commissioned, and who were invaluable in action. By dusk, A Company were forced back behind the Paddebeek, and the line consolidated. At great cost the 188th Brigade had advanced about 800 yards. The next day the two RMLI battalions were withdrawn into reserve. 1 RMLI suffered 10 officers killed and wounded and 270 other ranks, while 2 RMLI lost 8 officers and 391 other ranks. In this, just one of many battles fought by 1 and 2 RMLI on the Western Front, these two battalions lost more men from a total strength of around 1,170 than the Royal Marines suffered at the

Battle of Jutland out of their 5,700 participants. General Gough commanding Fifth Army sent a congratulatory message:

> Please convey to all ranks engaged in today's operations my very great
> appreciation of their gallant efforts; they have my sincere sympathy, as no
> troops could have had to face worse conditions of mud than they had to
> face owing to the sudden downfall of rain this morning. No troops could
> have done better than our men did today, and given a fair chance, I have
> every confidence in their complete success every time.[7]

One is left wondering why the attack was not called off. The maximum gain anywhere on the divisional front was less than 1,500 yards, and even that was pretty good for Third Ypres. The 188th Brigade alone lost 40 officers and 1,184 NCOs and privates, killed, wounded, and missing between 23 October and 7/8 November 1917. Missing in this battle and terrain almost invariably meant dead.

The last major action fought by the 63rd Division in 1917 was in the aftermath of the Battle of Cambrai. Here, after the first successful use of tanks in large numbers, General Byng's British Third Army made some spectacular gains. However, ten days later a German counterattack regained most of the ground they had lost: in one place the Germans nearly broke through, but were stopped and forced back by the Guards Division. At the end of December, the 63rd Division was holding part of a key feature known as Welch Ridge. 1 RMLI were on the right of the division with 2 RMLI in support. At dawn on 30 December the enemy attacked along the whole front of the division, dressed in white suits, as the ground was covered in snow. Using infiltration tactics, which they had employed for the first time on the Western Front a month previously, the Germans penetrated the defences at some points. 1 RMLI was out on a limb for a while when the battalion on their left was driven back. The 1st RMLI held throughout the day, and a spirited counterattack by the Anson Battalion during the night restored the situation. The enemy renewed the attack after dawn on 31 December, but were repulsed after fierce fighting, thanks largely to fine shooting by the 188th Brigade's RMLI Trench Mortar Battery, and RMLI Machine Gun Company.

In January 1918, the fourth year of the war, heavy snowfalls followed by thaw made life in the trenches miserable, and closed down large-scale operations. However, that same month plans were afoot in the Admiralty, which were to bear fruit in a daring raid on a port behind the enemy lines in Belgium. The Royal Marines were to play a leading part, and in relating their story we jump forward in time, interrupting the narrative of their activities on the Western Front.

9

Zeebrugge, 23 April 1918 (St George's Day)

St George for England

Vice Admiral Keyes

And may we give the dragon's tail a damned good twist.

Captain Carpenter of HMS *Vindictive*

By 1918 the German High Seas Fleet had been so successfully contained in its own home waters by the Grand Fleet that there was little prospect of it ever emerging. As in the Second World War, however, the U-boat posed by far the greatest maritime threat to the Allies, at one point in 1917 threatening to starve the United Kingdom into submission. The introduction of the convoy system had greatly reduced the U-boat menace by 1918, but submarines and coastal forces operating from Bruges were still a threat to the passage of shipping supplying the armies in France, and Allied shipping in the North Sea.

The outlets for German naval forces based eight miles inland at Bruges were, from their capture at the end of 1914, the ports of Zeebrugge and Ostend, connected to Bruges by two canals, each fitted with locks and therefore able to allow the passage of ships at any state of the tide. Here were housed about eighteen submarines and up to twenty-five destroyers, in specially constructed shelters that were the forerunners of the U-boat pens of the Second World War. They were immune to attack: another twenty-five years passed before bombs able to penetrate reinforced concrete, and aircraft capable of delivering them, were developed. Vice Admiral Keyes, commanding the Dover patrol, therefore devised a plan to block the canal exits at Zeebrugge and Ostend.

The 4th Battalion Royal Marines (4th RM) was chosen for the Zeebrugge force. This battalion had originally been raised to serve in Ireland, then in a state of unrest following the Easter Rising of 1916. It never served there, and was used to supply reinforcements for the RMLI battalions in France. Drafting from the 4th Battalion was stopped early in 1918, and by the end of February it had been brought up to full strength, and concentrated at Deal for six weeks' training. During the training period, the Adjutant General Royal Marines visited, and, without disclosing the objective, said that any man who did not wish to go could pull out. Nobody accepted the offer, so in effect the whole battalion were volunteers.

The battalion was organized especially for the raid, with three rifle companies, instead of the usual four at that time. Unlike a 'normal' battalion, it had a machine-gun section of two Vickers and four Lewis guns (in addition to the normal Lewis per rifle platoon), and a trench mortar section. This was manned jointly by the RMA and RMLI, and commanded by the only RMA officers in the battalion, Captain Dallas-Brooks and his second-in-command. It contained an unusual mixture of weaponry: one 11in howitzer, two 7.5in howitzers, two 1.5in pom-poms (firing 2-pounder shells), and two Stokes trench mortars. The adjutant of 4th RM was Arthur Chater, who had been so scathing about the GOC 52nd Division at Cape Helles, now just twenty-two years old, and a substantive captain. Before 1914, captains in the Royal Marines were in their mid-thirties. The casualty rate in the battalions in France, in particular, had improved promotion prospects beyond the wildest pre-war expectations.

Security was tight, in marked contrast to Gallipoli and several other First World War operations. Indeed, when King George V inspected the battalion at Deal on 7 March he was not let into the secret. The battalion were told that they were to join the 63rd Division for a raid on an advanced enemy ammunition dump in France. They would be required to mop up and hold the dump, while engineers prepared it for demolition. On completion, they would withdraw. A suitable piece of ground on the ranges at Deal was marked out with tapes, with the aid of air photographs of Zeebrugge. The area being simulated was the curved mole, a mile and a half long and eighty yards across at its widest part, protecting the harbour entrance of Zeebrugge. On the seaward side the Mole rose about thirty feet above high water. On the top was a raised pathway about ten feet wide, with a railing on the outmost side. There was a drop of about sixteen to twenty feet from the raised pathway to the Mole itself. At the seaward end of the Mole was a battery of what were thought to be three 4.1in guns (actually 5.9in, but referred to throughout this account as 4.1in), and one of 1.5in anti-aircraft guns. From here a continuation of the raised pathway led to the lighthouse. Six 3.5in guns were mounted on this section. There were three large sheds on the Mole: No. 1, the Seaplane Base at the shore end; No. 2 about two-thirds along, and No. 3 at the seaward end. In addition there was a submarine shelter on the harbour side, and sheds and concrete shelters for personnel. The Mole was connected to the shore by a wooden viaduct.

The mission of both the Zeebrugge and Ostend raids (no Marines took part in the latter) was to sink blockships in the entrances to the canal locks. All other operations were subsidiary to the mission, and were aimed at supporting it. One of these was to do as much damage to the Zeebrugge mole as possible in the time available. The parties storming the Mole were to destroy the batteries on the seaward end to prevent them firing on the blockships as they steamed into the harbour and towards the canal entrance. Having done this, they were to advance along the Mole towards the shore, carrying out works of destruction. Two submarines, crammed with explosives, were to be towed in to ram the wooden viaduct. Their skeleton crews would light the fuses and row to a pick-up by a destroyer before the charges blew the viaduct, preventing German counterattacks from landward. But most important of all, by attacking the Mole it was hoped that the enemy's attention would be diverted from the sinking of the three blockships, the old minelayers *Intrepid*, *Iphigenia*, and *Thetis*, in the canal lock entrance.

As well as forming the majority of the storming parties at Zeebrugge, the Royal Marines were also engaged in six monitors bombarding Zeebrugge and Ostend, and the RMA siege guns covering Dunkirk bombarded Ostend. The storming parties consisted of the three rifle companies of 4th RM (each 165 strong), and a seaman party of 6 officers and 150 men, divided into three groups of 50 each, as well as a demolition party of 50 seamen and 22 NCOs and men from 4th RM.

The storming parties were embarked in HMS *Vindictive* (Captain A. F. B. Carpenter RN), HMS *Iris* (Commander V. Gibbs RN), and HMS

Daffodil (Lieutenant Commander S. H. Campbell RN). The *Vindictive* was an old 6in-gun cruiser, specially adapted for this task. Her boat deck had been planked over, and broad ramps led up from the main deck below. On the port side of the boat deck fourteen narrow wooden brows, or gangplanks, had been fitted, designed to be lowered so that the outer end rested on the top of the Mole. The stormers would run up these, and drop four feet off the end on to the raised pathway. *Vindictive*'s foretop had been strengthened and raised to enable machine-guns to fire over the Mole. The *Iris* and *Daffodil* were Mersey river ferry boats, also adapted for the task.

The *Vindictive* was to tow *Iris* and *Daffodil* across the Channel, and after casting them loose to proceed under their own power she was to secure alongside the Mole, about two hundred yards from the seaward end. The *Iris* was to secure alongside the Mole ahead of *Vindictive*, while *Daffodil* pushed against *Vindictive*'s starboard side to keep her hard against the Mole. The *Vindictive* was to engage the battery by the lighthouse with her 6in guns, while Dallas-Brooks's howitzers and pom-poms, and the Machine Gun Section's Lewis guns, engaged the Mole from her decks, assisted by Stokes mortars manned by Marines and seamen. The 4th RM Stokes mortars and Vickers in *Iris* were also to engage targets on the Mole until ordered to land, which they would do up ladders carried for the purpose.

The seamen storming parties had a multitude of demanding roles. They were to man additional Stokes mortars in the ships, and land them on the Mole if ordered. They were responsible for lowering the brows on *Vindictive*, and placing the scaling ladders from *Iris* up to the Mole. They were to form the leading wave on to the Mole, fight their way out to the lighthouse and light flares as a navigational aid to the blockships. Three sections of seamen were to assist in attacking the 4.1in gun battery. Lastly, they were to cover the withdrawal of the ships with smoke bombs fired from Stokes mortars on board. The seamen demolition party, with Marines as porters, was divided into three sections, one to accompany the seamen destroying the 4.1 inch guns, and the other two under command of Lieutenant Colonel Elliot, commanding officer 4th RM.

Extracts from the 4th Battalion Operation Order Number 2, dated 8 April 1918, signed by Chater, give the tasks and concept of operations for the battalion:

I – DISPOSITION

    In *Vindictive*:   *Battalion Headquarters*
                            B [Portsmouth] Company
                            C [Plymouth] Company
                            Lewis gun section of Machine Gun Section
                            RMA Howitzers, Pom-poms and Stokes Guns [mortars]
                            [all under command of Captain Dallas-Brooks RMA]
    In the *Iris*:   A [Chatham] Company [Major C. Eagles DSO]
                            Vickers Gun Section
                            2 Stokes Guns [mortars]

II – The position to be attacked and held by the Battalion in this operation is the Zeebrugge Mole. The object of the attack is the destruction of the guns on the seaward end of the Mole.

III – The operation will be carried out in accordance with the instructions given while the battalion was at Deal [which were as rehearsed]:-

C Company (Major Weller DSC) less two platoons will carry out phase 1, and will disembark first [companies had drawn lots to be first to land, and C Company had won], and will establish a *point-d'appui* [base of operations] by occupying and consolidating the Mole to the West (shore) end up to and including the No 3 Shed and the AA battery, clearing up all points of resistance as far as point 600 [about one third of the way along]. Nos 11 and 12 Platoons under Captain Palmer will turn to the left and advance towards the battery [presumably the three 4.1in].

B Company (Captain Bamford) will then disembark and forming up under the cover of C Company attack along the Mole, securing the bomb ammunition dumps, shed and shelters as far as point 1200 [about two thirds along]; the end of this sector is to be held at all costs.

A Company (Major Eagles) when disembarked from *Iris* is to follow B Company and carry out the fourth phase, that is the occupation of the remainder of the Mole, including the aeroplane base, and attached quarters for aircraft personnel.

IV – Officers commanding units are to imbue their commands with the idea of carrying the operation through with the bayonet; rifle fire, machine gun fire, and bomb throwing are to be resorted to when necessary to break down enemy opposition.

V – The position of the most advanced unit is to be marked by the firing of Red Verey Lights. These will be the principal guide in the control of the covering fire afforded by the *Vindictive*.

VI – The seamen co-operating in the assault have orders to confine their movements to the raised path-way on the outer side of the Mole. They will endeavour to enfilade the three 4-inch [4.1in] guns from the footway. The success or failure of the attempt to silence these guns [by the seamen presumably] will affect the actions of the units carrying out phase 1 [C Company?].

VII – It must be firmly impressed on all ranks that the capture of the fortified zone at the seaward end of the Mole is the first essential to ensure the success of the entire enterprise, but that the task allotted to the Battalion does not end there; every endeavour must be made to carry out the later phases of the Operation. An elaborate scheme of demolitions has been prepared; this scheme can not be carried out unless demolition parties are covered by the Battalion. Nothing therefore except the strongest enemy opposition or the obvious lack of time must stop the advance along the Mole.

VIII – A number of torpedo craft, submarines, and other auxiliary craft including a Depot ship usually lie alongside the inner side of the Mole. It is expected that the majority of these will get under way during the aerial attacks [preceding the main attack]. Any craft found alongside must be cleared by units during their advance.

IX – [deals with timing for withdrawal]

X – [instructions for demolitions]

XI – [instructions for the Quartermaster to set up an ammunition dump on the Mole]

XII – [casualty evacuation instructions]

XIII – Battalion headquarters will be established in a favourable position on the Mole abreast of the ship. Reports should be sent to this position which will be indicated by a white flag.

It was a hugely complicated and ambitious scheme, with little margin for events not going to plan. The composition of the assault force, a mixture of seamen and Marines, was itself a curious, antique throwback to the nineteenth century, and a potential source of muddle and command and control snags. The clearing of craft alongside the Mole alone was a major task, and might have diverted large numbers of men from other more important duties. So much emphasis on attacking with the bayonet only, harking back to pre-1914 concepts, seems questionable. By now, infantry tactics on the Western Front stressed fire and move-ment with grenade and Lewis gun, and this would have been especially appropriate when fighting among buildings on the Mole. But few officers in 4th RM had any recent Western Front experience. We shall never know if Major Eagles, who had served with distinction in 2 RMLI in France, had anything to say on the matter.

Each man carried sixty rounds of ammunition and two grenades, and wore steel helmet, belt and ammunition pouches, bayonet, gas mask slung on his chest, a swimming 'belt' under his tunic, and rubber-soled gym shoes. Some had weighted clubs, or coshes, for close-quarter fighting. Each platoon had a Lewis gun, a flame-thrower, and two ladders and four ropes to enable them to descend from the raised pathway to the Mole. In addition Number 7 Platoon of B Company was to position heavy scaling ladders for the same purpose.

The embarkation of the battalion was planned to maintain security and deceive anyone who might be interested in their true destination. Chater:

> The Battalion left Deal by train on 6 April. At Dover we embarked in the transport *King Edward* as though for France, but at the Mouse Lightship we transshipped to the ferry steamer *Daffodil*. Arriving in the Swin in the afternoon, the Battalion transferred for accommodation to the old battle-ship HMS *Hindustan*, with the exception of C Company which went straight to HMS *Vindictive*.

4th RM embarked with 30 officers, 1 Warrant Officer, and 710 other ranks. Once aboard, all were meticulously briefed on the target for the first time. Each platoon was shown a model of the objective, and all officers and NCOs were given air photographs to study. Some NCOs made sketch maps for themselves from the air photographs. The bat-talion was to travel across the Channel, and land from *Vindictive*, except for A Company, which was to assault from *Daffodil*. The right combi-nation of tide, wind, and weather was critical for success, and this could be found on only five nights every two weeks. Because of adverse wind and weather conditions, the operation was postponed three times, twice after the force had sailed. Chater recorded after one of these postponements:

> One of the lessons learned from this abortive attempt was this: prior to our arrival, and without consulting us, the Captain of the *Vindictive* had announced that before the ship reached the Mole, a double tot of rum would be issued to all hands. As the operation was one in which all would need clear heads and steady hands and feet, we felt this to be a mistake: but there was no going back on it. We learnt however that the rum issue would need far closer supervision than had been given to it on 11th April.[1]

The strain of waiting for action can be imagined; particularly as, for security reasons, no one could go ashore, and they eventually remained embarked for sixteen days. There were now few days left when the state of the tide would allow *Vindictive* to be laid alongside the Mole, and the brows to reach the top at an angle which enabled men to run up them; and now tidal conditions meant that the length of time she could remain alongside would be reduced to about an hour and forty minutes. Chater:

> The first day of the second suitable period was Monday 22nd April [1918]. The order to carry out the operation was received at 1045 am. At 1.10 pm the Force sailed, and on a perfect spring afternoon and evening we approached the enemy coast. Towards dusk Wing Commander Brock was transferred by whaler from one of the destroyers to *Vindictive*. He was the pyrotechnics expert and brought with him a box labelled 'explosives – handle with great care'. This was hoisted on board and handled very gingerly. It was taken to the wardroom and found to contain several bottles of excellent vintage port, which were consumed with relish. Brock landed on the Mole and was never seen again.

So much for Chater's concern with keeping a clear head! He continues:

> At 11 pm the Battalion went to action stations. As the result of experience on 11th April, very careful precautions were taken to ensure that no man got more than his own ration of rum. In spite of this, one old soldier must have borrowed someone else's tot, for when I went round the mess decks with the Sergeant Major as the men were closing up, he shouted at us, 'We are just going over the top. We are all equal now'. I remember catching sight of the same man some three hours later, and thinking what a changed and sober man he looked.

The sea was beginning to get rough. The *Vindictive* slowed, as destroyers and motor launches pulled ahead to make smoke. Sergeant Harry Wright, Number 10 Platoon, C Company:

> Our little Sergeants' Mess was crowded. We hastily shook hands and then went out to get our men on to the upper deck, into the darkness. Rifles were loaded and bayonets fixed. No lights were showing on any of the ships, and everyone spoke in whispers. Our nerves were strained almost to breaking point. Would we get alongside the Mole without the Germans seeing us. We stood shoulder to shoulder, rifles in hand ready for the dash forward – not a movement, and only the noise of the propellers breaking the silence.

While the rifle companies were jammed in at their assault stations, the battalion's Lewis gunners crouched behind sandbags on the superstructure; Stokes mortars were set up on the boat deck and forecastle; Dallas-Brooks's 11in howitzer was on the poop, with one of his 7.5in howitzers forward and the other amidships on the port side. Two pom-poms and several Lewis guns were in the foretop under Lieutenant Rigby RMA. Meanwhile A Company took up their assault stations in the *Iris*. The demolition parties travelled in the *Daffodil*, and were to land across *Vindictive*. The air attack took place as planned and drove the enemy gunners to their shelters, but as the ships approached the Mole the wind shifted, blowing the smoke screens clear. A star shell burst above the approaching ships, floating gently down. Sergeant Wright:

> No sooner had that light died down than another went up. The silence was broken by a terrific bang followed by a crash as the fragments of shell fell in among us, killing and maiming the brave fellows as they stood to their arms, crowded together as thick as bees. The Mole was just in sight, we could see it off our port quarter, but too late. Our gunners replied to this fire, but could not silence that terrible battery of 5-inch guns now firing into our ship at a range of less than 100 yards and from behind concrete walls. A very powerful searchlight was turned on us from the sand-dunes of Zeebrugge.

Still 250 yards from the Mole the guns in *Vindictive*'s foretop opened up, the signal for all guns to start firing. The ship's 6in guns kept up the fire until the ship closed the Mole. The Stokes mortars remained in action until the brows were lowered. To cover the storming parties, the howitzers were ordered to open fire. Captain Dallas-Brooks went forward

to see why the 7.5in howitzer was not firing, and found the whole crew
dead or wounded. A volunteer crew of seamen from the ship's 6in guns
was in the process of bringing this howitzer into action. The 11in
howitzer on the poop kept up a steady rate of fire throughout, but the
amidships 7.5in was hit, damaged, and only brought into action just as
the ship was retracting from the Mole. The foretop, which protruded
clear of the Mole, was hit by a shell from a destroyer on the other side,
which killed or wounded everybody, although Sergeant Finch RMA
nevertheless kept his gun firing to the end of the battle. Captain
Carpenter was later to write of the foretop gunners, 'one cannot but
attribute the complete success of our diversion very largely to these
gallant men'.

Earlier, on his way to his action station with the CO on the bridge,
Chater had met Major Cordner, the second-in-command. To his surprise
Cordner announced his intention of joining the CO until the ship was
alongside. Chater always regretted not telling him more forcefully that
the CO and second-in-command should not be together. Chater:

> Although only 22 years old, I probably had a far more intimate experience
> of shell fire than either the CO or second-in-command. We were some
> distance from the Mole, and instinct told me to keep my head down. I
> suggested that my two seniors did the same, but either they did not hear
> me, or did not agree. They took no notice. A moment later a shell
> appeared to hit the front of the lower bridge beneath us. My two seniors
> dropped to the deck on either side of me. I grasped hold of them and
> spoke to them in turn, but neither answered me.

Chater found Major Weller commanding C Company, the next senior,
and told him he was now in command of the battalion. At five minutes
past midnight, Captain Carpenter laid *Vindictive* alongside the Mole, 300
yards further along than planned. Of the fourteen brows up which the
assault was to be made onto the Mole, only two survived the shellfire.
Chater found that the two platoons of C Company detailed to lead the
assault had suffered so many casualties that 'the platoons, as such,
appeared no longer to exist'. He ordered Lieutenant Cooke, of Number
5 Platoon, B Company, to lead. On reaching the Mole, Captain Bamford,
OC B Company, with Cooke's platoon, mounted an attack on it and
silenced a party of enemy riflemen who were near No. 2 Shed and firing
into the sub-units disembarking.

The plan was already beginning to unravel. Chater accompanied Cooke's platoon ashore,

> to investigate the height of the sea wall [the raised pathway], of which conflicting reports had been received, and the best means of getting down to the Mole and back again. I found there were no steps near to where the ship had been berthed, and that the height was too great to jump down. Returning on board, I gave instructions for hook ropes to be taken ashore and I made Sergeant Major Thatcher personally responsible that, after the men had landed, scaling ladders were placed and maintained in position. Without these ladders, no man who got down on to the Mole would have been able to get back on to the ship. Having given these orders, I returned to the sea wall, slid down a hook rope, and crossed over to number 3 shed on the far side of the Mole. My impression is that the sea wall abreast of the Mole was not under rifle or MG fire at this time, but the defenders were shelling the Mole and their shells were striking the sea wall and the sheds. Only the funnels and foretop of the *Vindictive* were visible over the sea wall.

Sergeant Wright, his platoon commander fatally wounded, found himself in command of the remnants of Number 10 platoon. With Lieutenant Lamplough's Number 9 platoon they dashed up the ramp onto the boat deck,

> passing our dead and wounded lying everywhere, finally crossing the two remaining gangways which were only just hanging together. Our casualties were so great before landing that out of a platoon of 45 only 12 landed. Number 9 platoon led by Lt Lamplough had about the same number.

Lieutenant Lamplough:

> On arrival at the brows I realised for the first time that the ship was berthed in the wrong position and we were abreast the centre of No 3 Shed and close to my objective. The ship was rolling quite heavily and the brows were at a considerable incline. We jumped down and onto the path inside the sea wall and down the ropes secured to the railings to assist us negotiate the 16 foot drop onto the floor of the Mole. I took my platoon to the shore end of No 3 Shed and established my position there before deciding what to do. During my landing there had been a tremendous amount of firing of every sort and the noise had been terrific, but the most encouraging, until unfortunately knocked out, was the firing of

the pom-poms from the foretop of *Vindictive*. We also saw the explosion of the submarine C3 at about this moment.

Submarine C-3, the only one of the two to arrive, destroyed the wooden viaduct, cutting communications with the shore. The second wave, the remainder of B Company, began to go ashore. Private James Feeney, Number 7 Platoon: 'in my anxiety to keep my balance on the see-saw of the gangway, I forgot about the rain of lead, and felt really comfortable when I put my foot on the concrete.'

The task of the leading wave of 4th RM, Weller's C Company, had been to deal with the battery at the seaward end of the Mole, assisted by the seamen storming party. Because the ship had berthed so far down the Mole, and C Company had taken such heavy casualties, some swift changes of plan were needed. Chater:

> I met Captain Bamford, B Company commander, whose totally unperturbed manner had the most reassuring effect on all who came in contact with him that night. Together we discussed the situation. All the men who belonged to units which were to have attacked the fortified zone [the seaward end of the Mole], now found themselves at No 3 Shed. No attack on the fortified zone had yet been made. As this was our principal objective, we decided to organize and attack along the Mole. This entailed attacking a prepared position across some two hundred yards of flat pavement devoid of any form of cover. Led by Captain Bamford the units [three of his platoons] started forward. They were well out in the open when the ship's siren was heard making what was taken to be the emergency recall signal. Captain Bamford therefore gave the order to withdraw.
>
> The signal arranged for the emergency recall was the sounding of the morse letter 'K' on the ship's siren. Although the siren was blowing it was not making this signal. We had expected to be ashore for one and a quarter hours, but we had been ashore for only forty-five minutes. As I was convinced that the recall was not really intended, I returned to the ship and went to the conning tower, where I found Captain Carpenter, and asked if we were to withdraw. Having been told the recall was ordered, I returned to the sea wall and passed the order to all those I could reach by voice or signal.

Meanwhile Lieutenant Lamplough's and Sergeant Wright's platoons had been clearing German dugouts, and Lamplough reported:

we did what we could to harass a destroyer alongside with what weapons we had available, and also dealt with a few Germans who came down the Mole close to the sea wall as if in an attempt to interfere with our scaling ladders. The whole time we were there German coast defence guns bombarded the *Vindictive* and Mole and a considerable number of shells burst at the base of the wall alongside the ship, not an encouraging prospect for our retirement.

At about 1250 am the recall was sounded and units commenced to retire, taking their wounded with them. My position being nearest to the shore end of the Mole, it was my duty to cover the retirement, and we left, only when, as far as I could see, none of our troops remained. When we got back to the wall, fortunately and to my great surprise, one of the scaling ladders remained, also one of the brows to the ship. On arrival on board I reported to the Captain [of *Vindictive*] that as far as I knew we were the last to leave. We learnt later that Captain Palmer [his company commander], 3 NCOs and 10 Privates failed to return and were taken prisoner.

As was Sergeant Wright, in the confusion over whether the signal heard was, or was not, the correct one:

We took it for the signal to retire and commenced doing so when the order was passed that it was not the retire signal and we were ordered back to our posts. We obeyed the order, and very shortly afterwards we had the terrible ordeal of seeing our only means of escape slowly move away.

He and the others left behind spent the rest of the war in a prisoner of war camp.

The *Iris* never managed to land Major Eagles and A Company. When Commander Gibbs put his ship alongside the Mole ahead of *Vindictive*, the grappling irons on her lines would not hold her. Two naval officers were killed scrambling up on to the Mole in an effort to secure her. The scaling ladders could not therefore be positioned. All this time the *Iris* was under heavy fire. One shell hit a group of 56 men, killing 49 and wounding the remainder. Gibbs was mortally wounded with both legs blown off. Eventually Lieutenant Spencer RNR, who took over command, decided to lay her alongside *Vindictive* and land A Company across her. But before she could be made fast, the recall was sounded. As she withdrew under fierce fire, a shell fell among the officers of A Company killing Major Eagles, and killing or wounding all the others

Malaya: Royal Marines commandos in a captured terrorist camp. Place and unit unknown.

Korea: a raiding party from 41 Independent Commando RM searching houses before blowing a stretch of track near Songjin, 138 miles from the Manchurian border, 10 April 1951. The Commando wore US equipment, but kept the green berets.

Training in the 1950s: Flannel Alley, a severe route on Chair Ladder, Porthgwarra, Cornwall. Commando Climbers from the Royal Marines Cliff Assault Wing.

Egypt 1952–4: a section of 45 Commando RM with their rucksacks, manpack frames, bazooka, and 2-inch mortar in Port Fuad about to bid farewell to the Canal Zone in 1954.

Helicopters flying 45 Commando RM into Port Said, 6 November 1956.

Troops of 42 Commando RM running out to Whirlwind helicopters on HMS *Bulwark* before landing in Kuwait, July 1961.

Cyprus 1954–9: Kykko Monastery in the Paphos Forest used as a platoon base at various times by both 40 and 45 Commando, and infantry battalions. The notice on the outer perimeter, 'Lazy S Ranch', is evidence that one of the platoons of Support Troop 40 Commando is in residence.

Cyprus 1954–9: a bridge on the road to Kykko Monastery. 'The mountain roads were narrow and mostly unsurfaced. Hairpin bends, cliffs, and steep slopes on both sides made them ideal places for ambush.' (p. 440)

Radfan: officers and men of 45 Commando RM, including a sniper scanning through his rifle-mounted telescope, looking down on the Wadi Taym from 'Cap Badge'.

Aden: the withdrawal. 42 Commando RM covered the airport from which most of the garrison was evacuated in RAF VC-10 aircraft. One of the last 42 Commando piquets lifted out of Aden, November 1967, in a Wessex helicopter. A sardonic grin from the section commander bids farewell to the 'Barren Rocks of Aden'.

Above: Northern Ireland: Marines of Z Company, 45 Commando RM moving into a cordon in Belfast in 1981. The man on the left is taking up a firing position from the 'wrong' shoulder. All troops serving in Northern Ireland were taught to fire from either shoulder to minimize exposing their body if they had to shoot round a right-handed corner. This man may be left handed anyway. Unlike the present-day SA 80, it was possible to fire the SLR off the left shoulder.

Opposite, top: Falklands War, 1982. Often captioned as the landings at San Carlos, this is actually the cross-decking of 40 Commando RM and 3rd Battalion The Parachute Regiment on 19 May 1982, two days before the landing on 21 May – LPD, LCUs and Sea King Helicopters.

Opposite, bottom: Falklands War, 1982: men of 45 Commando RM entering Port Stanley after the surrender of the Argentine forces. They walked from San Carlos.

Training in the early 1980s; recruits passing through the water obstacle on the endurance course at the Commando Training Centre.

Training: B Company 40 Commando emerging from a smokescreen to attack a hut during jungle training. The man in the centre is armed with a Light Support Weapon, which has replaced the GPMG.

Four members of the SBS dressed for a maritime counter-terrorist operation.

except one. The total casualties on board *Iris* that night, sailors and Marines, were 8 officers and 69 men killed, and 3 officers and 102 wounded.

While Chater was standing on the wall by *Vindictive* during the withdrawal, several men who passed him thought he was wounded and wanted to carry him on board:

> When I could see no more men approaching, I returned on board and reported to that effect. A few moments later the ship left the Mole.
>
> As the ship withdrew, we expected to be heavily shelled. Clouds of smoke were released aft, which hid us from the enemy and to our surprise we were not hit. As the danger from the enemy diminished I began to realize that my right knee was very painful. What had hit it I never knew, but it probably happened when the CO and second-in-command were killed.
>
> I discussed the operation with Bamford. We had failed to gain any of the objectives which had been laid down in our orders. We felt that our part in the operation had been a complete failure. We had lost a good many men with what seemed to us no result. We felt extremely despondent.

Private Feeney, back on board *Vindictive*:

> I shall never forget the sight of the mess-decks; dead and dying lying on the decks and tables where, but a few hours before, they ate, drank and played cards. In the light of day it was a shambles.

Chater:

> *Vindictive* reached Dover at 8.0 am and went alongside Admiralty Pier. On landing, I met Admiral Keyes. He told me the aeroplane had been over Zeebrugge that morning, and had reported the Canal entrance blocked. He said the operation had been a great success. I told him how we felt, and asked him to tell the men. The Battalion was falling in on the Pier to entrain for Deal. The Admiral came and told us his good news.
>
> I rang up the Brigade Major at Deal and said we were back: but both the CO and Second-in-Command had been killed. I think he did not believe me. The remains of the Battalion returned to Deal by train, and marched to the Depot. The task of licking our wounds, and accounting for the killed, wounded and missing began. Of a strength of about seven hundred and thirty, the Battalion suffered three hundred and sixty-six casualties, including seventeen officers of whom ten were killed. Next day

we were rung up by the Admiral's office at Dover, and told the Battalion was to elect one representative to receive a Victoria Cross for the Battalion, and that the Admiral wished to come over and announce the name of the person selected before the Battalion dispersed on 27th April.

On the afternoon of the 26th, the Battalion paraded in the Drill Field. I explained what was to be done, slips of paper were issued, the troops were told to break off for a few minutes to consult each other before writing a name on their paper and handing it in.

While this was being done, the [acting] CO and I went back to the office to complete the report, leaving Captain Bamford in charge to collect the voting slips and add up the result. Half an hour later he arrived at the office looking rather sheepish. He handed to the CO a list showing himself as having received the greatest number of votes. Second on the list was Sergeant Finch. We reported Bamford's name to Dover. [Bamford had won the DSO in the *Chester* at Jutland.]

Next morning, the Battalion paraded. When Admiral Keyes arrived, the CO and I met him. He told us that the Battalion was to receive not one, but two Victoria Crosses, and asked who was to receive the second one. After a moment's consultation with me, the CO said Sergeant Finch. This means of selection, although quite irregular, proved to very acceptable to all concerned. Had the voting for the Victoria Crosses been carried out according to statute, the officers would have elected one representative, and the other ranks the other. In that case, Finch would have still been elected, but I think the other officers would have chosen Cooke as their representative.[2]

For some extraordinary reason, it was decreed that in special honour of the remarkable deeds of the 4th Battalion, no other battalion should be numbered thus. So was lost an opportunity to maintain a living tradition.

Keyes was correct in telling Chater that the air reconnaissance had seen blockships in the Zeebrugge canal mouth. However, *Thetis* ran aground short of the canal mouth, and *Intrepid* was pushed from her correct block position when *Iphigenia*'s captain rammed her accidentally. Both ships were scuttled, but did not seal the canal mouth. Two attempts to block the Ostend canal were unsuccessful. However, nothing can diminish the courage of the Royal Marines and Royal Navy who took part in the Zeebrugge raid. In addition to the two VCs awarded to the Royal Marines, five were awarded to the Royal Navy. The operation reduced German confidence in the impregnability of their submarine bases. It restored the British public's faith in the Navy, after years of apparent inactivity in the North Sea, and what they perceived as the unsatisfactory outcome of the Battle of Jutland. Finally, the raid provided a much-needed boost to morale at a time when the war on the Western Front was going badly, and to this we must return.

10

The Western Front, 1918

THE SOMME, 1918: RETREAT

The Battle of St Quentin

There is a widely held misconception that there was only one Battle of the Somme, in 1916, and even that for most people means the events of 1 July of that year. In fact there were three battles: one in 1916, in which the Royal Marines' actions have already been described, and two in 1918, in which they also played their part. For the first three months of 1918, the 63rd Division took its turn as the right-hand division of V Corps in British Third Army, in positions east of the old Somme battlefields of 1916. For manpower reasons all brigades in the BEF were reduced to three battalions each, and 63rd Division was no exception. The 188th Brigade now consisted of the two RMLI battalions and the Anson.

As the war progressed some first-class battle-experienced officers commissioned from the ranks joined the RMLI battalions on the Western Front. Not all came from Royal Marines units. One such officer was Harold Horne, who had enlisted in the 6th Battalion Northumberland Fusiliers[1] in September 1914, fought with them at the Second Battle of Ypres, Hooge, and on the Somme, and risen to the rank of company sergeant major. After Army Officer Cadet training, Horne was posted to the RMLI, and reported to Chatham:

> besides myself there were another three ex-army cadets who formed the first batch of such recruits to the Marines. We were well received, and made welcome but, on parade, we were definitely given to understand that we had to drill in the Marine manner. We were to start with, put in the hands of a drill sergeant. The fact that I had been an army company sergeant major didn't count for much.

Some officers came from the fleet. Harold Horne:

> On 10th [January] Captain R. Poland took over C Company. He was a regular Marine officer who had been with the Grand Fleet at Scapa Flow most of the war. He was bored with the inactivity and applied to be transferred to the Naval Division. The same applied to Captain Campbell.

On 20 March, 188th Brigade was deployed with 1 RMLI in the front line, 2 RMLI in the support and counterattack line, and Anson in reserve. For some days heavy gas and conventional shell bombardments had indicated that the Germans were preparing an offensive. Recently the division had suffered about 2,800 casualties; one of its battalions was down to 150 all ranks, and the remainder were each about 500 strong.

Leave parties were rejoining the division as the storm clouds gathered. Among them was Private Polley, a Vickers machine-gunner, moving up to find his machine-gun company in the newly formed Machine Gun Battalion commanded by Lieutenant Colonel McCready RMLI.[2] Polley's company normally, although not exclusively under the new organization, supported the 189th Brigade. Polley was a machine-gun number 1, in charge of one gun, and the senior man in the returning leave party.

> I marched my little party off in the direction of the line. The snow had ceased and the sun broke through, and had we been going anywhere but to the trenches, we should have thoroughly enjoyed the march, but we were all a bit quiet. It did not take long to find our [company] HQ near Neuville. The majority of sections [four guns per section] were in the line, and were having, for all accounts a pretty rough time. All leave had been cancelled pending Jerry's attack. All conversation centred on the Big German Offensive, and although continual talk on a given subject breeds familiarity, familiarity with such a subject as the probability of being blown to smithereens does not make for confidence.
>
> A few reinforcements arrived, but the majority were detained at HQ filling belts [for the guns] during the day, and trudging up the line with ration limbers at night bearing on their shoulders the results of their day's toil.
>
> Enemy planes soared overhead at all times of the day and night. For some days we had been subjected to frequent gas attacks. All guns were ready for action. During the night of the 21st we captured several enemy scouts and learned that the attack was to commence in real earnest in the morning.

On 21 March, after a hurricane bombardment of short duration but great intensity, followed by storm-troopers attacking under the cover of gas and mist, the Germans launched Operation Michael, attacking with sixty-five divisions. Polley:

> At dawn the bombardment started, he opened with gas, and gradually worked round to high explosive. All troops were ordered to the dug-outs, and the infantry leaving double sentries on the firesteps and a pair at the head of the dug-out stairs, and a most unpleasant job it was. The enemy guns searched out almost every inch of ground and the trenches were knocked almost out of recognition. By 5 o'clock when 'stand to' was ordered, the barrage had grown to an intensity that was little short of terrifying. Their aircraft helped sweeping along the lines, flying very low and pumping lead into the trenches. Others paid full attention to our observation balloons, which they brought down in flames.
>
> Of the rest of the day's proceedings in front I know little for I was recalled to HQ very early [possibly for his gun to form a reserve, he does not say]. Here there was much ado sorting out sections for replacing casualties and arranging relays for [taking forward] ammunition.

Within hours the enemy had forced back British Fifth Army on the right of 1 RMLI, and also the brigade on their left. The 63rd Division were told by their Corps Headquarters that if a counterattack did not restore the situation they were to fall back on the Intermediate Line that night. The counterattack failed, and 1 RMLI fell back through 2 RMLI. The enemy followed up, and while Lieutenant Colonel Farquharson, the CO of 2 RMLI, was leading one of his companies up to stem the enemy advance he was mortally wounded. He had served with the battalion since Gallipoli, being adjutant at the evacuation. Further withdrawals were ordered by Corps Headquarters as the German tide swept forward on both sides of the division, mainly to the south in Fifth Army's sector.

Polley, moving back with most of his company through Neuville:

> As we were passing through the remains of the square, Fritz dropped a couple of heavies squarely in the middle. We scattered and lay flat. But in a few minutes reassembled and continued our march. We had entered the village by the sunken road and noticed with surprise that the artillery had their guns mounted, waiting for the enemy to attempt a further advance.

By 23 March the two RMLI Battalions had been withdrawn to a half-completed defensive position to the east of a high railway embankment in front of the village of Bertincourt. There was no wire, and the trenches were shallow. Unfortunately signs of digging were spotted by reconnaissance aircraft, of which the Germans had plenty, having temporarily wrested control of the air from the Allies. The two battalions were treated to a 'box barrage', as they feverishly worked to improve their positions. Polley:

> All along the roadside the big guns were in action. The gunners working like fiends and pouring with perspiration. Machine-guns joined in the inferno not very far distant. All desperately endeavouring to stem the enemy advance.

Throughout the afternoon the enemy pressed heavily, but for the moment did not threaten the 63rd Division directly. As darkness fell, the division could see large fires in parts of the front that had been evacuated, and the night was punctuated by explosions, as ammunition and supply dumps were burnt or blown up to keep them out of the hands of the enemy.

Others had found the stores useful. Polley, before they withdrew:

> We were up at dawn and found the Engineers [a neighbouring unit] had abandoned their canteen with its entire stock, and we had the finest breakfast ever eaten so close to the line. There were tins of salmon, several kinds of fruit, chocolate and a few bottles of beer, the latter did not appeal to me at that hour of the morning, but they went somewhere, so I suppose some of our number were not so squeamish.

Bapaume

By the morning of 24 March, counterattacks by other divisions having failed, the 63rd were subjected to a determined attack preceded by a heavy artillery bombardment. The leading companies of the two RMLI battalions bore the brunt of this attack in the 188th Brigade sector. Heavy hand-to-hand fighting ensued, during which a message arrived ordering a further withdrawal. Vain efforts were made to pull back the two companies, but lacking proper communications and good layback positions, and further impeded by fog, they were surrounded and taken prisoner. The remainder of the two battalions fought hard to make a clean break, with enemy on their right flank some two miles behind them. The whole front was now falling back, but fortunately the enemy immediately confronting the two RMLI battalions had become cautious and was slow to follow up.

The two battalions eventually went firm and, assisted by twelve Vickers machine-guns of the Divisional Machine Gun Battalion, they checked the enemy. The 189th Brigade had a similar experience, leaving Vickers machine-guns to cover the withdrawal. Polley:

> The Company halted and a hurried overhaul of men and guns took place. Gun teams were detailed and left for, where? Nobody appeared to know except the officers. The remainder of the company left for the Somme.

Because the 63rd Division was out of touch with its flanking formations, the Divisional Commander ordered a withdrawal of six miles. In three columns, each brigade with its own artillery and strong flank guards passed over the old Somme battlegrounds of 1916 to the north of Flers. Polley:

> On, on, on, until at last we linked up with the retreating infantry, and during this whole dreadful march we were shelled-shelled-shelled, and if there can be monotony in the expectation of death – then the very din of battle became monotonous. Eventually, it seemed like untold ages, we reached the open country of the Somme, and those on foot made it across the fields in the direction of Delville Wood, while the transport [mules, horses, and ammunition limbers] kept to the road.
>
> The sacrifice guns [left to cover the withdrawal] during the early stages were forced to evacuate their position. When it was found that the belt boxes with some ammunition had been left behind, the officer called for a couple of men to go back with him and get them. They never returned.
>
> We regained the road somewhere near Delville Wood, and the remnant of the company halted. Some of the company who had seen [the] previous fighting [on the Somme in 1916, Polley had not], called it Delville Wood, but to look at it, only a few dead stumps remained.

While on the march, orders were received to fall back further to a line east of High Wood, of First Battle of the Somme fame. The enemy following up attacked some of the gun teams and artillery transport. Hand-to-hand fighting ensued, and guns were lost. Throughout this move, enemy aircraft harassed the troops. The Germans continued to press, and the 63rd Division still could not maintain contact with its flanking formations, so the withdrawal continued. For one night the

188th Brigade held bridges over the Ancre, where they had fought so hard in 1916. Here the enemy was checked during the hours of darkness, so the brigade had a quiet, although mainly sleepless night, after five days and nights of non-stop fighting and marching.

When the German offensive started, Harold Horne was at the V Corps school midway between Albert and Doullens, where officers were brought up to date on the latest tactics. Orders were received to evacuate the school.

Mar 24: Palm Sunday.
Left the school by train via Achiet-le-Petit to Miraoument. Here we heard the Naval Division was fighting a rear-guard action somewhere to the east. Lieut Hotham and I set off on foot to try to find the Battalion. During this march we encountered many parties of stragglers seeking their units. Wild rumours were spread and continuous gun fire was heard in the distance eastwards. We found some Naval Division men returning from leave and collected them.

Mar 25
Left Pozières [where they had three hours' sleep in some deserted huts] for Albert, four miles of main road with much horses and mule transport as well as lorries. At Albert we found the Expeditionary Force Canteen was open, but had been evacuated so we managed to get a free breakfast and collected free supplies of biscuits and chocolate as we were hungry and had no rations.

In Albert we heard from a staff officer that the Royal Marine transport was believed to be somewhere in the Ancre Valley. Hotham and I found our battalion transport about 1½ miles away and at night went up with the rations and ammunition to the battalion in the ruins of Thiepval village.

Everyone was very weary, having fought rear-guard actions for three or four days and about 25 miles over the devastated country of the battlefields of 1916–1917.

In the early hours of 26 March the 63rd Division was ordered back across the Ancre, and the 188th Brigade, with 1 RMLI as rearguard, was clear without trouble by the early morning. Horne:

Mar 26
From Thiepval at 4.0 am we moved west about a mile, crossing the river Ancre to the road and railway between Mesnil and Hamel. Here the road runs alongside the railway which is on an embankment four or five feet

high. The road, river and railway are parallel, north and south. The river Ancre here is a double stream running through a marsh about five hundred yards wide. We were occupying the road, and using the railway embankment as a defensive parapet with the marsh and river in front. Beyond that, rising ground on which was Thiepval Wood and the ruined village.

Things were quiet during the day. Probably the Germans had not been able to get much of their artillery to keep pace with the moving battle. Towards dusk we saw a few of the German scouts on the slope on the other side of the marsh. After dark a small party came across and we had a hectic scrap for probably ten minutes – they on the river side of the railway and we on the road. Neither side had any hand grenades, so we fought it out with small arms at about ten yards range. They retired, leaving some dead and a few prisoners, mainly wounded in our hands.

The division was now on familiar ground, near the epic battle at Beaumont Hamel and Beaucourt. The troops were very tired after six days of heavy and continuous fighting and marching over the old Somme battlefields, which were badly cut up and very dusty. To add to their weariness, there was a shortage of water. The division had been told that here they must hold. That day the famous 'backs to the wall' order by the C-in-C, Field Marshal Sir Douglas Haig, was received.

The enemy attacked north and south of the division with the aim of cutting it off, but it held, with the assistance of a counterattack by another division. At midnight on that same day, after a brief bombardment, the enemy broke through on both flanks of 188th Brigade, which were held by 12th Division. The commander of 189th Brigade, Brigadier General de Pree, described the scene just as his brigade was going into billets, having been relieved by a brigade of 12th Division:

> an agitated officer with 30 men of the brigade which had relieved us arrived and said there were 2,000 Germans in Mesnil, and that they were marching on Engelbelmer. This was very awkward as the whole brigade [189th] had less than quarter of this number of very tired men.

De Pree was rousing out his men, when (as he continues):

> As it turned out, the enemy never came on, owing to a most gallant feat of arms by the 188th Brigade. When the news reached Brigadier General Coleridge [188th Brigade], he at once amassed his Brigade and arranged a counter-attack: the Anson to advance on Mesnil, 2 RMLI to clear Aveluy

Wood, and 1 RMLI in support. The attack was launched at 2.50 am and met with immediate success. The enemy in spite of their numerous machine guns, broke and fled in disorder, many screaming and climbing trees in Aveluy Wood in their panic. Fifty prisoners, and 13 machine guns were taken, and many killed.

In support, the 1st RMLI had the easiest part in this battle, as Horne, the veteran of many a fight, laconically relates:

We we relieved about midnight by a Lancashire regiment of another division [12th Division], and went to Martinsart, a village about 2,000 yards west of the railway. We were settling down to sleep in the damaged village, when, about 2.0 am we got the alarm that the Germans had broken through at the railway we had left and we had to counter-attack at the village of Mesnil about 1,500 yards NE of Martinsart. We went through Mesnil and down to the road and railway, but the enemy had gone and there was a gap in our line. We found the Lancs, and when they had re-established the line, we returned to Martinsart at daybreak.

Having restored the line by 0300 on 27 March, the 63rd Division handed it back to 12th Division. After further fighting to restore lost positions during that day, the two RMLI battalions were pulled back to rest billets for a couple of days. The German offensive was beginning to show signs of petering out. Harold Horne:

A very optimistic feeling developed among the troops as it looked as though the enemy had exhausted his offensive and we had held him. Things had quietened down – very little gunfire. His quick advance meant that his supplies and communications were difficult on account of the devastated country.

Between them the two RMLI battalions had lost 770 all ranks killed, wounded, and missing.

Aveluy Wood

After receiving reinforcements, 63rd Division relieved 2nd Division on the night 3/4 April, in the vicinity of Aveluy Wood. The positions occupied were incomplete, and improvement had not been possible because of the proximity of the enemy. Until the afternoon of 7 April both RMLI battalions were involved in confused fighting, stemming local attacks and throwing them back with counterattacks. At one stage the two battalions fought side by side when their commanding officers staged a counterattack which succeeded in re-establishing the line. Captain Newling, the second-in-command of 2 RMLI, personally led a company to clear a nest of machine-guns holding up his battalion, which led to the success of the counterattack which captured 55 prisoners and 10 machine-guns. He was awarded a bar to the MC which he had won at Gavrelle Windmill. For the March retreat and Aveluy Wood, the COs of 1 and 2 RMLI were each awarded a well-deserved DSO, and the commanders of 188th and 189th Brigades the CB for their skilful leadership in a month of hard fighting. A number of junior RMLI officers were awarded the MC, and 35 NCOs and privates the MM, as well as one DCM.

After another tour in the line at Aveluy Wood, the remainder of April was spent by the two RMLI battalions resting and refitting, or manning the reserve line. Because there were insufficient recruits in the Royal Marines reinforcement system, both battalions faced a grave manpower shortage; the 4th Battalion had taken most of the spare men at RMLI Headquarters in England. With great sadness it was decided to amalgamate 1st and 2nd Battalions into 1 RMLI. The 2nd Battalion The Royal Irish Regiment[3] arrived to take 2 RMLI's place in 188th Brigade. Horne, who had commanded C Company in the Aveluy Wood fighting, merely recorded:

> *April 29*
> 1st and 2nd Battalions Royal Marines amalgamated. Capt Poland took over from me as OC C Company.

From the end of April to mid-August, the division was in and out of the line in the Ancre Valley and 1 RMLI took part in the usual fare of raids, patrolling, and local attacks. Their periods out of the line were spent in training, but even out of the line the new weapon of air warfare could kill and wound. Harold Horne:

> *June 16*
> C Coy reorganised, now 234 strong. I was appointed Assistant Adjutant. Village bombed at night. CO (Col Fletcher) and Adjutant (Maj West) wounded. House opposite my billet destroyed and old woman killed.

The time of open warfare was about to begin, and new skills had to be mastered: cooperation with tanks and aircraft, and infiltration tactics, to name but two.

The German offensives which followed the great March push had been held. A magnificent victory had been gained by British Fourth Army at Amiens on 8 August, 'the black day of the German Army in the history of this war', according to General Ludendorff. The French Marshal Foch had started his offensive in July. The 63rd Division, up to strength, trained and fit, was ready to take part in some of the greatest victories in the history of the British Army.

THE SOMME, 1918: ADVANCE

The Battle of Albert: Logeast Wood

Polley and his fellow machine-gunners were sitting in a field as the division moved up to join the offensive, when

> a small mounted party entered, headed by a few troopers, one of whom bore a flag. They headed straight for where I was sitting, and as they drew near we made to stand, as we recognized our visitors as staff officers. One of them motioned to us to remain seated, and another addressing us asked us how we felt.
>
> 'All right sir', came the chorus in reply, and then we recognized to whom we spoke, it was Field Marshal Sir Douglas Haig. Most of us who had been 'out there' for some time knew that such a visit generally meant that those who were honoured, would shortly be in for a scrap, and one man voiced the thought that prevailed in most minds 'oh yes, we're all right for the bloody butcher's shop in the morning'.
>
> We were called together and told that the great Allied offensive had commenced, and that we were going over the top in the morning. Gun teams were ready and every available belt filled for the affair which we were told must be successful.
>
> By the afternoon everything in the way of preparation had been done, and a stranger entering the field (I call it a field, but it was a stretch of

open country) would have thought with a good deal of justification that he had entered a pleasure camp, instead of a gathering place for men who did not know whether they would be alive at the same time on the morrow.

Crown and Anchor[4] boards held most people's attention, and voices of the holders rang clear above the hubbub.

'Come on lucky lads, lay it on thick and heavy, Jerry will have you in the morning and then you won't be able to spend it'

'What about the old Mudhook [anchor]'

'Who's for the Sgt Major [crown]'

It was difficult to believe that many of the players would be lying stiff or perhaps maimed for life within 24 hours, but such is the spirit of the British Soldier, he never meets trouble half way, except when there's no trouble to meet, when he'll grumble and grouse as only a soldier can.

I was one of those fortunate enough to be detailed for Battle Personnel [LOOB], which meant following the Company after it had gone over.

The plan for the British offensive involved British Third Army attacking north of the Ancre towards Bapaume, while Fourth Army advanced to Peronne astride the Somme. The Vth Corps, of which 63rd Division was a part, was to force the passage of the Ancre. The division was given three successive objectives to take. To assist in the first objective, sixteen tanks were attached, and more for the second. During the night of 20/21 August, 1 RMLI marched up to their assembly position. Although the night was foggy, excellent navigation by the intelligence officer, who laid out white tape by compass in no man's land, meant that the battalion arrived on its jumping-off line on cue. The fog did not lift until noon, but well before this, at 0455 hours, the 63rd Division passed through 37th Division to attack. 1 RMLI supported by tanks overran the enemy advanced posts. But the two right-hand companies were held up by machine-guns firing from huts. A flanking attack was put in by C and D Companies, enabling the battalion to gain its objective, Logeast Wood, by 0800 hours, taking a 5.9in gun, 250 prisoners, and six mortars. The 2nd Royal Irish passed through towards the second objective, but lost direction in the fog. Major Poland, now the second-in-command of 1 RMLI, seeing the Mark V and Whippet tanks advancing, but without infantry support, took C and D Companies 1 RMLI and assaulted the second objective. To begin with the attack went well, but they soon encountered heavy fire from machine-guns and artillery. Most of the tanks were knocked out by enemy field guns firing in the direct role. Major Poland and Captain Andrews, one of the company commanders, were killed, and the other company commander wounded. The majority of the two companies pulled back, except for a small party under Lieutenant Stewart, who hung on until the enemy started to outflank them. Direct fire from enemy guns frustrated all attempts to go to their assistance.

During the day, 1 RMLI saw off three strong counterattacks. At 1730 hours the 2nd Royal Irish and the Anson attacked again, securing the second objective. At 0115 hours the following morning, the CO of 1 RMLI, Lieutenant Colonel Fletcher (back in command after being wounded in June), reported that he had learned from a prisoner that the enemy were about to attack at dawn. He had only 200 men left in his rifle companies, and had put his Battalion Headquarters in to fill the gaps in his position.

Polley was also in the vicinity of Logeast Wood, with the rest of the Battle Personnel escorting sixteen mules with limbers carrying ammunition and rations:

> By midnight we had reached Logeast Wood, and here the limbers were sent back after the ammunition and rations had been transferred to pack mules. Passage through the wood was impossible owing to its being very thoroughly wired. It had been an enemy stronghold, and barbed wire had been used in high quantities rendering the place one would have thought well nigh impregnable. This meant our making a detour by road so we struck off to the right.

In the darkness, the party, which was now quite large as it included gun teams moving up to occupy a new position, eventually found a way in to the wood,

> to be greeted by a few stray gas shells. We had, I suppose reached about the middle, when Fritz opened up and plastered the place with salvo after salvo. This caused the mules to bolt, leaving behind a trail of Ammo and rations as they went. Soon there was not a mule or transport man to be seen. The enemy was mixing his shells, gas and high explosive, and the latter were not only unpleasant in themselves, but great limbs were torn from trees and hurled for yards, and in some cases whole trees toppled and fell.
>
> I confess I became as jumpy as a cat, and wished myself anywhere but

in that wood. The place reeked of gas at first of the lachrymatory type which attacks the eyes, causing them to burn most painfully, and the nose to run in steady streams. I was between two stools, I must either keep my gas mask on and probably break my neck tripping over wire, or abandon my mask and risk whatever may happen to my eyes.

Polley chose to take his mask off, but fortunately kept the nose clip on and the breathing tube between his lips, because when he unwarily took a gasp of what he hoped was fresh air he inhaled instead phosgene (chlorine gas). He decided to collect what rations he could from those ditched by the mules, but gave up because he felt so sick after inhaling the gas. Utterly miserable, and lost, he crawled into a hole in a bank, only to be hurled out by a shell bursting nearby. He lay thinking, 'God what a place to finish up in,' when the bombardment, which lasted about half an hour, but 'seemed more like half a century', ended. He was found by a runner sent back by the officer in charge of the party. Having collected as many of the party as could be located, they pushed on and found the company gun position.

> I found my section sadly depleted, out of 24 who had gone up, about 8 remained to work the guns, which were mounted in shell holes in the open. It was still dark and the Lieutenant told the transport Corporal to dump whatever they had managed to bring up and clear off back as soon as possible, which they did with all speed. From our pit we could hear quite plainly the cries of the wounded lying out in front, but it was so dark that we could not see more than a yard or so.

After a most unpleasant night, and early morning, during which Polley was able to help a badly wounded lance corporal back to the dressing station, he was evacuated himself as a gas casualty.

At dawn the enemy put in a series of attacks, and at first they were repulsed. But at about 1330 hours a determined enemy thrust pushed back part of the division, and CO 1 RMLI could see units falling back through the centre of Logeast Wood. He rallied these units, with the assistance of his adjutant and Battalion Headquarters, and led them forward to restore the position. Fletcher was severely wounded in the leg, but refused evacuation until he was sure that the situation had been stabilized. Early on the morning of 23 August the division was relieved, and pulled back. The departure of Lieutenant Colonel Fletcher was a great loss to the battalion which he had commanded so successfully since

January. He was a gifted leader and trainer. He was awarded a bar to his DSO. Major Poland had been a subaltern in the *Warspite* at Jutland. Captain Andrews had commanded the platoon of C Company 2 RMLI covering the final withdrawal from Cape Helles.

The Battle of Albert: Loupart Wood and Le Barque

On the evening of 24 August, the 63rd Division was ordered to attack the following day, advancing alongside the New Zealand Division as part of the push on Bapaume. The first objective of 1 RMLI was a line of a trench known as Grevilliers Trench between Grevilliers and Loupart Wood. The next objective was another trench about 1,000 yards further on, and the final objective the eastern end of the village of Le Barque. Advancing in thick fog, the battalion gained its first objective by 0540 hours. During the battle, Private Brindley captured a gun single-handed with its whole crew, for which he was later awarded the DCM. Quickly passing through the intermediate objective, the battalion were firm on the final objective at Le Barque by 0630 hours, having captured 150 prisoners, two mortars, and six machine-guns, while the Anson consolidated astride the Albert–Bapaume road by 0745 hours.

The fog started to lift at 0900 hours, and the remainder of the division were stalled by heavy machine-gun fire on the outskirts of two villages, Thilloy and Ligny Thilloy. Meanwhile the enemy mounted strong attacks on 1 RMLI at Le Barque, all of which were repulsed with heavy casualties to the enemy. At one stage there were problems bringing up ammunition to resupply 1 RMLI so boxes were dropped by the contact aircraft. During this phase, Company Sergeant Major Windybank earned the DCM when he took command of his company when all the officers had been wounded or killed. He had joined the Royal Marines as a short-service recruit on the outbreak of war.

On 26 August the 188th and 189th Brigades attempted to infiltrate the enemy positions holding up the advance of V Corps. The GOC 63rd Division did not wish to attack Thilloy frontally. He tried to contain it, and pinch it out by sending in strong patrols to penetrate the village, but during the night the division was ordered to take Thilloy, so the 190th Brigade was assigned the task, with the other two brigades in support. After repeated attacks starting at 1100 hours two companies took part of the village. But they were eventually ejected by heavy counterattacks, and the assault was called off at 2100 hours. The brigades dug in. On the night of 27/28 August the division was relieved by 42nd Division, the 1st RMLI being sent to Miraumont to rest. The fighting had cost the battalion 5 officers and 46 NCOs and privates killed, 10 officers and 260 wounded, and 31 missing.

At the end of August the 63rd Division was transferred to XVII Corps under Lieutenant General Sir Charles Fergusson. The divisional commanders changed as well. Major General Lawrie Royal Artillery, who had taken over from 'that shit Shute' in December 1916, was relieved by Major General Blacklock King's Royal Rifle Corps.

THE SECOND BATTLE OF ARRAS, 1918

Battle of the Drocourt–Quéant Line

The Drocourt–Quéant Line was a strong heavily wired line south-east of Arras, forming a northern extension of the massively fortified Hindenburg Line. XVII Corps's objective was to gain a position from which to attack the village of Quéant from the north, as part of the Canadian Corps's advance on their left, and with VI Corps on their right. The initial XVII Corps objectives were assigned to other divisions, so 63rd Division's movements were dependent on these formations' success, or otherwise. The 188th Brigade had been briefed to take objectives which lay beyond and to the north-east of Quéant.

The approach of the division to its assembly areas involved a march of 17,000 yards (9½ miles) over broken country at night, but it was in position by Corps Zero Hour at 0500 hours on 2 September. At 0715 hours, General Blacklock learned that the Canadians had been successful, and issued orders at 0720 hours for 188th and 189th Brigades, consisting of one word: 'Move.' 1 RMLI moved off at 0745 hours with 2nd Royal Irish on their left. These swift responses and well-practised moves with the minimum of orders were far removed from the muddle of earlier days, Gallipoli especially. Careful briefing, well-trained staffs and units, experienced commanders at all levels, and good planning formed the key to success. Tactics were flexible, and commanders had learned to read the battle better, and avoid pushing ahead with attacks that had already failed.

At 1145 hours 1 RMLI were beyond the last line of the Drocourt system and wheeling to their right as ordered. The division had the bit between its teeth, and in spite of hard fighting, some in darkness, pushed on. Among the losses in 1 RMLI was Regimental Sergeant Major Weight, killed bringing up small-arms ammunition. His predecessor had also been killed. The next day the advance continued in fine weather until the 63rd Division was ordered to halt and hold the complete corps front just west of the Canal du Nord. Attempts to cross had failed. Fighting to gain possession of the canal bank continued throughout 5, 6, and 7 September, but the Germans still held the west bank. On the night of 7/8 September 63rd Division was relieved and moved back for rest and retraining, having suffered a total of 983 casualties, which by the standards of the time was low in the light of the tremendous gains. The 1st RMLI had 1 officer and 21 NCOs and privates killed, 4 officers and 130 wounded, and 17 missing (15 later reported killed).

Battle of the Canal du Nord

On 23 September 63rd Division was warned that it would take part in the attack on the Canal du Nord. The first phase was to capture the canal, the second to turn the Hindenburg Support Line from the north. In the 63rd Division sector the 190th Brigade was tasked to cross the Canal du Nord. It would be followed by 188th Brigade, which would pass through to the next objective. After this 57th Division would pass through and capture the high ground east of the Canal and River de l'Escaut.

The assembly area for 1 RMLI was Tadpole Copse. The 190th crossed the Canal du Nord, which had been drained by the enemy and was dry. At 0530 hours the 188th followed up without difficulty. After crossing, 1 RMLI wheeled to advance to high ground west of Bourlon Wood, from where it was to attack Anneux. The battalion attacked three companies up. They hit heavy opposition from a factory and Anneux itself. The Anson, which had tried to clear the factory, was repulsed. The first attempt by 189th Brigade to attack the factory from a flank also failed, until a heavy barrage was put down and, with the support of tanks, the factory was finally taken. As soon as this occurred, 1 RMLI were able to capture Anneux.

At 1845 hours the enemy counterattacked, and was beaten off. By 1930 hours all was quiet and food and ammunition was sent forward. Officer casualties were high. The battalion received a congratulatory message from the brigade commander: 'I am very pleased the RMLI can add Anneux to their laurels with a dozen guns and many prisoners.'

Crossing of the Canal de l'Escaut and Cambrai

The 63rd Division's task in the Canal de l'Escaut battle on 28 September was to follow up 57th Division, pass through after the 57th had secured the high ground east of the canal, and encircle Cambrai from the south. By 1500 hours the 57th Division had managed to get only small parties across the canal, and 63rd Division moved up to join in. After hard fighting, which continued well into the night, the Drake, Hawke, and Hood Battalions of 189th Brigade failed to establish themselves on the far bank. Eventually the Royal Marine Divisional Engineer Companies managed to set up two pontoon bridges, and by dawn two companies of the Drake crossed. By 1000 hours on 29 September the bridgehead had been enlarged. The 188th Brigade were ordered across and to leapfrog the 189th Brigade. 1 RMLI advanced with 2nd Royal Irish on their right, and the Anson Battalion in reserve. The enemy were still holding the outskirts of Cambrai in strength with machine-guns on the upper floors of houses. As the battalion worked forward, it had 3 officers wounded, 16 NCOs and privates killed, and 112 wounded. The following day, the 188th Brigade renewed the attack and were firm on their objective, an enemy trench system, by 1615 hours. As ever, they could not relax, because the inevitable counterattacks came in soon afterwards. Both 190th and 188th Brigades had experienced a difficult advance in the face of heavy machine-gun fire. On 1 October the 1st and 52nd Divisions pushed forward and on through the 63rd Division. At 2020 hours, having been relieved, 1 RMLI formed up and moved into a bivouac position near Anneux. The German Army, as always fighting with skill and tenacity, exacted a heavy price for these gains and successes. Victory against these superb soldiers was never easy. The battle between 27

September and 1 October had resulted in the division suffering a total of 2,817 dead, wounded, and missing. In 1 RMLI alone the casualties were 5 officers and 60 NCOs and privates killed, 10 officers and 258 wounded, and 56 NCOs and privates missing. The battalion was down to 200 all ranks, with only 2 rifle company officers and 7 in Battalion Headquarters and Headquarters Company fit to fight.

On 3 October British Fourth Army had broken through, and by the 5th the whole line of the St Quentin Canal and Hindenburg Defences were in British hands. On 29 September the 46th Division, of which Lieutenant Colonel Jerram RMLI was GSO I (de facto chief of staff), equipped with lifebelts from cross-Channel ferries, mats, and rafts had crossed the St Quentin Canal at Bellenglise, by swimming across and storming the German positions the other side.

THE BATTLE OF CAMBRAI, 1918

On 4 October the 63rd Division were told they were due for a rest and some leave. Some parties were about to set out when at 1830 hours that evening they were warned for further operations. The Divisional Commander was told that his objective was Niergnies, south of Cambrai, which would involve an advance of 5,000 yards. His was to be the leading division on XVII Corps's front. The division was to attack two brigades up, 188th on the right, and 189th on the left, with 190th behind 188th. The 188th Brigade was to advance on a one-battalion front, 2nd Royal Irish leading to capture the first objective. 1 RMLI was to pass through to assault the second objective, after which the Anson Battalion was to move through.

It is interesting to read the orders for this attack, the last major battle fought by 1 RMLI, drawn up by the adjutant, Operation Order No. 9, dated 7 October 1918. They are crisp, unambiguous, and clearly addressed to a battalion that despite heavy casualties still had a nucleus of battle-experienced officers and NCOs. For by now the company commanders, and most NCOs had been tutored in the hard school of the Western Front, and knew exactly what they were doing.

At 0400 hours on 7 October the 188th Brigade set out to march to its assembly area, arriving at 1850 hours. After a hot meal, 1 RMLI fell in at 1930 hours, reaching the jumping-off line at about 0330 hours the next morning, and had shaken out, ready to move at 0400 hours. At 0430 hours the attack was launched exactly on time. These timings in themselves reveal what a thoroughly well-trained and led battalion they were. They also give a clue to the lot of the infantry soldier in battle. He all too often crosses the start line after a long march under heavy load in rain or heat, probably without sleep for twenty-four hours or more, and sometimes without having fed for as long. In the case of 1st RMLI, good administration by their splendid Quartermaster, Captain Burton, at least ensured they were fed after their twenty-four-hour march.

The 1st RMLI followed 2nd Royal Irish in artillery formation, two companies up, two back. As they passed through 2nd Royal Irish, they shook out into attack formation, and advanced. At first progress was rapid, with few casualties. At the south edge of Niergnies and the cemetery on the road leading south-east from the village they encountered stiffening enemy resistance. With the help of tanks, the numerous enemy machine-gunners holding the cemetery were cleared, and the advance continued. Most of 1 RMLI's objective was in the battalion's hands by 0810 hours, and the last resistance was snuffed out by 0840 hours. Meanwhile, during the fighting by 189th Brigade to move into Niergnies, Acting Sergeant Carey RMLI, attached to Hood Battalion, led his platoon against a strong enemy post, capturing an officer and 60 men, before pushing on alone to capture an enemy machine-gun. Returning to his platoon, he led them forward again. For this he was awarded the DCM.

At about 0900 hours the Germans counterattacked with infantry and captured British tanks. This was the first time the division had been on the receiving end of armour, and found it most unpleasant. This did not deter them, however, even when seven enemy tanks emerged out of a sunken road, taking one of the British tanks with the division by surprise and without ammunition, forcing it to turn tail. Their defence against these seemingly invincible monsters was helped considerably because selected parties within the division had been trained to work captured guns and weapons. Lance Corporal Child of 1 RMLI engaged one tank, and when it was knocked out and the crew were attempting to remove the machine-guns, he forced them to retire, for which action he too was awarded the DCM; as was Acting Sergeant Insley RMLI, attached to the Machine Gun Company, who kept his two guns in action against shell and machine-gun fire from the tanks, finally putting one out of action when only 100 yards from his position. He took command of a large party of infantry who were wavering in the face of the tank attack, and led them back to their positions. He already had been awarded a MM and bar for previous actions. The CO of the Anson earned a third DSO for knocking out another of the tanks with a captured German anti-tank rifle. One tank was brewed up by the CO of the Hood Battalion, using a captured German gun, and another knocked out by the Divisional Artillery, again using a captured gun. In the end only two German tanks escaped.

During this German counterattack, 1 RMLI's forward posts were driven in for about 200 yards, but, with the assistance of a barrage, recaptured the lost ground by 1000 hours. The position had been restored largely through the leadership of Lieutenant Bareham, who was awarded the MC. He was a regular NCO who had been commissioned in 1916, and was typical of the excellent officers provided by many long-service NCOs in the Royal Marines at that time. Sad to report he was killed later.

During the afternoon the enemy were gathering for another counter-attack, so an artillery battery was sent up to Niergnies to deal with any tanks. At 1630 hours, after a heavy bombardment, the enemy attack came in at the junction of 63rd and 2nd Divisions. A battalion of the East Surreys[5] of the 24th Division had just arrived to relieve 1 RMLI, but the handover was delayed while the counterattack was being fought off. Eventually the counterattack was repulsed, ground lost was regained, and the planned relief of 63rd Division by 24th Division could proceed. At 0100 hours on 9 October, 1 RMLI marched back to their bivouac near Anneux. The battalion had captured two field guns, 12 machine-guns, and about 1,000 prisoners. They had lost 2 officers and 9 NCOs and privates killed, 4 officers and 116 wounded, and 14 missing. The division lost a total of 503 all ranks.

On 10 October the Commander of 188th Brigade sent a message to all ranks in his brigade:

I wish to place on record my great appreciation of the fine work done by the Brigade during the period 21st August to 8th October 1918.

Between these dates the Brigade has taken part in 5 general actions at:

> ACHIET LE GRAND
> LE BARQUE – THILLOY
> QUEANT – BOUCHE WOOD
> GRAINCOURT – ANNEUX
> NIERGNIES

and in minor operations near:

> INCHY and
> CAMBRAI

During these operations the brigade has suffered losses, but as soldiers it is our duty not to count our losses, but only to consider those inflicted upon the enemy. These are:

> over 2,000 prisoners
> 50 guns
> 240 machine guns
> 12 trench mortars
> many killed and wounded

This is an achievement of which you and your kinsfolk may well be proud and for which our gallant comrades, who have left us, have not laid down their lives in vain.

I am proud to command such a splendid Brigade and I look forward with confidence to its future efforts.

Cambrai was the last major engagement of the division. But it joined in the pursuit to Mons on 7 November; a very different kind of war from the hard slog of the past years. Although the enemy were pulling back, they still fought delaying actions and caused casualties; for 1 RMLI, 1 officer and 4 dead, and the CO, Lieutenant Colonel Sandilands, and another officer and 23 NCOs and privates wounded. Harold Horne:

Nov 8

Crossing the Belgian frontier. Arrived Angre 11–0 am but had to wait until our infantry cleared the Germans out. Left Angre 12–30 am for Audregnies where I arranged billets in the village. For HQ mess I went to the chateau on the outskirts. The butler answered the bell and invited me into the hall. He said 'Monsieur le Comte' would be pleased to accommodate the Colonel and staff. Day's distance 5 miles.

Nov 9

Day's distance 7 miles.

Nov 10

Left Sars-la-Bruyère for Bougnies, 5 miles due S of Mons. Battalion went into brigade reserve and later at night took over front line. Several casualties. The CO was wounded and Col Clutterbuck took over.

Early on 11 November 1 RMLI were about to put in an attack when they were told that hostilities would cease at 1100 hours. They could push on but were not to incur casualties. Harold Horne:

Nov 11

During the night of 10/11 the front line was NE of the village of Bougnies. About 6–0 [am] we got orders that an armistice would take effect from 11–0 am when hostilities would cease and all units would remain stationary on the line then reached.

The advance started at 7–0 am in a NE direction from the road north of Bougnies, passing the villages of Nouvelles, Spiennes, Harmignies to Villers St Ghislain, (4 miles SE of Mons).

At 11–0 am the Battalion was in open fields east of the village advancing in a north-easterly direction, having found no enemy in the village and being greeted by the villagers.

At 11 o'clock when we halted, an enemy rearguard who had been firing from a wood a few hundred yards in front sent up some coloured flares – a 'feu de joie' at the ending of the war.

The Quartermaster, Captain T. H. Burton MC, was the only officer to have served in the battalion continuously since the outbreak of war. He began as Quartermaster of the Deal Battalion, which became part of the 1st Battalion at Gallipoli. The colours of the Chatham Division were sent out to the 1st Battalion Royal Marine Light Infantry. One historian of the Royal Marines wrote: 'In their [the colours'] long history none brought them greater honour'.[6]

In all the fighting in the First World War none brought the Royal Marines as a whole greater honour than the RMLI battalions who had fought and endured at Gallipoli, and in France and Belgium, for over three and a half years in the primitive and unforgiving world of the infantry soldier. John Terraine, a leading historian of the First World War, never one to give praise lightly, said of the 63rd Division's record on the Western Front, against one of the finest armies in history, 'Its performance in battle was invariably first class'.[7] The price in dead, wounded, and prisoners, on the Western Front alone for the division was 1,683 officers and 34,992 other ranks, of which 96 and 4,020 were incurred just between 20 September and 11 November 1918, in the great advance.

On its return to England the battalion was disbanded. All the lessons about the need for properly trained, permanently formed units, with a real purpose in life were about to be forgotten until the next contest. The clock was turned back to the unsatisfactory days of pre-1914.

11

Russia, 1918–1919

After Lenin and Trotsky had signed a shameful peace whereby they betrayed their country and falsified its engagements to their Allies . . .

Winston Churchill, Secretary of State for War,
to the House of Commons 29 July 1919

If the trumpet give an uncertain sound, who shall prepare himself to the battle?

1 Corinthians

In the last eight months of the First World War, and for over a year after the Armistice of November 1918, British and Allied forces were engaged in an obscure and now largely forgotten campaign in Russia. The motives for Allied involvement in Russia are convoluted. Suffice it to say that on 3 March 1918, following the Russian Revolution and the Bolshevik coup which brought Lenin to power in October 1917, the Russians signed a peace treaty with Germany. Lenin's motive was to gain time for his revolution to take hold in Russia. He was indifferent to the consequences of this act of disloyalty to his country's Allies, one of them the release of a million German troops to participate in their great March 1918 offensive, which has been covered in the previous chapter.

Among the reasons given by Churchill to Parliament for British involvement in north Russia, in a speech whose opening phrases are quoted above, were the fear that the Germans would take advantage of Russia's weakness and seize Archangel for a submarine base, and that the large Allied ammunition and supply stores there and at Murmansk would fall into their hands. These supply dumps had been built up over the previous two years to support the Russian war effort against Germany. Apart from the fact that the Germans would be more likely to choose Murmansk in the ice-free Kola inlet as a submarine base, rather than Archangel which froze over every winter, it is questionable that they would base U-boats thousands of miles from the main Allied shipping lanes. More plausible is the hope that the threat of the Allies opening a front in this area would stop the Germans taking any more troops from the east to fight in France and Belgium; an aspiration that was realized. Following the Armistice in November 1918, it would have been logical to ask why the Allies did not withdraw their troops from north Russia. The British reasons for not doing so, given by the CIGS, Field Marshal Sir Henry Wilson, in a memorandum dated 1 December 1919, were two. The first was that the withdrawal of the whole force could not be guaranteed before the ports were iced up. This is hard to fault, since some of the force had to withdraw through Archangel. The second was that large numbers of Russians who had remained loyal to the Allied cause could not be 'precipitately' abandoned to the mercy of the Soviets.

The underlying reason for the presence of British troops in Russia after November 1918 was connected with the desire of all the Western powers to see the White Russian armies topple the Bolshevik government. Unfortunately both for the world in general, and the Russian people in particular, who were to suffer under the odious Lenin and his brutal successors for a further seventy years, British involvement, like that of the other Western Powers (France, Italy, Canada, Japan, and the United States), lacked clear purpose or commitment: 'Western public opinion was divided between the Whites and the Reds, while most of those in the middle, weary after four years of total war, were opposed to sending more troops abroad.'[1] Consequently some, although by no means all, of the British effort was muddled and half-baked. The White armies, rooted in the old regime, were psychologically hampered by a desire to turn the clock back to the old days. This made it difficult for the people to accept them as a serious alternative to the Bolsheviks. They were officers' armies, never managing to attract the support of the civilian population, or the private soldiers. 'There has never been such a top-heavy army in the history of warfare. Captains and Colonels were forced to serve as privates. Major Generals had to do with the command of a squadron.'[2]

A succession of Royal Marine contingents of varying size spent nearly two years in this confused and messy war.

NORTH RUSSIA

Murmansk, at the head of the Kola Inlet, and 100 miles from the Finnish border, had been completed only in 1916 as a port for the unloading of Western supplies to support the Russian war effort. It was linked by a single-track railway, via Petrosavodsk on the shore of Lake Onega, to Petrograd (St Petersburg). The ground in the Kola peninsula is mainly tundra, dotted with lakes, large and small. In winter it is frozen hard and covered in snow, and after the thaw it is a swamp. There were no major roads, only tracks. The political situation in 1918/19 makes even the Balkans in the late twentieth century look simple. The British (and Western Allies) supported the Red Guard Finns, who were anti-German, against the pro-German White Guard Finns. Among the Russians, however, the position was reversed: following the Bolshevik signature of the treaty with Germany, the Western Allies (including the British) supported the White Russians against the Reds.

The guardship at Murmansk since late 1917 was HMS *Glory*, with an unusually large Marine detachment. In March 1918 she was joined by HMS *Cochrane*. The two detachments were landed, and until the end of September took part in operations against the White Guard Finns who, acting in conjunction with the Germans, were threatening the railway and Pechenga Inlet. A number of skirmishes ensued. On one occasion, a flying column of about thirty Marines, equipped with two Lewis guns, mounted on sledges pulled by reindeer, with local guides on skis, was sent to attack a Finnish party about twenty-six miles away. The Finnish scouts retired in front of them as the Marines advanced. Having chased them as far as a river, the Marines bumped the main body, which turned out to be about 200 strong. Fortunately the two Lewis guns kept the Finns at bay as they tried to outflank the Marines on their skis. The reindeer drivers tried to bolt, but were persuaded to stay by a corporal threatening to shoot them. The Marines mounted the sledges and hastily withdrew. The threat of the Lewis guns kept the Finns from following up.

In May the Marines in the Kola Peninsula were augmented by a small

Field Force consisting of a 12-pounder battery manned by the RMA, an RMLI company, and a machine-gun section of Lewis guns. They were made responsible for the security of 500 miles of railway. After several months of minor operations, the RM Field Force were told they would spend the winter in Murmansk along with the British 236th Infantry Brigade, which had now arrived. Without warning, on 17 December, they were ordered to go 100 miles south to Kandalaksha to train for winter operations as a mobile column. They were issued with excellent Arctic kit designed by Sir Ernest Shackleton, specially prepared rations, and a pair of skis and sticks each. The force spent about a month learning to ski under a Marine officer and senior NCO who had been sent on a course to learn the art of cross-country skiing, or langlauf. Several pairs of snowshoes were carried by the force to replace any broken skis, since the snow was too deep for walking. Later it was decided to move the training camp to a port on the White Sea, with the unlikely name of Popoff. Here they learned to fire their rifles using their ski sticks as bipods, and to fire from skis on the move downhill. The temperature went down as low as 40° below zero, but thanks to good training and equipment cases of frostbite were few. Thus did the Royal Marines first encounter the rigours of Arctic training, as their successors were to do again some forty years later.

At the end of April, in high spirits, they left for operations against the Bolsheviks, or 'Bolos' as they called them. They joined a force of one company of French infantry and one company of the Slavo-British Legion (White Russians). The aim of the forthcoming operation was to enable the British commander, Major General Maynard, to gain control of all lines of approach to the Murmansk area from the south.

Their target was a large railway centre. On the way they encountered an armoured train, which they put to flight. They followed, assaulting the railway centre, alongside the French, with the Russians (who were useless) following in the rear, arriving in time to see the engine shed blowing up. They were on short rations because the enemy had destroyed twenty-seven bridges between them and their base. Some days later, the Royal Marines were ordered to follow up the retreating enemy down the line of the railway. Reinforced by a company of the King's Royal Rifle Corps (the 60th),[3] they pushed on. They met the armoured train again, but were able to take cover in the forest until a gun could be brought forward to deal with it. Continuing the advance, the force arrived in the proximity of a railway station and village called Medvyejya Gora on the north-western edge of Lake Onega. Here the Royal Marines alone attacked, and after several hours' fighting took the village and station, holding it until relieved by Army units.

The RM Field Force eventually embarked for home on 10 July 1919, having been congratulated by General Maynard. Although the actions in which they were involved were minor, and the enemy hardly first rate, they had done most of the serious fighting, and acquitted themselves admirably in very inhospitable terrain and weather. Certainly the official report to Parliament mentions the Royal Marines as having carried out most of the serious fighting, along with two British infantry companies.[4] Good training, careful preparation, and competent leadership must have played a part in this result. The story does not end there, because Maynard was subsequently extremely critical of the efforts of the RM Field Force in a telegram sent to the War Office. The Adjutant General Royal Marines (AGRM) riposted by demanding that the Army withdraw its remarks. The Army refused, and eventually the AGRM decided not to press the matter, because of bad news from North Russia involving another Royal Marines unit.

By mid-August 1919 it was becoming clear that the expectations of White Russian forces advancing from Siberia under Admiral Kolchak linking up with the Allied bridgehead around the White Sea were not about to be realized. Consequently the withdrawal of Allied forces from Murmansk and Archangel was ordered, and General Sir Henry Rawlinson was sent out as C-in-C North Russia to coordinate this tricky operation. To provide adequate covering troops to carry out his withdrawal plan a force comprising three infantry battalions, a machine-gun battalion, two batteries of artillery, engineers, and five tanks was despatched. In addition the 6th Battalion Royal Marines was sent at once to Murmansk, for use there or at Archangel.

This battalion had been formed to supervise a plebiscite in Schleswig-Holstein to determine its political future after the defeat of Germany – a not too demanding task in one of the most agreeable parts of Europe. The main requirements were seen as a high standard of spit and polish, including arms drill, and most training was geared to that end. The battalion had been formed in the old ad hoc pre-1914 way: 'fall in the men on the barrack square, from here to the left, right turn, to Schleswig-Holstein, (or wherever) quick march'. In a replay of outmoded practice, and hardly conducive to the battalion's cohesion, each port division provided a company: the RMA, A Company; Chatham, B Company; Portsmouth, C Company; and Plymouth, D Company.

Lieutenant P. R. Smith-Hill RMLI was a platoon commander in B Company. He wrote letters to his parents in diary form, with afternotes penned later on morale and the key personalities in his company:

> Morale was high. The allies had won the war and we had survived. Shore leave was given each evening.[5]
>
> The company commander [of B Company], Major Barnby, had spent most of the war in either the RN Air Service or the Royal Flying Corps. For him the command of an infantry company was not a promotion. Although Watts [Company second-in-command] had served in Gallipoli [commanding the Chatham Battalion Machine Gun Section], his only experience had been of trench warfare. The four subalterns [including himself] had spent the war in HM Ships. They were knowledgeable about naval gunnery, watchkeeping in harbour, and the man-management of RM detachments afloat. Most of the other ranks had corresponding experience at sea.

The remainder of the battalion was similarly devoid of skill in infantry fighting. The Commanding Officer, Lieutenant Colonel A. de W. Kitcat, had spent thirty-one years in the RMLI without seeing action ashore. Suddenly, in the middle of their leisurely training at Bedenham, the order came to embark in the transport ship *Czar*. The destination was not announced. Smith-Hill:

> *Sunday 3rd August*
> Even now [three days after embarkation] we do not know exactly where we are going. We know our destination is somewhere in Russia. The spirit of the troops is not too good.
>
> Cause 1. They were not given the chance of volunteering. The Adjutant General [professional head of the Royal Marines] vouched his word for them at the War Office.
>
> Cause 2. The CO Battn [Battalion] thought it wise not to pay the men the day before we left Bedenham to prevent us leaving drunks behind.
>
> Cause 3. The troops during the armistice do not like having to risk their lives on behalf of Russia. England would be a different matter.

On arrival at Murmansk the battalion was split up, with C Company being sent 200 miles south to Kandalaksha, and the remainder to Kem, another 150 miles further on. At Murmansk Smith-Hill heard the usual rumours and gossip that pervade any base area in a war zone. Smith-Hill:

> *8th August Thursday [sic: Friday 8 August, on arrival at Murmansk]*
> I heard from an RN Lieutenant today that the Italians cannot fight for nuts and that the British Army say they came as a garrison and refuse to fight and altogether tend [intend?] to turn Bolshevik themselves. 'The only people who fight out here', he said, 'are the Marines who will fight anyone' He went on to say that the only fighting casualties have been the Marines and that the Authorities realising that as the only real fighting units are Marines decided to have a few more of them. Hence us.

C Company spent about two weeks at Kandalaksha, during which time rumours were rife: they were going home, they would spend the winter in Russia, more troops were arriving to relieve them, and they would go south to Medvyejya Gora station to fight. The last proved to be correct. Rawlinson had directed General Maynard to mount an offensive south-west of Lake Onega in order to gain breathing space and elbow room to conduct the withdrawal without interference from the Russian Red Army. Having been told to expect a train the following day, C Company were surprised when

> at about 6 o'clock [that evening] a train full of troops arrived and had come to relieve us and we were to go on this train. Confusion reigned supreme. We expected them to arrive at about 4 am the next day. However by 10 pm we were all aboard.

While the train waited at Kem, en route, they heard rumours that the Portsmouth Company (C) had been caught while marching in fours by a 'Bolo' machine-gun. A letter written by Kitcat on 3 November 1919 to the Colonel Commandant of Portsmouth Division confirms that they were in column marching down the road, that he had been shot through the foot, and four men were killed and fifteen wounded. The company failed to reach its objective, the village of Koikori, and fell back, tired, hungry, and dispirited. In the letter Kitcat said, 'I have been given such an opportunity as has seldom fallen to the luck of anyone', and later:

> I did not think that I could have made such a hopeless mess of things. I suppose I was suffering from 'wind up' but I did not realise it.

> One thing stands out perfectly clear is that I am not fit to command
> troops either in the field or out of it.

Major Ridings RMA took command. The new concept of operations
for the brigade, of which 6th Battalion was a part, was for the main
thrust to follow the railway line to Lijma Station just to the west of Lake
Onega. The 6th Battalion, less the RMA Company which was dispersed
on duties up and down the railway line, was assigned to a flanking
operation, one of the objectives of which was Koikori, where C Company
had been repulsed. By 7 September it was in the vicinity of Svyatnovolok
about twenty miles to the west of Lake Onega and ready to move south
to attack Koikori and another village, some way off on another track,
called Ussuna. The Koikori force consisted of B and C Companies under
Major Strover of the Machine Gun Corps, while Major Ridings was to
take D Company to Ussuna. Why Ridings did not command the two
companies of his battalion, leaving the command of the one company
operation to the company commander, Major Nind, is a mystery. It was
to be the cause of much trouble. Morale was still not particularly good
in the 6th Battalion. Smith-Hill: 'the men were anxious that the officers
should not try to win any medals. They feared that the officers might do
something rash in action and their men might become unnecessary
casualties.'

D Company with Battalion Headquarters moved off to attack Ussuna
at 0600 hours on 8 September. Within sight of the village, they came
under fire. An attempt to outflank the enemy positions, and attack them
from the rear, led by Captain Burton, the Adjutant, failed. Why Burton
thought he should take on this task we shall never know; he was killed.
According to Smith-Hill: 'He was shot through the head. He had been
engaged in a sniping duel. He was very brave and cheerful, but of course
sniping duels were not his job.'

The attack was supported by Vickers machine-guns, and it was
thought on past experience that they and Burton's flanking move would
make the 'Bolos' run. They did not. Sergeant Mumford was sent forward
with a patrol to find out why. He got quite close, and returned to report
that the trenches were well constructed, fully manned, and with plenty
of wire in front. In accordance with instructions from Army headquarters
that 'operations should be taken slowly, casualties can and should be
avoided', D Company was ordered to go firm where they were for the

night, and push on in daylight. Hopes that the enemy would withdraw during the night were dashed the next morning when renewed attempts to take the village were met by heavy fire. D Company was pulled back slightly, and relieved by Russian troops after dark. In the light of the pathetically inadequate and uncertain orders from Army headquarters, and their lack of training, D Company had not done too badly. Mumford was awarded an MM, and an officer who had been wounded on another reconnaissance the MC.

Meanwhile the attack on Koikori had taken place. Led by a Russian guide, Smith-Hill's platoon provided the advanced guard. Neither Smith-Hill nor any of the other platoon commanders had a map. At about midday Smith-Hill, the guide, and a machine-gun officer climbed a small hill, from the top of which they could see the church in Koikori. Because he had heard a couple of enemy talking quite close to where they were standing, he went back and fetched up a section to clear the hill. The guide disappeared for a while, and on returning claimed to have shot one of the enemy. After establishing two Vickers machine-guns on the hill, one of them started to engage some trenches near Koikori church. This attracted immediate return fire from the enemy, wounding a machine-gun sergeant. At this Major Barnby ordered Smith-Hill to work forward, and Lieutenant Bramall to bring his platoon up alongside him. In a confused skirmish forward, Smith-Hill's two platoon scouts, privates Jenkins and Pyle, managed to get within grenade-throwing range of some enemy sangars. Pyle was wounded, all efforts to rescue him were to no avail, and he was taken prisoner. By this time both platoons were under flanking fire, and – far more worrying – being shot at from the rear, which at first Smith-Hill thought was from their own side. Smith-Hill returned to the hill, shouting for the firing to cease. No one answered him, and he was fired on, indicating that the enemy was occupying the ground in rear of the hill. At this moment Major Barnby was wounded in the wrist; and ordered the two platoons to retire. Smith-Hill's diary:

With the men I retired by compass through the forest until reaching the road. As I left the field of action, I noted that the time was 2.30 pm, the action had started at 12 noon. On reaching the road [at about the 15½ verst post – a verst is two-thirds of a mile] I ordered the men to return [north away from Koikori] to 12 VP [verst post] and report to HQ or any officer they might see. I myself, returned along the road to Koikoiri. At about 16 VP [a few hundred yards further south] I saw Major Williams, an army officer to whom I reported for orders.

Smith-Hill wrote later to explain some things not obvious from his diary:

The country in this part of Russia is covered by forest with thick undergrowth. Visibility is therefore bad. When withdrawing from the attack, I moved, as stated in the diary, by compass. This was necessary because we had to circle round obstacles such as patches of bog, ponds, fallen trees etc. and it was possible we would lose direction and end up in enemy territory.

Owing to the density of the forest it was necessary to employ Russian guides when we had to move any distance off the roads or tracks. It now seems certain that the guide who led us to the attack on Koikori was an enemy agent, who warned the defenders of our approach, and advised them to send men to occupy the small hill and engage us from our rear. Many of my men were shot in the back although they were facing the enemy. My servant Pte Davey was killed by a shot from our rear. We never saw the guide after the attack. Later we were ordered not to allow a guide to leave on his own and to warn him he would be shot if he attempted to do so. It was then too late. Pyle was repatriated several months later and saw the Russian guide fraternizing with the defenders of Koikori.

It seems to me now that the enemy knew all our movements and plans, and that our failures were largely due to bad intelligence and security on the part of higher authority.

When Major Barnby had been wounded and taken to the rear, Captain Watts would have become the commander of my Company. However, I did not see him and learned later he had been arrested. When back at Murmansk he was tried by Field General Court Martial.

On his return home months later, Pyle was awarded the DCM for his reconnaissance work, and loyalty and example to others as a prisoner of war of the Bolsheviks.

To return to Smith-Hill's narrative, having returned from reporting to Major Williams he found his company, reorganized them, and posted them in outpost positions to protect the road, after which he went to find and report to Major Strover. On his return, he found the company lined up on the road. When he asked them why they had left their positions, they replied that a major in the Machine Gun Corps (Strover) had told them 'to get the hell out of it', as they were not needed, and he would find someone 'who was of some use to man the positions'. The word had also been passed to them that men who did not wish to fight could march back.

From Smith-Hill's diary and from notes written later:

Major Strover had also telephoned to HQ informing them that he was sending the Marines out of it as he had no use for them, and asking that they should be neither fed nor clothed. It was said that he turned to a man standing near and asked if he was a Marine, and if he had heard what he, Major Strover, had said. On receiving the reply in the affirmative to each question he told the man to let the rest of his company know what he had said. I was also told that one man had been seized and kicked down the road for no specific offence.

On hearing this I at once went to Major Strover and informed him what was happening. *I also stated to him that any of his orders conveyed to the men through me would be obeyed.* [underlined in original]

I was informed in reply that the order re men retiring who did not wish to fight did not apply to the Chatham (B) Company – only to C Company, and that we were to sleep in our present positions. Major Strover told me that those who did not wish to fight would be marched back by Major Laing next morning. When I returned to my company, a party of men had left for the rear in accordance with orders they had apparently previously received.

9th September, Tuesday

At 9 am Major Laing addressed B and C Companies and asked for volunteers for the outpost line. About 16 NCOs and men volunteered from B Coy, and about 3 from C Coy. These were insufficient for the outposts required. The companies were dismissed. Major Laing then ordered me to accompany him to Report Centre [HQ?]. Lt Bramall also accompanied us. On my return with Lt Bramall to the Coy, I was told that about 50 men had left for Svyatnavolok [to the north, i.e. away from the front]. I reported this to Major Laing and Major Strover who ordered a message to be sent after them to the effect that they would be fired on if they attempted to enter Svyatnavolok. At about 5 pm I was sent alone to Svyatnavolok to take charge of the men who had marched back. (The men were not fired on). I found them quite glad to see me and friendly. As there were no NCOs I 'passed the word' that they were to fall in at 8 am next day.

10th September, Wednesday

At 8 am I found the men correctly fallen in, dressed, clean and standing to attention.

Later a stretcher party arrived carrying the body of Captain Burton, covered with a blanket. I searched the body for papers, but only found a map which was the only map I ever saw.

11th September, Thursday

Remainder of Coy arrived at noon and the 53 men rejoined their units.

15th September, Monday

at 9 am left Svyatnavolok to march to Med-Gora [his name for Medvyejya Gora Station].

The discipline of my platoon up to 8th September was good. I had no cases of insubordination while training or when in Russia. During the attack on Koikori the discipline and conduct of the men left nothing to be desired and no one left the scene of the action before receiving the order to retire. In my opinion the reasons for the failure of discipline were:

1. Exaggerated reports of casualties.
2. The absence of senior Company officers.
3. The lessening of morale and sullenness caused by treatment they received at the hands of Army officers.
4. The fact that they were given to believe that there would be practically no resistance on the part of the enemy and they need expect no casualties.

On 23 September 1919 the battalion was in Murmansk waiting to embark for England when 62 out of the total of 117 in B Company were suddenly placed under arrest, and taken off to be court-martialled. A day or so later, the battalion was addressed by Rawlinson, who told them that he thought little of them, but as there are no bad men, only bad officers, the commanding officer bore the main responsibility for their bad conduct. The court martial found 90 men of the 6th Battalion RM guilty of cowardice; 13 were sentenced to death, and others up to five years' penal servitude with hard labour. Rawlinson did not confirm the death sentences, and reduced some of the others to lesser terms.

Captain Watts was also court-martialled for using words calculated to create alarm and despondency by saying 'the whole bloody company is lost' or words to that effect. Smith-Hill was the prisoner's friend, but his efforts did not result in Watts's acquittal; he was cashiered and sent home. He joined the 'Black and Tans' in Ireland.

On Smith-Hill's arrival at Chatham station with his company,

> an orderly met us with a message from the adjutant asking us to wait until the Divisional Band arrived to play us back to barracks. [Traditional greeting to drafts arriving home from foreign service]. I felt we would never be forgiven if we allowed ourselves to be played back in triumph, so ordered the company to fall in quickly and reached barracks while the band was still getting ready to leave.
>
> I reported to the Commandant, Colonel Hamilton Maximilian Christian William Graham. No news of our disasters had previously reached him, so as my story unfolded, he was overcome. His tears made dark, pink spots on his pad of blotting paper.

Smith-Hill is clear that there was no mutiny and no cowardice. As he says:

> there was no case of any man refusing to obey a direct order to return to the line. There was a great deal of misunderstanding and frankly of bad discipline. The trumpet sounded an uncertain note.

It is hard to fault his arguments. Many Royal Marines units before and since have been thrown into far tougher fights at shorter notice, and under more adverse conditions than the 6th Battalion, and come through with flying colours. But an examination of the circumstances will almost always show that training and good leadership had prepared them for the hard knocks and setbacks of war, and so they were able to take them in their stride. The Adjutant General of the Corps should never have agreed to this battalion deploying; ultimately the responsibility for their disgrace lies with him. Let Smith-Hill have the last words:

> The officers did not shine and very few were subsequently promoted to more than one rank above the one they held in Russia. [Smith-Hill himself was an exception, rising to brigadier in the Second World War.]
>
> The other ranks suffered most and deserved it least. Those sent to penal servitude and those killed or wounded were the victims of the ineptitude of senior officers. They were transported two thousand miles by sea, and 450 miles by rail: they fought a minor action lasting two and a half hours – and returned home. They achieved nothing. They were like disgruntled, not vicious, children, in a strange land far from home.

Other Royal Marines performed better in Russia, both before and after the 6th Battalion's tour of duty. Some brisk little battles were fought by Royal Marines along the River Dwina, south of Archangel, in 1918 and 1919 until the evacuation on 30 September 1919, when the Royal Marines were among the last to leave. In particular the Royal Marines activities in eastern Russia and Siberia are in marked contrast to the sad little saga of the lacklustre 6th Battalion in North Russia.

EASTERN RUSSIA AND SIBERIA

The first British forces to arrive in Siberia and Eastern Russia were Marines and seamen landed at Vladivostok on 1 January 1918, from the cruiser HMS *Suffolk*, to protect the British Consulate and British refugees from Petrograd and Moscow against the depredations of the Bolshevik Red Guards. Here they found a Japanese force, landed to take advantage of Russian weakness, in the hope of annexing Russia's Far East. These small beginnings led to British participation on the side of the Russian anti-Bolshevik White Army in the civil war on the Volga Front.

Throughout the war large numbers of Czech soldiers deserted to the Russians from the Austro-Hungarian Army, and were formed into a Czech Legion numbering some 40,000 men. When the Russians signed the peace with Germany, the Czech Legion, who wanted to continue the fight against the Central Powers, eventually persuaded the Soviet Government to allow them to travel to Vladivostok, whence they would be transported to France to continue the war. In early 1918, while the Legion was actually in transit on the trans-Siberian Railway, Trotsky ordered their detention and disarmament. However, the local Red Guards were no match for the Czech Legion, who routed them. The Czechs took control of much of the line, eventually as far east as Irkutsk, at the southern end of Lake Baikal, as well as fighting on the Eastern Front west of the Urals.

Much of the area between Lake Baikal and Vladivostok was controlled by an unscrupulous warlord, Grigorii Semenov. The British paid him £10,000 a month to fight the Reds, and the French provided similar sums; a wasted investment, because Semenov conducted himself entirely in the pursuit of his own ends. He was also financed by the Japanese in order to create and maintain a state of instability, as part of their strategy to promote their ambitions in this region. He was highly successful, but it did the Japanese no good whatsoever.

The White government in Siberia was formed at Omsk under Admiral Kolchak, who at one stage in the civil war nominally ruled from Lake Baikal almost to the Volga; only nominally, because anti-White partisans actually controlled vast tracts of the countryside. Nevertheless, the Allies recognized Kolchak's government, and poured in supplies. Kolchak meanwhile mounted an offensive to the west, in the hope of linking up with White forces in north Russia around Archangel, and eventually capturing Moscow.

Kolchak appealed to the Allies for artillery, so a small detachment of Royal Marines were landed from the *Suffolk* with one 6in gun and four 12-pounders mounted on railway wagons. They gave valuable support to the Czechs on the Ussuri Front as far as Ufa, west of the Urals. When the detachment was withdrawn to Vladivostok, it was decided to form a British Naval Mission to help Kolchak form a Russian Naval Flotilla on the River Kama, a tributary of the Volga, and based at Perm, a large town just west of the Urals. The mission was headed by acting Captain Wolfe-Murray RN. On a visit to Vladivostok, Wolfe-Murray suggested that the guns used on the railway be mounted on vessels manned by British crews, and form part of the Russian Naval Flotilla. The British Admiralty agreed, provided sufficient volunteers could be found from the Royal Marine Detachment in HMS *Kent*, which had by then arrived at Vladivostok to relieve the *Suffolk*.

Captain Tom Jameson RMLI, the officer commanding the Royal Marine Detachment in the *Kent*, takes up the story:[6]

the proposition was put to the RM Detachment, and after several days interval each man was asked if he would volunteer for this expedition into Siberia. The Senior NCO (C/Sgt Bachelor) reported that of the total of 64 NCOs and Privates, 63 had volunteered. The odd man out was then in cells and had no vote. This response was somewhat surprising, for the Admiralty had just informed us of arrangements whereby *Kent* would be relieved at an early date by HMS *Carlisle*. Some 450 of the sailors were 'Hostilities Only' and it was a matter of urgency that they should return home considering that the war had ended nearly four months previously.

In outlining the service for which these Royal Marines had volunteered, due prominence was given to the following implications:

a. The ship was due to return home soon.
b. We would be involved in a civil war and little was known on which a forecast of the future could be made.
c. The vast country we were entering was still in the grip of the Siberian winter (35° below zero) with famine, disease and the language difficulty being only a few of the contingencies which we knew we would encounter.
d. Our base would be Vladivostok and the theatre of operations was likely to be in European Russia, west of the Ural Mountains, over 4,000 miles away from Vladivostok.

Whatever prompted so many to volunteer for further active service under these conditions at least it showed that the spirit of adventure was not lacking – in fact it was with an inspired mind that I formed and prepared the Detachment for the adventure that lay ahead.

We had little thought that we would travel some 10,000 miles before we saw Vladivostok again!

The strength of this small force was based upon manning the 6-inch gun and the four 12-pounders and consisted of:

    1 Captain RMLI
    1 Lieutenant (Mate) RN [i.e. a boatswain's mate]
    1 Gunner (WO) RN[7]
    7 NCOs RMLI
   22 Privates RMLI
    1 PO [Petty Officer] Armourer RN
    1 Sick Berth Attendant RN [medical orderly]
    1 Surgeon RNVR

Jameson acquired excellent winter kit for his force from the Canadians at Vladivostok. He laid in ample rations, calculating that he must take far more than at first might be estimated. He stocked twice as much weight in disinfectant as food to guard against the primitive hygienic conditions he foresaw. All these far-sighted precautions were to pay dividends, and did not escape the notice of his men, whose already high morale rose accordingly.

On 6 April 1919, the detachment set off by train for Omsk, 4,500 miles away. Because the Reds frequently cut the line, an engine and a wagon carrying spare rails travelled about a mile ahead of the train. At one station they saw the bodies of Reds who had sabotaged the railway hanging from telegraph poles, along with the local mayor, who had been assisting them. After a number of minor adventures, including saving a White Russian officer from being executed by one of Semenov's drunken Cossacks, the detachment arrived at Omsk on 16 April. At Omsk station, Jameson relates:

> [there] were some twenty parallel tracks, two for the trains moving east and west. The remaining tracks were completely filled with wagons of every variety, mostly cattle trucks, and each one filled to capacity. Troops lived in some, but the majority were occupied by whole families and it was quite obvious they had existed there throughout the winter. It is difficult to describe the utter filth and squalor that existed. Tracks were about twelve feet apart. The occupants of each wagon existed without water supply or any means of sanitation other than a hole cut in the floor, and for cooking and warmth a small stove in the middle of the wagon. These incredible conditions made one realise how crude these wretched people had become and wonder what would happen when the spring thaw set in.

On 28 April, the Detachment arrived at their destination, Perm. Here Jameson made contact with the delightfully named Admiral Smirnoff, commanding the Kama River Flotilla. He was given a Kama tug and a barge on which to mount the 6in gun. The tug was christened the *Kent*, and the barge the *Suffolk*, after the two cruisers. The paddle-driven tug, which the detachment referred to as the gunboat, was 170 feet long and 40 feet wide. The barge was even larger, and the 6in gun was dwarfed by it. Both vessels came complete with Russian crews. By now the ice on the river had practically disappeared, allowing the two craft to be brought alongside the bank, near the railway to enable the guns to be transferred from the wagons. The detachment and the local Russian workmen, and women, showed considerable ingenuity in fitting the 12-pounders, the 6in gun, and some Vickers machine-guns they acquired, constructing living accommodation, and armouring the vessels. When Jameson wanted to test the guns, 'Without hesitation I was given permission to carry out these tests against the hills on the other side of the river, and an assurance that the local inhabitants in that area were of no consequence.'

Rations supplied by the Russians were basic:

black bread, a loaf usually some eighteen inches across, meat in casks, often bear's meat which had been packed into the cask with ice and salt before the end of the winter, and potatoes. There was little variation and not infrequently the bread was sour, even moist and green at the centre of the loaf, whereas the meat had not always kept edible owing to faulty casks.

The tasks of the Kama River Flotilla were to support the White Army when they were fighting within range of the guns on the vessels, to cover any units crossing the river, and to attempt to engage and destroy Red ships and craft. Following the thaw, the river was anything from half a mile to two miles wide. On 14 May the two British vessels were in action for the first time, after which they were busily engaged until the end of June, when the Bolshevik advance put paid to the activities of this game little flotilla. Early in this period the *Kent* and *Suffolk*, with their sister vessels, were involved in a 'fleet action' with no less than eleven Bolshevik craft. The *Kent* opened fire at 8,100 yards, and eventually sank the Bolshevik flagship. Jameson: 'Her crew jumped on shore wearing white life-belts and provided an ideal target for our machine guns.' Having seen off the Bolshevik fleet, the flotilla came under fire from enemy guns sited in dead ground some way in from the river bank. *Kent* covered the withdrawal by laying a smokescreen and firing shrapnel on to the enemy gun positions.

At the beginning of June the Flotilla ran the gauntlet of Bolshevik gunners while passing the town of Sarapul. The bridge had been destroyed and the wreckage used to try to block the river. Fortunately a small gap remained. Jameson:

At 5.35 am the Flotilla, carrying barges and tugs appeared coming around the bend below the bridge. Targets were difficult to locate and enemy guns put down barrage fire on point after point upstream into which we ran unavoidably at maximum speed. Our 12-pounder guns swung on to targets and at point-blank range maintained a rapid rate of fire especially at targets on the water front. I pointed out a field gun firing at us through the back door of a house close to the edge of the water, and a shell blew house and all sky high.

This lively operation gave us a sense of satisfaction since it showed that though the standard of training and efficiency was sadly lacking in the White troops, the Bolshevik forces were not particularly skilful and let pass a brilliant opportunity of destroying the Flotilla.

The appearance of the Bolsheviks at Sarapul was, however, completely unexpected and threw the Whites into a panic. Colour Sergeant Taylor of the *Suffolk* went ashore with his dog for a walk, and described in his diary how he found 'the White troops in a filthy condition and their equipment in a deplorable state. Refugees were fleeing in every direction and the whole town in a ghastly turmoil.'

As neither side took prisoners, the panic at the approach of the Bolsheviks is understandable. The flotilla was getting under way, so the *Suffolk* left a tug to bring off Taylor. The crew of the tug fired four rifle shots to attract his attention, but he did not hear them above the din in the town. When Taylor eventually appeared the tug sent a boat in for him. The boat was about to be swamped by panic-stricken soldiers, when he pulled out his revolver and forced them back. Taylor:

> After I got into the boat, I found that our dog was still on shore, so I ordered the boat to put back, and then there was a real row. I had to threaten to shoot the whole damn lot of them if I had any more trouble. By this time the Reds were in the town and coming down the main street. I went back for the dog, and then there was some more fun. The dog was in for a skylark and as I went for him he ran away. The people in the boat were swearing, but they knew I would not come without him, so they helped me to catch him. We were away just in time, as we shoved off, the Reds were fairly close, their cavalry leading four deep.

Covered by 3in gun fire from one of the vessels, Colour Sergeant Taylor was able to regain the *Suffolk*.

A quiet period enabled battle damage on *Kent* to be repaired. It was followed by several days of activity, in which *Kent* and *Suffolk* engaged enemy batteries on shore in support of the White Army, as well as destroying a large ammunition dump, but by 15 June it was becoming clear that the Reds were gaining the upper hand. A few days later the British High Commissioner told Admiral Kolchak that the British Government could no longer recognize the Omsk Government, and that all British forces in Siberia were to be withdrawn. However, because no instructions were received from the Admiralty, the *Kent* and *Suffolk* continued their operations for a few days longer. Just before this Jameson had been awarded a high Russian decoration, which, to his disappointment, the British High Commissioner ordered him to return.

The British vessels had made their mark on the Bolsheviks, who reported that their naval manoeuvres on the River Kama were being seriously hampered by British 'destroyers'. The Bolsheviks sent a message over the radio from Moscow offering immunity from 'retribution' if the British discontinued their activities on the river. The British were about to discontinue their activities for a different reason: the river was getting too shallow for the larger vessels, and consequently the support they could give to the Army was severely limited. Jameson suggested to Admiral Smirnoff that the guns should be dismounted onto field mountings and the detachment should transfer to a land role. Smirnoff agreed, and Captain Wolfe-Murray duly telegrammed for field mountings to be sent from Vladivostok. But events were moving far too fast. On 20 June, with the Reds advancing rapidly, Smirnoff ordered *Kent* and *Suffolk* back to Perm to transfer their guns to their original Naval Armoured Train. After working round the clock for several days in the increasing chaos in Perm, the guns and remaining ammunition were shifted to the wagons. *Kent* and *Suffolk* were sunk by permission of Admiral Smirnoff.

The next hurdle was to find an engine to pull their train. Jameson:

We took an armed party to the repair sheds (the Motavileka Factory [at Perm] was the Swindon of East Russia) where we found all engines getting up steam. With firm determination we persuaded the Russians in charge to allot an engine and crew to our train, and with our armed guard on the footplate it reached and was attached to our train. About 6 am the next morning, 29 June, we pulled out of Perm with every wagon filled to overflowing.

The thirty-seven-strong detachment was packed into two wooden wagons, sleeping three deep. The next day the engine broke down with no prospect of repair, 300 miles from Ekaterinburg, and 1,000 miles from Omsk. They were busily working out what to do next when an engine appeared from the east. Admiral Smirnoff had heard of their escape from Perm, and when they failed to join him, sent the engine to investigate. On arrival at Omsk, Jameson offered the services of the Naval Armoured Train, but by now orders to withdraw altogether had been received from the British Admiralty. With the Admiralty's permission, Jameson handed over the guns and ammunition to the Whites.

He was told that a number of wagons containing bullion for transfer to the National Bank in Vladivostok had been attached to their train.

This was an extra worry, since the Bolsheviks would certainly take great pains to intercept the train if they learned about the bullion, and there was a high risk of attack during the 2,500 mile journey that lay ahead. Jameson found the Czech detachments along the railway very helpful with advice on the most potentially dangerous spots, and avoided travelling at night on these sections. This, and the evident alertness of his men, must have deterred potential assailants because they were left alone. They were delayed for several days by the wrecking of a train ahead of them, and from Irkutsk onwards the incidents of train wrecking were more frequent. With high summer another threat reared its head – typhus. Jameson:

> Hospital trains had been organised and were moving typhus victims away from the worst stricken areas. These trains could be identified when they stopped near our train by the discharging of corpses to the side of the railway. As soon as we became aware of such a train halting near us, I at once ordered our men into their wagons and to close all doors and ventilators to prevent mosquitoes from reaching them from the typhus train. I would then take a few armed men and visit the Stationmaster and demand that the distance between the trains be increased to at least half a mile. This invariably resulted in some excuse being given which might stimulate a bribe before an engine could be made available. The demand was then repeated and supported by an order to my men to load their rifles.

Fifty-two days after leaving Perm, their train rolled into Vladivostok. Jameson:

> It was a relief to feel that we had at last reached our destination and I can recall the surprise and thrill to find the band of the Middlesex Regiment at the station ready to lead us to HMS *Carlisle*. As we approached the ship the lower deck was cleared and we were given an extremely generous welcome by Commodore Carrington in the presence of the ship's company.

Happy to relate, Jameson was awarded a well-deserved DSO. Thanks to his leadership and initiative, in conditions of great uncertainty, surrounded at times by panic and fear among their allies, thousands of miles from assistance by their fellow countrymen, morale and discipline remained high. Among other decorations awarded to the detachment, the DSM was given to Colour Sergeant Taylor.

PART THREE

1920–1943

Say not the struggle naught availeth

12

The Twenty-Year Truce

In June 1923, as a result of postwar economies, the RMA and RMLI were amalgamated, and the ranks of gunner and private were changed to Marine. This reorganization logically led to the question being asked, what is the role of the Royal Marines? Any notions that they might be used to form an amphibious landing force were not encouraged by the reluctance of the Committee of Imperial Defence (CID) to consider such operations. The CID formulated defence policy for consideration by the Cabinet, and prepared the necessary plans in the event of war: combined operations (involving land, sea, and air, and including amphibious landings) did not figure in any plans in the interwar period. As late as 1938 the First Sea Lord told the Chiefs of Staff Committee[1] that he did not foresee a combined operation being mounted in the next war. The CIGS also said that there were no plans for a landing in the face of strong opposition. Curiously, despite this uninterest in high places, combined operations were regularly studied and exercised in the classroom at the three service staff colleges. In addition an Inter Service Training and Development Centre (ISTDC) was set up in 1938, rather late in the day, to study and develop the tactics and equipment needed for combined operations.

In 1924 a committee formed under the chairmanship of Admiral Sir Charles Madden to investigate the future role of the Royal Marines laid down the roles of the Corps in the following order of priority:

1. The Royal Marines are an integral and essential part of the Royal Navy. They are to provide detachments in war and peace for the larger ships capable of manning their share of the gunnery armaments.
2. They are to provide independent forces to join the Fleet on mobilization and to carry out operations for the seizure and defence of temporary bases and raids on the enemy's coastline and bases, under the direction of the Commander-in-Chief.

3. They will serve as a connecting link between the Navy and the Army, and will supply the Army in war with units for special duties for which Naval experience is necessary.

Well and good, but firmly in the 'blinding glimpse of the obvious' department and hardly an improvement on what had happened in the past. The bar to progress was priority one: manning a proportion of the guns of the fleet by men trained as soldiers, a role which should have been shed years before.

In order to meet the needs of priority two, the Madden Committee recommended the formation of a brigade-size Striking Force of four battalions, consisting of 1,800 full-time officers and men, to be augmented by 1,600 reservists on mobilization. The committee also recommended that a special training centre be established for the Striking Force, and it should carry out exercises with the fleet. There was a snag. As constituted, the Corps did not have enough men to do both priority 1 and 2 tasks. So unless these two priorities were reversed priority 2 would never be realized. Madden knew perfectly well that no funds existed to raise the additional manpower for a permanently constituted Striking Force. But he included his recommendation that such a force should be raised in his report, to leave the door open in case money could be found at some time in the future, or be required by the international situation. The international situation did demand it in 1940, and, as will be related, because no permanent properly trained and exercised Striking Force existed, various landing parties were cobbled together in the old way, while a Royal Marines Brigade was still in the process of being formed and trained. As a result the Royal Marines were in no position to play their rightful role in combined operations when war broke out, and for some years after.

Because no Striking Force existed, the staff college studies and exercises and the work of the ISTDC centred on the Army providing the landing force, rather as Fisher had done before the First World War. The Royal Marines were by no means seen as an amphibious force in their own right, as they are today, and their contribution to pre-Second World War amphibious planning was minimal. This was in marked contrast to the United States Marine Corps (USMC), which as early as 1900 had been tasked with providing the landing force in amphibious operations. Between the world wars, the USMC played the leading part in partnership with the US Navy formulating doctrine and developing equipment, including landing craft, for such operations. With the formation of the Fleet Marine Force in 1933, the USMC was well placed to play a starring role in the great amphibious landings in the Pacific, starting within nine months of America entering the Second World War.

The Royal Marines were called upon twice in the inter-war years to provide a force for overseas service. In January 1927, the 12th Battalion was formed in the old way at Portsmouth, and shipped out to Shanghai to help defend the International Settlement. After a year, it returned home and was disbanded. In 1935, because of a perceived threat by the Italians to the Mediterranean Fleet base at Alexandria, 1,600 Marines were sent out as part of an inter-service base defence force. The Marines manned 6in and light coast artillery, anti-aircraft guns, and searchlights, and provided signals, transport, and a landing company; hardly 'Striking Force' tasks. A year later they returned home, and were dispersed to their divisions. However, the seeds had been sown in the minds of the Admirals by this base defence assignment, which led to plans being laid for an MNBDO, or Mobile *Naval Base Defence Organisation* (author's italics), to be raised in wartime. The Royal Marines would provide the bulk of the manpower for this strange military enterprise with the long-winded title. Indeed the despatch of 1st RM Anti-Aircraft Battery to Alexandria in early 1939 was the first move in the raising of two MNBDOs. The bulk of Corps manpower when war came was now to be sidelined to a defensive, mainly heavy, coast and anti-aircraft artillery role, away from assault infantry; a backward step to the old heavy Blue Marines from the light Red Marines. The question 'Who would seize the bases for the MNBDO to defend?' was left unanswered; certainly not the one infantry battalion in the MNBDO. Most of the remainder of the Corps would be in gun turrets in ships. These tasks were in marked contrast to those planned for their USMC fellows in the Fleet Marine Force, spearheading the amphibious assault.

Between the wars, apart from the forays to Shanghai and Alexandria, which passed off without any incidents of note, the officers and men of the Royal Marines occupied themselves with routine on board ship or in barracks. Some officers, especially after the excitement of the war, and with promotion back to its paralytic pre-war pace, found settling down to the humdrum life impossible, and sought employment elsewhere. In 1921, Arthur Chater, aged just twenty-five, left England for loan service in the Egyptian Army. He was posted to the 14th Sudanese Battalion, stationed in Omdurman. In what was then called Anglo-Egyptian Sudan, the Army was part of the Egyptian Army, officered at senior level by the British. There were only two other British officers in the battalion. Within twenty-four hours, Chater found himself in command of 1,000 officers and men, the CO having been evacuated sick, and the other officer departed on four months' home leave. Chater:

> I had a great deal to learn. Apart from a dozen or so Egyptian officers, the officers, NCOs and men were all Sudanese. One never walked, but rode everywhere, even to and from the office. Early one morning, the Pasha, who had come over from Khartoum, was surprised to find me on foot drilling a squad of men. I explained that the best way to learn the Turkish words of command, was to do it oneself.[2] Most of the men were enlisted for life. When the Battalion moved station, the wives and families went with it. It was like a tribe on the move. The CO was the Tribal Chief.

He did not rate fighting quality of the Sudanese infantry highly, considering them pampered and spoilt, a bad imitation of poor British troops. 'They had lost the attributes of Africans, without gaining the qualities of British soldiers.' Later he managed to transfer to the Sudan Camel Corps, whose soldiers were 'tough, lightly built Arabs', and rode the 630 miles on a camel to take over his company, or 'idara'. It was rather more than a company, consisting of a troop of mounted infantry, a machine-gun section, an infantry company of four platoons, and enough mule and camel transport to make the unit fully mobile. No wonder Chater found life in the Sudan more exciting than supervising recruit training at the depot at Deal.

In 1924, following a mutiny by Egyptian officers in Sudan, they were ordered back to Egypt, and the British officers and Sudanese units of the Egyptian Army were formed into the Sudan Defence Force. In 1927 Chater was promoted to lieutenant colonel and appointed to command the Camel Corps. He was just thirty. Most officers in the Royal Marines and British Army in the inter-war period would be captains at that age, if they were lucky. Other Royal Marines officers would follow Chater into the Camel Corps. Chater went on to raise the Somaliland Scouts in 1941, and, as a major general, became Military Governor and Commander British Troops Somaliland.

For many Royal Marines officers of the inter-war period, if stationed in barracks, much time would be consumed 'counting socks'; at sea the less conscientious ones would be drinking pink gin in the wardroom, having completed their duties well before lunchtime, while their detachment worked in small parties around the ship. Other officers found fulfilment flying with the Fleet Air Arm. In 1930, Lieutenant W. H. N. (Norrie) Martin was appointed to the battleship *Royal Sovereign* in the Mediterranean Fleet based on Malta:

> It was just at the worst part of the depression and the fleet was severely rationed in fuel. As a result we spent a great deal of time in harbour. The Royal Marines detachment was about 250 strong with three officers, a Captain RM and two lieutenants, of which I was the junior. There was not much to do in those peaceful days in harbour. I was a watchkeeper and had to spend an awful lot of time on duty on the quarterdeck, which I felt was a dreadful waste of time.

Martin and his fellow Royal Marines officers were conscientious, and swinging round a buoy in Grand Harbour, Valetta, had one compensation; they could at least land the Royal Marine Detachment for infantry training, and this they did. Although it must be said that much of the training done in the 1920s and 1930s, by the Army and the Royal Marines, was half-baked. Financial stringency led to idiocies like troops being issued with football rattles in lieu of light machine-guns, and flags to represent anti-tank guns. The training was not improved if the officers running it had forgotten the old cry, 'time spent in reconnaissance is seldom wasted'.[3] Norrie Martin was to participate in one of these exercises:

> It was to be carried out by all RM detachments in the ships of the Mediterranean Fleet, and had been planned by the Fleet RM Officer [FRMO] on the Commander-in-Chief's staff. It was designed as a simple affair in which the Marines would storm ashore at first light, from ships' boats, and establish a bridgehead on the beach. After this had been done, there was to be a short advance inland, and then a withdrawal and re-embarkation in the ships in the late afternoon. All in all a nice happy day in the country, and a pleasant break from the ship routine.
>
> In the event the whole exercise was a disaster. The FRMO had, of course, not been able to visit the site before the exercise, and innocently planned the whole operation from maps which proved totally inaccurate.

At about 4.00 am on a very hot, airless June day all the Marines in the Fleet clambered into ships' boats and, just as at Gallipoli 16 years before, were towed ashore. When we reached the beach we found that there wasn't one, at least not the expected sandy, sometimes rocky, sloped beach. All there was for miles around was a narrow strip of very rocky ground, backed by the most forbidding looking mountains. Quite undaunted by this we set out up an appalling trail, which led into the mountains. It was nothing but the bed of a dried-up river, and strewn with rocks of every shape and size. Our two hand-pulled machine gun trailers had pneumatic tyres, and these were soon slashed to ribbons. The trailers which contained extra water and rations were left on the side of the track.

As the day wore on, the sun blazed down on us in the valley and it grew hotter and hotter. Very soon the men began to feel the effects of the heat, and many of them had to fall out by the wayside. Johnnie Phillips [his fellow subaltern] and I did our best to exercise strict water discipline, but with not much result. The great majority of our people managed all right because of our earlier training in Malta, but some detachments from other ships had as many as 50% casualties from the heat and awful conditions in the valley.

After we had battled our way about six miles up the track, which apparently led nowhere, word finally got through to us that we were to withdraw and re-embark. All we achieved was to walk a long way inland in frightful conditions, discover how useless our machine gun trailers were, and in a huge number of cases reduce our boots to tattered strips of leather.

Now we had to walk back by the same track. Johnnie and I were by this time carrying four rifles each, as the owners were in such bad shape. We finally got back to the beachhead, such as it was, and there were *Royal Sovereign*'s boats manned by a lot of laughing sailors.

Truly nothing had changed for the better despite Gallipoli. Whether it was this that decided Martin to go flying he does not relate, but at the end of 1931 he volunteered for a five-year tour of duty with the Fleet Air Arm. At that date the Fleet Air Arm had been manned and controlled by the Royal Air Force since 1918, and its squadrons were RAF units. The aircrew were provided by both the Royal Navy/Royal Marines and RAF. The Navy did not manage to prise the Fleet Air Arm out of the grasp of the RAF until 1937, leaving little time to make up the leeway after nineteen years of neglect. The ageing aircraft with which the Navy went to war in 1939 were the consequence of the low priority accorded by the RAF to the Fleet Air Arm. The RAF was wedded to the twin theories of its founder, Marshal of the Royal Air Force Lord Trenchard, the indivisibility of air power (that the RAF, and no one else, should own and direct all aircraft) and the invincibility of the strategic bomber. Consequently providing aircrew and aircraft for the Royal Navy was at best a diversion of effort, and at worst totally irrelevant to the RAF's perception of how it proposed winning the next war without any assistance from the Royal Navy and the Army.

The Navy did not help matters because it was dominated by gunnery admirals who had an insufficient grasp of what air power could do both to the enemy, and to them. Some Captains RN were in the same category, including at least one who was in command of a carrier at the outbreak of war. The Royal Navy, which had invented the carrier, entered the Second World War with six ancient carriers, one modern one, and more on the stocks, as well as obsolete or obsolescent aircraft; in all respects far behind the air arms of the US and the Japanese navies.

Norrie Martin joined HMS *Furious* in 1932, flying Blackburn Ripon torpedo bombers. The *Furious*, launched in 1917 as a cruiser-carrier, had been fully converted in 1925. The Blackburn Ripon was a biplane with a top speed of 116 mph, and ceiling of 13,000 feet. The other types flown by the Fleet Air Arm until the outbreak of war were not much better; the fastest was the Hawker Osprey, with a top speed of 176 mph.

Other Royal Marines joined the Fleet Air Arm for similar reasons as Norrie Martin, including two of the most famous Royal Marines to fly in the Second World War. Lieutenant Oliver Patch, finding watch-keeping and the custody of the ship's confidential books tedious, applied for the Camel Corps and the Fleet Air Arm, ending up in the latter. Ronnie Hay had always wanted to go to sea, and never wanted to be a Royal Marine, but ended up as one because he was too old for the Navy. Once at sea he found that 'Being a Royal Marine at sea is not the most exacting life. I volunteered to fly to get out of the Royal Marines.' The outbreak of war while he was still undergoing flying training increased his inclination to 'get out of the Royal Marines, because stories of the trenches put me off. In the Navy you get three meals a day, hot baths and all the comforts.' In fact he remained a Royal Marine for the duration of the war and beyond, and a very gallant one at that. Like some other Marines, he preferred the shipborne life, which in wartime was not always as comfortable as he makes out, and could, of course, be brought to an abrupt and unpleasant end by bombs, torpedoes, and shells, or in the case of the Fleet Air Arm by being shot down.

The more ambitious Royal Marines officers sat for the Army Staff College entrance exam, and if they passed and obtained a nomination, attended the two-year course. Some went on from there to Army staffs. They were a minority within the Royal Marines, and regarded as slightly offside to be so keen on their profession. Such an attitude in the 1920s and 30s was by no means confined to the Corps; in the Gordon Highlanders, for example, a request to attend staff college, rather than serving with the regiment, was frowned on.

In September 1931 the Royal Navy was shaken by a mutiny of eight ships' companies of the Atlantic Fleet at Invergordon. It was sparked off by appalling mishandling in the announcing of a pay cut imposed on the Armed Services by Ramsay MacDonald's all-party National Government in an effort to stop the run on the pound. Men who had joined in or after 1925 were on a lower rate of pay than those who had joined before that date, and who were on the 1919 scales. The Treasury plan was to cut the pre-1925 people to the post-1925 rate, a drop of about 25 per cent. Although pay scales differed depending on a man's qualifications, good conduct badges, and so forth, the case of Marine Fordham of HMS *Nelson* was typical:

> I had no badges [for good conduct], and a pay cut of 1 shilling a day out of 28 shillings a week meant a lot. I was married at the time. My wife got paid 7/6 a week by the Admiralty, which of course I had to supplement by a weekly allotment. Many people were buying furniture on hire-purchase agreements.

Because the cuts affected the older men, many of those it hit hardest were married with children, and financial commitments.[4] The Admiralty grant to wives was just enough to cover the rent.[5]

For some months there had been speculation in the press on the measures the government would take to alleviate the economic situation, which included cutting service pay. Various notions had been bandied about, such as a 10 per cent pay cut across the board; all pure guesswork, but highly unsettling. The naval periodical *The Fleet* had revealed that a reduction to the 1925 scale was being mooted in Whitehall, so it is fair to assume that the men of the lower deck were aware that their pay was under discussion. But the sailors took comfort from the thought that the Admiralty would fight their corner, and, that whatever the outcome, it would be communicated to officers and men before being passed to the press. They were wrong. When the Treasury heard that the Admiralty intended promulgating the new rates on 7 September, they objected and said that no details should be sent out until after the Budget. The Admiralty wetly caved in. Even then they could have passed the details by signal immediately after the budget, but did not. Instead of giving captains the opportunity of clearing lower deck and addressing their ship's companies to explain the pay cut, the Admiralty merely promulgated the facts in an Admiralty Fleet Order (AFO). Certain flag officers were also informed by letter. The AFO was sent to the fleet at Invergordon, and elsewhere, by mail.

The news of the pay cuts was learned by ship's companies in a variety of ways; few from the AFO, which arrived too late. Naturally everyone was aggrieved by this cavalier treatment by the Admiralty, and felt, with justification, that their Lordships did not care about the welfare of the men under their command. Some in the fleet picked up the news from the press. There were efficient arrangements for newspaper distribution at Invergordon, and the Sunday papers with headlines about the pay cut were in every ship by breakfast that day – before the arrival of the AFO. Lieutenant Commander Cobb, in HMS *Dorsetshire*: 'If the AFO had arrived that Sunday, we would have read it to our men at Sunday Divisions' (the parade of whole ship's company, held every Sunday). Those in HMS *Malaya* heard rumours of pay cuts while at sea on gunnery exercises. In the Marines' turret, it was suggested, in jest, that they should turn the guns on Ramsay Macdonald's house, which was within range of the practice area.

Although personal radios were a rarity then, and the practice of relaying BBC programmes over the ship's broadcast system was not so prevalent as it became later, some heard it announced on the BBC while still at sea before the weekend. By a twist of fate, the commander's writer (typist) in HMS *Norfolk*, a man called Hill, owned one of the few personal radios in the fleet. He and a close friend, Able Seaman Wincott, used to listen to dance music in Hill's cubby-hole almost every evening. Wincott was a very strong personality, a bit of a 'mess-deck lawyer', but also articulate and a born leader. He was not a Communist at the time, although he became one subsequently. According to Hill, when he heard about the pay cut on the radio he announced his ambition to bring about a fleet mutiny. Subsequently Wincott claimed credit for organizing the mutiny, but more recent evidence shows that his claims are exaggerated, although he was without doubt one of the principal ringleaders.

On the evening of Sunday 13 September there was a noisy meeting in the canteen ashore at Invergordon, which was attended by representatives from many ships. The meeting was addressed by a number of sailors, Wincott among them. One of the points made by several speakers touched a nerve in the married sailors – that as a consequence of the pay cuts their wives would have to turn to prostitution to make ends meet.

The next day, Monday, Wincott should have been Watch Aboard, but managed to get a substitute for his duty, and went ashore. Knowing that most of the ship's representatives would not be able to get leave that day, he says he took it upon himself to ensure that nothing went awry with the arrangements. As he had anticipated, he found a meeting in the canteen, following a football match, being addressed by a succession of hot-heads, including one sailor called Bond who, according to Wincott, was 'talking about marching to London. Followed by another called Drake, talking nonsense. I did not speak at this meeting. I went round to all present saying "don't forget 6 o'clock tomorrow".' Wincott did not need to address the meeting; by then the ringleaders had made their plans and were spreading the word in their messdecks.

The next morning, 15 September, at reveille, as planned, the ships' companies of *Nelson*, *Hood*, *Rodney*, and *Valiant*, followed later by *Norfolk*, *Adventure*, *York*, and *Dorsetshire*, refused to turn to and get their ships ready for sea to proceed on exercise. There was no violence, and no sabotage. The *Repulse*, *Warspite*, *Malaya*, and others sailed as planned. Ships that had been out on exercises did not join in the mutiny when they subsequently came in to Invergordon.

Marines on board ship did not live a privileged existence, and carried out much the same duties as seamen – gunnery, scrubbing decks, polishing brasswork, chipping paint, and hoisting out boats – in addition to providing guards of honour and landing parties, so they had as good a reason to be aggrieved as their blue-jacket shipmates. But on the whole the Marines, who also received the same pay as sailors, were to take the same cuts, and would be equally badly affected, remained loyal, turned to, and carried out their duties. Only in *Norfolk* did the whole detachment, less officers and NCOs, join the seamen. Despite subsequent statements to the contrary by *Norfolk* men, she was regarded by many in the fleet as a thoroughly troublesome ship, and Wincott's glib tongue may have had some part to play in the uncharacteristic reaction of her Royal Marines.

Most Royal Marines took a pride in being 'sworn men', because they took, and still take, an oath of loyalty to the sovereign on joining; sailors did not, and still do not. In the 1930s, and even later, Marines were quartered in what they called 'the barracks', a mess deck between the officers and the seamen; a relic from earlier times. Marines referred to sailors as 'pressed men', which of course they were not, but this little conceit gave the Marines a sense of their own superiority. Their one concern, subsequently often expressed, was that being 'sworn men' they would have to put down the seamen by force, a prospect they did not relish. There were isolated instances of junior Royal Marine officers and senior NCOs suggesting that detachments should fix bayonets and sort out the seamen. Fortunately cooler heads prevailed. So, as at Spithead in 1797, the mutiny was not put down by using the Marines to suppress it by force of arms. Such action would have had disastrous, and long-lasting consequences. The Navy's discipline had to come from within, not be imposed by an outside force.

Without exception Naval and Marine officers, whether their own pay was being cut or not, sympathized with the men over their shabby treatment at the hands of Treasury and Admiralty, and felt desperately sad that matters should have come to such a sorry pass. Eventually all ships were ordered to their home ports, and the mutiny ended by 1900 hours on 16 September, as soon as sailors were told where their ships were bound. Subsequently the ringleaders were quietly dismissed the service: Wincott went to Leningrad in 1934, and lived in the Soviet Union thereafter, except for a visit to England in 1974. Morale and discipline in the fleet were soon restored, not least by the appointment of the 'sailor's admiral', Admiral Sir John D. ('Joe') Kelly, to command the Home Fleet. On 21 September, in an almost complete climb-down, the Government announced that the men on 1919 rates were to receive their current scale less 10 per cent. A great injustice was averted.

Despite much rumour and speculation, the mutiny was not the result of a Communist plot. According to Wincott, the Communists tried to establish 'a foot in the Navy, but failed'. The accuracy or otherwise of his information hardly matters. With hindsight Wincott and his fellow ringleaders did the Navy a service. The mutiny was the lance that pierced the boil of discontent before the poison invaded the whole body. The Navy entered the Second World War eight years later with its morale and fighting spirit unimpaired, to face the sternest test in its long history.

As war loomed in September 1939, in only one respect was the Navy less prepared than it had been in 1914: its equipment. There were far too few ships for the tasks that lay ahead (especially convoy escorts), its anti-aircraft gunnery systems were below par, and its aircraft were obsolete. The Royal Marines were 12,390 strong, with only just over 1,000 reservists waiting in the wings. Conscription had been announced in April of that year, and men were flooding into the Army, but none had yet joined the Corps. The huts at Lympstone where they would be trained had not yet been completed.

13

1939–1940

When the United Kingdom declared war on Germany on 3 September 1939, the fleet had top priority for Marines. In a replay of 1914, the Grand Fleet's successor, the Home Fleet, was based at Scapa Flow. The defences there had been dismantled in the inter-war period, and the work done to replace these was the genesis of the RM Fortress Unit, and the RM Engineers. RM anti-aircraft batteries were raised, and deployed within the United Kingdom: eventually these formed into anti-aircraft brigades, some of which later became part of the MNBDOs (Mobile Naval Base Defence Organisations). An RM Siege Regiment was formed after the fall of France, to shell the enemy coast across the Channel. In line with the Madden Report of 1924, the RM Brigade was ordered to form. In early 1940 orders were given to form the full MNBDO, initially consisting of over 2,000 officers and men, and rising to well over 5,000, commanded by a major general. This defence organization had priority for men and resources over the RM Brigade. However, neither was operational on the eve of the German invasion of France in May 1940.

Despite the array of land force units being thrown together by the Royal Marines in the early part of the war (of which those above are only a sample), most of the action for the first three years was seen by the sea-going Marines. The first three and a half years of the war were the most perilous in the long history of the Royal Navy. There was no phoney war from September 1939 to May 1940 for the Navy, nor were there, as there were for the Army, years when the majority of a greatly expanded Army was out of action, training for the battles to come. RAF Bomber Command took the battle to the Germans from early in the war, but it was 1943 before the Army or Bomber Command began their toughest fighting and taking their heaviest casualties. By then the Royal Navy had fought its most desperate battles, and suffered most of its losses in the heavier ships in which Marines served, including all five battleships/battlecruisers, and all five carriers sunk during this period.[1] Unlike the other two services, the Royal Navy fought from the very beginning to the very end of the war.

One of the first RM Fleet Air Arm pilots into action was Lieutenant Griffiths, who was dive-bombing a U-boat west of the Hebrides, and had the tail of his Skua blown off by his own bomb because of defective fusing. He and another Skua pilot, who had a similar experience in the same attack, were later picked up by the submarine, and spent the rest of the war in German prison camps.

The first major naval action of the war took place on 13 December 1939. Commodore Harwood's Force G, consisting of the 8in cruiser *Exeter* and the two 6in light cruisers *Ajax* (flag) and *Achilles*, intercepted the German 11in pocket battleship *Admiral Graf Spee* (Captain Langsdorff), 150 miles off the estuary of the River Plate. The battle lasted most of the day, during which *Exeter* suffered the most damage, as *Graf Spee* concentrated her 11in guns on her, while firing at the two cruisers with her 5.9in guns. But all ships were hit, the Marine turrets in both *Exeter* and *Ajax* being disabled. Lieutenant Ian De'ath RM was later awarded the DSO. By late afternoon, both the light cruisers were almost out of ammunition, and Harwood pulled them back to shadow *Graf Spee*. At about midnight, *Graf Spee* entered the neutral port of Montevideo in Uruguay. By international law, the British could not follow, and prowled outside. The damage to *Graf Spee* was not serious. Only one of her six 11in guns was out of action, and she had 36 dead and 60 wounded, whereas half the British cruisers' main armament was disabled. Then followed a game of bluff. By a clever use of signal traffic, and deliberate breaches of security by their embassy staff in Montevideo, the British successfully fooled Langsdorff into believing that the fleet carrier *Ark Royal* and battlecruiser *Renown* were in the offing, instead of several days' steaming away. Fortunately Langsdorff was not in the mould of the great fighting captains of the Royal Navy, such as Vian, or Warburton-Lee, or he might have sortied and crushed the cruisers. Instead he scuttled his ship and committed suicide.

In January 1940, Lieutenant Ronnie Hay and other Fleet Air Arm pilots were returning overland via Paris from deck-landing training in the Mediterranean.

> Walking down the Champs Elysee, we stopped to gloat over a captured ME 109 on display. We were rather shocked to see how good it looked, and that we would have to fight it.

For the next three years the Fleet Air Arm fought in obsolete aircraft against superior German and Japanese types. The British aircraft industry seemed unable to produce high-performance aircraft capable of operating off carriers. The Fleet Air Arm had to wait for American naval aircraft before it could face the enemy on equal, and finally better, terms.

Spring 1940 brought little to celebrate. On the morning of 9 April the Germans invaded Denmark and Norway. Denmark, totally unprepared, surrendered by lunchtime. The Norwegians fought back with spirit, although simultaneous landings at Oslo, Kristiansand, Stavanger, Bergen, Trondheim, and Narvik taxed their limited and unprepared military resources to breaking point. Both France and Britain reacted by sending forces to Norway, landing in three places: in central Norway at Namsos and Andalsnes, each side of Trondheim, and in north Norway at Narvik.

The first Allied troops to land were Marines from the cruisers *Sheffield* and *Glasgow*, whose task was to secure the harbour and road bridges at Namsos in advance of the force under Major General Carton de Wiart, arriving two days later. As soon as the main force arrived, the Marines were re-embarked in their ships. At Andalsnes, a few days later, a force formed by the Royal Marine Detachments of *Nelson*, *Hood*, and *Barham*, then refitting in the United Kingdom, landed from four sloops. They had a more ambitious task than the Namsos party. Having covered the disembarkation of the main force, they were to hold the landing place and railhead at Andalsnes.

Whether on ship or shore, the Allies were subjected to almost continual air attack. The Germans had seized the key airfields in Norway, and quickly gained air superiority. The British troops, who were neither trained nor equipped for winter warfare, were incapable of moving off the roads, and were easy targets for air attack. They were also outclassed by the German Mountain Division, which formed the core of the invading force. In under ten days the Allied forces in central Norway were pushed back, and evacuated through Namsos and Andalsnes. The Marines in both ports, who had been subjected to frequent air attacks, were the last to leave.

At Narvik the German General Deitl was left holding the town with about 4,000 men, half of them sailors, against 24,000 Allied troops, including the best Norwegian formation, the 6th Division, and French Alpine troops. The RM Fortress Unit had set up on the island of Harstad. In the Fortress Unit was a young 'Hostilities Only' officer, Second Lieutenant Stewart. After one month's training he had been sent to join the RM Fortress Unit, employed erecting defences at Scapa, and based on the transport ship *Mashobra* which was carrying landing craft, trucks, and other equipment for landing operations. He was appointed to the transport company. After some weeks *Mashobra* was sent to Norway. On arrival, Stewart was told

> to take a naval steam pinnace and guard the mouth of the fjord against submarine attack. I had a few men and a Lewis gun, some petrol cans, and some 5 lb charges. I was told if I saw a periscope I was to fire at it with Lewis gun, drop the empty petrol cans over the side so they look like depth charges and drop the 5 lb charges at the same time. We were only there for a night.
>
> We then moved up to Harstad. *Mashobra* was bombed. We kept a chart, and when I left the ship to go ashore, we had had 83 bombs within a 100 yards. The transport company went ashore to help the RAF build an airstrip. We could see the ships lying in the fjord under attack. We had no air protection other than an ancient Walrus.

Eventually, after long delays, an attack on Narvik was mounted on 27 May, the town was taken, and the Germans pushed back to the Swedish frontier. Despite this success, the German invasion of the Low Countries and France eventually forced the Allies to withdraw their troops and ships. The withdrawal under air attack was as chaotic as all that had gone before. Lieutenant Stewart:

> We were told to evacuate. We drove back to Harstad. *Mashobra* had been holed by a near hit, and she had been beached. Our CO told us we had been offered a trip back in the carrier *Glorious*. But he had said that the place of honour could go to the RAF. We were to make our own way back. So we separated, found ships returning home, and collected food and blankets from the *Mashobra*. The transport company managed to get on board a French ship that was going to Scapa. The trucks went on other ships. The men slung hammocks in the hold. The officers slept on deck. By the time we reached Scapa we had nearly run out of food. The French

could supply little food. We were down to a few tins of bully beef and gallons of rum.

It was lucky for Stewart that he did not travel back in the *Glorious*, because thanks to obtuseness on her captain's part, the carrier was caught and sunk with 1,474 of her ship's company on the way home by the battlecruisers *Scharnhorst* and *Gneisenau*. There were only 37 survivors.

Most Marines in this, the first amphibious campaign of the war, were manning guns in the battleships, battlecruisers, cruisers, and especially the anti-aircraft cruisers that faced the fury of the Luftwaffe in the narrow fjords. However, a few Marines had taken part in Fleet Air Arm attacks on key enemy targets. The first of these was on 10 April, the day after the German invasion of Norway, when 800 and 803 Squadrons in Blackburn Skuas attacked enemy shipping in Bergen. At that time the Skua, designed as a fighter/dive-bomber, was one of only two monoplane types with the Fleet Air Arm, and obsolete before it came into service. The other was the equally disappointing Roc. Captain R. T. Partridge RM, commanding 800 Squadron:

We took off and formed up over Hatston [in the Orkneys]. With a full load of fuel and a 500-lb semi-armour-piercing bomb, we were overweight and unstable. Going across [the North Sea] in the dark the two squadrons got separated. I was in the following squadron, and we arrived over the Norwegian coast as dawn was breaking. Bergen lies quite a long way up a fjord. We followed this up, and circled over the harbour, looking for the target and the other squadron. We saw neither, until my observer said 'there they are', and we saw a single Skua, which turned out to be the last aircraft of the other squadron in a steep dive, attacking a cruiser lying alongside a pier in the harbour.

We closed in, I put the squadron in line astern, and we dived down-sun, following very closely on the tail of the last Skua of the previous squadron. The ship stood out very clearly and appeared to be trying to get underway. There was one anti-aircraft gun on her quarterdeck firing steadily, but apart from that very little opposition from the ship itself. I dropped my bomb which was a near miss on the starboard bow, climbed away, and made my getaway out to sea to the RV for the rest of my squadron. The remainder dived down but I did not see how they did, but we joined up off the coast of Norway and started our trip back to the Orkneys.

The sortie had been successful. They sank the cruiser *Königsberg*, the first major German warship sunk by air attack in the Second World War, and the first warship sunk in action by dive-bombing. Partridge was awarded the DSO.

Others among the small band of Marines in the Fleet Air Arm were also busy. Norrie Martin, now a flight commander in the *Ark Royal*, was flying Swordfish biplanes, nicknamed 'Stringbags'.

This was to be our first air operation in which we might expect determined opposition from the air and the ground. I was a bit scared, but when I realised my flight was looking to me for leadership, the adrenalin started pumping, and I was no longer afraid.

810 Squadron was flown off to bomb frozen lakes where German aircraft were landing, or, alternatively to bomb Trondheim airfield. Flying conditions were very bad over Norway on April 25th – snow, clouds and very mountainous terrain made it impossible to find the lakes we were supposed to bomb. So we proceeded to our alternate target of Trondheim airfield.

On arrival over the airfield at about 6,000 feet, we could see many fires on the ground, which told us the other squadrons had been there already. We attacked in line astern and were met with fairly heavy and accurate flak. We each had six 250-lb bombs and eight 25-lb anti-personnel bombs. I was fourth in line and dropped my 250-lb bombs in the hangar area. I then climbed up to make a second attack with my 25-lb bombs. After my first attack I lost sight of the rest of the squadron.

The flak was most impressive – red and green tracer. It was hard to realize that I was being fired at. I remember laughing and saying to my observer, 'They are trying to hit us'. He wasn't very amused. As I made the second attack, the flak seemed heavier. This of course was because the rest of the squadron had dropped all their bombs in one salvo and gone, leaving me as the only aircraft in the area as a target for the flak.

I made my getaway and flew down the fjord and out to sea, when I became aware that we were very short of fuel and hadn't enough to get back to the ship. I suppose I had been hit during the attack and the fuel had leaked. Mercifully, I saw a destroyer escorting a merchant ship about ten miles to the north, so I decided to ditch alongside her.

I ditched with the aircraft nose-up 70 degrees, and stalled in from about 10 feet. The dinghy came out at once and I stepped in without getting my feet wet. The Stringbag floated for about 40 seconds, and my

Observer and Airgunner clambered over the centre section of the plane into the dinghy.

He and his crew were picked up by HMS *Maori*, and taken to Scotland. Here, along with other aircrew who had ditched and been picked up by destroyers, they picked up a replacement aircraft and flew to Hatston in the Orkneys to await *Ark Royal*'s return to Scapa. As soon as she arrived:

We landed on '*Ark*' and almost at once proceeded to the Narvik area. We had a tumultuous welcome on board, as most of us had been given up for dead. We arrived off Narvik and began intensive flying operations, mainly so far as 810 Squadron was concerned, to endeavour to put out of action the railway running from Narvik to the Swedish border. This carried the iron from Sweden to Narvik, from whence it was shipped to Germany [or would be once Narvik was back in German hands].

On return from one of these raids, in which he and Captain Skeen RM each led a section, he broadcast an account to the ship's company:

We split into two sections and proceeded independently to our pre-arranged targets. Captain Skeen's section went up to a large railway bridge near the Swedish border, and each aircraft carried out two attacks on this objective and on a tunnel nearby. One pilot obtained two magnificent hits right on the middle of the track on the bridge, and Captain Skeen placed a bomb salvo into the mouth of the tunnel. My section went to a place called Hunddallen where we were greeted by the pleasing sight of a train standing in the railway station. This we attacked and I managed to hit the train with a 250-lb bomb. It caught fire and the front half overturned. We were greeted by flak and machine-gun fire, but although two aircraft were hit there was no damage to personnel.

Ronnie Hay flew Skuas and Rocs from *Ark Royal* off Norway. His first sortie was to dive-bomb Trondheim, followed by fighter patrols over Andalsnes. His first kill was a Heinkel III in the Namsos area; a good effort since the Skua was slower, and had only four forward-firing machine-guns, and a rear gunner with a First World War vintage Lewis gun. Hay and his fellow aircrew were not issued with maps, only charts, which were fine for making a landfall from the sea, but useless once over land. He also flew defence of the fleet missions in the Roc, which had no forward-firing guns, just a four-gun powered turret in the back; his job was to shoot down shadowers. On one occasion he saw a JU 88 about 20 miles away. As he was lower than me, I thought I could dive and catch him. When I was quite close he spotted me. I saw a puff of exhaust smoke as he increased power, and I knew he would outrun me. The only way to get my guns to bear, was to tip right forward and invert my aircraft, telling my gunner to fire when he saw the enemy. My gunner pulled the trigger, and after one round had a stoppage. All four guns were useless.

The arrangements for air defence were elementary, there was no radio control, and no radar. On one occasion on coming back to *Ark*, she was steaming cross-wind. I flew alongside, and when they saw me, she turned into wind. After landing, they said 'where have you been?'

As a consequence of the German occupation of Norway, Marines landed to secure the Faroe Islands and Iceland, to forestall the enemy. These small unopposed operations were successful, ensuring that the Allies, not the Germans, had the use of these islands as air and sea bases. This was to prove absolutely crucial in the Battle of the Atlantic.

The Royal Marines played a very minor part in the Battle of France in May and June 1940. However three small parties were involved in the last days of the campaign. On the evening of 11 May, the Chatham Division was told to provide 200 men for 'a defensive role in an unknown place'. They were selected in the old makeshift way, some of them reservists, and under Major Mitchell they were taken to Dover and embarked in two destroyers, where they learned their destination was the Hook of Holland. Here they were to hold the port for the arrival of a force which would land and advance to the Hague, the seat of the Dutch Government. The destroyers landed them, and departed at high speed, leaving the Marines with four machine-guns, two Lewis guns, and their rifles. Having flushed out some German snipers from nearby houses, probably airborne troops, all was quiet except for air raids, and in the evening, three enemy aircraft dropping parachute troops some distance away.

The next morning the force arrived, a mixed battalion of Irish and Welsh Guards. At this stage a German mechanized column began to advance on the Hook from Rotterdam, fortunately too late to prevent the Queen of the Netherlands from reaching the Hook and embarking in the destroyer *Hereward* for England. No sooner was the Queen safely away than the Germans comprehensively bombed the town. The German mechanized column halted and dug in about 2,500 yards from the

Marines. The planned advance to the Hague was now redundant since the Dutch Government had gone. After some further minor adventures, the Guards and Marines left in three destroyers the next day, under heavy air attack.

On 23 May another hastily mustered company left Chatham for Boulogne to cover the naval parties demolishing port installations. The Boulogne party managed to withdraw without casualties once their task was complete, arriving back at Chatham in the early hours of 24 May. They had not been back long when the Royal Marine Office in London ordered another party to be formed. It was commanded by Captain Courtice, who had been second-in-command of the Boulogne party, and consisted of 2 other officers and 85 NCOs and Marines, some of whom had also just returned from Boulogne, organized into two platoons and a Vickers machine-gun section (two guns), and a signal section. At 0023 hours on Saturday 25 May Courtice and his men were landed at Calais, already occupied by the British 30th Infantry Brigade.

This brigade was hardly in a better state than Courtice's force. The Queen Victoria's Rifles (QVR), a TA battalion, had left its transport and signals vehicles behind on orders from higher authority. Two-thirds of the men had rifles and the remainder pistols; but the battalion had none of the forty-three Bren light machine-guns it was supposed to have. The two regular battalions were not much better off. The 1st Battalion The Rifle Brigade (1 RB) had unloaded only half its transport and ammunition when the ship left for England. The 2nd Battalion King's Royal Rifle Corps (2 KRRC) had landed without eighty of its Bren guns, and the remainder had been loaded in a vessel that never arrived. The anti-tank battery had only eight guns instead of twelve. There was no artillery. 3rd Royal Tank Regiment (3 RTR), which had been fighting a delaying action against 10th Panzer Division south of Calais, had a handful of tanks out of the forty-eight with which it landed. The 10th Panzer Division had already started to attack the town with generous artillery and air support when Courtice's party arrived.

At first Captain Courtice's company was sent to assist French Marines to defend the Citadel, the old fortress in the middle of the old part of town. After a day of confused fighting, often under heavy air bombardment, most of Courtice's party established a defensive position in the area of the North Quay, along which the railway lines run to Boulogne station, between the port and an artificial lake. One of his platoons was about 300 yards back from the North Quay, in the dunes in support of 1 RB, and covering the approaches to the pier from which any evacuation would be most likely. Most of the British troops expected to be evacuated that night. But the War Cabinet decided that they should stay to draw off as much as possible of the German armour pressing up against the Anglo-French perimeter round Dunkirk, some twenty miles to the east. The Germans decided to continue the attack on Calais, instead of merely masking it while they dealt with the Dunkirk perimeter; it has been suggested that since the British Arras counterattack had inflicted losses on Rommel's 7th Panzer and the SS Totenkopf Divisions a few days before, the Germans were ultra-sensitive to any tank force on their flanks, perhaps unaware of just how few tanks 3 RTR had left.

Two hours after first light, supported by the artillery of XIX Panzer Corps, 10th Panzer Division renewed the assault, and by 0800 hours had taken the old town (Calais Nord). By early afternoon, the Marines' positions on the North Quay were under heavy attack and they were forced back. By 1800 hours it was all over. Captain Courtice, Lieutenants Hunter and Bruce, and all but twenty-one of his party were captured. Those that got away did so thanks to the initiative of Sergeants Mitchell and East. Both NCOs had been sent out by Courtice the previous night to locate Marines cut off in the day's fighting. On Mitchell's return at first light, he could not locate Courtice, who had withdrawn from his original position. Meanwhile East, after assisting wounded into boats towed in by minesweeping trawlers, was sent to find the brigadier commanding 30th Brigade with an important message. Eventually the two NCOs found themselves separated from their party, each with a group of Marines and soldiers. Mitchell, having spent most of the day bringing in wounded under mortar, artillery, and air bombardment, escaped with about 164 others in a small Royal Naval vessel that had grounded on the mud by the pier. As they were trying to refloat her, two bombs dropped nearby, and the waves caused by the blast floated her off. East, who had been similarly engaged assisting wounded during the day, joined with a party of others who had eluded capture, and hid from the Germans under the pier. As a small naval motor yacht, the *Gulvar*, passed close inshore that night, looking for survivors, East signalled with a torch. The *Gulvar*'s captain, concerned about fire from enemy guns on the pier, shouted through his loud-hailer that he could not stop, but would make one close pass, and the men would have to swim for it.

Four officers, and forty-seven Marines and soldiers, including East, made it to the yacht. Sergeant Mitchell was awarded the CGM, and East, for gallant service at Calais and Boulogne, the DSM.

One casualty of the withdrawal from Dunkirk, in which Marine units played no part, was Lieutenant Colonel V. C. Brown RM, who was the GSO 1 (chief of staff) of Montgomery's 3rd Infantry Division, the most efficient formation in the BEF. 'Marino' Brown, as he was called by Montgomery, was a highly proficient officer – he would not have lasted long under Monty if he had not been. His death was a great loss to the Corps: given Monty's interest in his protégés, had 'Marino' Brown lived, he might have become Chief of Staff of Eighth Army, or achieved high rank in some other capacity with the Army, perhaps commanding a corps or at least a division. Two other Marines who would play distinguished parts later in the war also served with the Army in France. Major B. W. 'Jumbo' Leicester was brigade major of the 8th Infantry Brigade in Monty's division. As with 'Marino' Brown, he would not have lasted long had he not been up to 3rd Division's exacting standards. He had served in the Sudan Camel Corps before the war, and was a graduate of the Army Staff Course at Camberley. Captain J. L. Moulton was a GSO 3 operations in GHQ BEF, and was involved in organizing the evacuation from La Panne and Dunkirk. He had escaped the tedium of pre-war Marine life by flying for four years in the Fleet Air Arm, and attending the Army Staff College.

Fleet Air Arm Marines also played a minor part in the Battle of France. Following the success of German dive-bombers, 801 Squadron was ordered to destroy a canal bridge near Nieuport, in Belgium. The RAF was to provide fighter escort. On arrival 801 Squadron could find no sign of a bridge, so bombed the canal. Hay:

> after pulling out, we thought we saw our RAF escort. When they got closer, we saw iron crosses on the wings, about a dozen ME 109s. I got chased half way across the Channel. Four of us got shot down. The camouflage of naval aircraft over water when viewed from above is pretty good. We had a tight turning circle because we were so slow. Every time the enemy got on my tail, I turned towards him and fired, and immediately turned back on course. He had a big turning circle, and took several miles to catch me each time. I did this about ten times. I was heartily relieved when he broke off the attack, perhaps because he was running short of fuel. I had about twenty holes in my wings.

The imminent fall of France led to the Prime Minister, Winston Churchill, writing to the Chiefs of Staff on 5 June 1940: 'I look to the Chiefs of Staff to propose me measures for a vigorous, enterprising, and ceaseless offensive against the whole occupied German coastline.' The War Office sent out letters asking for volunteers to join a special force for mobile operations. Those who responded were formed into Commandos. These did not include the Royal Marines, although the Adjutant General Royal Marines, General Sir Alan Bourne, was appointed the first Director Combined Operations (DCO), and the RM Brigade was placed at his disposal for operations. However, as events would show, the Army hijacked the concept from the outset. Bourne managed to set in motion a number of projects that would bear fruit in the future, but hardly surprisingly found being both Adjutant General RM and DCO impossible, and asked to relinquish the job of Adjutant General. Churchill, however, decided to give the DCO post to his friend Admiral of the Fleet Sir Roger Keyes, and Bourne was made his deputy, but only temporarily.

The name 'commando', which describes both the unit and the individual, was the brainchild of Lieutenant Colonel Dudley Clarke, the Military Assistant to the CIGS. He had been brought up in South Africa and read Denys Reitz's book *Commando*, describing the guerrilla operations of the Boer Commandos against the British in South Africa from 1900 to 1902.[2] To begin with, the term was regarded with suspicion by those responsible for paperwork in the War Office, and they referred to them in official documents as Special Service troops, SS for short. When it was pointed out this acronym had originated with Hitler's infamous black-shirted Schutzstaffeln, the term Special Service for units was discontinued, but, perversely, Commando brigades were called SS brigades until the last year of the war.

The RM Brigade never took part in any of the raids planned by Bourne, Keyes, or their successors. At the end of August, the brigade was sent on the aptly named Operation Menace, an attempt to bring the Vichy French garrison of Dakar in West Africa into the war on the British side. In the event the brigade never landed, because the garrison declined to change sides. The farce that ensued has been parodied by Evelyn Waugh in *Men at Arms*, his fictional account of his short time in the Royal Marines, thinly disguised as the Royal Corps of Halberdiers.

By the time the brigade returned from Freetown, where it had been languishing after the *opéra bouffe* Menace, the formation of a complete Royal Marine division had been approved, consisting of three brigades:

— 101st RM Brigade: 3rd and 5th RM
— 102nd RM Brigade: 1st and 2nd RM, and 8th Argylls
— 103rd RM Brigade: 7th, 8th, and 9th RM, plus 10th RM later

For most of its existence, the RM Division was deployed with 101st and 102nd Brigades in Scotland, and 103rd in cadre form at Dalditch Camp near Lympstone in Devon. The division was earmarked for a number of operations which never materialized, but which also kept any of the brigades from being used on raids, as originally envisaged. This idleness was partly self-inflicted by the Royal Marines themselves. One senior Marine staff officer expressed the view to the Director of Naval Plans that the RM Division should not be 'turned over to the Army' as happened in the First World War. The fact that the RMLI battalions and the Howitzer and Anti-Aircraft Brigades on the Western Front had been the only Royal Marines fighting on the main point of effort in the First World War seems to have escaped the officer who made this remark. The burden of his complaint was that the Marines had to raise a special battalion for the Zeebrugge raid, because the already formed battalions were fighting in France. In the cold accounting of war, the Zeebrugge raid, however gallantly conducted, was a minor affair, with very little impact on the outcome of the First World War; very different from the Western Front, where the war was ultimately won. Whether or not the staff officer concerned thought that the RM battalions in the First World War should have sat around doing nothing for four years on the off-chance of a raiding task coming up, he does not say. But that is the implication of his remark. In fact, as we shall see, it was only when the Royal Marines became involved alongside, or in conjunction with, the Army on the main point of effort, in the principal theatres of war, that the years of frustration and waste for the Corps ended. The Royal Marine battle 'to keep their amphibious force firmly in the Royal Navy's jurisdiction, to be used for operations which did not entail remaining in an Expeditionary Force when more suitable employment arose',[3] turned out to be a sterile pastime for a number of reasons; not least because the Navy was not interested in, and had no plans for, unilateral amphibious operations. Furthermore the most suitable employment for fighting men is marching towards the sound of the guns, not picking and choosing where they will fight.

After a year of frustration and disappointment, 1940 ended on a cheerful note for a small handful of Royal Marines. On the night of 11/12 November the air strike against the Italian Fleet in Taranto harbour was launched from HMS *Illustrious*. Originally the *Eagle* was also to have taken part, but she had been damaged in action off Calabria, so some of her aircraft were transferred to *Illustrious*. Twenty-one aircraft in two waves were launched from *Illustrious*, at 2040 hours and 2100 hours on 11 November. They achieved complete surprise, sinking three battleships at their moorings. The raid was led by Captain Oliver Patch RM. The C-in-C Mediterranean Fleet, Admiral Sir Andrew Cunningham, wrote:

> The 11th and 12th November 1940 will be remembered for ever as having shown once and for all that in the Fleet Air Arm the Navy has a devastating weapon. In a total flying time of about six and a half hours carrier to carrier, twenty aircraft inflicted more damage upon the Italian Fleet than was inflicted on the German High Seas Fleet in the daylight action at Jutland.

14

The Mediterranean and Atlantic, 1941–1942

The inactivity and boredom experienced by the ship's companies of the Grand Fleet for most of the First World War was in marked contrast to the busy life in destroyers in that war. Throughout the Second World War the whole Royal Navy, including capital ships, was kept at full stretch. This great effort, of course, encompassed the Royal Marine Detachments embarked in some seventy-six ships at the outbreak of war, and in many more by its end nearly six years later. The years 1941 and 1942 were hectic and perilous in the Mediterranean and Atlantic, with great losses of ships and men, and with the entry of Japan into the war at the end of 1941 the resources of the Royal Navy were spread even thinner, into the Indian Ocean and East Indies.

Royal Marines crewed a main armament turret as well as a share of the secondary armament in every battleship, battlecruiser, and cruiser. They also manned a heavy anti-aircraft battery of two twin barbettes in most carriers. Since 1916, the action station for the musicians of the Royal Marines band was in the bowels of the ship, in the Transmitting Station (TS) – every ship from the smallest cruiser upwards had a band, and playing their musical instruments was secondary to the vital task of operating the fire-control table in the TS. This table was the forerunner of a computer, and the musicians were in effect the human microchips manually making the correct connections in order to produce a firing solution. The sequence of events in arriving at this solution, was, in outline, as follows (the details and numbers of men involved of course varied depending on the class and type of ship).

In the gun director high above the bridge two operators followed the movement of the target through their telescopes, and in doing so trained the director around following the target, irrespective of where their own ship was pointing. A third operator in the director took a continuous reading of the range of the target using an optical rangefinder. Through a system of electrical circuits, the movement of the two telescopes in the director actuated pointers on dials on the fire-control table in the TS far below, giving the movement of the target relative to their own ship, and the target's elevation. As the range-taker spun the screws on his rangefinder to match the images of the target, the range was transmitted to the table in the TS. Simultaneously other information was being fed into the table, such as the outside air temperature, the barometric pressure, wind direction and speed, the temperature of the guns (as they heated up, their ballistic characteristics changed), the speed of their own ship, and the rotation of the earth relative to the ship's heading. All this information would be linked in so as to affect the needle settings which constantly altered on the numerous dials on the table as the ship changed course and speed. As the host of pointers on the table moved, each musician who monitored a small clutch of dials would turn the relevant handle on the table to keep a second pointer over the first. Turning the handles to follow pointers generated two final settings, which were transmitted through electrical circuits to the turrets. Here each turret trainer swivelled the turret to place his pointer in his dial over the one being controlled from the TS, while each gun layer elevated or depressed his gun by following the pointer on his dial. Each gun out of, say, three in a turret, would have different characteristics, demanding minute variations in how much each was elevated to hit a target at a given range; this would have been pre-calibrated and the gun layer's pointer adjusted accordingly.

The firing solution computed by the TS enabled the guns to be aimed in such a way that twenty or so seconds after the guns fired, shells and target would arrive in the same piece of sea. The target might be twelve or more miles away, steaming at 25 knots on an oblique course relative to the firing ship, which itself was moving at 30 knots, as well as rolling and pitching.

As each gun was reloaded, all the crew had to do was to snap shut the gun-ready interceptor switch, closing the electric circuit in the firing system and lighting a lamp in the director. When all gun-ready lamps were lit, the gunnery officer fired all guns together by pressing the trigger on a master pistol-grip, as soon as the downward roll of the ship levelled all guns. The accuracy of the ship's gunnery depended in great measure on the training and skill of the musicians in the TS. C. S. Forester, who is hardly a fan of the Marines, is correct when he wrote about the TS of a light cruiser in action:

> round the table of the Transmitting Station it was necessary that there should be discipline and courage. Trembling hands could not keep those pointers steady, nor cold minds distracted by fear be alert to follow the aimless wanderings of the guiding needles so that the guns above could continue to hurl forth their broadsides every ten seconds. Down here, far below the level of the sea, the men were comparatively protected from shell fire, but not far below their feet was the outer skin of the ship, and around them were the bunkers of fuel oil. Mine or torpedo might strike there, engulfing them in flame or water. Other compartments of the ship might be holed, and the sea pour in as the ship sank slowly; in that case it would be their duty to remain at their posts to keep the guns firing to the last, while above them there were only the difficult iron ladders up which they might eventually climb to precarious life.
>
> The Marine bandsmen were perfectly aware of all this – they were far too intelligent not to be.[1]

The Royal Marines bands lost a great many men at sea in the Second World War, and their casualty rate in proportion to their total numbers was high. Several ships sank before anyone in the TS could get out, including the battleship *Barham* and the cruisers *Neptune* and *Gloucester*, in which every member of the Royal Marines Band was lost; and in other ships only some musicians escaped.

The introduction of gunnery radar as the war progressed speeded up range-taking and spotting, but while greatly improving the chances of a hit with the first salvo did not diminish the importance of the TS. Ship-to-ship gunnery was complicated enough, anti-aircraft gunnery even more so, as the target was moving in three dimensions at a much higher speed than a surface target.

It is impossible to cover every action at sea at which the Royal Marines, including the Band Service, were present; to do so would require an account of the activities of every capital ship and cruiser of the Royal Navy in the Second World War. Marines were present at triumphs such as the stunning victory over the Italian Fleet off Cape Matapan, and the Second Battle of Sirte in which cruisers under Rear Admiral Vian saw off a 15in Italian battleship, two 8in heavy cruisers, a 6in cruiser and ten destroyers. Marines also played their part in the events leading to the sinking of the battleship *Bismarck*, during the course of which every member of the Royal Marine Detachment and band was lost in the *Hood*.

CRETE, 1941

In May 1941 Marines fought at sea and ashore in the battle for Crete. Since the Italian invasion of Greece in October 1940, the British had used Suda Bay in Crete as an advanced naval base for ships taking part in the Greek campaign. In January 1941 it was decided to send MNBDO 1 out there to fulfil the role for which it had been raised (defending naval bases), and to raise a second MNBDO in England. MNBDO 1 arrived in Egypt via the Cape, just as the British were evacuating Greece following the successful German invasion. Troops were urgently needed to defend Crete, which was rightly forecast as being next on the German invasion agenda. Some 27,000 troops evacuated from Greece, mainly New Zealanders and Australians, but also British and Greek infantry, had been deposited in Crete to join the British garrison. Some of these troops were in a low state of morale, and many were without much of their equipment and weapons, including 104 tanks, 40 anti-aircraft guns, 292 field guns, 1,812 machine-guns, about 8,000 vehicles, and most of the signal equipment, all of which had been lost in Greece. The lack of radios was to be critical in the forthcoming battle. There was only enough shipping for about half MNBDO 1 to be transported to Crete, whither their commander, Major General E. C. Weston, had preceded them. Their task, in Churchill's words, was to turn Suda Bay into 'a second Scapa'.[2]

Originally Weston was charged with the command of all Allied forces in Crete, which became known as CREFORCE. At the end of April 1941, Major General Freyberg VC, the GOC of the New Zealand Division (CO of the Hood Battalion in the RN Division on the Western Front in the First World War), took over command of CREFORCE, and Weston took over the Canea sector of the island's defence. Eventually the MNBDO was deployed with most of the 2nd AA Regiment around Suda, Canea, and Heraklion, coast gunners at Maleme and Rethymno, and S Searchlight Battery and Regimental Headquarters of 11th Searchlight Regiment, without its lights, in the Suda area. The Searchlight Battery was to have taken over equipment from an Army searchlight battery, but was deployed as infantry, equipped only with rifles and Lewis guns.

The commander of S Battery was Major (later Major General) R. W. Madoc RM. His battery, which was about 400 strong, had spent the latter half of 1940 on anti-invasion duties in an infantry role in the area of Deal in Kent. The battery mounted some 40 Lewis guns at various points all over the ship taking them from Alexandria to Crete. As they approached the island just after sunset, a German aircraft overflew them, possibly without having seen them, and was shot down by massed Lewis gun fire. This was a good start, but about the only thing to go right from then on. The island had been comprehensively bombed for some days before S Battery's arrival. Madoc:

> We did not know Crete was about to be invaded. On arrival, I was told by General Weston that invasion was imminent. Suda Bay was a shambles, with beached and sunk vessels all over the place, including the cruiser *York*, sunk by an Italian explosive motor boat.

On the same ship as Madoc was Gunner Whelan Royal Artillery, attached to the 11th Searchlight Regiment, who took a pretty jaundiced view of being in a Marine unit. They landed in the middle of an air raid, bowed down with rifle, full marching order, canvas bag with sun helmet, and two kit bags each.

To begin with S Battery was deployed to defend Suda village and the Royal Navy Headquarters. Madoc was ordered to select searchlight positions around Suda Bay, but there was no evidence of any searchlights becoming available. At night there was more danger from trigger-happy troops than from the enemy. Any sign of a light, from a match to a cigarette to dimmed headlights, drew fire, mainly from Australians. On the morning of 20 May, Madoc was having a shave and wash when he saw the German parachute drop west of Canea. Soon afterwards he was ordered to move towards Canea in trucks, to keep south of the town, but told nothing else. He took up a position south-west of the town, but had no contact with the enemy. Whelan: 'Air activity was still intense, but now we tended to ignore it, except when it became too close and we were directly fired on.' Various groups of people came through the position, including Cretan civilians, and some drunk sailors looking for 'the bloody battle, mate'. Later, a drunken Australian appeared,

> dragging a Greek civilian, aged about forty, with an automatic pistol pointed at his head. 'This is a bloody Fifth Columnist', the Australian cried, 'and I'm going to blow his bloody brains out'. I hastily advised him that we were military police [not true], and that prisoners were our responsibility. The Aussie stumbled off presumably to find more spies, but most likely some more drink.

Meanwhile other parts of MNBDO 1 had been in action elsewhere in the battle against German paratroopers at Maleme, Rethymno, and Heraklion. By 27 May the battle for Crete had virtually been lost, and Freyberg, the commander of CREFORCE, gave the order for the troops in the Canea–Suda area to withdraw over the mountains to Sphakia on the south coast for evacuation by sea. The 14th Infantry Brigade at Heraklion, including about 160 MNBDO anti-aircraft gunners, ignorant about conditions in the west of Crete, thought that the Germans were beaten. So they were somewhat surprised to learn that the Navy would take them off on the night of 28 May. Thanks to the discipline and training of the British regular infantry battalions in this brigade, the withdrawal and evacuation went without a hitch. When daylight came, the destroyers packed with troops were dive-bombed by Stukas for six hours. Over 360 soldiers were killed, and about the same number seriously wounded. The majority of the Heraklion force dead were killed at sea during the voyage to Alexandria, not in contact with the enemy ashore.

At Rethymno the two Australian battalions continued to deny the airfield to the enemy until overwhelmed by superior force. The withdrawal to Sphakia began in chaos, and continued that way. In the darkness parties of men and vehicles cut in from side tracks, mixing in with units already on the main road, and splitting them up. Madoc:

> Every vehicle was packed with demoralised troops. A truck was broken down on the pass [at the highest point on the track over the mountains], blocking the route, and preventing ambulances loaded with wounded from driving down to Sphakia. The occupants of the broken-down truck refused to move. Eventually we got them out at gun point, and pushed the truck over a cliff.
>
> Finally we reached a check point at a village about 11 miles north of

Sphakia, which became known as 'Water Point Village', here there was some semblance of order.

The withdrawal was followed up by troops of the German 5th Mountain Division, who had been flown in to the airfields secured by their parachute brethren. The tactics employed by these well-trained troops were to advance to contact, and on bumping and identifying Allied positions to send mortars and machine-guns to high ground on either flank, to cover the subsequent attack, again if possible from the flank. In common with most German troops throughout the Second World War, even these mountain troops did not operate well at night. But as over half of CREFORCE, including the MNBDO, were not infantrymen, they lacked the training to take advantage of the Germans' inadequate night-fighting skills.

Although the Luftwaffe continued to strafe troops on the road to Sphakia, the intensity of German air activity tailed off after 27 May. That day saw the last of the series of heavy air strikes on land, because most of the Luftwaffe's VII Air Corps was withdrawn from Greece and the Aegean to prepare for the invasion of Russia. But the German air onslaught on shipping did not slacken.

On 28 May Major Garrett, a staff officer at MNBDO Headquarters, told Madoc that he had been ordered to form a rearguard to protect Sphakia just north of 'Water Point Village', and that Madoc was to be his second-in-command. The 2/7th Australian battalion, part of 19th Australian Brigade, was out in front of them as a screen. The MNBDO rearguard force was about 400 strong, a mixed bag formed into four companies made up from the remnants of MNBDO units on Crete.

All that day and the next, the MNBDO rearguard was shot up from the air, but had no contact with enemy ground forces. By the night of 29/30 May, Madoc remembered,

> All British and Greek troops, including Female Greek Nurses, had passed through our position, and we were ordered to withdraw from the area of the village. We still had had no contact with the enemy.

The plan was for the 2/7th Australian Battalion to withdraw through the MNBDO rearguard, after which they would pull out too. Madoc, his batman, driver, and one other officer were the last to leave. He found the MNBDO force astride the top of the pass above Sphakia, deployed among rocks. It was impossible to dig in. Here they were to form the ultimate rearguard. Major General Freyberg had his HQ located in some caves above Sphakia, about a mile from the village. The commander of 19th Australian Brigade, under whose command the MNBDO force had been placed, was on the beach. Madoc:

> The MNBDO was to remain until everyone had gone. We just hoped we could hold off the Germans until the evacuation was complete, and then get off on the last boats. The morale of the troops passing through on the road was not good. Where we were was OK, as was our morale. We had steep mountains on one side and a sheer precipice on the other. The enemy mortared us. We had no mortars, only our rifles and Lewis guns. We were short of water and food.
>
> On 31 May, Garrett sent me down to Sphakia village to try to find supplies. I was also to recce the route for our withdrawal. I took four men with me. It was a three hour trip each way. The village of Sphakia was a shambles; looting of stores was rife, and there were no troops available or willing, to help us take supplies back up the hill. On my return Garrett told the company commanders to be prepared to withdraw that night. During the day, the Germans had tried to outflank us.
>
> Suddenly, at 2030 we were told to withdraw immediately.

They were ordered to form a protective screen round General Weston's HQ, in the cave which he had taken over from Freyberg, who had been evacuated on Churchill's orders. Freyberg was Ultra-indoctrinated and could not be allowed to fall into German hands. Madoc was told to report to Weston, who told him that only 100 of the MNBDO force would be evacuated that night. The remainder would remain behind, as that was the last night of the withdrawal. As Madoc and Garrett were, in Weston's words, 'specialists', they were to be among the lucky ones to get away. Madoc returned to Garrett and told him what Weston had said. Together they chose the 100 to go. Madoc:

> We went and joined the column on the narrow track leading down to the beach. Control was very difficult. A number of Army Commandos pushed through and jumped the queue shouting 'make way for Layforce'. They said they had orders to form a beach defensive line. I sent my Adjutant, Captain Gale, on to the beach to say we were coming. I never saw him again. He got away in a ship. When we arrived [at the beach], we saw the last three ships move out. It was only about 2.30 am, but quite light. We

had missed them. This was the worst shock of all. The chaps in the rearguard were going to be dumped. I felt numb.

The Army commandos referred to by Madoc came from two battalions and the headquarters of Layforce, commanded by Colonel Robert Laycock, a brave and competent soldier. An account of Layforce's somewhat frustrating, inglorious, and chequered career up to their arrival in Crete has no place in this book.[3] It was an ill-starred formation, and by May 1941 many of its soldiers were cynical after almost a year of disappointment. They had been sent to Suda expecting to raid German airfields on Greece. Their arrival coincided with the withdrawal to Sphakia. Some of them gave a good account of themselves during the initial stages of the withdrawal. Others did not. Just before he left Crete, Freyberg told Laycock, 'You were the last to come so you will be the last to go.'[4] This was confirmed by Weston, who ordered him to remain until the MNBDO rearguard and 2/7th Australian Battalion got away. In fact, two days before this, New Zealanders being evacuated in HMAS *Perth* found some Army commandos skulking on board. Laycock, his headquarters, and most of his men got away, and it is probable that the Army commandos who pushed past Madoc were Laycock's party. At the last moment he probably bamboozled Weston into authorizing his evacuation, just when Weston was about to lay on him the responsibility for surrendering the remainder of CREFORCE. It is a measure of Laycock's personality that he persuaded Weston to change his mind, not least giving Layforce priority over his own Marines. Weston was flown out by a Sunderland flying boat that night. Laycock passed the task of capitulation to one of his battalion commanders. This 'devil take the hindmost' attitude was a feature of some special service forces during the Second World War, and is not entirely unknown in Special Forces to this day.

Whelan:

The night before the remains of the Company were helping to hold the last sensible defensive position on the route to the little port from which the Army was being evacuated. Wisely the Germans had not attacked us frontally as we guarded the head of the winding road which descended rapidly by hundreds of feet to the sea.

We were ordered to leave the position and made our way in the darkness to the little port. From our eyrie we had seen little sign of life on the narrow coastal strip below, and it was assumed that the job was done, and that only we of the rearguard were left to be embarked. As we marched onward our progress became slower and slower, and I became aware of shadowy crowds around us, and halts that became progressively longer as the night wore on. Eventually our progress came to a complete halt, so I lay down and fell asleep. When I woke the sun was up, and I could see there were hundreds of men around me – some of them engaged in trying to smash up rifles and bren guns.

None of our group had got away, and I soon met up with the Major [Madoc] and some of his officers together with a few dozen Marines. The Major suggested that the only sensible thing we could do was to clean the sweat and dust of the past few weeks off ourselves. We were on our way to the water's edge when he was hailed by another officer from the same Corps [The Royal Marines] who said that a derelict landing craft could be made serviceable, but there was no fuel. It was as a result of this news that we searched [were sent to search] for diesel oil and thereby missed the last boat.

The officer who sailed in charge of the last boat was Major Garrett. Madoc:

> I got a message that Garrett was leaving in the LCM [MLC], offering me a place. I had to decide to go with him or stay with the troops. I decided to stay, as there were over 1,000 MNBDO people altogether left behind.

Madoc was the senior officer of the MNBDO left on Crete, and his honourable, courageous, and entirely correct decision meant that he spent the remainder of the war in a prison camp.

The Royal Navy suffered 1,828 dead and 183 wounded during the battle and evacuation of Crete. Three cruisers and six destroyers were sunk; four battleships, six cruisers, and seven destroyers were damaged. There were Marines on all the cruisers and battleships.

Garrett had set off at 0855 hours, having got the MLC's twin engines going, taking with him 4 officers and 134 other ranks, including 56 Marines. They found diesel, water, and rations before slipping. There was a slight mist which must have hidden them from the Luftwaffe, who were bombing Sphakia as they slowly motored out on one screw (the other was fouled). After three hours they reached a cave on Gavdopula Island, where they freed the cable fouling the port screw, and topped up their water containers from a well.

That night they sailed, and made reasonable progress despite continuous engine breakdowns. By the third day they were down to a sixth of a pint of water per man per day, and the engines had broken down beyond repair, possibly because of unsuitable or contaminated fuel. They rigged sails, but the MLC was so unhandy under sail, and with such little steerage way at 1¼ knots, which was all they could make, that to tack they had to put men over the side to push her head round by swimming. They tried to attract the attention of passing ships and aircraft by burning fuel oil, but to no avail. They were passed by another MLC, which had insufficient fuel to tow them, but said it would report their position. On the eighth day two men died. On the evening of 8 June they sighted the coast of North Africa, finally beaching seventeen miles west of Sidi Barrani in Egypt. After reaching the road just inland, they were collected in trucks belong to the 1st RM AA Regiment, MNBDO.

The other MLC, under the command of 2 naval officers, with about 60 troops, including 2 Marine officers, made it too. Some time after passing Garrett's MLC they ran out of fuel, and like him had to rig sails from blankets on boathooks and spars. They made the coast at Sidi Barrani the day before Garrett.

After Crete, MNBDO 1 was refitted, and many of its units sent to the Indian Ocean before the Japanese attack. The Coast Regiment and other units mounted guns at Diego Garcia, the Seychelles, and Addu Atoll, and remained to defend them, particularly Addu, which became a highly secret fleet base.

The latter half of 1942 was to see the Royal Marines involved in three raids, one at Bordeaux successful, the others, at Dieppe and Tobruk, disasters.

DIEPPE, AUGUST 1942

In late November 1941 a message went out to all Royal Marines establishments and Royal Naval ships asking for Royal Marine trained personnel to volunteer for special duties of a hazardous nature. At last, a Royal Marine Commando was to be formed. The host of volunteers that responded reported to Deal, where their CO, Lieutenant Colonel J. P.

Phillipps, was waiting for them. He had recently finished the course at the Army Staff College, Camberley, where he had summoned Captain Peter Hellings to help him sketch out the structure of the Commando. Together they had decided that it would be organized into a headquarters and three rifle companies each of three platoons, rather than the five smaller rifle, or fighting, troops which the Army Commandos had adopted. Quite why the Army decided on this curious organization is a mystery: one suggestion heard by the author is that some of the early Army Commando COs were gunners or cavalrymen, who did not understand companies, and opted for troops, with which they were more familiar. The troop was an unwieldy set-up, but as we shall see, the first Royal Marine Commando, and all the others, were eventually to adopt the five rifle troop establishment, and keep it until 1961.

At Deal, stringent medical and physical tests weeded out the faint hearts, and interviews with the CO or the second-in-command, Major R. D. Houghton, acted as yet another filter. Training was rigorous, and even more men were returned to unit (RTU) as the tests got tougher and tougher. At first it was thought that the Commando would be employed in the Far East or Pacific, but this was later changed. Although the Army had by now set up the Commando Basic Training Depot at Achnacarry in Scotland, Phillipps, an independent-minded officer, decided to carry out his training based at Dorlin, on the shores of Kentra Bay. Eventually some of the Commando spent some time on an 'acquaint' at Achnacarry, where only live ammunition was used on exercises, and the excellent twelve-week course produced a first-class Commando soldier.

In May 1942 the Commando moved to the Isle of Wight to join the Special Service (SS) Brigade. Here most men lived in billets, being paid 6s 8d a day with which to pay their landladies for food and accommodation. Out of this sum, the landlady was required to provide breakfast and supper, as well as a packed meal for lunch. By now it was clear that some cross-Channel operation was afoot, but the target was still kept secret while training continued apace. The target was Dieppe, and it was to be the largest and most ambitious raid conducted in the Second World War, and involved some 5,000 men of the Canadian 2nd Infantry Division, three Commandos (3 and 4 Army Commandos, and the Royal Marine Commando), and 50 US Rangers (the US equivalent of Commandos), as well as 237 warships and landing craft, including 8 destroyers, supported by 74 squadrons of aircraft, of which 66 were fighter squadrons.

The intelligence was scanty. The beach gradient was calculated from a holiday snapshot. The locations of German strongpoints were known, but gun positions on the headland cliffs overlooking the beach were missed. German strengths and deployments were not known. The plan was for attacks by two Canadian battalions, landing at Puits and Pourville, on headlands on each side of the town, followed by the main assault by Canadian infantry and armour on the beach in front of the town of Dieppe. This was to be followed up by a further Canadian battalion landing at Pourville, and passing through to link up with armour landed over the main town beach. Two coastal batteries further out on each flank, at Varengeville and Berneval, were allocated to 4 Commando and 3 Commando respectively. In the original plan these batteries had been assigned to two parachute battalions, but the problems of finding days when the weather and tidal conditions were suitable for both parachute operation and seaborne assault persuaded the planners to substitute Commandos for parachute battalions. The substitution was not made until after the first attempt at the raid in early July had been cancelled because of adverse weather for the parachute part of the operation. By that stage, everyone had been briefed, and the raid should have been cancelled for good, instead of being allowed to go ahead a month later. Even before that 'security was abysmal', according to James Hill, then commanding the 1st Parachute Battalion.[5]

The task allocated to the Royal Marine Commando, landing after the Canadians, was to force an entrance to the harbour in the gunboat HMS *Locust*, followed by the remainder of the Commando in French fast patrol boats called *chasseurs*. Once inside they were to destroy the dock installations, capture prisoners and intelligence material, and cut out any craft that could be used by the Germans as invasion craft. The intelligence material was apparently held in a safe in the Dieppe port offices. This safe was to be the special objective for a Marine who had been a safe-blower in civilian, or rather criminal, life, before the war. In all, the Commando had a pretty full programme to meet. Why invasion craft should have concerned anyone at this stage in the war is a mystery.

Surprise was lost when a small German convoy exchanged fire with part of the force out to sea off Puits and Berneval, alerting the batteries there. 3 Commando got some men ashore, and using their initiative kept the battery occupied by sniping with small arms. About half the Commando landed on an adjacent beach, and were all killed or captured. At Puits the Canadians were landed late, and never got off the beach. 4 Commando landed successfully without being fired at and captured and held the Varengeville battery, the only unit to take its objective that day. At Pourville the Canadians were landed in the wrong place, although the follow-up battalion did succeed in penetrating further inland than anyone else, before being driven back by the Germans. The main assault by two Canadian battalions and twenty-seven tanks was a disaster. The supporting fire by destroyers alone was far too light to have much effect on the concrete defences. Most tanks slithered, stripped their tracks, and bogged down on the shingle beach, where they were sitting ducks for anti-tank guns. Those that did get off the beach were stopped by concrete roadblocks. The Canadian infantry were slaughtered.

As HMS *Locust* approached the harbour, it became clear that the German guns in the cliffs had not been silenced, and that there was absolutely no possibility of the Royal Marine Commando carrying out its task. The landing force commander, Major General Roberts, the GOC Canadian 2nd Infantry Division, was embarked in HMS *Kelpy*, but could not see the beach because of the smoke-screen laid by the ships in support of the landings. Acting on incorrect information, and unaware of the mayhem on the main beaches, he ordered the Royal Marine Commando to land on one of these beaches (White), in support of the Canadian infantry battalion. The Commando was to pass through the town and attack batteries on the cliff on the east headland from the south. One can imagine the utter chaos this last-minute change of plan must have brought in its train. The CO had to transfer his Commando from the *Locust* and the *chasseurs* into landing craft which had been used in the earlier waves, and brief them on the new task, in very short order.

Captain Peter Hellings, commanding A Company, reported later:

The Commando started to move towards the shore, it being about 1130 hours, smoke was provided by the *chasseurs*, who accompanied us within 500 yards. Shell fire opened on the boats almost immediately, at about 4,000 yards increasing in intensity as the range shortened. The fire appeared to consist of 3-inch to 4-inch mortar bombs, or a similar size, intermingled with low-angle gun fire of about 4-inch and tracer shell of about 2 lbs which may have come from tanks. The range was shortening and rifle and LMG fire was becoming apparent, the *chasseur* being no longer able to support the force owing to the depth of water.

The MLC in which we had embarked had done the main landing and was in need of repair, one engine being out of commission and the deck of the MLC was washing down with water [awash]. Owing to one engine being out of commission and the other very hot, steering was difficult, and our speed reduced which resulted in an ever increasing distance between boats. Just prior to reaching the shore, and while in thick smoke, we broke down, which may have been the result of a near miss, or the overheating of our engine. The engine was started after about two minutes, and we proceeded on toward the shore out of the smoke in time to see the Colonel's MLC, and an ALC containing Captain Deveraux and one platoon, and Major Houghton's ALC arrive under heavy mortar and MG fire. Fire was intense and any attempt to reach the houses [in the town] would have been most hazardous. Colonel Phillipps stood up in his MLC and waved the remaining boats to return to the cover of the smoke. One ALC was extracted, the Colonel's MLC turned broadside on and I believe from survivors' reports, caught fire.

My MLC at this stage received a hit close to the stern which finished any attempt at steering, leaving us some 300 yards off shore. Smoke was used in quantity and we were able to increase the distance [from the beach] by about 200 yards before the engine finally went. After some period, a *chasseur* took the MLC in tow and returned to *Locust*, where the company were placed on board and told to await orders. I reported to Commander Ryder who sent me to General Roberts. I reported that White and Red Beaches were held by the enemy.

Most of the Royal Marine Commando's landing craft had been hit and disabled. Meanwhile two other landing craft had already beached, under heavy mortar and machine-gun fire. The one which had taken in Major Houghton blew up almost immediately after the troops had landed, probably because it contained all the explosives for the demolition tasks in the harbour, and had taken a direct hit by a mortar bomb. Those of the Commando who got ashore were all killed or taken prisoner. The remainder were picked up by *chasseurs* or other craft.

Marine McConkey was in a craft behind the Colonel's, which was hit just after being waved off.

I swam away from our landing craft and made for a big buoy, but after looking back saw Will McKnight still clinging to the side of the craft. So I and a marine called Jack Cowan swam back, and in no uncertain language asked him why he was waiting for the craft to blow up. He said, 'I canna swim, Mac'.

I said, 'You can't sink either, you've got a Mae West on'.

At that moment a scaling ladder was floating by, and we grabbed it and towed Willy McKnight out to sea. Willy shouted, 'You're going the wrong way Mac'.

'Shut it, we're going home', I replied.

We got picked up by HMS *Berkeley*, who put us down below and rigged us out with gear. Then one of their Oerlikon crew were hit. The skipper asked can anyone use an Oerlikon. My mate Knocker White, an anti-tank gunner, went on deck and blazed away. We were hit six times. At one stage we went aground picking up survivors, but got off and returned to Portsmouth at about 4 knots, under air attack for much of the way.

The Royal Marine Commando, which had embarked at a strength of 370, suffered 23 dead and 76 wounded. There is no doubt that the casualties would have been much more severe had it not been for Phillipps waving some of the craft back from this suicidal mission, an action which cost him his life.

Casualties for the raid were heavy: 3,367 Canadians were killed, wounded, or taken prisoner, and British landing force casualties, including the three Commandos, totalled 275. The Royal Navy lost 1 destroyer and 33 landing craft, and suffered 550 dead and wounded. The RAF lost 106 aircraft to the Luftwaffe's 48. The German ground force casualties were 591.

Much has been made since about the fact that the Dieppe raid was a necessary precursor to the great amphibious operations that were to follow, in terms of lessons learned, and experience gained, all of which were to pay dividends. Mountbatten in particular pursued that line all his life. But since he, as Chief of Combined Operations, was responsible for mounting the operation, one can only comment: 'He would, wouldn't he.' Certainly the disaster pointed up the need for much heavier fire support in future, special arrangements to land armour, and intimate fire support right up to the last moment while troops crossed the waterline (the most dangerous place on the beach) and closed with their objectives. However, it did not need a debacle like Dieppe to learn all this and more. The Royal Marine Major General Sir Leslie Hollis, who was secretary to the Chiefs of Staff Committee, and deputy head of the Military Wing of the War Cabinet with direct access to Churchill, judged that the operation was a complete failure, and that many lives were sacrificed for no tangible result.

The Royal Marine Commando returned to the Isle of Wight, and having been brought up to strength with reinforcements got on with life. One of those reinforcements was a young officer, who wrote later:

> Fit young men are surprisingly resilient in moments of stress and their recuperative powers when combined with a spirit of adventure are incredibly rapid. A newcomer to the Commando in September 1942 would not have suspected that they had just survived a very tough battle indoctrination. The men were in good heart, their laughter was spontaneous and their morale unshakeable.[6]

Meanwhile, splendid news: another Royal Marine Commando was being formed. Things were beginning to look up in the Royal Marines after the early frustrating years. The two Commandos were dubbed Royal Marine A Commando and Royal Marine B Commando. A little later A became 40 RM Commando and B became 41 RM Commando. At about the same time the green beret was issued. Curiously, at first, it was unpopular, the colour being judged effeminate. But soon it became a headdress to be worn with pride, as it is today.

In England, as 1942 came to an end, the prospects for the Royal Marines may have been getting brighter, but in the Mediterranean there was still much muddle and waste.

THE TOBRUK RAID, 13 SEPTEMBER 1942

Among the units of MNBDO 1 left in the Middle East after most had been sent to the Indian Ocean was 11th Battalion RM, whose official, if uninspiring, role in the MNBDO was Land Defence Force. While the MNBDO was engaged elsewhere, the 11th Battalion had spent some of the time practising for raids. In April 1942 the Battalion's B Company took part in a minor raid on what was thought to be a radar station on the small island of Kupho Nisi, off the coast of Crete. Fortunately the island was lightly held by Italians, because the operation had a similarity to a number of previous amateur amphibious efforts right back to Dardanelles days. This was not the fault of the battalion, but of lack of proper equipment. The force was rowed ashore and recovered in ship's boats from the destroyer *Kelvin*. No beach reconnaissance had been carried out beforehand, but fortunately the landing was preceded by Lieutenant Commander Clogstoun-Wilmott RN, who later founded the Combined Operations Pilotage Parties (COPPs) which carried out beach surveys before the North African, Sicily, Italy, and Normandy-landings. He sounded the bottom with an oar to find the channel through the offshore reefs. Without his efforts, daylight might have found the whole force stranded on the rocks. At the cost of three wounded, the force overwhelmed the opposition, captured the building which was supposed to house the radar, discovered no radar, and withdrew, bringing with them some equipment and documents.

The battalion's next, and final, operation was at Tobruk, about 300 miles behind where Rommel was confronting the Eighth Army at Alamein. Rommel received most of his supplies through Tobruk and Benghazi. If these ports could be damaged, he might be forced to rely on Tripoli, 1,200 miles to the west, as his main port, just as he was expending supplies at a vast rate fighting off the British attack at Alamein, scheduled for October. Accordingly the British made plans to attack Benghazi and Tobruk. The attack on Benghazi does not concern us, but the operations had three aspects in common: the raids were on far too large a scale, the plans were too complicated, and security was so poor that the intended targets were common knowledge in the bars in Cairo.

The aim of the raid on Tobruk was to destroy oil tanks, ammunition dumps, repair facilities, and harbour defences and installations. Tobruk was to be attacked from seaward and from inland. The force approaching from inland was led by Lieutenant Colonel Haselden, who had been operating in the Western Desert in a clandestine role for years, mainly with the Long Range Desert Group (LRDG). He was to drive into Tobruk in three trucks carrying ninety commandos (mainly ex-Layforce Number 8 Army Commando), and Special Air Service soldiers (SAS), disguised as British prisoners of war, with their weapons hidden. Their 'escorts' were mainly German-speaking Palestinian Jews in German uniforms. This force would be led to the outskirts of Tobruk by an

LRDG patrol under Captain David Lloyd Owen, which would seal off the road after Haselden's party had set off. Under cover of an air raid, Haselden's group was to capture coastal and flak guns to the south of the harbour, and hold a bridgehead there. Offshore would be two destroyers, *Sikh* and *Zulu*, eighteen MTBs, three MLs, eight *Hunt*-class destroyers, and the anti-aircraft cruiser *Coventry*. On an Aldis lamp signal from one of Haselden's party, about 350 men of 11th Battalion RM, and men from other units, including sappers, would land from *Sikh* and *Zulu* and some of the MTBs. Together with Haselden's party, they would destroy the designated targets in Tobruk. On completion, the whole force, less the LRDG, would withdraw by MTBs and destroyers. On receiving a radio message from Haselden, the LRDG patrol was to attack a radio direction station, remove a vital piece of its equipment, and cut communications before withdrawing. For the landing, the 11th Battalion RM, travelling in *Sikh* and *Zulu*, would transfer to wooden lighters, of which only one in three had an engine; each powered lighter towed two engineless craft.

The operation by Haselden was a failure. Although his men captured some of the coastal guns, they were quickly retaken by a garrison much stronger and more alert than had been expected. Haselden was killed sometime during the night. Although the attack from landward may have taken the garrison by surprise, the approach from seaward did not. As *Sikh*, *Zulu*, and the MTBs approached, the searchlights which had been pointing skywards at the departing RAF bombers swung down and picked out the ships offshore. The first wave of 11th Battalion had already been launched. The sea was quite rough, engines failed, and craft broke up, drowning some of the occupants. The CO's craft started to founder, and his one radio failed to work, so he could not warn the two destroyers that things were going badly wrong. They had closed the beach to cut down the journey for the lighters returning to collect the second wave. When the searchlights dipped down, *Sikh* and *Zulu* were caught in the beams, as were the first wave of 11th Battalion RM, or those still afloat, 800 yards from the beach. Only seventy Marines under Major Jack Hedley made the shore, two miles west of the correct beach. They put up a stout fight, in the course of which Hedley, a Bisley champion pistol shot, accounted for five of the enemy with five rounds of his revolver. By 0830 hours there were only twenty-one Marines alive, and still evading capture, ashore. Hedley led them to some caves intending to lie up for the rest of the day and make for their own lines, 300 miles away, after dark. They were discovered and captured just after nightfall. Hedley was told by the garrison commander that the Germans had been expecting them.

Sikh was so badly damaged she was scuttled. *Zulu* and *Coventry* were sunk by bombing on the return to Alexandria, as were six out of the twenty-one MTBS and MLs. Only ninety Marines returned to Egypt. Outside the town Lloyd Owen's LRDG patrol waited for the signal that never came, so at dawn, he gave the order to withdraw. They got clear, despite driving right through a huge German Army camp, where they waved to the occupants, who waved back. Apart from Lloyd Owen's patrol, only eleven others who went into Tobruk by land or sea got out. Of these only five made the British lines over two months later.

Nearly everything about the Tobruk raid had been chaotic, and the seaborne landing the worst of all. Apart from all the other cock-ups, it seems inconceivable that anyone would regard landing troops on an enemy-held coastline in towed lighters as a serious operation of war. That they did so is an indication of the sorry state of amphibious thinking, or lack of it, in the Middle East at the time. The 11th Battalion was reconstituted, and from 1943 to late 1944 was in Ceylon and India, where it saw no action, before returning to the United Kingdom and disbandment.

THE BORDEAUX RAID, DECEMBER 1942

The raid on shipping at Bordeaux in December 1942 was carried out by a Royal Marines unit with the cover name of Royal Marines Boom Patrol Detachment (RMBPD). This unit with the long-winded name grew out of a wish by the Combined Operations Development Centre (CODC) to develop an explosive motor boat for British use. One of these craft manned by Italians had damaged the cruiser *York* off Crete. The CODC was one of Mountbatten's brainchildren; it was formed after he took over from Keyes as DCO, and changed his title to Chief of Combined Operations (CCO). The officer in charge of the wildly optimistic explosive motor boat project, which never saw action, but consumed much research time and effort, was Major H. G. 'Blondie' Hasler RM. Earlier he had sent a paper on small boat attacks on shipping to Mountbatten's Combined Operations Headquarters (COHQ). They had turned it down. As part of his trials unit, and to rescue the explosive motor boat driver after it had been launched on the final run-in to the target, Hasler acquired some canoes. In the end the RMBPD went to war in the canoes, not explosive motor boats. The cover name was chosen because the unit trained off Southsea near the boom that stretched to Seaview on the Isle of Wight to protect the Solent. It was hoped that anyone seeing them at work would conclude that they were maintaining the boom, which was also a good cover for the RMBPD's diving training.

Originally the RMBPD trained in Folboats, a canoe designed for civilian pleasure canoeing before the war. These had also been used in the early days by the Army's Special Boat Sections (SBS). At that time there is no record of any Marines serving in the SBS, and it did not become a Royal Marines unit until after the war.[7] Hasler developed special canoes for use by the RMBPD, which were much more robust than Folboats, could be dragged over mud and shingle, and were more seaworthy. With timbered decks and keels, they could be collapsed for stowage in a submarine.

The targets for the RMBPD's first raid were German ships in the Bordeaux–Bassens dock some seventy-one miles up the Gironde River. These were fast blockade runners, plying between French ports and the Far East, bringing in vital supplies such as tin, tungsten, and rubber, and taking back specialized equipment for the Japanese. So far many of them had escaped being sunk by British submarines. Bombing the docks would have caused too many civilian casualties, and an attack by commandos was ruled out so far up the Gironde. The area was well defended, and some estimates put the number of troops to carry out the task at around 20,000. After the Dieppe fiasco that August, the COHQ planners were chary about large-scale raids against such targets. They gave the task to Hasler. His canoeists were to be launched from a submarine nine miles off the mouth of the Gironde, paddle up the river, which would take several days, place limpet mines on the ships, and escape overland, using the already established escape system for shot-down aircrew set up by MI9 working with the French Resistance.

Attaching a limpet mine from a canoe requires practice. When the canoe comes alongside the ship, one canoeist holds his craft in place against the tide or current, by clamping on to the metal hull of the target with a strong magnet. The trick is to avoid a loud 'clunk' as the magnet attaches itself. Meanwhile the other canoeist lowers a pre-fused limpet mine down the side of the hull using a steel hook. Again, avoiding a 'thunk' as the limpet fixes itself is advisable, but not always achievable. After fixing the limpet, the canoe is paddled, or allowed to drift, to the next target. One section of the RMBPD under Lieutenant MacKinnon trained for the task in the River Thames and in the Clyde (the unit was divided into two twelve-man sections, plus headquarters and administrative staff). At first Hasler was forbidden to go on the raid by Mountbatten, but after a great deal of discussion Hasler managed to persuade him that it would be bad for morale if he did not lead this first, and highly dangerous, operation, by the RMBPD. Mountbatten insisted on one amendment to the plan: six canoes were to go, not three as originally envisaged.

Captain Stewart was the training officer with the section. He and Hasler were the only members of the RMBPD who knew the location of the target:

> We planned off aerial photographs. But several days would elapse after the final briefing before their arrival at Bordeaux. So the ships might have moved berth. We also tried to find lying-up places on shore for the canoes as they went up river. We thought it best for the canoes to go in two sections [two half sections]; one [half] section one side of the Gironde and one on the other. We didn't realise there was a tidal race at the mouth of the Gironde. We should have done.

Hasler and MacKinnon's section embarked in HMS/M *Tuna* on 30 November 1942. They were not briefed on the operation until they were aboard. Five canoes were launched from *Tuna* on Monday 7 December 1942, south of the mouth of the Gironde River in the Bay of Biscay. One by one each fully loaded canoe, with its crew already sitting in it, was hoisted outboard and lowered into the sea by means of a steel beam fitted into the barrel of the submarine's gun. *Catfish* (Major Hasler and Marine Sparks), and *Cuttlefish* (Lieutenant MacKinnon and Marine Conway) headed for the west bank at Bordeaux, *Crayfish* (Corporal Laver and Marine Mills) and *Coalfish* (Sergeant Wallace and Marine Ewart) for the east bank at Bordeaux, and *Conger* (Corporal Sheard and

Marine Moffat) for the north and south quays at Bassens. The sixth canoe, *Cachelot*, crewed by Marines Ellery and Fisher, also heading for Bassens, was damaged in the torpedo hatch and could not be launched.

After three hours of paddling, the five crews saw the white water of a tide race ahead: short, steep waves breaking on the shallows as the flood tide pushed in. Hasler rafted everybody together to give some advice on how to cope with this unforeseen hazard. *Coalfish* (Wallace and Ewart) apparently failed to get through the first line of surf, and was never seen again. *Conger* capsized on the second line of breakers. The canoe was scuttled, by slashing the canvas hull. Corporal Sheard and Marine Moffat were each towed by *Catfish* and *Crayfish* to within a quarter of a mile of the shore on Pointe de Grave, where the lighthouse marks the entrance. The light had been suddenly switched on, and was so bright they all thought they must have been seen. The two men set off to swim ashore, but they never made it. The others set off, but were almost immediately swept by the tide towards a small pier, with three small German warships alongside. They could not paddle out to sea against the tide, and there was nothing for it but to slip under the pier, hoping they would not be spotted. On the far side, *Cuttlefish* (MacKinnon and Conway) was missing. It was fortunate that Mountbatten had ordered that the force be doubled, because as far as Hasler was concerned they were now down to two canoes out of six. Actually there were still three, because, although Hasler did not know it, MacKinnon and Conway had succeeded in negotiating the pier, and were paddling hard up the Gironde; but they never made contact with him.

At their first lying-up position, in the reed beds by the village of Vivien de Medoc, Hasler and his three men were spotted by French villagers. Hasler told them they were British, and they must have kept the secret, for no Germans appeared. In fact, the Germans knew something was afoot, because their radar had spotted *Tuna*, and Wallace and Ewart had been washed ashore near a coastal battery and captured. Under extreme Gestapo interrogation, Wallace managed to stick to his story that only two canoes were taking part in the operation, and that the other had been damaged and left behind in the submarine. Neither he nor Ewart revealed the target. Two days later they were shot. Triumphantly the Germans announced on the radio that they had foiled an attack at the mouth of the Gironde, to the consternation of the staff of COHQ.

After dark, Hasler's two canoes set off to paddle to the next lying-up position, twenty-five miles upriver. With 300lb of kit in the canoes, it was a hard paddle, water froze on the decks, and they only just made it after avoiding a small German convoy which overtook them in the darkness. They escaped detection all that day and the next night, 9/10 December, as did MacKinnon and Conway, who were also paddling all night and lying up by day. Halfway through the next night Hasler's party had to stop and lie up on a small island, to wait for slack water after the ebb. It was nearly full daylight before they could find a place to lie up, twelve miles from their targets. The fourth night they found a good position in reed beds on the river bank opposite the Bassen Sud, which contained two ships, and here Hasler gave orders for the attack. They would take the last of the flood tide up through the docks, which would allow them to catch the ebb for their escape downriver. *Catfish* (Hasler and Sparks) would go up the west bank quays, and *Crayfish* (Laver and Mills) the east bank. With limpets set for 9 hours and 15 minutes, they launched the canoes at 2115 hours.

Drifting with the flood, after the moon had set, Hasler and Sparks, using single paddles to cut down their silhouette, placed all their limpets: three on a large cargo ship, two on a mine destroyer (a *sperrbrecher*), two on a smaller merchantman, and one on an oil tanker. Alongside the *sperrbrecher* they were illuminated by torchlight, and heard the footsteps of the deck sentry above them. They froze, bent forward with faces pressed to the canoe's deck. The canoe drifted down the ship's side, as the sentry above leaned over trying to make out what the log-shaped object was. Finally, after several heart-stopping moments, the canoe drifted into the shadow of another ship.

As Hasler and Sparks paddled downstream as hard as they could go, they heard paddles behind them. They stopped, and Corporal Laver and Marine Mills in *Crayfish* told them they had found the east quays empty, and floated down on the now ebbing tide to place four limpets on each of the ships opposite their last lying-up position. Together they forged on down river, finally separating before landing to attempt their escape overland in pairs. Since leaving *Tuna* they had paddled ninety-one miles.

Four ships were damaged, and in dock for several months, although according to German reports they were empty at the time. The damage to the *sperrbrecher* was negligible, perhaps because her sides were especially designed to withstand underwater explosions. The other limpets probably failed to explode, or perhaps they fell off before detonation. Hasler and Sparks returned to England in April 1943 through the Resistance escape line 'Marie-Claire'. Only after the war was the fate of the other crews discovered. As already related, Sergeant Wallace and Marine Ewart had been shot a few days after being captured. Of *Conger*'s crew, Marine Moffat's body was washed ashore, but Corporal Sheard's body was never found. Lieutenant MacKinnon and Marine Conway had pressed on for three nights after becoming separated from the others, until their canoe was sunk by an underwater obstacle. They landed and set off to make their way home via Spain. Helped by local people, they had put about thirty miles between themselves and Bordeaux, and were hidden in a hospital, when they were betrayed, arrested by the French police, and handed over to the Germans. On arrival in the prison, they found *Crayfish*'s crew, Laver and Mills, under interrogation by the Gestapo. These two, still in uniform, had walked about twenty miles before being arrested by the French police. How long the four held by the Germans survived cannot be established for certain. At the end of December 1942 the Swiss Red Cross reported to the British that Mac-Kinnon and Conway were prisoners. The burial certificates of all six men shot by the Germans were annotated, 'found drowned in Bordeaux harbour'. But it is probable that they were shot in March 1943, since German records state that men captured after the Bordeaux raid were shot in accordance with Hitler's infamous Commando Order of 18 October 1942, kept secret by the Germans at the time, part of which read:

> From now on all men operating against German troops in so-called Commando raids in Europe or in Africa are to be annihilated to the last man. This is to be carried out whether they be soldiers in uniform, or saboteurs, with or without arms; and whether fighting or seeking to escape; and it is equally immaterial whether they come into action from ships and aircraft, or whether they land by parachute. Even if these individuals on discovery make obvious their intention of giving themselves up as prisoners, no pardon on any account is to be given.

The order specifically excluded enemy soldiers taken prisoners in open battle, in large-scale attacks, major assault landings, or airborne operations. Neither did it apply to aircrew who baled out.

General Jodl, Chief of the Operations Staff of the Oberkommando der

Wehrmacht (OKW – German Armed Forces High Command), and one of Hitler's closest military advisers, took some pains to keep this order secret. His directive on 19 October 1942 included the passages below, which are a clear indication of a wish to cover up a monstrous edict:

> This order is intended for Commanders only and is under no circumstance to fall into enemy hands.
>
> The Headquarters mentioned in the distribution list are responsible that all parts of the order, or extracts taken from it, which are issued are again withdrawn and, together with this copy, destroyed.

*

Our story has taken us into early 1943, a watershed year in the course of the war, as it was in the history of the Royal Marines. Before recounting the great changes that came about, we must turn the clock back, to the activities of Marines in the Far East when the Japanese storm burst on 8 December 1941.

15

The Far East: Burma and the Indian Ocean, 1941–1942

On 2 December 1941, before the Japanese entered the war, Force Z (the battleship *Prince of Wales*, the battlecruiser *Repulse*, and four destroyers) arrived at Singapore. Churchill hoped that Force Z would deter the Japanese attack, or failing that keep several Japanese capital ships occupied looking for them, rather as the German *Tirpitz* lurking in the Norwegian fjords was doing to the British Home Fleet. On 6 December, two large Japanese convoys were sighted off southern Indo-China (modern Vietnam), on a western course, apparently heading for Malaya. Early on 8 December the first of many Japanese air raids hit Singapore. The Japanese also struck the US base at Pearl Harbor, sinking four battleships, and damaging four, two of them very badly. The same morning Japanese troops landed at Kota Bharu on the east coast of Malaya, and Singora on the Kra Isthmus in Siam (Thailand).

Admiral Sir Tom Phillips, commanding Force Z, decided that he must try to destroy the convoys landing these troops. He was uncertain of the Japanese surface ship strength, but in fact was heavily outnumbered. He was even more unaware of the Japanese air capability. He correctly assessed they had no carriers in the South China Sea, and, basing his calculations on British experience in the Mediterranean, considered the landings at Singora to be well outside the range of land-based aircraft. Phillips, who up to now had spent the Second World War driving a desk in the Admiralty, and had never endured air attack, was about to suffer a series of rude shocks. Force Z sailed from Singapore in the evening of 8 December. Early the next morning he was told by signal from Singapore that the RAF would not be able to provide air cover because the airfields in northern Malaya were being evacuated. He pressed on.

At about midday on 9 December, Force Z was sighted by a Japanese submarine and was subsequently shadowed by aircraft launched from their cruisers. Phillips, realizing he had been spotted, had a change of heart, and turned south. Had he held his course at full speed all night he might, just, have got away. That night, 9/10 December, a Japanese submarine spotted him again. In the early morning, Phillips received reports – false as it turned out – of another landing, at Kuantan. He decided to alter course to the south-west to attack this landing. The landings were, after all, 400 miles from the nearest Japanese airfields, and he was unaware that their aircraft were capable of operating out to three times that distance. Learning that reports of the landing at Kuantan were false, he now steered north-east to investigate a supposed sighting of a steamer towing landing barges. All this fiddling about ended at about 1000 hours when one of his destroyers reported being under air attack about 150 miles *south* of his position. At last he turned south-west again at full speed. At 1113 hours, the first wave of Japanese dive-bombed Force Z.

Repulse was damaged by this attack, but could still steam and fight. The next strike, by torpedo bombers, hit *Prince of Wales* with two torpedoes. She lost electrical power, and with her rudder jammed steamed in a circle. *Repulse* was hit by four torpedoes, and began to roll over. While two destroyers were picking up 796 of *Repulse*'s crew of 1,306, the Japanese finished off *Prince of Wales*. She sank at 1320 hours, taking Phillips and her captain with her. Out of her ship's company of 1,612, the destroyer *Express* rescued 1,285. Twenty-seven Marines from the *Prince of Wales* and forty from the *Repulse* lost their lives. The survivors from detachments of both capital ships were rescued, and taken to Singapore where initially they were used on static guard duties, and as a mobile reserve.

On Christmas Eve a platoon from *Prince of Wales*'s Marine detachment was detached from guard duties, sent on a week's jungle training, and, in early January, despatched by train to join Major Angus Rose of the 2nd Battalion the Argyll and Sutherland Highlanders. Rose had been detached to carry out some behind-the-lines operations from Port Swettenham on the west coast of Malaya, while it was still in British hands. On 28 December Roseforce, using boats of the Perak Flotilla, landed some 140 miles up the west coast of Malaya to attack the lines of communications of the Japanese 5th Division, fighting twenty miles to the south. Roseforce set up ambushes, and destroyed a number of trucks.

The most satisfying coup was the killing of two senior Japanese staff officers in their cars. On completion of this operation, Roseforce withdrew to Port Swettenham. Two days after their return, enemy aircraft sank the flotilla's depot ship and most of the craft; this, and the rapid Japanese advance, brought Rose's behind-the-lines activities to an end. The Marines were therefore employed on demolition tasks, and at one stage helped cover the Army's retreat, before being returned to Singapore at the end of January.

On 31 January the 2nd Argylls, led by their pipers, were the last over the causeway connecting Singapore to the Malayan mainland. Thanks to the dynamic commanding officer, Lieutenant Colonel Ian Stewart, it was the only British, or Indian, battalion to have done any proper jungle training in the whole of Malaya Command. The Argylls had fought aggressively, and given the Japanese a bloody nose on more than one occasion, but had lost heavily, particularly at the Slim River Battle. On arrival in Singapore, the battalion was brought up to a strength of 250 all ranks by officers and men who had been wounded and sick, or had been detached. The other two battalions in the 12th Indian Infantry Brigade, the 5/2nd Punjabis and 4/19th Hyderabads, were inexperienced, poorly trained, and badly led by their equally inexperienced British officers. They had performed badly in the battle for Malaya, and their morale was so poor they were almost useless.

On 2 February, the 2nd Argylls were reinforced by the 210 Marines of the combined detachments of *Prince of Wales* and *Repulse*, formed into two companies: B Company from *Repulse* commanded by Captain Lang, with Lieutenants Hulton and Davis as platoon commanders; and C Company from *Prince of Wales*, commanded by Captain Aylwin, with Lieutenants Sheridan and Verdon. As both detachments were from Plymouth Division, the composite battalion, officially designated the Marine Argyll Battalion, became known as the 'Plymouth Argylls', after the football club of that name.

It was a happy coincidence that the commander of the 12th Indian Infantry Brigade was the son of Major General Paris, who had commanded the RN Division from 1914 to 1916. Both he and Stewart gained the confidence of the Marines. The latter wrote of them: 'It is scarcely necessary to say that they were troops of the highest quality, and the Argylls are indeed proud that it was to the 93rd (2nd Argylls) that the Marines asked to come.'[1]

On 8 February the Japanese assaulted across the Johore Strait, on the north-west coast, catching General Percival, the British Army commander, on the wrong foot, mainly because he thought the terrain there unsuitable for an amphibious landing. Expecting the attack on the northeast coast, he had deployed his troops accordingly. So instead of encountering the fresh British 18th Division, now sitting in the northeast sector, the Japanese met Australians who had suffered heavily in the retreat. The battle for Singapore was fought and lost in the north-west, where the Australian commander, Bennett, had been dilatory in using the time available to prepare his division's positions properly, or make a sound plan.[2] Bennett's handling of his division once battle was joined and the performance of his brigade commanders were equally inept. They were not helped by the indiscipline of the Australians, particularly recent reinforcements; large-scale desertions started before the Japanese landing on Singapore Island took place, and by the end of the battle some 8,000 of Bennett's troops had deserted.[3]

On 9 February, 12th Indian Infantry Brigade was ordered forward, the Plymouth Argylls to a position near Tengah airfield, which was in Japanese hands. The next day the Japanese attacked the battalion's position. Aylwin was wounded in the wrist in this battle, but remained with his company. At around this time Paris gave orders to his brigade to pull back, and this uncovered the left flank of the Australian defences, which unravelled from north to south. The Plymouth Argylls withdrew to a position south of Bukit Panjang, just east of the Bukit–Timah road. It was now the turn of the Australians to expose the flank of Paris's brigade, and enemy tanks were soon moving down the Bukit–Timah road. The Plymouth Argylls established a roadblock on the road and in the rubber plantation east of it; without their efforts the road to Singapore would have been open. Stewart ordered the battalion to remain silent and use only the bayonet on infiltrators.[4] Before dawn the CO ordered the battalion back to the brigade RV, a dairy farm about a mile to the south, as a prelude to a further withdrawal into Singapore. The two Argyll companies were cut off, and while the CO waited for them at the RV, Paris, unknown to him, took the two Marine companies via the golf course to Tyersall Camp some six miles further south. Eventually the two Argyll companies fought their way out, and rejoined at Tyersall. Here the Plymouth Argylls spent the final days of the fighting for Singapore. Stewart and some of his officers were ordered out of the

besieged city by General Wavell, so that their jungle experience would
be available for the fighting in Burma. Command devolved onto Captain
Lang RM.

The performance of this battalion in the dying days of the Malayan
campaign was one of the brighter spots in this otherwise shameful
episode, which culminated in unconditional surrender of the Singapore
garrison to a numerically inferior Japanese force on 15 February 1942.
Throughout the battle for Singapore, the Plymouth Argylls stood firm
while others – mainly, it has to be said, Australians – ran back through
their lines, deserted, and forced their way onto ships in the harbour. The
surviving Marines went into captivity with their Argyll comrades in
arms, spending the next three and a half years in the atrocious conditions
of the Japanese prison camps. Twenty-four Marines of the Plymouth
Argylls died in the battle; the majority have no known grave.[5] About
twenty Marines escaped from Singapore, just after the surrender, but
only two were successful; the remainder were captured or died on
remote islands.

The fall of Malaya made possible the Japanese invasion of Burma,
which began before Singapore surrendered. In early January 1942,
Marines of 1st RM Coast Regiment in Ceylon were asked to volunteer
'for service of a hazardous nature', the usual phrase in the Second World
War. Five officers and 102 NCOs and Marines were selected, and after
three weeks' infantry training embarked in the cruiser *Enterprise*. Once
aboard they learned their destination was Rangoon. The party was
commanded by Major D. Johnston RM, with Captain H. Alexander RM
as his second-in-command. Johnston gave his force the suitably aggressive name Viper, and divided it into three platoons and a headquarters.
As events would show, Johnston was a spirited and tenacious officer,
who must have been like a fish out of water in a coast regiment. On
arrival at Rangoon he was briefed on a number of highly impractical,
one might almost say crack-pot, tasks, which need not concern us; they
were never carried out, being overtaken by events, as the Japanese
advance into Burma was too fast.

About a week after his arrival, Johnston was told to form a flotilla for
river work. At the same time a most valuable officer was attached to
Force Viper; Lieutenant Penman, Burma RNVR, a senior engineer with
a teak company, who spoke passable Burmese and Hindi, and was a
keen yachtsman. He was joined a few days later by Sub-Lieutenant

Wikner, Burma RNVR, a construction engineer. Johnston put him in charge of repairing vessels, and armour-plating them.

The types of vessel in Force Viper varied, as some craft used in the early days were found to be unsuitable, and others were tacked on later, but for much of the time the Force Viper flotilla was organized as follows:

> Number 1 Platoon – launch *Doris*, motorboats *Alguada* and *Xylia*
> Number 2 Platoon – launch *Stella*, motorboat *Snipe*
> Number 3 Platoon – launch *Rita*, motorboat *Delta Guard*
> Stores   – *Ningpo*, a double-decker

They were an unprepossessing collection, varying from 40 to 75 feet long; the slowest had a maximum speed of five knots, the fastest eight. The motorboats were manned entirely by Marines and carried two Brens each; each launch carried one Vickers, five Brens, and one 2in mortar. As well as carrying Marines, the launches still had their Chittagong Lascar crews. These 'Chitta', as the Marines called them, who came from what is now Bangladesh, had not been paid for a month, were naturally disgruntled, and wanted to return to India. Penman ensured their loyalty by his leadership. After about two weeks' training, the Force was employed on river patrols in the Rangoon area, in the mouths of the Irrawaddy, assisting with maintaining law and order in the docks. By now the Japanese had crossed the Sittang, the last major river obstacle on their route to Rangoon. Referring to this period in his comprehensive report, Johnston comments on

> an increased feeling of insecurity in Rangoon. The question was not if but when the city would be evacuated. The Governor's broadcast that Rangoon would be a second Tobruk was not taken seriously. Arson and looting was on the increase and large fires were constant in the town. In the docks area Brens were used to keep looters in check.

The Burmese, who occupied the heartland of Burma, welcomed the Japanese as liberators, and did all they could to speed the British on their way. The Kachins, Karens, and Chins, who lived in the more remote outer regions of the country, loathed the Burmese, as they do to this day, and on the whole supported the British.

On 7 March, as Rangoon was being evacuated, Force Viper was ordered some 120 miles up the Irrawaddy to Prome. Here they were to operate on the left flank of 17th Indian Division, who were withdrawing in contact with the Japanese between Rangoon and Prome. Before leaving the Rangoon area, Force Viper assisted with the destruction of dock and oil installations, including one refinery containing 20 million gallons of aviation fuel. Finally they took Army demolition parties out from Rangoon to where a seagoing ship was waiting to take them to India. As Force Viper motored up river, they stopped to burn or smash any boats they passed to keep them out of Japanese hands, or sank them in the channels to bar the enemy's progress. At one stage, while setting fire to some rice boats, Johnston's legs were burned. They later turned septic and were very painful. He never allowed this to cramp his style.

Force Viper's first contact with the enemy, on 17 March, occurred when cooperating with Major Mike Calvert's Commando company, formed mainly from staff and students at the Bush Warfare School at Maymyo, near Mandalay. Calvert, who ran the school, and was later to make his name with Wingate's Chindits, was tasked to carry out demolitions at Henzada, south of Prome. The *Rita* escorted Calvert's craft, the *Hastings*. Johnston, who lent Calvert some Marines to assist with demolitions, heard the story from him the next day.

The two ships had arrived at Henzada that morning, and *Hastings* had secured to the bank while *Rita* lay off. Calvert sent a section ashore as advance party and when they got 200 yards across a field towards the village, a Burmese in civilian clothes told them to surrender as they were covered by machine guns from all directions. They gave him an 'unprintable' reply, whereupon the enemy appeared in large numbers and they had to fight their way back to the river.

Hearing heavy firing, *Rita* pulled out to midstream waiting for targets to present themselves, which they soon did in large numbers. She drew most of their fire which she returned with the Vickers and five Brens, the rest firing Tommy guns. Vickers-man [sic] Lance Corporal Marriott got right among the enemy [with his fire]. Mortar shells then began to fall and *Hastings* pulled out, but had to go back twice to pick up the rest of the party. Rae, the skipper, handled the ship well from an exposed position forward very coolly. Eventually both ships made off up river without being hit by mortars. Commandos lost one marine and two of their men. *Rita* had two slightly wounded. They had plenty of hits, including two through the ensign, but the Jap bullets had poor penetrating power, being stopped by a rolled blanket and a tin of sausages.

Some days after the Henzada operation, some Burmese were caught with Japanese grenades hidden in their clothing. They reported that over 100 enemy had been killed at Henzada. After which, Johnston commented: 'They were treated as spies, taken ashore and shot. They took their fate stoically.'

The Force had its problems and limitations. For lack of suitable radios, 'communications with the Army were almost nil', according to Penman. Often the Force would be left operating downriver while the Army retreated, and were fired on by their own side when returning upstream. It was the dry season, so the river level was dropping all the time, and the channels changed frequently. The Burmese cut away buoys and removed crossing marks on the banks. The river current was deceptive, giving no indication of twists and turns in the channels as these meandered from bank to bank. The Force had to rely on sounding poles and the skill of the Chittagongi serangs (boatswains). The launches were slow, vulnerable, and because of their draught restricted to the main channels. The side creeks were inaccessible to them. In the early days the motorboats, manned by enthusiastic Marines, would, in Johnston's words,

> behave like a pack of unruly hounds, dashing off whenever they had a chance to chase country boats up creeks, usually ending up aground. Then a party would have to strip off and go over the side to push the boat off. They had to be discouraged as the Japs might literally have caught them with their pants down.

Johnston soon found that operating large underpowered boats on the open expanses of a river imposed severe tactical limitations: surprise was very difficult to achieve, especially as accurate navigation by night was almost impossible. He was forced to adopt a mainly defensive role. As Johnston and Penman have recorded, the Force was lucky that the Japanese never succeeded in positioning one of their heavy mortars or an artillery piece at a place where the channel ran close to the bank, and ambushing the craft as they slowly chugged upstream. On the other hand, the Japanese never made tactical use of the main river while Force Viper patrols were operating. Possibly they overestimated the strength and capabilities of the Force; the bloody nose inflicted on the enemy by just two boats at Henzada, in the early part of the Japanese advance up the Irrawaddy valley, may have reinforced this view.

The Force's next major contact with the enemy occurred at Padaung, a village a few miles south of Prome and on the other bank of the Irrawaddy. Again the Force was operating with commandos, about a platoon, this time under command of Lieutenant Colonel Musgrove, who had been told to hold Padaung to stop the Japanese crossing to the east bank where 17th Division was fighting a fierce battle. Number 2 Platoon (Lieutenant Fayle), number 3 Platoon (Lieutenant Cave), a Vickers section (two guns), and the commandos were landed, while the flotilla remained by the shore, awaiting their return. Johnston rode in to the village on a bullock cart because of his burned legs. On arrival, Musgrove sent out commando patrols. The Burmese villagers appeared smiling, and selling bread and chickens. There appeared to be no enemy in the vicinity of the village. Cave's platoon was told to patrol the river edge. Fayle's platoon was sited in reserve around Force Headquarters, which had been established in a bungalow in the police compound on the edge of the village. Musgrove told all officers that if they got detached they were to take their parties off into the hills, strike north, and turn back to the river a good way north of Prome.

The strands of what followed are difficult to disentangle from the various accounts by participants, some recounted years after a confused battle at night in the middle of Burma. Just after midnight the Japanese, who had been hiding in houses in the village all day, attacked the compound from the south, by the light of a brilliant tropic moon, screaming and shouting, with fixed bayonets. When the uproar started, Fayle, armed with a Tommy gun, rushed down to the compound and let go to right and left, killing a number of the enemy. The remainder vanished after reaching the northern limit of the compound, and all went deathly quiet. But Fayle was cut off from most of his platoon, and in the ensuing lull could find only Corporal Winters, Marine Shaw, and a Commando soldier.

Fayle's party then saw a large party of Japanese marching down the road behind them, and lay low under some huts which were on three-foot-high stilts. Shortly afterwards, a herd of cattle was driven through the compound, but Fayle's men held their fire. Suddenly, a horde of screaming Japanese charged through the compound. Luckily Fayle's little party of four had considerable firepower, two Brens, and two Tommy guns. They blasted the Japanese, and threw grenades. A voice shouted in good English, 'Surrender or we'll shoot.' Marine Shaw answered, 'Fuck off.' A torch was shone, which Corporal Winters greeted with a burst of fire. The torch and its owner vanished. The Japanese charged again, but were mowed down and eventually went to ground, while Fayle's men hurled grenades at them. By now the moon was setting, the Japanese seem to have been given a bloody nose, and Fayle decided to take advantage of the darkness and the lull to withdraw. Covering each other they moved north as ordered, eventually reached the river, and boarded the boats at about 0930 hours. Johnston was astonished to see them, as he thought they were lost.

According to Johnston, after expending most of their ammunition the headquarters party and the bulk of Fayle's platoon were ordered to withdraw by Musgrove. Fayle's little party was still fighting at this stage, and this probably allowed the main body to slip away unhindered. Fayle was awarded the MC, and Winters and Shaw the MM. There was no sign of Cave's platoon, or the Vickers section, and Johnston assumed they had made their way into the hills. In the morning, the *Rita* stood off Padaung and laced it with machine-gun fire for half an hour. As Johnston recorded, 'This relieved their feelings but had no visible results.' About half the Commando platoon got back. Force Viper had 1 officer and 35 NCOs and Marines missing. Later in the day the launch landed two Burmese to reconnoitre Padaung, who reported that the enemy had over 100 casualties and had taken all day to bury them. They also said that the Japanese had strung up Marine prisoners and bayoneted them. How accurate the enemy casualty count was we shall never know. Johnston assessed it as 'about 40'. In a confused battle, indeed in most battles, it is usually impossible to say until well afterwards, sometimes if ever, what the true figures of enemy casualties are. Certainly the Japanese were hit hard, or they would have overrun Fayle's little group. Several men reported hearing terrible screaming during the withdrawal to the river. The bayoneting of prisoners story was confirmed some days later when a Commando sergeant with three bayonet wounds came in. He reported that he and eight or nine other Commandos and three Marines had been lined up for bayoneting. He and a Marine had broken away. He had no news of what had happened to Cave's platoon.

Following the threads of the fate of Cave's platoon is even more complicated than the rest of the Padaung story, because there were so few survivors – three or four. When the battle started at the village compound, Cave tried to take his platoon in to join the rest of the force.

Almost immediately they ran into a large body of Japanese between them and Padaung. Following his instructions, Cave headed for the hills, with the aim of striking north before turning east to the river. Sometime during the night he fell and damaged his compass. The next day they met six Gurkhas, who were also cut off from their unit. That night, hungry and lost, they followed a road, and at dawn were about to lie up nearby when they heard the sound of transport. To their relief it turned out to be three empty 15-cwt trucks belonging to a Sikh transport unit heading for Prome. They had some rations which they shared with Cave's men. Morale rose when they realized that they had been heading in the right direction after all.

Cave had some trouble persuading the Sikhs not to move on the roads by day, and thus avoid the attentions of the Japanese Air Force. Having spent half the day under cover, the Sikhs must have decided to ignore Cave's advice, because they set off in the mid-afternoon, and were attacked by two Japanese aircraft. One truck was damaged beyond repair, the other two had bullet holes and flat tyres, but were still runners. About twelve men were killed, and about four wounded. Fortunately the aircraft did not make a second pass. They loaded up in the remaining two trucks, and after a few miles met a party of Burma Police who told them that Prome was strongly held by the enemy.

Cave decided to abandon the trucks and head north to bypass Prome. The story becomes confused from this point for several weeks, because the only known witness spent a long time delirious with malaria. A number of the party died of their wounds, and others of malaria. The Sikhs deserted. At the end of May the party, now numbering ten Marines, including Cave, and three Gurkhas, was somewhere between Prome and Alanmyo (about fifty miles north of Prome). The survivor's account puts them at Toungoo, on the Sittang, nearly a hundred miles *east* of Prome, which seems unlikely. Wherever it was, one night they encountered the Japanese in some strength. During the ensuing action two of the Gurkhas slipped out to silence a machine-gun, and returned with two severed ears to prove they had done so. Later they were mortared and Cave was hit in the knee by shrapnel. The next morning, with four of the party badly wounded, the Japanese overran them. The Japanese herded them onto trucks and eventually they ended up in a camp at Mogok, about seventy-five miles north of Mandalay. It is possible that Cave died from gangrene soon after arrival. It seems that they were subsequently moved to Katha, about 150 miles north of Mandalay. Here, according to one survivor of Cave's party, the camp was overrun by Stilwell's Chinese, and the prisoners released. Certainly the Chinese were operating in that area at the end of 1944, although not under Stilwell, who had been relieved. The prisoners were eventually flown to Assam and on to India.

Padaung, and the first close-quarter encounter with the ferocious Japanese and their bestial habits, was a sobering experience for Force Viper. Colour Sergeant Harry Wonfer, the Force Sergeant Major, and a regular of over twelve years' service, commented: 'the men, mostly young fellows, who up to then had regarded the expedition as good fun, began to take things more seriously.'

After Padaung the Force retired to Prome, and while operating there and for the remainder of their time on the river came under fire from the bank several times. They often returned the fire to good effect. The retreat gathered momentum as the Japanese pressed ruthlessly forward, swinging in behind units and formations, forcing them to withdraw. By now the whole of southern Burma was lost, and the Japanese were considerably strengthened by having Rangoon as a logistic base. By contrast the British had to march up the centre of Burma without a line of communication or base, withdrawing all the time towards India, whose sole overland connection to Burma at that time was a cart track. It was only a question of time before the whole of Burma fell.

By 15 April Force Viper was at Magwe, over 100 miles north of Prome, ferrying a brigade across the river, which took three days. Two vessels of the flotilla were several miles downstream when news came that the Japanese were in Magwe. The channel ran within a few yards of the shore, and these vessels were fired on as they chugged upstream. The flotilla was machine-gunned from the air for the first time at this time, killing one Lascar. The *Ningpo* was lucky, being hit about 200 times.

Two days later the flotilla was off Yenangyaung. Johnston went ashore with Marine Clift to try to make contact with the Army. Wonfer: 'Johnston was a man like Calvert, and few Marines were keen on accompanying him on his jaunts, as he plunged into the jungle regardless.' Penman disagrees, saying that Johnston was a first-class leader, 'but not a belligerent one-man band like Calvert. In short a disciplined Marine'. His loyalty and regard for Johnston is admirable, and well deserved, but despite Penman's disparaging remarks, Calvert became an

outstanding fighting soldier, and far and away the best brigade commander in Wingate's Chindits.

Yenangyaung was a major Burmah Oil Company oilfield, and a huge
pall of smoke hung over the town as demolitions were fired by the
retreating British and Indian troops. While Johnston was ashore, Marine
Clift came rushing back to the Flotilla shouting that the Japs were
coming. Penman:

> It was useless to wait for the Major, so I warned the hospital ships [craft
> being used to evacuate wounded], and got under way myself, returning
> once hurriedly to pick up some of the demolition party. I signalled for
> the rest of the fleet, which were anchored above the town, and we all
> proceeded upstream. The Japanese brought up mortars and opened fire
> on us, but we got out of range on time. Three aircraft strafed us with
> machine gun fire, but there were no casualties. The Japanese had come
> round to the back of Burdiv [1st Burma Division – the flotilla was now in
> support of this division], and made a roadblock on the road to the north.
> Johnston got out on a tank, and eventually rejoined us at Myingyan.

Johnston's report on this period (he refers to himself as J, which the
author has amended so the text reads in the first person):

> I got in a car whose driver was also looking for HQ, and went north
> through the town, till we were stopped as there was a Jap roadblock 200
> yards further on. Retired and found Div HQ just south of the town. They
> had just been informed of the roadblock and I was unable to get any
> instructions for the flotilla, so I returned to the beach. Here I found
> considerable confusion, troops pouring up from the south and down
> from the north. The flotilla had pulled out from the bank and were being
> bombed and machine gunned from the air. I collected a few British troops
> with a bren gun and took up a position on a hill overlooking the north
> part of town. Later the adjutant of the Inniskilling Fusiliers came along
> with more troops, and I turned over my party and returned to Div HQ.

Johnston does not mention how he got out, but Corporal Winters
heard from a wounded man that he had led some Cameronians in three
bayonet charges against the Japanese before commandeering a tank and
breaking through the roadblock. This would certainly be his style. HQ
1st Burma Division was extricated from Yenangyaung by a Chinese
regiment that attacked from the north, clearing the Japanese roadblock.
Johnston rejoined his Force on 26 April, having been away for nine days.

The morale of the Lascar crews had borne up well, but at Myingyan it finally cracked, mainly because of the unpleasant experience of being strafed from the air. While at Myingyan a small double-decker launch was capsized by a dust storm and of eleven Marines on board, only four were saved. The confluence of the Chindwin and Irrawaddy rivers is near Myingyan, and the Lascars, knowing that the way back to India lay up the Chindwin, refused to go up the Irrawaddy any further. In fact this did not matter, because the way out for everybody lay up the Chindwin. As it was shallow, only the *Alguada* and two small motorboats could navigate upstream; before destroying and sinking the launches and bigger boats, Force Viper ferried 1st Burma Division across the Irrawaddy at Sameikkon, and covered the crossing. After this, the Lascars were sent out to India.

Force Viper withdrew up the Chindwin, where it did good work in support of the Army, including firing on Japanese crossing in boats to attack Monywa, through which the British were withdrawing. At Kalewa the last waterborne tasks were undertaken by Force Viper. The boats were taken up to Sittaung and destroyed, and the Force marched out over the hills to India. It was a nightmare march over a track littered with the corpses of refugees and soldiers who had succumbed to cholera and malaria. The Marines marched out with the rearguard, the 48th Infantry Brigade, and so were at the very tail of the retreat, with the exception of the rearguard battalion of the brigade. Fortunately the Japanese did not follow up. The monsoon had started, and their logistics were tenuous after their long advance. Except for patrols, they stayed on the east bank of the Chindwin. The water points on the march out were fouled by their predecessors, and the Marines strained the disgusting mud through their handkerchiefs.

The Marines marched into Dimapur, the railhead, with their rifles at the slope, and all their weapons in good order. Here a staff officer demanded they hand over their weapons. The Marines refused, and eventually were allowed to keep them. After a few days, they were evacuated to Calcutta by train, and later to Colombo. Out of the total of 106 all ranks in Force Viper, 58 got back to India: nearly half of the gallant band were dead, or prisoners. Some epic little fights had taken place in the last few days, particularly when Monywa was attacked. One was that fought by Lance Corporal Parratt and Marine Lough, last seen firing a Bren at Japanese motor transport accompanied by tanks.

The Japanese certainly rated Force Viper highly, paying them the compliment of broadcasting a threat to 'roast and cut into small pieces' any of them who were caught. It could be argued that without Force Viper the Japanese would have been free to use the river far more than they did, and crossings by large numbers of British and Indian troops, certainly in the later stages of the retreat, would have been far more difficult, if not impossible.

*

Over two years elapsed before the Royal Marines encountered the Japanese on land again, although they continued to engage them at sea and in the air. After HMS *Exeter* was sunk in the Battle of the Java Sea on 28 February 1942, her Marines spent the rest of the war in Japanese prison camps along with their shipmates. Survivors from the cruisers *Dorsetshire*, *Cornwall*, and the ancient carrier *Hermes*, all sunk off Ceylon in early April 1942 by Japanese carrier-borne aircraft, were landed in Ceylon. Marines of the Air Defence Brigade in Ceylon played an important part in defending Colombo and Trincomalee from the attentions of aircraft from the same Japanese carrier force.

The battleships, carriers, and cruisers of the Eastern Fleet also carried detachments. The Royal Marine Detachment of one of the Eastern Fleet's First World War vintage 'R' class battleships, the *Ramillies*, was in action ashore in May 1942, but against the Vichy French, on Madagascar.

The island of Madagascar, a Vichy French colony, lay off the convoy routes from Britain to the Middle East and India via the Mozambique Channel between Madagascar and the east coast of Africa (the Mediterranean route was far too hazardous in 1942). For the Japanese to attack these routes from bases in Burma, except by submarine, was difficult: the distances were too great. If, however, they could seize a good harbour within striking distance it would be a different matter. Such a harbour existed, the port of Diégo-Suarez and Vichy French Naval Base of Antsirane (now Antseranana) on the northern tip of Madagascar. To pre-empt the Japanese, a landing was planned. To this end a division, Force 121, was put together for the task, under the command of Major General R. G. Sturges, who commanded the RM Division. To the intense disappointment of the 101st and 102nd Brigades of the RM Division they were not included in the Madagascar force. Sturges took with him a skeleton headquarters from the RM Division, and 29th Independent

Infantry Brigade, the 17th and 15th Brigade Groups, and 5 Army Commando.

The assault was to be made by 29th Brigade and 5 Commando on the west side of the Diégo-Suarez peninsula, about twelve air miles from the base and port. These were situated about seven miles inside a large, almost land-locked, natural harbour, whose narrow entrance was on the east side, and protected by coast defence batteries. Batteries were also sited near the port and naval base.

The other two brigade groups were to carry out follow-up landings to capture the remainder of the island after Diégo-Suarez had been taken. Air support was to be provided by the Fleet Air Arm from the carriers *Indomitable* and *Illustrious*. The naval task force commanded by Rear Admiral E. N. Syfret included, as well as the carriers, the battleship *Ramillies*, the cruisers *Hermione* and *Devonshire*, five assault ships with landing craft, and several destroyers. The planning for the operation, codename Ironclad, had been efficient and speedy, as was the operation itself – in marked contrast to some of the earlier efforts in this war, and some yet to come, which were covered in the last chapter. On 5 May 1942, the naval task force arrived at the lowering positions for the three assault beaches, 9,000 miles from Britain and only seven weeks after the Chiefs of Staff had proposed the operation.[6]

The first wave of landing craft touched down on the west side of the peninsula, 5 Commando on the northern of the two beaches at 0430 hours, followed an hour or so later by 29th Brigade on the southern one. Ten minutes after the Commando landing, the planned diversion began. The cruiser *Hermione* fired star and smoke shells off the most likely landing beach on the east side of Diégo-Suarez. This was followed about forty minutes later by the Fleet Air Arm striking the harbour and airfield, destroying all the French aircraft and denying the garrison of any means of air reconnaissance. There was little opposition from surprised and weak defences, and the troops pushed across the peninsula with ease.

On the northern axis of advance, 5 Commando had seized its objective, Diégo-Suarez town, by 1700 hours. On the southern route 29th Brigade, after an eighteen-mile approach march, had run into the southern defences of Antsirane, consisting of artillery, pillboxes, and an anti-tank ditch. The French beat off a brigade attack at dawn on 6 May. Another attack was planned for 2030 hours that night, with the support of one of the follow-up brigades. As a diversion, General Sturges asked the Navy to land Marines in the rear of the French at Antsirane. Fifty of *Ramillies'* detachment, under Captain M. Price RM, transferred to the destroyer *Anthony*, which made a high-speed passage round to the entrance of Diégo-Suarez bay. At 2000 hours, she steamed at full speed in pitch darkness in choppy seas, through the narrow entrance, under fire from every battery that could bear. She fired back with a will, and shot out the only searchlight that picked her out. In a strange harbour, in the dark and in a strong wind, *Anthony*'s captain had problems laying her alongside the jetty. Finally, in a brilliant feat of seamanship, he went stern-on to the jetty, holding her there just long enough for the Marines to race ashore. Their orders were to attack everything except the barracks and the magazine, which were known to be strongly held, but within half an hour they were in possession of both of them, with only one casualty to themselves.

At 2030 hours the main force attacked from the south, and by 0100 hours on 7 May had reached the docks and linked up with the Royal Marines. The dashing attack by Price and his men had prevented heavy street fighting and the consequent casualties and damage to the town. The official report credits them with having created a 'disturbance in the town out of all proportion to their numbers'.

At 1040 hours on 7 May, Admiral Syfret with *Ramilles*, *Devonshire*, *Hermione*, and four destroyers shelled the batteries covering the entrance to the bay. In ten minutes the defence collapsed. That afternoon the British task force steamed into the bay. The rest of the 900 mile coastline of Madagascar dominating the Mozambique Channel was still in Vichy French hands, and they declined to surrender: a two-month campaign, from September to November 1942, was necessary to subdue them. The Royal Marines played no part in the subsequent landings and fighting ashore in Madagascar, although they were, of course, manning guns in ships supporting those landings. But they could take a pride in their key role at Antsirane as part of an operation which Churchill described as 'a model for amphibious descents'.[7]

PART FOUR

1943–1945

REORGANIZATION – A NEW DIRECTION AND PURPOSE

16

The Great Reorganization and Marines in the Mediterranean: Sicily to Anzio

Prime Minister to General Ismay, for COS Committee   3 June 42

I have heard nothing of the Royal Marine Division since the Royal Marine brigades [sic] went with the Dakar expedition. What are the plans for its employment? Is it to be used in 'Sledgehammer' or 'Roundup' [plans for the invasion of North-West Europe]? If not might we not offer it to General Wavell? There should be good opportunities for well trained, lightly equipped amphibious troops in his area in the near future.[1]

Despite the Prime Minister's personal interest in mid-1942, another year was to pass before the future of the RM Division was satisfactorily settled, and it had suffered years of frustration already. In mid-1941 the division, together with 29th Independent Infantry Brigade and the Special Service (Commando) Brigade, was warned off for an operation to seize the Canary Islands if Spain entered the war on Germany's side: U-boats could not be allowed use of these islands with their easy access to the Atlantic trade routes. Other projected operations followed, none of which came to fruition. At the time of the Madagascar operation, which included the 29th Brigade, the Army suggested to the Admiralty that the RM Division be put on the regular establishment, and be made part of the expeditionary force for the various invasion plans being contemplated, North Africa being the first. The Admiralty refused; the Army lost interest, withdrawing its units, and the division lost its operational status. The Royal Marines brought in the 9th and 10th Battalions, and the Admiralty offered the division to Eisenhower for the

North African invasion. It was all to no avail, the division never became operational again.

In hindsight this was fortunate. Had an RM Division taken part in the great amphibious operations that still lay around the corner when all this juggling was going on it would no doubt have acquitted itself well, but it would not have saved it from precipitate disbandment the minute the war ended.

Meanwhile huge numbers of officers and men were still tied up in the two MNBDOs. Number 2 arrived in Egypt in early 1943, and some of its units were eventually deployed for the Sicily operation, but unemployed thereafter. MNBDO 1 trained in India for amphibious operations in the Arakan, in Burma, which never came to pass, partly for lack of landing craft. Again, with hindsight, this was probably fortunate since the MNBDOs were backward-looking, Blue Marine-type 'heavy' formations of coast and anti-aircraft gunners, including a large HQ Wing of 'cooks and bottle-washers'. Rather than assault troops, these were supporting and follow-up outfits; worthy but unglamorous, hardly something Royal Marines want to be labelled – and susceptible to instant disbandment once peace broke out.

With the war entering its fourth year, the Corps had over half its strength in formations which had seen little action so far, and had little prospect of doing so. The potential waste of thousands of first-class people, both in terms of numbers and talent, was unacceptable. Matters came to a head in early 1943, when Mountbatten told the Marines that the RM Division must convert its battalions to the Commando role or face total oblivion. At the same time the First Sea Lord needed a huge number of men to crew the mass of landing craft required for the invasion of Normandy, just over a year away. Eventually the decision was made by the Chiefs of Staff to break up the RM Division and the two MNBDOs, and reallocate the manpower to Commandos and landing craft.

The AGRM, Major General Hunton, must take much of the credit for pushing this decision along, against the entrenched views of some of the more traditional, old-style Marine officers of the time, who saw no need to change the Marine way of doing things which had been good enough for the last 279 years. This small reactionary element could not, or would not, see that times had changed, and it was simply not good enough for over half the Corps to have no prospect of taking part in the war because there was no employment for them while they clung to outmoded organizations and practices. It was a case of adapt or die. This historic decision was the turning point of the Corps's fortunes in the Second World War, and in its whole history. Today, the majority of its talent is employed in Commandos and landing craft.

By 1943, Marines were not strangers to landing craft. The MNBDO had developed the LCM before the war, and landing craft were included in its landing and maintenance units. Marines already manned the guns in flak and support landing craft, and had taken part at Dieppe in this role. Although the total crewing of landing craft was new to the Royal Marines, they took to it well, and the Navy issued an order in August 1943 giving Marines full powers of command of all types of landing craft, from the smallest up to and including LCTs. Not all landing craft were crewed by Marines by any means, but there were flotillas of all-Marine landing craft, as well as mixed Navy/Marine flotillas. The only task not undertaken by Marines in even the smallest landing craft in the Second World War was maintaining and operating the engines.

Marines even ventured into the territory of the Royal Armoured Corps, albeit only briefly. The RM Armoured Support Regiment was formed to man obsolescent Centaur tanks for the Normandy landings. Originally these tanks, without drivers, were intended to travel in LCTs, firing their guns as they approached the beach. When the LCTs beached, they were to remain embarked, still firing, like stranded pill-boxes, from the waterline, or thereabouts. General Montgomery heard of this crass notion, told the Royal Armoured Corps to provide drivers, and decreed that the tanks were to go ashore, and continue the battle on and up the beach. The chance to fight ashore was welcomed by the RM tank crews. It was a fortunate decision, because the most dangerous place in an opposed amphibious operation is the waterline and one tarries there at one's peril. Only one part of the ill-starred MNBDOs was kept, when the 5th RM Anti-Aircraft Brigade was formed for service under 21st Army Group in North West Europe, using units from both MNBDOs.

When the decision to disband the RM Division was announced in July 1943, the two Royal Marine Commandos, 40 RM and 41 RM Commandos, were taking part in the Sicily landings with the Middle East Special Service Brigade, later 2nd SS Brigade, under Brigadier Laycock, who had, following the disbandment of Layforce in the Middle East, returned to Britain, and then taken the Commandos out to the

Mediterranean with him. Seven more RM Commandos were formed
from the RM Battalions of the RM Division, as follows:

Battalion	Commando
1 RM	42 RM Commando
2 RM	43 RM Commando
3 RM	44 RM Commando
5 RM	45 RM Commando
9 RM	46 RM Commando
10 RM	47 RM Commando

and in February 1944, after serving in Sicily as a beach brick of MNBDO 2:

7 RM	48 RM Commando

The conversion of the RM Division Battalions into Commandos
was not universally welcomed by the Army commandos, not least in
the higher echelons. Brigadier the Lord Lovat, who had commanded
4 Commando in the brilliantly executed assault on a German battery at
Dieppe, and who had recently been appointed to command 1st SS
Brigade, refers in his book *March Past* to the obvious limitations of an
untried formation of 5,000 officers and men, none of whom had
Commando experience or knew what close quarter fighting was about.
Brigadier John Durnford-Slater, who commanded 3 Commando with
considerable success in Sicily and Italy, complained to the CCO that
'units of conscripted Marines could not be expected to maintain the high
standards of shock troops'. These sentiments were proved to be wrong.
Others thought that the Marine Commandos through their lack of battle
experience were appropriating to themselves prestige that they had not
won.

Turning RM Battalions into Commandos was not just a matter of
changing the name and carrying on as before. A Commando was about
half the strength of an infantry battalion, so half the officers and men
became surplus to requirement. They went to landing craft and back to
sea. All RM commandos underwent the course at the Commando Basic
Training Centre at Achnacarry, where about a third of the course,
whether Army or Marines, usually failed. This quickly sorted out the
faint hearts, and others who lacked the necessary physical and mental
attributes were given the opportunity to vote with their feet, or were
posted elsewhere. The manpower shortfall in RM Commandos after the

weeding-out process was made up with volunteers for 'hazardous duties' from within the Corps, so in effect the RM Commandos that converted from battalions consisted of men who wanted to be in these units, and even the originals transferred from the battalions were volunteers in all but name. The Army commandos did not see it that way, and made adverse comments on the Marines' lack of operational experience, saying that they were not volunteers.

There is an analogy here with the parachute battalions of the 6th Airborne Division, who were formed by turning infantry battalions into parachute battalions. They were accused by the 1st Airborne Division of not being volunteers, and the author has heard ex-Army commandos make similar disparaging remarks at the expense of the 6th Airborne Division. In fact the 6th Airborne Division became one of the finest divisions in the British Army in the Second World War and second to none, including any Army Commando.

On the question of operational experience, it was hardly the fault of the Royal Marines that the newly formed RM Commandos lacked this, since the traditional role for which the RM Brigade had been formed in 1940 had been usurped by the Army Commandos. As one distinguished Royal Marine Commando officer, and author, remarked on the Army Commandos' operational experience:

> Marines felt, and usually tried not to say, that, while there was much to admire and envy in the well-publicized efforts of the Army commandos, not all of it was above criticism and some of it was positively amateurish.[2]

Fortunately this potentially explosive mixture of Army and RM Commandos was all put into Special Service Group under the Royal Marine Major General Sturges, whose firm but wise leadership was responsible for making the concept work. The four SS Brigade commanders also had a part to play in the successful outcome.

*

When General Sir Bernard Montgomery's Eighth Army invaded Sicily on 10 July 1943 the role assigned to 40 and 41 RM Commandos was to land on the left flank of Canadian 1st Infantry Division, to clear enemy machine-gun positions and hold the flank until the Canadians were firmly ashore. 41 RM Commando (Lieutenant Colonel B. J. D. Lumsden

RM) was to land first and hold the beachhead, to be known as Commando Cove, through which 40 RM Commando (Lieutenant Colonel J. C. Manners RM) would also land. Each would then advance to their own objectives: 40 Commando to the west, and 41 Commando to a gun battery on Punta Castellazzo, dominating the beaches over which the Canadian 1st Division would land. Each Commando would be launched from its own transport ship (40 from the *Derbyshire* and 41 from the *Durban Castle*, which were liners converted to carry 20 LCAs each, at davits). By now all Commandos, RM and Army, had reorganized into five rifle troops, each of three officers and sixty-three men. Rifle troops were further sub-divided into two sections, each equivalent to an understrength platoon and commanded by one of the troop subalterns, except in 40 RM Commando, which had originally been organized in companies, where each rifle troop was sub-divided into two platoons. A heavy weapons troop of two 3in mortars and two Vickers medium machine-guns had been added to each Commando to increase firepower.

The weather was fine and sunny on D–1 of the Sicily landings, but by the time the convoys carrying the assault forces approached the lowering position for the LCAs, the wind had risen and the swell had broken into steep waves. As the LCAs were lowered crammed with troops they swung wildly on their cables, crashing against the ships' sides, but without serious damage in the case of both 40 and 41 RM Commandos. On the run-in sheets of spray drenched the commandos, as their LCAs dug their blunt bows into steep seas, and the craft soon stank of vomit. A craft carrying part of A Troop, 41 RM Commando was swamped, sinking about 400 yards offshore, and the Marines had to swim in. Although there was some fire on the last hundred yards of the run-in, fortunately there was little opposition, because both Commandos were landed on the wrong beach. But they pressed on inland, and by 0500 hours both had secured their objectives after despatching about 50 Italians and taking over 100 prisoners. They had expected to encounter coast-defence guns, but found none; 41 RM Commando suffered 9 killed and more wounded, from machine-guns sited in pillboxes. After two days, both Commandos were withdrawn into reserve, to await further operations. Although warned off for an amphibious hook up the east coast of Sicily, six miles north of Catania, this move was subsequently cancelled, when Montgomery changed the axis of advance of Eighth Army to bypass the town. A German air raid on shipping in Augusta harbour killed 13 officers and men, and wounded 58 of 40 RM Commando, putting two rifle troops out of action. Fortunately there was time before the next operation to reorganize. Montgomery decided that the Commandos should be kept for the forthcoming invasion of Italy.

As noted earlier, the last battalion to convert to the Commando role was the 7th. The story of this battalion's vicissitudes is a microcosm of the unhappy state of the Corps in the first half of the Second World War. Originally formed as part of the RM Division, it was sent by the Admiralty to guard naval ammunition dumps in South Africa. On arrival, the South Africans refused to allow the Battalion to undertake garrison tasks on South African territory. At the same time units were being formed in the Middle East for logistic duties in the forthcoming amphibious operations in that theatre. With a number of administrative sub-units tacked on to an infantry battalion, and given the unglamorous name of Beach Bricks, these necessary but humble organizations were responsible for moving stores, ammunition, and fuel out of landing craft and ships and across the beach, then despatching them forward. The 7th Battalion was spare, and became the nucleus of Beach Brick Number 31, which, after about six months' training in Egypt, landed as part of the Sicily invasion force. The 7th Battalion worked on the beach for several days as part of Beach Brick 31, before being plucked out without warning and sent forward some seventy miles to join 51st Highland Division in the valley of the Dittaino River, inland from Catania. The second-in-command of 7th Battalion, sent ahead for orders, was briefed to cross the dry river-bed, about three and a half miles west of the left flank of the division, and attack weak Italian positions on high ground commanding the road and railway which ran along the far bank. The second-in-command reminded the Divisional Commander that the Battalion had done no infantry training for over a year, and asked for time to reorganize and sort out the Battalion. His request was refused.

Later that afternoon, the leading company arrived, and the company commander and his platoon commanders scanned the ground over which they were to attack, through their binoculars. Beyond, and dominating their objective, was a large hill feature where they saw large numbers of soldiers wearing uniforms of a type, including distinctive ski caps, that marked them out as Germans. When relayed to the staff of 51st Highland Division by the CO of 7th Battalion, who had now arrived, this information was greeted with scorn, and he was told that he was mistaken. With the self-regarding clannishness of all veteran formations, the 51st Highland Division may well have regarded these outsiders and tyros with contempt. The 7th Battalion officers lacked the self-confidence engendered by battle experience to challenge this response.

In the event, bearing in mind their inexperience and lack of training, the Battalion did quite well. Starting after dark, the Battalion moved out, A and B Companies leading. B Company reached its objective and took about 150 Italian prisoners. A Company was stalled on the railway line. The two rear companies remained in reserve near the river-bed. With the onset of daylight the Germans on the high ground flayed the Battalion with multi-barrelled 20mm cannon, 81mm mortars, and 88mm guns. The Battalion's small arms were totally outclassed. The sole artillery support allocated to the Battalion, two 3.7in howitzers, were forced by their short range to deploy on forward slopes where they were easy meat for the 88s. Two anti-tank guns, the Battalion's 3in mortars, and three tanks also in support suffered the same fate at the hands of these powerful and deadly guns. Eventually, after a day of enduring several casualties at the hands of the German gunners, the Battalion was withdrawn to its start line positions, where it spent the next nine days under shell fire, suffering more casualties. There were indeed Germans on the position, the best part of a regiment of the crack Hermann Goering Division.

The CO of 7th Battalion was sacked, and his immediate replacement did much to restore the Battalion's morale. The blame for failure should not be laid at the door of the CO, even less on the officers and men of 7th Battalion. Rather it lies with the Corps commander who allowed this untrained and totally inexperienced battalion to be attached to 51st Highland Division, and with the Divisional commander, who appears not to have been interested in the fate of his latest reinforcement. Indeed one of his own battalions had suffered a similar experience the day before, when it ran up against strong German positions, which should have told him something about the situation in the Dittaino valley. Most of all, the blame lies with the Admiralty and Royal Marines who both before the Second World War, and for the first four years following the outbreak of war, allowed so many Royal Marine formations and units to drift purposelessly without a proper role. This unblooded battalion experienced a nasty shock on the Dittaino River, and it would take good leadership to restore confidence among those of its officers and men who later formed part of 48 RM Commando. Having spent the remainder of 1943 in the Mediterranean Theatre, the Battalion was sent back to England to form the nucleus of 48 RM Commando, an altogether more fulfilling role, and fortunately, on arrival they acquired an outstanding CO, Lieutenant Colonel J. L. Moulton.

*

For the invasion of Italy, Special Service Brigade was split. 3 Army and 40 RM Commandos and Major 'Paddy' Mayne's 1st Special Raiding Squadron (SRS) were allocated to Operation Baytown, the crossing of the Strait of Messina to the toe of Italy by Lieutenant General Dempsey's British XIII Corps, while 2 Army and 41 RM Commandos were to operate under command of British X Corps, which formed part of US Fifth Army under Lieutenant General Mark Clark for Operation Avalanche, the assault on Salerno.

For Baytown, 40 RM Commando and 3 Commando were placed as a floating reserve under the command of 231st Independent Infantry Brigade, Brigadier R. E. Urquhart.[3] Dempsey's Corps, having landed on the toe of Italy, at Reggio, advanced up the west coast. He decided to speed up his advance by a left hook at Pizzo by Urquhart's Brigade, landing at the small harbour of San Venere three miles outside the town. 40 RM Commando and part of number 3 were to precede 231st Brigade, landing at 0230 hours on 8 September to secure the beach and seize San Venere.

Despite minor snags, 40 RM Commando's landing went well, and was unopposed. However, as Urquhart's Brigade was in the process of landing, the beachhead came under fire from two batteries of 88mm guns, causing some 40 casualties to the Marines. Urquhart ordered Manners to deal with the 88s, and two troops of 40 RM Commando overran the guns after an air strike had been called in. Having taken prisoners and withdrawn, two further air strikes were directed at the batteries by the Commando to destroy the guns. Two Commando rifle troops, X and Y, were then sent to assist 1st Battalion Hampshires,[4] who were engaged with a German battlegroup on the outskirts of Pizzo. As the two troops approached, they came under mortar and machine-gun fire from high ground outside the town. X Troop was ordered to send a patrol forward, led by Lieutenant T. D. Morgan. His section approached along the railway line, and just as they emerged from a tunnel they bumped into a German patrol outside the railway station; a brisk close-quarter battle ensued. Morgan took his rear group round to a flank, and engaged the German main body in the station, killing an officer and six soldiers. While Morgan was moving forward again, his patrol came under heavy machine-gun fire from positions beyond the station. With one missing and two wounded, Morgan decided to withdraw.

Later that day the Germans put in a counterattack supported by armoured cars. The Hampshires pulled back their two leading companies, and called for naval gunfire. The first rounds fell among X and Y Troops' positions, but a quick adjustment soon had them falling in the right place, and the attack was beaten off. The next day the Commandos and 231st Brigade linked up with 5th Infantry Division, the leading formation of XII Corps coming up from the south. That day news was received of the Italians' unconditional surrender; the Germans, however, continued fighting. The two Commandos were withdrawn into reserve.

Meanwhile, 41 RM Commando had been experiencing some very hard fighting at Salerno. The purpose of the landings there was to seize Naples, and this task was allocated to the British X Corps landing on the left of US VI Corps, both part of Lieutenant General Mark Clark's US Fifth Army. The direct route to Naples, some thirty-five air miles from the beaches on the Gulf of Salerno, went through Salerno and the village of Vietri sul Mare (Vietri), and then through two narrow defiles at La Molina and Nocera, north of Vietri. The Commandos with Laycock's SS Brigade Headquarters were to land at Marina, where a battery enfiladed the western end of the beach. From here they were to march inland to seize and hold the La Molina defile until British 46th Infantry Division, advancing from the beachhead, linked up. Three battalions of US Rangers were tasked to seize the Nocera defile.

On 9 September 1943, both Commandos landed unopposed. 41 RM Commando found Vietri almost clear of enemy, except for about twenty Germans left behind when the others withdrew. As the Marines were padding silently through the village, a 155mm self-propelled gun came along the street. The Marines ambushed it, killing the driver and capturing its crew of twelve. 2 Commando (Lieutenant Colonel J. M. T. F. ('Jack') Churchill) and Brigade Headquarters then occupied the village, while 41 RM Commando continued the advance to La Molina. On the way they came across a German tank whose crew were asleep by the road. They were killed, and a Marine dropped a grenade down the commander's hatch, which detonated the ammunition stowed in the turret. The demolition section blew up the railway line and removed the German charges on the road viaduct, while the rest of the Commando dug in astride the road.

The main body of Fifth Army was having a much busier time to the south of Laycock's men. The Germans, by a process of deduction, had correctly anticipated that landings would take place on the beaches south of Salerno, and had taken steps accordingly. But not foreseeing the landing by Allied Special Service troops to gain control of the road to Naples, they had denuded this area of troops. Headquarters SS Brigade had established radio contact with the 46th Division and learnt that the leading brigade was ashore but held up on the far side of Salerno. Troops of German XXXVI Panzer Corps, in particular 16th Panzer Division, were in good positions in high ground overlooking the landing beaches, and were responsible for delaying 46th Division in Salerno. The Germans, as usual, were counterattacking, and attempting to push 2 Commando out of Vietri, although on this first day these were mainly probing attacks: two tanks were driven off by anti-tank guns and PIATs, as was an infantry attack which followed. The enemy in the vicinity of La Molina were also becoming bolder and more aggressive, and tanks probed 41 RM Commando's position. The LCAs that were carrying both Commandos' large packs and the balance of the first-line ammunition not on the men were unable to land thanks to heavy mortar fire on the beaches. Fortunately the Commandos were able to be supplied with food and ammunition from within the beachhead, but had to fight in light order for the ensuing nine days.

At about last light, some armoured cars of the Divisional Reconnaissance Regiment reached 41 RM Commando's positions, and passed through. Before long they were back with an Italian prisoner, and confirming patrol reports from the Commando that enemy armour was no more than a mile or so from their positions. Despite being so close, that night no enemy bumped the Commando's patrols spread across their front, possibly because, as so many veterans of the war have observed, the Germans were not particularly good at fighting at night.

The next morning, by which time the armoured cars had withdrawn, the Special Service Brigade was told that the 46th Division was so busy fighting off German counterattacks that it could spare no troops to reinforce the Commandos. After a mortar bombardment, dismounted infantry from the 3rd Panzergrenadier Division attacked 41 RM Commando's position. The Commando let them come within twenty yards, and blasted them with Brens, rifles, and Tommy guns. But large numbers of panzergrenadiers were able to infiltrate along gulleys between the rifle troop positions. Marine Kelly was in a section forward of A Troop's main position on a vineyard terrace:

> The Germans were very well camouflaged, their fieldcraft was good, and they kept up a good rate of fire all the time. I could hear the rounds thumping off the wall in front of me. The grapes on the vines were being chewed off by the bursts of fire, and dropping down on me. It reminded me of the firing range, when the rounds were hitting low on the bank in front of the butts. Quite suddenly we were taking casualties, as mortar bombs dropped all round us. I was scared. It would have been better if I could have seen something.

Q Troop counterattacked just as A Troop was being overrun, driving off the Germans. But Q Troop commander and one officer were killed, leaving nineteen-year-old Lieutenant Peter Haydon in command. Although wounded, he refused to be evacuated. They beat off another attack, Haydon accounting for several enemy with his rifle, although weak from loss of blood, and wounded for a second time. He was subsequently awarded the DSO, the youngest RM officer to be awarded this decoration in the Second World War.

During the day, Lumsden was wounded by a mortar bomb, and handed command over to Major Edwards. The enemy attacks continued, the main threat developing along a ridge (Dragone Hill) on the left of and overlooking the Marines' positions, thus threatening 2 Commando in Vietri. Laycock asked for and got some infantry reinforcements, and these were enough to release three troops of 2 Commando to seize the vital ridge. That night was quiet, and the next day two more infantry companies reinforced the Special Service Brigade, so that night both Commandos were pulled back into reserve. However, the following day (12 September) the enemy counterattacks on the 46th Division were renewed, and the situation in the beachhead became very serious. To release their infantry to assist 46th Division, both Commandos were ordered back into their old positions, albeit with narrower frontages. By now each Commando was down to about 300 all ranks: 41 RM

Commando's casualties, dead, wounded, and missing, were 11 officers and 74 NCOs and Marines, and 2 Commando's 1 officer and 33 other ranks.

At first light on the 13 September a full-blooded attack came in, cutting off the two forward troops of 2 Commando, which held their ground. The enemy managed to infiltrate back onto Dragone Hill, and the situation hung in the balance. Artillery fire helped stem the enemy, but they also managed to seize ground overlooking 41 RM's Vickers machine-guns. The commander of the machine-gun section, RSM Tierney, led a counterattack, which drove off the enemy, but he was killed.

X Troop was sent over from 41 RM Commando to assist one of the troops of 2 Commando mount a counterattack on Dragone Hill, under the command of Churchill's second-in-command, Major Lawrie. During the assault, Lawrie was killed, and Major Edwards of 41 Commando took over, and cleared the hill. This was the decisive moment of the battle in this sector, because there were no more German counterattacks here. 2 Commando lost 22 dead and 55 wounded, and 41 Commando had casualties too. The fighting on the rocky terraces and vines was often confused, and the enemy mortar fire accurate. Kelly:

> The action was so fluid that one day a German mortar forward observer officer just walked forward shouting, perhaps looking for his men, and the troop officer shot him at point blank range. The slightest movement brought down mortar fire. My Bren's bipod had one leg shattered by shrapnel, and the other sheered off.

On 14 September both Commandos were pulled out for a twenty-four-hour rest, before being moved to Mercatello, two miles east of Salerno. Here they came under the command of one of the brigades of the British 46th Division. A very serious threat had developed following the German seizure of four features overlooking the village of Piegolelle, a high crag, and three hills known as the Pimple, Whitecross, and Point 339 (spot height 339 metres – over 1,000 feet above sea level). They overlooked the beachhead and it was highly likely that a determined push from this direction would cut the precarious Allied toehold in two. 2 Commando was ordered to take Piegolelle and the 'Pimple', while 41 RM Commando was to take Point 339. On the night of 15/16 September, after a hard night march, involving at one stage scrambling up the steep vineyard terraces, each seven feet high, and fifteen feet wide, 41 RM

Commando occupied Point 339, without encountering opposition. The feature became known as 41 Commando Hill.

Starting at last light 2 Commando mounted an operation to clear the valley leading to the other two features occupied by the enemy, by advancing in six parallel troop columns, like a partridge drive by a Commando-strength fighting patrol. Many of the Germans, unable to see their enemy, surrendered without a fight. 2 Commando, having reached and cleared the village of Piegolelle and the Pimple, returned to their start line with 136 prisoners, more than the whole of 46th Division had taken so far in the battle. It was a pity they did not stay on the Pimple, because on their return they were ordered back to take it. By now, although it was still night, visibility had improved, the clearance operation had not been one hundred per cent successful (hardly surprising in the darkness), and the enemy had reoccupied the feature and were thoroughly alert. The 2 Commando attack stalled with heavy casualties, including the Duke of Wellington, one of the troop commanders. The Commando consolidated in Piegolelle, and managed to link up with 41 Commando. During 16 September the enemy made several efforts to knock both Commandos off their positions, but they held firm under increasingly heavy mortar and artillery fire.

The 138th Brigade of 46th Division was ordered to take the Pimple and Whitecross Hill, but without warning this was changed and 41 RM Commando were told to take on the task. At 0200 hours on 17 September the Commando moved from 41 Commando Hill to their start line. On arrival they were treated to an artillery concentration from the 46th Division's guns, firing at a high rate and lasting over ten minutes; not the first nor the last time that an artillery programme designed to hit the objective has by mistake fallen on the troops it was supposed to be supporting. Kelly in 41 Commando recorded, 'We suffered more casualties from our own fire than from the enemy.' The fire killed eight of the Commando, including the CO, Major Edwards, and wounded twenty-two. P and Y Troops nearly got onto the summit of Whitecross Hill, but all the officers were killed or wounded. The NCOs led another assault, but short of ammunition, and outnumbered by the now thoroughly alerted defenders, the attack was called off. B Troop's attack on the Pimple was also beaten off with heavy loss. Carrying their wounded with them down the steep terraces, 41 RM Commando pulled back into Piegolelle.

On the night of 18/19 September both Commandos were withdrawn to Sicily to rest and reorganize. After nine days of almost continuous fighting, both were reduced to about half strength. They had come through a tough test of their courage and tenacity in battle, against first-class troops. The Commandos were the only troops who took their initial objectives on time and both had made a major contribution to holding the beachhead on more than one occasion when disaster threatened and the whole landing seemed doomed. 41 RM Commando's efforts in particular gave the lie to the disparaging remarks levelled at the Royal Marines by Army commandos back in England. 41 RM Commando's losses at Salerno were about fifty per cent, amounting to 49 dead and some 150 wounded. Officer casualties were worse: out of 27 officers, 21 were killed or wounded, nearly 80 per cent.

The day after the Commandos were withdrawn, British Eighth Army linked up with Mark Clark's Fifth Army, and Naples fell eleven days later. After arriving in Sicily, Laycock handed over to Lieutenant Colonel T. B. L. ('Tom') Churchill, and left the theatre to take over from Mountbatten as CCO, on the latter's appointment as Supreme Allied Commander South East Asia Command (SEAC).

On the other side of Italy, the other half of what was now 2nd SS Brigade, 3 Commando, 40 RM Commando, and the SRS, all under the command of Lieutenant Colonel Durnford-Slater, and depleted by battle casualties, was being briefed at Bari for an amphibious hook at Termoli, 120 miles further up the coast. The British 78th and Canadian 1st Divisions were encountering increasingly stiff German resistance north of Foggia, and Montgomery was concerned that the enemy might turn the Bifurno River line, some twenty miles to the north, into a strong defensive position. By capturing Termoli just north-west of the mouth of the Bifurno the German defences would be outflanked, and the lateral road from Naples to the east coast would be opened up for Allied use. The terrain in Italy favoured the defence. The central spine of the Apennines limited east–west movement to a few passes, and numerous rivers ran from the spine to each coast, presenting a succession of potential obstacles to the Allies advancing north between the coasts and the mountains.

It was thought that Termoli would be held by the administrative units of German 1st Parachute Division, who were facing 78th Division. British intelligence was unaware that 26th Panzer Division was resting in the vicinity after the Salerno battles.

Dempsey, the commander of XIII Corps, ordered Durnford-Slater to land west of Termoli, capture the small fishing port and town, and link up with 11th Brigade of 78th Division advancing from the south-east. Durnford-Slater planned that 3 Commando would land in LCAs, followed by his Headquarters also in an LCA, to establish the beachhead. 40 RM Commando and the SRS would follow in four LCI(L). 40 RM Commando would pass through the beachhead to capture the town and port. The SRS was to establish a block on the road into Termoli from the north-east, reconnoitre south-east along Route 16, up which 11th Brigade would come, and seize and hold the road and rail crossings over the Bifurno. The LCI(L) towed the LCAs most of the way, and stopped to allow 3 Commando to transfer into them from the larger vessels; challenging, but successfully accomplished, in the moderate swell. Thanks to the shallow draught of the LCAs, 3 Commando had a dry landing. 40 RM Commando and the SRS had an exceedingly wet one in six feet of water when the LCI(L)s grounded fifty yards offshore. The radios were drowned and useless, so all information had to be passed by runner, and it proved impossible to bring the Vickers machine-guns ashore.

For the initial part of the operation, the CO, Manners, divided 40 RM Commando into two groups, Q, P, and Y Troops under himself, and A, B, and X under Major Peter Hellings. Manners' group was to capture the town, while Hellings's took the port, and established roadblocks on the two main roads out of town.

Y and P Troops had a tough fight for the railway station, after which some of the German prisoners said that they were an engineer party and revealed that the station and water tower were already prepared for demolition. As a test of their good faith, these prisoners were kept in the station until all the charges were located and defused. Q Troop secured the railway bridge after a brisk close-quarter battle. In a nearby building, several German parachute troops were taken prisoner, including the commander of the battle-group defending the area.

Meanwhile A Troop, having cleared the port, moved along the beach to the south, and came under fire from houses to their right. Corporal Humphrey had spotted the source of the fire, and told his troop commander, Captain Ephraums, who, taking Humphrey and Sergeant Haslett with him, tried to reconnoitre the enemy position prior to a troop attack. As they turned up a side street they came under fire;

Ephraums was killed and Haslett wounded. Despite this, Haslett brought up his men and overran the enemy.

By first light the town was secure, and soon afterwards the enemy counterattacks began. Snipers from 1st Parachute Regiment also infiltrated the town and gave some trouble. 40 RM Commando's X Troop sprang a very successful ambush on seven trucks and a staff car driving towards Termoli, blissfully unaware of the Commando's presence. They contained among other things canteen stores including a large consignment of cigarettes. B Troop ambushed some parachute soldiers, two more trucks, and two motorcycles. The SRS had discovered the rail and road bridges demolished, but while down by the river found a battalion of Lancashire Fusiliers[5] preparing to cross on a pontoon bridge.

At this stage, 40 RM Commando was ordered to set up a strong defensive position to the south of Termoli. The leading troop on the way to the new location suddenly ran into a strong enemy position. Captain Marshall ordered his leading sections to fix bayonets and charge firing from the hip. The German resistance folded. In the early afternoon armoured cars and personnel carriers of the 56th Reconnaissance Regiment arrived in town, a sign that 11th Brigade could not be far behind. Durnford-Slater pulled in 3 Commando and the SRS to form a reserve, leaving 40 RM Commando to protect the perimeter of the town. Later that afternoon, the Lancashire Fusiliers and four Canadian tanks crossed the river, but had not succeeded in making contact with 40 RM Commando before nightfall. For the rest of the day there were contacts with small pockets of enemy, and reports of Germans forming up in strength to the south-west of Termoli.

That night, the second without sleep, was spent by 40 RM Commando patrolling, and bringing in more prisoners. At midnight more reinforcements from 78th Division arrived at Termoli by sea, consisting of Headquarters 36th Brigade, 8th Battalion Argyll and Sutherland Highlanders, 6th Battalion The Royal West Kents,[6] and some of 11th Brigade. Early the next morning, Durnford-Slater was told that his task would finish by 0830 hours. No sooner had the two battalions of 36th Brigade starting deploying than a German counterattack appeared imminent. An attack on the Argylls' position was broken up by 40 RM Commando's mortars, and although the town was bombed, there were no further attacks that day. Unfortunately, heavy rain had caused the Bifurno River to flood, and swept part of the pontoon bridge away. The flow of reinforcements into Termoli by road dried up. That evening a prisoner was brought in from 26th Panzer Division, and before first light on 5 October enemy armour could be heard approaching from the south. After dawn, the Luftwaffe bombed the town. The Germans started shelling the town, and the building occupied by Durnford-Slater's HQ was hit, causing casualties, but he was unscathed.

Throughout the afternoon German armour and infantry tried to penetrate the defences from several directions. They pushed back the Argylls, some of whom withdrew through 40 RM Commando's positions. Some attacks were beaten off by artillery fire from the guns of 78th Division south of the Bifurno and an air strike, both requested by the CO of the Reconnaissance Regiment over his radio link to Divisional HQ. At 1700 hours about eleven German Mark IV tanks with infantry could be seen forming up opposite 40 RM Commando, which were under shell and mortar fire, the preliminary to an attack. The Army crews of two 6-pounder anti-tank guns attached to the Commando ran off under the strain of the mortar fire, and the guns were manned by Marines from B Troop. For unknown reasons the German attack was not pressed home, possibly because the light was fading. As usual, enemy activity died down with the onset of darkness.

An attack out of the perimeter was planned for the next morning by the Lancashire Fusiliers and London Irish Rifles from 40 RM Commando's positions. The Germans had other ideas, and, preceded by artillery fire and low-level attacks by aircraft, infantry and armour headed towards P Troop, 40 RM Commando. The attack was beaten off with the assistance of anti-tank guns. Next it was the turn of A and Q Troops and the SRS to come under attack. But again the enemy was stalled by steady fire from the Marines and troopers. Q Troop had a ding-dong fight for possession of the cemetery, and eventually, after the battle had ebbed and flowed back and forth, the Germans were ejected. In the early afternoon the planned attack through 40 RM Commando's position eventually took place, supported by fire from A and Q Troops, the Commando's mortars, and the 6-pounder anti-tank guns, still crewed by Marines. The Germans put up little resistance, and pulled back. Later, 40 RM Commando and the SRS were withdrawn into the town. The following day Generals Montgomery and Dempsey came to congratulate the SS Brigade on a job well done.

The operation was a classic amphibious hook to restore momentum to the battle. Surprise was total, and responsible for the quick capture of the town and harbour with relatively low casualties. The commandos subsequently held the perimeter for five days against armour and well-trained panzergrenadiers and parachute soldiers until sufficient force could be built up to push the enemy back. Among the well-deserved awards, there was a DSO for Manners, an MC for Hellings, and an MM for Corporal Usher. 40 RM Commando was withdrawn to Molfetta to rest and recuperate.

Some reorganizations took place following the Termoli operation. 43 RM Commando (Lieutenant Colonel Simonds) and 9 Commando (Lieutenant Colonel Tod) were sent out to the Mediterranean to join 2 SS Brigade, while 41 RM Commando, 3 Commando, and the SRS returned to England in readiness for the invasion of Normandy the following year.

At the end of December 1943, 40 RM Commando was trucked across the Apennines to Castellammare on the western side of Italy, where they found 43 RM and 9 Commandos. Here they learned that 40 RM Commando was to come under command of British 56th (London) Division, part of British X Corps, under Mark Clark's US Fifth Army. The Division had been given the task of crossing the Garigliano River as a prelude to Fifth Army's taking Cassino and advancing to Rome. The crossing was to be by two brigades, about two miles apart, with 40 Commando split between them. Force One, under Captain Ecrepont, consisting of B and Q Troops and an artillery FOO party, was to operate with the 169th Infantry Brigade. Captain Marshall, with A, P, and X Troops, formed Force Two under command of the 167th Infantry Brigade. The Commando tasks were to exploit beyond the objectives of the leading infantry battalions, penetrate the German positions, attack communications, and cause as much mayhem as possible. The country was broken with hills, mountains, ravines, gulleys, and fast-flowing rivers swollen with winter rain. Extensive German demolition work had destroyed, or mined, roads, railways, tunnels, and bridges.

Preceded by the 2nd/6th Battalion The Queen's Royal Regiment,[7] Force One crossed the Garigliano in assault boats at 2030 on 17 January 1944. The 2nd/6th Queen's had marked a route through the minefield for the commandos, who advanced quickly until the tape ran out near an orchard. Three Marines stepped on mines before the cleared track could be found. At this juncture they came under fire from an enemy machine-gun. A successful attack by the leading section eliminated the gun, taking one prisoner. By now daylight was approaching, and Ecrepont ordered his men to dig in. He linked up with 2nd/6th Queen's and both prepared for the expected counterattack. However, except for shell and mortar fire during the ensuing day, they were left alone. That night some aggressive patrolling by Force One netted a total of thirty-eight prisoners.

Force Two had an altogether more difficult time. Moving behind 8th Battalion The Royal Fusiliers, they came under heavy artillery, mortar, and machine-gun fire as soon as they crossed their start line. The far bank of the river was mined, and progress was slow. Corporal Usher of X Troop was hit in the thigh and in the shoulder. He lay out all night, and when evacuated the next day he was found to have frostbite. The lead scout of A Troop was killed by a mine, which blinded Sergeant Shea. As next senior, Corporal Humphrey took over. A little later, a stick grenade landed next to a Marine alongside him, and as Humphrey tried to kick it away, it exploded, blinding him and wounding him in the shoulder. A Troop continued to take casualties as it pressed on in the darkness towards the objective, Monte Salvatito. Having consolidated with 8th Royal Fusiliers, Captain Marshall waited for daylight before clearing Monte Salvatito and establishing an artillery OP there which proceeded to harass the enemy for the next three days. The clearance of some troublesome enemy machine-gun posts in the vicinity was also successfully achieved.

That night, 18/19 January, the 167th Brigade planned a further advance on to Monte San Cosmodamiano. This feature was dominated by Monte Rotondo. Force Two was ordered to infiltrate the German lines, seize Monte Rotondo, and attack traffic on the roads north-west from Castelforte, one of the Divisional objectives and still in enemy hands. After dark, Force Two split into section-strength patrols to move at thirty-minute intervals on to Monte Rotondo where they would rendezvous. After an exhausting night, climbing up, down, and around steep rocky outcrops and making diversions to avoid enemy posts, only part of the Force arrived on Monte Rotondo. Without sufficient men to hold the feature, Captain Marshall decided to carry on with his second task, of attacking the road. Having shot two motorcyclists, and destroyed two field guns, they ambushed a column of vehicles and two armoured cars. Some of the vehicles got away, but one armoured car was disabled.

After establishing a roadblock, a Mark IV tank approached, and was seen off after being set on fire by a 77 anti-armour grenade. This drew the attention of three more tanks, who fired as they approached, wounding two of Marshall's men. Clearly believing the commandos were hardly a challenge, a German officer dismounted and said in excellent English, 'Come here, I have orders for you.' He was answered with a burst of Bren fire. This defiance notwithstanding, Marshall judged it was time to withdraw. He jumped on the back of one tank, engaging the crew with his Colt .45in automatic through the hatch, while his men dashed across the road into a thickly wooded gully, taking their three wounded with them. Marshall jumped down and ran after them. With three wounded and ammunition running low, Marshall decided to lie up for the day, and make for their own lines after dark. Just before dawn on 20 January, Marshall's group regained the British lines, having endured being shelled by their own side en route.

Meanwhile Force One had been busy patrolling, capturing more prisoners, to bring their score up to forty-six, for the loss of one killed, five missing, and ten wounded, and on 21 January they were pulled back into Brigade reserve while Force Two put in some more aggressive patrols. German mines were a constant threat, and Troop Sergeant Major Malcolm was killed, and seven Marines wounded by S-mines. On 23 January both Forces were withdrawn into Corps reserve, and had a chance to rest, and enjoy a hot meal and a wash. A few days later, 40 RM Commando, all together again, was employed in the line as normal infantry until 21 February. Three MCs and five MMs were awarded to 40 RM Commando for its work behind the lines at the Garigliano.

While 40 RM Commando had been fighting and patrolling north of the Garigliano River, 43 RM Commando and 9 Commando had landed at Anzio, some fifty miles south of Rome and north of Cassino, where Fifth Army was stalled. The Anzio landings, Operation Shingle, were ordered by General Sir Harold Alexander, the overall Allied Land Force Commander in Italy, in order to cut the line of communication to the Germans facing Fifth Army on the Garigliano and Rapido Rivers. Alexander hoped the Germans would pull troops out to face this new threat, thereby enabling Fifth Army to break out. As a long shot, Alexander thought that Rome might be taken as well. In the event, Major General Lucas's US VIth Corps, consisting initially of the British 1st and US 3rd Infantry Divisions and part of US 1st Armored Division, was not nearly strong enough to accomplish such an ambitious task. The German reaction was much quicker than the Allies had anticipated, easily outpacing the Allied build-up, and soon had the VIth Corps pinned in the beachhead. Lucas has since been criticized for not taking Rome. As Major General Lucien Truscott, the commander of US 3rd Infantry Division, a *beau sabreur*, and the best commander at the operational level in the US Army, remarked, 'We would have got into Rome, and stayed there as prisoners of war.'

When 43 RM and 9 Commandos stepped ashore shortly after midnight on 21/22 January 1944 this all lay in the future. There was no enemy resistance on the beach, and they plodded inland through muddy going. Soon after midday they had taken their objective, high ground inland dominating the US beaches. The following morning they made contact with the US Rangers, and were withdrawn by LST to Naples. The Commandos had not seen the last of the infamous Anzio beachhead.

Soon after their arrival in Naples, 9 and 43 RM Commandos were warned for an operation by the Commander of X Corps to extend his bridgehead over the Garigliano. They would be under command of British 46th Division. Their objective consisted of three peaks, Monte Tuga (2,000 feet), Monte Ornito (2,400 feet) and Monte Faito (almost 3,000 feet). The hills were bare, rocky, boulder-strewn, and without any cover. Their precipitous sides were guarded by scree slopes. The assaulting Commandos' assembly area was in a river bed, 300 feet above sea level, so any approach to the objective would involve a climb of at least 1,700 feet. Digging was impossible, the only cover would have to be provided by building rock sangars. Mules could only climb halfway up Monte Tuga, and supplies would have to be carried the rest of the way.

The reconnaissance by the two commanding officers, Tod and Simonds, was dogged by mishaps, including thick mist obscuring the objective, and the attack was postponed for twenty-four hours. After several changes, the final plan was for both Commandos to march round the flank of Monte Tuga until they were north of Monte Ornito. Having taken Ornito, 43 RM Commando would strike south to capture another feature, Point 711, while 9 Commando went north-east of Ornito and seized Monte Faito. 43 RM Commando set off at 1830 hours in bright moonlight. They were fired on by mortars and machine-guns, but pressed on. After a long and exhausting climb, A, B, and D Troops of the Commando, led by Captain John Blake, seized both Monte Ornito and Point 711. C Troop mopped up behind, taking casualties from enemy bypassed by the leading troops and concealed in the broken ground. Over thirty prisoners were taken, but clearing the two huge objectives with only one Commando was very difficult.

Number 9 Commando came under such heavy fire from Monte Faito that Tod, who had been wounded, decided to call off the attack that night, and pull back to Monte Ornito. Brigadier Churchill concurred with this decision, and assessing that Faito was strongly held, augmented by troops falling back from the other features, decided that until he was reinforced Monte Faito would be too hard a nut to crack. Meanwhile the two Commandos were to probe the enemy with aggressive patrols. As the day progressed it became clear that the Germans were about to mount a counterattack, and at 1600 hours it materialized. The main weight fell on 43 RM Commando, which managed to beat it off, although the enemy closed to grenade-throwing range. The two Commandos were relieved that night. Brigadier Churchill was congratulated by the Corps Commander, commenting on the courage, endurance, and enterprise of his men in very difficult conditions. In the end it was to take several months before Monte Faito was finally taken, after being captured and lost six times during the Cassino battles.

On 23 February, the day after 43 RM Commando and 9 Commando arrived back in Naples, 2 SS Brigade was ordered to send one Commando to join 2 Commando on the island of Vis in the Adriatic. Churchill selected 43 RM Commando for this, and followed soon after with his Brigade Headquarters. A few days later, the situation in the Anzio beachhead became so serious that 40 RM Commando, which had just arrived in Naples, and 9 Commando were sent in to reinforce VI Corps, now commanded by Truscott. 40 RM Commando came under command of British 169th Brigade, and 9 Commando under British 167th Brigade. Both Commandos operated on the left flank of the beachhead. Here for three weeks they operated in and out of the line, patrolling and taking part in local attacks in rain and mud, in the extremely unpleasant and dangerous conditions of the Anzio beachhead. Their positions were overlooked by the Germans on higher ground, and subjected to heavy shelling and mortaring. On 22 March 40 RM Commando was withdrawn to Anzio, and two days later, having been joined by 9 Commando, they were both taken in LCIs to Naples. From here both Commandos were eventually to move to the Adriatic to rejoin their brigade.

As well as the RM Commandos, other Marines had of course been operating in the Mediterranean in 1943, in ships and landing craft. The Royal Marines were beginning to play a full part in the war after the doldrums of the earlier years. The events of the rest of 1944 and into 1945 saw even greater efforts on their part.

17

North-West Europe, 1944–1945

The extreme gallantry of the Royal Marines stands forth

Winston Churchill[1]

The Normandy Landings on 6 June 1944, and the subsequent fighting in the bridgehead, saw the greatest single effort by the Royal Marines in the Second World War. They provided the following:[2]

4th SS Brigade (Brigadier B. W. ('Jumbo') Leicester)
— 41 RM Commando (Lieutenant Colonel T. M. ('Tim') Gray RM)
— 46 RM Commando (Lieutenant Colonel C. R. Hardy RM)
— 47 RM Commando (Lieutenant Colonel C. F. Phillips RM)
— 48 RM Commando (Lieutenant Colonel J. L. Moulton RM)

In Brigadier the Lord Lovat's 1st SS Brigade (3, 4, and 6 Army Commandos)
— 45 RM Commando (Lieutenant Colonel N. C. Ries RM)

Two Armoured Support Regiments in Centaur tanks
RM gunners in fifty-four landing craft providing supporting fire
Three flotillas, each of ten LCAs, firing 'hedgehog' mortar bombs
Two-thirds of the crews of assault craft, and most of the crews in the build-up phase following the assault
About half the men in the obstruction clearance units
About half the men in three minor landing craft headquarters
Three port parties, with camp staffs, military police, hard parties, and signals
RM detachments in twenty-two bombarding battleships and cruisers

Some 17,500 Marines took part in the initial phases of the liberation of North-West Europe. Later the 5th RM AA Brigade, the 116th Infantry Brigade RM, and RM Engineers also participated, which (counting men brought in to replace casualties, especially in the Commandos) brings the number of Marines who fought in this campaign to well over 25,000. Space does not permit coverage of all the units, craft, and ships in which Royal Marines participated in the campaign, so pride of place will be given to the Commandos, with some mention of the part played by landing craft.

From left to right on and behind the one Canadian and two British beaches, the two SS Brigades would land behind the leading waves of infantry and armour in the assault divisions, and then move out ahead, or to the flank, of these divisions to carry out a number of tasks. In Lovat's 1st SS Brigade, 4 Commando was to clear Ouistreham, while the remainder quickly pushed inland to link up with Major General Richard Gale's British 6th Airborne Division, which would have seized the crossings over the River Orne and Caen Canal during the night of 5/6 June. This brigade would then form part of the left flank of the 6th Airborne bridgehead east of the Orne.

The Commandos of Leicester's 4th SS Brigade all had independent tasks on D-Day. 41 RM Commando, landing on British Sword Beach, was ordered to destroy coastal defences in the area of Lion-sur-Mer, and advance west to link up with 48 RM Commando advancing east from the Canadian Beach (Juno), after which the two Commandos would eliminate a strongpoint at Petit Enfer. 48 RM Commando, having landed at St-Aubin, had first to destroy coastal defences at Langrune. 47 RM Commando, landing on the right-hand British Beach (Gold), was tasked with capturing Port-en-Bessin, some six miles west of Arromanches. 46 RM Commando was to remain afloat on D-Day ready to assault two coastal batteries east of the Orne at Houlgate and Berneville, should these start to threaten the landing beaches.

All the Commandos, except for 4 and 47 RM, which landed in LCAs, were embarked in Landing Craft Infantry (Small), or LCIs (S). An LCI(S) was a 110-ton craft, not unlike an MTB in appearance. It could carry 100 men and had a crew of 17. It had a wooden hull and upperworks, with large, unprotected tanks containing high-octane fuel. The commandos landed down gangplanks pushed over the bows on rollers. Even when the bows of the LCI (S) grounded, the swell lifted the stern, and the gangplanks sea-sawed, often tipping heavily laden commandos into the sea. Originally designed for raids, these craft were unsuitable for assault against defended beaches.

LCAs could also have their mishaps, and on the run-in they were slower and less seaworthy than LCIs (S). One of the trickiest times, especially in a seaway, was when being lowered from davits on the ships which had brought them across from England. Just after the LCA skippered by Corporal Tandy RM had settled on the water, the steering wheel and engine telegraphs were snagged by the hook on the wire hanging from the davit-head, which ripped them off as the craft dropped on the swell. At this stage it would have been understandable if Tandy had bowed gracefully out of the contest on the grounds that it was too difficult to take a landing craft the fourteen miles round trip, under fire, with a load of troops on the run-in, and in marginal weather conditions, with no steering wheel and no means of communicating with the engine room. Instead, Tandy lowered himself over the stern, and steered the craft with one foot on the rudder, and the other on the rudder guard, shouting engine orders to the mechanic in the tiny engine room through the hatch on the after deck of the craft.

Landing in any sort of craft in the second, or subsequent, waves could sometimes be more hazardous than being in the first. A member of 3 Commando remembered that D-Day was to be his eighth landing, and, 'I was most unhappy about it, because it was to be my first in daylight and the first time we were not first in. We were due to land after the hornet's nest had been disturbed.' His craft was holed on the run-in and he was one of the few survivors. The nineteen-year-old Lieutenant Alex Sudborough of 45 RM Commando landed with B Troop, the CO, and part of Commando Headquarters, in LCI(S) 518:

As we hit the beach, I went forrard to see if the brows [gangplanks] had been shot over their rollers. The party of seamen – four or six – were a mass of duffel-coats, steel helmets, teeth, jaws, brains and blood. There was a sweet sickly smell, stronger than all the cordite, grease, and oil normally present in almost any small craft in action. I saw a rope trailing in the sea. Shouting, 'Follow me', I swung myself over the side into what I expected to be three or four feet of water. In my panic, I had not ensured that the rope was made fast inboard; the loose end snaked across the deck as I, gripping the rope, neatly dropped like a plummet into a six-foot shell hole which the tide had covered. I was well and truly stuck in the sands of Normandy with eighteen inches of water over my head.

Help was quickly forthcoming. An RAMC medical orderly waded into the water and dragged me ashore to the cheers of the men in the craft who had the sense to make their exit in a more dignified way. Wading to the water's edge, I could not help noticing the numbers of battle-dressed bodies, all face down, gently floating on the tide line surrounded by a pinkish tinge. The sound of the Adjutant's hunting horn made me gather my wits, impressing on me the need to make for the Commando RV.

While 4 Commando fought to clear Ouistreham, the rest of 1st SS Brigade, led by 6 Commando, made for Benouville, and the bridge over the Caen Canal. Although 6 Commando tried to bypass or infiltrate enemy positions, it had to overcome a number of strongpoints and a gun battery to allow the remainder of the brigade to follow; but it covered the six and a half miles in three and a half hours, a remarkable fighting advance for lightly equipped troops with no artillery support. Lord Lovat and his piper reached the bridge at Benouville (later called Pegasus Bridge) at 1430 hours, with 45 RM Commando, followed by 3 Commando. The bridge was still under fire from pockets of enemy overlooking it, which resulted in several casualties, including Ries commanding 45 RM Commando. The second-in-command, Major W. N. (Nicol) Gray RM, immediately took over command. He was the elder brother of the CO of 41 RM Commando, and had been a land agent before the war. He was not initially popular with the Commando, having commented unfavourably on their performance at the Combined Training Centre at Dorling, when he was Chief Instructor. He commanded for the rest of the war, and proved to be a brilliantly successful, highly respected, commanding officer. 45 RM Commando had also lost their Intelligence and Signals Officers, and despite the 6th of June being a quiet day for them, their total casualties were 4 officers and 44 other ranks, dead, wounded, and missing, although some of the latter rejoined some twenty-four hours later.[3] Among those missing were Lieutenant Winston and his MOA (batman), Marine Donald, who had parachuted into Normandy with the 9th Parachute Battalion to act as liaison between the two units in the Merville area.

By nightfall the 1st SS Brigade, less 3 Commando which had been despatched to Ranville, had taken up positions on the left flank of 6th Airborne Division, along a ridge which gave observation over the landing beaches, and had to be denied to the enemy: 6 Commando in the Le Plein–Breville area; 4 Commando at Hauger; and 45 RM Commando in the village of Merville. Originally, 45 RM Commando had been ordered to occupy the nearby battery, which had been attacked the night before by the 9th Parachute Battalion, in case the Germans had reoccupied it – which they had. But just as the Commando was about to attack, Lovat ordered them to ignore the battery, and hold the village because it was more important to deny the north end of the Amfreville ridge to the Germans. In the early hours of 7 June there was a further change, and the Commando was pulled in towards the rest of the 1st SS Brigade, and occupied positions in an orchard just north of Hauger, close to 4 Commando. Later that morning, another change of plan, and 45 RM Commando was ordered to seize coastal defences at Franceville, right on the eastern extremity of the Orne estuary. Although Lovat was reluctant to overextend his Brigade position, Gale overruled him. Franceville had originally been a D-Day objective for 45 RM Commando, and everybody had been briefed on the task in the staging camps back in England. Lovat said after the war, 'Nicol Gray had been given an awkward assignment.'[4] Two troops of 3 Commando were sent to attack the Merville battery to prevent the enemy from interfering with the Commando's move to Franceville. A Forward Observer Bombardment (FOB) was attached to 45 RM Commando to spot for naval gunfire. As the Commando moved up the road from Hauger, they were subjected to harassing fire from artillery and mortars, which destroyed their mortars. To avoid this fire, a section of A Troop and the two signallers carrying the rear link sets to Brigade HQ took a different route from the remainder, and the Commando lost communications with Lovat. 3 Commando's attack on the battery failed, but once 45 RM Commando reached Merville village they were in dead ground, and safe from small-arms fire from the battery. The section of A Troop and the signallers met the survivors of the 3 Commando attack on the battery, and returned with them to Le Plein, whence they were eventually reunited with their own Commando.

Franceville was a small coastal holiday resort, its villas situated mostly north of the coast road, but with some to the south of it. The plan for attack was unchanged from that given out in England: C Troop (Major Rushforth) was to protect the Commando's left flank, while B and E Troops advanced to attack beach defences on the sea front, after which A and D Troops were to pass through, turn right and attack further beach defences to the east. The main road running north through the centre of Franceville was codenamed 'Piccadilly'. HMS *Warspite* fired a pre-planned bombardment on the coastal fortifications north of Franceville with her 15in guns, at 1705 hours the Commando advanced, and

Warspite switched target to the eastern defences. At this stage the radio set providing communications between the FOB party in their OP and the Commando was smashed; the Marines were now without any form of fire support.

> As the troops moved north towards the coastal defences they came under fire from, and then were attacked by German positions in the villas and small copses on the eastern outskirts of Franceville. In this area there was no clear physical dividing line, fields of vision and fire were mostly limited to the distance between one building and its near neighbours, and sometimes walls and hedges impeded movement and further restricted observation. In this sort of terrain even a battle-hardened unit would have had difficulty coping with an attack on its flank during an advance, but 45 was in its first action and lack of operational experience soon became apparent. From troop level downwards control became less and less effective, as groups of men and individuals moved out of sight and hearing control was often lost. Those not caught by the German attacks from the flank moved on towards their objectives, but by that stage troops had become intermingled and there was confusion and uncertainty.[5]

The troops east of 'Piccadilly' were caught up in this chaos, and as one of the participants wrote later, 'no accurate, or coherent account of the fighting which took place east of Piccadilly is available nor is it possible to produce one now'.[6] Many accounts speak of confusion and uncertainty. Marine Harris of A Troop, part of which was continuing with the advance, while others faced an attack from its right flank, recalled:

> We had taken up a position by some concrete anti-tank blocks which appeared to be part of a line of them leading to a pillbox. All the action seemed to be taking place behind us – we felt very confused, wondering what was happening. I only saw Lt Thomas and Capt Grewcock once: I think they were defending the right flank in the wooded area.[7]

Marine Walker of D Troop:

> We went into the first house to attack from the back gardens. Lt Gale and seven others got over to the second house. I was one of them when we came under fire. I am sorry to say only I and Mne Murray escaped by crawling round the back porch of the house. Lt Gale, Sgt Nutter and all the others were killed. Ted Murray and I got back to the rest of the

section. We decided that we would go and attack from the front of the house. As we moved from the front of the house, we came under fire again and more were killed or wounded.[8]

Gray, realizing that the three troops east of 'Piccadilly' were about to be overwhelmed, ordered them back to the western side. Meanwhile Rushforth's C Troop, west of 'Piccadilly', was having a very quiet time, when he was summoned by radio to join the main body of the Commando. Here he was ordered to counterattack the enemy, who were threatening to surround the Commando by seizing the cross-roads that dominated the entrance to Franceville. He briefed his Troop:

> I told my men to fix bayonets and recall the satisfaction of giving this order. I had heard of the Chindits bunching all their automatic weapons in front when in close contact with the Japs in Burma, so called all those in C Tp with automatic weapons, Brens and TSMGs [Tommy guns] to form a group on my right and left. This worked well for us. We then set off to find the enemy. At one point we were stopped by a thick box hedge. I got my troops to throw me bodily on top of it and thus forced a way through.[9]

C Troop's counterattack was successful, although Rushforth was wounded as he reached the gardens of the school which dominated the area. Much of the fighting took place at close quarters in and around the school and the playground. But 'the aggression and determination shown by Maj Rushforth and his men, and their secure hold on the position they had won undoubtedly saved 45 from further severe casualties and possible destruction.'[10]

Gray realized that the area held by the Commando was far too small, and totally inadequate as a defensive position, and he ordered a withdrawal to Merville that night. The next morning the two missing signallers turned up at Merville, along with a message from Brigade HQ that supplies and reinforcements would be sent up as soon as possible. This was followed at 0830 hours with a message that no supplies or reinforcements would be forthcoming and that Merville must be held at all costs.

Starting at 0930 hours the Germans put in a series of attacks supported by artillery and mortar fire, and self-propelled (SP) guns. These were beaten off, but by afternoon the shortage of ammunition in the Commando was critical. At 1700 hours Lovat ordered Gray to withdraw back into the brigade position at Amfreville after dark. With several hours of daylight left, the enemy mounted another attack, during the course of which Gray shot a German with his rifle, while his orderly shot another with a pistol. Although the German advance was slow, possibly because they had taken a bloody nose in the previous hours, it was methodical, and supported by SP guns, to which the Commando had no response, since its PIAT ammunition had run out. By 1830 hours the CO ordered the withdrawal to start.

To begin with, the enemy harassed the Commando, but a brisk action by E Troop on the flank of the withdrawal saw them off. As the Commando withdrew, tense and exhausted after the previous three days' experiences, many were prone to go to ground needlessly, until, 'seeing Nicol Gray walking across the field as though he was on a parade ground and of course his attitude of "nothing to worry about, men", percolated to the rest of the commando and we all sauntered likewise' remembered one of the Commando.[11]

As 45 RM Commando entered 4 Commando's position at Hauger they were greeted with a cheer. The 1st SS Brigade had been under heavy attack while 45 RM Commando had been fighting out on a limb, and unable to come to its assistance. But, the stout defence of Merville by the Marines had reduced the strength of the enemy troops available to attack the brigade position. Gray was awarded the DSO, along with three MCs and four MMs to 45 RM Commando. Lovat wrote to Rushforth in 1980: 'Franceville can not have been a healthy place and 45 RM Commando did a fine job holding up the Hun's advance along the coastal road while the Brigade dug in on the high ground.'[12]

The Commando had thirty-five killed between 6 and 8 June. Along with the rest of 1st SS Brigade, it spent the whole period of the Battle for Normandy under command of the 6th Airborne Division, and in the fighting between 9 June and the end of August lost another thirty-three dead.

*

The 4th SS Brigade had a tougher landing than 1st SS Brigade. 41 RM Commando was landed some 300 yards west of the intended beach, and some of the rifle troops took heavy casualties on the beach, from artillery and mortar fire as they paused to blow gaps in the uncut wire. Marine Kelly was still in A Troop, 41 RM Commando:

On the back of my pack I had a section of radio aerial with a blue A Troop pennant. I heard Colonel Gray [T. M. Gray – Nicol's brother] shouting 'all commandos this way', he had found a gap in the wire. He shouted at me, 'wave that', pulling my aerial section out of my pack. I gave only a couple of waves, not wanting to get shot. He snatched it off me, and kept waving.

41 RM Commando's objectives at Lion-sur-Mer consisted of a strongpoint and a fortified chateau. The CO had divided the Commando into two Forces (numbers 1 and 2), each to deal with one of the objectives. However, because of the casualties taken on landing, including the commander of Force 2, the CO took both Forces under his command. Finding the village of Lion-sur-Mer deserted, the Commando advanced to attack the strongpoint. All the FOB's signalmen had been wounded and their sets destroyed on the beach, so it was impossible to call for naval gunfire support, and in addition the entire FOO party had been wounded and all three AVREs supporting the Commando were knocked out. Without any support the Commando could make no progress, and as the enemy were about to mount a counterattack the CO ordered a withdrawal to a more defensible line. The strongly held chateau beyond the village was later reinforced by tanks and infantry, remnants of an attempted counterattack by 21st Panzer Division to break through to the coast. With both the strongpoint and the chateau as possible jumping-off places for German counterattacks on the beachhead, it was important that 41 RM Commando hold this exposed flank. By now the Commando had suffered 123 casualties, nearly a third of its fighting strength, so it was reinforced by two infantry battalions from the 9th Infantry Brigade. The next morning, while waiting to move forward, a concentration of anti-personnel bombs from three rogue Heinkels fell on the orchard where Commando HQ was situated, killing 4, and wounding 9, including the CO. The adjutant Major J. A. Taplin took command, the second-in-command having been killed the day before. When 41 RM Commando advanced again, with 2nd Battalion the Lincolnshire Regiment,[13] they found the chateau had been abandoned, and the Lincolns captured the strongpoint.

48 RM Commando, in LCIs (S), suffered heavy casualties landing on the Canadian beach. They would have been worse had the CO, Moulton, not previously trained his Commando to fire 2in mortar smoke from

the bows of their craft during the run-in to the beach. Although the resulting smoke-screen shielded the craft from direct enemy fire, beach obstacles and shrapnel holed the wooden hulls, killing and wounding troops and crews. Most craft did not beach square on to the waterline, and the heavily laden troops were very exposed as they scrambled down the steep bow gangways, which pitched and lurched in the swell, and as they waded through waist-deep water. Some commandos were unceremoniously thrown off head first into the sea. Some were swept off by the swift current and drowned while trying to swim ashore from broached craft.

Although Moulton was wounded by fragments from a mortar bomb, he directed his men to the assembly area, to find that he had only 50 per cent of his Commando before even beginning his allotted task. All the planning, attention to detail, and array of equipment involved in an amphibious operation ultimately have but one purpose: to put a force ashore where they can start fighting. Amphibious techniques are a means to an end, not an end in themselves.

48 RM Commando moved through St-Aubin, where the Canadians were fighting to overcome a major strongpoint, and advanced to Langrune, two miles east. Here the Germans had established a strongpoint consisting of a block of old houses, and streets full of wire and mines. Despite meagre supporting fire, consisting of one 3in mortar and a handful of tanks, one of which threw a track and blocked the road for the others, the Commando made several attempts to overcome the strongpoint.

Eventually Brigadier Leicester, expecting a German counterattack, ordered Moulton to halt and take up defensive positions. The next day, 48 RM Commando captured Langrune. The first two days had cost the Commando 217 all ranks dead, wounded, and missing, out of a strength of around 450. It is worth pausing in the narrative to reflect that the nucleus of 48 RM Commando had been found from 7th Battalion RM, and other units from the Mediterranean MNBDO. The Commando's disastrous landing, and casualties, on D-Day and D+1, were potentially far more shattering to morale than the 7th Battalion's experience the previous year on the Dittaino River. But good training, understanding leadership, especially by Moulton, and, perhaps above all, a sense of purpose enabled the Commando to weather the storm, and go forward to achieve their mission. In part their morale had to do with pride and fulfilment that comes with being valued, being among those entrusted with an important role as part of a great national enterprise. A far cry from the aimless wanderings and wasted years that preceded the conversion to Commandos.

In capturing Port-en-Bessin, 47 RM Commando had perhaps the most daunting task of any in either SS Brigade. The approach to the port involved a march of about ten miles beyond the forward line of friendly troops. It was important to secure Port-en-Bessin early as the junction point between the British and American sectors, and because it had been selected as the terminal for PLUTO, the pipeline under the ocean through which fuel would be pumped directly from England to France. The port was strongly defended, and dominated by three hills: a tough proposition for a Commando whose fighting strength was under 450 all ranks. After studying the problem, the CO decided to land on Jig Green Beach, after it had been secured and cleared by the 231st Brigade of British 50th Infantry Division, and move through German-held country to attack the port from the landward side.

The Commando embarked in fourteen LCAs from two LSIs, and the run-in was uneventful until about 2,000 yards from the beach. Major Paddy Donnell, then second-in-command:

It became obvious that Jig Green beach was deserted except for four support tanks under heavy fire. At about this time a 75 mm battery on the high ground above Le Hamel opened accurate fire on the LCAs. The CO ordered a turn to port and all craft in some disorder, started running east, parallel to the beach. At least one craft was hit and sunk, and it soon became a case of every craft for itself. The beach was crowded with craft and all types of vehicles and equipment, mostly wrecked or swamped. Each craft picked its own landing place. Very few had a dry landing; most grounding offshore, in some cases on obstacles in water so deep that the only way ashore was to dump equipment and swim. One craft at least ran onto a mine, and had its bows blown off. Of the fourteen craft, only two returned to the LSI.

The landing was a shambles. The Commando was spread over a frontage of some 1,500 yards. As planned the Commando moved west, in groups of boat-loads, along the road running parallel to the beach towards the RV, the church in Le Hamel. It became obvious that Le Hamel was still in enemy hands, and 231 Brigade was heavily involved clearing the town.

Donnell made contact with the commander of 231 Brigade who suggested they swing south to avoid Le Hamel, before returning to the original route. By now it was possible to take stock.

The CO, four officers and 73 other ranks were missing, practically all the bangalores and 3in mortar bombs had been sunk. X and B Troops were reasonably dry and equipped. A Troop were complete, but had lost most of their weapons. Q and Y Troop had each lost a craft load [about 30 men each]. There was only one Vickers and one 3in mortar out of four of each, and the latter was without a sight. Commando HQ was almost complete, but all the wireless sets were doubtful starters.

The Commando set off under the second-in-command. As they were moving round Le Hamel, the CO appeared, riding on an ammunition sledge behind an SP gun. That night, after overcoming or bypassing pockets of enemy, the Commando established a firm base on Point 72, part of the high ground about two miles south of Port-en-Bessin. Many of the Marines were now armed with German weapons, and there was no shortage of ammunition for these.

The next day, 47 RM Commando attempted to contact the American artillery whose support figured so prominently in the plan for the capture of Port-en-Bessin; to no avail. Eventually communication was established with 231 Brigade and ships offshore, including the cruiser HMS *Emerald*. The attack started at 1600 hours, supported by naval and air bombardment, smoke from one of 231 Brigade's field batteries, and the one Vickers and one mortar without a sight. The fighting in the town was confused and bitter. Having secured one feature dominating the town, the eastern feature was captured at the second attempt by about midnight. The troop commander, Captain Cousins, having found a route through the wire, was killed leading the attack. The next day the Commando was relieved; of the 431 who had embarked in the LCAs on D-Day, 276 remained. The accumulation of setbacks the Commando had encountered, such as losing weapons and equipment on landing, might have tempted less well-trained and led units to withdraw from the fight on the grounds that it was all too difficult. General Montgomery visited to congratulate them, before they moved with HQ 4th SS Brigade and 48 RM Commando, to come under command of 6th Airborne Division, which was holding the left flank of British Second Army, east of the Orne.

Before this, 46 RM Commando, which had not been required to deal with the batteries at Houlgate and Bennerville, was instead ordered to land on Juno Beach (Canadian) on the morning of D+1 to capture a strongpoint at Petit Enfer. This task was accomplished by that evening. By this time 41 RM Commando had moved into the area from Lion-sur-Mer, and the two Commandos, joined subsequently by 48 RM Commando, surrounded a complex of two radar stations at Douvres, which were heavily wired and mined, with subterranean defences fifty feet, and four storeys, down – reported to have taken three years to build. The complex originally contained 238 men, three 50mm anti-tank guns, three 50mm guns originally designed for use in Mark III tanks, six 20mm flak guns, and twenty machine-guns, mortars, and flame-throwers. On the evening of D-Day it had been reinforced by one company of 192nd Panzergrenadier Regiment of 21st Panzer Division, following an abortive attempt by two battlegroups of that division to counterattack to the coast. It held out for ten days, providing the Germans with important information, as its telephone lines remained intact.[14] The GOC of I Corps, Lieutenant General J. T. Crocker, ordered that the radar station be masked, by covering it so the enemy could neither reinforce nor evacuate it.

After a couple of days, 41 RM Commando found itself the sole custodian of the radar station, as both the other Commandos were sent elsewhere. By 12 June, it seemed that the smaller of the two radar stations had been evacuated, so a twenty-man fighting patrol from A Troop was sent to reconnoitre it. Crocker ordered that the patrol was not to take unnecessary casualties, and should abort the operation if the enemy were still present. A party with Bangalores blew a gap in the outer wire, and AVREs fired petards at the bunkers. Neither provoked a response, so the patrol moved in to blow a gap in the inner wire. By now there had been more changes in 41 RM Commando. Marine Kelly:

Lieutenant [T. M. P.] Stevens took over what was left of the Troop. He turned out to be the finest soldier I have ever known. He was a brave man. There was no way you could refuse to do what he wanted, because he would not ask you do anything he wouldn't do himself. He had complete disdain for danger.

We went in at night as a big fighting patrol with bangalore torpedoes, led by Lieutenant Stevens. If the volume of fire was very heavy, we were

to turn back. The enemy opened up with tracer, [from four locations]
and we returned to the RV, a large crater.

Eventually, on 17 June, supported by forty-four AVREs and flail tanks,
and a heavy bombardment from 7.2in guns, 41 RM Commando captured
the radar complex.

On 11 June, 46 RM Commando was placed under command of the
Canadian 3rd Infantry Division. The divisional commander still had a
dangerous gap between two of his brigades, and to close it he had to
clear the 12th SS (Hitler Jugend) Panzer Division from the Mue valley,
west of Caen. 46 RM Commando was given to the Canadian 8th Infantry
Brigade, and ordered to clear the Mue valley from the village of Barbière
to the twin villages of Rots and Le Hamel (not to be confused with the
village of the same name on the coast), north of the Caen–Bayeux road.
For this operation Hardy was given A Squadron of the Fort Garry Horse,
a troop of the RM Armoured Support Regiment (Centaurs), a section of
sappers, a field regiment (25-pounders), and a Vickers machine-gun
company.

The first three phases of the attack, involving clearing some woods
and the villages of Cairon, Lasson, and Rosel went well, and the
Commando re-formed for the fourth phase. Information about the
strength of the enemy in Le Hamel and Rots was sketchy, but an attack
by the Canadians earlier in the day had been thrown back. Hardy
planned a two-pronged attack, with A and B Troops holding the left
flank just short of Rots, and supporting Y and S Troops assaulting Le
Hamel. S Troop, without its mortars and machine-guns, was fighting
as a rifle company. Once Le Hamel was secure, A and B Troops were
to take Rots. Major Lee, who was coordinating the attack by Y and S
Troops, reported later:[15]

Y and S closed to within 150 yards of the artillery concentration and then
assaulted in line through the waist-high corn. The tanks plastered the
north-east and north-west sides of the village with their Besas and 6-pdrs.
There were five enemy machine guns in weapon slits about 100 yds
forward of the village on the axis of the assaulting troops. These held their
fire until Y and S Troops were 100 yards away and then let fly. Without
hesitation the assaulting troops went in, firing their rifles, Brens and
Tommy guns from the hip. There were two hedgerow obstacles to cross,
one of which was lightly wired, but the attack went on. While we were

crossing the last obstacle, 30 yards from the enemy FDLs, the Boche flung their grenades and turned to run for the defended houses in the village. A number of them were shot down before they could reach the village.

Y and S Troops were now engaged in fierce street fighting for two hours. The enemy were, according Major Lee,

well camouflaged, and obviously very well trained. They darted about from house to house, changing their positions all the time. Except on one occasion when confronted with a Sherman [tank] at close quarters, they showed no inclination to surrender. Their morale was obviously high.

Eventually Le Hamel was taken, including two 88mm guns. A and B Troops now advanced into Rots. While A Troop was dealing with a Panther tank, which caused some casualties, B Troop found itself being engaged from both flanks and rear. At the same time a tank vs. tank battle was in progress in the main street, in which the Shermans were coming off worse, as their 6-pounder (75mm) guns were no match for the Panthers' 88mms. B Troop took severe casualties trying to outflank the village; however, with the support of X and Z Troops, accompanied by a 17-pounder Sherman, the enemy were forced to withdraw. Two Panthers were destroyed, and by 2000 hours the village was captured.

46 RM Commando's advance of seven miles had outstripped that of friendly units on their flanks, so Hardy was ordered by the Commander of the 8th Brigade to withdraw to Cairon. At Le Hamel and Rots the Commando had run into an SS panzergrenadier company of 26th SS Panzergrenadier Regiment and a Panther company of 12th SS Panzer Regiment, as well as the Divisional Escort Company, all from the Hitler Jugend, a far tougher nut to crack then any of the enemy encountered in the coast defences. The congested Mue valley and all the ground to the north-east were under observation. 46 RM Commando took 60 casualties including 20 dead. The Fort Garry Horse lost six Shermans.[16]

A few days later Major General Keller, the GOC Canadian 3rd Infantry Division, wrote to Brigadier Leicester:

Just a note to thank you, your staff, and your Commandos for the excellent work you carried out for us and also for your loyal and enthusiastic co-operation during the successful assault [on D-Day and subsequently].

During these last few days I must ask you to congratulate for me Lieut-
Colonel Hardy and his 46 Commandos, for their thorough dealing with
the enemy in and along the river line (Rots and Rosel): my R[egiment] de
Chauds [Chaudière] buried 122 Boche done in by your chaps.

Be assured we appreciate all this and will deem it an honour to be
fighting alongside and preferably with the Royal Marine Commandos.[17]

On 12 June, Brigadier Leicester was ordered to take 47 and 48 RM
Commandos across the Orne to occupy defensive positions in the
Hauger and Sallenelles area on the left of 1st SS Brigade. 46 RM
Commando followed on completion of their battle in the Mue valley. 41
RM Commando continued to mask the radar station at Douvres, until
they were given sufficient support to capture it. Then they joined 4th SS
Brigade across the Orne. The Commandos of both SS Brigades remained
under the command of 6th Airborne Division on the left flank of the
British sector of the Normandy bridgehead.

In early August, the 4th SS Brigade was relieved in the Sallenelles area
on the northern end of the 6th Airborne Division perimeter, and moved
to Troarn, at the southern end in preparation for the breakout. On 17
August the 6th Airborne Division, with both SS Brigades still under
command, was given the task of protecting the left flank of Canadian
First Army as it drove forward out of the Normandy bridgehead to the
River Seine. The Division's objective was the mouth of the Seine, and to
reach it they had to cross several other rivers. Gale drove his division
hard, marching and attacking both by day and night. The actions of
45 RM Commando in 1st SS Brigade and the Commandos in 4th SS
Brigade, astride the axis Troarn–Dozulé–Pont l'Evêque, give a flavour of
this advance, the last act of the Battle of Normandy.

In order to start the breakout, the 6th Airborne Division had to cross
the River Dives and its flooded valley. The crossings were overlooked by
the Brucourt feature some two miles beyond the river. The sausage-
shaped ridge, rising to about 400 feet at the western end, lay north of,
and dominated, the intended divisional axis. B Troop, 45 RM Commando was sent on the orders of Brigadier Mills-Roberts, Commander
1st SS Brigade, to reconnoitre this ground, and Major De'Ath led a
daylight troop-strength patrol out. By probing forward and drawing fire,
he was able to get a rough idea of the enemy locations on the western
end of the Brucourt ridge. The next morning, De'Ath led another patrol

to gain intelligence of the crossing places of the smaller rivers east of the Dives. His information enabled Mills-Roberts to finalize his breakout plan, which consisted of a brigade night infiltration in single file. This was successfully carried out, and as the historian of the Commandos in the Second World War comments:

> The tactical handling of the brigade had been perfect; it had slipped through all the lines of the enemy and had reached the heart of his position undetected, although every man had at one moment to cross a bridge covered by a German machine gun post less than a hundred and fifty yards away.[18]

Once on the feature, the main priority was to dig in as quickly as possible in readiness for the counterattack. At first light the first attack came in, and it, and the subsequent three, was beaten off. Ammunition was becoming short, and the supply jeeps had to negotiate country still held by the enemy, but at about 2300 hours, just after dark, they got through to the brigade, with most welcome rations in addition.

To begin with 4th SS Brigade were out of contact with the enemy. On 19 August the 5th Parachute Brigade, having captured the village of Putot-en-Auge, had been forced off high ground, known as Hill 13, beyond the village and dominating the approaches to Dozulé. Leicester was told to restore momentum to the advance. He ordered 46 RM Commando to clear Hill 13 that night.

While Hardy was briefing his troop commanders, a mortar bomb landed close by, wounding the adjutant and a troop commander and three other officers. Brigade Tac HQ was close by, and Leicester ordered Lieutenant P. R. Kay, his Liaison Officer, to report to Hardy, who asked, 'Are you armed?' When Kay replied in the affirmative, he was told, 'You will lead Z Troop this evening.'

After dark, 46 RM Commando set off in single file led by Hardy and his Intelligence Officer. Arriving at the top of the hill, they rushed the Germans, and after some brisk fighting, some of it hand-to-hand, most of the enemy fled. Hardy shot a German at a yard's range as he lunged at him. In the morning a number of enemy were found hiding in dug-outs, still shocked by the suddenness of the Commando's night attack. An officer prisoner who had fought in Africa and Russia said that he had never seen such a well-conducted night attack, and admitted that his unit was taken completely by surprise and had had no intention of giving up the hill so easily. The casualties sustained by the Commando during the assault were 1 killed and 2 wounded, but a further 17 were caused by shelling before and after the attack.[19]

Meanwhile, 3rd Parachute Brigade had taken over the lead and was approaching Dozulé some miles beyond Putot-en-Auge. Gale, wanting to cut the German escape road east of Dozulé, ordered Leicester to send a Commando to secure a hill on the far side of the village, by infiltrating through, or round, the German defences. The task was given to 48 RM Commando. Leicester also ordered 41 and 47 RM Commandos to follow in 48 Commando's tracks, and they would mount a brigade attack on Dozulé from the south. Starting at first light on 20 August, the outflanking operation by all three Commandos went well, although not without some casualties.

The 4th SS Brigade's next objective was Pont l'Evêque. The Germans were dug in on high ground on the far side of the River Touques, which is to the west of the town. The brigade having been ordered to ford the river that night, the Germans pulled out. The brigade moved through the burning town, and continued the advance. In an outflanking operation 46 RM Commando captured enemy positions south of Beuzeville, where 5th Parachute Brigade had been held up. Hardy was wounded but remained in command, and the second-in-command and 11 of the Commando were killed, and 37 wounded. About two enemy companies had been encountered by 46 RM Commando, in a battle that their historian reckoned the toughest since Rots.[20] Hardy was awarded a bar to the DSO earned for the Rots battle. Earlier a written message from Gale was received by Leicester, which read: 'Brigadier Leicester, you will pursue the enemy relentlessly into the night.'

Moulton's Commando were starting to eat their suppers that night when he was told he was to lead the whole brigade, less 46 RM Commando, to penetrate some five miles to the village of St-Maclou. By candlelight he gave his orders, dividing the route into 'legs', and giving each 'leg' to a troop commander to learn by heart, and take it in turns to lead. It was so dark that only the next morning did the Commando jeep drivers learn that a particularly bad bump they had driven over coming into the farm where Commando HQ was situated was in reality a dead German.[21] In the early dawn, the brigade entered the village unopposed – the enemy had fled.

Chilly, unshaven and longing for sleep, we looked forward to a good billet in the chateau; but, an hour later, Brigade ordered us out to make way for them; and we had to find ourselves other billets in the village. That evening, someone in Brigade opened a drawer, booby-trapped by the departing Germans, and two men were seriously wounded; 48 took it as the intervention of divine justice and laughed unkindly.[22]

Now the 6th Airborne Division and the 1st SS Brigade were withdrawn to England, while 4th SS remained in France under the command of I Corps. Both SS Brigades spent more time in contact with the enemy in the Normandy campaign than any other British formation – eighty-three days. Of the five RM Commandos in the Battle of Normandy, 46 RM Commando alone suffered 170 casualties. The fighting record of the RM Commandos in Normandy, especially feats such as 46 RM Commando's battle in the Mue valley against the finest German troops, proved that the critics of the Marines were wrong. The operational experience of many of their detractors had been limited to raids against second-class coastal defence troops, and however good for morale these may have been at the time, they actually achieved very little in the cold accounting of war. What separated the 'men' from the 'boys' was performance in 'real' fighting as part of the main point of effort in-theatre. If any doubts lingered, they should have been stilled by General Richard Gale's judgement that he rated 4th SS Brigade during the pursuit to the Seine as one of the finest brigades he had ever had under command. Much of the credit for this must lie with Brigadier Leicester, a brilliant soldier and tactician who showed an outstanding ability to cope with a fluid battle. His control of his strong-willed COs was masterly. That very tough soldier, Lieutenant Colonel Dawson, after his 4 Army Commando had transferred from 1st SS Brigade to Leicester's, once referred to the 'joyful privilege of serving under "Jumbo"'. Royal Marines today have Leicester, and his COs – along with their opposite numbers in 45 RM Commando and RM Commando in other theatres – to thank for the fact that after the Second World War the Commando role became an exclusive Marine preserve. Had they failed, it is likely that the Corps as a whole would by now have disappeared from the order of battle of the UK's defence forces.

*

On the conclusion of the Normandy campaign, some changes took place
in the SS brigades. 45 RM Commando returned to England with 1st SS
Brigade, which had been warned for service in the Far East, but in the
end returned to North-West Europe and spent the rest of the war in that
theatre. 4th SS Brigade, having crossed the Seine, remained in the area
of Le Havre until it moved forward to take part in operations to contain
the German garrison of Dunkirk; 46 RM Commando was switched to
1st SS Brigade, its place in 4th SS Brigade being taken by 4 Commando.
In the autumn of 1944, the SS Brigades changed their names to
Commando Brigades.

From Dunkirk, the 4th Commando Brigade moved to de Haan, near
Zeebrugge, on the Belgian coast. Here, Kelly, now a corporal, remembers:

> We used the huge German coastal defences as a training area. We threw
> grenades like a cricket ball, rather than lobbing them. There was a feeling
> about Arnhem going around, we were told that our next operation would
> be successful, and that they would not attempt another Arnhem.

The next task for 4th Commando Brigade was the assault on the
Dutch island of Walcheren at the mouth of the Scheldt estuary. Although
the port of Antwerp had been captured early in September 1944 with its
dock installations more or less intact, the port could not be used until
the River Scheldt had been swept of mines along its fifty-mile length.
After savage fighting, the banks of the Scheldt leading to Antwerp had
been captured by the Canadian II Corps with, under command, the
British 52nd (Lowland) Division, but the approaches to Antwerp from
the sea were dominated by German batteries built into the dunes of
Walcheren, in massive concrete emplacements, protected on the landward side by minefields and smaller emplacements, from Flushing
(Vlissingen) in the south to the extreme north of the island. So long as
these batteries remained intact, minesweepers could not enter the river.
There were thought to be about 10,000 German troops on the island,
but more could have been driven by the Allied offensive in Holland over
the causeway that linked the island with the mainland at South Beveland.

The capture of the batteries by the 4th Commando Brigade was the
final phase of the operation to clear the Scheldt. Walcheren was a saucer-
shaped island, whose rim consisted of high dunes of loose, soft sand,
passable to men on foot only. The gap in the dunes on the western edge
was filled by the Westkapelle Dyke. Behind this natural and man-made

rampart lay the flat polder, all reclaimed land below sea level, strewn with farms and small villages. At the instigation of Lieutenant-General Simonds, commanding Canadian First Army (in the absence of General Crerar), the Westkapelle Dyke was breached by bombing. Simonds had foreseen that the Germans would partially flood the saucer, leaving the embanked roads and dunes above the water, making the attacker's job more difficult. By flooding the saucer completely, the Germans would be denied the use of the roads, but the British, who had amphibious vehicles and craft, which the Germans lacked, would be able to penetrate the gap in the dyke, and go where they chose, attacking positions from the rear. After a series of attacks by heavy bombers, the dyke was breached in three places and about three-quarters of the island was under water, pinning the garrison to the saucer's rim, and Flushing, Middleburg, and some smaller towns. In the west the rim was no more than 250 yards wide.

The GOC Canadian II Corps planned a three-pronged attack. Two brigades of the 52nd Division would attack from the east across the Walcheren–South Beveland causeway. 4 Commando was to assault Flushing in LCAs from the south bank of the Scheldt under cover of darkness, followed up by the 155th Infantry Brigade of the 52nd Division; after the capture of Flushing, it was to revert to command of 4th Commando Brigade. The main body of Leicester's 4th Commando Brigade was to assault Westkapelle two hours after first light, supported by Captain Pugsley's Naval Force T, consisting of landing craft squadrons, and twenty-five support landing craft of the Support Squadron Eastern Flank, to provide intimate fire support. The guns in all these craft were manned by Marines, who also provided some of the crews and skippers. Also in support were the 15in gun battleship *Warspite*, and the monitors *Roberts* and *Erebus*. Artillery support from the south bank of the Scheldt was available on call. The plan for the assault on Westkapelle included air bombardment of the batteries. As in Normandy five months earlier, this was largely ineffective: of the twenty-five heavy guns only three 150mms were put out of action.

Landing at 0540 on 1 November 1944, 4 Commando cleared the enemy from fortified houses overlooking the 155th Brigade's landing area and attacked the German positions in the western end of Flushing. It was to take three days' hard fighting by 4 Commando and the battalions of the 155th Brigade before the whole town was cleared, after which, as their signals sergeant remarked, 'We were sent along the dunes to rejoin the Marine Commandos. We had thought we had been given the toughest job, but theirs turned out to be far worse.'

The assault plan for Westkapelle was for 41 RM Commando to land on the north shoulder of the gap in the dyke, and advance north, clearing strongpoints and batteries, including the large battery W 17 at Domburg. 48 RM Commando was to land on the south shoulder and push south, eliminating defences including battery W 13, and as far as Zoutlande. Here 47 RM Commando would pass through, dealing with batteries further along, including W 11 and W 7, eventually to link up with 4 Commando advancing north from Flushing. Only 41 RM Commando had armoured and AVRE support. The craft allocated to 4th Commando Brigade were a considerable improvement on those used in Normandy: most of the brigade was to land from LCTs in Buffaloes, backed up and supported by Weasels, DUKWs, and Terrapins. The Buffalo, or Landing Vehicle Tracked (LVT), its official name, was an American invention, and could swim ashore, cross the beach, and depending on the going motor or swim to the objective, all without having to disembark its load, unlike conventional craft which unloaded close to, or on, the waterline, the most dangerous place in any water-borne operation. It was the most potent amphibian in the array of vehicles available to the British in late 1944. The DUKW (pronounced Duck) was an American six-wheeled amphibious truck, taking its name from the initials of its maker's code. The Weasel had originally been designed as oversnow vehicle, and as the 52nd Division had already discovered, proved inadequate in the flooded, sandy terrain of Holland. The Terrapin was an inferior British version of the DUKW.

Originally the first waves of the two leading Commandos, 41 and 48, were to land in the highly unsuitable LCI(S)s. Moulton, still command-ing 48 RM Commando, remembered what he and his Commando had experienced in Normandy when these craft were used in an assault, and made strong representations to Leicester and Pugsley that his whole Commando be landed in amphibians from LCTs. His tenacity and integrity were rewarded and his request was granted.

When the 4th Commando Brigade sailed from Ostend at 0315 on 1 November the weather was rough, but moderated later. Leicester and Pugsley, travelling together in HMS *Kingsmill*, were authorized to post-pone the assault if sea state and visibility were such that the operation

Royal Marines crew a four-barrelled pom-pom anti-aircraft gun on board a battleship.

Lieutenant General T. H. (later General Sir Thomas) Hunton, the Adjutant General Royal Marines, taking the salute at the march past by of a guard provided by 43 (RM) Commando wearing their recently awarded green berets on completion of the Commando Course at Achnacarry.

Italy: General Montgomery visits 40 (RM) Commando at Termoli the day after the battle. L to R: Lieutenant Colonel Manners (CO), Captain Maude, General Montgomery, Lieutenant General Dempsey GOC XIII Corps, Lieutenant T. D. Morgan.

Often captioned as A Troop 41 (RM) Commando on D-Day, 6 June 1944, in fact this picture was taken in April 1944 on the last day of Excercise Fabius at Littlehampton: the sergeant in the foreground still has the dust cover on his rifle, and he and others are grinning at the cameraman. Lieutenant T. M. P. Stevens RM, the Troop second-in-command, is standing up. On D-Day he took over when his Troop Commander was wounded, and led A Troop thereafter. On 6 June 1944, 41 (RM) Commando lost 123 dead, wounded or missing out of a strength of 450.

A Centaur tank of the Royal Marines Armoured Support Regiment taking part in 50th Division's operations near Tilly-sur-Seulles in mid-June 1944, at least fifteen miles inland from the beach. In the original plan for D-Day in Normandy, these Centaurs were to have been left immobile on the beach, until Montgomery ordered the Royal Armoured Corps to provide drivers.

The Adriatic, Sugar Beach Sarande: an LCG engaging a troublesome German battery with its two 4.7-inch guns.

Walcheren, November 1944: an LCT and Buffaloes approach the gap in the dyke at Westkapelle.

A film still of a Buffalo driving down the ramp of an LCT at Walcheren. The techniques and equipment for amphibious assault had improved out of all recognition in the thirty years since the first picture in this book was taken. Now, some fifty-six years later, there are no comparable armoured amphibians in the British inventory.

Film still of troops whose craft were sunk or disabled at Walcheren, and swam or waded ashore.

Walcheren: gun in Battery W 17, with control tower behind. The guns in W 11, W 13 and W 15 were in thick concrete casemates, unlike the ones in W 17, and were much less vulnerable to air bombardment and shellfire. Despite this, on 1 November 1944, HMS *Warspite* fired over three hundred 15-inch shells at W 17 without putting any of its guns out of action.

Italy: Marines of 40 (RM) Commando making dummies in preparation for the deception operation on the River Reno as part of Operation Roast, the Battle of Lake Comacchio.

Italy: follow-up troops of 2nd Commando Brigade crossing the River Reno during Operation Roast.

Burma: troops of 3rd Commando Brigade wade ashore into the mud at Myebon, January 1945.

Burma: Marines examine Japanese mines after landing at Myebon.

Right: Germany: Marine Laidler of 45 (RM) Commando hoists the B Troop flag 'Bash on Regardless' in Osnabrück, April 1945.

Below: Germany: Marine Moyle of 45 (RM) Commando, standing among captured flak guns, looks back over the Elbe, crossed by 45 and 46 (RM) Commandos as part of 1st Commando Brigade on 28 April 1945.

was unlikely to succeed. Before dawn Pugsley received the success signal from 4 Commando indicating that they were ashore. A little later he was told by signal that because of fog on the airfields it was unlikely that the force would get any air support or air spotting for the naval and artillery bombardment. Although at this stage of an amphibious operation the final decision whether or not to proceed was his, as naval force commander, he consulted with Leicester, and both agreed to go ahead. As the naval bombardment began, twelve Typhoons appeared overhead, despite the earlier news about the airfields being fog-bound. But it became obvious that the air bombardment had failed to silence the German batteries north and south of the gap in the dyke. Pugsley ordered the assault to go in. The landing craft of the Support Squadron Eastern Flank closed to engage the batteries.

Edited extracts from an official pamphlet issued some six months later by the Royal Marines to keep all units in the picture on the doings of their Corps give some idea of what these support craft faced.

The Germans held their fire, opening up at between 3,000 and 4,000 yards with very accurate fire. As H-hour approached (0945), three Landing Craft (Gun) closed to 2,000 yards of an especially active battery north of the gap in the dyke, steering parallel to the beach and firing as hard as possible. Reversing course, they closed to 800 yards, bringing their Oerlikons into action as well as the main armament. Three other Landing Craft (Gun) engaged a battery south of the gap in similar style.

Other support landing craft went in to attack the beach defences. They were received with heavy fire of all calibres. One was set on fire. One was hit below the waterline, but the damage control party partly plugged the hole with hammocks. At 0945 she came under very heavy fire. She made smoke and went full ahead, but the battery had her measure. She was hit astern, a near miss filled bridge and upper deck with water, two hits forward blew away her bows and the forward magazine. Finally at 0950 hours she received a direct hit in the main magazine, which blew up approximately 100,000 rounds of 2-pounder and Oerlikon ammunition. Most of the crew were blown into the sea. There were 29 survivors. The enemy fired on their floats and rafts at about 1,500 yards range, so they paddled away from the beach, to be picked up 45 minutes later by another craft.

Large support landing craft closed zigzagging at top speed. They repeatedly closed the beach, engaging targets, but without much effect against the heavy concrete of the enemy pillboxes. One was hit, caught fire in the magazine, and had to be abandoned. Two were badly damaged.

The Landing Craft (Gun) beached north and south of the gap to engage the pillboxes. One about 30 yards from the target which she engaged with armour piercing shot. The kedge [a small anchor] was dropped; this probably saved the craft from broaching-to as the tide ran at about 6 knots parallel to the beach. The craft kept up a hot fire for the next 20 minutes until both turrets were out of action, owing to small-arms fire through the sighting ports. As far as could be seen, no penetration of the pillbox, which had no slits facing seaward, was achieved, but it was neutralised while the first flight [of troop carrying landing craft] got ashore. It appeared that the garrison panicked, for one individual ran out out into the open, to be cut down by fire. The craft was hit in several places by 150mm and 200mm shells, mostly astern, as she was so close in that the German guns could only just train on her. She retracted at about 1000 hours and when about 800 yards offshore, sank by the stern. Casualties [in this craft] were amazingly light, two dead and four wounded. The other Landing Craft (Gun) was last seen ablaze on the beach. No survivors were picked up.

Out of the twenty-five craft of the Support Squadron Eastern Flank, only four remained fit for action. Their self-sacrifice, which drew the fire of the batteries, was not in vain. Casualties among the landing craft and commandos during the run-in of the first two waves were light. The touchdown of the leading LCI(S)s of 41 RM Commando north of the gap was twenty-seven minutes late, as 48 RM Commando landed south of the gap. As 41 Commando's LCI(S)s ran in, the water around their craft appeared to those watching to be deluged by a shower of rockets from a Landing Craft (Rocket) (LCT(R)), whose missiles fell short. In fact they fell between the leading waves of 41 and 48 Commandos, but until it was established over the radio that 41 Commando's leading wave had suffered no casualties from this mishap, Moulton wondered how the leading wave of his Commando would fare on its own. He describes his run-in and landing:

Shells were now falling near us and splinters coming inboard. I watched with peculiar detachment the flashes of the dyke battery, as we came closer to it each minute. One of the rocket craft [LCT(R)] exploded in a sheet of flame, hit while reloading. Then we were close in under the dunes. The Oerlikons of the tank landing craft [LCT] and the Polsen guns of the Buffaloes, projecting above the sides of the tank decks, swept the radar station and other likely looking bits of concrete and sand with a satisfying clangour, and our craft checked smoothly as she took the beach. Down ramp. Out churned our first Buffalo with its load of troops, then the others, then Ronnie [Adjutant] and I in our command Weasel. The Weasel splashed into the water gap, swam perhaps fifty yards, the tracks bit sand, and up the beach we went into the shelter of the dunes. This was the way to land – dry shod, plenty of fire power, very few casualties, and my wireless set with me, working to Skinner [Second-in-Command], to bring in my reserve where I wanted it.[23]

In 41 Commando, Captain Stevens's A Troop objective was Westkapelle tower at the end of the main street of the town. In this part, only the road was above the water. Kelly:

About two-thirds the way there, I saw movement in a top window. I shouted 'top window' and fired at the same time. There was a burst of fire in reply, and they shot someone at the back of the Troop. Most of my section ran for cover in the houses at the side of the road, straight into deep water, leaving Captain Stevens and I in the middle of the road. Stevens tried to blast the enemy out using a PIAT, but could not get the round into the top windows.

Although a Sherman tank came up and fired at the tower, winkling out the enemy involved climbing the narrow staircase, which the Germans had blocked with wire. Stevens took a German speaker from 10 IA Commando,[24] and walking out into the road, shouted to the enemy to surrender, repeating the words as the German speaker uttered them. The bluff succeeded, and the enemy artillery OP surrendered.

After the initial euphoria of landing, and clearing 48 Commando's first objective, a radar station, without difficulty, Moulton told de Stacpoole, his senior troop commander, to go on with Y Troop and attack W 13. The enemy resistance stiffened as the Germans recovered from the shock of the bombardment, and Moulton was greeted with the news that Major de Stacpoole was dead. His troop's gallant attempt, without supporting fire, against one of the concrete battery positions had failed. Meanwhile Moulton learned that the second wave had been caught on the waterline as they beached. One craft was hit, disabling the Buffaloes. Other Buffaloes and Weasels were hit on the beach as the German gunners zeroed in. Follow-up Buffaloes were blown up on anti-tank mines, passed over by the leading Buffaloes because they were drifted over with sand, but scraped away by the tracks of successors. Most Buffaloes brewed up immediately when mined. After much delay caused by radio sets failing, and further casualties, Moulton managed to arrange a fire plan from artillery firing from across the Scheldt, and an air strike by ground-attack Spitfires on the battery that was holding him up. By now one of his Troops, Z, had no one left unwounded above the rank of corporal. Weapons jammed with the fine sand, a constant feature of fighting in the dunes, his Commando attacked under the supporting fire, and burst into the battery position. A brief bout of close-quarter fighting followed. Lieutenant Albutt of B Troop was faced by a German at close range; both tried to fire, but their sub-machine-guns were jammed by sand. Albutt hurled his weapon at the German, and Sergeant Stringer shot him. As X and B Troops reached the guns inside the emplacements, the gunners surrendered: 'Big fit men, they had little desire to mix it with the commandos in close-quarter fighting.'[25]

With the onset of darkness, 48 RM Commando went firm for the night, evacuated their wounded, searched for the missing, mostly dead, and commanders found time to grieve. Moulton:

First I came to Derek de Stacpoole. He was propped half erect, in a shallow German trench; it looked as if he had been shot trying to get a look forward or perhaps leading an attack. Ten yards in front was a German in rather a similar position; possibly they had shot each other simultaneously. Now I had time to mourn his loss; the pitcher had gone to the well too often; and Jumbo's and my plan to send him to safety had come to nothing. [They had planned to send him to Staff College and save his life.] A gallant, handsome Irish gentleman and most admirable soldier, we owed much to the standards he had set. Bare-headed and hunched against the cold wind I stayed a little while, then moved on.

In a hollow in the dunes, I found David Winser [medical officer]. He and his RAMC orderly were lying with the bandages still in their hands, where the mortar bombs had caught them as they dressed the wounds of Davies and his telegraphist. The bodies, the bandages and the mortar-bomb tails in the moonlight made a tragic tableau which told the whole story. I stayed there too, and thought of David's help and support during the weeks of training and months of battle;.... of the brilliant promise of his life.[26]

As in Normandy, the landing of 47 RM Commando was, through no fault of theirs, less than satisfactory, and mainly in the wrong place, north, not south of the gap in the dyke (several hundred yards of swiftly flowing water, under fire). All four LCTs carrying the Commando were hit as they beached or neared the beach. As B Troop's LCT, shared with Commando Headquarters, lowered its ramp, a shell passed through the driver's compartment of one of the Buffaloes, killing the driver and radio operator, but not exploding until it exited the far side of the vehicle, bursting under a Weasel carrying a flame-thrower, which brewed up. From this LCT, only the Troop Commander's and the CO's Buffaloes got ashore. The remaining vehicles caught fire, and the men swam to the beach. On arrival the troop mustered some twenty-eight all ranks out of the sixty with which it had started.

The remaining LCTs carrying 47 RM Commando drifted to port and beached on the left-hand side of the gap. Eventually, using Buffaloes, the four rifle troops of the Commando were ferried across the gap, and concentrated in the assembly area at 1900 hours, where they should have been at 1400 hours at the latest.

Setting off the next morning, 47 RM Commando passed through 48 RM Commando south of the village of Zouteland and moved towards their final objective, a large battery (number W 11), the last between Westkapelle and Flushing. By the time the Commando had overcome smaller enemy positions on the way to the battery they had already suffered casualties. At 1700 hours, the Commando advanced to their objective, about 1,000 yards away, first having to take two intermediate positions this side of it, an anti-tank ditch and a searchlight platform. Their first attack nearly succeeded, but with heavy casualties, including all five rifle troop commanders, and two TSMs, in an hour. The anti-tank ditch and searchlight platform were secured, and in some confusion two troops badly short of men got into part of the battery position, although not into the casemates. Eventually the two troops were collected and withdrawn by subalterns and sergeants to the searchlight platform, some 400 yards back. Here the second-in-command, Major Paddy Donnell, and the Adjutant, Captain Paul Spencer, organized the defence for the night.

By now Leicester was being reminded by the Canadian IInd Corps of the urgency of making progress towards Flushing. Moulton pressed him to allow 48 RM Commando to take over the task of capturing W 11 in the morning, after Phillips, rightly, had refused to continue that night. 47 RM Commando had had an unsettling two days, beginning with its chaotic landing followed by the repulse of its initial attack on W 11. As Moulton remarked later:

> If the problem had been set in a promotion examination or staff college exercise, there could only have been one answer, one or both of the fresh units [41 and 48] should have been used the next day to go through 47 and renew the attack. Any student suggesting that 47 should be required to do so would have been in trouble.[27]

However, battles are not as simple as staff college exercises, and brigade commanders have to take account of the morale of all their units, which includes the effect that decisions which could be interpreted as lack of faith in a particular unit might have on their future performance. As another great brigade commander of the Second World War, James Hill of the 3rd Parachute Brigade, once remarked, 'battalions [and commandos] are like children, they have their good points and their bad.' Also like children, they must be encouraged, not rejected, and sometimes their feelings must be nurtured, regardless of what the 'book' says. Leicester decided to use 47 RM Commando, reinforced by a troop of 48 RM Commando.

After looking at the ground in daylight, Phillips decided that as the dunes were wider here than elsewhere, he would use A Troop of 48 RM Commando on his flank to provide supporting fire. Although this troop came under fire on their way forward, they managed to establish themselves in a good position from where to carry out their task. The first attack by 47 RM Commando gained part of the battery, and it took a second assault by two troops under the command of the adjutant, Captain Spencer, to penetrate the higher ground in the position. At this point, under fire and attack from several directions, the Germans asked for a truce under a white flag to clear their dead and wounded. After some tense moments, Phillips, through his German-speaking interpreter, talked them into surrendering. Captain Reg Wiltshire, commanding the Buffaloes supporting the Commando:

> After a few 'Sieg Heils', they were eventually marched to the point to drop their arms. They realised they outnumbered us considerably and had been tricked, but it all passed off OK, and we could breathe again. I think it

was one of the best spoofs of the war, and Phillips did it without batting an eyelid.

41 RM Commando had captured the two batteries between the north of the gap and the small town of Domburg by nightfall on 1 November, the first day of the landing. Here, with 10 (Inter-Allied [IA]) Commando, two troops of 41 Commando were left to prevent any counterattack from the north-east rim of the 'saucer', while the remainder of the Commando joined in Leicester's number one priority task, the clearing, south of the gap, of batteries commanding the Scheldt so the mine-sweepers could start working. In the event 41 Commando assistance was not required, 47 and 48 Commandos had taken all the batteries to the Flushing Gap, and linked up with 4 Commando. As Moulton wrote: 'That afternoon, sitting on the dunes back at W 13, I watched the first minesweepers sweeping the channel to Antwerp.'[28]

Leicester sent 41 Commando back across the gap on 4 November, with orders to clear the remaining two batteries north-east of Domburg, W 18 and W 19. In the early afternoon of 5 November, following a pause to arrange artillery and air support, A and B Troops, with two Shermans, moved to a position among minefields in the dunes from which to support Y Troop, who would make the assault. Haydon, commanding Y Troop, who had won a DSO at Salerno, said as he was being helped on with his equipment, 'This time a VC or bust.'[29] Haydon and one of his subalterns was killed as the troop was fighting in the battery position. Captain Stevens brought up his A Troop, took command, and finished the task of taking the battery itself by nightfall. Clearing the concrete defences took the Commando most of the night.

The next morning, 41 RM and 10 (IA) Commandos continued the advance towards the final battery, W 19. Minefields made progress slow. Two days later, Leicester, having brought 48 RM and 4 Commandos across to Domburg, planned a brigade attack: 41 RM and 10 (IA) left, 4 Commando right, and 48 in reserve. 4 Commando, moving in darkness against light opposition, infiltrated past W 19, and got near the end of the dunes on the east coast of the 'saucer'. Here the CO, Lieutenant Colonel Dawson, found the local German commander willing to negotiate a surrender of the 4,000 German troops in that area, including those manning W 19. The battle of Walcheren was over. Although many others had taken part, the gallantry and élan of the Royal Marines commandos assisted by Royal Marines landing craft gunners in capturing the huge shore batteries led Churchill to write the comment quoted at the head of this chapter.

This was the last full-scale battle for 4th Commando Brigade, although those involved did not know it at the time. The Brigade was to spend the remainder of the war in Holland, first in the area of the eastern Scheldt, and then on the River Maas. They were not idle, being involved in many brushes with the enemy on raids, patrols, and minor actions. But it seems a waste of such well-trained, battle-experienced troops to use them in this way, rather than in operations to cross the Rhine and advance to the Baltic.

While in Holland, Moulton came up against old-style Royal Marines bureaucracy. His RSM, Travers, was actually only a substantive corporal, and one of his troop sergeant majors, McGowan, a substantive Marine. On writing to Plymouth Division, asking if Travers could be at least promoted to substantive sergeant and McGowan to substantive corporal, he was told this was impossible because Travers was very junior as a corporal, and that McGowan had not passed his recruit's gunnery course. However, if he reduced McGowan to Marine, and sent him back to Plymouth to do the course, he might be promoted to corporal. The impasse was eventually sorted out. But Moulton had encountered the resentment felt by some, but by no means all, old-fashioned sea going Marines of the 'upstart' commandos, whose promotion prospects were better – not surprisingly, since they were doing most of the fighting.

*

1st Commando Brigade, which included 45 RM and 46 RM Commandos, was in England in early January 1945, expecting to be shipped to the Far East, when its orders were changed, and it was sent at short notice to Holland. The catalyst for this move, the German Ardennes offensive, was fizzling out, but it was thought that Antwerp might still be vulnerable to Special Force raids. More important, the advance into Germany would include the crossing of the Rhine, followed by a series of smaller but still formidable rivers. Commandos would be useful to spearhead these crossings. Lieutenant Colonel Nicol Gray still commanded 45 RM Commando; his brother Tim, having recovered from wounds suffered in Normandy as CO 41 RM Commando, was now in command of 46 RM Commando, for Hardy had been sent to take command of the 3rd Commando Brigade in the Far East.

On 22 January 1945, 1st Commando Brigade came under command of the 7th Armoured Division, which was undertaking a limited offensive east of the River Maas, from the area of Sittard, with the object of driving the enemy back behind the River Roer, and clearing the country between the two rivers. The brigade, supported by a squadron of tanks, was given the task of clearing the enemy from the division's left flank between the railway and the River Maas and capturing Maasbracht, Brachterbeek, and Linne.

On the night of 22/23 January, 6 Commando crossed the Juliana Canal over the ice and moved on to Maasbracht, occupying it without meeting any opposition. On a cold, clear morning 45 RM Commando passed through 6 Commando and reached Brachterbeek, which was also clear of enemy. The leading troop, A, was ordered to advance to the railway station south-east of Brachterbeek.

As they moved over open ground they came under fire from the station to their front, as well as from their left flank; the latter from enemy positions lining the Montfortebeek dyke and a machine-gun in a windmill beyond the dyke. Most of the leading section found cover behind some potato clamps, but Lieutenant Cory and two men were left wounded out in the open. Despite the firefight still continuing, Lance Corporal Harden RAMC, A Troop's medical orderly,

insisted that he should go to attend to the three wounded men, fearing that they would soon die if left lying in the snow. He moved out alone across 120 yards of open ground, putting dressings on each man and then carried one man back to safety. As he moved around bullets could be seen striking the snow close to him, and on his return he was told not to go out again until tanks or smoke could be organised to cover him. Unwilling to wait for this, he obtained two volunteer stretcher bearers, Marines J. Haville and R. Mason, to assist him to bring in the remaining 2 casualties. Returning on his third trip under fire with Lt Cory, LCpl Harden was killed. For his outstanding gallantry and devotion to his duty, LCpl Harden was awarded a posthumous VC.[30]

Announcing the award to the House of Commons on 13 March 1945, the Secretary of State for War said, 'I do not remember ever reading of anything more heroic.'[31]

A Troop could not be extracted by daylight, and attempts by tanks
and artillery to assist came to naught. The key to unlock the impasse was
Montfortebeek dyke. E and B Troops were ordered to obtain a foothold
on the dyke by advancing under cover of an embankment east of
Brachterbeek. This advance was checked when the leading section of E
Troop came under fire from a position on the embankment. Day, OC
B Troop, decided to move to the left to outflank the enemy position,
which meant crossing a marsh. One section, commanded by Lieutenant
Riley, was despatched to find a way over this obstacle, and soon
afterwards caught about a dozen Germans withdrawing from positions
on the embankment. Riley attacked them, killing three and taking five
prisoner; the others fled. Hearing the sounds of action, the remainder of
B Troop moved speedily forward to take advantage of this setback to the
enemy, and took up a position in a wooded gully, later dubbed Riley's
Gully, to the north and on the flank of the Montfortebeek dyke. After
dark, B Troop saw off an attack by about forty Germans approaching
Riley's Gully from the direction of the windmill, and called down artillery
fire on the dyke in case a counterattack was mounted from there as well.
In the morning, 6 Commando took over 45 RM Commando's positions,
and subsequently that day cleared the Montfortebeek dyke from north
to south, using Riley's Gully as a jumping-off point.

Later that night, 45 RM Commando received a signal from Brigadier
Mills-Roberts, who had taken command of 1st Commando Brigade
when Lovat was wounded after the first six days of the Normandy
campaign. Mills-Roberts was not easily satisfied, and his message read:

> Special Order of the Day. To all ranks of 45 RM Commando. The
> Divisional Commander congratulates 45 RM Commando on their valu-
> able work today which has been of great importance in driving back the
> enemy on the Divisional front. Well done Royal Marines. You put up a
> fine show today and I'm very proud of you.[32]

The next task given to 45 RM Commando was to meet the 7th
Armoured Division's requirement for information on the enemy in the
area of Merum, a small village close to the River Maas, and halfway
between Linne and Roermond. The only way to approach Merum, some
two miles behind the German positions north of Linne, was the River
Maas, but this could not be used until Belle Isle – the name given to a
small island in the Maas opposite Linne – was captured. On the night of

27 January, D Troop crossed the Maas to Belle Isle in canvas assault boats, but in bright moonlight the boats were spotted by a German sentry, and surprise was lost. There was no preliminary artillery bombardment before D Troop's approach as it was considered that a silent attack would enable B Troop an element of surprise in their subsequent raid on Merum that same night. Having lost surprise and faced with an entrenched position, manned by numbers almost equal in strength to the attacking force, D Troop was badly hit and the survivors withdrew across the river. D Troop lost eleven killed, thirteen wounded, and six missing.

The 1st Commando Brigade's task as part of Operation Plunder, the crossing of the Rhine by Montgomery's 21st Army Group between Rees and Wesel, was to seize Wesel following an attack by RAF Bomber Command. Mills-Roberts decided that 46 RM Commando would lead the crossing with Brigade Headquarters, and establish a bridgehead two miles downstream from Wesel, into which the rest of the brigade would be ferried. From here, led by 6 Commando, the brigade would march across country to Wesel.

Following the bombing by seventy-seven Lancasters, and after a comprehensive artillery bombardment by six regiments of the intended touchdown point on the opposite bank, at 2100 hours on 23 March 46 RM Commando crossed the 300-yard-wide river in Buffaloes. One drifted off course and was hit by shells from the supporting barrage, but the remainder touched down on the far bank about four minutes later. The Commando landed to find the enemy dazed by the bombardment, and secured the bridgehead in thirty minutes, having taken twenty-two casualties, including nine killed, the majority in the Buffalo hit by friendly artillery in the first wave. The remainder of the brigade followed in Buffaloes and assault boats. At this stage the bombers attacked Wesel a second time; two hundred aircraft delivering more than 1,100 tons of high explosive. Day:

> We clambered aboard our Buffalo (at a briefing Derek Mills-Roberts had said that Hannibal had crossed the Alps on an elephant and we could tell our grandchildren that we had crossed the Rhine on a Buffalo!) and quickly began to lurch towards the river ... The crossing was noisy but uneventful. Overhead, Bofors guns were firing tracer to mark the flanks of the assault, and to our left a Buffalo, hit while landing the first wave of Tim Gray's men [46 Commando] was still blazing. By now the [second]

bombing of Wesel had started and as we moved to our forming-up area in the bridgehead, we could feel the impact of the bombs as they crashed on that unhappy town. 6 Commando were crossing in storm boats, several of which broke down, and they also came under fire as they made their way to the bridgehead.[33]

During the advance through the rubble and shattered streets of Wesel, Nicol Gray was wounded but remained in command for the next two days. In the morning the commandos were treated to the sight of more than 1,500 Dakotas, followed shortly after by nearly as many tug aircraft towing gliders, carrying the British 6th and United States 17th Airborne Divisions to the Dropping Zones and Landing Zones on the high ground east of Wesel. A link-up with the airborne troops soon followed, and one of the many bridges across the Rhine was built that night. 1st Commando Brigade had done well, at a cost of ninety-five casualties.

The brigade now took part in the advance to the Baltic, coming under command of several different divisions in turn. In the process they crossed three more rivers, the Weser, Aller, and Elbe. For the Weser crossing, 45 RM Commando was temporarily detached and under direct command of 11th Armoured Division. A company of 1st Rifle Brigade had already seized a small bridgehead across the Weser at Stolzenau, but were unable to make progress against the enemy, part of 12th SS Panzer Division Training Battalion. 45 Commando was ordered to cross and capture the small town of Leese about 2,000 yards from the bridgehead. Major Blake, in command in the absence of Gray, decided on a flanking movement, using the river bank for cover, once they were across. The Germans had good observation from a railway embankment, and soon realized what the Commando was up to. They moved troops up to the river bank and after advancing for half a mile, the leading troop, D, was engaged in hand-to-hand fighting. Day's B Troop was about halfway along the long column, of the kind all too familiar to all infantry soldiers and often referred to as the battalion or commando snake:

The Luftwaffe now made one of its rare appearances and some thirty aircraft, including a few Stukas, attacked the Royal Engineers at the bridging site. Having dropped their bombs, the Stukas flew along the river attempting to machine gun us. Fortunately their aim was poor but the hail of bullets striking the water a few yards away was distinctly unnerving. The unfortunate sappers were also being shelled and some of this hate came in our direction. For the first time I experienced air-bursts, shell which exploded about thirty or forty feet in the air, spraying fragments over a wide area, and I developed a hearty dislike for this type of weapon.[34]

As the commando snake wended its way along below the bank in fits and starts, the battle at the head of the column ebbed and flowed.

One German leapt over the bank and landed on the edge of the river almost on top of Dudley Coventry. Dudley, the very strong, tough A Troop Commander, reacted instinctively and hit him very hard with his fist. The German was killed by this blow, a fact confirmed to me by our Chaplain, Reg Haw, who, as always, was well up with the action, ready to tend any casualty, friend or foe.[35]

At one stage the Germans threatened to cut the commando snake in half by attacking the Tac HQ, of signallers and intelligence personnel. Corporal Harris, one of the German speakers attached to 45 Commando from 10 (IA) Commando, seized a Bren and hose-piped the attackers. Joined by other members of the Tac HQ, the attack was stopped. Harris was wounded in the eye, and awarded the MM for his gallantry. After advancing further, the Commando halted and dug in. Later they were told that the remainder of the brigade would join them that night, but lack of boats prevented any further crossings of the Weser, so the Commando, somewhat out on a limb, were ordered back into the original bridgehead. The following night, the rest of the brigade crossed the river, and retraced 45 Commando's route along the river bank. The going was difficult with marshy ground, streams, thick hedges, ditches, and a steep railway embankment. The town was taken with little opposition by 0700 hours. As so often, a bold night operation against the Germans paid off.

The crossing of the Aller was not without incident. Although not as formidable an obstacle as the Rhine or Weser, the surrounding country-side was thickly covered with dense woods and undergrowth. 'A little bit of Burma in the middle of the bloody Reich,' as one Marine in 46 RM Commando put it.[36] 1st Commando Brigade was tasked with securing a crossing for the 11th Armoured Division. Mills-Roberts decided to cross on the railway bridge, rather than attempt a frontal assault on the road bridge. After leading the whole brigade across the railway bridge, which the enemy failed to blow completely, 3 Commando patrolled to the road bridge, about a mile and a half away, reporting that it was held in strength. Subsequently 6 Commando successfully captured one end, but found that the bridge had been blown two hours previously. While 6 Commando was digging in, the enemy counterattacked in strength, and 46 RM Commando sent to assist, beat them off. The next day, 45 and 46 RM Commando were ordered to 'beat back' through the woods between the two bridges, to flush out strong enemy forces who had infiltrated them. The sappers had started to build a Bailey Bridge to replace the road bridge, and the bridgehead had to be held. The enemy, later established as a Marine Fusilier battalion, was about to counter-attack the brigade when the two Commandos encountered them. Mills-Roberts, realizing that the 'beat' would not succeed in reaching the railway bridge, ordered the two Commandos back. But no further enemy counterattacks were put in that day; 45 and 46 RM Commandos had forestalled, and stopped in its tracks, a very strong counterattack just as it was about to roll in on the bridgehead. The following day, with the Bailey Bridge built, the 11th Armoured Division crossed, the bridgehead was expanded, and the enemy ejected. The Commando Brigade had badly mauled two Marine battalions, 12th SS Panzer Division Training Battalion, and an anti-tank battalion equipped with 88mm guns.[37]

1st Commando Brigade's last operation of the war was the crossing of the Elbe, this time under command of 15th Scottish Division. The brigade was ordered to capture the town of Lauenburg and bridges across the Elbe–Trave Canal. The Elbe at the crossing place was as wide as the Rhine, but with the added disadvantage of steep ground, 150 feet high, on the far side. Originally a comprehensive bombing programme followed by a parachute assault by 5th Parachute Brigade was built into the plan for the crossing, but bad weather caused both these to be cancelled. The brigade would cross in Buffaloes two miles downstream from Lauenburg. The bridgehead would be seized by 6 Commando, and 46 Commando was to lead the brigade into Lauenburg. 45 Commando was to take the southern part of the town, and B Troop was to capture some flak guns on high ground at Furstengarten, overlooking the proposed bridging site. Day:

> As the routes and other problems in the marshalling area were rather complex, all Troop Commanders were taken to the site one evening before the operation to do a reconnaissance, under strict orders to do

nothing which might attract the attention of the enemy. This turned out to be something of a farce as throughout our visit we were harassed by the enemy, a German bull which chased us from field to field.

We moved to the marshalling area, close to the river, soon after midnight in the early hours of 29th April, and sat around for about two hours in drizzling rain while our artillery pounded the enemy defences. 6 Commando came under fire when they crossed the river but by 3 am when it was our turn, the enemy guns shelling the crossing had been silenced. Once up the cliff, we followed the white tape and reached the outskirts of Lauenberg before dawn without incident.[38]

Surprise was complete and resistance was negligible. When B Troop arrived at the flak gun site they took it without casualties to themselves. There were ten dead Germans on the site, and Day's men took fifty prisoners. Two days later, 30 April, 11th Armoured and 6th Airborne Divisions passed through on their way to their meeting with the Russians on the Baltic coast. As far as 1st Commando Brigade was concerned the war was over. In six weeks they had advanced from the Rhine to Neustadt, near Lübeck on the Baltic.

*

Other Royal Marines had also fought as infantry in North-West Europe. By autumn 1944 the Army manpower problem was so acute that pressure was exerted on the Navy and RAF to provide infantry reinforcements. The RAF Regiment, many of whose units were doing very little sitting around airfields in the United Kingdom that no longer need guarding, provided individual replacements in infantry battalions. The Royal Marines demonstrated their versatility by forming two standard infantry brigades from landing craft crews and MNBDO people who were now no longer needed. The first of these brigades, 116th Infantry Brigade, Royal Marines joined 21st Army Group on the River Maas in February 1945. The brigade was commanded by Brigadier C. F. Phillips, lately of 47 RM Commando, and consisted of the 27th Battalion (Lieutenant Colonel N. H. Tailyour RM), the 28th Battalion (Lieutenant Colonel J. A. Taplin RM – who was only twenty-three years old and had made his name in 41 RM Commando), and the 30th Battalion (Lieutenant Colonel T. K. Walker RM). The NCOs and Marines in these battalions were good material. An army officer wrote of the 27th Battalion, 'I was struck by the physique of the men and bearing of the NCOs. It impressed me as it had been many months since I had seen the same in the Army. They were very lucky to have material like this, and, if well led, it was bound to be a good unit.'

As they would shortly show they were well led by their CO, but the standard of some of the other officers, especially the company commanders, was not impressive. Although keen and willing to learn, they appeared to be unable to 'get things going'. This was not their fault, they had possibly been too long away from that most testing of roles, infantry soldiering, if indeed they had ever been in Commandos or battalions. They had some very fast catching up to do in the art of 'taking a grip' of their commands at the tactical level, to use the vernacular. Phillips noticed the same, telling the officers of the 30th Battalion that some of them would not be filling similar appointments in an infantry battalion of the British Army – by implication they were unfit to do so.

Most of the 116th Brigade spent the time on the River Maas in defence, patrolling, and engaged in minor operations. Although at this phase of operations in Holland the policy of British I Corps, of which 116th Brigade formed a part, was not to cross the river, but to hold while operations progressed elsewhere, most of the officers and men, particularly in 27th Battalion, were keen to get to grips with the enemy, and crossed several times on raids. On 12 April, 27th Battalion was detached to command of XXX Corps for operations to capture Bremen. The Battalion was told that it would be grouped with a United States Navy Seabee unit to prepare the port for American use.[39] When it became clear that the battalion would not be used in the assault, Tailyour asked Phillips for permission to seek work elsewhere. Tailyour went to Canadian II Corps Headquarters, where according to an officer who accompanied him, they were 'greeted with joy'. The Canadian 4th Armoured Division, who were advancing towards Oldenburg, had used up all its motorized infantry 'stopping off' the side roads on its axis, and could certainly use another battalion.

The role of the battalion was primarily to protect the flank of the Canadian 4th Armoured Division, and often found itself out on a limb, deep in enemy territory, as the armour thrust forward. Here it was vulnerable to counterattack and the division gave them a squadron of tanks and platoon of Vickers machine-guns from the Divisional Machine Gun Battalion. Even though the end was not far off, German resistance could be fanatical, depending which troops were involved. Each night a comprehensive programme of patrols was carried out, while the armour went into laager, refuelled, and rearmed in preparation for the next day's advance. As the battalion report comments:

> The strain of moving and fighting by day, and patrolling by night unrelieved over a period of 10 days was great, and it speaks highly for the standard of training and morale of Officers, NCOs and Marines serving in the Corps that they were able to do this during their first real active role. This fact was commented on by Comd 10 Cdn Inf Bde, and the GOC 4 Cdn Armd Div, who sent a formal letter of appreciation of the service rendered by 27 RM.

The letter read:

> *Headquarters*
> *4th Canadian Armoured Division*
> *Germany*   5 *May* 45
>
> Dear Tailyour
>
>   I wish to congratulate you and your battalion on your fine efforts during the recent operations.
>
>   I have long known your Corps by reputation and have now myself seen evidence of the basis for that reputation. The vigour, skill and enthusiasm shown by your officers and men was noted and appreciated throughout the division.
>
>   I am only sorry we could not have had your help earlier. I was proud to have you in the 4th Division.
>
> C Vokes
> Maj Gen

Tailyour was awarded the DSO, one of his company commanders the MC, and several MMs were awarded to NCOs.

When hostilities ended, the 116th Brigade was deployed on naval tasks but under Army administration, because Phillips had a low opinion of the Navy's ability to administer a land force. Much to his chagrin his brigade was split up providing guards on German ships, submarines, port installations, and naval establishments, which he rightly regarded as a return to the bad old pre-war days. His objection to this is clear from a memorandum he wrote to Rear Admiral Muirhead-Gould:

> Through no fault of its own, the Corps has suffered many vicissitudes and much frustration in this war. [To put it mildly – author.] Officers and men are disappointed that there has been another change in their tasks.

Essential to morale, discipline and performance that they should retain
their entity as battalions under their own officers. Battalions should not
be split between ports.

I urge that 116 Inf Bde RM be regarded in exactly the same way as
would a military [i.e Army] formation earmarked for this duty with the
Royal Navy.

In other words he was asking for a change of attitude from old-style
naval officers who were accustomed to regarding Marines as a pool of
labour for all manner of tasks such as chipping paint and dockyard
sentries, which they would not dare foist upon an Army unit. It is
possible that Phillips's words fell on deaf ears, for he wrote at the time
of a visit to the Naval Officer in Charge of North Sea Ports:

Had lunch with his Chief of Staff (Capt Moir RN) and NOIC [Naval
Officer in Charge] Wilhelmshaven (Capt Conder RN). Found the latter a
bit difficult, mainly due to his ignorance of military affairs. I'm afraid that
Tailyour will spend most of his time attending to this and resisting
Conder's efforts to turn his bn [battalion] into an RM det [detachment]
afloat.

I said that I thought the RMs were oversubscribed for the tasks. Both
Moir and Conder regarded this as heresy.

The second RM Infantry Brigade, the 117th, arrived too late to take
part in any fighting, and was also assigned to naval duties in the ports.
But at least as related in this chapter, and those that follow on the
Adriatic, Italy and Far East, some Royal Marines were in their rightful
place, in the fore-front of the battle.[40]

18

The Adriatic, Aegean, and Italy, mid-1944 to May 1945

The first quality of a soldier is fortitude in enduring fatigue and hardship: bravery but the second.

Napoleon Bonaparte

After the Italian surrender on 8 September 1943, the Germans re-established control over the main road and rail communications in mainland Yugoslavia, and by the end of the year had placed garrisons on the Dalmatian Islands, with the exception of Vis, which lies furthest west. Tito accepted the offer of Commando support for the joint defence of this useful base, so in January 1944, 2 Commando, under Lieutenant Colonel ('Mad') Jack Churchill, landed on the island. They were joined at the end of February by 43 RM Commando, and at the beginning of May by 40 RM Commando.

It was not long before reconnaissance parties, helped by local partisans, went out to observe the movements of the Germans on the other islands. In March, as a result of their reports, Churchill took 2 Commando, supplemented by the Vickers section from 43 RM Commando, on a well-planned attack on Solta. After a strenuous night approach march, the assault troops used the cover of darkness to take up positions around Grohote. Shortly after dawn, six Kitty Hawks carried out a bombing and machine-gun attack on the village before the commandos dashed in. The whole garrison of just over a hundred was accounted for, and brought back to Vis, for the loss of two commandos killed and a few wounded.

The first joint operation involving 43 RM Commando and two battalions of partisans took place shortly afterwards on Hvar, where eighty Germans were captured, and about fifty killed. Captain Hudspith was awarded the MC, three Marines were wounded, and two were missing. The partisans suffered four killed (one a woman), and fourteen wounded. Further ambushes on German patrols, boarding party sorties from MTBs and MGBs on German coastal shipping, and reconnaissance operations followed. British sappers supervised the construction of an airstrip on Vis, which provided a forward base for fighters, and enabled damaged Allied bombers to make emergency landings. Together with crews who baled out before their aircraft ditched, the lives of 1,936 airmen were saved.

By this time, Brigadier Tom Churchill had arrived with his Brigade Headquarters, and in May he took the whole of 2 and 43 RM Commandos, one troop from 40 RM Commando, and other supporting units on six LCIs to Mljet, but this operation was not a success. Four of the ramps on the LCIs jammed, taking some time to free, and there was only one narrow track up from the beach, so disembarkation and movement off the beach was very slow. For once the partisans did not use tracks up the steep hills, and the heavily laden commandos had to force their way through dense, tangled scrub. Twelve Spitfire fighter-bombers roared in at 0615 hours, on cue, but the commandos were still miles away. They did not arrive until midday, to find that the Germans had retired to strongpoints on the north coast, which were supported by fire from batteries on the mainland. The return to the landing beach was one of the most exhausting tests of endurance many of the commandos had ever experienced.

It was during Brigadier Tom Churchill's absence in England, briefing the Special Service Group on the activities of his brigade, that his elder brother Lieutenant Colonel Jack Churchill led a major (for this theatre) operation on the island of Brač. The Germans had mounted a big offensive against the partisans in western Bosnia, including a well-planned attack by parachute troops on Tito's headquarters at Drvar. They failed to capture Tito, but severely dislocated his operations. As well as large-scale partisan diversions, and some 1,000 Allied air force sorties from Italy, Tito asked the Allies for a large-scale operation on the Dalmatian coast, or islands, to distract the Germans from their mission of destroying his partisans. Tito ordered his forces on Vis to participate in these operations. Consequently, it was decided to attack Brač, in an operation codenamed Flounced, to prevent the Germans taking troops from Dalmatia to reinforce their forces in Bosnia, and to make them move troops from the mainland to the islands.

The enemy on the island were about 1,200 strong, from the 738th Regiment of the 118th Jäger (Mountain) Division, two batteries of artillery, and a company of pioneers, divided between four locations. The main position consisted of about 500 men manning a complex of mutually supporting strongpoints to the south of the village of Nerežišća. Each was sited on top of a hill, with good observation and clear field of fire all round, and supported by four 105mm guns. The OP for the main position was sited at Vidova Gora, some four miles to the south-east of Nerežišća, on the highest hill on Brač. It overlooked the entire island (less valleys and other dead ground), could bring down fire more or less anywhere, and could control gun positions on the mainland as well as on the island. It was well fortified, and protected by a minefield. At Selca on the eastern end of the island, some fifteen miles from the main position, were another four 105mm guns and a garrison of 400 men. At Supetar, on the north-west coast, was a further position manned by 280 men.

The joint British/partisan plan called for four separate forces to deal with the four enemy locations. North Force of 500 partisans would be responsible for cutting the Nerežišća–Supetar road, and eliminating the Germans in Supetar. OP Force, consisting of one company of 2nd Battalion the Highland Light Infantry (HLI) with partisan guides, was to assault and destroy the OP before the main landing took place. Both these forces would land from schooners on the night D–2/D–1, and lie up by day, closing their objectives after dark.

On the night D–1/D-Day, two further forces would land. East Force of 1,400 partisans would land at Bol, about halfway along the south coast, to cut the Nerežišća–Selca road, and eliminate the Germans at the eastern end of Brač. Main Force, under Colonel Jack Churchill, consisted of 43 RM Commando, P and S Troops of 40 RM Commando (P Troop acting as porters), and two captured Italian 47/32 anti-tank guns manned by 10 Troop Raiding Support Regiment. In addition there were 1,300 partisans, who were not under Churchill's command, but would conform, more or less, to the agreed plan. Churchill's force and the partisans would land on three beaches five miles south-west of Bol, and attack and destroy the main position south of Nerežišća. The artillery support for Main Force consisted of one troop of partisan 75mm guns and a battery of eight 25-pounders of the 111th Field Regiment with gun positions in Bol. In addition there were six Browning machine-guns of the Raiding

Support Regiment. In reserve on Vis were A, Q, and Y Troops of 40 RM Commando, and 2 Commando, although most of the troop officers of the latter were on a parachute course in Italy. East Force was also given artillery support, and because they were operating out of range from the landing place at Bol were provided with jeeps and trailers for their guns. Rocket-firing Hurricanes were also in support, and fighters on call at Vis. The US Army Air Force (USAAF) was to bomb Split and Makarska on the mainland once the operation began, to hinder German reinforcements being lifted to Brač.

D-Day was 2 June, and as planned, the OP Force and North Force were landed without being detected on the night 31 May/1 June. The next night, the OP Force attacked, but failed because the defenders' position, in stone-walled sangars surrounded by mines and wire, was too strong. Two officers were left wounded in the minefield. However, these two managed to organize a second assault, which rescued them, but made no progress. The next attempt was called off because the HLI was running out of officers, NCOs, and steam. The OP Force kept up harassing small-arms fire on the enemy to distract them. North Force managed to block off the port of Supetar, but not to penetrate the defences.

After dawn on 2 June, and following an attack by rocket-firing Hurricanes, 43 RM Commando and the partisans attacked the main position, but stalled on the minefields. Another cause of failure was that the limited artillery support for the Commando and the partisans was dispersed, and therefore ineffective because the attack came from two directions. A repeat performance in the afternoon was called off because the partisans were not ready. Meanwhile another attack on the OP had been beaten off. Finally the RAF Hurricanes blasted the OP with rockets, and the garrison of only twenty men surrendered. Well sited in hardened defences, behind a skilfully laid minefield, they had held off over five times that number. However the OP was now in Allied hands, and the 111th Field Regiment used it for the rest of the operation. The news from East Force was also encouraging: the partisans had captured Selca, killing about 130 Germans and capturing some 100 together with their 105mm guns.

That night Colonel Jack Churchill made another plan, in which both 40 RM and 43 RM Commandos would assault the main position, assisted by partisans. Manners and his three rifle troops, along with 300 partisans and two 25-pounder guns, were summoned from Vis, arriving at Brač at 0345 hours. After a further reconnaissance, the plan was modified to the two Commandos attacking Point 622 at last light, while the partisans harassed Points 542 and 648, without attempting to capture them. Even this half-hearted move on the part of the partisans was not achieved without much argument and persuasion. All this toing and froing, coupled with radio problems, and a 40 Commando runner losing his way, resulted in Churchill's orders failing to reach Manners in time, while garbled radio orders to 43 RM Commando plus the fact that their CO, Simonds, did not know that 40 Commando were on Brač, led him to believe that his Commando was to attack alone, supported by partisans on his flanks.

43 RM Commando attacked Point 622 on cue, but were counter-attacked almost immediately, and Simonds lost contact with his B Troop. Hard fighting ensued, in which two of the assault troop commanders were killed and the other wounded, as well as three other officers and several NCOs. With a casualty list of 13 killed and 53 wounded from a strength of 135, and with ammunition running low, Simonds decided to withdraw.

Manners meanwhile was walking to Brigade Headquarters to find out what his Commando was supposed to do, having picked up a 'stand by to move' order on the radio at 1800 hours and then silence. On the way he met Churchill, who rapidly gave Manners the gist of the plan, and accompanied the three troops of 40 Commando to the start line. On arrival at 2130 hours Churchill decided to save time by briefing the three troops himself. He said that he not been able to contact 43 Commando on the radio, but it was likely that it had already taken the hill. In his opinion the Germans would be tired and short of water, and that a noisy, vigorous attack would succeed. Manners gave further orders on how the rifle troops would deploy. As 40 Commando advanced, it ran into B Troop 43 Commando in captured enemy trenches well up the hill. The Troop Commander said that he had been held up by mines and mortar fire. They had lost both subalterns and the TSM; the Troop Commander was killed a few minutes later. Churchill and Manners did not, however, assess the mortar fire as serious enough to cause any delay, and of mines there was little sign – merely a two-strand barbed-wire fence. Manners ordered the assault to start. Lieutenant Beadle, second-in-command of Y Troop, later wrote:

The night which up to this point had been moderately quiet, was suddenly shattered by the shouts of the men of 40 RM Commando as they advanced up the hill with bayonets fixed and firing from the hip. The harsh crack and whine of exploding grenades was accompanied by the sound of bagpipes played by Lt Col Churchill as he and Lt Col Manners urged the men forward.[1]

Churchill wrote later: 'Y Troop, 40 Cmdo [sic] were magnificent, all in line, and shouting and firing from the hip as if on the assault course at Achnacarry.'[2]

40 Commando soon cleared the top of the hill, and fired the success signal, two green Very lights. As if this was the cue, the Germans counterattacked. 40 Commando was very thin on the ground, having suffered several casualties on its way up the hill. This counterattack was beaten off, and six more Germans were taken prisoner. But there was no sign of 43 Commando, and while Manners was moving about the position to consolidate the defence he was badly wounded in the arm. Churchill applied a tourniquet using a handkerchief, and propped him by the side of Captain Wakefield, one of his brigade staff, who was critically wounded. Heavy mortar and machine-gun fire heralded another counterattack. Runners were sent to try to locate 43 Commando. As the enemy approached, and Manners, although weak from loss of blood, prepared to fire his revolver at them, a mortar bomb burst in the middle of his group, killing Wakefield, wounding Manners again, and killing a Marine who was going to Churchill's assistance. A group of about thirty Germans approaching the position were stopped by Y Troop firing rapid. As other Germans tried an outflanking movement, Churchill attempted to bring 43 Commando back by playing 'Will ye no come back again' on his pipes. It is doubtful if anyone in 43 Commando recognized the significance of the pipes, and those who heard them took them to be connected with some unplanned HLI initiative. Eventually, following a shower of grenades, one of which stunned Churchill, his little group was overrun by the enemy.

Major Maude, the second-in-command of 40 Commando, rallied Q Troop and part of 43 Commando's B Troop, and following reports that both A and Y Troops were running low on ammunition, and realizing that he was about to be outflanked, ordered a phased withdrawal to the start line. Both Commandos withdrew to the beach just after dawn. The withdrawal of the whole force, including guns and partisans, was conducted by the Royal Navy in full daylight without interference from the enemy. The RAF maintained a CAP overhead throughout, and shot down two ME 109s which attempted to attack the craft returning to Vis. A small party of 2 Commando, in what Tom Churchill described as the 'bloody silly idea of rescuing Jack Churchill and other prisoners', remained on Brač for a while in the hope of finding commandos or partisans who might have evaded capture. These would-be rescuers lost a further twenty men, captured while having a rest. The following night a 40 Commando patrol was landed on Brač for the same purpose. MGBs mounted a seaborne ambush off Supetar to intercept any German attempt to take off prisoners from there. All these efforts were in vain.

Manners died of his wounds two days later. He was sadly missed. Nicknamed 'Pops', he was an inspiring leader and fine soldier. Brigadier Tom Churchill judged him to be the best commando leader in the brigade – by inference including his own brother. Beadle was one of those taken prisoner, having been wounded, knocked unconscious by blast, and assumed to have been killed. Tactically, Operation Flounced was a disaster, for apart from the loss of two talented and experienced commanders, Manners and Jack Churchill, another 14 officers and 111 other ranks were dead, wounded, missing, or prisoners of war, and the partisans suffered 206 casualties all told. It failed because of the two uncoordinated attacks resulting from a communications breakdown, and an overall lack of control by the force commander. Strategically, however, this operation, and those that preceded and followed it, kept the Germans tied down on the islands, using troops they could ill afford to spare.

Lieutenant Colonel R. W. Sankey DSC RM took command of 40 Commando. He was a tough, ebullient, impressive man, who had been Royal Marines heavy-weight boxing champion when younger, and still looked the part. He had joined the Corps as a Marine in 1932, winning the King's Badge as the best recruit in his squad. Over-age for commissioning from the ranks under the rules in the 1930s, he became an NCO before leaving to pursue a civilian career. He re-enlisted in 1939 and was commissioned in 1940. Before coming to 40 Commando, he had served in the 11th Battalion, being promoted to command it after its disastrous Tobruk experience. 40 RM Commando was moved to Italy and on to Malta to allow it to be rebuilt and retrained. Sankey had a difficult job, and the Medical Officer wrote: 'It required tremendous moral courage and stamina to recreate 40 Commando. The first superb vitality had been shot out of it and a few splendid chaps who could not readjust from the magnificent free-wheeling days were returned to UK. Others gave him their full support.'[3]

By mid-August 1944, 43 RM Commando had been left by itself on Vis, both 2 Commando and HQ 2nd SS Brigade being sent to Italy. Led by its CO, Simonds, 43 Commando mounted a successful raid on Hvar in August, following which Simonds went home, at his own request. He was replaced by Lieutenant Colonel McAlpine of the Black Watch. He had commanded 6 Commando in Tunisia, been invalided sick, sent to command the Holding Commando at Wrexham, and had pulled strings to get back to operational Commandos. On 11 September, with no warning, 43 Commando was embarked in LCIs and taken to Brač. Partisan intelligence had reported that the Germans were withdrawing, and it was decided to try and catch the last two groups of enemy on the island. Partisans were landed, but failed to stop the enemy making their getaway to the mainland. Meanwhile 43 Commando had landed on the south coast of the island, and while slogging the ten miles to its first objective was attacked by RAF Spitfires, luckily with no casualties. The Commando was not involved in the fighting which resulted in the surrender of the final German garrison in the south-west corner of the island.

Only two days after the return to Vis, 43 RM Commando was ordered to Šolta, the island immediately to the west, where again there were indications that the Germans were about to withdraw. The landing was at night and, lacking artillery, the Commando had to rely on its own 3in mortars and Vickers machine-guns for support. Each officer and man carried either two 3in mortar bombs (10lb each), or a belt of Vickers ammunition, in addition to his normal battle order including ammunition for his personal weapon, Bren magazines, and grenades. At daylight C Troop, under Captain Loudoun, deployed first, and under machine-gun and mortar fire occupied a forward OP. When D and E Troops advanced in daylight over the bare slopes towards two strongpoints on the two highest hills on the island they came under mortar and machine-gun fire, so the two troop commanders, Captains Gourlay and Parkinson-Cumine, wisely decided to take cover among the rocks, and wait for nightfall before moving closer. The night approach was enlivened by having to negotiate a minefield, but without casualties. In daylight it was discovered that the safety strings on the mines had not been cut by the enemy, by which time D and E Troops had entered the enemy position to find that the birds had flown. Here they spent two extremely unpleasant days under mortar fire from German positions on the island, and shelling by heavy guns on the mainland. Chilling winds and torrential rain added to the miserable conditions. The bad weather not only prevented craft bringing in artillery from Vis to support the Commando and made air support impossible, it also prevented a resupply of rations. It did, however, frustrate German attempts to escape by sea.

Shortly after dawn a couple of days later both troops were ordered to capture Rogač, a small harbour on the north coast, having moved into position on hills overlooking the objective the day before. As they began to move down three Marines in E Troop had a foot blown off by German schu-mines. One man was killed and five similarly wounded in A Troop, and as the sapper officer with A Troop prodded his way forward to reach the casualties, his foot was blown off. It was impossible to spot the small wooden schu-mines among the bushes of lavender, thyme, and rosemary, and knowing that prodding a way through would take hours, E Troop commander and his troop subaltern, Jenkins, each led a single file of men, telling them to tread exactly in the footsteps of the man in front; the wounded were carried out on their comrades' shoulders. Luckily the troop reached a road without further incident. The sapper officer and the two troop commanders were awarded the MC for their leadership that day.

When the two troops reached the harbour, they found five demoralized Germans. Over a hundred of their comrades had embarked in lighters, and had subsequently been sunk by two MTBs. There was no more action on Šolta, and after being returned to Vis the Commando left for Italy a month later.

*

By early autumn 1944, the Germans were beginning to withdraw from Greece through Albania into Yugoslavia to avoid being cut off by the Russian Army advancing from the east. Accordingly, the Commander Land Forces Adriatic decided that the town of Sarandë, which lay on the main road north from Greece through southern Albania, should be captured. As well as denying this route out of Greece to the enemy, the garrison on the island of Corfu, some eight miles off the coast of Albania, would also be cut off. 2 Commando landed in Albania first, with part of the Raiding Support Regiment. They discovered that Sarandë was held by at least 500 enemy, and there were 1,200 at Delvinë, seven miles to the north-east. Clearly reinforcements would be needed, so 40 RM Commando and another troop of the Raiding Support Regiment were ordered across from Italy. The country was very challenging. High mountains rose steeply from the shore up to 2,000 feet, and the valleys were choked with scrub and woods. There were few paths, and the rocky terrain consisted of countless spikes up to nine inches high, so close together that one's boot got jammed between them, and so sharp that teetering about on top was extremely painful, even in army boots. The river beds proved to be unsuitable avenues of approach, as they consisted of a jumble of enormous boulders with matted undergrowth on the banks. The only possible access to the hills from the beach (Sugar Beach), was along what came to be called Commando Valley, about three miles as the crow flies, considerably more on foot, and blocked at the halfway point by a 400 foot rock outcrop, with two smaller rock formations beyond, before the valley debouched onto the plain where the road ran north from Sarandë. It was impossible to use transport, either of the wheeled or animal variety, to take supplies up from the beach, so everything had to be manpacked, including water.

After landing at Sugar Beach, 40 RM Commando established OPs on various features overlooking Sarandë from the north, as well as conducting reconnaissance, and assisting 2 Commando with protecting the beachhead. More guns arrived to support the two Commandos and the partisans who were based north of Commando Valley. As soon as the British guns started harassing Sarandë and the Sarandë–Delvinë road, an artillery duel began. The Germans responded at first with 75mm and 105mm guns, and quickly raised the ante with 88mm and 150mm guns, including coast batteries of 150mms based on Corfu, the latter firing on Sugar Beach and Commando Valley.

A few days after the arrival of 40 RM Commando, it poured with rain nonstop for eight days. Commando Valley became a river, and everybody was soaked. The overabundance of water solved the problem of man-packing water to forward positions, but caused many exposure casualties to men without any cover from the elements (even groundsheets had been left in Italy). Some 150 men from both Commandos were evacuated to Italy with trench foot, and over 200 whose feet had swollen so much they could not get their boots on were treated at Sugar Beach. Hardest hit were the manpacking parties. Brigadier Churchill ordered that the OPs should be thinned out to about eight men each. LCIs were brought in and provided hot meals and drying-out facilities. These measures, and an improvement in the weather, resulted in the two Commandos being ready for offensive action by 6 October. Churchill, in what was called Houndforce, now had 400 men of 40 RM Commando, 350 of 2 Commando, 500 Albanian partisans, and 130 men of the 1st Paratroop Company RAF Levies, as well as a force of Pioneers. These last were most welcome because they relieved the Commandos of the detested manpacking task.

Meanwhile the Germans had been rapidly evacuating Corfu, and their troops were moving through Sarandë and Delvinë into Yugoslavia and northern Greece. Churchill ordered an attack on Sarandë on 9 October. 40 RM Commando was to advance south to clear two beaches, Zebra and Italian Beaches, followed by swinging left to clear a feature called Point 261, and on to clear Sarandë. On its left would be 2 Commando advancing south to take a strongpoint and clear a coastal battery. A partisan force of 200 men would deploy on 2 Commando's left to take enemy positions on the Sarandë–Delvinë road. The RAF Parachute Levies would land at Parachute Beach, south-east of Sarandë, and establish a blocking position on Point 164 due south of the town. A force of 350 partisans would mount a diversion at Delvinë, while Lieutenant McNab and ten men of the New Zealand Engineers equipped with pyrotechnics would simulate a brigade attack near Shian, about halfway between Sarandë and Delvinë. The purpose of these latter two operations was to divert the attention of the large Delvinë garrison away from the attack on Sarandë. It was a somewhat risky plan, because as the two Commandos moved south they would expose their left flank and rear to attack from Delvinë, and might get cut off from their base at Sugar Beach; furthermore, if the estimates of enemy strengths in the Sarandë area were inaccurate, Houndforce might be heavily outnumbered. It should also be borne in mind that the Germans were excellent soldiers, who almost invariably gave a good account of themselves, and – it can never be stated too often – they were troops with whom you took tactical liberties at your peril.

At 0430 hours, after a thirty-minute bombardment by the guns of Houndforce to cover the move of both Commandos, 40 Commando crossed its start line. The leading troops ran into cross-fire from a series of interlocking enemy machine-guns, necessitating each to be cleared by fire and movement. In tough, gutter fighting in the darkness, occasionally lit by star-shells fired by a Royal Navy destroyer in support, the Marines fought their way on to their first objectives. While Q Troop held Point 261, X Troop with sapper support cleared paths through the minefields on Zebra and Italian Beaches, to enable ammunition to be brought in there, short-circuiting the tortuous route from Sugar Beach. By now both Q and X Troop Commanders were dead, two platoon commanders had been wounded, and the Brigade Royal Engineer Officer was killed during the mine clearing of the two beaches.

By midday, 2 Commando had captured the gun battery, and the partisans had captured Jaste, a village south-east of Sarandë. The RAF Levies had an unopposed landing at Parachute Beach and had seized Point 164, taking several prisoners. P, X, and Y Troops of 40 RM Commando now had the hard nut of Sarandë to crack. As they advanced through wire entanglements and anti-personnel minefields towards the western end of the town, they came under mortar and machine-gun fire, and as they got closer they were held up by machine-guns in the houses on the outskirts, and from high ground overlooking the town. Machine-guns in a hospital about 400 yards away also caused considerable trouble. OC P Troop, Captain Marshall, was badly wounded in the head, and the MO had his head cut by a mortar fragment but continued tending the wounded.

Lieutenant Colonel Sankey called for fire support from a Royal Navy frigate; with this and fire from his own 3in Mortar and Machine Gun Platoons, as well as covering fire from A and Q Troops, he ordered P, X, and Y Troops into the assault. With three of his troop commanders dead or wounded, he was well to the fore, and during the fight-through led at least three of the attacks himself. It took four hours of bitter street fighting before the garrison of 750 men surrendered – the same number of men in Sarandë alone as the two Commandos' total strength. More prisoners were taken when schooners packed with troops from Corfu arrived that evening, including the Garrison Commander, who, as Beadle remarks in his history of 40 Commando, 'suddenly found himself without a job'. Sankey was awarded a well-deserved DSO. Captain

Marshall, who had been awarded the MC for his leadership at Termoli, and a bar at the Garigliano, died of his wounds.

At first Churchill hoped to billet his commandos in Sarandë, but Lieutenant McNab quickly found a series of cunningly concealed booby traps. He also suspected that the Germans had buried large charges under the roads in the centre of town, because he found some time-delay fuses, but no charges. Churchill ordered everybody out, and the following day the centre of town almost disappeared in a gigantic explosion. A second explosion in the undamaged part of town caused even more devastation the following day.

40 Commando was sent to Corfu to take the surrender of the remainder of the garrison and to prevent civil disturbance. Meanwhile the Germans abandoned Delvinë. Just after this Brigadier Tom Churchill was ordered by Land Forces Adriatic to follow up the retreating Germans. He pointed out that he had no transport, the Germans would blow every bridge and had swept the country bare of supplies, and, having been ordered to leave 40 Commando in Corfu, with 9 and 43 RM Commandos engaged elsewhere, he only had 2 Commando for the task; he was not therefore in a position to comply. Land Forces Adriatic sitting at their desks in Italy did not agree. Churchill offered his resignation, which was accepted, and he was relieved by Lieutenant Colonel Ronnie Tod of 9 Commando. Thus did 2nd SS Brigade lose the services of a gallant and experienced commander thanks to the inflexi-bility of Land Forces Adriatic, whose commander and staff were not held in high regard by anyone with whom they came in contact. On return home, Churchill was immediately given command of an infantry brigade.

Although 40 Commando was greeted with great enthusiasm by the Greek population of Corfu, the situation soon turned sour, the Marines finding themselves in circumstances that would be all too familiar to their postwar successors. On the island both the pro-Communist National People's Liberation Army (ELAS) and EDES (the non-Com-munist, anti-monarchy, National Republican Greek League) were repre-sented in strength, armed and hostile; civil war appeared imminent. The civil population was also fearful of an invasion by ELAS from mainland Greece, their apprehension fuelled by some 8,000 refugees from ELAS persecution. Firmness and tact were called for, and, led by their CO, 40 Commando displayed both qualities in abundance. Within a month, the main body of the Commando was withdrawn to Italy, leaving two troops under the second-in-command, Major Matters. Soon they too were recalled to Italy, but trouble rapidly broke out again, and Sankey returned with his whole Commando. He disarmed both ELAS and EDES, and formed a National Guard from the non-political elements. Within two months all was quiet and the Commando returned to Italy. During their time in Corfu, what would now be called 'hearts and minds operations' by 40 RM Commando had played an important part in restoring normality to the island. The Commando controlled food supplies, suppressed the black market, donated their rations to the hospital, the mental home and the orphanage, encouraged the workforce to clear war damage, and assisted with children's education.

While 40 RM and 2 Commandos were fighting in Albania, and 9 operating in Greece, 43 RM Commando was engaged in mainland Yugoslavia. Its presence was occasioned by a plan to harass and inflict casualties on the German XXI Mountain Corps as it withdrew through the mountains of Montenegro in southern Yugoslavia. With Tito's partisans engaging them at one end of the long column, and the Albanians likewise at the other end, the participation of Allied troops with artillery and air power might wreak havoc on the corps. Accordingly a force consisting of 111th Field Regiment Royal Artillery, elements of the Raiding Support Regiment, 43 RM Commando, and six Hurricanes with an RAF Regiment Squadron to protect their airstrip were sent to Dubrovnik. The force was called Floydforce, under the command of Brigadier O'Brien-Twohig.

On arrival, the British noticed that their reception was distinctly chilly, unlike the friendly relations they had enjoyed with the partisans on Vis and in the Dalmatian Islands generally. This period marked the start of Tito's open alignment with the Soviet Union, as the Red Army approached, although he had never made any secret of where his loyalties lay. As a result he became less and less enamoured of the Allies operating on Yugoslav soil. He was determined that the liberation of Yugoslavia should be seen to be a home-grown effort, and, unknown to the Allies at this time, he also had designs on Trieste, which he hoped to incorporate into postwar Yugoslavia. However, he was still beholden to the Allies for matériel, and it was only his lack of artillery that led him to agree to Floydforce coming over at all.

XXI Mountain Corps had a choice of three routes north out of Montenegro: along the coast; inland through Nikšić to Sarajevo; or a wide swing further inland, to the north-east and north through Višegrad. Captain Loudoun's C Troop with a battery of 25-pounders was sent to assist the partisans blocking the coast road in the area of Risan and Ledinice, and later B Troop was sent in further north to act as a longstop. Loudoun taking a party on a roundabout route blew the road culvert about two miles south of Risan. As the demolition was in full view of the gunner OPs, and within range of the 25-pounders, any attempts at repair would attract shell fire. Eventually, holed up in Ledinice, the Germans surrendered after heavy shelling. The coast road was no longer open to XXI Corps.

A and E Troops were sent to operate on the inland road to Nikšić. Here E Troop saw the execution of two Chetniks by Tito's partisans, evidence of the bitter civil war being fought while the country was still occupied. The Chetniks had been formed by Drazha Mihailović, a royalist Yugoslav Army officer, to resist the Germans. For a while they were the resistance organization favoured by the Allies, until Tito's partisans, who were more active, gained the undivided support of Churchill, and Mihailović was abandoned. Despite the Titoist propaganda, the Yugoslavs spent more time and energy fighting each other than engaging the Germans and Italians. Most of the 1.2 million Yugoslavs who died in the Second World War perished at the hands of other Yugoslavs.

The bridge south of Nikšić was prepared for demolition should the partisans fail to hold the Germans, but they switched to the north-eastern, most inland route. Relations with the partisans became increasingly strained. On one occasion it took ten days for authorization to arrive from Belgrade for British guns to shell an enemy concentration. Fraternization with the partisans, which had been easy and friendly on the Dalmatian Islands, was stamped on by political commissars. Even during the happier times on Vis, any fraternization with the many women partisans had been taboo. The penalty for sexual liaison between male and female partisans was death for both parties. Females found pregnant were executed. The commandos were forbidden to have anything to do with the women, other than required in the line of duty.

At this time Lieutenant Colonel Riches arrived to take command; McAlpine had succumbed to malaria again, the initial cause of his evacuation from Tunisia. Riches found his Commando dispersed, and often under command of other units; highly unsatisfactory for any CO,

especially a new one who must if he is to be effective quickly stamp his
personality on his unit. The winter conditions were severe in the
mountains, with deep snow and high winds making life on the bare,
rocky slopes very unpleasant. The Commando was not equipped with
cold-weather kit. It says much for their stamina and mental and physical
robustness that the sick rate was so low. In view of the unwelcoming
and increasingly ungrateful attitude of the partisans, it also speaks
volumes for the commandos' discipline and the leadership of their
officers and NCOs that they did not openly express the view that the
Yugoslavs should be left to their own devices, whatever the outcome –
although they were perhaps not yet fully aware that the Yugoslavs already
had the result they wanted: a clear run to a postwar Communist
Yugoslavia.

Plans were made to fly in part of the Commando and four guns to
Berane on the route now being taken by the XXI Corps. This was
cancelled by bad weather. The same force was sent to help the partisans
further south on this route. But just before Christmas it became
increasingly obvious that the partisans were unwilling to allow Floydforce
to gain any more kudos in the forthcoming victory, and 43 Commando
was eventually withdrawn to Italy.

*

Before returning to Italy with the 2nd Commando Brigade, as it like the
other SS Brigades were now called, we must wind the clock back in
the narrative to briefly mention the exploits of a small Royal Marines
sub-unit in the Aegean, the RMBPD (Royal Marines Boom Patrol
Detachment).

There were other Marines in the Mediterranean and Middle East in
ships and notably in landing craft. Many of the latter, in particular, took
part in the operations described in this chapter, and others for which
space can not be found. After the raid on Bordeaux described in Chapter
14, from which only Hasler and Sparks returned, the RMBPD section
which had not been on the raid eventually went out to the Middle East
under Captain Pritchard-Gordon. Here it came under command of
Raiding Forces Middle East, which ran raiding operations in the Aegean
– by mid-1944, with great events unfolding in Italy and France, a
backwater. Following the capitulation of Italy the previous year, the
Germans had rapidly moved in to fill the vacuum in the Aegean. Because

most of the Allied resources had been taken away from the Middle East theatre to prosecute the war elsewhere, the British lacked the means to eject them, so they confined themselves to harassing the enemy by raiding and generally making a nuisance of themselves. By this time raids in this theatre were mainly carried out by Jellicoe's Special Boat (SB) Squadron, an offshoot of the Special Air Service (SAS), since the other major player in the Aegean, the Long Range Desert Group, was now operating in Italy and the Adriatic.

The SB Squadron was planning a raid to eliminate the garrison on the Dodecanese island of Simi, just off the coast of Turkey, but the operation could not go ahead until two ex-Italian destroyers, manned by Germans, had been located and eliminated. Lieutenant Richards with five men and three canoes of the RMBPD were based in a camouflaged caique just off the Turkish coast about forty miles east of the island of Leros. On the afternoon of 16 June 1944, a Royal Navy Fairmile Motor Launch (ML), Number 360, arrived with recent air photographs of Portolago Harbour on Leros, showing that not only were there two supply ships anchored there, the *Anita* and *Carola*, but also the two destroyers, a flak craft, and some smaller escorts. ML 360 embarked Richards's section and their canoes, and launched them off Leros. Richards and Marine Stevens were in *Shark*, Sergeant King and Marine Ruff in *Salmon*, and Corporal Horner and Marine Fisher in *Shrimp*. Corporal Horner picks up the tale:

In our canoes we had our sten gun and fighting knife, camouflage nets, twenty-four hour ration pack, water, and eight magnetic limpet mines. We hadn't screwed down on the delay device; a butterfly nut on top of the limpet which crushes an ampoule of acid. The strength of the acid determined the time taken for it to eat through the capsule and release the firing pin. We had four and a half hour delay ampoules, which depending on the temperature would detonate the limpet half an hour either side of the designed delay time.

We followed each other underneath the shadow of the cliffs before we got to the entrance. Lt Richards told us to screw down on our limpets. I was ordered to go in first, the others to follow at fifteen minute intervals. We used single paddle, the lowest position. We passed the boom boat, and paddled over the boom.

As we got into the harbour and were approaching our target's position, we could see it looming up. The stars made the strip midstream like the beam of a searchlight. To the right and left under the cliff was quite dark, as was the naval base. Right in the centre the *Anita* [Horner's target] was lying fore and aft. We were approaching her stern, and when we were two to three hundred yards off, a motor boat came across our bow. The sailors were shouting and singing. It seemed like a liberty boat returning to their base.

As we started moving moving towards *Anita*'s stern, we saw three or four men standing by the guard rail looking straight down on us. They shouted. There was nothing we could do. If we were caught, the raid would have to be aborted.

Horner remembered being told that a German special unit called the Brandenburgers patrolled the harbour from time to time. Whether or not this was true, he called out, 'Brandenburger Patrola!'

We were now alongside, and they were still shouting at us. What seemed to be a Jacob's ladder started coming over the side and they were shining a torch. I called 'Patrola' again and proceeded to the bow [of the target] and over to the shadow of the cliffs. There we stayed silent and waited. We really thought we had opened up a hornet's nest. But nothing happened. It was very quiet, and we decided that we couldn't go up a further mile-and-a-half to our other targets, and the best thing we could do was get away to the lie-up position at Kalymo Island two to three miles away.

We negotiated the boom successfully. We remembered to get rid of our limpet mines which were live, we set course for our lie-up position. Finally, after rejecting one sea cave because there was a net across the entrance, we got off on a rocky inlet, got our canoe out, unloaded our stores, and put the canoe in the crevasse of some rocks and covered it with the camouflage net. Taking our weapons, personal camouflage nets, rations and water bottles, we climbed the steep earth and found a large overhanging rock. From here we could see Leros and the coast of Turkey. As dawn came up we saw a canoe go by below. We knew we would have to go the same way that night to make contact.

During the day there was a lot of activity and aeroplanes flying around. We heard bangs coming from Leros. There was activity on the cliffs above us. We were told later there was a pillbox up there, and the noise could have been a patrol. But we were safe where we were.

The sea cave we had almost gone into turned out to have been a hiding place for Greek fishermen, because patrol boats fired into it to flush them out. One or two patrol boats went by our lying-up position but nothing happened.

At about 11 pm we made our way down to our canoe and paddled in the direction of the other canoe. I made contact using our bird call. It was Lt Richards and Mne Stevens. We made contact with the ML using a walkie-talkie. As we paddled out, we heard Sgt King on his walkie-talkie saying he was coming in. We were all picked up, and the ML proceeded to its hide-up in a bay on the Turkish coast.

Lt Richards had attacked the destroyers, and Sgt King the escort. Although badly damaged they didn't sink. However, when they were on tow to Piraeus harbour for repair, they were sunk by the RAF.

In hindsight, Horner believes that he should have approached from the dark bow. However, his quick thinking, and avoidance of capture, allowed the other two canoes to approach the targets and complete the mission. Marine Stevens:

> No sooner were we in [the harbour] than we heard a shout, we learned later it was Horner. We fixed about six or seven limpets, including three on the destroyer. Although a man looked down on us from one of the ships, and urinated over the side all over us, he didn't see us. We canoed out of the harbour and lay up on a little island. We arrived as dawn was breaking. We saw a canoe going by, and it was Fisher. We camouflaged our canoes using nets over chicken wire. You could make various shapes with the chicken wire, a rock for example. We heard the limpets going off that day. During that day a machine gun opened up. You could hear the bullets richochetting all around, and we thought they were aiming at us. But it was fishing boat that was the target. We contacted the ML on the walkie-talkie. On the way out we met King and Ruff. We learned later that King had sunk one Destroyer and we the other.

Lieutenant Richards was awarded the DSC, and Sergeant King and Marine Ruff the DSM for this remarkable effort. As Pritchard-Gordon remarked, this was one of the rare occasions when six men went out and six came back. Although they were used in the raiding role subsequently in the Aegean, this was the last successful ship attack (the principal reason for their existence) they carried out. It was also perhaps the most successful ship attack by the RMBPD in their four years of life as a unit, because it had a direct relevance to a forthcoming battle. Thanks to the RMBPD the Simi operation could now go ahead, and was highly successful.

*

In the year since the 2nd Commando Brigade had been away from Italy, the Allied Armies, the US Fifth and British Eighth, had captured Rome, overrun a succession of German defensive lines, and, at the end of 1944, halted about fifty miles south of the River Po. Here the Allied Supreme Commander Mediterranean, Field Marshal Alexander, decided they would wait for the spring weather before continuing the offensive. The British Eighth Army held a line running from the southern end of Lake Comácchio in the east to the foothills of the Apennines. At the seaward end the line ran more or less along the south bank of the River Senio, a tributary of the River Reno, and along the eastern leg of the Reno which flows to the sea just south of Lake Comácchio. The lake, really a forty-square-mile lagoon with salt pans in the north-east, is separated from the Adriatic by a spit about seven miles long from north to south, and between one and two miles wide. The lake, silted and shallow over much of its area, was six inches lower than usual as there had been less rain and snow than average during the winter. Much of the lake was only a few inches deep, and seldom more than six feet. Just north of the spit the Valetta Canal flows into the Adriatic at Porto Garibaldi. At its southern end the River Reno curves right across the spit in an L shape, to its estuary the Foce del Reno, leaving a narrow 'tongue' of land between its eastern bank and the sea. The spit was dotted with shallow water pans, and two canals cut through from the lake. One, the Bellocchio Canal, ran east–west across the spit, the other formed an L shape east from the lake and then north to the Valetta Canal at Porto Garibaldi.

The terrain in the whole area was flat, low-lying, and open, and criss-crossed by canals and dykes, with small clumps of trees dotted about. The best going lay to the west of the lake and astride Route 16 running north-west through Argenta. To the west of Argenta the River Reno and two canals bounded a large area of low-lying land flooded by the Germans. The gap between the lake and this flooded area, the Argenta Gap, was the axis chosen for his advance by General McCreery, commanding British Eighth Army. As part of his plan, he wanted to use 2nd Commando Brigade to seize the spit and clear the enemy from that area, and to deceive the Germans that the main thrust of the spring offensive would be along the coast, before the main body of the Eighth Army assaulted through the Argenta Gap. The spit was believed to be held by about 1,200 men of the Turkoman Division, of Russian origin, stiffened by German units. The area was well entrenched and fortified, although there appeared to be few positions sited to defend the spit from an attack across the lake. Consequently, the Commander of V Corps, under whose command 2nd Commando Brigade was operating, suggested that an attack on the spit across the lake would be the best approach. Brigadier Tod agreed, but also wanted to attack up the 'tongue', followed by an attack up the spit, accompanied by a feint on the western side of the base of the spit.

By now Tod had his own brigade together again, 2 and 9 Commandos, and 40 RM and 43 RM Commandos. In order that his brigade would be familiar with the ground, and to accustom them to working with standard Army formations after their lengthy sojourn in the Balkans either on their own or with a rather unconventional mix of units, Tod asked that his commandos should spend some time in the line over-looking the Reno and the lake. Here they relieved infantry battalions and renewed acquaintance with the standard fare that is the bread and butter of infantry in the line in contact with the enemy: patrols, sniping, and exchanges of shell and mortar fire. Being able to study the ground was to pay dividends later.

Tod's orders to his brigade for Operation Roast were that 2 Commando was to cross the lake, land on the spit north of the Bellocchio Canal, take two bridges over the canal codenamed Amos and Peter (all the defended localities and key points had been given biblical names), and hold the line of the canal. 9 Commando was to cross the lake and clear the south-west half of the spit. 43 RM Commando was to attack north up the 'tongue', cross the Reno estuary, and swing down to clear the south-eastern half of the spit. 40 RM Commando was given three tasks: first, to mount a feint crossing of the Reno; second, to put in a troop strength assault supported by a troop of tanks from the North Irish Horse to clear the north bank of the Reno in the south-west corner of the spit; third, to provide the brigade reserve and hold the existing line. After the southern end of the spit was clear, 2 and 43 RM Commandos were to advance north and seize the southern bank of the Valetta Canal, with 2 Commando on the lake side of the spit, and 43 Commando on the Adriatic side. Once these two were firm on their objectives, 9 Commando would pass through and take Porto Garibaldi. There were 150 guns in support of 2nd Commando Brigade's operation. The various crossings would be made in a mixture of LVTs, as had been used at Walcheren (which for some reason were called Fantails in Italy), Weasels, storm boats, and assault boats. It was an imaginative plan exploiting manoeuvre by the use of boats and LVTs, and involving attacks from several directions to outwit the enemy; designed to keep him guessing the direction and timing of the next assault.

Reconnaissance by the Special Boat Service and a Combined Operations Pilotage Party (COPP) in Folboats had established the depths of the lake. An artificial dyke constructed of stakes ran across it. COPP Folboats with lights would mark the gaps and places where it was awash. Because the lake was so shallow, the storm boats being used by 2 and 9 Commandos would have to be carried for about 500 yards through the mud, then floated and pushed for another 1,000 yards before the eighteen commandos each carried could embark. The storm boats were heavy, each weighing three-quarters of a ton, and carrying them took all eighteen men, plus another seven to bring the paddles and outboard engine. 43 RM Commando was allocated four LVTs, five assault boats, four rubber dinghies, a troop of Kangaroos of the 4th Queen's Own Hussars,[4] two troops of Churchill tanks of the North Irish Horse, and a platoon of Royal Engineers. A Kangaroo was a Sherman tank from which the turret had been removed, and carried about eight men – an early form of armoured personnel carrier. The attack by 43 RM Commando was timed for midnight 1/2 April, as 2 and 9 Commandos landed (H-Hour), so the enemy would be surprised by being hit in two directions at once. At least, that was the grand conception, but things rarely go to plan in war.

The move of the LVTs and commandos to their start lines and boat launching points was covered by artillery harassing fire, RAF bombers circling overhead, tanks moving on the road just behind the front line, and 40 RM Commando playing Wagner through loudspeakers. The shallow water and thick mud caused serious delays to 2 and 9 Commandos: their LVTs bogged down, and the order to transfer their passengers to boats added to the confusion. As the time for H-Hour passed, 43 RM Commando's leading troops, A and B, ahead of their Commando, and in danger of being caught out in the open unless the attack got underway, knew they would have to get back to the Commando main body before daylight. The COs of both 2 and 9 Commandos wanted to postpone the operation to the following night, but Brigadier Tod, seeing that at last the boats were afloat, and appreciating that conditions the next time would not improve, courageously gave the order to continue. Fortunately the generous artillery support available meant that smoke could be laid on to cover the daylight assault. With storm boats lashed together, and towing assault boats, the two Commandos set off. One boat's engine failed entirely and its passengers had to paddle the whole way across. 2 Commando had to drag all their boats across the dyke. But with typical guts and élan, they pressed on, and by about 0530 hours were ashore and tackling their initial objectives.

At last, at 0500 hours, 43 RM Commando got the order to move. By this time A and B Troops had started to come back to join the main body before sun-up, but they were turned around just in time. E Troop on the west flank could hear the sounds of 40 RM Commando's diversion as they floated assault boats containing dummy figures across the river, and men crouching in slit trenches on the south bank fired rifles in the boats by pulling on string attached to the triggers.

43 RM Commando's A and B Troops advanced over the open ground to the enemy strongpoint on the tongue – Joshua – held by a company and well defended with machine-guns, some of which continued to fire, holding up A Troop, despite the artillery supporting the attack. German guns, mortars, and multi-barrelled rocket launchers were ranged on the tongue in anticipation of seaborne landings, rather than on the back-door approach by 2 and 9 Commandos. B troop arrived first, and entered the left-hand side of the position, followed by A Troop assisted by D Troop (the reserve for this part of the operation), which had been travelling in Kangaroos, but after these bogged down the men de-bussed and continued on foot. By 0730 hours Joshua was taken, along with thirty prisoners and several enemy dead.

While 43 RM Commando made preparations to cross the Reno from the tongue, A Troop 40 RM Commando, under Lieutenant Marsh, crossed the river some five miles inland in LVTs, supported by Churchill tanks, and turned right to take strongpoint Mark in the flank. Before reaching their objective they encountered a deep dyke, much wider than expected. Royal Engineers and commandos covered the bottom with fascines (bundles of sticks). At first the tanks bogged in and could not climb out. This necessitated bringing forward more fascines, which took until about 1330 hours, before A Troop could get on the move again. Working forward in two groups the troop cleared enemy slit trenches between the dyke and Mark. At this stage Marsh was wounded and

Lieutenant Seales took over. The radios, as they so often do, now chose to give trouble, and the only way of communicating with Commando Headquarters was through one of the supporting tank's radios. One of the LVTs bogged in, and one was disabled by a mine. In the final assault on Mark, two Marines were killed and six wounded to add to the four earlier casualties. Undoubtedly the relatively low casualties in clearing this position were due to the support provided by the tanks, although two of the three never made it to the objective. There were, however, further dugouts along the north bank of the Reno at Mark still left uncleared late that afternoon, so E Troop of 43 RM Commando was sent south to assist, and the position was finally taken by 2000 hours.

Much earlier in the day E and C Troops had successfully crossed the Reno from the tongue at two crossing points. C Troop, whose task was to set up the main ferry crossing for the whole Commando, had a difficult time under artillery fire. Two of their assault boats had been holed by shrapnel while being carried, still folded, on Kangaroos. While C Troop assembled the boats (holed or not), and inflated rubber dinghies, they were hidden by smoke laid down by artillery, thickened up by the Commando's mortars. C Troop also rigged up a fully rehearsed system of ropes to ferry not only themselves but also B and D Troops across, but not without loss: four of the eight Marines manning the ferries were killed, and one seriously wounded. E Troop were supposed to cross in LVTs, but the steering in the troop commander's LVT jammed, and it went round in circles for some time, before bogging in at the foot of the far bank. None of the other LVTs managed to climb the bank, so E Troop staggered through the heavy estuary silt, sinking up to their thighs under their heavy loads, before scrambling up the bank. Here the troop found itself exposed in the open on a bare flood plain, shorn of its LVTs and without armoured support, because the tank commanders decided that the river was too deep even for water-proofed Churchills to wade across. Ahead of them, Acts, an enemy company position with an 88mm gun and 47/32 anti-tank gun, stood out starkly as the objective for B, D, and E troops. As they closed, the gunners put down first high explosive on Acts, followed by smoke to cover the final phase of the assault. The three troops swept past the position under the cover of the artillery smoke and cleared each bunker from the rear, tossing grenades into the entrances.

The clearing of Hosea I and II, to the south of Acts, by B, D, and E

Troops followed, and the enemy started surrendering in large numbers. With the south-eastern part of the spit in their control, 43 RM Commando had now taken all its objectives. However, 9 Commando had been held up on Leviticus, and was unable to proceed to its next objectives, Matthew I and II, so 43 RM Commando was ordered to take them. The enemy positions were well protected from the sea, the way the Commando was coming, but with the assistance of generous artillery support both were taken. That evening, the Commando, except for E Troop, was ordered north to Peter bridge, in preparation for the next day's advance, where it was joined by E Troop at about midnight.

The spit up to the Bellocchio Canal was now held by 2nd Commando Brigade. The next phase, an advance to the Valetta Canal by 2 and 43 RM Commandos, ordered for 1100 hours, was postponed until 1400 hours because the armour that was to support 2 Commando had difficulty moving forward to join it. The only bridge over the Bellocchio Canal capable of taking armour, Amos, had been blown before 2 Commando could seize it the day before, so an Ark bridging tank had to be brought up over which the tanks could cross. 43 RM Commando's route, which was straddled by two extensive marked and wired-in minefields, would have been unsuitable for tanks and could only be negotiated on foot by way of a narrow sandy track, replete with the footprints of departed Germans, that ran northwards through the low scattered scrub and the mines. 43 RM Commando accordingly moved forward in a long single file, with C Troop at the head of the snake, closely behind shifting concentrations of supporting artillery fire. There was no enemy to be seen until a track debouched into a cleared area of ground 100 yards or so short of the canal bank. On its near side were groups of soldiers, looking confused. The leading section of C Troop, coming one by one from the track exit, shook out into a loose extended line and went for the Germans. Some raised their hands in surrender. Some fired a few rounds. Some seemed indecisive. There was a brief period of milling around, and then several Spandaus opened up simultaneously, firing at close range from the Porto Garibaldi houses. The Marines and Germans round them dived for the nearest cover. Corporal Tom Hunter, from a completely exposed position on top of a heap of rubble, took on the Spandaus with a Bren gun. It was a self-sacrificial intervention that allowed many of his friends to reach a precarious temporary safety. Hunter fired methodical bursts at the muzzle flashes of the Spandaus until he was shot through the head. For this selfless act of gallantry, coupled with an outstanding performance throughout the battle, Tom Hunter was posthumously awarded the Victoria Cross, the only Royal Marines VC of the Second World War.

For the remainder of the daylight hours, C Troop, and E Troop on their right, were stuck behind sparse cover close up to the Valetta Canal. Any overt movement attracted a stream of Spandau fire. An accurate low-level bombing attack on the houses by Hurricane fighter-bombers, and some equally accurate gunner shelling, brought some amelioration; and shortly after nightfall, both troops were pulled back to join the Commando.

Clearly a large set-piece attack would be needed to cross and take Porto Garibaldi, so 9 Commando was not brought forward. The Commandos held the line until relieved by 24th Guards Brigade the following night, and pulled back to rest at Ravenna. The Army Commander sent the following message to Brigadier Tod:

> My best congratulations to you and all ranks of your force on your most successful operation which has captured or destroyed the whole enemy garrison south of Porto Garibaldi. Your operation demanded very careful and detailed planning and skill in execution. All ranks have shown a splendid enterprise, endurance and determination to surmount difficulties. Your success has helped the whole army plan. Well done indeed.

The 2nd Commando Brigade had indeed done well, taking 946 prisoners, and eliminating the equivalent of a brigade of three infantry battalions, with artillery, anti-tank guns, and three companies of heavy machine-gunners.

2nd Commando Brigade's next task was to take part in a series of operations to eliminate the enemy holding Menate and Longastrino on the west side of Lake Comácchio, as a prelude to the Eighth Army offensive through the Argenta Gap. For this 40 RM Commando was placed under command of the 169th Brigade of the 56th Infantry Division, to lead the assault across the Argine Dyke and Menate Canal on the night of 10/11 April 1945. 40 Commando's objectives were to capture the bridge and pumping station at Menate, and exploit along the Strada del Pioppa. Three battalions of the Queen's Royal Regiment from the 169th Brigade would follow in LVTs: the 2nd/5th would cross the bridge to capture Menate and the 2nd/6th were to capture Longastrino;

the 2nd/7th were in reserve. The area between the dyke and the western side of the lake had been flooded by the Germans blowing a gap in the dyke. As it curved to converge on the Menate Canal very close to the Commando's objectives, Sankey decided to use the dyke as the approach route. The gap blown by the Germans would be crossed in rubber boats carried by the leading troop. There was sufficient light from the moon screened by a thin layer of cloud to make movement reasonably easy. Delays crossing the Reno made it necessary to move along the dyke at a brisk pace, alternately doubling and walking. At the gap, the boats were laid side by side in the manner of a pontoon bridge, and about half the leading troop had crossed when a mine detonated on the far side, wounding the troop commander, one of his troop subalterns, and ten men. As the wounded were being evacuated, more mines were found. Lifting them would take too long and be too hazardous, so the surviving troop officer ordered the trip wires to be cut. So far the noise had not attracted the enemy's attention.

Sankey forced on with Y, P, and X Troops at best speed towards the bridge. Just before dawn Y Troop reached the point where the dyke converged with the canal, where it came under fire. OC P Troop, Major Porter, decided to cross to seize the bridge, supported by fire from the bank. By now the enemy were engaging the dyke with artillery, mortars, and machine-guns. Eventually P Troop managed to cross, while Y Troop engaged the enemy to draw their attention away from the crossing. Both troops were taking casualties, which increased as the light improved. P Troop's support group for the assault on the bridge were picked off one by one, Lieutenant Wedgewood being wounded for the second time, but continuing to return fire with his .45 automatic pistol. The leading section of the assault group crossed the bridge, but almost immediately the enemy counterattacked with infantry and a self-propelled gun. The whole of the assault group were killed and wounded; Marines Harwood and Mullens were taken prisoner. Fortunately, it was discovered later, small-arms fire had cut the wires to the explosive charges on the bridge, so the enemy were unable to blow it. Some of the German infantry and the SP gun moved to the pumping house.

Suddenly LVTs with 2nd/5th Queens appeared, and the Germans on the bridge panicked. With commendable speed, Harwood and Mullens picked up weapons and demanded the enemy's surrender. The Germans did so. However, fire was still coming down on P Troop, causing more casualties, killing several, including Porter and Wedgewood. As X Troop were moving to cross the Canal, they came under enfilade fire from Spandaus on the canal edge and a house a little further on. At that moment the radios stopped working. OC X Troop, Captain Belbin, sent a runner back to Tac HQ asking for air or artillery support. No sooner had he returned than four Spitfires ordered by Sankey roared overhead and rocketed the house and pumping station. Under cover of this fire, Belbin swam across the canal towing a line made up of toggle ropes, and the rest of the troop followed. According to the Commando's historian, this was the first time that 40 Commando had used toggle ropes in action, having carried them in battle for nearly three years, since August 1942.[5]

Captain Belbin led the assault on the house and pumping station. Nineteen prisoners were taken, and the SP gun, which was turned against the remaining German positions. Q Troop was sent to take over the bridge and power house. The enemy put up a stiff fight, and the troop lost twelve casualties. A Troop was brought up with the remnants of P and Y Troops, along with LVTs carrying the 2nd/5th Queens. Patrols from X Troop captured a fortified house and fourteen more prisoners, but took more casualties supporting 2nd/5th Queens. The fighting continued until 2100 hours, while the Queens cleared Menate and Longastrino. Just after dark Belbin, his MOA (batman/orderly), and Captain Pook were walking to attend the CO's O Group when they entered an unmarked minefield and detonated a mine, wounding all three. A stretcher party going to their assistance detonated another mine, causing more casualties, one of whom subsequently died.

The war in Europe was nearly over and the fighting at Menate, 40 RM Commando's last battle in the Second World War, had been arduous and costly, with twenty-seven killed and forty-five wounded. As the first RM Commando to form, 40 Commando's performance in battle had added lustre to the laurels of the Royal Marines, and contributed to the high regard in which the Corps was held by outsiders; an esteem which owes much to the fighting record of all the RM Commandos.

The last major battle fought by Marines in Italy was 43 RM Commando's involvement, with 2 Commando, at the Eighth Army's breakthrough at Argenta. Just north-west of Argenta two canals from the west bend sharply south-east close to the River Reno, and all three run parallel together for three miles south to Bastia. They were separated by dykes about thirty yards wide, each with terraces on either side of a higher central embankment, bare of cover, so it was impossible to avoid being sky-lined. Helped by accurate artillery fire and preliminary bombing from the air, 2 Commando managed to capture the three bridges across the canals and the Reno just west of Argenta. Here they withstood four counterattacks by units of the 42nd Jäger (Mountain) Division.

43 RM Commando was ordered to clear all the embankments northward up to the sharp bends on the night of 17/18 April, in conjunction with a major night attack by the 78th Infantry Division, just east of Argenta. Once again the Marines were deprived of direct tank support: at the start of the advance the leading Churchill was badly damaged by a Tellermine and slewed across the only inclined track from the terrace up to the central embankment, blocking the route for the following tanks. A and B Troops came under heavy fire from a German 88mm gun, Spandaus, and rifles. Captain Nunns was wounded in the leg for the third time, but continued to lead his troop, and brought back some prisoners. On the western terraces both D and E Troop commanders were wounded by Spandaus, dug in on the flanks of the central embankment. Captain Parkinson-Cumine was hit in the chest by a burst at close range, puncturing one lung, and detonating some rounds in a bandolier in one pouch. One Spandau round knocked off the shoulder from a 36 grenade in his other pouch, but the lever did not fly off, so the grenade did not detonate. He survived. Lieutenant Jenkins took over D and E Troops, and he too was fortunate. A point-blank shot from a slit trench immediately below him hit the edge of an iron gate he was rounding, and he received splinters of metal in his neck. From on top of the embankment he managed to subdue the two Spandau positions, and the enemy platoon on the objective was taken prisoner. Subsequently he was awarded the DSO, very rare for so junior an officer.

After being heavily shelled the next day, 43 RM Commando carried out another advance on the night of 18/19 April, to secure the western flank up to the bends so that the 6th Armoured Division could advance safely through Argenta towards Ferrara. The Germans had withdrawn, and the following day the advance continued westwards, 2 and 43 RM Commandos leapfrogging through each other and mopping up prisoners, until they reached the Malinella–Ferrara road on 21 April, where long columns of surrendered Germans were marching south. The Eighth Army had fanned out to the north, and the 2nd Commando Brigade was withdrawn to Ravenna. 43 RM Commando lost six Marines killed, and four officers and nineteen other ranks wounded; a heavy price to pay considering that the rifle troops were down to about thirty strong after the Comácchio battle.

On 2 May they heard the news that the Germans in Italy had surrendered. The Army Commander sent a signal to the brigade:

> After your successful spit operations, your troops showed a magnificent fighting spirit combined with skill and enterprise in difficult operations, which enabled V Corps to break out of the Argenta defile. This success was the decisive phase of the whole battle. Well done.

The end of the war in the remainder of Europe was only six days away.

19

South-East Asia and the Pacific

3RD SS BRIGADE ARRIVES

In early December 1943, Brigadier Nonweiler, the commander of 3rd SS Brigade, arrived in India ahead of his commandos to discover what Admiral Mountbatten, the Supreme Commander South East Asia Command (SEAC), had in store for his formation. He was not happy with what he heard. There was little chance of 3rd SS Brigade being used for major amphibious operations for at least a year; most of the available landing craft were earmarked for the Normandy landings, and any spare for the Mediterranean. It might be possible to mount operations for a single Commando, or less; one Mountbatten had in mind was a seaborne version of long-range penetration on the lines of Wingate's brigade-size expedition earlier that year. Nonweiler was not over-enamoured of that idea, nor should he have been. The sole credit from that foray had been publicity. On the debit side, a third of the force were missing, and few of the survivors were ever fit to take part in operations again.[1]

The brigade set sail from Scotland on 15 November 1943, consisting of 1 Commando, with battle experience in North Africa; 5 Commando, which had landed in Madagascar; 42 RM Commando (Lieutenant Colonel Leathes RM); and 44 RM Commando (Lieutenant Colonel Horton RM). The ship carrying 1 and 42 RM Commandos was hit by a bomb in the Mediterranean, and put into Alexandria for repairs, while the ship with the other two Commandos pressed on arriving in Bombay in mid-December. By the time 1 and 42 RM Commandos caught up a month later, 5 and 44 RM Commandos were already involved in preparations for Operation Screwdriver.

Following the offensive by Indian XV Corps which captured Maung-daw in the Arakan, the Japanese riposted with Operation Ha Go, which stopped XV Corps in its tracks. But the Japanese failed to gain any of

their objectives, and were beaten off with heavy losses. On the orders of
the Corps Commander the two Commandos landed from old and creaky
landing craft, all that were available, in the rear of the Japanese near the
village of Alethangyaw, well to the south of where XV Corps was fighting
along the Maungdaw–Buthidaung road. 44 RM landed half an hour
before midnight, and set out for Alethangyaw. Here it fought a confused
battle, encountering the Japanese, and their habits, for the first time. On
one occasion, the Japanese dragged a wounded Marine out into a paddy
field where he lay all day, in the hope that his comrades would come
out into the open to rescue him. He was brought in by villagers that
night. At first both Commandos admitted to being taken in by the tricks
familiar to all soldiers fighting in Burma: snipers tied to trees, orders
shouted in English, making a noise in one direction and coming in on
another, and screaming in the night to tempt a retaliation to expose
the position of defences and machine-guns. They joined conversations
on the radio in order to identify commanders' voices for future reference, in the hope of passing false orders on some later occasion. One
such attempt was made when a fluent English-speaking Japanese came
up on 44 RM Commando's command net during the Alethangyaw
battle, asking for the CO to pass a message. Horton sharply retorted
that he was busy, to receive the reply, 'Thank you, I now know your
voice.'

However, the commandos were aggressive and did not play into the
Japanese hands by sitting like tethered goats waiting for a tiger. The
trick, as they learned, was to hit back hard and quickly, to keep the
enemy off balance. Patrolling out at first light to clear Japanese away
from the perimeter of the defensive 'box' in which each Commando
spent the night became second nature. They discovered that the Japanese
were not invincible, did not like fighting at close quarters, and, despite
their enjoyment of bayonet practice on tethered prisoners and chopping
off their captives' heads, greatly feared being on the wrong end of a
bayonet themselves. When, as planned, 44 RM Commando withdrew
from the Alethangyaw operation back to its landing craft, the Marines
were delighted to hear the Japanese screaming and shouting as they
attacked an empty position.

No sooner had the situation in the Arakan been restored than the
Japanese Fifteenth Army attacked across the Chindwin River, attempting
to seize Kohima and Imphal, the British bases in Assam. Here, the

stubborn and skilful defence by IV Corps eventually ended in the Japanese reeling, defeated and starving, back across the Chindwin. However there were some tense moments, so 5 and 44 RM Commandos were pulled out of the Arakan, where they had been patrolling south of Maungdaw, and hastily despatched to Silchar, a vital communications junction to the west of Imphal that could not be allowed to fall into Japanese hands. April to August was spent patrolling the monsoon-soaked hills of Assam, before being sent to Ceylon, where they found 1 and 42 RM Commandos, who had been undergoing jungle training there. By now Lieutenant-Colonel H. D. Fellowes RM had relieved Leathes as CO of 42 RM Commando.

The whole brigade was now together at last for the first time since leaving Scotland nine months earlier. In early November 1944, it was sent to the Teknaf area, the southern tip of present-day Bangladesh, as a base for a series of small raids along the Arakan coast. These gave 1 and 42 RM Commandos a chance to practise their jungle skills against a live enemy for the first time; a valuable period getting the measure of the Japanese. Unlike British units in the early days of the war against Japan, none of the commandos were tossed into battle in circumstances where the Japanese held all the cards, without adequate training, or a chance to 'blood' themselves. After some ten months during which they spent weeks and sometimes months living and operating in the jungle, they were ready for more testing times. By now Nonweiler had left, and his place was temporarily taken by Colonel Young, lately commanding 3 Commando in Normandy, until Brigadier Campbell Hardy arrived from 46 RM Commando in early December 1944, to command the 3rd Commando Brigade, as it was now called.

FLYING MARINES

The Commandos were not the only Marines in South-East Asia Command and the Pacific. There were of course Royal Marine Detachments in the Eastern Fleet, and later in the British Pacific Fleet (BPF) as well. In the carriers of these two fleets there were a small number of Royal

Marine aircrew. In all theatres, the Royal Marines aircrew had made a
name for themselves out of all proportion to their numbers. For example,
in the Mediterranean and North Africa, Major Newson had been
awarded a DSO and DSC for attacks on enemy shipping both at sea and
in harbour, and Major Oliver Patch, who was awarded the DSC for
leading the raid on Taranto in 1940, was later awarded a DSO for a
successful attack on Italian warships at Bomba Bay on the Libyan coast.
Some eight Royal Marines officers served in various aircraft carriers as
Commander (Flying), the senior aviator aboard a carrier, commander of
the air group embarked, and the captain's adviser on air matters. Perhaps
the most distinguished and certainly the most senior Royal Marine
aviator of the Second World War was Lieutenant Colonel Hay DSO DSC
RM, who has already appeared in this book. He served in most theatres,
and having made a name for himself in the early part of the war
continued flying right up to the end.

In January 1944, ninety-two aircraft of the combined air groups from
HMS *Illustrious* and HMS *Indomitable* attacked Pangkalan in Sumatra,
destroying thirty-two Japanese aircraft. Major V. B. Cheeseman RM,
leading 1770 Firefly Squadron, was shot down, but rescued. The raid
owed its success to the Air Coordinator, Hay, who as wing leader of the
Victorious air group was flying in a Corsair, and directed the attacks. He
was now the senior aviator in the Eastern Fleet, including Royal Naval
aircrew.

In January 1945, while Admiral Sir Philip Vian was en route to
Australia to form the nucleus of the BPF, with four carriers, the
battleship *King George V*, three cruisers, and ten destroyers, he shaped
his course to pass within striking distance of oil refineries at Pelembang,
Sumatra. Hay was the Combined Carrier Air Group Commander under
Vian. Events had moved on since the desperate early days of the Fleet
Air Arm, when aircrew flying in obsolete, underpowered, undergunned,
unsuitable machines had gallantly taken on great odds, and in many
cases paid with their lives for the years of inter-war neglect of the Fleet
Air Arm. Now they flew American Hellcats, Avengers, and Corsairs,
designed for carrier work; splendid aircraft. The British-made Firefly
fighter-reconnaissance aircraft had also been designed for the Fleet Air
Arm, but was originally a temperamental beast and took a long time to
come into service. The Seafire used for defence of the fleet was a naval
version of the Spitfire, short-ranged and designed for the defence of

Britain. It did not have the endurance to stay in the air for long periods, which forced the carriers to keep turning into wind to recover and launch aircraft, slowing down the speed of advance of the fleet. Nevertheless, things were definitely looking up, as Hay remembers, describing the Pelembang raids:

> The Pelembang oil refineries were in two locations. An attempt by B-29 Superfortresses had failed. These were the most important oil refineries in Dutch East Indies. There were Hellcats, Corsairs, and Avengers, from four carriers [forty-three Avengers and eighty fighters]. Each Avenger bomber carried 4,000-lbs of bombs. This was the first time that the Navy had attempted attacking a strategic target. It was a two day raid, and I shot down four Japanese on the two days. We lost about 5% of aircrew. The results were very important and put out the oil refineries. At the time only the Navy could do it [because of range from friendly airfields], except the B-29s who had failed. We never had any trouble fighting the Japanese. We could outclimb them. For the first time in the war, except when I was doing sweeps in Spitfires over France, I was totally in command of the air. There was no aircraft that could touch me. The Corsair was a tremendous aircraft. It was a relief that they [the enemy] were getting the treatment we had to endure at the early part of the war. When I was told I was crazy to volunteer to go back to flying, I said, 'I'm senior enough and being flying long enough to keep out of harm's way. All I'm going for is rank and more gongs'. I never got touched. I was told by Admiral Vian that I was not to go ground strafing. I didn't take any notice. After Pelembang on to Sydney.

As well as the destruction of the oil installations which supplied about three-quarters of the Japanese aviation fuel, some 130 Japanese aircraft were destroyed, for the loss of 48 Fleet Air Arm aircraft from all causes, of which fifty per cent were deck-landing accidents. Nine aircrew fell into the hands of the Japanese, who executed them just before the war ended.

By 'on to Sydney', Hay is referring to the main base for the BPF, whose forward base was Manus in the Admiralty Islands. Hay describes what it was like in the BPF for the aviators. As senior aviator he kept an eye on his aircrew, caring for them as a leader should.

> When I came across one of my chaps whose chum had been shot down, I would get his flight commander and Squadron commander to speak to him, and give him a shot of whisky, and send him off to have more with

his mates, and tell him to go to bed early, and to be on duty the next morning. It worked.

We were all in fear and trembling that Vian would be a bash-on-regardless Admiral. We were wrong, he was eager to learn about the air, and not like a destroyer captain. I got on very well with him. He was an astonishing bloke and had a terrifying appearance. But he was very kind. He consulted me on all air matters, I was his air 'admiral' so to speak. When I said some of us have been in continuous ops for a year, whereas the USN aviators only had to do six months tours. He sent a signal to the Admiralty that he insisted that none of his aviators should do more than the Americans, and threatened to resign if he was not allowed to do this. This must have been a bombshell among the Admiralty and caused some replanning of aircrew training. I had been doing 18 months non-stop.

The first big operation for the BPF was Operation Iceberg, the assault on Okinawa. The BPF was one of the two covering forces, the other being Admiral Mitscher's Task Force 58, itself divided into four task groups, each as big as the BPF. Mitscher's carriers embarked 1,218 aircraft to the BPF's 218.[2] Still, the latter constitutes more aircraft than any Royal Marine officer has ever been responsible for coordinating, or is ever likely to, and this was Hay's job. The BPF was allocated the task of neutralizing the Japanese airfields on Shakashima Gunto. Hay:

I did the tasking based on my recces. I went twice a day. I took photos to see what damage had been done, and re-task accordingly. After Iceberg One we attacked Formosa. Had fun shooting up a railway train. Japanese were more or less spent, and concentrating on defending their mainland and islands close in to Japan.

The BPF also endured Kamikaze suicide attacks:

Particularly nasty when you have a full deck range of fully fuelled aircraft, all bombed up, and turning into wind. I looked across, and saw *Indomitable* being hit. I was in *Victorious*. I was on the outboard side of the deck range. The ship was turning hard to starboard, and there was the sea straight beneath me. If they had hit with a full deck range, we would all have had it. Fortunately we weren't hit while we were on deck. I was first off, being leader, and I was glad to go. *Victorious* was hit three times by Kamikazes by the end of the war in the Pacific. But it didn't stop us operating. *Formidable* was hit and had a huge hole, she was out of action for only four hours. I left before the end of the campaign. My 18 months in the Far East was over.

The officials behind their desks in the Admiralty in their inimitable fashion managed to make a mess of the pay scales:

> The sailors [and Royal Marines] were on UK rates of pay. When ashore in Ceylon you received Living Overseas Allowance, when drafted to sea, you took a pay cut. So there was much discontent. All the officers were on the sailors' side. They were penalised to fight the enemy.

Life at sea in the Pacific in ships designed to operate in the North Atlantic was not comfortable, and aircrew need sleep if they are to be on top line:

> We were nearly always doing in excess of 20 knots, and sometimes at 30 knots to launch aircraft. The ships were not air-conditioned. At night time with ship darkened, scuttles closed, it was very hot and humid, which was not healthy. The noise was very loud, with fans and machinery. It was difficult to sleep in that sweaty dreadful din. There was no 'hard liers'.[3]

THE SPECIAL OPERATIONS GROUP

In June 1944, as part of the preparations for a series of amphibious operations being planned by SEAC, the activities of all the small units in the theatre involved in beach reconnaissance and other advance-force operations were brought under command of the Special Operations Group (SOG), based in Ceylon with Mountbatten's SEAC Headquarters. The units involved were the COPPs, the SB Sections, which in those days were SAS not Royal Marines units, the Sea Reconnaissance Unit (SRU), and later Detachment 385.

Detachment 385 was a Royal Marines unit trained in Ceylon by Lieutenant Colonel Hasler, the founder of the RMBPD, which became operational in February 1945. The 122 strong detachment consisted of canoeists and parachutists. It is probably among the least-known units of the Royal Marines in the Second World War, possibly because its existence was short and its performance was patchy. Of the eighteen operations it carried out, eight were failures. Three of the remaining ten were only partially successful. Of the seven deemed to have achieved their mission, four involved setting up dumps on the coast of Thailand and Malaya, and at least two others involved deception operations whose effectiveness it is hard to assess. This low success rate was partly due to the very different operating conditions found in the Far East compared with North-West Europe or the Mediterranean. Much basic data available in Europe, coastal pilots, even tourist guides such as Michelin, and holiday snapshots, did not exist in the Far East. The distances to the targets were greater. Mangrove swamp, mud, and uncharted shallow reefs made the approaches to many beaches difficult, as did the numerous small fishing boats, sampans, and other local craft. Many of the people, Burmans, Malays, Thais, Sumatrans, and Javanese, were either cowed into submission, or still collaborating openly and willingly with the Japanese.

The biggest disaster was Operation Copywright (sic) on 9 March 1945, whose mission was to land on Phuket Island off the west coast of Siam (modern Thailand). Thailand was occupied by the Japanese and neutral. Up to this point in the war the Thais would almost always turn over prisoners to the Japanese, but as the war progressed, and Japan was clearly losing, the Thais became more flexible in this matter. The task of the Copywright party was to obtain intelligence on (a) 'certain named aerodromes', and (b) the seaward approaches for underwater gradients to the two fathoms line (six-foot line) and a rough test of the bearing surface.[4]

The beach survey information at (b) was, and still is, required for any amphibious landing. The beach gradient determines how far offshore landing craft will beach, and therefore how far troops and vehicles will have to wade, and through what depth of water. The bearing surface gives an indication first of the trafficability on the beach both above the waterline and on the stretch over which the vehicle will have to wade, and second whether wheeled and tracked vehicles, including possibly armour, will cope without laying trackway. All pretty standard by this stage in the war after years of experience, and lessons learned from cock-ups caused by not obtaining this sort of information before committing a force to a landing. Standard maybe, but usually difficult and hazardous to obtain. The gradient was, and still is, obtained by swimming in to the beach from a canoe launched from a submarine or ML, planting a stake to which is attached a cord with pellets at six-foot intervals, swimming out again along this cord on a designated bearing, and taking soundings at every six-foot interval along the cord, using a weighted line with a lead pellet at each foot, and recording the depths on a matt-white slate using a chinagraph (grease) pencil. The bearing information on the beach is obtained by using an auger to bring back samples of mud, sand, or whatever the composition of the beach. The physical difficulties of doing all this at night, in addition to navigating to exactly the right part of the beach, and locating the parent submarine or ML on return can be imagined: add enemy sentries and patrols, and possibly searchlights and patrol craft, as well as the need to leave as little evidence as possible of having visited a particular beach, and it can be seen that great skill and courage were, and still are, required to carry out a beach survey.

Three canoes were used by the party on Copywright, crewed by Major Maxwell and Corporal Atkinson, Major Mackenzie RE and Marine Brownlie, and Flight Lieutenant Brown RAF and Colour Sergeant Smith. HMS/M *Thrasher* launched the canoes on 9 March at 1910 hours, having spent the previous day scanning the target through the periscope. The point of release was a little under two miles from the intended landing positions. The submarine remained in the vicinity until midnight in case the party encountered difficulties. For the next five nights she returned to the RV. She also went to a second RV ten miles west of the recovery position each morning at 1000 hours. On 15 March (D+6) it was decided to abort the pick-up attempts. The report contains the bald statement 'The recce party did not return'.

After the war Major Mackenzie, Flight Lieutenant Brown, and Corporal Atkinson were repatriated, and were able to give some information about the operation. The party landed according to plan, and began their reconnaissances. On D+2 it became apparent that Thai patrols had seen the canoes, because later a strong patrol arrived, and after a short battle the party, or that part of it in the hide at the time, escaped. For the next six days the party waited in the area of the escape RV (an alternate RV on shore). During this time they met a Japanese patrol and in the ensuing battle Marine Brownlie was killed and Colour Sergeant Smith seriously wounded. Following the clash with the Japanese, the party rendezvoused at the escape beach. The next day the party split up and eventually some ten days later Mackenzie, Brown, and Atkinson gave themselves up to the Thais, and were removed to Bangkok. Here they learned that Atkinson and Smith were prisoners of the Japanese. Mackenzie was interrogated by the Japanese and handed back to the Thais and was well treated throughout.

Allied interrogation of the Japanese revealed that Major Maxwell and Colour Sergeant Smith, along with Flying Officer Tomlinson, who was shot down during a carrier-borne raid on Sumatra, were beheaded on 20 July 1945, only twenty-five days before the end of the war with Japan. According to the Japanese intelligence officer, Captain Ikoda, 'we tried to get information from them but in vain'. No details of the tortures used are known. Ikoda admitted, 'I beheaded Tomlinson, and ordered Lt Kajiki to behead Major Maxwell and Sgt/Maj [sic] Smith, showing the way of beheading.' Although this is of little consolation to the next of kin of these three gallant men, they were clearly highly regarded by the Japanese if they were beheaded in this manner, rather than being bayoneted to death or shot. One other member of Detachment 385 was executed by the Japanese, Major R. M. Ingleton RM, captured in late 1944 while he was lent to the Australian Services Reconnaissance Department for Operation Rimau, an attack on shipping in Singapore harbour using motorized submersible canoes in a repeat of the successful Operation Jaywick.[5] The operation was a disaster and there were no survivors.

Operation Carpenter III, in May 1945, on the east coast of Johore, was one of Detachment 385's successes.[6] The sixteen-strong party led by Lieutenant R. T. Onslow RM had the task of extracting twelve men, including downed aircrew, and landing arms and provisions for Force 136 in Malaya. Force 136, part of the Special Operations Executive (SOE), carried out clandestine and sabotage operations in the Far East. In Malaya, it mainly trained and supplied the Malayan Peoples Anti-Japanese Army (MPAJA), an almost exclusively Chinese, rather than Malay, guerrilla organization, which the Royal Marines were to meet in rather different circumstances some five years later, during the Malayan emergency.

Onslow's report states that after landing in inflatable boats launched from the submarine *Thule*,

> We hit the beach after about 20 minutes to be greeted by Major Hart, the Australian liaison officer, three US airmen, six Englishmen, five of whom had been in since 1942 (it was now 1945), and a large mob of highly excited and warlike guerrillas. The latter pulled the boats, Marines and all,

up on to the beach and took everything they could lay their hands on into the jungle, which was only about 15 yards from the beach and very thick. Everything, including our personal weapons, went, and it took a lot of persuading to make them understand that we were not prepared to part with them.

The stores we took ashore ranged from anti-tank rifles and small steam generators to tooth brushes, and included a case of Scotch whisky which I nursed all the way to the beach.

The party with their passengers returned safely to the submarine and were taken to Perth in Australia. The six Englishmen were three sergeants who had volunteered to stay behind after the fall of Singapore, two privates, the survivors of a party of twenty-two who had escaped into the jungle at the same time, and a planter in Malaya before the war. All had been looked after by the MPAJA.

In total, the detachment lost eleven officers, NCOs, and Marines on operations, killed, missing, or captured. One of them was Major Johnston, who had commanded Force Viper. He was killed during an abortive attempt to 'snatch' a village headman and a member of the Japanese garrison of a village on the Bassein coast of Burma. Had the war with Japan lasted as long as predicted, into 1946 or even 1947, it is likely that Detachment 385, having learned many lessons, and improved its techniques, would have played an important part in the series of great amphibious operations that were being planned as part of the strategy for defeating the Japanese. Unbeknown to the detachment, and indeed anyone in the Far East Theatre, there were few major amphibious operations yet to come, but the 3rd Commando Brigade was to be involved in three of them.

THE 3RD COMMANDO BRIGADE AT AKYAB, MYEBON, AND KANGAW

While IV and XXXIII Corps followed up the Japanese retreat from Imphal and Kohima in the offensive that would take it to Rangoon via Mandalay, XV Corps was ordered to drive the Japanese 28th Army out of the Arakan. The Arakan Yomas north of Kangaw is a rugged range of jungle-covered mountains rising steeply to 6,000 feet and impassable to vehicle, guns, or any fighting formation of troops. The only practicable escape route for the Japanese was down the north–south coast road. If this could be blocked, they would be trapped between the mountains to the east and the coast, fringed with a network of chaungs (tidal creeks) and mangroves to the west. They could then be destroyed between the hammer of the 81st and 82nd West African Divisions and the anvil of the 3rd Commando Brigade and the 25th Indian Division. Accordingly, the Corps Commander, Lieutenant General Christison, decided to use 3rd Commando Brigade in a series of outflanking assaults from the sea. The first place chosen was Akyab. However, by the time the brigade was about to land, news came that the enemy had gone. Christison told them to go ahead anyway, because it would be a good rehearsal.

An officer who fought in Burma in 44 RM Commando wrote:

In general the Arakan consists of tangled jungle-covered hills, only wide enough on top to deploy three or four men in line. The steep slopes run down to a narrow coastal strip of paddy-fields or mangrove swamps, which are highly malarial and heavily infested by the most virulent type of mosquito. The hills and coastal strip are intersected by hundreds of tidal creeks (or chaungs), which are often many miles long, but are mostly unfordable and offer very few landing points: and such that existed were strongly defended by the enemy. Since there is not a single beach along the 100-mile stretch of coast from Taungup to Akyab, these chaungs constituted the only means of access to the hinterland.[7]

Christison hoped to destroy the Japanese 28th Army before it could withdraw into the Irrawaddy valley. As part of his plan he decided to land 3rd Commando Brigade on the Myebon Peninsula, which dominated several chaungs and rivers, including the Daingbon Chaung, used by the Japanese. This would protect the left flank of the approach up the Daingbon Chaung by the 3rd Commando Brigade.

The beaches selected were on the southern tip of the Myebon Peninsula. Brigadier Hardy had examined the beaches from an ML, and noticed a line of thick coconut tree stakes offshore. A gap in these was blown by a COPP, using delayed action charges timed to detonate just before H-hour to preserve surprise, creating a gap about twenty-five yards wide for the landing craft. On the morning of 12 January, 42 RM Commando landed under cover of a thick smoke screen laid from the air, followed by 5 Commando. There was little opposition, but Lieutenant, as he was then, Banks remembered: 'One machine-gun on the beach would have made mincemeat of us as we slowly floundered ashore. However, the artillery did get the gap in the offshore coconut tree stakes registered and we all had to run the gauntlet.'[8]

The main enemy was the soft mud, and as the tide receded follow-up waves of troops found it worse, so when the time came to land tanks of the 19th Indian Lancers[9] it was decided to open up another beach for them. 1 and 44 RM Commando were supposed to land just to the left of the first beach, but by mistake their craft landed them on the original one. By then the tide was out, and they were faced by 400 yards of mud, much of it covered with about a foot of water. The scientists at SEAC headquarters had deemed that the mud would be firm. They were wrong. The troops floundered through mud into which they sank up to their waists and even chests, with a foot of water on top of that. The medical officer of 44 RM Commando said:

> In vain we tried to stand upright and keep essential equipment dry. Officers and men were seen sprawling in the mud which somehow seemed to remove boots and socks from some. Men formed scrums and managed to push towards the beach: some scrums collapsed wholesale and took some minutes to re-emerge from the sludge and re-form. The last man out was a subaltern who staggered back time and again to rescue men and equipment from the morass. It was only after he had washed in the water of a bomb crater that we discovered who he was.[10]

It is hardly surprising that it took the two Commandos some three hours to cover the 500 yards from landing craft ramp to dry ground. Fortunately both 5 and 42 RM Commandos were already ashore holding the beachhead, or it could have been a very different story.

The next day, after 5 Commando had taken a hill to the south of the village, 42 RM Commando entered Myebon without opposition. The enemy were discovered in possession of three small hills, which 42 RM Commando took with the assistance of A Squadron 19th Lancers, but suffered casualties, including their CO, Lieutenant Colonel Fellowes. The second-in-command, Major H. H. Dales, a South African, took over. After 1 Commando had cleared enemy at the north end of the peninsula, more patrolling and mopping-up operations by the whole brigade completely cleared the Myebon Peninsula. Two prisoners were captured, unusual in itself, since the Japanese rarely surrendered. They revealed that there had been 250 Japanese on the peninsula, of whom only about forty got away, so the brigade's casualties of five killed and thirty wounded were surprisingly light.

Now that the British held the Myebon Peninsula the only route out to the Arakan Range for the Japanese lay through the village of Kangaw to the east of Myebon. An approach due east from Myebon led across three chaungs, and would take too long. An approach using the waterways to the north-west of Kangaw was too obvious and would prejudice surprise. It was decided to take the long way round, due south from Myebon, and north up into the Daingbon Chaung. This northward leg would be a trip of eighteen miles up a waterway whose banks might be held by the enemy. Again Hardy made a personal reconnaissance of the landing area – beach is hardly an applicable term for the mangrove-ridden swamp.

> It was anticipated that the Kangaw landing would be heavily opposed, and great care was taken to find a suitable point for the assault. In chaung warfare, the selection of landing-points always presents a problem, for points suitable both from a naval and from a military point of view are rare; and where these do exist, they are usually dominated at a close range by jungle-covered hills. The large navigable chaungs are intersected by a great many minor ones, and this prevents landings from being made on a broad front. It is necessary to find a gap in the mangrove banks through which a landing can be made into the paddy-fields and care must be taken to ensure that the ground beyond is firm enough to support not only infantry, but tanks and artillery as well.[11]

Hardy's plan was for 1 Commando to land first to seize Hill 170 between Daingbon Chaung and the village of Kangaw. 42 RM Commando would land next and establish a bridgehead with two smaller chaungs on their left and right, nicknamed Thames and Mersey. 5 Commando would land, pass through 42 Commando's bridgehead and assist 1 Commando in its task. 44 Commando, once ashore, would be brigade reserve. Squadrons of 224 Group RAF were in support of the operation. Direct support of the landings would be provided by a troop of 25-pounder guns mounted on Z lighters (flat-decked metal pontoons), and the sloop HMIS *Narbada* lying off Myebon. Most of 25 Indian Division's artillery, a troop of 6th Medium Regiment RA (5.5in guns), and 'Auntie', a 7.2in howitzer, also in the Myebon area, were in support. On D+1 the 8th Hyderabad Battalion and a troop of the 19th Lancers would join the brigade.[12] Very little was known about the enemy in the area.

The hazardous passage up the Daingbon Chaung passed without any reaction from the enemy, other than some shelling near the end of the journey, where the Japanese had one section of the chaung 'nicely registered', according to Banks, and 'It was sheer luck that no LCA received a direct hit. I certainly heard shell fragments rattling against the side of my LCA.'[13]

The terrain at Kangaw was to have an important effect on the battle. The hills that were to figure so prominently in the fighting, such as Milford and Pinner, were long, narrow, tree- and scrub-covered hog's backs, and Hill 170 was similar. Separating the hills by 300 to 400 yards was flat paddy, firm except at the beachhead near the Daingbon Chaung, where the ground was soft. During daylight the open ground was under Japanese observation, and they shelled any worthwhile targets that presented themselves, so movement across the paddy had to be circumspect. At night the Japanese infiltrated these areas.

1 Commando was able to secure most of Hill 170, except for a stubborn small pocket on the northern side. 42 RM Commando established the bridgehead, and 5 Commando came in as planned and moved to assist 1 Commando. 44 RM Commando was ordered to push on to Milford, to the east of Hill 170. During the night the Japanese counterattacked 1 Commando from their toehold on Hill 170, but were beaten off after a brisk close-quarter battle. The next morning 44 RM Commando was ordered even further east, to Pinner. The 8th Hyderabads landed and took over 42 RM Commando's positions in the beachhead, releasing it to defend Milford, vacated by 44 RM Commando. The troop of tanks joined 1 Commando at the northern end of Hill 170.

An officer of 44 RM Commando wrote:

from our newly dug positions (on Pinner) we could see clearly the heights where the enemy was in strength guarding the Kangaw pass. An uncanny stillness pervaded the lifeless scene in front of us. We sensed some conspiracy in the hills above Kangaw. It was too quiet. Just before dusk we stood to, and afterwards settled down, silent and uneasy, in our trenches.

Suddenly, at 2000 [GMT], a mortar opened up on our northern flank: two men were wounded, one of them seriously. There was a pause for about 20 minutes. A heavy vehicle and numerous mules could be heard clearly moving across the moonlit paddy from the direction of Kangaw, but the foliage was so thick that we could see nothing of this from our positions.

Commands in Japanese were audible from below the hill and we could hear them getting their weapons into position. A red Verey light shot up from the paddy and the main attack started. First an MMG [medium machine-gun] opened up on our left flank sweeping our forward trenches; heavy shellfire followed from guns in the paddy which blasted us at point-blank range. Together with mortaring, grenades and machine gun fire, the barrage was deafening. The Japs swarmed up the hill and, as we could not hear movement, they succeeded in getting close to our positions before opening up with their small-arms fire. On the forward slope, they advanced fanatically into their own shellfire which must surely have killed some of them. Most of the damage to us was caused by shells striking the trees and spraying our trenches below with fragments. The shells which landed on the forward slope killed the Marines guarding this part of the hill. They died grimly with their weapons in their hands. Reinforcements were brought up from the reverse slope to fill the gaps. Every shell flash from the paddy virtually coincided with the detonation on our position and sent clouds of choking dust and splinters into the air around us and a reek of cordite. Under cover of this deafening frontal fire, other Japs quietly crept up the flanks to lie in wait until the barrage stopped.

After what seemed an age, orders to cease fire were heard whereupon the Japs on the flanks put in what they hoped was a surprise attack with grenades and machine gun fire. Rifle fire from various snipers cracked round the perimeter. The Marines held their fire until the Japs were seen within a few yards of our trenches and then let them have it; hand-to-hand fighting with the bayonet followed.

Wave after wave tried to get into our outer defences but without success, apart from some snipers who managed to get into the trees. They were soon dislodged. The only other intruder was a large porcupine which, badly shaken, staggered into a trench alongside the RSM, leaving a few quills in the regimental hide, before he managed to expel it. 44 [RM Commando] suffered 26 killed and 44 wounded.[14]

At one stage a Japanese shouted 'Play the game, Johnny Commando – come down here and fight.' Some comic immediately replied, 'Send your pals away and I'll come right down and sort you out, you little yellow bastard.' As the moon went down, a voice shouted, 'All right, we'll be back in the morning.' 'Tata for now,' replied the comic. They were back just before dawn, but it was a half-hearted affair compared with the night's effort. 44 RM Commando was relieved by the 8th Hyderabads and 42 RM Commando, and pulled back to Hill 170.

The Japanese artillery barrages in the Kangaw battle were among the heaviest in the whole of the Burma campaign. Banks:

> When we in 42 Commando took over the shallow scoops on Pinner, in which 44 Commando had taken a battering the night before, we hacked like mad in the rocky terrain to get a bit deeper down. That night we got the treatment from the Japanese guns, and it was the most frightening night of my life.

The ground on Pinner was hard compacted gravel and it was partly due to the difficulty of getting a reasonable depth down that 44 RM Commando suffered such heavy casualties. As one of 42 Commando's troop commanders commented later:

> It took the powerful incentive of self-preservation to drive us into this inhospitable ground. There was also the danger of tree-bursting shells, a peculiarity of the war in Burma, which I had earlier experienced when attached to the 11th East African Division in central Burma. A shell would explode on hitting an overhead branch, and the fragments would strike straight down into one's trench. One therefore had to dig a cave sideways once down a certain depth, and I spent many a long hour at night in this occupation, picking away with the point of a bayonet.[15]

While 42 RM Commando was on Pinner the Japanese positioned on two hills, one of which commanded the road at Kangaw, were subjected to a massive air bombardment. The commander of B Troop remembered:

> Right on time the bombers appeared, flying at about 10,000 feet at a guess, making their run from the sea towards the mountains and therefore passing directly over the brigade's positions. In order to hit their target they obviously had to release their bombs well before they were

over it and, standing on Pinner, we saw through binoculars the bombs leave the first wave of planes, wobble slightly, steady, and point downwards – apparently straight at us. Many thoughts flash through the mind at such moments: they were American bombers, and we regarded the Americans as poor map readers and careless on detail; each hill looked much like another and even a good navigator could confuse them; what use would our pathetic little slit trenches be? Useless or not, we all dived for them. A few seconds later the thunder of heavy bombs exploding half a mile away began, and we raised our heads. The bombers were still passing overhead, wave after wave, their bombs were falling right on target.[16]

The brigade was ordered to hold where it was, and not move forward. From 25 January for four days and nights Hill 170 was subjected to heavy shelling. The next day, the 51st Indian Brigade landed and took over Milford and Pinner, allowing 44 RM Commando to be withdrawn to the beachhead. Two days later, the 51st Indian Brigade mounted an attack on Kangaw, and on two hills to the east which not only dominated the village, but – more importantly in view of the overall Corps plan – the road into the hills. By nightfall one of the hills was in their hands. 5 Commando, now under command of the 51st Brigade, patrolled the road and Kangaw, and laid ambushes, but there was no sign of the enemy using the road.

On 30 January the Commando Brigade was ordered to start thinning out the next day. 44 RM Commando was withdrawn, 5 Commando remained on Pinner. 1 and 42 RM Commandos were on Hill 170, waiting orders to withdraw. Here 42 RM Commando's B Troop was positioned between the beachhead and the hill, and the terrain was so wet the Marines could not dig in at all.

We struck water after a foot or so, and had to build roofless igloo-like structures upwards with mud 'bricks'. We experienced heavy shelling here particularly at night, but many of the shells failed to detonate in the soft mud, landing with a whine and a dull thud.[17]

The Japanese needed to keep the road open for their escape, and planned to recapture Hill 170 and cut off the 51st Indian Brigade, forcing it to release its grip on the road. At 0545 hours on 31 January after a heavy artillery bombardment the enemy delivered a determined assault on the steep wooded northern ridge of Hill 170, held by 4 Troop, 1 Commando, and tanks of the 19th Lancers.

> Two of the Shermans got out, though one was damaged, but the third was destroyed by an engineer suicide squad armed with pole charges and the crew killed. Twenty-six Japanese engineers were killed and most of the remainder were wounded.[18]

At 0630 hours the enemy, having occupied some old weapon pits, launched an attack on 4 Troop. Two hours later the forward section was overrun, and the troop was desperately short of ammunition. The remnants of the troop held on to the rest, inspired by Lieutenant Knowland, who was attached to 1 Commando: after firing a 2in mortar from the hip and killing a number of Japanese he finally fell mortally wounded surrounded by enemy, spraying them with a Tommy gun, killing or wounding a further ten. He earned a posthumous Victoria Cross that day. Counterattacks by part of a platoon of W Troop, 42 RM Commando could not regain the position.

At 1015 hours, Hardy came up and decided to use X Troop 42 RM Commando to restore the position on the northern part of Hill 170. At midday the attack went in supported by a Sherman tank. But X Troop could get no further than the remnants of 4 Troop, and eventually joined them in their positions. Part of 6 Troop of 1 Commando made a try at regaining the lost ground, but failed with 50 per cent casualties, joining 4 and X troops in their slit trenches. Hardy ordered that there would be no more counterattacks until after last light. But the battle raged on, both sides utterly spent, hanging desperately to blood-soaked slit trenches. As Bren gunners were hit, another man rolled in to take his place; behind one gun twelve men were hit one after the other. The Commando mortars brought down fire right in front of their own positions, and the 25-pounders not much further out. In the opinion of the Deputy Brigade Commander, Colonel Young, the Japanese were so ferocious in their attack that 'The Bosche would not have stood it', and he had fought them often enough in Italy and France. He was convinced that no British soldiers ever fought better. The CO of 5 Commando was wounded bringing one of his own troops forward to assist on Hill 170, on Hardy's orders. Just before last light fighter-bombers roared in and blasted the Japanese positions. The Japanese attacks ceased, leaving a few snipers; the enemy appeared to have shot his bolt, for the moment anyway. The CO of 1 Commando sorted out the muddle of troops from three Commandos on Hill 170. At first light, 5 Commando put in a full-blooded Commando attack to finally clear the position.

The Japanese dead lay thick, 340 of them. The commandos took a total of four prisoners. Ten officers' swords were picked up. One officer of 42 RM Commando killed four Japanese and was wounded four times. Several commandos were found well forward and dead among Japanese, having fought on alone. Some were found wounded but alive, pinned under the bodies of dead Japanese. All this took place in an area of about two acres. The 3rd Commando Brigade on Hill 170 alone lost forty-five dead and ninety wounded.

> The battle, in which both sides had suffered very heavy casualties, had been comparable in ferocity with the battle of the 'Admin Box' in the previous February, and with the battle of Kohima. By hitting the enemy at a very sensitive point, we had brought him to battle in strength, for, at the height of the action in the Myebon–Kangaw area, the Japanese were using the equivalent of a full fighting division, as well as divisional and army troops. In the Kangaw battle, they lost at least 2,000 men killed, 16 guns, 14 large motor craft, and a considerable amount of other equipment.[19]

The Corps Commander wrote a special order of the day to the 3rd Commando Brigade:

> The Battle of Kangaw has been the decisive battle of the whole Arakan campaign and that it was won was very largely due to your magnificent defence of Hill 170.

In the opinion of many who were at Kangaw, Brigadier Campbell Hardy was a key factor in winning the battle. Although he had only taken over the brigade shortly before the Akyab operation he immediately inspired confidence. The morale of the troops was high, and they knew they could beat the Japanese, but he added that extra fillip whenever he appeared. He personally led the assault waves of three successive commando attacks at Myebon, on a one-troop front. Captain Codrington recalled:

> One morning following a busy night, Hardy arrived to see how we were getting on. He walked round B Troop's position, all was in order, morale was good, and as he left, I had expected a few words of commendation

for withstanding the shell-fire and ferocious onslaughts. Not at all. All he said was, 'Codrington, some of your men have not shaved this morning'. I thought on reflection that this remark was an example of true leadership, just right to bring a note of normality into what until then had seemed a stressful situation.[20]

Lieutenant C. N. C. Carryer of X Troop, 44 RM Commando wrote to his mother: 'Our Brigadier is absolutely marvellous, and everyone has complete confidence in him. He is always up at the front, and the troops say he goes in first to see how many Japs are there.'

As with Leicester in North-West Europe, the high reputation gained in battle by Hardy was to be a decisive factor when the question of the Commando role's being given exclusively into the care of the Royal Marines was under discussion after the war. Given the records of the two RM brigade commanders, and those of the commanding officers, no one could argue convincingly that the green beret ethos was not safe in Royal Marine hands.

The brigade moved back to India to prepare for Operation Zipper, the invasion of Malaya. The invasion took place, but only after the Japanese had surrendered after the dropping of two atom bombs, at Hiroshima and Nagasaki. Zipper was carried out in a tactical fashion, with all the trimmings and fingers on triggers, just in case there were any Japanese who were not inclined to obey their God Emperor's order to surrender. In the event not a shot was fired. The war was over, and in every theatre the Royal Marines had been in the forefront of the battle.

Had the Japanese not capitulated when they did, the Royal Marines would have played an even greater part in their defeat than of the Germans in Normandy the previous year, having prepared to provide the Marine element for:

> Two Army/Marines commando brigades
> The landing craft of three naval assault forces
> The 34th Amphibious Support Regiment RM
>   (tracked amphibians mounting rocket projectors)
> One Small Operations Group
> Six Mobile Landing Craft Bases
> Sixteen Mobile Naval Bases
> 10,000 Royal Marine Engineers

The Marine detachments in the ships of the British
Pacific Fleet and the East Indies Fleet.[21]

No sooner had the guns stopped than the 'rats' were nibbling away
again at the Royal Marines.

PART FIVE

1945–1999

FIGHTING PEACETIME WARS

The finest troops in the Empire.
I did not know how the Royal Marines did it.
But you always do.

Field Marshal Slim to the Commandant General Royal Marines, 1950

Introduction to Part Five

At the end of the War in Europe, the Royal Navy had 120 major warships (battleships, carriers, and cruisers) and over 1,000 landing craft in commission. All the major warships had Royal Marine Detachments, and many of the landing craft were crewed by Marines. By 1948 the Corps had reduced from a wartime strength of over 74,000 to about 13,000, of whom some 2,200 were in the Commando Brigade, and several hundreds in landing craft, but only 2,000 in ships' detachments. As the number of ships reduced, so the number of Marines serving at sea in their traditional role would decrease. This imbalance of sea and Commando service was viewed with suspicion by the Navy, which wanted to revert to a pre-war concept for the Marines: top priority to ships' detachments, gunnery, and all that went with it. A committee set up to review the structure of the Armed Forces as a whole recommended complete disbandment of the Corps, but the Admiralty countered with a plan to reduce the Royal Marines to a strength sufficient to provide ships' detachments.

Fortunately, while this depressing notion was being considered in the Admiralty, a new Commandant General Royal Marines was appointed, Lieutenant General Sir Leslie Hollis. Wise in the ways of Whitehall after spending the wartime years as Secretary to the Chiefs of Staff Committee, and working closely with the War Cabinet, he was well equipped with influence and friends in high places to fight the Marines' corner. By making cuts elsewhere, notably dispensing with the Chatham Division, he persuaded the Admiralty to retain the Commandos. Had the battle gone the other way, with fewer and fewer major ships in commission as the years went by, the Royal Marines would have ceased to exist by the early 1960s at the latest.

In company with the other services, the Royal Marines had National Servicemen in their ranks, at this time and until the 1960s. The Corps had fewer in proportion to overall numbers than any other service – it had 30 per cent National Servicemen and 70 per cent long service regulars, whereas the Army for example had a mere 30 per cent regulars, many of whom were only three-year men anyway – and was fortunate in the quality of its National Servicemen, who were not only given a longer training than elsewhere, but whose standard was higher. Although without conscription the recruits would not necessarily have wanted to spend time in the armed services, by joining the Royal Marines they opted for the toughest training, and in that respect were volunteers in all but name. All regular recruits and young officers joining postwar, and National Servicemen, had to complete the Commando course, qualifying for the coveted Green beret, except the few going to blue-beret postings (ships and landing craft). Many National Servicemen demonstrated their commitment by joining the Royal Marines Forces Volunteer Reserve (RMFVR, later Royal Marines Reserve – RMR) before call-up, to guarantee themselves a place in the Corps. As the author can testify, once in a Commando it was impossible to distinguish between a National Serviceman and a regular. In return a Royal Marines National Serviceman probably had as rewarding a period of service in terms of job satisfaction as anybody in the Navy, Army, or Air Force, and considerably better than most.

At the end of the war against Japan, the 3rd Commando Brigade was sent to Hong Kong in what was then known as an Internal Security (IS) role. In December 1945, all RM Commandos were renamed Commandos Royal Marines. By early 1946 six Commandos Royal Marines had been disbanded (40, 41, 43, 46, 47, and 48), and by January 1947 1 and 5 Commandos as well, along with all Army Commandos, their place being taken by 45 Commando RM, which had arrived in Hong Kong in early 1946. 44 Commando RM changed its name to 40 Commando RM, so that the Commandos in what was now 3rd Commando Brigade Royal Marines each represented a Second World War theatre of operations in which the RM Commandos had served with such distinction – 40 Commando, the Mediterranean; 42 Commando, the Far East; and 45 Commando, North-West Europe. The decision to change 44 to 40 had been made by the then Commandant General Royal Marines, General Sir Thomas Hunton, but much pressure to do so had been exerted by 44 Commando's CO, Lieutenant Colonel Houghton MC RM, a founder member of 40 Commando, who was back from prison camp after being captured at Dieppe. From henceforth in this story, with no need to differentiate between RM and Army commandos, the RM will be omitted from the title when referring to any Royal Marines Commandos.

Another rationalization, as we would now call it, involved the numerous amphibious special forces units born in the Second World War, the COPPs, RMBPD, SRU, Detachment 385, and SBS (both Special Boat Service and Special Boat Section). Royal Marines who had served in these units were all lumped together in the Combined Operations Beach and Boat Section (COBBS), at Appledore, the Army members of these units having gone the way of their fellows in the Commandos, either back to their parent regiment or, more often, civil life. Although COBBS was under the command of Hasler, an influential figure was Lieutenant Peter 'Pug' Davis DSC RM, who had commanded assault landing craft in the Adriatic, and earned the DSC landing commandos and partisans on the Yugoslav islands and mainland. He was the last commander of the RMBPD, and was to become the father of the modern SBS, although Hasler was responsible for drawing up the proposals for the skills needed for the COBBS and how it should operate. In mid-1947 the COBBs moved to Eastney, the Alma Mater of naval gunnery training for Royal Marines since the old Blue Marine days, and spiritual home of the seagoing Marines.

At this stage, a part of the Corps, as one author of an SBS history relates,

> were dubious about the entire Commando concept. The Royal Navy still had many large ships and it was felt by a number of Royal Marines ... that the right rig and place for a Royal Marine was in best blues and white gear, guarding the keyboard on a battleship, not 'playing pongos' in a green beret, let alone poncing about in canoes.[1]

This attitude was to persist for several years, and especially towards the Commandos.

In 1948 the COBBS was renamed the Small Raids Wing (SRW). In 1949, the SRW formed the first operational Special Boat Section: 1 SBS. At the same time the Soviet threat to Western Europe was beginning to harden, and the Western Allies' operational plan involved trading space for time, by withdrawing across West Germany, back to and behind the River Rhine. As part of this concept, a detachment of the SRW called the RM Demolitions Unit was deployed with the RN Rhine Squadron for demolition tasks: in stay-behind parties destroying bridges, up to 6,000 barges, and other shipping. In 1950–51 Davis was serving in the Rhine Flotilla, where initially the only other RM officer was Lieutenant Colonel N. H. Tailyour. Together the two Marines formed the RM Demolitions Unit into 2 SBS, and then 3 SBS. Having commanded both 2 and 3 SBS in Germany, Davis returned home to command 1 SBS. These sub-units were the basis of what became Special Boat Company (later Squadron and now Service). In the 1950s these consisted of a headquarters and six sections: 1 SBS based at Eastney, 2 and 3 SBS in Germany, 4 and 5 SBS consisting of RMFVR canoeists, and 6 SBS with the 3rd Commando Brigade in Malta.

In the four years following the end of the Second World War, the Royal Marines took the shape that was to persist until the end of the century. Although there were many changes, mostly for the better, over the following fifty years, the major and premier fighting formation in the Royal Marines remains the Commando Brigade, supported by landing craft and landing ships, with the SBS supporting both, and engaged on independent operations, either with or without the SAS. The seagoing requirement for traditional ships' detachments withered away and disappeared as big ships vanished from the Royal Navy's order of battle. For a time, in the late 1950s, and through to the mid-1970s, reverting to late eighteenth and early nineteenth century practice, small Royal Marine Detachments were embarked in frigates, mostly stationed in the Gulf and the West Indies – this did not always prove a happy arrangement. The Marines replaced seamen, and were therefore even less able to be spared for other duties such as landing parties than in the old battleship and cruiser days, because without them the ship's husbandry (chipping paint, scrubbing decks, cleaning brasswork, and painting) suffered.

The second half of the twentieth century was a busy time for the Royal Marines, along with the rest of the Armed Forces.

20

Counter-Insurgency
before 1960

The Royal Marines are, I think, the most remarkable body of men
I know.

Mr J. P. W. Mallalieu MP, House of Commons, 6 March 1952

PALESTINE

After nearly two years in Hong Kong, 3rd Commando Brigade was sent
to Malta to form part of Britain's strategic reserve in the Near and
Middle East. In January 1948, 40 Commando was despatched to Palestine, to be followed later by the other two Commandos in the brigade.
British troops had been deployed in Palestine since the end of the First
World War, but the garrison had been greatly increased following the
end of the Second World War, as strife between Jews and Arabs became
increasingly bitter.

The roots of the internal security situation in Palestine lay as far back
as 1917, when the British government, aware of the need to make a
gesture which would ensure the continued support of the American
Jewish lobby and its money for the war effort, announced in the Balfour
Declaration (a letter from Lord Balfour, the British Foreign Secretary, to
Lord Rothschild) that it would look with sympathy on the concept of a
national home for the Jews. The Declaration included a caveat which is
often conveniently forgotten: 'it being clearly understood that nothing
shall be done which may prejudice the civil and religious rights of
existing non-Jewish communities in Palestine . . .'

At the end of the First World War, Palestine, which had been part of
the Ottoman Empire, was mandated by the League of Nations to Britain
to administer. The overwhelming majority of the population were Arabs,
and the term 'national home' had not been intended, at least by Balfour,
as is made clear above, to mean taking over territory from the existing
occupants to create a new country. The terms of the Mandate embodied
the terms of the Balfour Declaration and invited immigration by Jews.
By 1939, the number of Jews living in Palestine had multiplied from
50,000 in Turkish times to around 500,000, and in response to Arab
pressure and violence the British limited Jewish immigration to a
maximum of 75,000 over five years, after which there would be no more
without the consent of the Arabs; Palestine after all was their country.
Following the Second World War, the terrible experiences of the Jews at
the hands of the Nazis, the huge numbers who were homeless, and the
prospect of a fresh start in Palestine vastly increased the demand for
immigration. Naturally there was worldwide sympathy for the Jews, and
from America in particular, with its large Jewish population, considerable
support, both moral and financial. American politicians ignored or
flouted the wishes of American Jews at their political peril.

At the end of 1945, the Jewish Agency, which dealt with Jewish affairs
in Palestine, decided to mount a campaign of violence and propaganda
to persuade the British government to lift restrictions on immigration,
and to gain worldwide support for Zionism, the concept of a Jewish
national home in Palestine. To begin with, the majority of British troops
arriving in Palestine were sympathetic to the Jews; a substantial number
of the officers and other ranks had fought in North-West Europe and
had seen at first hand the horrors of Nazi treatment of Jews. Some had
been wounded, and had seen their friends killed fighting Nazism, so they
were astonished to read Jewish newspapers labelling them 'Gestapo'.
Soon many British troops were eyeing the Jews with distaste. One
medical officer with the British 6th Airborne Division remarked, 'I was
impressed by the Jews, some behaved just like the Nazis. They had
clearly learned a number of tricks from the Germans.' On the whole, the
troops came to sympathize with the Arabs.

There were four Jewish para-military organizations. The Hagana was
the underground national army, raised mainly for defence, and usually
moderate compared with the terrorist groups. The Hagana became
virtually a Jewish National Army, in which the majority of able-bodied

males and a large number of females were obliged to enlist and give part-time service. Within the main organization of the Hagana was the Palmach, consisting of full-time regular soldiers, well trained and disciplined and led by good officers, one of whom was Moshe Dayan. These two were the 'official' Jewish forces tasked by the Jewish Agency to carry out acts of sabotage. There were two other groups, who took their orders solely from their own leaders: the Irgun Zvia Leumi (IZL) and the Stern Gang, or Fighters for the Freedom of Israel (FFI) as they preferred to call themselves. '"Stern Gang" has been the name sponsored by the alien government of oppression in this country,' said the FFI in a letter to the newspapers, in a revealing example of 'terrorspeak', which others including the IRA have not been slow to follow. The 'government of oppression' was of course the British, doing its best to ensure that the Arab majority had a say in the future of their country.

Both IZL and FFI were extreme, the latter the more vicious of the two. The Jewish employed classic terrorist tactics: murder and sabotage, which they hoped would result in overreaction by the troops, thus alienating the population against the British Army; and a propaganda campaign waged in Palestine and worldwide which, coupled with riots, sabotage, and general disorder, would persuade the world at large and the British government in particular that the country was ungovernable. Intelligence was poor, and it was impossible for the British troops to take the initiative; they could merely hold the ring while first the British government, and then the United Nations (UN), tried to find a settlement acceptable to both Jews and Arabs. Looked at from the perspective of the late 1990s, it was a hopeless task. Much of the terrorist activity was between Arabs and Jews, jockeying for position after the British left. The Jews were determined to set up a Jewish state in someone else's country, the Arabs were equally determined they should not. The Jews were fortunate that they had to contend with the long-suffering and usually good-humoured British soldiers and Marines. Ironically, the Israelis have faced a similar situation since the end of the 1980s, and are getting poor marks for the standards of training of their troops in Internal Security and their restraint.

Eventually, Britain's patience wore out. She submitted the issue to the UN for arbitration, and declared that she would withdraw, handing over responsibility to the UN. At this stage 40 Commando, still commanded by Lieutenant Colonel Houghton, arrived at Haifa with the task of keeping the port open to allow the evacuation of some 10,000 British troops, and hundreds of thousands of tons of military stores built up since the occupation of Palestine in 1917. The Commando's first task was to strengthen security, which was woefully inadequate. Lieutenant P. R. Thomas, then the mortar officer, wrote later:

> Day One gave a foretaste of things to come. A bomb destroyed an Arab house bordering Wadi Rushmiya, the no man's land between Arab and Jew, resulting in an exchange of fire. Order was restored by a patrol of 8/9 Para at the cost of one soldier wounded. An hour later two Palestine Policemen were shot outside No 3 Gate. Their bodies were recovered and the gate closed by 40 Cdo in the face of a large crowd of angry Arabs. Sadly both policemen were ex-Marines. The Palestine Police Force was a fine, brave body of men who bore the brunt of the terrorism. Their Inspector General was Col Nicol Gray DSO who had commanded 45 Commando in NW Europe. He had recruited many ex-Marines, and afterwards took a number on to Malaya.[1]

Both Jews and Arabs were involved with gun-running and smuggling arms and explosives through the port, and stealing from lighters and warehouses. One ship's manifest included tractors destined for Jewish settlements, which on inspection proved to be armoured half-tracks, half-heartedly painted to look like agricultural tractors. These were impounded. Thomas: 'eight Jews were found running a dump for goods stolen by Arabs. . . . a rare example of inter-community co-operation.'[2]

The use of vehicle bombs was widespread. The Jews were the first to use them, initiating a terrorist tactic employed worldwide, often in present-day Israel on the inventors. In one example a bomb in a military truck in 40 Commando's area killed five Jews, set fire to twelve Jewish vehicles, and damaged several Jewish-occupied buildings. The Jews struck back using a British Army 3-ton truck with Airborne Division markings, and driven by a man disguised as an Airborne officer, who parked the vehicle and was driven away in a jeep. The truck detonated killing eleven Arabs and wounding thirty-one. The Jews fired mortar bombs from Mount Carmel into the Suq, the Arab part of town; the ranging bomb fell about fifty yards from 40 Commando's Headquarters. Jewish snipers killed Arab workers in the port and in villages nearby. The Arabs retaliated by killing the drivers of any Jewish truck they could lay their hands on. British troops were the jam in the sandwich between these two communities. Neither Arabs nor Jews cared whether their targets were armed or not. In one incident, twelve unarmed Arabs including a small girl were shot by snipers. Meanwhile an American media mogul, Ben Hecht, declared that 'he had a song in his heart for every British soldier killed in Palestine'.[3]

Lieutenant Thomas's Mortar Platoon was responsible for manning two Staghound armoured cars. Each had a powered turret mounting a 37mm gun and a co-axial .30in Browning machine-gun. Originally intended as static pillboxes, the Commando soon had them in running order. Many servicemen were offered bribes by the Jews to hand over their equipment. Thomas:

> I was offered £8,500 [about £200,000 today] to be paid into any bank in the world if I would leave a Staghound unattended for a few minutes at a nominated corner. I informed the CO who told me in no uncertain terms that if I lost one of those Staghounds he would never want to see me again.
>
> Sgt R. R. Dodds (later Lt Col Dodds DSM MM) stalked and disposed of a sniper firing from behind a sheet of armoured plate using a PIAT. The Jews were so impressed they put up the price of PIAT bombs.[4]

Two mortar platoon corporals, Maill and Dennis, were offered more.[5] There had been predictions that the conflict in the port area would increase once the orange season ended and all the fruit had been exported; both communities were involved in citrus farming, and it was not in either's interest to do anything to impede the commerce in oranges. The prediction was fulfilled when the Haganah announced its intention of taking over Haifa to 'restore peace and order'.

Thomas:

> The Irgun and the Stern Gang were given the task of capturing the village of Deir Yassan on the road to Jerusalem. Enraged by the tenacity of Arab resistance, when the village was eventually captured on 8 April 1948, every inhabitant was massacred; a total of 245 men, women, and children.
>
> By 20 April the situation in Haifa became critical and it was decided to withdraw all British troops from Haifa and let the two sides fight it out. 40 Cdo was left to hold the port. Overnight in Operation Cockpit, the fighting troops moved out to hold strongpoints on Kingsway [a major street in Haifa]. The CO reported operation completed at 0617 hours. At 1000 hours the Jews opened fire on the Arabs. I was patrolling Kingsway

and Bank Street in a Staghound at the time when two British police were caught in the crossfire. We gave covering fire while some gallant Jews in a bus recovered the casualties. Unfortunately one policeman died later. At about the same time Lt Tony Seed was shot in the back and head when a Jewish Bren gunner fired a deliberate burst at our forward positions. Cpl Earp took two Marines and eliminated the gunner, for which he was awarded the MM.

At 0522 hours on 22 April the fighting increased in intensity and the Jews started mortaring the Suk [Arab market]. A number of bombs fell in the east of the port, and some hit the tented camp housing the Mauritian Pioneers, who were employed as dock labour, causing 20 casualties. . . .

Confusion broke out among the Arabs, and many panic-stricken men, women and children carrying pathetic bundles of belongings massed outside No 3 Gate begging to be let in. I will never forget nor forgive the Jews, who had already won the battle for Haifa, for sending down a hail of murderous fire on the unprotected mass. The CO ordered the gate opened on humanitarian grounds. While helping these refugees, Lt Peter Pitman and our doctor, Surgeon Lt Mike Cox were both wounded in the legs. I brought up a Staghound, zeroed the gun on the wall of a house and fired a number of HE rounds at a row of binoculars watching from the GPO building. Firing stopped, and the CO said the telephone lines to Cdo HQ were hot asking us to desist. We learned later that the Commander of the local Haganah broke his leg running down the stairs.[6]

The shooting and mortaring continued until it became clear that the Arabs wanted nothing except to be evacuated from Haifa. Eventually all except some 2,500 Arabs in Haifa were taken away by sea to Acre or Lebanon; 40 Commando were responsible for evacuating some 12,000. The Jews, in full control of the port, dictated terms, which included disarming any remaining Arabs, their weapons to be held in trust by the British until 15 May, the day on which the Mandate was to end. Meanwhile thanks to 40 Commando's efficient control of the security situation, the military evacuation was on schedule. Following the complete stoppage of work in late April, the tempo picked up and daily totals being loaded reached 1,000 tons on several occasions, the record being 1,421 tons on 25 May.[7]

As the day for the final British evacuation drew near, the GOC was concerned that extremist Jewish groups would take the opportunity to attack the troops as they withdrew. So the remainder of 3rd Commando Brigade was ordered to Palestine. 45 Commando, which had been training in Libya, arrived first and took over some of 40 Commando's positions in Haifa, while 42 Commando was sent to Jerusalem to cover the withdrawal of the British High Commissioner. 45 Commando did not stay long, as the tension in Haifa eased with the impending cessation of the Mandate, but 40 and 42 Commandos remained to cover the evacuation of the last British troops from what was now the Jewish state of Israel. At 0400 hours on 30 June the British rearguards began thinning out from the dockyard at Haifa: covered by tanks of 4/7th Dragoon Guards the final elements of 1st Guards Brigade embarked, followed by 42 Commando. 40 Commando established a small perimeter round the LST HMS *Striker*, where Commander 1st Guards Brigade handed over command to the CO, Lieutenant Colonel Houghton. All ships except *Striker* proceeded to sea. Houghton pulled in his forward troops, and as they embarked they were covered by a mortar section from the forecastle of the LST. Houghton reported to the GOC, 'Withdrawal of British Troops in Palestine completed. 40 Commando Royal Marines, the last unit to leave is now embarked.' *Striker* sailed.

All the Commandos received the congratulations of the Board of Admiralty for their work in Palestine, but 40 Commando had borne the brunt and been there longest. The work of 40 Commando, under the leadership of Lieutenant Colonel Houghton, arguably had a more tangible and enduring outcome for the future of the Royal Marines than bouquets from Whitehall. Hitherto Commandos had been considered too 'gung ho' for internal security duties, or in today's parlance 'peace enforcement', but 40 Commando's outstanding record in Palestine changed that perception, and possibly ensured the continued existence of the Corps and the employment of Commandos in the many similar operations which followed.

MALAYA, 1950–1952

The commandos of the 3rd Commando Brigade spent from July 1948 to May 1950 in Malta, Libya, Cyprus, and Hong Kong. In May, the brigade was ordered to Malaya, where Communist-inspired violence had reached crisis point. When the Japanese surrendered in August 1945, the Malayan Peoples Anti-Japanese Army (MPAJA), based on the Malayan Peoples Communist Party (MCP), which was recruited exclusively from the Chinese population, and equipped and trained by the British, was some 7,000 strong. In December 1945 the MPAJA was disbanded and ordered to hand in its weapons. Some members did, but about 4,000 did not. Their leader Chin Peng was awarded the OBE and took part in the Victory Parade in London in 1946. The MPAJA had, meanwhile, renamed itself the Malayan Peoples' Anti-British Army (MPABA), later the Malayan Races' Liberation Army (MRLA), a classic example of Communist 'double-speak', since the 'Army' included no Malays. This 'Army' moved into pre-prepared jungle camps near Chinese squatter villages, from which it was supplied.

The Chinese formed about 38 per cent of the population of Malaya, the Malays around 49 per cent, and the Indians some 12 per cent. The remaining 1 per cent were aborigines and Europeans, the latter mostly British rubber planters and businessmen. In general the somewhat easy-going Malays, most of whom had supported the Japanese, resented the near monopoly that the hardworking and entrepreneurial Chinese exerted on the economy. By the end of the Second World War most of the Chinese population had been born in Malaya, but regarded China as their cultural and political home, and China was a Communist country by 1949. The Chinese not only inhabited Chinatown in every Malayan city and town, but some 600,000 of them farmed 'squats' on the jungle fringes, where they had moved during the Japanese occupation in an attempt to escape Japanese brutality. Controlling these squatter encampments was to be one of the keys to the campaign.

Immediately after the fall of Japan, Britain attempted to reimpose colonial rule by forming the Union of Malaya. In 1948 this was changed to the Federation of Malaya. On the Malay Peninsula Singapore, Penang, and Malacca formed the Straits Settlements, a British colony, until 1946, when Singapore became a separate crown colony. The other eight states, each ruled by its own sultan, formed the Federation of Malaya, a dominion; the British exercised control through a British Resident in each state, and a British High Commissioner at Kuala Lumpur overseeing the whole.

After forming the Federation, the British Labour Government announced its intention of granting independence to Malaya, including

the Straits Settlements, but only via Dominion status. The problem was
how to frame a constitution fair to all parties, and ensuring a post-
independence democracy. While negotiations were underway, the all-
Chinese MCP decided to mount an uprising and drive the British out,
after which they would impose Communist rule on the majority Malay
population.

Thus began the bitter and protracted campaign, lasting from 1948
to 1960. The Malay Peninsula is 700 miles long and 200 miles wide,
and was ideal guerrilla country. Except for parts of the coastal plain,
it was covered by thick jungle, mixed with mangrove swamp in the
coastal areas. A north–south spine of mountains running up to 7,000
feet was covered with primary jungle, whose 200 foot high trees formed
a canopy under which there was little undergrowth, and through which
it was reasonably easy to move. There were also extensive areas
of secondary jungle, in places where the slash, burn, and move on
agriculture of the aborigines and Chinese squatters had destroyed the
primary jungle, allowing thick undergrowth, thorns, and tropical 'bush'
to spring up; these and grass over head height made movement
extremely difficult, and sometimes almost impossible. The rubber plantations were regularly cultivated, and, on the whole, provided little
obstacle to troops on foot. Numerous streams and rivers flowed to each
coast from the central spine, and crossing these, combined with almost
daily tropical downpour, meant that troops in the jungle were seldom
dry.

The swamps, streams, and even wet grass harboured myriads of
leeches; small enough to get through a boot lace hole, they swelled with
the blood of their host, and were best disposed of by applying some salt
or the end of a lighted cigarette. At halts to 'basha up' for the night a
hunt for leeches was usually possible, because in the heavy smoking
1950s the far stricter rule about smoking in the jungle at any time,
enforced by some units in the latter part of the campaign, had yet to
come. When lighting cigarettes on operations was not possible it was
best to let the leeches sate themselves and drop off naturally. The
thought that occurred to most men from time to time, of a leech
crawling into their penis, and once engorged with blood being stuck
there for ever, had to be pushed to the back of the mind. Some wore
condoms, which for obvious reasons usually fell off. A far bigger threat
to health was malaria. Every man took a Paludrine tablet daily. Anyone

who caught malaria and was found by medical tests to have failed to take his Paludrine was charged and punished.

By March 1950 it was clear that the security forces in Malaya were losing the war. The Chinese Communist terrorists (CTs) were killing 100 civilians a month, and operating in large groups of over 100 strong. CT losses had been replaced from the Chinese population. One major reason for the British lack of success was the logistic help given to the CTs by the squatters; the other was the lack of a coordinated plan, including intelligence gathering. The appointment of Lieutenant General Sir Harold Briggs as Director of Operations, in overall charge of Army and Police, in April 1950 proved the turning point.

He decided to resettle the Chinese squatters into new villages, which would be guarded to isolate the inhabitants from the CTs, and then to improve the standard of living of the resettled squatters to wean them off Communism, and provide a source of intelligence. He also planned to clear the country systematically from south to north. To assist in implementing the Briggs Plan, the Army Commander, Major General Boucher, requested the reinforcement of Malaya by the 3rd Commando Brigade, once again commanded by Brigadier Hardy.

The brigade sent a party of officers and NCOs ahead by air to the Jungle Warfare School at Johore Bahru, at that time commanded by Lieutenant Colonel Michael Calvert, who had commanded a Chindit column in Wingate's first behind-the-lines operation in Burma, and a brigade in the second. The brigade's Tactical Area of Responsibility (TAOR) was Perak State on the Thai border of north Malaya, an area about the size of Wales, with tin mines and rubber estates on the lower ground in the west and dense jungles in the mountains to the east. The CTs had safe camps in Thailand, and crossed the border to rest or train, and to resupply and reinforce their guerrilla groups. 40 Commando had the biggest TAOR, around Kuala Kangsar in the north of Perak, while 42 Commando was in the centre around Ipoh and 45 Commando at Tapah in the south of the state. 40 Commando's TAOR was less populated than the other two, and included the seventy miles of the Lenggong–Grik road, which ran towards the Thai border. Most troops were deployed along the road, with bases at Grik and Lenggong. The road was bordered by rubber plantations, which gave way to secondary and finally primary jungle. Most CT camps were situated in deep jungle well away from the road, but occasionally they would mount ambushes on the road, so vehicles drove in convoy with armoured car escorts. In an effort to discourage the CTs, likely ambush areas were sometimes treated to 'prophylactic' fire; a largely nugatory exercise.

To begin with there was little contact with the CTs as patrols flogged through the jungle. Time after time, patrols would find abandoned camps, or just signs of CTs, or 'bandits' as they were also called. The key to success was good intelligence, and this can only be built up over a protracted period. Many patrols were accompanied by Iban trackers from Sarawak on the island of Borneo. Their ability to track and give advice on the best route to follow was invaluable, especially in the early days before the Marines had found their feet in the jungle.

Successful patrolling was always punishing mentally and physically, demanding cunning, patience, and fortitude. Napoleon's dictum quoted at the beginning of Chapter 18 applied in the jungle as in most other campaigns. Contacts were usually fleeting and unexpected, often following weeks, and sometimes months, of slogging through the jungle. Following a track could be fraught with danger, leading straight into an ambush. Movement off tracks might be as slow as 200 yards an hour. Unless a night ambush was to be laid, the patrol would stop well before dark and move away from its route. After posting sentries and erecting poncho shelters or 'bashas', a meal would be eaten. If the patrol was judged to be near possible CTs, food would be eaten cold to avoid the giveaway smell of cooking. Basing-up near water was a give-away, so a patrol might have to be sent to collect water, and having collected the water it would have to be sterilized with tablets before drinking. Just before dark, another ritual: the anointing of all exposed skin, including the scalp under the thickest hair and under rolled-down sleeves with insect repellent, and taking the daily Paludrine. The jungle nights were twelve hours. Even the most exhausted men could not sleep for that long. Success in the jungle campaign was a matter of inuring men to the discomfort, and learning to cope with the environment, so that operating in it became second nature; to conquer the tendency to allow survival to assume greater importance than finding and dealing with the enemy. Clothes ripped on the thorns, the canvas jungle boots rotted and had to be replaced frequently. The men who spent long periods on patrol were pale from lack of sunlight; bronzed men with sun-faded jungle boots were the base 'wallahs'.

The Commando Brigade soon picked up the rhythm of jungle warfare, and by October 1950 had killed or captured more CTs and destroyed more camps than in any other TAOR. But by December the number of successes dwindled, possibly because the CTs had discerned the Commandos' methods of operating. By changing the operational pattern and above all by persistence, the Commando Brigade slowly built up its success rate again. In particular the resettlement programme was beginning to pay dividends. In January 1951, Hardy was succeeded by Brigadier C. F. Phillips, who had commanded 47 RM Commando and the 116th RM Brigade in North-West Europe. As 1951 unfolded the success rate mounted, often as part of a follow-up of a CT ambush or contact. In these situations, the Iban trackers were essential, and it helped even more if a 'turned' CT (known as a Surrendered Enemy Person – SEP for short) was also with the patrol.

On 2 April, a 40 Commando patrol was ambushed by CTs. The patrol commander, Lieutenant Coop, and a corporal, were killed, and one Marine wounded. As the patrol moved to outflank the CTs, they withdrew, and the follow-up lost contact. Another patrol followed the trail but without success. Some days later a patrol led by Lieutenant J. J. Moore with an SEP as guide searched through the same area:

> The SEP claimed that he could lead us to a place where supplies of rice etc. were left for pick-up from a small hut in the clearing, which we tried to identify from maps and air photographs. His directions were somewhat vague, and when we set forth from this place it very quickly became apparent that he was not taking us any where near where we had expected, but since he was adamant that he this was a route used by his group of CTs, I continued along it.
>
> As dusk approached, we were about to enter the edge of the jungle from a rubber estate we had been traversing. To our flank, about thirty yards off, a strip of thicker cover ran down into the rubber, and this made me feel very uncomfortable – I felt as if all the hairs on the back of my neck were standing on end. Having quickly checked with the SEP that the route lay strait into the jungle forty or so yards ahead, I moved the patrol in to the strip of thick cover, and instructed them to prepare a rapid ambush on the track we had been following. I was still moving along the position giving directions to the blokes on fields of fire etc. when three CTs appeared exactly where the SEP said they would. We all froze and watched as they walked into our killing ground, though we were not yet ready for them; the Bren gunner was a yard in front of

me squatting behind his gun getting magazines out of his pouches for instance.

One of them spotted us, which both the Bren gunner and I saw, but before he hit the ground, the gunner had flattened himself behind the gun and got off a burst which hit the CT in the groin. Of the three CTs in the killing ground, only one got away, while others engaged us for a while, not very accurately from the edge of the jungle, before fleeing. By the time we had cleared the scene of the ambush, it was almost dark (night falls very suddenly in Malaya), so we could not mount a follow-up that night. There was much rain in the night, and the next morning's efforts did not find the remainder of the party.[8]

The Commandos also took casualties in road ambushes and shoot-outs. The fiery Welsh Troop Sergeant Major (TSM) of 40 Commando's B Troop, 'Dai' Morgan, attempted to penetrate a CT camp with a patrol dressed to look like Chinese; a highly risky gimmick. The disguise was spotted, and the patrol ambushed by forty CTs, killing a Marine, and wounding the TSM and a corporal. Marine Lowrie covered the patrol's withdrawal, while Morgan moved the patrol out of the killing ground. Morgan then led an outflanking attack, killing four CTs, and the remainder fled into the jungle. He followed up, and found and destroyed a large camp. Both he and Lowrie were awarded well-deserved DCMs.

A patrol led by a corporal from Y Troop of 42 Commando had its patience and soldierly skills rewarded when ambushing a track running alongside a pipeline from tin mines situated in the jungle. They were dropped off by transport well away from the objective, and approached the ambush position by a roundabout route so that their intentions would not be compromised. They laid up some distance away the first night, and approached on the second day, crossing a high ridge through thick jungle and wading several streams. They halted near the pipeline and the corporal ordered them not to cook, as the smell of the hexamine burners and cooking food would cling to the foliage for hours, and be smelt a long way off. Each man carried two water bottles, which would have to last him all night and the next day if necessary; there would be no patrolling for water. They ate a meagre meal of cold food – each man carried the minimum to save weight. While they were eating, the corporal crawled to reconnoitre the track. When he returned he gave his orders. The whole patrol would mount the ambush all night, since there were too few of them to have one half in a lying-up area while the others watched (in any case a bad practice, as moving about to relieve men on watch is a giveaway).

The ambush was set with each group connected by string to give warning of the approach of CTs. The Bren firing was to be the signal for everyone to open up, and the corporal was sited by the Bren gunner. Nobody passed through the position all that night. In the morning Malays and Aborigines walked past, the patrol lay still. The sound of voices talking in Chinese, totally different in pitch from Malay, had the outer rifleman tense up, and grasp his string more tightly. Two Chinese with rifles and bundles came round a bend in the track. The patrol allowed them into the killing area, and the Bren gunner opened fire, killing one instantly and the other as he tried to make a break for it. They were couriers making for a base beyond the tin mines. Their identification was made possible by the patrol lugging the bodies to the police station; hard work. The more usual practice of merely bringing back the heads had recently been banned as a result of questions in the House of Commons.

Many of the successes in Malaya resulted from correct drills following a contact. One such action took place when X Troop, 40 Commando was sent to 45 Commando's TAOR in south Perak. The troop was committed to long patrols over a number of weeks, in the course of which two sub-sections under Lieutenant Langley spotted an unoccupied CT OP in a tree. Recent track marks led from the tree to a waist-deep patch of mangrove, in the centre of which was a thicket of bush and high grass. As the leading scouts started to wade across to the thicket, machine-gun fire from CT positions killed Corporal Ireland, and wounded Langley and Marines Alexander and King. Langley put in an immediate counterattack with part of his patrol covered by the remainder. The CTs abandoned their positions dug in on the perimeter of a camp with accommodation for eighty terrorists. Alexander died of wounds while being casevaced.

40 Commando also took part in the first operation in Malaya involving the Malayan Scouts Air Service Regiment, as Calvert's newly raised 22 SAS Regiment was called at the time.[9] Lieutenant Pennell and half of A Troop with twenty-five police spent seven days penetrating a remote area of northern Perak, where the inhabitants of a village were totally under the control of the CTs. As planned, just before Pennell

arrived a squadron of the Malayan Scouts was dropped by parachute into a clearing close to the village – the first airborne operation to be carried out in Malaya.

In May 1952, after two years' outstanding service, the Commando Brigade left Malaya bound for Malta, having accounted for two hundred and twenty-one CTs killed or captured. It had suffered thirty-three dead, and won forty awards for gallantry, not including sixty-eight mentions in despatches.

MALTA AND EGYPT, 1952–1954

On arrival in Malta, the Commando Brigade once more assumed the role of Middle East strategic reserve. Here, under its new commander, Brigadier J. L. Moulton, who had commanded 48 Commando in North-West Europe, the brigade retrained in amphibious skills not practised since the end of the Second World War. One of the Middle East plans inherited by the 3rd Commando Brigade involved the evacuation of British citizens from Alexandria. Moulton watched the Army brigade, whose task this had been, carry out an exercise to practise the operation. Moulton judged it a 'very bad exercise', and told the Second-in-Command Mediterranean Fleet that the plan was useless. At this juncture, the Amphibious Warfare (AW) Squadron consisting of two LSTs, *Striker* and *Reggio*, and two LCTs, *Bastion* and *Sallyport*, arrived in the Mediterranean on a visit. Moulton reworked the plan and persuaded the C-in-C Mediterranean, Admiral Lord Louis Mountbatten, to 'shanghai' the AW Squadron, and to extend its stay in-theatre for the next two years. In fact the squadron was to stay for rather more than two years, and with the Headquarters ship, HMS *Meon*, was to provide the transport for many an amphibious exercise until the mid-1960s. Moulton put the brigade through its paces on several amphibious schemes, but being a practical soldier, and not content with merely brushing up landing skills, which are not an end in themselves, he included two testing exercises in the Sinai Desert, one in which the brigade provided the infantry element of an armoured division, and the other against the

16th Parachute Brigade. These were followed with another hard exercise in Cyprus, again with 16th Parachute Brigade.

In hindsight, Moulton's 'hijacking' of the AW Squadron, and his steering the 3rd Commando Brigade back to amphibious operations while not forgetting the primary role of his formation, to fight in the land battle, was crucial in the never-ending struggle to retain the Royal Marines. His guiding hand was to continue to be essential in securing the Corps's future roles, long after he had relinquished command of the 3rd Commando Brigade.

As part of the plan for the evacuation of British subjects from Alexandria, the SBS carried out a reconnaissance of the private harbour there in which King Farouk of Egypt had kept his large motor yacht. Lieutenant Emslie and Sergeant Moorehouse paddled to a position near the harbour entrance in two canoes. Leaving their number twos in the canoes, they swam in. While by one of the jetties, they thought they were spotted by a sentry. Emslie swam out to his canoe, but Moorehouse hid under the jetty, and having ditched his reconnaissance kit, swam to the emergency RV. When no one turned up to extract him, he disposed of his equipment, and handed himself in to a coastguard, saying that he had fallen overboard from a ship, and swum ashore. He was handed over to the British embassy the same day. Although Moorehouse had acted correctly, this unsatisfactory operation was to have repercussions some years afterwards.

In May 1953 the brigade was ordered to the Suez Canal Zone, where one of many crises in Anglo-Egyptian relations, brewing since 1951, was coming to a head. The British presence in the Canal Zone dated back to General Wolseley's invasion of Egypt, then part of the Ottoman Empire, in 1882, after which the British effectively ruled Egypt for the next seventy years. Britain's principal concern in staying in Egypt was to retain control, in partnership with the French, over the Suez Canal, the lifeline to the Empire in India, the Far East, Australia, and New Zealand. As one author remarked, referring to Britain's occupation of Egypt,

> Egypt had been transformed from a Levantine shambles to a prosperous modern state.
>
> Nevertheless the Egyptian people were not happy. They might grudgingly concede that the British had acted fairly, and administered the country well and without lining their own pockets, but the very presence

of the British in their country running their Army and public affairs, was an insult to their national pride.[10]

In 1952, King Farouk of Egypt was deposed, and replaced briefly by Colonel Neguib, who in his turn was ousted by Colonel Nasser, a politician of genius. The British granted full independence to Egypt and withdrew their forces, but announced their intention under the terms of the 1936 Anglo-Egyptian Treaty to retain control of the Suez Canal Zone until 1956. The Canal Zone was a valuable British base strategically situated to supply and reinforce the Near and Middle East, and consisted of a number of large military depots, some dating back to before the First World War, the Headquarters of Middle East Command, and some 83,000 British soldiers. The Egyptian government riposted by abrogating the 1936 Treaty, and ordered her troops and police to harass the British in the Canal Zone. The main trouble was caused by the 'fedayeen' or 'freedom fighters', often the Egyptian police in disguise, and took the usual form of ambushing vehicles, attacking camps and depots, and shootings. Although service in the Canal Zone was marked more by boredom than danger, it was hazardous enough by the standards to which the British public has become accustomed by the end of the twentieth century: in just eighteen months between October 1951 and March 1952, fifty-four British servicemen were killed and sixty-nine seriously wounded. No campaign medal was ever issued, a source of mild surprise to this day among soldiers and Marines who served there.

Operations mainly took the form of static guards on vital installations, and patrolling. The big stores depots, with their stocks of ammunition, weapons, and vehicles, and other attractive kit such as watches, binoculars, and rations, were magnets to 'fedayeen' and pilferers alike. The perimeters were several miles long, and in the days before night-vision equipment, infra-red intruder alarms and other devices became commonplace, could only be covered by mobile patrols, with sentries at key points. Ambushes laid just outside the wire on likely approaches, to catch infiltrators, or 'fedayeen' taking pot-shots at patrols and sentry sangars, were hazardous because of the mixed minefields (anti-personnel and anti-tank) laid to protect some of the depots during the Second World War: the sand had drifted over the markers, and exposed some mines, while burying others deeper. One troop commander ordered one of his subalterns to lay an ambush outside the wire of one of these depots, and overrode all protests, saying that any mines would be buried so deep as to be harmless. Even when the nineteen-year-old officer in question was backed by his section sergeant, a highly experienced and fully qualified Assault Engineer, the troop commander would not be budged from this idea. The patrol tiptoed out of the perimeter, praying that they would not tread on an anti-personnel mine. They lay out on the bare sand all night, the visibility quite good in the bright starlight, but no 'fedayeen' or other infiltrators approached. In the morning, the troop commander drove out into the minefield, 'told you so' written all over his face, until one of his rear tyres was shredded by an anti-personnel mine; he was lucky it was not an anti-tank mine, or he would have been blown sky high. The patrol tiptoed out even more carefully.

Amenities in the Canal Zone were almost non-existent and opportunities for relaxation in pleasant surroundings nil. Those in 42 Commando and 45 Commando, based by the Great Bitter Lake and at Port Fuad respectively, could wistfully eye the wives and daughters of the French Canal Company employees disporting themselves on the adjacent beaches. Although the females concerned appeared to grow more attractive and nubile as the months went by, it was a look but don't touch situation. 40 Commando at the aptly named Sandy Camp at El Ballah, was denied even these diversions. It was therefore with relief that when the Anglo-Egyptian Suez agreement was signed at last, in August 1954, the brigade was ordered back to Malta.

In the autumn of 1954 it was decided to send 42 Commando back to England, to reduce ratio of overseas to home service in the Royal Marines as a whole. The Commando would be held ready to reinforce the brigade at short notice. In the meanwhile the other two Commandos trained in North Africa and in the Mediterranean, based on Malta – but not for long, for trouble was festering in Cyprus.

CYPRUS, 1954–1959

The island of Cyprus had been ceded to Britain by the Ottoman Empire at the Treaty of Berlin in 1878 for use as a base. In 1914 Turkey allied herself to Germany and the British annexed Cyprus. In 1915 the British offered it to Greece as an inducement to come into the war against the Turks; the Greeks refused. Cyprus became a crown colony in 1925. The population was split, as now, into Greek and Turkish communities. Both retained cultural and religious links with Greece and Turkey, and the Greek Cypriots outnumbered the Turkish by four to one. From 1878 the Greek Cypriots had demanded *énosis*, union with Greece, which was and is unacceptable to Turkey: the island is very close to Turkey's southern coast, and the idea of such a strategically sensitive place in the hands of Turkey's most hated enemy was anathema. Furthermore, Turkey had no wish to see the Turkish minority ruled by Greeks. The *énosis* movement gained momentum until in 1954 the Turks threatened to invade to protect the Turkish minority. The position was further complicated because both Turkey and Greece were members of NATO, so the Alliance was in danger of being weakened by this quarrel, and, if matters took a turn for the worse, a three-sided war might break out involving Britain, Greece, and Turkey on the sensitive southern flank of NATO. Seeing Britain had no intention of precipitating such a situation by granting *énosis*, and with the tacit support of mainland Greece, the extremists on the island formed a terrorist organization known as EOKA, Ethniki Organosis Kuprion Agoniston, or the National Organization of Cypriot Fighters. Its aim was similar to the Jewish terrorists', to attract world sympathy by provoking the British into acts which would be seen as repression of a downtrodden race seeking self-determination. Command of EOKA was given to a passed-over Greek colonel called Grivas, who had fought in the Greek Army in the Second World War.

Greek Cypriot anti-British sentiments were sharpened when it became clear that following the loss of the Suez Canal Zone base in 1956 the British would transfer many of their assets to Cyprus, including the headquarters of the C-in-C Near East: an additional incentive for the British to hang on to the island. Initially EOKA confined itself to rioting and fomenting strikes and other disorders. Things soon took a turn for the worse as EOKA became more active: shootings, bombings, and assassinations quickly became commonplace. Grivas acquired a substantial quantity of arms and ammunition following a raid on a British store in Famagusta. Before this, the two Commandos and Brigade Headquarters were among other reinforcements ordered to the island.

Cyprus, in those days before mass tourism and deforestation, was a

beautiful place, particularly in the two mountain ranges. In the centre of
the island, Mount Olympus in the Troódos range rises to nearly 6,000
feet, and has sufficient snow in winter for skiing. Pine forests covered
the sides of the steep scree-covered mountains. Moufflon, the large wild
mountain sheep, could sometimes be seen on the higher and more
inaccessible slopes. Except for the odd forester or shepherd the forests
were deserted. To the west of Mount Olympus, the Paphos Forest
covered the hills as they descended in rolling waves to the sea at the
legendary birthplace of Aphrodite. In the centre of the Paphos Forest,
Kykko Monastery dominated one of the few north–south roads. The
Greek Orthodox Church, steeped in intrigue for centuries, was deeply
implicated in support of EOKA. The Kyrenia range in the north, along
the panhandle, is lower but more dramatic. The sharp peaks give a
Disney castle effect, rising almost straight out of the sea in places. The
central plain between the two ranges is dry and dusty, dotted with low
hills, cultivation, and lemon and carob trees. Vineyards cover the lower
slopes of the Troódos mountains and Paphos hills. The mountain roads
were narrow and mostly unsurfaced. Hairpin bends, cliffs, and steep
slopes on both sides made them an ideal place for ambush. The villages
cling to the sides of the mountain, and in the main valleys. A vehicle
approaching can be seen for half an hour or more as it winds its way
seemingly interminably towards its destination. Only towards the end of
the campaign were there any helicopters, and travelling in a vehicle was
usually an invitation to be ambushed. Patrols stayed out for days and
nights at a time. Ambushes would be set at night by likely forest tracks.
Villages would be cordoned off by men marching all night over the
mountains and arriving before day-break. Boots wore out in a few days
on the razor-sharp scree. Hot in summer, bitterly cold in winter,
soldiering in the Troódos and Paphos was tough and demanding,
Kyrenia only marginally less so, and the two Commandos were to spend
much of the next four years in these mountain ranges.

On arrival 40 Commando was based in the Limassol area, and
operated in the Paphos Forest to the north and west. 45 Commando
mainly operated in Kyrenia, where its operations were so effective that
EOKA eventually concentrated its main rural efforts in the Troódos/
Paphos area. The majority of casualties throughout the campaign were
suffered by Greek and Turkish Cypriots killing and wounding each
other, but there was a steady trickle of casualties in the two Commandos

along with the other troops in the island. When the outgoing CO of 40 Commando, Lieutenant Colonel T. M. (Tim) Grey, was travelling in a Champ with his successor, Lieutenant Colonel D. G. Tweed, they narrowly escaped injury when a bomb exploded just behind the vehicle. A few days later Major Maude was badly injured and Lieutenant Dick killed when a bomb landed in the latter's lap as they were travelling to a meeting with the Chief of Police and District Officer at Paphos.

There were also successes, usually as a result of speedy reactions following a contact, or good patrolling, professional soldiering, and a measure of luck. Sometimes the larger, set-piece operations paid off, more often they did not – such as the ill-fated Operation Lucky Alphonse. It was thought that Grivas was holed up in a valley deep in the Paphos Forest. 45 Commando and several battalions, including 3rd Battalion the Parachute Regiment (3 Para), were ordered to cordon off a large area.

To be effective a cordon had to be set up quietly, and completely surround the area as quickly as possible. If the quarry suspected what was happening he would slip away. Long approach marches, often at night, were usually necessary. Accurate map reading was difficult, and the steep scree made quiet movement almost impossible. Once the cordon was in place, patrolling within it started. Navigation had to be good so that a patrol did not wander into another's patch and be shot for their pains. At night it was better to stay and listen and watch for movement, so the patrols would set ambushes within the cordon. Cordon operations had to be capable of being sustained for days and even weeks. Men in the cordon had to be in sight of each other, or at least cover the ground between each other by observation and fire. It was not good enough to have a ring of men with each man on his own: if a group of terrorists attempting to break out attacked a lone soldier they might overcome him, particularly at night. Often complete sections were allocated positions in the cordon. OPs and ambush positions would be forward of the section position, to which men returned to eat and sleep. Well-trained troops usually changed their positions after dark, in case they had been under observation by terrorists during the day and the position had been compromised.

These operations in the forest were expensive in troops, and if they were to be successful demanded a very high standard of soldiering. The Commandos and Parachute battalions were in their element. Others

were not so good, and the larger the operation the more chance there
was of dozy sentries, chattering and cooking in section posts, and patrols
'bimbling' through the forest in a dream.

Operation Alphonse started well. A hide was found, and the chances
of catching Grivas, or at least some of the leading EOKA players, looked
good. A patrol of C Company of 3 Para got very close to a group of
terrorists when the clink of boot on scree alerted them and the group
fled. Shots were fired, but shooting with a bolt-operated number 4 rifle
at a jinking target among trees is not easy. There were no hits.
Examination of the hide showed that the patrol had almost netted Grivas
and his immediate staff. However, no reports came in from the cordon
indicating attempts to break out, and it was assumed that he was still
somewhere inside. After that it went from bad to worse, and a few days
later disaster struck: a huge fire swept through the tinder-dry forest. Its
cause has never been established, but it is likely that it was the result of
someone's idea of trying to flush out the terrorists by mortar fire, and
45 Commando's mortars were certainly engaged on this task at the time.
Twenty-one officers and soldiers, mainly from the Gordon Highlanders
and Royal Norfolks,[11] but including two of 3 Para, were burnt to death.
Captain Meadows of 45 Commando organized the rescue of many
soldiers, carrying one for over a mile, and moving a burning armoured
car.

In July 1956 the two Commandos and Brigade Headquarters were
withdrawn from Cyprus for the Suez operation, which is covered in a
later chapter, but in 1957 and 1958 both 40 and 45 Commandos carried
out tours in Cyprus, the final one being in 1959 by 40 Commando. Most
of the time in Cyprus post-Suez was spent in the Troódos Mountain–
Paphos Forest area, but 45 Commando in 1957 formed a Heliforce,
which consisted of Commando Tac HQ and two rifle troops and a flight
of four Fleet Air Arm Whirlwind helicopters. No great successes were
achieved by Heliforce, although some valuable lessons were learnt. One
sad incident occurred when using helicopters to put in the cordon round
a suspected terrorist group in the Panhandle. After the insertion, Tac
HQ heard the radio message 'Contact, opening fire'; jubilation was
followed by despondency when it transpired that one stick, dropped in
the wrong place in the darkness, had walked into a section on the
cordon, which opened fire, killing Sergeant Baldwin and a Marine, and
wounding two more. On another occasion during a night insertion, the

CO, Lieutenant Colonel Jack Richards, was last out, roping down. He was near the end of the fifteen-foot rope, when the helicopter took off – in those days no crewman was carried to pull in the rope, and the helicopters flew back to base with ropes dangling. Richards was faced with the choice of trying to hang to the rope during the fifteen-minute flight back to Nicosia over the Kyrenia Range, or dropping off quickly. He chose the latter, and speared in from about twenty feet, breaking both legs.

The longest cordon operation of the campaign was Operation King-fisher, in which 40 Commando took part, with several other battalions, in 1958. Once more, Grivas was the prey. The Commando, which was dispersed in troop bases in the Paphos Forest and Troódos, had to be concentrated at night and driven to drop-off points, then marched in by night to establish the cordon. Several days were spent moving in tightening the ring. But as before, the sheer unwieldiness of a large cordon operation was self-defeating. On one occasion, a patrol from the Machine Gun Platoon of S Troop, engaged on ambush operations inside the cordon, was fired on by a section of the cordon manned by part of a company of 1st Battalion the Argyll and Sutherland Highlanders, commanded by Major Mitchell, later of Aden fame. Luckily, the patrol was crouching in a gully, and the bullets cracked harmlessly over their heads. Despite the cordon lasting six weeks, and every square yard of ground being searched, Grivas was never found, although it has been subsequently established that he was inside when the operation started. Bad soldiering and ill-discipline somewhere in the cordon had enabled him to escape.

S Troop 40 Commando had more success later in the same tour with a snap cordon during Operation Matchbox, an extensive affair involving several units cordoning a number of villages in the Paphos and Limassol areas, followed by searches. After several days of nugatory cordon operations, the troop commander decided that the terrorists must now be thoroughly alerted, and any that had not already escaped might have gone to ground in the villages. The next village allocated to S Troop was Platinistassa, and it was to be a daylight operation. The Troop commander reasoned that putting in a cordon in the traditional manner, by approaching from several directions, on foot over the hills, from outside the village, would take too long, and might allow any terrorists hiding up to make a break for it. However, if the cordon could be put in very quickly and was too tight for terrorists to break they might not have time to hide properly, and there would be ample time to carry out a thorough search. Accordingly part of the troop drove through the village, as if heading for another further on, and at the given codeword over the radio, the Marines leapt out of their vehicles at both ends of the village, and raced round to form a tight cordon. A man was seen dodging through the houses, and was arrested at gun point by an alert Marine. A search revealed a couple more, and the accompanying police identified them as a group of notorious bombers, wanted for many months.

Soon after this, 40 Commando was summoned back to Malta, where the whole Brigade, including 42 Commando sent out from England, was assembling. Unrest in the Near and Middle East was threatening the governments of several Arab countries with whom the British had treaty arrangements, including Libya (then ruled by King Idris, friendly to Britain), Jordan, and Iraq. In the event the 3rd Commando Brigade was not committed, although the 16th Parachute Brigade spent several months deployed in Amman in Jordan, and the US Marines landed in Lebanon. During this period, King Feisal of Iraq was assassinated, an event which eventually led, after a series of dictators, to the present regime.

While 40 Commando was deployed in the Troódos Mountains and Paphos in 1959, the Zurich agreement was signed. This created the independent Republic of Cyprus, renouncing both *énosis* and partition into separate Greek and Turkish states. In addition, British Sovereign Base Areas (SBAs) were established, in Akrotiri, Limassol, and Larnaca. The Zurich agreement was overturned in 1974 when the Turks invaded northern Cyprus, initiating partition as it exists today, but leaving the SBAs untouched. Both 40 and 41 Commandos were involved in the events of 1974, the latter having been re-formed in March 1960.

21

Korea

Gentlemen, we are not retreating. We are merely advancing in another direction.

Major General O. P. Smith USMC

Just as the 3rd Commando Brigade was deploying in Malaya in June 1950, North Korean troops crossed the 38th Parallel into South Korea. The armed forces of the Republic of Korea (ROK) were in no state to hold an invasion by over seven well-trained and equipped North Korean divisions, and they fell back rapidly in confusion. The United States deployed ground forces from its occupation troops in Japan, as well as naval and air forces. In addition to carriers and cruisers, the British deployed the 27th Infantry Brigade from Hong Kong, consisting of the 1st Battalions of the Middlesex Regiment[1] and the Argyll and Sutherland Highlanders (the third battalion in the brigade, 1st Royal Leicestershire Regiment,[2] was left behind). The British land force contribution eventually included the provision of the majority of the troops in 1st Commonwealth Division, including the GOC, the headquarters, an armoured regiment, artillery, engineers, signals, five infantry battalions, and logistic units. All the forces participating in the Korean War, against the North Koreans and later the Chinese, came under the auspices of the United Nations (UN), under the command of General Douglas MacArthur, and United States forces, land, sea, and air, greatly outnumbered all the others combined.

The first Royal Marines to take part in the Korean War were those in ship's detachments bombarding the coast and carrying out raids. Altogether some seven cruisers and seven carriers took part in the Korean War, and all carried Royal Marine Detachments. In August 1950 Admiral Sir Patrick Brind, C-in-C Far East Fleet, offered to provide Admiral C. Turner Joy USN, commanding all UN naval forces off Korea, with a small force to raid the North Korean coastal communications. Only sixteen seamen and Marines volunteered from the Far East Fleet, and about half of them were eventually returned to their ships by the CO of 41 Commando as unsuitable. Meanwhile, the British Chiefs of Staff in Whitehall had been discussing the deployment of troops to Korea, amid some disagreement. The First Sea Lord, having heard of Brind's offer to Joy, and embarrassed by the feeble response in the fleet, announced that he had made arrangements to form a new Commando, 41 Independent Commando Royal Marines, to serve in Korea in a raiding role. But he also wanted to send 3rd Commando Brigade from Malaya, reminding his colleagues that it was part of the Royal Navy, and therefore his to dispose of. He was especially influenced in this by news that a United States Marine Division was being formed for operations in Korea. The CIGS and the CAS opposed the move of 3rd Commando Brigade from Malaya, saying that operations in Malaya were as important as countering Communist expansion in Korea. The Secretary to the Chiefs of Staff Committee recorded that First Sea Lord then withdrew, presumably having lost the argument; no more was heard of redeploying 3rd Commando Brigade from Malaya to Korea.

Major, Acting Lieutenant Colonel, D. B. Drysdale RM was ordered by the Commandant General, Sir Leslie Hollis, to form a 300-strong Commando in two weeks from volunteers within the Corps. Drysdale had been Hardy's Brigade Major in Burma, later taking command of 44 RM Commando. About 100 of 41 Commando paraded at Bickleigh on 16 August and flew to Japan on 1 September, arriving at Camp McGill south of Tokyo the following day. Here they were joined by a reinforcement draft of young Marines, including some specialists, from a draft due to join the 3rd Commando Brigade in Malaya, taken off the troop transport *Devonshire* in Singapore, and flown to Japan.

The country over which 41 Commando was to fight was described by a British soldier:

> it presented a hostile environment for military operations ... The winters were prolonged and very severe. Temperatures were frequently over 40°F below freezing, and accompanied by Siberian winds ... In summer the temperatures crept up to 105°F and more, and the humidity was high.[3]

There were few roads or tracks. The terrain was hilly, many features rising over 3,000 feet, mainly rocky and bare higher up, the lower slopes were covered in shrubs and small trees. In summer the luxuriant growth on the steep hillsides impeded sweating soldiers as they toiled up, often under heavy loads. Paddy fields dotted the wider valleys. The sides of the narrower defiles were often precipitous. Malarial mosquitoes and rats which spread other diseases abounded. Locally grown products could not be eaten raw because of the extensive use of human faeces as a fertilizer. In the shimmering heat of the summer the whole countryside stank.

The enemy, at first the North Korean Peoples' Army (NKPA), and later the Chinese Communist Forces (CCF) as well, were tough, fanatically brave, and masters of camouflage and fieldcraft. They attacked relentlessly in waves, often at night, screaming and blowing bugles. In defence they dug extensive fieldworks concealing and providing overhead cover for guns to an extent which astonished Western armies fighting in Korea, but would not have surprised the French in Indochina, faced by equally industrious human moles. The Chinese in particular were adept at long approach marches by night, and infiltration, and their attacks were skilfully conducted by fire and movement. Hardy and frugal, they relied on a minimal line of communication and supply.[4] They maintained large armies in the face of overwhelming air power.

By 4 August, the Americans and South Koreans had been forced back to a perimeter around the port of Pusan. Meanwhile MacArthur was planning the great amphibious hook at Inchon, the port for Seoul (the capital of South Korea), now in North Korean hands. Royal Marines played a small part in this landing, being involved in a deception operation. Lieutenant E. G. D. Pounds RM, who had volunteered for 41 Commando and was appointed C Troop commander, arrived at Camp McGill ahead of his troop, where Drysdale promptly put him in command of the volunteers from the fleet mentioned above. Here they were joined by three Marines from 41 Commando, which had also arrived, and were dubbed Poundsforce. The force joined the Raider Company of the US Army and embarked on the frigate HMS *Whitesand Bay*, commanded by Lieutenant Commander J. V. Brothers RN, and sailed for their first operation. On the night of 12/13 September they landed from inflatable boats on Robb Island and Kongsoon on the mainland without difficulty, and conducted beach reconnaissances, deliberately leaving tell-tale signs of their presence before withdrawing. The main assault would follow two nights later, to the north. Poundsforce withdrew under inaccurate machine-gun fire without casualties, but the Americans on Robb Island had two killed. The Inchon landings were completely successful, and by 20 September Poundsforce had moved in to join the main body at Kaesong airfield north of Seoul, along with the Raider Company. For about ten days the Force patrolled the hills and fought minor actions. After being withdrawn they went to join the main body of 41 Commando at Camp McGill, where everybody was training for three raids against the east coast railway between Ch'ongjin and Hungnam, which carried supplies to the North Koreans from Russia and China. The Commando was equipped entirely with American kit and weapons, retaining only their green berets.

Two raids were to be made from two American Assault Personnel Destroyers (APDs – destroyers modified as fast surface transports, and able to carry landing craft), the USS *Wantuck* and USS *Horace A. Bass*. The third was to be from the US submarine *Perch*, which had been modified to carry 160 raiders. On the night of 1/2 October B Troop of 41 Commando landed in ten inflatable boats from the *Perch*, to attack the railway line south of Ch'ongjin. The raiders, led by Drysdale, carried their demolition charges through the surf, laid them on the line, and pulled the fuses; they detonated as the party withdrew. During the move back to the beach the troop became involved in a running battle, and had one man killed.

The next targets consisted of a railway tunnel and large culvert just south of Songjin, and another railway tunnel in Kyongsong Man, twenty miles south of the port of Ch'ongjin. On the night of 6/7 October C and D Troops, commanded by Captain L. G. Marsh and Lieutenant Pounds, under the command of Drysdale's second-in-command, Major D. L. St M. Aldridge, embarked in the APDs *Wantuck* and *Horace A. Bass* to attack the tunnel at Kyongsong Man. They were accompanied by US Naval officers of an Underwater Demolition Team (UDT), and the British journalist and Socialist MP Tom Driberg, a correspondent for *Reynolds News*. Again the troops came ashore in inflatables, on this occasion towed to within 500 yards of the beach by Landing Craft Personnel (LCP(R) – the US equivalent of the LCA). After paddling a further 200 yards, the reconnaissance boat under Lieutenant Thomas beached, and, checking that all was clear and the surf could be negotiated, he signalled in the remainder with a torch. Both troops were landed on the correct beach thanks to good radar vectoring of the LCP(R)s from the destroyers. The parties moved off to their objectives, and having located them, the business of humping some two tons of explosives through the surf and up from the beach began. The raiders allowed two trains to pass before starting to place the explosives, having sited a bazooka to destroy any further trains that appeared while this was in progress. By 0100 hours all was in place, the fuses pulled, and the Marines withdrew to their boats. They were back in their LCP(R)s when with a mighty roar and an orange burst of flame the charge blew. The line was blocked for weeks. There was one casualty, Corporal Babbs, a wartime RMBPD man, now SBS, killed on the beach and later buried at sea. There was nearly another, as Lieutenant Pounds relates:

> I had detailed Corporal Ridout to help isolate the beachhead by cutting any wires on any poles in the vicinity. This he did with great enthusiasm, including a high-powered electric cable which knocked him down the pole. He, being a boxer, shook his head and got on with the job. However the cable fell across my withdrawal route. As my boat had broached to during the landing (because Tom Driberg wasn't sufficiently agile [and did not disembark with the necessary speed]), I was saturated and being the last man to leave the objective, had the misfortune to walk on to the cable. The result was spectacular, with sparks flying everywhere. Luckily my signaller, Marine Condron, came back, and reversing his rifle, fished the wire off me. This did not prevent me from taking part in the next raid.[5]

A similar raid was carried out the next night by C and D Troops, further along the coast, when a tunnel and bridge were attacked. On this occasion the Reconnaissance officer swam the last 100 yards into the beach to check the surf before signalling the force in. With the manpower available to the Communists such damage was probably soon repaired, but it did disrupt supplies from the USSR only 100 miles up the coast.

This was an encouraging beginning for 41 Commando, but when Drysdale returned to Camp McGill from the raid mounted from the *Perch* he found that the opportunities for coastal raids were fast diminishing. The UN forces, having comprehensively defeated the North Korean Army, were advancing fast to the Yalu River, the border with China. Until now, Drysdale had resisted pressure to attach his Commando to the 1st US Marine Division; now, if he did not join the division, the British Marines would miss the action. Unfortunately,

the Marine Division was already embarked for a landing at Wonsan
on the east coast, as part of MacArthur's plans for a general advance to
the Yalu. There was no room in the landing ships, and no task for 41
Commando. If Drysdale did not play his cards right, his Commando
would spend the rest of the war on occupation duties. He decided to
switch to training in conventional war, rather than raiding, and wait
to see what fate would bring.

By the end of October the training was finished. The 1st Marine
Division had landed at Wonsan, and having found the ROK Capital
Division had preceded them had gone further north to Hungnam, which
was still miles from the Yalu. Major General Smith, the divisional
commander, had objected to being ordered to rush forward to the Yalu
like the rest of General Almond's US X Corps, who had also landed at
Wonsan, and under whose command he had been placed. Almond had
ambitions to destroy the remnants of North Korean forces in the Chosin
Reservoir area in a swift Patton-like advance, for by now the Chinese
had entered the war on the side of the North Koreans; but although they
had attacked the US Eighth Army on the western UN axis in late
October, by early November they had withdrawn and apparently faded
out of the picture. Smith harboured no illusions, and guessing that the
Chinese would be back wished to keep his division concentrated, and
did not want to advance to the Chosin reservoir until he was ready. He
advanced slowly, concentrating his attention on improving the road
behind him, and securing his exposed line of communication back to
Hungnam, the nearest port, with outposts on the high ground overlooking the route. He improved his base at Hagaru-ri just short of the Chosin
Reservoir, including building an air base that would take C-47s. By 23
November, despite Almond's impatience, Smith had established a firm
base for further operations in the frigid barren wastes round the Chosin
Reservoir some 4,000 feet high, with peaks in the surrounding mountains
up to 7,000 feet. The winter had arrived two weeks before, and was to
bring snow and sub-zero temperatures driven by screaming winds from
Siberia, causing night temperatures of –24°F (–31° Celsius), freezing
vehicles, weapons, and feet.

Meanwhile Drysdale had asked Admiral Burke, the Chief of Staff to
Joy, for help. Burke sent a signal to Smith: 'British 41st Royal Marine
Commandos available and anxious to join your division earliest. Suggest
this excellent unit be employed.'[6] As the official history relates:

There was no reply for ten days. General Smith was anxious to have 41 Commando but X Corps headquarters [Almond] was miffed at being bypassed. Trivial objections to the attachment had been raised.

'This need not deter us', Admiral Burke remarked to the British naval attaché, Commander J. M. D. Gray, RN, 'They [41 Commando] are being sent to the 1st Marine Division as replacements – this will get over the difficulty'.

It did. The Commando embarked on the USS transport *Jackson* for Hungnam on Thursday 16th November.

The Chinese army re-entered the scene on 25 November, starting by crushing a ROK corps, followed by attacks all along the front, including X Corps's sector. As Eighth Army withdrew towards Seoul, X Corps was ordered to pull back to a perimeter round Hungnam and eventually to re-embark and abandon North Korea. The 1st Marine Division was cut off at the Chosin Reservoir. The Marines had advanced beyond the narrow Toktong Pass and secured Yudam-ni on the eastern arm of the Reservoir. The base at Hagaru-ri, on the southern tip of the Reservoir, was garrisoned, and Smith had kept his 1st Regimental Combat Team (RCT) at Koto-ri and Chinhung-ni, as lay-back positions. Because all the infantry companies not engaged on other tasks were at Yudam-Ni, and Divisional HQ had an enormous perimeter to guard to encompass the expanding runway, Smith was desperately short of infantry.

41 Commando arrived at Koto-ri on 28 November, bound for Hagaru-ri and eventually Yudam-ni. The Chinese were attacking Yudam-ni, and the road from Koto-ri to Hagaru-ri was cut. Lieutenant Thomas served in 41 Commando from the beginning to the end of its time in Korea, commanding the Heavy Weapons Group of four American 81mm mortars and four Browning .30in medium machine-guns, and wrote later:

> Early next morning HQ 1 Mar Div [1st Marine Division] order that Task Force Drysdale totalling 922 men and 141 vehicles comprising: 41 Independent Commando, G Coy 3 Bn 1st Marines USMC, B Coy 31st Infantry USA and elements of HQ personnel and the Divisional train [trucks carrying supplies], be formed to fight its way to Hagaru [sic] at the southern tip of the Chosin Reservoir.[7]

The Commando and G Company took the first two features commanding the road, but enemy on two more stopped any advance after the column had covered two and a half miles from their start point. At 1350 hours Drysdale was reinforced by seventeen tanks from D Company 1st USMC Tank Battalion. With air and armoured support, Force Drysdale pushed on another mile and a half. By now it was dark, and further delays were caused by the tanks pausing to refuel. At this stage, Drysdale received a radio message that it was vital that the column get through that day 'At all costs'. His very sensible tactics of clearing the high ground as he advanced would take too long, and he took the only decision he could. He mounted his men in the trucks and pressed on. Unfortunately by an oversight the tanks had not been placed under his command, and their commander, with strange notions of tactics, insisted on leading the column, instead of, as Drysdale wanted, providing support throughout its length. Thomas:

> About halfway to Hagaru [sic] the MSR [main supply route] entered a defile where the CCF closed in and split the column, leaving one Heavy Weapons section, the Assault Engineers and elements of Commando HQ with most of B Coy and Div HQ [personnel moving up to reinforce the Div HQ], who fought throughout the night, strung out in a number of defensive perimeters. Subsequently the Heavy Weapons section led by Cpl E. Cruse, found its way to Hagaru-ri badly frostbitten and seven of the Cdo HQ personnel were led back to Koto Ri by the Assault Engineer officer, Captain P. J. Ovens, after slipping out of the perimeter while surrender terms were being negotiated in the early hours of 30 November.
>
> Meanwhile the remainder of the column forced on under sporadic fire until under a mile from Hagaru [sic] it was stopped by concentrated mortar and small-arms fire within sight of the USMC Engineers working under floodlights to construct a 2,900 foot runway out of frozen earth. The MSR was blocked by an abandoned tank and several vehicles were set on fire.[8]

By now Drysdale had been lightly wounded, and other casualties included two officers killed (including Captain Parkinson-Cumine, missing presumed killed, who had served in 43 Commando in the Adriatic and Italy), and three officers seriously wounded. Eventually, nearly ten hours after leaving Koto-ri, the advance elements of Force Drysdale reached Hagaru-ri, to a warm welcome from the USMC. The rear of the convoy, supported by a second tank company, managed to return to Koto-ri.

The last vehicles to enter the four mile defensive perimeter at Hagaru [sic] were a 2½ ton truck and Heavy Weapons 30 cwt, both loaded with wounded and led by the Heavy Weapons officer. Force Drysdale had suffered 321 casualties and lost 75 vehicles. Less than 100 of 41 Independent Commando got through, and 61 became battle casualties [over a quarter of its original strength].[9]

All through the night, parties came in to Hagaru-ri having evaded the Chinese; some, unfortunately, shot approaching the perimeter. But the effort had been worthwhile, the force that reached Hagaru-ri was vital to the survival of that part of the Marine Division out on a limb and with the Chinese in overwhelming strength.

When General Almond was summoned to Tokyo, where MacArthur had decided that X Corps should withdraw to the Hamhung–Hungnam area as part of the general withdrawal of all UN forces across the whole of North Korea, he realized that for most of his Corps this would be reasonably easy, because the formations on the east coast were not engaged. For the 1st Marine Division, extended from Koto-ri to Yudam-ni, and surrounded in pockets by a total of seven Chinese divisions, it was very different. Yudam-ni was seventy-eight miles from Hungnam, eight from Hagaru-ri, and eighteen from Koto-ri. At X Corps headquarters there were gloomy forecasts that Yudam-ni and Hagaru-ri would be overrun by the attacks being mounted each night; evacuation seemed out of the question.

General Smith refused to abandon a single man. He ordered a withdrawal from one strongly held position to the next. As many wounded as possible were collected at Hagaru-ri and flown out from the air strip he had prepared in advance. Any equipment or weapons that could not be taken out would be destroyed – nothing would be left for the Chinese. Smith's iron will was responsible for what one author called, 'the basis for the legend of the retreat from the Chosin, perhaps the only really creditable American military performance of that winter campaign of 1950.'[10]

Beginning on 1 December, the 5th and 7th Marines at Yudam-ni had to fight their way south into the Hagaru-ri perimeter, clearing the road for their vehicles. They were supported by the US Navy and Marine Corps Air Wings from seven carriers. The US Marine pilots would never let down their fellow Marines fighting on the ground. The two regiments battled on in the bitter weather; battalions leapfrogging each other, under mortar and artillery fire wherever the enemy weapons could be brought to bear.[11] Even those Marine fighter-bombers that were tasked on other missions would keep some ordnance spare for a crack at the Chinese fighting their brothers-in-arms below. After checking in over the radio with the FAC on the ground, on arrival over the battle area, they would under his well-practised direction roll in and blast the enemy on the hillsides with cannon, rocket, and bombs. When low cloud made air support impossible the Chinese attacked the column, sometimes blocking the road for hours with wrecked vehicles. The first men of the Yudam-ni force entered the perimeter at Hagaru-ri on the afternoon of 3 December, the last on the evening of the 4th. Fifteen hundred wounded came in with the two regiments. Thomas:

> members of 41 Independent Commando who were privileged to go out to the perimeter to meet them [5th and 7th RCT] will have an abiding memory of the splendid US Marine Corps infantry marching into Hagaru [sic] alongside their wounded after fighting for a week in numbing sub-zero temperatures driven by the screaming north wind.[12]

A total of 4,342 wounded and severe frostbite cases were flown out of Hagaru-ri, including 25 Royal Marines, and 537 reinforcements were flown in. About 1,000 walking wounded and less severe frostbite cases remained, and many of both were detailed off as drivers for the next phase of break-out, releasing the original drivers as riflemen.

While 5th and 7th Marine Regiments were fighting their way south, Hagaru-ri was attacked by the Chinese Twentieth Army. 41 Commando was allocated the role of mobile reserve within the four-mile perimeter. Between midnight and 0630 hours on 30 November/1 December, a series of attacks managed to establish an enemy toehold on the perimeter on the south-east corner. 41 Commando was ordered to retake a key feature occupied by the Chinese, and Lieutenant G. F. D. Roberts was sent with B Troop, now down to twenty-seven all ranks, to G Company, 3rd/1st Marines, from where he would make his assault. G Company had come north with Force Drysdale. Roberts found the company commander, Captain Sitter, although wounded, still in command, but concerned that the Chinese would break right through in strength at any moment. The only reserve available to G Company was a dozen or so men of Battalion Headquarters under the battalion intelligence officer. Together Roberts and Sitter made a plan for fire support to B Troop. Just before 0400 hours, B Troop moved forward in the darkness, and assaulted the enemy position, taking it with grenades and small arms, losing three wounded in the process. Soon after the onset of daylight, the Marine Air Wing piled in on the Chinese ringing the perimeter. Unknown to the garrison of Hagaru-ri, the CCF had shot their bolt that night, their 58th and 59th Divisions taking about 5,000 casualties in two large scale assaults.[13] Sitter was later awarded the Congressional Medal of Honor.

41 Commando had already participated in other sorties from the Hagaru-ri perimeter, playing a full part in its defence, when on 6 December it was involved in the ten-mile fight out to the south. The divisional plan was for 7th Marines to lead, and 5th Marines with 41 Commando attached to form the rearguard.[14] Before moving, their USMC comrades noted with amazement that 41 Commando paraded shaved, with their weapons ready for inspection (some accounts include 'and with boots polished', but this was impossible because they were made of rubber). Smith had hoped to clear the whole of his division from the perimeter by nightfall, but darkness found the rearguard still fighting off the Chinese at Hagaru-ri, and 41 Commando had to move back into the perimeter to protect the artillery firing in support of the divisional advance guard; here they fought off the Chinese in the darkness, as they put in screaming attacks. Eventually the Commando could turn round and retrace its steps once again. As the rearguard left, they destroyed dumps of stores and ammunition. The Marine Division took their dead with them, to the fury of X Corps staff; but in a mood of sheer bloody-minded determination on the part of the US Marines that the entire division, dead or alive, would escape the clutches of the Chinese, they ignored Almond, whom they despised. As 41 Commando passed the blackened wrecks of trucks from Force Drysdale's battle on the way up to Hagaru-ri a week earlier, known as Hell Fire Valley, they recovered some of their own dead, and most welcome, at Koto-ri, Captain P. J. Ovens rejoined with seven members of HQ Troop, who had evaded capture when the Chinese had cut the column on 30 November. The journey by the 10,000 men of 1st Marine Division in the face of attacks by seven CCF divisions took thirty-eight hours to complete.

The division plus its various attachments at Koto-ri now numbered 14,000; 41 Commando's strength had been brought up to 150 all ranks by the addition of Ovens's team, and others that had managed to trickle in. On 8 December, in darkness and heavy snow, the breakout to Hungnam began. 41 Commando was tasked with holding the high ground overlooking the MSR during the night to guard against enemy infiltration.[15] The Chinese had blown the bridge over the thirty-foot wide gorge in the Funchilin Pass. The divisional engineer officer overflew the gap in a light aircraft, and proposed that bridging should be dropped in sections, by parachute, into the Koto-ri perimeter. Of the eight sections dropped, six survived the impact and were sufficient to bridge the gap. The Marines pressed on into the Hamhung perimeter held by I ROK Corps and the US 3rd and 7th Divisions, and the rearguard was complete by 11 December.

41 Commando arrived late on 10 December, having turned back to relieve 3rd Battalion 1st Marines in the Koto-ri perimeter, before resuming the twenty-three-mile march to the Hamhung bridgehead. From here the Royal Marines were taken in trucks and open railway cattle trucks to a tented camp in Hungnam '.... in a sea of mud but after a 23 miles march over the mountains and without sleep for 72 hours, we could not have cared less!' On the 12th, Colonel Drysdale noted, 'Whole unit embarked in USS *General Randall*, with remainder of 5th [Marine] Regimental Combat Team, 5,000 in a ship designed to carry 2,000 but it had sheets, baths and plenty of food'. They set sail for Pusan, and then Masan.[16]

The 1st Marine Division had come out fighting, bringing its wounded and most of its equipment. In the process it had inflicted a major defeat on the CCF.[17] The march to the sea became part of the USMC legend. Drysdale wrote in his report, 'the admiration of all ranks of 41 Commando for their brothers-in-arms was and is unbounded. They fought like tigers and their morale and esprit de corps is second to none.' For this action the 1st US Marine Division and attached units were awarded the Presidential Unit Citation. 41 Commando was not listed in the original citation, but subsequent representations by the US Marine Corps resulted in 41 Commando's inclusion.[18]

41 Commando had suffered 93 casualties, and was sent back to Japan to re-fit and re-train. Here, with its strength eventually raised to 300 by reinforcements, the Commando made preparations for a series of coastal raids. By now, the United Nations had been driven south of Seoul, had recovered, and were back near the 38th parallel, the original border of

North and South Korea. Here, or hereabouts, despite outbreaks of fierce fighting, the line stayed until the truce was signed in mid-1953. Operations here did not involve 41 Commando, and hence do not concern us. Raids on the west coast of Korea were mostly deemed impractical because of the large tidal range, so the majority of such operations were confined to the east coast, and attacks on the railway line.

The British official historian of the Korean War contends that the Commando was grossly misemployed. He gives as a reason:

> the local intelligence organisations were a law unto themselves. . . . and did not want the commando as a rival. Admiral Dyer USN was unwilling to allow Drysdale or his successor Lieutenant Colonel Grant, to engage in enterprises without the most detailed scrutiny and control of his plans. As a consequence, these highly trained Royal Marines were restricted to a handful of small reconnaissances and minor raiding tasks, performed in an exemplary manner and at minimum cost, and occasional fire control ashore for the daily bombardment of targets in the Wonsan area. Otherwise, they were stuck in garrison duty on the Wonsan harbour islands until December 1951, after which they returned home.[19]

After their gallant efforts with 1st Marine Division at Chosin, and in the epic march to the sea, the service of 41 Commando in 1951 might be seen as an anti-climax. It is not how members of the Commando see it themselves.

> It always seems a pity that the Chosin do has overshadowed our raiding role, which is what we were sent [out] for. 41 carried out 12 major (troop and above) landings on the enemy coastline, with a further nine smaller operations within Wonsan Harbour during our 16 months in-theatre. I don't know how this compares with WWII units, but I believe it was quite creditable.[20]

In the author's opinion, the record compares very well with units in the Second World War, being as good as any, and better than most.[21]

The first of the post-Chosin raids, a major affair at Sorye Dong, took place on 7 April 1951. The Commando was embarked in the LPD USS *Fort Marion* and the APD USS *Begor*; a cruiser and two destroyers provided gunfire support, and two carriers provided air support. First to land were D Troop in two LVTs, to establish the beachhead through which the Assault Engineers and remainder of the Commando landed. Earlier raids, both in Korea and in the Second World War, tended to attack culverts and bridges, which can easily be repaired, and tunnels, in which roof falls can also be repaired quite quickly – unless a train is caught in there which delays proceedings. At Sorye Dong it was decided to wreck a section of embankment, using over half a ton of TNT in sixteen bore holes to produce large craters, and repeating the process in the craters, blowing a gap a hundred feet wide and sixteen feet deep. On completion fifty-five anti-personnel mines were laid to catch the repair gangs. The Commando was ashore for eight hours, and although there were reported to be two divisions fifteen miles north of the beachhead, there was no enemy activity other than a few stray shots.

Following the Commando's return to Japan there was talk of a possible return to the 1st Marine Division. As by now the division was operating as a normal infantry formation in the line, it is hard to see how the lightly equipped Commando could have been used to advantage in a situation akin to First World War trench warfare. A radical reinforcement (to double its strength), reorganization and re-equipping programme would have been necessary to enable it to take its place in the line. Difficulties had been experienced before, and would again, with Commandos organized into troops of sixty all ranks relieving British infantry companies of over a hundred, and the rifle troops in 41 Commando were only about forty-five strong. US rifle companies were nearer two hundred strong. The problem might have been overcome by using the Commando as an additional divisional reconnaissance battalion with the US Marines, who understood these things, in contrast to a British division of the time, which did not.

In the end it was decided to keep to the raiding role for 41 Commando and for this purpose establish a base on Yo-Do Island, within Wonsan Harbour, some sixty miles behind enemy lines. Wonsan is a large natural harbour, some ten miles deep and five miles wide at the entrance. Much of the harbour had been swept of mines and United Nations ships patrolled regularly, bombarding, and dominating the whole sea area. Many of the islands were garrisoned by ROK Marines. 41 Commando's task was not only to garrison but to raid, and accordingly over the following months the rifle troops fanned out from the original base on Yo-Do to occupy bases on other islands.

The enemy, despite having lost control of most of the offshore waters, was not supine. The ROK Marine garrison on the island of Hwangto-Do some two miles off the coast was overwhelmed by an enemy raid from the mainland. The island was reoccupied by Lieutenant Walter and a force from D Troop, and used as a base from which to harass the mainland using the Commando's 81mm mortars and a 75mm anti-tank recoilless rifle (RCL). Fire controllers from Heavy Weapons Group also landed on occupied and unoccupied smaller islands, such as Umi-Do, which was only 300 yards from a troublesome battery of enemy 76mm guns used against bombarding ships. From their OPs the mortar fire controllers and naval gunfire observers would bring down fire on suitable targets; Umi-Do was too close, so when Lieutenant Thomas laid up on this island he drew a panorama, and sent this out to a carrier from which an air strike was launched on the enemy battery. He did not trust overhead fire from US Naval gunnery that close.

Canoe patrols from B and C Troops made six canoe raids on Hodo Pando, the peninsula forming the northern arm of the harbour. These raids were not without loss: Lieutenant Harwood and Sergeant Barnes were killed on one of them. A landing craft broke down and was driven ashore on the southern side of the harbour, and TSM Day of B Troop with four others were taken prisoner.

Two more raids were mounted from the *Wantuck*, both on the railway south of Songjin. The first was partially successful in that mines were laid on the road by which enemy troops moved by truck, and explosions were heard as the troop was withdrawing. But the railway was not damaged because the party detailed off to set charges in the tunnel was fired on, compromising surprise. It was assumed by 41 Commando that since the earlier raids, the enemy was having to divert increasing numbers of troops to guard the railway line. This assumption was borne out when the reconnaissance for the second raid, a repeat of the first, found the area heavily guarded, and the operation was aborted. Four raiders led by Lieutenant Walter in two canoes tried landing in the vicinity of Sorye Dong, the scene of the earlier success, and were fired on; again the raid was aborted.

Two raids on 30 November and 1 December between Songjin and Hungnam, both accompanied by the new CO, Lieutenant Colonel F. N. Grant, were similarly frustrated by opposition met on the beach. Operations in Wonsan Harbour continued, and plans were being made for raiding to continue for the rest of the winter. However, at higher level there were ill-informed comments along the lines that the Commando was wasting its time on defensive operations, and that raids would be impossible in winter. These statements ignored the fact that raids were already being conducted in winter, and that Grant was making plans to increase both tempo and punch with the assistance of some 800 ROK Marines who had been put under his command. If raiding in winter was difficult, it would not be expected by the enemy, so, following the military precept 'don't be predictable', much more could have been made of the raiding capability and expertise of 41 Commando had those at higher level with influence over the unit's future operations possessed a little imagination and intellect. An intelligent deception plan, perhaps painting the threat of using the whole of 1st US Marine Division to conduct major landings following up 41 Commando, might have tied down even more troops than the already large numbers pinned down by 41 Commando's efforts. Grant had begun conducting raids using the ploy of descending on the coast where the enemy was not present, by landing on difficult rocky sections, instead of the obvious, and consequently well-guarded, beaches. Without warning, the Commando was ordered to withdraw. The last raid by Walter and Dodd, now promoted to TSM since Palestine days, was Operation Swansong. On 15 December 1951, they paddled in canoes two miles up the enemy-held coast of Hodo Pando, and destroyed craft at Changguok Hang.

Opinions have been expressed that the Commando could have been used to better effect on the west coast by the British Task Force commander, Rear Admiral Scott-Moncrieff. One suspects that some of this may be generated by irritation on the Admiral's part at the Commando being under command of the US 7th Fleet instead of forming part of his 'empire'. The record of the raiding operations on the west coast does not bear out the contention that Scott-Moncrieff would have used them any better than on the east coast. However: 'As a consolation prize, he drew in the last of the Commando's reinforcement draft and attached its officers and men to his fleet Royal Marines.'[22] On which one can only comment, some consolation prize to be transferred from a Commando to a ship's detachment, to spend hours as a keyboard sentry, scrubbing decks, chipping paint, and polishing brasswork.

As a relief from these housemaidly tasks, the Royal Marine Detachments in the cruisers took part in bombardments and some raids on the west coast. Most of these were to seize prisoners for information, and to identify targets for bombardments. A US Army organization, codename Leopard, was responsible for running agents in North Korea and obtaining information on coastal defences. Its agent network never extended deep into North Korea, and in the opinion of Farrar-Hockley few of the American officers running Leopard had any experience of the work involved.[23] The term 'cowboy outfit' seems to fit them perfectly.

The Leopard chief controller asked the captain of HMS *Ceylon* (Captain G. A. Thring RN) to raid an area just to the north of Choppeki point to capture prisoners from an isolated detachment of the NKPA. A company was formed, consisting of two platoons of Ceylon's Royal Marine Detachment, and one of stokers. Accompanied by the destroyer *Charity* (Commander J. A. C. Henley RN) and frigate *Rotoiti* (Commander B. E. Turner RNZN), *Ceylon* ran in towards the beach, bombarded the target area for twelve minutes, and launched the first platoon in an LCVP she carried. The leading platoon landed without opposition, but as they moved inland to a position on a ridge from which to cover the remainder they were hit with mortar and small-arms fire. With support from the ships' guns, they withdrew to the beach, re-embarked and withdrew, taking their seven wounded with them. It is likely that this fiasco was the result of Leopard's information being faulty, or more likely a betrayal, since the organization contained several double agents. The main problem with many of the raiding operations both on the east and west coasts seems to have been a lack of coordination at theatre level to ensure best use of the assets and avoid conflict between the plethora of agencies and operators.

Those who had served over a year in 41 Commando were shipped back to England, arriving in February 1952. The Commando had achieved much, apart from earning the respect of the USMC, a legacy that continues to this day. Its raiding tied down large numbers of troops on the sole railway line on the east coast taking supplies from Russia and China to Communist troops fighting United Nations forces. Wonsan was a key road and rail focal point for north–south traffic, and the east–west road system. The enemy could not ignore the presence of 41 Commando sitting just off the coast and constantly raiding. Furthermore, during the numerous landings carried out by the Commando, the teams saw frequent signs of bombing and naval gunfire which had not damaged the target despite contrary, and often exaggerated, claims. Raiding was more positive, and reduced what is now called collateral damage. Experience shows that in all wars, right up to and including

Kosovo in 1999, air and naval gunfire bombardment rarely live up to the expectations generated by their practitioners; Korea was no exception.

In addition to the thirty-one dead, the Commando left twenty-nine as prisoners in Korea; for these the fight went on until mid-1953. Of these, nine were known to have died as POWs, and one was presumed to have done so. Eighteen were repatriated, and one, Marine Condron, who had been Lieutenant Pounds' radio operator, elected to remain. Falling into the hands of the North Koreans or Chinese was something for which no British or American serviceman had been given the slimmest of briefing or training. Recent experience was confined to the usually correct behaviour of the Germans towards POWs, and arbitrary bestiality of the Japanese. The North Koreans were brutal and lived up to their reputation, gained in Second World War Far East POW camps, as worse than the Japanese. The Chinese were better disciplined, and at the soldiers' level more humane than the North Koreans.[24] Neither was a signatory to the Geneva Convention, and they

> shared the view that military forces fighting against the Communist cause were by definition, war criminals, political sinners. But they were sinners who should be given the opportunity to be brought to repentance by political education to join the struggle against imperialism and the capitalist camp.[25]

POWs were subjected to incessant indoctrination, including 'confessions' to 'war crimes' in front of their comrades. The slightest lack of cooperation on the part of the POW was met with punishment, torture, food deprivation, and withdrawal of the already grossly inadequate medical facilities. Very few POWs escaped, and none from the camps in the very north of the country, where the majority were held. Great efforts were made to recruit POWs to the Communist cause. We should not criticize those who succumbed. Farrar-Hockley, the author of the official history of the Korean War, a POW himself, surviving two and a half years of captivity with great courage, and one of the leading lights in resisting, and escape attempts, wrote:

> Herein lay another stimulus to accept the captor's requirements: survival. Most prisoners had witnessed deaths on the march, and deaths in the camps due to lack of basic necessities. Those who had survived on starvation rations came to recognize that the captor had the power anytime to cut, even to withhold altogether, food. All dreaded becoming

sick because medical care was lacking everywhere except in special sites [where a very small number of POWs, mainly Americans, who co-operated fully were housed].[26]

Farrar-Hockley said of Marine Condron, who elected not to be repatriated:

He had a good reputation among his fellow prisoners. His genuine interest in Communism had never persuaded him to betray others – indeed he had often helped sick and wounded comrades. After some years in China, he returned home without any penalty.[27]

Marines Hicks and Murphy were awarded commendations for their exemplary conduct as POWs. Now, as a result of the Korean experience, the briefing of servicemen in conduct after capture is part of training.

On arrival back in Plymouth, 41 Independent Commando was disbanded, to be reformed in 1960.

22

Suez, 1956

Six weeks after the last British troops left the Canal Zone on 13 June 1956, the Prime Minister, Anthony Eden, told the Chiefs of Staff to prepare plans to return. This turn of events was brought about by Nasser's decision to nationalize the Canal, as a means of funding the building of the Aswan Dam, a project which the Americans, British, and French had refused to support. While the politicians negotiated, to try to find a way to counter Nasser's move, the British and French prepared a force to take the canal back into 'international control', effectively Anglo-French control. The hope was that Nasser would thereby be toppled from power. The Americans sat on the fence, more concerned with the Presidential election, in which Eisenhower was running for a second term, at the end of the year. Although 3rd Commando Brigade had been brought back to Malta from Cyprus, and 42 Commando sent out to join it from England, one of the main problems was the lack of sufficient amphibious shipping immediately available and in commission, for the brigade and all the necessary follow-up units. The AW Squadron still consisted of the headquarters ship HMS *Meon* and the LSTs *Anzio* and *Reggio*, two LCTs, and Motor Launch 2583, commanded by Lieutenant A. C. J. Sharland RM (the only Royal Naval vessel commanded by a Royal Marine officer at that time). Such LSTs and LCTs that remained from the Second World War, eleven years earlier, had been mothballed, sold, or scrapped. Time had to be spent gathering together and commissioning mothballed ships, and finding crews.

There were a number of other problems. Not until mid-September was it decided that the landings would take place in Port Said; until then Alexandria was the initial objective, followed by an advance to Cairo, and on to Suez after defeating the Egyptian Army. Eden rightly decided that a major battle in a large port followed by the occupation of Cairo would not be acceptable to world opinion. However, the Port Said option was second best in every way for a number of reasons, not least logistical. Once ashore at Port Said, the British and French would have to deploy down a causeway twenty-eight miles long and in places less than 300 yards wide, with a salt marsh on one side and the Suez Canal on the other, before they could move onto the desert for the last seventy-one miles to the southern end of the canal. Two roads (the Treaty Road and the Canal Road), one railway, and the Sweetwater Canal shared the space on this causeway; only one road was fit for tanks. Port Said was also seventy miles from Abu Sueir, the nearest airfield capable of accepting high-performance aircraft. General Stockwell, who had been appointed to command the joint Anglo-French land force, said: 'Port Said is like a bottle with a very long neck, and we will have to extract the cork and squeeze the neck before enjoying the rich juices of the bottle.'

The plan was pedestrian. First the British and French air forces would spend six days destroying the Egyptian Air Force on its airfields, a very necessary prelude to an operation of the kind being contemplated. On the seventh day an amphibious assault would be followed after half an hour by a parachute assault. All this was fair enough. The place selected, with everybody landing at Port Said, was not. Brigadier Butler, the commander of 16th Parachute Brigade, protested strongly and argued that a proper use of the parachute forces should be made by dropping his brigade at Ismailia, about halfway down the canal, and the French parachute force under General Massu at Port Tewfik at the far end, and landing the 3rd Commando Brigade and the French amphibious force at Port Said, all simultaneously. Thus all three main points on the canal would be seized at one blow. He was overruled because the Government were fearful that the British would overextend themselves. The Government appeared to have ignored the fact that the bulk of the Egyptian Army would be engaged with the Israeli army in the Sinai Desert, thanks to Franco-British collusion with Israel, described later.

Most of the equipment used by the 3rd Commando Brigade at Suez, along with all other British formations, was still of Second World War origin: the 1940 Sten gun and the bolt-action number 4 rifle were still in service. Major Billett, then a young acting corporal in A Troop, 40 Commando, remembers: 'It was ironic that we should land with the old No 4 rifle as we had been using the new 7.62mm FN rifle on operations in Cyprus.'[1] 106mm recoilless (RCL) anti-tank guns had to be borrowed from NATO stocks because the ammunition for the new anti-tank gun, the BAT, had not yet been cleared for use in hot climates. The Commando Brigade had no organic anti-tank guns (i.e., of its own) at this time, and 17-pounder anti-tank platoons from two infantry battalions were attached to two of the Commandos to provide an anti-armour capability. 45 Commando, which was to assault by helicopter (of which more later), was issued with 106mm RCL. A universal theme in many British reports following this operation is astonishment that the Egyptian Army was better equipped: for example, they had the Kalashnikov AK47. However, what the British lacked in equipment, they made up for in the quality of the men who were to carry out the assault. The commandos and parachute soldiers were fit, well trained, well led, and thoroughly worked up as teams after operations in the demanding terrain of Cyprus. With the élan and enthusiasm of their kind, they did not allow the problems to bear down too heavily.

The plan for the amphibious assault, made by Brigadier R. W. Madoc, the commander of 3rd Commando Brigade (who had been in the rearguard at Crete in 1941), had to be changed several times to keep in step with the overall scheme being produced by Stockwell. The brigade had carried out no amphibious training for nearly a year, and even that had not included exercising with tanks, naval gunfire and air support, LVTs, and helicopters. These supporting arms and equipment had to be included in rehearsals. A number of skills needed brushing up, including waterproofing vehicles, and fighting in built-up areas.

In 1956, only eleven years after the end of the Second World War, at least half of the troop commanders in the three Commandos, and the more senior NCOs, had battle experience in one of the theatres in that war, and some of them in Korea as well. Second Lieutenant N. F. Vaux had just joined 45 Commando on their return from Cyprus: 'My troop commander [Captain L. G. Marsh] had fought through World War Two, been wounded twice, and had the MC [earned in Korea]. The TSM had an MM, at least two of the troop sergeants had significant commando service.'

At first, as part of the 'land at Alexandria' option, 40 Commando rehearsed landings onto a four-foot-high quay along ladders from an LCT. Billett: 'On one occasion we climbed our ladders only to find US sailors on a ceremonial parade, who ran for their lives!'[2] Unfortunately the captains of ships were not allowed to be privy to the plans, and some objected to these seemingly strange manoeuvres. Mercifully this ploy was dropped when the Alexandria plan was discarded in mid-August. The amphibious assault had to be launched from Malta, because the harbour and port facilities at Cyprus were inadequate and the water too shallow for the larger amphibious ships. But both the French and British parachute assaults were to be mounted from Cyprus, so the troops, and, more important, the headquarters of the formations carrying out the two most critical parts of the operation were situated over 1,000 miles apart during the planning and rehearsal phases. The LVTs from the 1st LVT Troop, Royal Armoured Corps were driven by men recalled to the colours, who had last driven these vehicles at Walcheren and the Rhine crossing in the Second World War. Gathering together all the equipment and formations for the operation took so long that the force would not be ready until early September. The French 10th Airborne Division had to be extracted from operations in Algeria and shipped and flown to Cyprus, while the 3rd Commando Brigade and 16th Parachute Brigade had to be relieved on operations in Cyprus. Although the Parachute Brigade stayed in Cyprus, the soldiers had to carry out refresher parachute training in England. Finally, the RAF had only enough aircraft to drop one battalion at a time, and even that in two waves.

The plan was finally settled as follows: 40 and 42 Commandos would land either side of the Casino Pier at Port Said at 0645 hours local 0445 hours Zulu (GMT), H-Hour being thirty-five minutes after sunrise, 40 Commando landing left and 42 Commando right, with the leading two troops of each commando in LVTs, the remainder in LCAs. The landing was to be preceded by naval gunfire and air strikes to destroy and suppress beach defences. The French seaborne assault on Port Fuad, across the canal from Port Said, would start at 0700 hours local, followed by 3 Para dropping on Gamil airfield, west of Port Said, and 2ème Régiment Parachutiste Coloniale (2 RPC) dropping on Port Fuad, followed later by 1er Régiment Étranger Parachutiste (1 REP). 45 Commando was to land by helicopter in the area of the Interior Basin some two miles inland from the beaches over which the other two Commandos were landing, and three miles east of the DZ for 3 Para. 45 Commando's objectives included two bridges at Raswa which carried the Treaty Road and Canal Road, over a canal between the interior basin and the main canal, the only roads out of the top of the 'bottle' leading to the 'neck'. At least one had to be captured intact to enable the Franco-British Force to advance to seize Port Tewfik at the southern end of the canal. After 40 and 42 Commandos had established the beachhead, 6th Royal Tank Regiment (6 RTR, with Centurions) would land in support of the advance out of the beachhead: 40 Commando along the Bund, alongside the canal, to capture the four shipping basins, while 42 Commando advanced along the Shari Mohammed Ali (Mohammed Ali Street: in some accounts, Rue Mohammed Ali), the main road through the centre of town, to link up with 45 Commando. After that the three Commandos would each be responsible for controlling a part of the town. At least that was the grand conception.

The lift for 45 Commando was provided by the Joint Experimental Helicopter Unit (JEHU), consisting of six Whirlwind Mark 2 and six Sycamore Mark 14 helicopters, and eight Whirlwinds of 845 Naval Air Squadron (NAS). A full rehearsal could not be held in Malta because of security. Which, as this was the first time ever, in the world, that any unit had carried out an amphibious assault by helicopter against a live enemy, hardly made things easy for the CO, his officers, and men.

The SBS had originally been tasked to carry out reconnaissance of the beaches and provide terminal guidance – their traditional advance force role. However, in the end, possibly harking back to the abortive operation in which Emslie and Moorehouse had participated some four years earlier, it was decided that secrecy might be compromised if anyone was detected near the beach before D-Day. This was despite the fact that in the aborted Alexandria option the SBS had a far more risky task, a relic of the Second World War, to dive and cut the harbour boom, for which they practised diving to fifty or sixty feet on oxygen, and aimed to cut the wires securing the boom using special equipment developed for the operation by the Admiralty Materials Laboratory.

On 28 October, appropriately the day celebrated as the Corps birthday, in commemoration of the raising of the Admiral's Regiment on that date in 1664, the 3rd Commando Brigade was ordered to embark for yet another exercise. In twenty-four hours the 178 officers and 2,300 NCOs and Marines were embarked in the headquarters ship HMS *Meon*, eight LSTs, and nine LCTs, many out of reserve in the Clyde, and sailed from Grand Harbour the following day. Only when the ships did not turn to port on clearing Grand Harbour to head for the beach exercise areas but steamed straight on did the Marines know that the operation was on at last.

Once at sea, briefings began. Lieutenant Mayo RM, a twenty-year-old

National Service officer in Captain H. B. Emslie's A Troop, 42 Commando kept a diary:

> *Wednesday, 31st October*
> 10.30 am wardroom full of maps. We heard 5 minutes ago that we are definitely going in for an assault landing on Port Said. My outward reaction is one of studied indifference and mild discussion of whys and wherefores. Underneath there is a tautening feeling.

45 Commando sailed in the carriers HMS *Ocean* and *Theseus* on 2 November – being faster than the AW Squadron they would catch up. The remaining helicopters were embarked in *Theseus*. Vaux:

> We embarked on HMS *Ocean*, which had been adapted in a basic way for helicopter operations. Our troop's task was to take the bridges in the inner basin. If the Egyptians had their wits about them, we felt they would defend them in strength. We wondered how these flimsy looking helicopters, with inexperienced pilots would cope. Another problem was that during the five days on passage, we had to rehearse a lot of rudimentary things that nowadays would be commonplace in an LPH [Landing Platform Helicopter]. We had to work out the routes along which to move large numbers of men loaded down with equipment through long, narrow passages cluttered with pipes, and up through hatchways that have to be closed down in action stations, except for a small manhole-sized opening. Getting formed bodies of men on to the flight deck in the right order and time was quite difficult. On D-Day it seemed to work quite well.

In addition to the carriers taking helicopters, the Royal Navy provided two more to provide air support, *Eagle* and *Bulwark*, as well as two cruisers, *Jamaica* and *Ceylon*, and eight destroyers, *Daring*, *Duchess*, *Diamond*, *Decoy*, *Delight*, *Chieftain*, *Chaplet*, and *Chevron*. In addition the cruiser *Newfoundland* was stationed in the Gulf of Suez to provide fire support when the British and French arrived at the southern end of the canal. There were Royal Marine Detachments on all the carriers and cruisers. Supporting the French were one battleship, one carrier, and five destroyers.

By now the plan had been changed yet again. Madoc had been told by Stockwell that the helicopter assault on the two bridges was cancelled; the bridges would be captured by part of 2 RPC and a detachment of the Guards Independent Parachute Company with sappers from 16th

Parachute Brigade. 45 Commando would now be brigade reserve, landing by helicopter when ordered by Madoc into the beachhead, and
advancing on foot to link up with the parachute troops at Raswa.
Whether the casualties at Raswa had the helicopter operation gone ahead
would have been heavier than those suffered by the parachute soldiers in
the event is impossible to say. 42 Commando's task was also modified to
advancing only as far as the southern edge of the town to prevent
infiltration from the Arab quarter, or shanty town, and linking up with
40 Commando. These changes had to be communicated to the brigade
and the supporting ships, involving signals to some twenty ships in all.

The picture was further complicated by the collusion of France and
Israel in a joint plan, a plot which eventually the British joined. The
Israelis would invade Sinai, and when they approached the canal the
French and British would land to interpose between the Egyptians and
Israelis posing as peacemakers, thus occupying the canal. On 29 October
the Israelis started their advance. For public consumption both the
British and French governments expressed dismay and demanded that
the Israelis and Egyptians disengage immediately. The Israeli advance
went rather faster than planned, and by 4 November it became apparent
that there was every chance that it would close up to the canal before
the amphibious part of the Anglo-French force was within range of Port
Said, in which case the Egyptians might surrender, removing at a stroke
the need for a landing to interpose a force between them and the Israelis
in the name of peace; and furthermore, relieved of the necessity to face
the Israelis, the Egyptians might reinforce Port Said. In that event, and if
the British and French landing went ahead it might run up against more
than the three battalions, a few flak guns, the coast artillery, and four
SU-100 assault guns the Egyptians had in Port Said. The French and
British amphibious forces were at sea and the speed of the AW Squadron
was such that there was no chance they could land before 6 November.
Action was required at once. A bold decision was taken to drop the
British and French parachute soldiers just after dawn on 5 November.
They would be on their own for twenty-four hours and no friendly ships
would be within gun range. Without artillery, their only support would
be from the air, and the few mortars, machine-guns, and anti-tank guns
they could take with them. Stockwell had not known about the collusion
with the Israelis, so was taken by surprise at this turn of events. Had he
been forewarned, and with the knowledge that the Egyptians could not

possibly reinforce their forces in the canal area while fighting the Israelis at the same time, he might have agreed weeks before to Butler's plan to seize three key points at once, and the outcome of the operation might have been very different. The politicians, Eden in particular, were to pay for their deviousness and lack of trust in their military commanders. Unfortunately so were the British people and several soldiers and Marines.

At this juncture, it was decided at very senior level in Whitehall to limit the naval gunfire support to below 6in calibre, to minimize damage in the town. At one stage the dithering in high places led to doubts whether there would be any fire support at all for the seaborne landings. Madoc was told only sixty minutes before H-Hour that he would get naval gunfire support for his brigade. Some of the indecision was the result of efforts by Brigadier Butler and the French paratroop commander, Colonel Joubert, to arrange a ceasefire.

The parachute assaults on 5 November went well, and during the night of 5/6 November Butler and Joubert contacted the Egyptian commander at Port Said, El Moguy, promising that in return for the surrender of the garrison, the air strikes and naval bombardment planned for the morning would be cancelled. At one point it seemed that El Moguy would acquiesce. But at the last moment he got through to Cairo by telephone, despite Butler's efforts to cut all the lines, and was ordered to continue the fight. To bolster El Moguy, Nasser told him that World War Three had started, the Russians were raining bombs down on London and Paris, and thousands of Soviet troops were on their way to Egypt. The Soviet Consul in Port Said told El Moguy that he should turn the town into another Stalingrad, and hold out until the arrival of massive reinforcements of Russians, who would sweep the British and French into the sea. He was so convincing that El Moguy was persuaded to order that crates of Russian AK47 assault rifles be opened and issued to anyone volunteering to take part in defending Port Said.

Lieutenant Mayo's entry for 5 November included the thoughts:

Well there are only a few hours left now. We shall land at 0446. I am quite calm now. Pray God I many do whatever is needful at dawn, and in the day to come.

Later. Eight hours to go till H-Hour, and we have just heard that the

Egyptian C-in-C has asked for an armistice to discuss surrender terms. We are still at the moment to go in as planned, but I imagine the landing will be unopposed and we shall merely take over the town. I can't help admitting I am very disappointed. It's a dreadful anti-climax for all concerned, though I suppose for the sake of humanity one should be pleased. It is certainly a tremendous triumph for Sir Anthony Eden. This is the reaction after six days of preparing oneself psychologically to a battle frame of mind. Everything is very uncertain, and it is still quite possible there may be a fight. We shall soon see.

Meanwhile the amphibious force was approaching. Vaux:

I went up on deck to see the last gathering of major ships I ever expected to see, including a French battleship [Jean Bart], and several carriers. It was just daylight. I remember a breezy naval officer giving a running commentary over the Ship's broadcast, in a very up-beat way, saying that all was going well, and the enemy were running away.

The word about the cancellation of any naval gunfire support over 4.5in had not been universally well received. Billett in 40 Commando:

This change of plan upset some. I remember an argument with a National Service marine in the breakfast queue whether we should land or not – he hoped it would be called off – I told him that for once we were doing what we were paid for and he should concentrate on what he had been briefed to do – and support his mates. This was an odd incident, for the NS marines had done an excellent job in Cyprus and they brought a wide degree of skills to the Corps.

After breakfast we made our final preparations and were allowed on the upper deck to see the effects of the bombardment and air cover. The noise was incredible, as was the smell of spent propellants and burning oil from the refineries. Our Troop Commander, Captain R. H. 'Dickie' Grant pointed out landing point and first objective, before leading us down to the tank deck to embark in our LVTs. The bow doors opened and out we went into the noise of a full-scale amphibious invasion.[3]

Mayo started his entry for 6 November with:

Well, I appear to be still alive, though I rather think I am lucky to be so. Reveille was at 0215. Breakfast was not the tense, silent meal I had expected. In fact it was kidneys and bacon, and everyone almost light hearted. I really do think that most people were glad to be going in, though it was thought there would be little or no opposition, with talks of armistice and surrender.

Captain Oakley, commanding B Troop, 42 Commando, was scheduled for the leading wave of LVTs from the LST *Suvla*, with his two subalterns Lieutenants Hudson and Westwood, the latter a National Service officer. Later he wrote:

Only a handful of B Troop had seen action before, and one section consisted almost entirely of National Servicemen. Weapons were checked and ammunition distributed, many discovering for the first time how much live ammunition and mortar bombs weigh. The order was passed to go down to the tank deck to embark in our LVTs, each of which could carry 30 men, swim at about five knots and run up the beach on their tracks. Perhaps we would not get wet feet that morning.

Circling in our pre-positioned assembly area like so many ducklings around a mother duck, the marines whispering to each other, checking their watches. They showed 0425 hours and were set to Zulu Time (GMT) which made timings seem very unreal that day. I saw the LVTs of A Troop (Captain Emslie) joining our circle for it was fast approaching time for the run in.

The minutes ticked away and the sun's rays gathered strength. Then, suddenly with a roar that rent the Mediterranean stillness, the 4.5in guns of our supporting ship HMS *Decoy*, and her fellow destroyers opened up as she steamed parallel to the coastline. This was our signal to start the run in. Below my feet, I heard the LVTs engines roar into life as we started the approach – we were barely a mile offshore, but it would be only minutes before we touched down. Marines nervously fingered their webbing and equipment as they waited. We had been assured that there would be no mines on the beach, but it was not clear what Egyptian opposition we might meet. We knew we would have to overcome some five rows of beach huts, many of which we could already see burning.

To my left I could see the long line of Buffaloes [LVTs], firstly with A Troop, then with 40 Commando in the distance nearer to the town of Port Said. To my right I could see our two destroyers, *Decoy* and *Chaplet*, their battle ensigns taut at their masthead, almost obliterating their superstructure, their guns pounding the shoreline. I glanced eastwards towards the statue of de Lesseps guarding the entrance to the Suez Canal, not realising that this statue would be blown up by Egyptian dissidents within a fortnight.

With only 400 yards to go I could clearly see the shells landing on the beaches. A couple of Fleet Air Arm Sea Hawks swooped down from the cloudless sky and straffed the beach in front of us. With 100 yards to go to the waterline, I felt the LVT's tracks grind against the bar, grip the sand and majestically lift out of the water. We felt naked and exposed, a sitting target for any enemy near the beach. But the Royal Navy's sea and air bombardment had done its job and there was no resistance there. Above the din of the engine I could hear the occasional sniper shot and ricochet reminding us that this was no exercise. The bombardment now lifted to the second row of objectives.

The Sergeant Major ordered the rear ramp to be lowered as soon as we hit the beach so that disembarkation would be swift. Fifty yards short of the beach road we stopped and the marines felt the soft touch of sand on their feet. They fanned out into defensive positions prior to tackling their first objectives. Leslie Hudson's sections' first target was a large oriental building with a huge solid oak door. It was securely locked. Taking every possible precaution, Hudson ordered the assault engineers to lay a pole charge against the door. Retiring to a safe distance, the AEs lit the fuse and the door disintegrated in small pieces. As the dust cleared, a small dilapidated Egyptian, obviously the caretaker, emerged from a nearby ditch waving the key.

The Marines stormed the building, some clearing the ground floor, others taking the huge staircase in their stride. Next door Westwood's Marines were doing a similar job dealing with a large block of luxury flats.

It was now 0535 hours by our watches and we saw with much relief the tanks of 6 RTR roll up the beach. Our LVTs were being refuelled and mustered along the seafront road as C and X Troops passed through us to take the blocks of houses further inland. Many of our marines took the chance for a quick brew up as breakfast seemed an age ago. We had taken no casualties and the marines were in good heart. However, bad news was in store as an uncontrolled air strike mistook some of our supporting anti-tank gunners from the Somerset Light Infantry for enemy and strafed them with disastrous results.[4]

The run-in of 40 and 42 Commandos' LVTs and LCAs was preceded by ten minutes' bombing by RAF Canberras and strafing by Hunters. Two destroyers alone, *Diamond* and *Duchess*, fired a total of almost 1,400 rounds of 4.5in HE at the beach, and at H–5 the Fleet Air Arm struck the beach just ahead of the leading wave of LVTs. Although the leading wave of both Commandos was fired on as the LVTs ran in and clanked up the beach, there were few casualties. The machine-gunners in trenches under the beach huts may well have been taken by surprise, and shocked by the fire support, cowered in their positions. But some of them recovered when the follow-up waves came in, and there were casualties among troops landing from LCAs. However, the sight of tanks landing must have been too much for them and machine-guns found abandoned in the beach huts told their story – their gunners had legged it. A young officer of 42 Commando was bending over his dead Marine runner when he felt a kick up the backside, and his TSM told him to get moving, now was not the time to mope over his runner, that could come later. Fortunately the beaches were not mined. As related earlier, there had been no checks by the SBS before the landing for fear of compromise should the reconnaissance go awry.

40 Commando's objective was the complex of basins around the Canal Company offices, Navy House (once Admiralty property), and the Customs Houses. It was intended that follow-up troops and armour would be unloaded in these basins once secure. Captain Grant's A Troop and Major Willasey-Wilsey's X Troop of 40 Commando cleared their initial objectives, a block of flats and some buildings. Billett of A Troop, running in in an LVT:

> The Egyptian guns, which had started to range on us were silenced [by the bombardment], but not before one unlucky driver was shot by a direct hit through the small windscreen of his LVT.
>
> On the beach the ramp at the rear of the craft was lowered and we [disembarked and] took off at a smart pace after Sgt Reg Weeks through burning beach houses and across a large open area to our first objective. When we reached the first building I thought I had been shot as something hot and stinging nicked my neck. We cleared the buildings as we had been trained to do, but shooting locks off with a Mark 5 Sten is not to be recommended as you are in danger of getting your own back. When we had taken the building we covered P Troop as they took over the point and led the other troops from 40 Commando out of the beachhead.[5]

The second wave in LCAs, consisting of B, P, and Y Troops with Commando Tac HQ, came in on cue. Captain Morgan's Y Troop captured the Liberation Barracks south of the de Lesseps statue, while Captain Marston's B Troop cleared the Fishing Harbour area, on the outer end of the canal. With the Fishing Harbour clear the LCT *Bastion* carrying the attached anti-tank platoon, from 1st Battalion the Royal Berkshire Regiment,[6] landed their 17-pounder guns, towed by Stewart carriers. 11 Troop, C Squadron 6 RTR was soon ashore also, and Lieutenant Gardner's P Troop with the Centurions in support advanced as far as the Port Police Station. 40 Commando's advance continued with Captain Grant's A Troop being sent to release the British Consul from house arrest. The buildings en route had to be cleared room by room, followed by placing coloured air recognition panels on each roof to warn the Fleet Air Arm that they were now in friendly hands. The Consulate square was held by Egyptian infantry, and took some time to clear, killing twenty-three and capturing fourteen. Billett:

> The rest of that day was spent house fighting to clear the Egyptian army out of the buildings. It was nerve-wracking stuff, snipers and grenade throwers were everywhere. When you broke into a house it was hard to distinguish the soldiers from civilians. I remember vividly crossing from the roof of one building to another. The only way across was a brick wall nine inches wide and twenty feet long – that may not sound much – but we were about six stories up and under sniper fire at the time.[7]

Captain Morgan's Y Troop now took the lead, and, with tank support, cleared as far as the Suez Canal Administration Building. Captain Marston's B Troop pushed on past Y Troop and ran into stiff opposition in the Customs Houses. These consisted of long sheds with a warren of offices and cubby holes off the main corridor. Lieutenant McCarthy, leading the attack, was killed almost as soon as he entered the building. Lieutenant Ufton followed up, and was clearing through to the end of the building when he was also killed by an enemy soldier hiding in the last office to be searched. Seventeen Egyptians were despatched, two were wounded, and a third was found hiding in a cupboard.

Major Willasey-Wilsey's X Troop pushed on past B Troop to clear the rest of the Navy House Quay beyond the Customs Houses, supported by tanks. The Egyptians put up strong resistance, and an air strike was called in just before last light. Navy House was not finally cleared until midday the following day. Two officers and six Marines of X Troop were wounded in the fight, and seventeen Egyptians were killed and ten taken prisoner. X Troop raised HMS *Reggio*'s white ensign over Navy House. It was discovered that the basins and the approaches to them in the canal had been blocked by ships sunk by the Egyptians, so plans to use the basins for the main offload had to be cancelled. Instead, the Navy unloaded the LSTs in the Fishing Harbour cleared by 40 Commando early in the operation.

42 Commando's next task was to dash south through the town, to secure the Nile Cold Storage Depot and the Port Said power station on the southern outskirts. Oakley:

At 0630 [hours] we climbed back into our LVTs, this time leaving the rear ramps lowered for a quick exit if necessary. I was well aware that this phase would not be easy as the Egyptian Army, most of whom had discarded their uniforms for native djellabahs, were likely to have taken up sniping positions on the flat roofs of the taller buildings. While I was in the cockpit with the driver and his mate, the marines sat in the well of the LVT with their backs to the sides, facing inwards. David Westwood and Sgt Maj Casey, with a bren gunner, sat at the rear with their feet dangling over the ramp. The plan was to move with a Centurion leading, then my LVT, then a tank, LVT, and so on. B Troop led, with A and X Troops following with the CO's rover, the Vickers medium machine guns and some assault engineers. The land speed of the column was governed by the speed of the LVTs, about 15 mph.

With a roar of engines the snake-like column moved off along the sea front, turning inland down one of the widest streets in Port Said, the Shari Mohammed Ali. The time was still only 0645 [hours], and as we rolled into enemy territory, the adrenaline started to flow and nerves became tense. My leading tank, commanded by Lieutenant Peter Hetherington, a National Service RTR officer, seemed to gain on us and we felt unprotected.

Suddenly as we passed one of the many cross streets, there was a burst of machine gun fire, confirming that the enemy were still very much alive. The tall buildings on either side of the road seemed to engulf us and our eyes were on the roofs looking for opportunity targets. Another burst of machine gun fire hit the vehicle causing it to swerve momentarily, and a scream came from one of the Marines sitting in the well. Cpl Jim Peerless groaned and said 'I've been hit', and as he turned over the blood oozed from his buttocks. Only then it dawned on me what had happened. When we left Malta, such was the secrecy, that we had thought we were off on just another exercise. Each LVT had the facility for armoured plating to be lowered into the side skins of the vehicle, but that took several hours with a crane and was unpopular with the crew. The awful truth that the sides of the vehicle were not bullet-proof came as a severe shock to morale. The bullet that hit Peerless had come through sides like so much paper.

As we hurried through the streets that looked so serene in the morning light, there was a cry of 'grenades'. I looked up and saw the disappearing face of an Egyptian who had just thrown a grenade from some seven storeys up. His aim was impeccable and he judged the speed of our vehicle well. But luck was on our side. Instead of exploding in our midst, the grenade landed at the feet of my rugby-playing subaltern [Westwood], who kicked as the grenade hit him and rolled it into the road behind us. Splinters caught Sgt Maj Casey in the head. Our Royal Naval sick berth attendant bandaged him quickly and efficiently, but Casey was not amused that he could not wear his coveted green beret.

I could now see the Cold Storage plant in the distance, and beyond that our target as the cut-off troop [far troop to cut off attempts at infiltration]. I warned the marines to prepare to disembark, but to my horror the leading tank rolled relentlessly on. Suddenly it turned into the front gate of an Egyptian Army camp, which to my intense relief had been evacuated. As we came to a halt, the marines fanned out into defensive positions. As the engines were switched off, there was an uncanny silence. My signalman called up commando headquarters to report our situation, and I was relieved to hear that A and X Troops had taken their objectives against very spirited opposition, but snipers were still causing a nuisance. I tried to contact Hetherington in the leading tank, but he remained firmly locked inside. The training manual tells you that you call him up on the radio, but that did not work. The second immediate action was to use the telephone on the back of the tank, but after whirring the handle many times, no answer was forthcoming. As I gingerly climbed on to the tank to attract his attention, its gun fired and I was thrown back on to the ground. Eventually, I tried again, and this time Hetherington raised the hatch an inch and a half, and said, 'Sorry old boy, I think I've made a mistake'. He had indeed fired a round into the distant prison making a large hole through which, we learned later, many prisoners escaped.

Meanwhile Leslie Hudson had called for a casevac helicopter for the Sergeant Major, Cpl Peerless, and Mne Chaffey, who had also been wounded. Casey removed the dressing from his wound, put his green beret back on, and refused to go, saying he was quite all right. It is sad to relate that he was killed in Cyprus about six months later.[8]

A Troop's LVTs were the last in the line of vehicles in the dash down the Shari Mohammed Ali, except for a troop of tanks bringing up the rear. Mayo's LVT was slower than the rest, and got left behind, so the enemy was able to concentrate their fire on him:

A lot of windows held snipers, and side streets too. From them until we got out at the other end there was continual boil of fire. We kept shooting all the time, half the time not at anyone in particular, because moving as we were it was difficult to catch more than a fleeting glance of the Egyptians. However, it must have done something to distract them, and their aim must have been pretty poor. There was the continual crack of bullets passing by, but luckily it is difficult to tell just how close they are – lucky that is for our peace of mind. Suddenly in the middle of a lot of firing from a house on our right I felt a sharp sting on my right arm, just where it was bent at the elbow next to my side. The bullet slightly tore my [camouflage] smock and left a small red blister on my arm, without even breaking the skin. It must have passed about an inch in front of my body. There was no time to think of this, for at the same moment Thistleton and a sergeant of the Tanks [RTR] in command of the LVT, who were standing with me on the platform at the front, all three of us actually touching each other, both turned to me with a look of shock and surprise on their faces. Thistleton the bren gunner had been hit. The tank sergeant made a sort of inarticulate noise and pointed to his chest which was already soaked in blood. I shoved Thistleton in the bottom of the craft where someone started helping him. He was quite conscious and behaving terribly well, trying to refuse morphia, and insisting he drink only from his own water-bottle. He had a shot through his left shoulder, another in his chest which didn't seem to have come out, and a third in his thigh. The sergeant had been hit by what we afterwards discovered from a hole in the LVT to be a .50 calibre round in the right chest. I opened his shirt, put on a field dressing and gave him morphia. I thought he was dead then, or else he died in the next minute or so. I don't think he felt anything. My hands were covered with his blood, and I shall never forget the sweet, hot smell of it. It required an effort of will to stand up again from the comparative safety of kneeling down to deal with him, and the cowardly sense of relief it brought.

After X Troop had captured the power station, and A Troop, after a stiff fight in the markets, the cold storage depot, 42 Commando cleared the last remnants of opposition and went firm on its objectives. Mayo had another lucky escape, clearing an office building:

I was standing in the hall, when a burst of fire came through the door of a room just up a corridor, in which it seemed three or four Egyptians had locked themselves in. Marine Ditchfield had a pocket of his smock ripped out by a bullet which didn't touch him. Someone tried to throw a grenade through a stove-in panel [in the door], but hit the top of the door with it, and it bounced back into the passage. There was a marked increase in activity, and somehow every body managed to get behind a corner somewhere before it went off. As second one was thrown in but failed to explode. A third followed. I was waiting for the explosion, when suddenly it appeared on the floor a couple of yards away rolling gently towards me, having been thrown out by the Egyptians – a good effort on their part I must say. With a four second fuse that didn't give me much time, and I was diving for the floor, when it went off. Simultaneously I felt a sting on my left cuff, and a fairly healthy sort of crack on the back of my head. I put my hand out, and when I failed to find my brains gushing out realised it was nothing very bad, though there was a fairly convincing stream of blood. Someone told me to get behind the hull of the tank, and Doc Milton [troop medic] fixed me up with a field dressing. It wasn't hurting at all except in a sort of incidental way. I had been hit a glancing blow which had merely sliced open a chunk of scalp, and started a much needed haircut. I discovered a rather more purposeful looking bit later that night in my breakfast [ration pack], having gone through my pack and one mess tin. An inch lower and it would have been that far into my back.

I suppose I must have looked rather worse than I was, as when I said I would go upstairs with 1 and 2 sections to clear the rest of the house, I was told rather brusquely by Hamish [Emslie] to stay where I was. The characters in the locked room had been dealt with by an 80 (phosphorous) grenade.

Meanwhile the clearing went on. Mayo:

The TQ [TQMS] 'Lofty' Impett was hit in the side, luckily not too bad a wound, the bullet having followed round the ribs and come out again. He was carried in and remained in good spirits till later in the afternoon when he was evacuated by LVT.

45 Commando, Madoc's floating reserve, was called in from *Ocean* and *Theseus* at H+55 minutes. The CO, Lieutenant Colonel Tailyour, flew in ahead of his Commando to reconnoitre the intended LZ, a sports stadium. As the helicopter settled down in a whirl of dust Tailyour got out, when it became clear to him that the LZ was under small-arms fire, of which the pilot was blissfully unaware, being unable to hear any

external noises thanks to his 'bone-dome' and earphones. The pilot was about to take off when Tailyour scrambled back in, just as enemy infantry started closing in. He switched the LZ to the open ground near the de Lesseps Statue, near the outer end of the canal, on ground already cleared by 40 Commando.

The troops jammed into the scratch collection of helicopters used by 45 Commando took up every available space. Each of the ancient Sycamores could carry three men. Two sat with their legs dangling outside, each cradling a 106mm anti-tank round. One sat in the middle, holding on to the belts of his comrades, to prevent them pitching headfirst out of the helicopter. Between his legs were six mortar bombs. The Whirlwinds, without seats or doors, to save weight, and with minimum fuel for such a short flight, could just stagger off the deck with six men in each. With them, on an unofficial visit, and unknown to the Chiefs of Staff and others in the hierarchy in Whitehall, came the Commandant General Royal Marines, General Sir Campbell Hardy – determined to be there, as over a third of the Corps was at Suez.

Vaux remembers that just before he boarded his helicopter the officer who had hitherto been giving an optimistic running commentary on the ship's broadcast changed the tone of his remarks.

He ominously declared that, 'the first wave ashore should expect heavy opposition'. A few minutes later off we lumbered, and a few minutes later we were on the beach. When you land in sand you see nothing at all, just whirling dust and noise from the rotor blades. It can be very disorientating, and we were doing this for the first time. We got out, and ran forward away from the helicopter, and went to ground as we had been trained. When the dust cleared, I looked up and saw a pair of feet, obviously belonging to someone standing looking down on me as I lay there. I realised from the puttees he was wearing he must be British. In fact it turned out to be my friend Roger Learoyd the Brigadier's assistant. He said, 'How nice to see you Nick, get your chaps up and walk to the road and you will find everybody's waiting for you.' We mustered on the main boulevard and could hear shooting ahead and to the side, so clearly the war was still on.

Despite the helicopters being capable of carrying only tiny payloads (by today's standards), 415 men and twenty-three tons of stores were landed in eighty-three minutes. The losses of helicopters was far less than the planned ten per cent. 45 Commando was ordered to move to the west, to the right of 42 Commando, towards the shanty town and a link up with 3 Para advancing from Gamil airfield. As they were moving along the main boulevard, Vaux's troop was alongside Commando Tac HQ:

> I noticed that there was considerable friendly air activity overhead, and felt very reassured. I saw a FAA Sea Fury flying low towards us, I thought he was encouraging us; going to do a victory roll or something. He comprehensively straffed my troop, and the Cdo HQ. Several people were killed, the CO Norman Tailyour was badly wounded. We were thrown into confusion, demoralised, and deeply shocked; it was a frightening and devastating experience. Whether the pilot had been given the wrong co-ordinates or just mistaken us for enemy, I don't know. Subsequently, we discovered that he had queried his instructions several times. It was also one of those moments when order is either restored or you lose it altogether; and is when training and leadership count for so much. I remember the Adjutant [Captain E. G. D. Pounds], realising that his CO and other officers had been badly wounded, and seeing that the CO's signaller had been mortally wounded by a cannon shell, turning to a marine and saying, 'Take the radio set off Marine Fowler, put it on and come with me'. This made everyone realise this is what you had to do, you had to get on with it.

The air strike had caused seventeen other casualties besides the CO, who remained in command for a while, but was then evacuated under protest back to HMS *Ocean*. Some of the less experienced Marines in the follow-up waves waiting on the flight deck were somewhat shocked that their first sight of a wounded man should be their own CO.

Among the wounded were men in 7 Section, B Troop, one of them a National Service Marine who recalled:

> Cpl Mike 'Sticks' Mead grazed on the thigh, and Lofty Sharplin with a minor wound, were the lucky ones. More unfortunate were Johnny Gotobed and 'Tuffer' Smith with hospitalisation wounds; but most unlucky of all were myself and Errol Ireland whose leg injuries resulted in amputations. 'Sticks' carried on with the aid of a first field dressing, but was later snaffled by the SBAs, and was hustled back aboard the carrier to rejoin his wounded comrades. To say that he was annoyed would be an understatement, but he was later awarded the Military Medal for his bravery that day.[9]

Meanwhile 45 Commando, now under Major R. Crombie, advanced.
Vaux:

We moved forward, entered the grounds of Government [Governate on
some maps] house which looked just like you would expect a Government
house to look like; immaculate lawns and raked gravel. Just as I was
looking at this, round the corner appeared what looked like an immaculate soldier with a rifle over his shoulder; actually I suppose he was a
Government House guard. I realised he was coming to report to me. The
corporal of the nearest section was hell bent on killing him. I prevented
that. He did speak some English and handed over Government House to
me. It was deserted and totally untouched. As I was walking through the
hall, the phone rang, it was irresistible, I picked it up and a muffled voice
in Egyptian spoke to me. I apologised for not speaking Egyptian. But said
if he could speak English may be I could help.

He said, 'you are English?'

'Yes', I replied.

'You are soldier?'

'No, I am a Royal Marine actually'.

He said, 'My God', and put the phone down.

After that things got a bit more serious, and we moved into town, and
got into some quite hard street fighting. What made life infinitely easier
for us was the armoured support of 6 RTR. The tanks could use their
smoke, machine gun fire and main armament to help us get on. You
could talk to the tank commander on the telephone on the back, rather
than on a useless radio which kept breaking down. The tank commander
who was a World War 2 veteran kept on saying 'Isn't this fun. For God's
sake this is what we should all be doing'. I didn't want to say, but felt
'this isn't fun for us behind the tanks with bullets whining all round us'.
We advanced to the end of the more sophisticated part of Port Said and
halted on the outskirts of Arab town, a huge, sprawling mass of shanties,
and small houses. We secured for the night. In order to form a proper
defence, we withdrew to the middle of the European part of town. Many
European, mainly French, people who were still in the houses in the part
from which we had withdrawn, pleaded with us to stay. Several of them
were massacred in the night. All of that part of town was looted. There
were sporadic attacks by Egyptians. Afterwards we found plenty of
weapons and ammunition, of which there was no shortage. The town
caught fire in parts. Some of the police horses got out, and ran terrified
up and down the streets.

Mayo:

We ate a meal when it was just dark, our first since 2.30 that morning, but even so we were more thirsty than hungry. We only had our water bottle, and had to watch that, as it was uncertain when we would be able to get more. The local taps were all dry.

The plan for the break-out from Port Said on the morning of 7 November involved an advance guard of 2 Para, who had landed from LSTs in the Fishing Harbour on the afternoon of the 6th, and a squadron of 6 RTR driving south over the Raswa bridges at best speed. The battalion would be followed by General Massu, in overall command of the main body, some on the road, and some in craft on the Suez Canal. Waiting in Cyprus was the 3rd Battalion of 2 RPC, ready to drop since first light that day on Qantara, a third the way down the canal, and the whole of 1 RPC to drop on Ismailia, halfway down, once the advance got under way. The squadron of 6 RTR, but without 2 Para, crossed the bridges at Raswa, advanced to El Tina, about fifteen miles south of Port Said, and waited.

The advance had taken a long time to wind up. Stockwell had reserved to himself the right to order the breakout, but the previous day the Egyptian Garrison commander, El Moguy, had approached Brigadier Madoc asking for a ceasefire. Madoc said he was not empowered to agree to one unless the conditions set by Butler the previous night (including a complete surrender of weapons) were adhered to, and sent him to the Italian Consul to negotiate the terms. The position was further confused on the evening of 6 November, when Eden lost his nerve and announced a ceasefire before the terms had been agreed on the ground by the commanders on the spot.

Oakley heard about it from his CO when he reported that there appeared to be no enemy to the south:

> we learnt with dismay that a temporary cease-fire had been ordered by our government back in London. We felt deflated and let down as we knew we could complete our aim of taking over the whole Suez Canal. Leaving A and X Troops in position, I rather sadly led my troop back down the Shari Mohammed Ali to the beach houses, still being made uncomfortably aware that no-one had as yet told the Egyptian sniper of the cease-fire.[10]

Mayo had also heard on the evening of 6 November, when

at about 1030 [2230 hours], Hamish shouted over from the main building
that an armistice and cease-fire had been agreed on at the highest level
for all active forces in the Middle East. This was to come into effect at
midnight.

At 0900 hours on 7 November, Stockwell came ashore by boat with
his French Deputy Commander, General Beaufre, to assess the situation.
After nearly being shot when he was landed in the wrong place, he made
his way to Madoc's headquarters. Here he borrowed a vehicle to drive to
the Italian Consulate, where he understood the surrender negotiations
were to take place. The Egyptians did not turn up. Unfortunately he
spent so much time on these fruitless surrender negotiations, out of
touch with his two brigade commanders, Butler and Madoc, that the
moments seeped away.

Politically, Eden had already pusillanimously sold the pass, thereby
attracting the ordure for no visible gain. But all was not lost. Provided
Eden had kept his nerve, and using the excuse that the Egyptians had
not agreed to a ceasefire, there were a number of military options to
enable Stockwell to carry on and finish the job. Possibly the best of these
would have been to order either 2 Para or 45 Commando to be lifted by
helicopter to El Tina to marry up with 6 RTR. Indeed an opportunity
had been lost the day before; instead of tying down 45 Commando
clearing the town, the LVTs could have been used to take the commandos on to El Raswa, leaving the town clearing to 1 Para, who having
arrived off Port Said in ships were sent back to Cyprus to prepare for a
follow-up parachute operation. Eventually 2 Para motored down the
road to El Tina to find the 6 RTR Squadron leaguered up for the night.
A swift altercation took place between Lieutenant Colonel Bredin and
the squadron leader before the Centurions were moving. Bredin wanted
to make Qantara before he had to stop, but was halted at El Cap.

Many Marines in the 3rd Commando Brigade first heard of the
ceasefire over the BBC World Service before they were told officially, but
by whatever means they were told, there was a general feeling of disgust.
Everyone was totally confident that, within three or four days they would
recover the canal, and utterly defeat the Egyptians. Vaux:

> We were told we would be relieved by the UN in a few days. However,
> there was law and order to be maintained. By now the French had come
> across from Port Fuad. Because I could speak French I was seconded to

the French Foreign Legion for a couple of days. This was fascinating because in those days the troops were mainly German World War II veterans, who had been fighting in Indochina and Algeria. They were the most experienced troops I have ever met. Not all their officers had so much experience, but they were all from the top of the class from St Cyr. Their discipline was different from ours, informal, but hard, if you did not pull your weight. They were clear that the priority was protecting themselves, and that everybody else, including civilians, came a long way second. They did not believe in minimum force. I was with a company who were issuing flour to the civil population. When it looked as if a riot might start as the crowd jostled for their rations, the French company commander spoke to his Sergeant Major, and his men immediately shot six people who were identified as stirring up trouble. It sorted the problem out. When I gently remonstrated with the company commander, he said, 'which would you rather have. Kill a few now, or more later?' It was a difficult question to answer.

We eventually began to patrol a road quite far south of Port Said, near where the road came in from Cairo. As I was travelling south to relieve another troop on a road alongside a lake [Lake El Manzala], I heard firing ahead. When I queried this over the radio to Commando HQ, I was told to get on with it, and stop being difficult. When I arrived there certainly was a problem, the troop were firing at two small dhows, across the lake; claiming that they had been fired on first. Although by the time I arrived, there was no fire in reply from the boats. Our Egyptian interpreter hailed the boats, and discovered that the passengers were European, and some were women. They were all journalists, so it turned out. We had to wade out to the boats, where we discovered that two of the Egyptian crew were dead. Among the passengers was a truculent American woman reporter, who promised to report the incident to the President of the USA personally. There were also two Russian journalists who, convinced that they would be shot without further ado, clung to the others. We carried them all carefully ashore on our backs. We subsequently had to have a comprehensive course of injections because the Sweet Water Canal through which we had waded, is a misnomer if there ever was one.

A Troop 40 Commando had similar experiences of the hard-nosed crowd-control methods of the French. Billett:

We were joined later that day by a troop of AMX 13 tanks of the French Foreign Legion. We provided infantry protection for them in patrol operations which included a memorable food riot. Hanging on to an

AMX 13 as it raced through the streets had not been covered in our infantry/tank co-operation training, but we were quick learners. The Legionnaires were quite ruthless; they aimed their tanks straight at a crowd of rioters – who quickly got out of their way. We then dismounted and drove them off the street at bayonet point.[11]

After keeping law and order in Port Said, the two assault brigades, 3rd Commando and 16th Parachute, were relieved by infantry battalions and left for Malta and Cyprus over the period 14 to 28 November, 42 Commando being the last assault unit to leave. To this day the Suez operation is frequently tagged a military fiasco. It was nothing of the kind. It was a political fiasco. The servicemen did all that was asked of them, reacting swiftly to changes of plan resulting from indecision in high places; committed to battle with obsolete equipment, the result of indifference and parsimony by ministers, Socialist and Conservative alike. Eden, having decided to topple Nasser against the advice of his Chiefs of Staff, did not have the will to see it through. Britain's standing in the world, and with the Arabs in particular, plummeted. British casualties were 22 killed and 97 wounded. Of these, the Commando Brigade had 9 dead and 60 wounded; some of the latter would have died had they not been casevaced to the ships by helicopter. The French lost 10 dead and 30 wounded.

Let a Royal Marine have the last word:

Dickie Grant had trained A Troop hard. For us 'The Saints' (so called because Leslie Charteris was the favourite author of Captain Mike Ephraums MC RM who was killed at Termoli in 1943 while commanding A Troop), the pay off was that we sustained only minor casualties. My pay off came later. I was promoted to corporal.[16]

23

Somewhere East of Suez, 1960–1968

Ship me somewheres east of Suez, where the best is like the worst,
Where there aren't no Ten Commandments an' a man can raise a thirst:

Rudyard Kipling

COMMANDO CARRIERS AND LANDING SHIPS: BATTLES IN WHITEHALL

To understand some of the background to the struggles for the survival of the Royal Marines and Amphibious Warfare after Suez, and the procurement of the amphibious ships which played, and still play, such a significant part in the life of the Corps, it is necessary to interrupt the narrative and briefly cover the paper battles that took place, mainly in Whitehall, in the late 1950s.

When Moulton finished commanding the 3rd Commando Brigade in 1954, he became the Major General Royal Marines (MGRM) at Portsmouth. Mindful of his experiences as Commander 3rd Commando Brigade, and the deficiencies of the AW Squadron, and being the man he was, he was determined to improve the Amphibious Warfare capability rather than be content to sit back in what was a not too demanding job in agreeable surroundings. His attention was drawn to the US Navy's decision to convert the carrier *Thetis Bay* into a helicopter carrier (in American: Landing Platform Helicopter – LPH) for use by the USMC. Moulton credits Ronnie Hay, who had been Vian's air wing commander in the East Indies and the Pacific, and had subsequently transferred to the Royal Navy, with suggesting that the British should do likewise. Moulton formed a special team, which included two of his staff officers, both of whom had distinguished records as pilots in the Second World War, to examine the concept. Moulton had been in the Fleet Air Arm pre-war, so he and his ex Fleet Air Arm officers could 'talk air language to the Headquarters of Flag Officer Air (Home), at Lee on Solent', just across Portsmouth Harbour from Moulton's own headquarters, and joint studies by the two headquarters took place. Moulton:

> laid on a fictitious [classroom, or cloth model] exercise as an operational demonstration of how an actual problem in Arabia could have been handled with an LPH. We produced it at all the staff colleges, and in Whitehall attended by the First Sea Lord and CIGS. At Camberley we were met with criticism from the Commandant, Nigel Poett, protecting the airborne role, and saying the helicopter was very vulnerable.[1] As Marines we were lucky to have access to the Fleet Air Arm. The RAF didn't like helicopters in those days.
>
> The second round of these exercises coincided with the Suez operation, and of course helicopter operations were carried out there. The operation helped push on the LPH idea very well. At Port Said the helicopters were used [*unimaginatively* – author] as 'flying landing craft'. My concept was deeper penetration. The Whirlwind was a primitive stop-gap, but I knew that the Wessex helicopter was on the drawing board. I visited Yeovilton and Westlands on a number of occasions, and based my ideas on the Wessex. The USMC had used helicopters in Korea, and had already commissioned the first LPH. The French had used helicopters in Algeria, and I consulted them. My concept was to avoid landing where the enemy were located in strength.

Eventually, in 1957, the Admiralty, influenced by the success of the helicopter landings at Suez, approved the conversion of the light fleet carrier HMS *Bulwark* to what was originally called the Commando Carrier, then Commando Ship, and finally, some years later, the LPH. In 1961, the conversion of an additional light fleet carrier, *Albion*, was approved.

In September 1957, Moulton went on to become Chief of Amphibious Warfare (CAW) in the Ministry of Defence, where he reported direct to the Chief of the Defence Staff and was in an altogether more powerful position to exert influence on behalf of the Royal Marines than as

MGRM Portsmouth. When he visited the first amphibious exercise carried out by *Bulwark*, landing 42 Commando into the Libyan desert (still a friendly country and where British troops trained), the 'enemy' were provided by an armoured car squadron. In his opinion, the armoured cars, with their longer range weapons and mobility, would have won. As a result he persuaded the Vice Chief of the Naval Staff that artillery should be attached to Commandos; thus the Commando gunner idea was born.

He did not find his task as CAW easy. The three single-service headquarters were still very independent, and not interested in Amphibious Warfare. Moulton:

> The Army had two jobs: post-colonial and the British Army of the Rhine (BAOR). The former took priority in their affections, they clung to the garrisons, and bases tenaciously. The Amphibious Warfare concept and carrier task forces were rivals and a threat to the Army's aspirations to hang on to these garrisons. The Director Royal Armoured Corps was only interested in BAOR.
>
> Several views prevailed in the Royal Navy.[2] The overwhelming majority were pre-occupied with anti-submarine warfare (ASW) in the North Atlantic. The LPH was irrelevant in this context. The politicians on the other hand viewed the Royal Navy as useful for policing the withdrawal from Empire, which was popular with the Fleet Air Arm, [*and in some respects played into the hands of the Amphibious Warfare lobby* –author], but not with the ASW fraternity.
>
> The RAF had the deterrent, the V Bombers, which were viewed by them as a continuation of the Trenchard strategic bombing vision. The RAF also took the line that any small-scale intervention would be by air.

Furthermore, in their efforts to 'dagger' the Royal Navy in general, and carriers and the Amphibious Warfare concept in particular, the RAF was not above discreetly rearranging the geography of the Indian Ocean to support its argument that it could move aircraft and troops to any part of the Far East and Western Pacific from a string of air bases stretching from Cyprus, via Aden, the Maldives, and Australia. Suez, according to Moulton, got Amphibious Warfare 'a bad name'. The vision of the AW Squadron chugging along to Port Said was at odds with the 'glitzy' artist's impressions of transport aircraft in the calendars and other sales material produced by the aircraft industry which the airmen plugged on all possible occasions.

Moulton saw that any new amphibious ships must be large enough to carry troops as well as heavy vehicles, including tanks, and equipment. They must also have the speed and range to operate with units of the fleet, particularly the LPH. Soon after he became CAW, he was authorized by the Vice Chiefs of Staff (V/COS) to carry out design studies in conjunction with the Director of Naval Construction for possible future amphibious ships. In Moulton's view the answer lay in the Landing Platform Dock (LPD), a British invention; although none had been built in Britain, the USN had used them in the Pacific, at the tail end of the Second World War. By the late 1950s, according to Moulton, 'no one in Whitehall had heard of them'. He was able to interest the Army's Director of Movements in the concept of moving tanks about by sea, but not, perversely, the Director Royal Armoured Corps. In the end, with much encouragement by Moulton, the Director of Movements' staff designed the Landing Ship Logistic (LSL), originally for Army use. This had a beaching capability so that it could be used as a follow-up ship in an opposed landing.

By 1959 the concept of LPDs working with the LPH was a feature of Amphibious Warfare presentations given by the Amphibious Warfare HQ (AWHQ), at the Joint Services Amphibious Warfare Centre, but as far as the British were concerned LPDs existed only in the imaginations of the presenters. Although there was support in many quarters for the renewal of the UK's amphibious shipping, there was also a substantial body of opinion in Whitehall which strongly discounted any future requirement to land tanks or any heavy equipment across a beach, against opposition. After two years as CAW, Moulton was becoming depressed at the failure of the Joint Planners in Whitehall to produce an agreed paper on the priority, if any, to be given to Amphibious Warfare. Even Mountbatten, the Chief of the Defence Staff, was not convinced that the LPD was necessary, and Moulton was contemplating early retirement when he had, in his own words, 'two strokes of luck'.

At the beginning of 1960 the Chiefs of Staff decided to move the AW Squadron to Aden to be on hand to lift tanks to Kuwait in the event of Iraqi aggression. Moulton persuaded the C-in-C Middle East (an RAF officer) of the advantage of stationing a half squadron of tanks afloat in an LST at Bahrain. This seaborne tank force proved particularly valuable when President Kassim of Iraq threatened Kuwait in July 1961 (as described later), because two LSTs with tanks embarked happened to be in Bahrain for the changeover at the time. The second stroke of luck, and the clincher in obtaining permission to build the LPDs (*Fearless* and *Intrepid*), was a brilliant thirty-minute presentation laid on by Moulton to Harold Watkinson, the Minister of Defence (at his invitation), and the Chiefs of Staff. He included a US Marine in his presentation team to give the audience ten minutes' worth on what the Americans were doing. In his words:

> This was the turning point. Mountbatten [*still not a convert*] was CDS, Watkinson was courteous and receptive [*unlike his predecessor Duncan Sandys (pronounced Sands) – known to servicemen as 'shifting Sandys'*]. Charles Lambe was First Sea Lord. In the absence of the Chief of the Air Staff, his Vice-Chief did not dare depart from his brief, and the CIGS [Chief of the Imperial General Staff] was Frankie Festing who had commanded 29th Independent Brigade at Diego Suarez in the Madagascar operation. The Chiefs of Staff were taken aback by what the USMC were doing. The Chiefs were unaware of the technology of Amphibious Warfare in 1959, and still thinking in terms of 1944. There had been no study of Inchon in the UK – nobody was interested.

The presentation did much to shift the logjam in Whitehall. Moulton seized the initiative, bypassed the system, and sought approval from the V/COS individually, for AWHQ to submit their own paper on Amphibious Warfare, including a requirement for the LPD. The paper was approved in Whitehall quite quickly, and Moulton's determined and persistent advocacy was rewarded when the subsequent Defence Estimates included the first LSL, RFA *Sir Lancelot*, and first LPD, HMS *Fearless*, to be commissioned in 1965. Without the amphibious ships, there would be no amphibious role for the Royal Marines. Thus the Royal Marines today owe their continued existence in great part to Moulton; as doughty and wily a fighter in Whitehall as he had been on the battlefield.

On 14 March 1960, 42 Commando embarked in HMS *Bulwark*, the first LPH, and she sailed for the Far East, conducting trials in the Mediterranean on passage, the first of which Moulton witnessed, as related earlier. By this time 41 Commando had started to re-form, and the raising of a fifth Commando, 43, was authorized. Both were to be based in the UK. Although both deployed out of the country on exercises, and in 41 Commando's case briefly to East Africa, and later to the Mediterranean and Northern Ireland, neither figured in the East of Suez years 1960 to 1971, in which the other three Commandos played such key roles.

Throughout the 1960s the LPH was a most valuable amphibious asset, even though some captains regarded the embarked Commando as a large ship's detachment, or at best 'the main armament' to be directed by him. Although uttered with the best intentions by naval officers, this phrase was merely a version of Fisher's dictum 'the Army is a projectile to be fired by the Navy'. Whereas in fact the LPH, and every other amphibious ship for that matter, is *in support* of the embarked force, however large or small, and, within the limits of navigational safety and operational common sense, exists solely to enable the embarked force to engage in the battle ashore to a plan designed by the land component commander, or landing force commander. Most of the problems were ironed out by mutual goodwill, but resurfaced again from time to time, and no doubt will continue so to do.

ADEN AND SOUTH ARABIA

In April 1960, 45 Commando moved to Aden, where it spent the next seven and a half years on operations in South Arabia and Aden colony. The officers, NCOs, and Marines spent a minimum of a year in 45 Commando, being sent back to UK on completion of their tour, followed by tours in one of the other two overseas Commandos. Some people carried out two or more tours, usually at their request.

Most of the region of the coast of south-west Arabia is mountainous, up through the Yemen and the Hejaz. Sixty miles north of Aden, and in the mountains thirty miles from what used to be the border between the Western Aden Protectorate and Yemen, lies the Radfan, astride the Aden–Yemen road. This unsurfaced road follows the wadi bottom, climbing almost imperceptibly until it snakes up the pass on to the Dhala plateau at 6,000 feet. Grim black volcanic mountains stretch from horizon to horizon. Clusters of stone-walled houses make up the scattered villages, each house like a miniature fort with no windows, and sited for defence. Small watch towers crown the tops of some of the ridges. Scrub and camel thorn are the only natural vegetation. All the mountain people in the Protectorate were, and still are, fiercely independent. To carry a rifle, then a Lee Enfield, now an AK47, is a sign of manhood. The tribesman, rifle on shoulder, held by the muzzle, cartridge belts and curved dagger at his waist, owed allegiance only to his tribal ruler, and then only when it suited him. Blood feuds, inter-tribal warfare, and tolls exacted from passing travellers were a way of life. Courage and strength were admired; conciliation, a sign of weakness, was treated with contempt. The Quteibi, the self-styled 'Wolves of the Radfan', were among the most truculent; brave, excellent shots, adept at fieldcraft, with an eye for ground.

The British had never bothered to administer the sheikhdoms, sultanates, and emirates that made up the Aden Protectorates. Each ruler administered as much of his state as he could without interference by the British. Foreign affairs were the province of the British government, and political officers resided in each state to see that British interests were not threatened. The exception was Aden itself, which was a British colony.

In the early 1960s most of the states and Aden colony, renamed Aden State, were joined into the Federation of South Arabia with their own federal parliament responsible for the internal affairs of the Federation. The tribal rulers had always been encouraged to keep a small armed force for internal policing known as the Federal National Guards (FNG). Overall peace was maintained by tribesmen recruited into the Federal Regular Army (FRA), officered at first by the British, but with an increasing number of Arab officers. To back up the FRA, British battalions were stationed in Aden, and 45 Commando in Little Aden about fifteen miles to the west. In scenes reminiscent of the North West Frontier of India, Marines and soldiers, Arab and British, patrolled, piquetted, and manned outposts at scattered points in the mountains. Live ammunition was always carried, even when peace nominally reigned, and the RAF Hunters flew top cover over convoys when they were passing through the most dangerous stretches of the Dhala road. The tribesmen were wont to take a shot at a passing convoy or patrol, sometimes just for the fun of it.

The British intended that the Federation should become independent. There was, however, considerable opposition to the Federation from several quarters. Britain had lost a good deal of influence and prestige in the Arab world after her agreement to setting up the State of Israel; her reputation fell further after the Suez campaign, and any steps she took in this part of the world were subject to Arab criticism. To the north the Yemen had always coveted the Protectorate, and saw no reason to renounce her claim just because of a change of name. In 1962 the Imam of Yemen was overthrown by General Sallal, an Egyptian-backed republican revolutionary. The many Yemeni and pro-Yemeni elements in Aden State gave their enthusiastic support to Sallal's regime.

President Nasser of Egypt, the self-appointed leader of Arab aspirations, had plans for the Federation, hoping to prise it away from the British sphere of influence and install a puppet regime under his control, as he had done in Yemen. The trade unionists and merchants in Aden State deeply distrusted and feared the tribesmen and their rulers, to whom they were joined in a shotgun marriage. In their eyes the rulers were undemocratic, and the tribesmen savages. The rulers for their part eyed the trade unions, deeply penetrated by Yemenis and Nasserites, with distaste, and the tribesmen regarded the fat merchants, bankers, and soft town dwellers with scorn. In the background, supporting Nasser in the hope of rich pickings in the form of influence once the British had been kicked out, waited the Russians. By the end of 1963 the stage was set for trouble.

Before this 45 Commando had been involved in the bread and butter of soldiering on a tribal frontier for two and a half years. In summer 1961 there had been a break from patrols, picketing, and Dhala convoys. The Iraqi dictator General Kassim laid claim to Kuwait, and massed his armour on the border. In response, HMS *Bulwark* sailed from a visit to Karachi and her helicopters flew 42 Commando into Kuwait airfield, while 45 Commando were flown by RAF Britannias, Hastings, and Beverleys, the latter via Bahrain, into the same airfield, while (as already related) two LSTs sailed from Bahrain and landed a squadron of tanks in Kuwait.

The fly-in by the RAF did not go without incident. 45 Commando's mortar platoon was most put out to discover that the baseplates for their mortars had been offloaded by some RAF 'erk' at Bahrain in favour of beds for RAF aircrew, whose personal comfort always seemed, to the Marines anyway, to take precedence over operational imperatives. Until the baseplates could be located and flown forward, the mortars were so much scrap metal. The RAF's stock with the Commando plummeted further when the Marines found that all their picks and shovels had been deemed 'unsafe' loads, and had been unloaded for repacking, so they too arrived in Kuwait well after the Marines. When the Commando arrived in its defensive position, the Marines had to dig in using their mess tins. Fortunately the sandy soil was reasonably soft. The Marines wondered if the RAF was fighting on their side or Kassim's. Despite all these snags, the operation was a success, the two Commandos took up positions on the Mutla Ridge, and some days later Army reinforcements arrived from Kenya, Bahrain, and even the UK. Kassim backed down and the crisis was over.

One of the matters highlighted when battalions relieved Commandos during the Kuwait operation was the incompatibility of the Commando organization, of five rifle troops of around sixty men each, with an infantry battalion consisting of three or four rifle companies, each of three platoons of thirty-five men and totalling over a hundred men. This problem had been encountered before, during the Second World War and after. Rifle troops were fine for raiding, the original task of the early Commandos, but being divisible into only two manoeuvre sub-units were tactically unsound in a conventional battle. It was decided to take the long overdue step of reorganizing the Commandos into three rifle companies, support company, and headquarters company.

On 4 January 1964 there was a mutiny in the Tanganyikan Army. 41 Commando was flown from UK to neighbouring Kenya, but the expected mutiny there did not materialize. However, President Nyerere of Tanganyika requested British assistance in suppressing the mutiny in his army. The Middle East strategic reserve, 45 Commando, was embarked in the strike carrier HMS *Centaur*, which happened to be close to Aden, and carried some anti-submarine helicopters. When the carrier arrived off Dar-es-Salaam, it was discovered that the ammunition loaded for the Commando consisted mainly of blank; the depot at Aden had sent the wrong nature of ammunition out in lighters to the carrier. By an oversight it had not been checked before being stowed in the ship's magazines. This somewhat embarrassing situation was partially overcome by using ship's stocks of 7.62mm rounds held for the ship's Royal Marine Detachment which, like the Commando, was armed with the SLR, and issuing the .303in number 4 bolt-operated rifles, with appropriate ammunition, normally allocated to the ship's seamen landing platoons, to make up the balance. Fortunately, there was no fighting ashore, and the commando was able to augment its stock of 7.62mm ammunition from the lavish supplies held by the Tanganyikan Army. However, there were some red faces for a while. When 45 Commando landed in the ship's helicopters, some fire was directed at Z Company, but a 3.5in rocket from one of the company's rocket launchers into the guardroom roof at Colito barracks soon had the mutineers streaming out with their hands up. Companies were sent up-country to round up other bands of mutineers, and calm was restored. 45 Commando was relieved by 41 Commando from Kenya and returned to South Arabia, where a far more serious threat had arisen. Soon afterwards 41 Commando left for UK with the thanks of the Presidents of Kenya and Tanganyika, soon to be Tanzania, ringing in their ears.

On 10 December 1963, a bomb attack on the British High Commissioner in Aden signalled the beginning of a terrorist campaign in Aden State, while up country the Quteibis, having been forbidden to exact tolls from travellers on the road to and from Yemen, had been defying the Emir of Dhala, their ruler, by shooting at convoys and mining the Dhala road. The civil war in Yemen was in full swing, and President Nasser, who was still heavily involved, saw the chance to foment trouble in a British protectorate and gave the tribesmen his support in the form of weapons and training in the Yemen. Following a successful operation by the FRA, the federal government decided that further action was needed and called on Britain to assist under the terms of the agreement between the two countries.

A force was assembled, very much in the manner of a pre-war punitive expedition on the North-West Frontier of India. As one officer who took part commented: 'The big difference was the old India hands knew about mountain warfare and the Aden gentry didn't.' Dubbed Radforce, the 'expedition' included 45 Commando, FRA battalions, and artillery. By now, March, it was the start of the hot season in South Arabia. As the sun gains height, stepping out from the relative cool of a stone building is like opening an oven door, the glare striking like a blow. Even some distance from habitation the smells of goats, donkeys, and cattle pervade the shimmering air. At midday the temperature in the sun rises to 110°–120° Fahrenheit. There is little shade and Marines and soldiers carried strips of hessian to provide shade by day, and a rough blanket by night. With the onset of darkness, the temperature drops, but start marching and thirst sets in. Water was to be a constant problem because there were few local sources. The ration was two gallons per man per day for drinking, cooking, and washing. Almost every gallon had to be carried by the troops or flown in by the tiny helicopter force.

The CO of 45 Commando, Lieutenant Colonel T. M. P. Stevens, who had won an MC in 41 Commando in Normandy, decided that night infiltration of enemy-held ground would pay dividends – the tribesmen did not enjoy fighting at night. As part of the overall plan to cut the tribesmen off from their cultivated areas and their routes to the Yemen, 45 Commando was ordered to capture the high ground on the north side of the Danaba Basin on 30 April. Stevens was given B Company, 3 Para under command. His plan was to march at night to seize two features, 'Rice Bowl' and 'Sand Fly'. B Company 3 Para would parachute in the same night into the Wadi Taym and seize 'Cap Badge'. Unfortunately the DZ marking party provided by 22 SAS was discovered the day before, the ten-man patrol was cut off by about a hundred tribesmen, and it had to fight its way out supported by air support from RAF Hunters. The patrol turned up at Radforce HQ in the morning of 1 May, but the commander and one trooper were left behind; subsequently their heads were displayed on spikes in the Yemeni capital of Sa'ana.

Just before last light on 30 April, following three weeks of patrolling, the three rifle companies and Tac HQ of 45 Commando dropped off from trucks on the road north of Habilayn and silently lay up to wait for darkness. They were accompanied by some of Support Company, manpacking mortars and Vickers machine-guns. The long snake of heavily laden men marched steadily through the darkness, along the bed of the Wadi Boran, and split, Z Company heading for 'Sand Fly', X and Y Company for 'Rice Bowl'. When Brigadier Hargroves, the commander of Radforce, received a radio message from the SAS patrol that it was in trouble and the DZ could not be marked, he cancelled the drop and ordered B Company to come up to Habilayn, the Radforce camp north of Thumier, by truck. Because 45 Commando would be very exposed forward on 'Rice Bowl' without B Company on 'Cap Badge', he tried to tell Stevens by radio to halt on 'Sand Fly' and an intermediate feature, 'Coca Cola'.

As the Commandos marched, a garbled radio message from Hargroves, changing the plan, was received at Tac HQ at about 2235 hours; but only at midnight, when Stevens and X Company were traversing higher ground on the wadi on the flanks of 'Coca Cola', did the message get through in its entirety. By the light of shaded torches, Stevens and OC X Company, Major M. Banks, an accomplished mountaineer, studied air photographs of 'Coca Cola', looming 1,500 feet above them. The route would be difficult, especially for men carrying mortars and Vickers. Banks, with the Recce Troop (many of them trained climbers), led the way up a steep ravine leading up the side of the mountain, before reaching a steep face. He led up this face, a difficult feat in the dark, without previous reconnaissance. Fortunately, just in case, he had brought a length of manila rope with him. Once he had established this rope at the top, X and Y Company and Tac HQ hauled themselves up. Two hours before first light, 250 men of 45 Commando were on 'Coca Cola', and below them in the dawn they could see the Danaba basin surrounded by rock ridges over 1,000 feet high, and 'Cap Badge' 9,000 feet high off to their east.

It was a splendid achievement, to react to a change of plan, received at midnight, and climb a strange mountain in the dark in under four hours. Few other troops could have done it. Banks's skill and his free-spirited approach to orders played a key part in the success. Apart from his experience as a mountaineer, he had studied and instructed in the art of soldiering in mountainous terrain. As far as he was concerned the Radfan was a familiar environment, whereas to what he calls 'flat earth soldiers' it was 'intimidating'. Furthermore, as a mountaineer he knew that about 40lb is the critical load when going uphill. 'Go seriously above this and you cease being a soldier and become a beast of burden. With lamentable ill-discipline I therefore ignored all orders and made my company travel light and fast. It paid off.'[3]

Four days later the Commando with B Company 3 Para still under command again marched by night to secure 'Cap Badge', their original objective, via the Danaba Basin. When Major Banks was told that the next objective was Cap Badge,

> I suggested that I conduct a night reconnaissance of a direct but steep descent into the Danaba Basin. Having confirmed the feasibility of this descent, I would, with a small team of climbers, descend to the Basin the following night, cross it and nip up Cap Badge. With the benefit of hindsight, this would have worked a treat.[4]

However, his suggestion, which involved a far shorter route, was over-ruled, and instead the whole Commando descended to the west of 'Coca

Cola', at dusk, into an assembly area, which took time, and having had a meal the companies set off. From the basin, X Company was to climb the south-west ridge while Y Company secured 'Gin Sling', a feature on the end of the south-west ridge, but affording a 'foot on the ground' for the Commando, from where it would be possible to support either X Company or B Company. The latter were to approach 'Cap Badge' by the longer but apparently easier route through the Wadi Taym, and up on to the southern face of the feature. Y Company had a steep climb up onto 'Gin Sling', but were established on the top with Commando Tac HQ an hour before first light. X Company travelled light and fast, scaling steep rock slabs, but, like Y Company, were unopposed and found empty summit sangars that had clearly been occupied very recently. In fact both companies outsmarted the tribesmen, who had spent the night in the village below, by surprise. As the Commandos moved into position they saw lights below indicating that the tribesmen had been alerted, were off their charpoys, and were moving about. Any tribesmen who climbed the ridge in daylight received an unpleasant surprise and were swept off in a hail of fire.

B Company were still marching, for the going was harder than anticipated, and the soldiers were overladen. On two occasions the parachute soldiers had to lie up while tribesmen went by. Daylight found the company on low ground dominated by the village of El Naqil, below 'Cap Badge'. The tribesmen, smarting from their reverse at the hands of the Marines on 'Cap Badge', opened fire on B Company from the houses and the lower slopes of the mountain. The company commander led one of his platoons to clear a small fort while the rest of the company assaulted the village. Having driven the tribesmen out, a group cut in behind the leading soldiers in an attempt to assault them from the rear. These tribesmen ran into an ambush by the rear element of the company, under the second-in-command. All the tribesmen were killed. The company consolidated in the village. Snipers in the foothills above the village engaged them, positioning themselves so they were in dead ground to the commandos on 'Cap Badge'. The company called in Hunters to strafe the tribesmen's sangars, to good effect. Two Beaver light aircraft dropped water and ammunition to the parachute soldiers. Meanwhile the company second-in-command was killed assisting a wounded soldier, one soldier was killed, and six more wounded.

Stevens ordered up his reserve company, Z, now off 'Sand Fly' and back in the Commando assembly area. An RAF twin-rotor Belvedere helicopter, taking more than its approved load of twenty-two men, took the leading troop forward to rope down below X Company's positions on 'Cap Badge', in a position from which they could give covering fire while the remainder of Z Company flown in subsequently negotiated the three-hour climb down 1,500 feet to take in the rear the tribesmen who were causing B Company so much trouble. By mid-afternoon the enemy had made off, and Z and B Company wearily climbed 'Cap Badge', arriving at dusk, as far as B Company was concerned after an eleven-hour march and ten-hour battle. El Naqil was renamed Pegasus Village. The Commando and B Company spent another three days patrolling, and found that the tribesmen had abandoned the Danaba Basin, before returning to base camp.

The next two weeks were spent reorganizing Radforce. Brigadier Blacker and Headquarters 39 Brigade were brought out to command with substantial reinforcements including Lieutenant Colonel Farrar-Hockley, the CO of 3 Para, with his A and C Companies. 3 Para was ordered to secure the ten-mile-long Bakri Ridge, whose south-eastern spur dominated the Wadi Dhubsan 3,000 feet below. After a night approach march, the battalion established itself on the Bakri Ridge and began clearing along its length, which took another four days before reaching the final spur, which was called Arnold's Spur, after CSM Arnold, who captured it. Following the clearance of the village of Quedeishi on the highest point of the Bakri Ridge, the battalion had the whole ridge in its hands. 3 Para was now ordered to descend into the Wadi Dhubsan, to prove to the tribesmen that the wadi was not impregnable, as they thought. Farrar-Hockley was told to stay for only twenty-four hours, because maintaining the battalion in the wadi would be difficult. He was given X Company of 45 Commando to reinforce his battalion for what was in effect a raid. It was a wadi too far, and in retrospect a pointless operation.

The battalion approached by the most obvious route, straight down from Arnold's Spur, where the whole battalion had been clearly visible for some time. At first all went well. Major Banks's X Company was to have been lifted forward to join and pass through 3 Para's leading company. The night before, Banks had pointed out that 'come the dawn, the nature of the ground dictated that we would descend into the valley far too quickly to allow time for piquets to work their way along the difficult and intricate rock of the containing ridges above us.'[5]

When adverse weather conditions ruled out the use of helicopters, X Company was ordered to descend from the ridge on foot, which it did. It arrived at about 0630 hours to be ordered on to the objective, which unfortunately lay *beyond the cover of C Company's piquets*, and X Company came under fire from high ground which had not been piquetted. Altogether there were about fifty to sixty tribesmen with rifles and at least six automatic weapons. X Company, through no fault of its own, was pinned down in the open. Farrar-Hockley flew forward in a Scout helicopter, which had got as far forward as Battalion HQ, in now clear weather. His pilot overshot X Company and the helicopter was hit several times. The pilot managed to keep it airborne long enough to land just forward of the leading Commandos, who rushed to cover the occupants as they hurriedly deplaned. Small-arms fire continued to smack into the rocks and side of the wadi, where Captain Brind, second-in-command of X Company, had been carried, badly wounded in the stomach while trying to lay out panels to point Hunters towards the enemy positions. Eventually, fire from two 5.5in guns and strafing by Hunters with cannon induced the tribesmen to withdraw.

It is arguable that the guns and rockets hit nothing. A tribesman's fire position often consisted of an inconspicuous coffin-shaped hole, roofed over with stones and with a small firing slit.

> You could almost trip over one before you saw it. Therefore Hunters and 5.5 guns had nothing at which to aim. The tribesmen withdrew, probably on concealed lines of retreat, as was their wont, after they had enjoyed their target practice. There is no way they would be so silly as to indulge in set piece battles with our superior numbers and fire power.[6]

The next morning the battalion withdrew up Arnold's Spur, and was flown out, leaving X Company on the Bakri Ridge until relieved by the FRA the next day. Some who took part in this operation, both paratroopers and Marines, find it hard to see the point of ordering the battalion into the Wadi Dhubsan, and an old lesson was relearned; ignore at your peril the holy mantra of mountain warfare: *piquet the heights*.

45 Commando was to spend much time in the Radfan over the next three years, and carried out nine more tours there, which, as well as patrolling, involved many engagements with the tribesmen (an up-

country tour was usually about four to six weeks long). For example, the Commando carried out 305 night patrols in June and July 1965 and 66 in February and March 1967, and some innovative ambushes were rewarded with success. Over these years the Marines experienced the frustration and stress of being under fire without always being able to reply effectively. Manoeuvre without covering fire was always dangerous. Locating the enemy was difficult enough, let alone bringing effective fire to bear on tribesmen in deep caves. Artillery was often imprecise, and not always successful. Fighter ground-attack aircraft were more frightening (to the enemy) and efficacious, but were not always available. To get moving again the Marines often had to rely on their own firepower resources. The GPMG (general-purpose machine gun), in action for the first time, was a great success. Its rate of fire, considerably greater than the Bren, produced a stream of bullets that could 'claw' their way through sangar walls, and greatly assisted in winning firefights. The 3.5in rocket launcher did not succeed in blasting holes in the solidly built watch towers. Marines relearned the old lessons, practised on exercises, but only brought home under fire: the importance of battle discipline, silence on patrol at night, good weapon handling, and fire orders – and when you stop, build a sangar (time-consuming, back-breaking, thirsty work: thirst was a constant companion).

As well as tours up country, 45 Commando had since September 1964 increasingly been involved in Aden town, or State, itself, as urban terrorism there increased. Urban terrorism attracted the attention of the UK press to the detriment of the up-country operations, not least because Aden town was more accessible to the bars of the Crescent Hotel, the Ledra Palace, and the Aletti (where some but by no means all journalists had their perches) than the grim mountains of the Radfan and the dusty Dhala road.[7] In Aden, if they were lucky, they could file a story between one drink and the next. The battleground in Aden State consisted of the squalid Arab town of Sheikh Othman, on a flat dusty plain north of the drowned volcano crater and the stinking salt pans of Aden harbour. To the east of Aden harbour, on the peninsula, lay the international and RAF airport, and the complex of Khormaksar. South of these were the Westernized shopping and residential area of Ma'alla, and, nestling within an old volcano crater, the largely Arab business, banking, and residential town, aptly called Crater, which was the oldest of the complex of towns that made up Aden State.

The political scene had changed since 45 Commando arrived in 1960. Until early 1966, the British government had always said that it intended maintaining base facilities in Aden and honouring defence treaties with states in the Federation, even after independence, which it anticipated granting in 1968. However, in 1966 the British government, Labour since 1964, pulled the rug out from under the Federal government. Even while the Radfan campaign was still in progress plans were being hatched in Whitehall for the withdrawal from South Arabia. In February 1966 the Defence White Paper announced that Britain would neither maintain defence facilities nor respect her treaties with the Federation. This came as a bombshell to the rulers. They had reluctantly agreed to the Federation in return for assurances that Britain would continue to defend the Federation after independence. They were now to be left to their fate, labelled British stooges, with 60–70,000 Egyptian troops in the Yemen. From this moment the people of South Arabia, townsmen and tribesmen alike, whether originally hostile or not, had no incentive to cooperate with the British in a smooth transfer of power. Nasser made it very clear what fate awaited anyone who collaborated with the British. He had been on the point of withdrawing from the Yemen, but now proclaimed that his troops would remain for five years.

The British government was given a practical lesson in the futility of negotiating from a position of weakness. The incidence of terrorism in Aden and guerrilla warfare in the mountains rose immediately. There were two organizations opposed to the Federation: the Front for the Liberation of Southern Yemen (FLOSY) and the National Liberation Front (NLF). FLOSY's power base was in Aden itself, among the trade unions, and the Yemenis in Aden, and was supported by Egypt. The NLF broke away from FLOSY in late 1966 and was supported mainly by the mountain tribes. Egypt withdrew support from the NLF soon after the break with FLOSY. Both organizations fought bitterly against each other to build up their power base in readiness for the day the British left, and both carried out attacks on British servicemen and civilians.

In July 1966 the Federation was given another example of the spinelessness of which Britain was capable in the swinging sixties. Two MiG fighters from Yemen attacked a small town in the state of Beihan, injuring four tribesmen and damaging a number of houses. The Emir, with the full support of the Federal government, demanded action by Britain under the terms of the defence treaty. To their consternation,

Britain refused and deferred the matter to the UN. The outcome surprised no one, not least all of the rulers of the Federation. The UN, having debated the matter for two weeks, including hearing a submission from the Yemenis that the Beihanis had been seeing unidentified flying objects, asked the Secretary General to settle the dispute – in effect, do nothing. The message to the rulers was clear: Britain was not to be trusted ever again. By early 1967, 45 Commando, along with all other British units in Aden and the rest of South Arabia, found itself keeping peace in a country that had been thoroughly stirred up by decisions emanating from Westminster, and within nine months would be abandoned by the government that was largely responsible for the mess. In the process the Marines and soldiers stood a good chance of being killed or wounded.

Many terrorist attacks in Aden involved either hand-thrown grenades, or Blindicides, a rifle grenade of Belgian manufacture. Cordons and searches, foot and vehicle patrols were the staple diet of the Marines on the streets. The withdrawal, originally planned for early 1968, was brought forward to 29 November 1967. To assist in covering the final phases, 42 Commando was brought from Singapore to Aden in the LPH HMS *Albion* on 11 October, and took up position in the defence line known as the 'Pennine Chain', north of the peninsula. Here the Commando and 1 Para, recently withdrawn from Sheikh Othman, kept Khormaksar airfield out of range of the terrorist small-arms fire, but not terrorist mortars. By now 45 Commando had abandoned its camp in Little Aden, home for seven years, and moved into Ma'alla. The NLF and FLOSY had meanwhile engaged in a bloody battle for supremacy. The FRA, now the South Arabian Army (SAA), came off the fence on 6 November and declared for the NLF.

One by one the units were flown out. 45 Commando, the second last to leave, went in thirteen C-130s at midnight on 28/29 November; the last British troops in Aden, 42 Commando, left by helicopter to *Albion*. Offshore during the pull-out steamed HMS *Bulwark*, with 40 Commando and 7 Commando Light Battery embarked, and with the strike carriers HMS *Eagle* and *Victorious* in the offing, ready to provide air support should all go wrong at the last moment. So all three Commandos were involved in the operation to ensure that the withdrawal was as bloodless as possible – for the British.

40 Commando and 7 Commando Light Battery were back again off

Aden in *Albion* with the strike carrier battle group in early 1968, when it seemed that the increasingly chaotic situation accompanied by a complete breakdown of law and order might necessitate the withdrawal of British and other friendly nationals. In the event the Commando was not required. But it was able to demonstrate the value of a force that could 'poise' out of sight of land, ready to be used if required, needing no diplomatic clearance for the use of bases or airfields, and deniable if necessary – until the moment came to land.

BRUNEI AND BORNEO, 1962–1966

> One of the most efficient uses of military force in the history of the world.
>
> Denis Healey, Secretary of State for Defence

On Sunday 9 December 1962, Captain J. J. Moore, OC L Company 42 Commando, was in his room in the officers' mess at Simbang in Singapore writing Christmas cards when a Marine came in and said that the Colonel wanted to see him. The Colonel, Lieutenant Colonel E. R. Bridges, asked Moore how quickly he could move his company. The two other rifle company commanders were on picnics or water-skiing, and messengers were scouring Singapore to get them back. L Company, about half a troop light, was flown to Brunei airport, arriving during the evening of 10 December, to be joined later by a section from Support Company with two Vickers machine-guns. The cause of this hasty move was an insurrection in Brunei.

Kalimantan, part of the Republic of Indonesia, forms about three-quarters of the huge island of Borneo; the remainder consists of East Malaysia and the Sultanate of Brunei. Sukarno, President of Indonesia since independence from the Dutch in 1949, had long dreamt of bringing Malaya, Brunei, Singapore, and the British Borneo colonies into a Greater Indonesia. His first attempt at doing so by force was in Brunei in December 1962. At this stage the Federation of Malaysia was merely a gleam in the eye of Tunku Abdul Rahman, the Prime Minister of Malaya.

He realized that only by joining together Malaya, Brunei, and the British colonies of Sabah and Sarawak could he hope to resist Sukarno's expansionist schemes. From mid-1961, under the Tunku's guiding hand and with full support from the British, the concept of federation looked increasingly likely. However, the Sultan of Brunei was not convinced that joining the Federation was in his interest, and Sukarno seized the opportunity to make trouble. On 8 December 1962 pro-Sukarno dissidents calling themselves the North Kalimantan National Army (TNKU) rebelled against the Sultan, who asked Britain for assistance.

The TNKU had attacked the Sultan's palace, the British Residency in Brunei Town, and other places in the Sultanate including the oil town of Seria and the town of Limbang across the border in Sarawak. In Brunei Town the attackers had been beaten off, but in Limbang the TNKU had taken the British Resident, Richard Morris, and all other British people in the vicinity hostage and was holding them in the police station. Fortunately the rebels had failed to secure the airfields, otherwise the outcome might have been very different.

By the afternoon of Saturday 8 December, two companies of 1/2nd Gurkha Rifles had been flown in and were occupying Brunei Town. On Sunday, 1st Battalion the Queen's Own Highlanders[8] arrived, followed then next day by L Company 42 Commando and by 1st Battalion The Greenjackets.[9] Under the totally unrealistic contingency plan for reinforcing Brunei, Plan Ale, a hastily cobbled together headquarters under Brigadier Glennie was flown out to take charge of the situation. Eventually both Headquarters 3rd Commando Brigade and 99th Gurkha Brigade were sent out. Most of the trouble spots were quickly sorted out, except Limbang, only accessible by river, or helicopter, of which at that stage there were none in Brunei with the necessary range. The urgency to rescue the hostages at Limbang was sharpened when it was learned that the TNKU had murdered some hostages at Bangar, and threatened to treat those at Limbang likewise.

Moore with eighty-seven of his company arrived at Brunei airport, just as it was getting dark on Monday evening.

> I went into the airport buildings and telephoned the brigade headquarters to inform them of my arrival and find out what I could do. I spoke to the BM, who said that due to the uncertainties of the situation, and to avoid the possibility of a 'blue on blue', I was to stay at the airport overnight

and was to report to him in the morning with a view to using the whole company to guard the British Residency. He received some quite unjustified but forceful comments upon the folly of employing the best sub-unit available to him to do a job which could easily be accomplished by a dozen policemen, and I settled the company down for the night in the airport buildings.

At dawn the next morning, as I was half-way through shaving, one of my Marines came and told me that there was a brigadier outside who wanted to see me. This turned out to be Pat Patterson [commander 99th Gurkha Brigade, which had now arrived]. Just the sight of him raised my morale at once. Having briefly explained that he had come to take command of the operation, he told me to:

1. Start thinking how to rescue the hostages in Limbang, which task I was to hand over to Robin Bridges [his commanding officer] as soon as he arrived, or carry [it] out, whichever was the sooner.
2. Find accommodation for the Commando in Brunei Town, and take that over as well as requisitioning transport, both road and water, for the unit's use.

I went to the police station to find out what I could about Limbang, sent my 2ic (Peter Waters) to find a Hotel, and senior Troop Commander (Paddy Davies) to look for river craft. Having obtained the one air photograph available, and a 500000:1 scale map of that part of Borneo, Robin Bridges arrived, so I handed the Limbang requirement over to him, and went to find some vehicles. When I returned with these, the CO handed the job back to me, to be carried out that night.[10]

The information on Limbang was sparse. Although the air photograph was a help in identifying buildings, Moore had no idea of the strength and deployment of the rebels; except that there were thought to be about 150 of them, with some automatic weapons but mostly armed with shotguns, a potent weapon in a built-up area at close quarters. Moore spoke to a policeman who had been up-river in a launch to take a look, but

not being trained as a soldier, he could tell me little other than he had been fired on by automatic weapons from near the police station and elsewhere. He did not know how many hostages there were, nor where they were located. He thought there were about half a dozen; there turned out to be 14 in at least four locations.

I reasoned that the rebels would use the hostages as a human shield, and that the best way to avoid this would be to knock out their command post before they had time to get organised. It seemed logical that they would have their HQ/CP in the Police Station, and might well have the hostages there in cells. This being a brick building, any innocents who were there might gain some protection from our fire. I therefore planned to go straight for the Police Station in the hope of taking the heart out of the enemy before they could get organised to fight us off, or harm any of the hostages. The hospital was also a brick building, but most of the others were wooden. Once the Police Station was in our hands, I planned to move south to clear the rest of the Government buildings before tackling the town.[11]

Moore went to the waterfront in Brunei and met the Senior Naval Officer, Lieutenant Commander J. J. Black RN, who commanded two minesweepers, HMS *Fiskerton* and *Chawton*. He had located two Z-Lighters, flat-bottomed craft looking rather like large landing craft, with a wheelhouse aft, one of which was carrying two yellow-painted bull-dozers. Black's minesweeper provided crews for the lighters. The first lieutenants of the minesweepers commanded these craft, with a stoker PO, a leading hand as coxswain, and a midshipman as second-in-command. Captain Mouton, the Brunei Director of Marine (a combination of the head of the Brunei River Authority and harbour master), navigated from the leading lighter, although, according to Moore, 'his knowledge of the leads through the Nipa swamp seemed as sparse as my map'.

Moore's Vickers, LMGs, and SLRs would outrange the rebels at over 100 yards, and be able to bring down a far heavier weight of fire, but at close quarters the rebels would outnumber his men and be able to bring more weapons to bear. The town lay on a bend in the river, and was built on a waterfront site cut out of the jungle, about a thousand yards long and a few hundred wide. L Company sailed from Brunei on the night of 11/12 December. In the first lighter, commanded by Lieutenant D. O. Willis RN, was Moore, 5 Troop, his reconnaissance group, and part of company HQ, with the Commando Intelligence Sergeant attached. The Vickers, the remaining troop and a half, and company main HQ, were in the second lighter. Moore aimed to arrive at the town at first light, and as the craft came round the bend in the river all the street lights went out. Moore thought they had been spotted, but in fact, as he discovered later, they had been extinguished because dawn was breaking. When the little flotilla was 300 yards from the police station, 'it was exactly like an ant heap with people running everywhere'.[12]

The Intelligence Sergeant shouted in Malay through a loudhailer, telling the rebels that the rebellion was over, and they should lay down their arms. The rebels replied with an LMG, some SMGs and about 100 shotguns. The Vickers fired back instantly, allowing the leading craft to beach thirty seconds later, but two Marines were killed in the leading craft, and the troop commander, Lieutenant Davies, was hit as his men poured ashore. Sergeant Bickford, the senior section commander, took over, and cleared the police station with two sections under Corporals Lester and Rawlinson.

The remaining section was still aboard the leading craft when the helmsman was hit and it drifted off the river bank. Lieutenant Willis grabbed the wheel from the wounded helmsman and drove the lighter back towards the bank, but it broached 150 yards upstream between the hospital and the British Resident's house. In the second craft, Waters, the company second-in-command, was wounded, so CSM Scoins took over and asked the lieutenant in command of the lighter to 'pull out of line a bit, Sir please, so we can get a better arc of fire for the machine-guns'. To which, as he did as asked, the naval officer replied, 'Sar'nt Major, Nelson would have fucking loved you.' A compliment treasured by Scoins.[13]

Lieutenant Willis, on Moore's orders, closed the bank and landed the third section of 5 Troop under the troop sergeant, MacFarlane, to clear the shoreline back down to the police station. When Moore found the craft stuck fast, he landed, and found that MacFarlane had cleared the hospital and rescued Morris, the Resident. The jungle at this point came down to some forty to fifty yards from the river, just behind the hospital, and MacFarlane and two Marines were killed in the process by shotgun fire at close range.

Morris told Moore that there were about 300 rebels in town, and where the other hostages were being held. Moore set about organizing his company clearing the rest of the town. The CSM landed the other two troops, and Moore, discovering that the two young troop commanders had never done any house clearing, even in training, talked them through the procedure, and then set them off to do it for real. By the afternoon another eight hostages were freed. By last light there were still rebels within the town, two of whom were killed that night. The next day the town was finally in L Company's hands. The rebels' losses were 15 killed and 50 captured from a force of 350, for the loss of 5 NCOs and Marines killed, and 7 wounded. Moore was awarded a bar to his MC, and Corporals Lester and Rawlinson the MM. This battle, with actions by the Queen's Own Highlanders at Seria and the Green Jackets at Miri, broke the back of the rebellion, although it took until May 1963 to clear the last pocket of rebels.

The remainder of 42 Commando arrived on 12 December, followed by Brigade HQ, and 40 Commando landed from *Albion* at Kuching on 14 December. Both Commandos spent some weeks patrolling, but by April 1963 the whole brigade had returned to Singapore. Within weeks it was back in Borneo. While mopping-up operations in Brunei were in progress, Sukarno announced a policy of confrontation towards Malaya 'because they represent themselves as accomplices of neo-colonialist and neo-imperialist forces pursuing a policy hostile towards Indonesia'. At the same time, groups of volunteers began to cross the border into Sabah and Sarawak, carrying out acts of sabotage and attempting to subvert the inhabitants. On 16 September 1963 the Federation of Malaysia came into existence, without Brunei, but, until 1965, including Singapore. Sukarno immediately broke off diplomatic relations with Malaysia. The number of incursions by company-sized bands of Indonesian irregulars increased until in early 1964 the Indonesian Army took control of operations.

Major General W. C. Walker, GOC 17th Gurkha Division, an officer who had spent his whole military service with the Gurkhas, and had served in Burma and Malaya with distinction, was initially in overall command of operations to mop up the Brunei rebels, and remained in Borneo until March 1965. As Director of Borneo Operations (DOBOPS), he was technically subordinate to the Malaysian National Operations Committee after Federation. To begin with he thought of the security situation in Borneo in terms of the Malayan emergency, and that the main 'enemy' were the Clandestine Communist Organization (CCO), whose insurgents, stationed in Kalimantan known as Indonesian Border Terrorists (IBTs), were supported by an unknown number of Indonesian regulars.

In East Malaysia, as Sabah and Sarawak had become following Federation, the British, Malaysian, and other Commonwealth forces faced a major problem. Borneo is in the centre of the Indonesian archipelago, and there are several small Indonesian islands between the

Commonwealth main base in Singapore and the main ports in East
Malaysia. The terrain along the 900-mile-long border with Kalimantan,
like all of Borneo, is some of the most inhospitable in the world, and is
altogether 'bigger country' than that described in the chapter on the
Malayan campaign. Except for patches of cultivation, and extensive
mangrove swamps, the island consists of huge mountain ranges, deep
valleys, and rolling plateaus covered with dense tropical rainforest,
interspersed by large and frequently fast-flowing rivers. These sometimes
provide a means of movement by boat, but just as often they are an
obstacle to movement. Even if their course is more or less in the desired
direction of travel, rapids and falls, except near the sea, can make all but
the shortest boat journey a considerable undertaking. There were in the
mid-1960s few roads outside the towns and larger villages, and almost
all were on the coast. A few logging tracks penetrated a little way inland
in areas where timber was being felled. In the steamy heat, trudging up
and slithering down the sometimes near vertical hillsides, often through
thick secondary growth, heavily laden Marines and soldiers could take
several hours to cover even a mile. On one occasion it took a Gurkha
patrol three days to cover 5,000 yards; a helicopter covered the same
distance in three minutes.[14] Leeches and leptospirosis in the rivers and
streams and scrub typhus ticks in the few drier areas added to the
natural discomforts and dangers of the patrolling Marine and soldier,
without taking into account what the enemy might do.

The Marines and soldiers were based in a series of jungle forts at
intervals along the border and usually a few miles back. These were not
intended to form a stop line to incursions, but acted as a base from
which troops patrolled and sortied to ambush and harry the Indonesians.
A fort occupied by a company or troop was usually sited on high ground.
The defences included barbed wire and punjis (pointed bamboo stakes).
Trenches and bunkers were dug and most bases had at least one 3in
mortar (later 81mm), or a 105mm pack howitzer. The jungle forts were
supplied by helicopter, or in the case of the bigger, more far-flung ones,
by air-drop from Beverley and Argosy aircraft, or by Twin Pioneers
which could cope with very short strips. Everything came by air, from
sandbags to live chickens in crates. Somebody had the idea of saving
parachutes and packing by throwing the chickens out to fly down under
their own power, but as they could not be briefed on the correct LZ this
method was discontinued. Life in the dank, musty bunkers was boring

Except for the steam pinnace, the Royal Navy's 'techniques for amphibious assault had hardly progressed beyond those used . . . over a century earlier' (see p. 44). RMA Battalion being brought ashore at Ostend, August 1914.

RMA in the infantry role in defensive position in a ditch outside Ostend, August 1914. They are wearing sea-service blue uniforms and that military abomination, the Brodrick Cap, named after, although not invented by, the Hon. William Brodrick, Secretary of State for War (1900–1903), and worn by the Army and Royal Marines. The Royal Marines retained it for sea-service dress after the Army had abandoned it.

RMLI armoured car mounting Maxim gun in Antwerp, October 1914, with fox terrier mascot.

Gallipoli: wounded from ANZAC being brought off in a lighter.

Gallipoli: Gully Ravine Cape Helles opposite Y Beach, taken later in the campaign, well after 25 April 1915.

Gallipoli: the old battleship HMS *Albion* ran ashore on a sandbank off Gaba Tepe on 24 May 1915. She was hit by over a hundred shells. Here HMS *Canopus* attempts to tow her off. Eventually, by firing all her heavy guns together, *Albion* unstuck, and got away.

Gallipoli: the 1st Battalion RMLI trenches at the extreme right of the French line, taken over in December 1915.

Gallipoli: ANZAC from seaward.

The Grand Fleet at sea.

Western Front: an RMA gunner with a 15-inch howitzer shell.

Western Front: loading the RMA 15-inch howitzer 'Granny' near Arras, 11 September 1917.

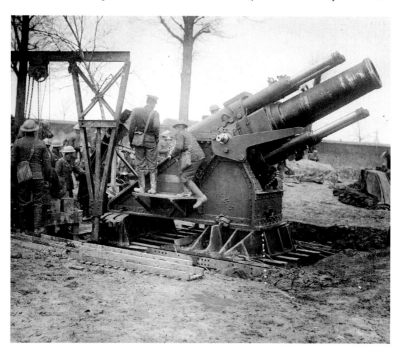

Western Front, Battle of Arras 1917: RMA gunners with a captured German field gun, at Feuchy.

Western Front, Ypres 1917: a typical German pillbox, with German dead outside.

Western Front, the First Battle of Bapaume: machine gunners move through Aveluy,
25 March 1918. The third man from the front in the file nearest the camera is carrying a
tripod on his shoulders; the barrel of his gun is carried wrapped in a tarpaulin by a man
out of sight behind him. The remainder are similarly loaded with liners of ammunition
and condenser cans as well as rifles. This could be a section of four gun teams.

Western Front, the Battle of the Drocourt–Quéant Line. Quéant was where the
63rd (RN) Division broke through the Hindenburg Line, September 1918.

HMS *Vindictive* after her return from Zeebrugge, showing the bridge, the foretop, and on the right a hut specially constructed for a flame-thrower. Below the hut can be seen some Stokes mortars. The crew of the foretop included Sergeant Finch RMA, awarded the VC by ballot. What look like clusters of old mattresses are 'splinter mats', rigged in an attempt to cut down the number of flying metal splinters.

Russia: Bolshevik prisoners with RMA guards, Murmansk, 1919.

for the Marines left behind to defend them while the remainder were out on patrol, and it was not long before they were looking forward to their turn to go out 'jungle bashing'. Except for their one week of rest and relaxation (R&R) in Singapore, and perhaps a few days in the Commando base, Marines and soldiers usually spent the whole of their six-month tour in these jungle forts or out on patrol. A typical routine would be eight to twelve days out on patrol and four days defending the fort; one troop would be in while the rest of the company was out. Time in the fort not on sentry duty would be spent cleaning up after the last patrol, washing, and shaving off beards (shaving cream and soap give off a distinctive smell easily detected by sharp-nosed enemy soldiers). As in Malaya, jungle boots rotted after a few days on patrol and thorns tore the sweat-soaked jungle greens: rotting and torn equipment and clothing would be exchanged for new, and preparations made for the next sortie, including the relentless search for means of cutting down weight. Toothbrushes were cut in half, rations sifted and repacked, and only the bare minimum taken. The more experienced the Marine, the fewer creature comforts he took.

Patrols sometimes walked direct from their jungle fort to their task, returning on foot. On other occasions they would be taken by helicopter. This saved time and energy, but in some situations there was a risk that the clattering helicopter would reveal the patrol's location to a watching Indonesian. So, as a rule of thumb, patrols were usually landed one valley away from their objective. Unless they were landed into another base, a village or on one of the rare open patches such as a dry river bed, the only way of getting down through the jungle canopy was by roping down from the helicopter as it hovered overhead. A pick-up by helicopter often necessitated cutting sufficient space for it to descend. Explosives, special hand saws, and sometimes buzz-saws were lowered through the 100–200 foot jungle canopy from a helicopter, and Marines became adept at the rapid clearance of helicopter landing points for the extraction of patrols and casualty evacuation. As in Malaya, patrolling was mentally and physically exhausting, but more so, as patrols were out longer, and the terrain was more challenging. The operational environment encountered in Malaya, such as the risk of following a track or path, and the routines for basing up and so forth, also applied to Borneo, and were greatly improved. With the successful Malayan campaign only four years past, there was a wealth of experience to draw on. The highly motivated all-volunteer Gurkhas, and British Marines and soldiers rapidly became peerless jungle fighters. Operations in Borneo were well planned, subtle, and executed with finesse.

Despite some excellent work by British and Gurkha troops, by the end of 1963 the Indonesians still held the initiative and crossed the border when and where they pleased. In early 1964 the war really began to hot up, and the Indonesians changed tactics. The Indonesians in Borneo were far better equipped, and more aggressive and dangerous than the CTs in Malaya. Some Gurkha officers who had fought the Japanese in Burma, including Walker himself, rated the Javanese, Sukarno's best troops, on a par with the Japanese. Not everybody agreed with this assessment, but whereas in a contact the CTs normally ran away if counterattacked, or ambushed, even if they outnumbered their attackers, the Indonesians fought back, and company-sized battles were not uncommon. The Indonesians were not guerrillas, but well-equipped soldiers operating from behind their own frontier, and well supported by artillery and mortars, provided they were within range. They established bases, usually near the border, from which they sortied to raid Commonwealth bases; something the CTs in Malaya would never have seriously contemplated. Perhaps the most ambitious attack was on 27 April 1965, by at least two companies of Indonesian regulars against the base at Plaman Mapu occupied by one platoon of B Company 2 Para, the other two platoons being out on patrol. The attack was beaten off by the aggressive soldiers of B Company led by the CSM, and the close support of mortars and guns.

By mid-1964, estimates of Indonesian strength in the border garrisons were well over 22,000. In places where there were no suitable sites for bases adjacent to the border, the Indonesians went to considerable lengths to get their troops to the border on their side over great distances, then to the target, and out again. They often did this by river, and intelligent anticipation by the British enabled them to work out where the Indonesians would cross and what routes they would use, for without air superiority the Indonesians could not use helicopters to lift troops across the border, whereas the British used helicopters extensively in the follow-up of Indonesian parties after incursions and raids. An astute estimate of where a raiding party was heading to cross back into Kalimantan would enable cut-offs to be placed by helicopter.

In March 1964 the 2/10th Gurkha Rifles encountered an Indonesian raider battalion, and some days later the 'Black Cobra' Battalion. Fierce firefights took place on both occasions, quite unlike contacts with the IBTs. From then on the war changed from a platoon or troop commander's war to a company commander's war. In August 1964 the Indonesians mounted a seaborne and airborne attack on the Johore coast of Malaya. Although successfully mopped up, it was clearly time to take the initiative. That same month, under pressure from Walker, the British government agreed to cross-border operations by British and Gurkha troops. These, codenamed Claret Operations, were usually carried out by a force of at least company strength, only within range of their own artillery support, and against Indonesian bases which had been located and well reconnoitred by either SAS or reconnaissance patrols from the unit tasked with the operation. In this way the Indonesians could be forced to pull their bases back, making their incursions more difficult.

To begin with only the Gurkhas were allowed to mount Claret Operations, and then Walker extended the clearance to British battalions on their second Borneo tour. Royal Marine Commandos, with their great experience, took part in several. These operations were graded Top Secret, and outside those who had taken part, and a few commanders and a handful of specially 'Claret Cleared' staff officers, nothing was known about them until the mid-1980s, even within the armed services, let alone the public. The fact that they were concealed from press and public for twenty years was a remarkable feat, and speaks volumes for the integrity of the Marines and soldiers of the time, rather different from the – admittedly few – soldiers today who rush into print to describe even the most secret operations at the first opportunity. The British government was not at war with Indonesia, and at the time would deny that any British soldiers had crossed the border. The guidelines for Claret Operations, known as the 'Golden Rules', were:

— Every operation to be authorized by DOBOPS himself.
— Only tried and tested troops to be used.
— Depth of penetration to be limited and the attacks must only be made to thwart offensive action by the enemy. No attacks were to be mounted in retribution with the sole aim of inflicting casualties on the foe.
— No close air support will be given to any operation across the border, except in the most extreme emergency.

— Every operation must be planned with the aid of a sand table and
thoroughly rehearsed for at least two weeks.
— Each operation to be planned and executed with maximum security.
Every man taking part must be sworn to secrecy, full cover plans must
be made and the operations to be given codenames and never
discussed in detail on telephone or radio. Identity discs must be left
behind before departure and no traces such as cartridge cases, paper,
ration packs etc. must be left in Kalimantan.
— On no account must any soldier taking part be captured by the enemy
– alive or dead.

In 1964, 40 Commando was based in the Tawau area on the south-
east coast of Sabah, very different from the situation in Sarawak, which
had a land border with Indonesian territory. The Commando's task was
to prevent infiltration into the 150 square miles of mangrove swamp and
waterways surrounding Tawau, and into the bay itself. To assist the
Commando, the SBS operated in this area carrying out waterborne
reconnaissance missions in canoes and raiding craft in and among the
islands. The border with Kalimantan ran across the large Tawau Bay,
and Indonesian Marines were deployed in brigade strength on their side
of the border, including Nunukan Island, close to the border. The
Indonesian Marines manned an OP on Sebatik Island, south of the
logging town of Tawau, and north of Nunukan Island. Half of Sebatik
Island was in Sabah, and the other half in Kalimantan.

In December 1964, a typical shallow-penetration cross-border operation was carried out on Sebatik Island by Lieutenant R. A. M. Seeger
and a fifteen-man fighting patrol from B Company of 40 Commando,
the first offensive cross-border operation the Commando carried out.
Seeger had recently been sent to the Commando from the SBS, it being
normal form in the Royal Marines for an officer or other rank to
intersperse Commando and SBS tours. His account, written some years
later (in the third person), tells the story:[15]

The Indonesian Marine OP, manned by four or five Marines from
Nanukan [sic], was 500 yards over the border by the mouth of a river.
They operated quite openly, and lived in an atap hut at the back of a
small beach. Supplies and reliefs came by small boat. There were no
obvious defensive measures such as earthworks, wire, or trenches, but the
jungle and mangrove reached down to the water's edge on both sides of
the beach. To the west of the beach the foliage was less dense, and a

narrow sandy strip only thinly covered by trees and scrub ran for about 75 yards before thick vegetation began again. This strip offered an alternative landing place from the sea and an indirect approach to the position. Counter-observation on the OP was maintained by a patrol boat permanently anchored mid-way between the island and the mouth of the Serudong. Earlier in the year, 1 SBS had carried out a clandestine reconnaissance of the OP. Two men had swum ashore from a boat and crawled to the edge of the hut.

Seeger was ordered by his company commander, Captain Bacon, to select fifteen men, the number that would fit into two Gemini inflatables, and he

immediately began an intensive programme of inflatable handling and close-quarter shooting. The attack plan was as follows. A 'parent craft', the *Bob Sawyer*, would be provided by the Tawau Assault Group – a waterborne river and sea patrol force drawn from Support Company. It would simulate a routine move through the northern waters of Sebatik Island and under cover of darkness launch three Geminis at the north-west tip. The inflatables would paddle down the shoreline to the border, where one would wait as emergency support, while the other two moved forward into Indonesian waters to beach at the end of the sandy strip. Once ashore, the patrol would close silently on the hut, and kill any enemy there. If they were fired on while still approaching the landing point, they would abort the raid, and return under outboard engine power to the parent craft. Once the boats were beached, however, any enemy reaction would be counter-attacked and fought through to a finish. The support Gemini could start its engine as soon as shooting began, and could, if signalled, reach the enemy position within minutes. The cover story for the raid was a waterborne patrol, broken down engines, and an accidental drift on to the enemy beach.

The *Bob Sawyer* left Kalabakan late in the afternoon of 8 December, and released the Gemenis as planned. With the support Gemini were Captain Bacon, as overall operational commander, a signaller for communication to Commando HQ and the parent craft, a coxswain, a GPMG team and several riflemen. In the assault Geminis were Lieutenant Seeger, his Troop Sergeant – Sergeant Costley, and the other picked Marines from 6 Troop. These included Marine Allen with the GPMG, a close quarter assault group with SMGs under Corporal Tomlin, and a stand-off/cut-off group of two riflemen. The latter had torches fixed to their SLRs as a simple night vision device for accurate shooting.[16] They were both leading scouts and good rifle shots.[17] Lieutenant Seeger as the front man on the approach carried a number of grenades.

The three Geminis reached the border without incident. There were whispered goodbyes and good lucks, and the craft separated. After watching the assault Geminis disappear into the darkness, Captain Bacon checked the readiness of his support craft and settled down to wait for the planned H-Hour. To his surprise and alarm, shooting began long before this – within about twenty minutes of the assault boats' departure.

Seeger had beached his boats and was part way along the sandy strip when an automatic weapon opened up on his half left. It fired high and the rounds passed harmlessly over the patrol. For a moment there was a stunned silence before the patrol returned fire. Seeger shouted out instructions to spread out left and assault forward. Sergeant Costley and Marine Allen moved up from the rear to give supporting fire from the right flank. At this point Seeger stumbled and fell. He later found that a bullet had gone through the flesh of his elbow, but whether the fall was caused by the shock of this or tripping over a mangrove root, he could not tell. Where the bullet came from was questionable also; it could as easily have come from his own side as the enemy. Getting to his feet, Seeger moved forward across several patches of open ground. Fire was still being exchanged, and despite the darkness, he experienced sensations of colour and brightness, and a curious feeling of treading on air. Suddenly the shape of a hut loomed into view. Seeger stopped and crouched in the cover of some trees. Shouting a warning 'grenades' he threw two at the front of the house. Sergeant Costley and Marine Allen, moving parallel with Seeger, were now thigh-deep in water, and hearing the shout, took the only cover available, submerging under water with their weapons held aloft. Even then some grenade fragments hit their bodies. Allen surfaced and opened up with his GPMG as Seeger followed up his grenades, with fire from his SMG. He changed magazines rapidly so a continual stream of 9mm rounds preceded him to the front of the hut. A camp fire was burning lighting the darkness and enabling Allen to engage moving enemy with his GPMG.

The remainder of the patrol had been held up by the narrow approach and surrounding vegetation. Now with a rush they caught up Seeger and fanned out across the beach. Two enemy dead were sprawled out near the fire, hit by grenade, SMG or GPMG. Another body was spotted by the hut. A fourth man had been seen stumbling, possibly hit, into the outer darkness. There was not time to search for bodies or examine injuries. Following shouted orders to return to the boats, the patrol retraced their footsteps at speed, scrambled into the inflatables, pushed out to sea and started motors. As they did so, enemy reaction began, small arms fire from high ground to the south-east passed overhead, and mortar fire from Nanukan began to fall in the area of the OP. Captain Bacon greeted the boats with relief and led a hurried last leg to the *Bob Sawyer*. She had closed on the action as the shooting started so the return journey was not long.

The patrol was transferred to the Governor's boat (a motor yacht, the *Petrel*), and here

> in comfort the raiders were able to stretch out and sleep or celebrate success with cans of Tiger. On board were Lieutenant Woodham in command and Surgeon Lieutenant Wilson, the MO. Wilson and his medical assistant, cheated of major injuries of interest, seized upon Seeger's elbow and made what they could of this.

Seeger was awarded the MC and Costley and Tomlin were mentioned in despatches.

As well as surveillance operations in the Tawau area, the SBS was engaged in similar OP work at the other end of Borneo, in Sarawak. In addition it carried out reconnaissances for possible retaliatory operations on the Indonesian coast at various places. On a number of occasions submarines were used to take the SBS teams to a point offshore of the target. At this stage there was no covert way to launch the SBS from a submarine: the boat had to surface, as in the Second World War, and the inflatables or canoes were floated off the casing. Captain David Mitchell RM, commanding the SBS in the Far East, and Commander John Moore RN, the Commander of the 7th Submarine Squadron (SM 7), worked out and practised a solution involving putting out SBS operators, two at a time, from the escape chamber while the submarine was still dived. They breathed from air bottles attached to the casing of the submarine until the whole party was complete, at which they switched to an oxygen close-circuit breathing system, which leaves no bubbles on the surface, for the swim in to the target. This worked well in the warm waters of the Far East, but had to be refined for operations in colder climates.

By February 1965, new weapons were beginning to be issued to troops in Borneo, such as the American Claymore anti-personnel mine, a curved slab of explosive that threw out a devastating cone of steel balls, and could be detonated either by a switch or trip-wire. The American AR-15

Armalite (the civilian version of the rifle adopted by the US forces as the M16) replaced the SMG, and by the end of the campaign most SLRs. The Armalite was not only lighter, but fired automatic, which the SLR did not, and had a far greater stopping power than the 9mm SMG. The British actually received the Armalite before the US forces in Vietnam. The American M-79 grenade launcher, which discharged a 40mm HE round 100 yards, was a distinct improvement on the British Energa grenade launcher.

Commandos and SBS were not the only Marines to serve in the campaign. Royal Marines officers piloted some of the naval helicopters, far and away the best medium-lift squadrons in Borneo. In April 1965, two Sioux AH-1 helicopters arrived to join 40 Commando, the first of the Commando air troops, attached to all Commandos.

In September 1965, 40 Commando was back in Borneo, this time in Sarawak, in the area of Serian. Jungle operating techniques were by now vastly more skilled than in the old Malaya days, and the first tours in Borneo. Seeger:

> Gear was personalised and cut to the minimum. The dehydrated ration packs which were good and already lightweight were even further reduced. Cutting [*as seen in the movies, where patrols hack their way through the jungle*] rarely occurred, and never on the move. When we stopped for the night I would allow one to two minutes of cutting only, (done all together at the same time) to prepare our camp site. Swiss Army knife saw blades were invaluable here as you could saw silently before or after the time allowed for chopping. We moved off at dawn, and kept going until dusk, stopping for breakfast well after dawn, and for supper well before dusk. This reduced the risk of a following enemy catching you in an unprepared state. Tracks were rarely used, and all communication was in whispers or silent signals. Small patrols used hammocks and slept on the sides of steep hillsides or other awkward ground. This further reduced the chance of being caught by an enemy patrol. Para cloth track suits were worn at night, and wet clothes put back on in the dark in time for the dawn stand-to or move off. Gear was organised into three lines – survival items in the pockets, essential operating equipment (water, ammo, etc) on the belt, and the rest in the small pack. Belts were made by ourselves out of air-drop straps with buckles, so that they could not suddenly unclip and come off. Olive green trousers and shirts were painted to achieve better camouflage, and cam cream worn on face and hands. Maps were unmarked and all waste carried in plastic bags.[18]

D Company, under the command of Lieutenant Seeger, mounted Operation Freefall, a cross-border attack on an Indonesian camp at Apuk. Seeger:

> On the morning of 6 September [1965], company HQ, 1 Troop (Lieutenant Taffinder), and 2 Troop (Lieutenant Binnie) moved south from Kujang Sain along the border to a point where it hooked west into Indonesian territory. The ground here was steep, offering good communications and defensive fire positions for a fighting withdrawal. For these reasons it had been chosen as a forward base for the operation. 3 Troop (Lieutenant Linn) from A Company at Plaman Mapu had secured it the day before and would hold it until D Company's return. D Company spent a relaxed night guarded by 3 Troop sentries, and at first light the next day bade goodbye and stepped across the border into the unknown jungle.
>
> They were carrying rations for seven days and an average supply of ammunition. Riflemen had three magazines and a bandoleer [50 rounds], GPMG teams carried 400 linked rounds, and every man a grenade. Gear had been cut to the minimum – a para cloth sleeping bag, a poncho, a spare pair of socks, a face veil, water bottles, a mess tin, personal sundries and a generous supply of mosquito repellent. Each section carried two waterbags and a small machete. Personal equipment was organised into the usual three lines, and the only 'documents' carried were identity discs, blank notebooks, and clean maps. Lavatory paper was unmarked and each man had a plastic bag for sweet papers, spent matches, cigarette ends, and food wrappings. The company's cover story was a routine border patrol whose commander had got lost.
>
> Intelligence reports had indicated an Indonesian position at Apuk but there were no firm details. Information on the ground was meagre, and had been gleaned from inadequate air photographs and maps. D Company's first task was to find the enemy.
>
> The first day was slow and tiring. Direct progress proved impossible. There were large tracts of open ground and groups of civilian workers, round which awkward and painstaking detours had to be made – no easy task with a line of 60 men. After some searching, a secure and concealed harbour area was found near to a convenient stream and on top of a small hill. The plan was to stay here for two days while a reconnaissance patrol, specially picked for their experience and fitness, established the location and activity of the enemy.
>
> The patrol chosen by Lieutenant Seeger comprised himself, Lieutenant Wells-Cole, Company Sergeant Major Wilson, and Sergeant Adamson.

For speed and stealth they carried belt order only – water bottles, ammunition and cold rations for 24 hours. They were armed with Armalite rifles. They soon found themselves with the same problem as with the company on the first day – open or cultivated ground, villagers and workers. The need for cautious concealment, detours, and back-tracking, aggravated the job of looking for the enemy camp, and by nightfall their information was as inconclusive as ever. Soldiers had been seen moving in the village, but they had come across no sign of a permanent position.

That night it rained, and the patrol started off again in the dawn stiff, cold and anxious. There was only limited time to complete their task. All turned out well, however, and by 0800 hours the enemy position had been found. It was on an isolated piece of high ground by an east-west bend in the river which flowed past Apuk. Steps ran down to the water from what appeared to be the main entrance. A series of bunkers, communication trenches and atap buildings clustered round the flat summit. Alongside the river ran a frequently used track leading, it was assumed, to the village. The position was observed for an hour, and with the ground knowledge gained on the move out, fast progress made back to the company harbour.

In the jungle everything is relative. To the patrol, the company base seemed the height of comfort and security. They drank, ate and relaxed, before settling down to planning the company follow-up. It was to be simple and straight-forward. Packs would be cached in the stream-bed near the harbour area, and the company would close on the enemy position by the patrol's return route. Near the enemy camp they would split, each troop following its own path north and south of the river to the final assault position. The only complication was mortar and artillery fire which was to come down fast and less than 100 metres in front of the forward sections. By the end of the afternoon, preparations were complete. Coded radio messages had been transmitted, O Groups and briefings conducted in hoarse whispers, and all weapons and ammunition carefully checked, cleaned and stowed.

Next morning, 10 September, the company set out as planned for the enemy camp. As they drew near, a lone civilian was sighted heading towards them through the trees. The lead scout gave the danger signal and the sign for an indigenous local. Quickly the marines faded into the cover of the jungle scrub. The local walked unhurriedly past but without apparently noticing anything. Another alarm came from an energetic domestic pig on the left flank.

Three hundred metres short of the enemy position, a rear Company HQ was dropped off as a withdrawal rally point. A few minutes later the Troops split. Seeger, and Sergeant Adamson led Lieutenant Binnie's troop towards the point from which they had observed the camp the day before. Lieutenant Taffinder took 1 Troop across the river and over unreconnoitred ground towards a parallel position 50 metres north. Behind the leaders in each file walked GPMG gunners and Energa grenadiers – just in case contact was made earlier than expected. Seventy metres behind the planned firing positions and on a slight rise Seeger dropped off his MFC [Mortar Fire Controller], Corporal Holland, FOO, Bombardier Livingstone, HQ Signaller, Corporal Hathaway, and a rifleman escort. He, himself, carried on with Binnie to spring the assault. Some 50 metres short of the river, and about 70 metres from the first enemy bunker, they halted. Binnie spread his sections out in extended line. The far left one went slightly further forward with the Troop Sergeant – Preece, and Sergeant Adamson of the reconnaissance patrol. Weapons in the aim, safety catches off, the troop settled down for H-Hour.

Number 1 Troop meanwhile were having difficulties with the unknown ground and a large gap in the trees. They were still on their approach in a long single file. Back at the enemy camp a bathing party walked out of the front entrance down to the river. Other movements could be clearly seen in the position. Then just before H-Hour, a large well-built Indonesian soldier began to climb the steps to the camp. Unable to resist this target, Seeger opened the proceedings with a single shot from his armalite. The soldier catapulted forward hit by the simultaneous fire of a 2 Troop GPMG and a dozen or so SLRs. The weapons on the south side of the river raked the bunkers, sentries, and moving personnel at the edge of the camp. North of the river, only Taffinder and one GPMG team were ready. The rest of the Troop broke into a run firing on the move. As the troop's second GPMG team crossed an exposed gap, they saw three enemy 30 metres to their right coming down a ridge from the camp. They opened fire and killed them but not before one tried to throw a grenade. Luckily for the GPMG gunners it hit the back of the leading enemy and exploded against him. The CSM who should have been at the rear HQ but had accompanied 1 Troop, directed Marine Porter, a newly joined young marine with an energa, to fire at one of the forward bunkers. To his satisfaction, it scored a direct hit. Lieutenant Wells-Cole, who had stayed where he had been told, in the Company rear HQ, watched with interest as enemy return fire began to burst through the trees above him. Ahead of him in the forward HQ, the MFC and FOO had brought down white phosphorous markers and were giving their corrections [to the mortars and guns over the radio] for a close engagement of the enemy.

The first shot had been fired at 0953, and two minutes later Seeger gave the order to withdraw. Now reluctantly, the sections began to pull back. There were sharp explosions from enemy grenades and 2in mortars. Just too late a machine gun began to kick up earth where the troops had lain. Machine gun fire followed 1 Troop back across the gap. On target, 105mm shells and 81mm mortar bombs began to burst among the enemy fire positions. The transition from days of silence to sudden uninhibited noise was startling. Men called out or talked in excited release, commanders shouted orders, radio operators tried to make themselves heard, and a vengeful Marine Kennedy from 1 Troop shot the pig that had caused alarm on the way in.

Lieutenant Wells-Cole and the CSM (who had hurried back to his post), checked the company through the rear HQ and saw it shake back into the discipline of jungle silence and single file. Seeger moved up into the lead, and Corporals Finn and Cudbertson, the assault engineers, fired the Claymore Mines they had rigged to cover the withdrawal. The mortars and artillery fired their final rounds and except for the heavy breathing of men moving at speed and the squelch of jungle boots in the mud, all was quiet again. Seeger expected a follow-up, and shouts and noise of movement suggested a sortie from the camp, but nothing developed. The company reached the border without interference, and by the end of the afternoon, were back in Kujang Sain.[19]

In March 1966 L Company (Captain J. Smith) and M Company (Captain Thomas Seccombe) of 42 Commando took part in an ambitious Claret Operation, to raid an Indonesian camp at Sedjingan. After marching from their respective company bases at Biawak and Samatan, in western Sarawak, the two companies rendezvoused the day before the proposed attack nearly two miles away from their target. A very successful close reconnaissance led by Lieutenant Clark of L Company was carried out. At one stage, Sergeant Pearce got to within five yards of Indonesian sentries without being spotted. Later, while lying up behind the enemy camp, an Indonesian urinated on the bush behind which Pearce was crouching; again, he escaped detection.

As a result of Clark's report, it was decided that L Company would attack the camp at first light, while M Company ambushed the likely enemy withdrawal routes. This necessitated M Company moving into position in full daylight the evening before, which they managed without detection. The next day the attack went in as planned, both parts of the operation being successful, and the Indonesian Army sustaining considerable casualties. During L Company's withdrawal, Lieutenant Clark, whose reconnaissance had been so critical to the success of the mission, was hit by a stray round and killed; his body was evacuated by helicopter. This attack in strength by 42 Commando undoubtedly had a considerable effect on the morale of the Indonesian troops in the area, especially as Sedjingen had been garrisoned by members of the Siliwangi Division, one of the crack formations of their army.

This Claret Operation was merely one of the seven Seccombe took part in during that six-month tour in Borneo, and not the largest either. He promised his company that on all Claret Operations he would not return across the border without all his men, be they alive or dead.

In March 1966 General Suharto replaced Sukarno in a coup, and secret peace feelers were sent to Kuala Lumpur, but meanwhile cross-border incursions, again by the IBT leavened by Indonesian regulars, continued. Although Claret Operations were halted, the British continued to reconnoitre across the border to give warning of incursions. On 28 May 1966, cross-border activity ceased, and on 11 August the end of Confrontation was ratified.

As one study of Claret Operations has commented:

> One of the key ingredients in bringing the Indonesians to the negotiating table were Claret Operations. They pushed the Indonesians 10,000 yards or more back from the border, from where viable incursions simply could not be launched. When pressure was eased, the Indonesians went back on the offensive. Militarily, Claret was able to stop the Indonesians. Politically, the secrecy of Claret allowed the Indonesians a face-saving way of backing down once military aggression proved fruitless. Both tactically and strategically Claret was an excellent example of war as a continuation of policy by other means. It was successful because of strict control by policy makers and because the operations were conducted by highly trained, physically fit and well led troops.[20]

Although several British infantry battalions served in Borneo between 1962 and 1966, the brunt of the campaign was undoubtedly born by the eight Gurkha battalions, and 40 and 42 Commandos. Between December 1962 and September 1966, there was almost always one Commando in Borneo, and on more than one occasion both were there. The Gurkhas lost 43 killed and 87 wounded, and the two Commandos, 16 and 20, compared with a total for all fifteen British infantry battalions of 16 killed and 51 wounded.[21] 40 Commando, the last Commando to serve in Borneo, arrived in May and left in September 1966. The Royal Marines had been in at the beginning, and were there to the end.

*

Royal Marines officers on loan to the Sultan of Oman were engaged on operations east of Suez long after the Commandos were withdrawn to the United Kingdom. Starting a couple of years before the British withdrawal from Aden and until 1975, the Sultan's Armed Forces (SAF) fought a hot, bloody, and uncompromising war in the Dhofar, at the western end of the Sultanate. The soldiers, NCOs, and junior officers of the SAF infantry battalions[22] and artillery regiment were Arabs or Baluchis. The COs and company commanders were officers on loan from the British Army and Royal Marines, as well as ex-officers on contract, including British, Southern Rhodesians, South Africans, and Australians. Five Royal Marines lost their lives in the Dhofar, among them a contract officer, Captain A. W. Woodman RM, who was mortally wounded assaulting a series of caves in a wadi, and brought down fire on his own position to save his men. Another contract officer, Captain H. B. Emslie MC, was hit by a rocket from an anti-tank weapon while in his vehicle; the largest piece of him picked up was his finger.

Initially there were no helicopters, and little support of any kind. Air support was provided by some Beavers and a handful of piston-engined Provosts. The drill for dropping napalm on the enemy consisted of rolling a barrel of it out of a Beaver, followed up by a Provost firing tracer or a rocket at the liquid as it lay on the target. Water resupply was sometimes reduced to dropping blocks of ice in sandbags, preferably into an acacia bush so the bag did not burst, and pouring the melted ice into one's chuggal (water bag). The medical support to a rifle company consisted of a Baluchi lance-corporal with a medical bag. Casevac was by mule.

The SAF was poorly equipped with number 4 bolt-action rifles; the enemy had AK47s. Southby-Tailyour usually carried a 2in mortar on patrol, and his first action on contacting the enemy was to fire two HE bombs in the general direction of the enemy; it was more effective than a pathetic spatter of fire from bolt-action rifles. He bought 150 sets of disruptive-pattern trousers for his company from Millets in Dover while back on his mid-tour leave. He was not the only officer to privately equip his men.

The terrain was testing, mountainous like the Radfan, but with the added hazard that many of the wadis, especially near the coast, were choked with luxuriant growth brought on by the heavy rain in the monsoon. The enemy were tough, ruthless Communist guerrillas trained by the Chinese, who infiltrated from the old Eastern Aden Protectorate, which became Southern Yemen (now part of the Yemen), and Dhofari tribesmen who had been subverted. To begin with the Chinese stayed on the Yemen side of the border, but Southby-Tailyour found a dead Chinese on the battlefield as early as 1968. The Yemenis thought nothing of liquidating tribesmen who would not join their cause. The British officers were under no illusions what would happen if they were captured: torture followed by beheading.

Southby-Tailyour was one of a number of Royal Marines on loan to the SAF who were awarded the Sultan's Bravery Medal (the equivalent to the British DSO) for his gallantry in one of his many actions; on this occasion he led his company in a bayonet charge. Not many officers since 1945 have taken part in bayonet charges, and especially not in 1968, which is widely, but incorrectly, proclaimed as being the one year since 1945, up to the time of writing, that the Army and the Royal Marines saw no action.

This hotly contested, and almost unheard-of, war, was vitally important to British interests, and indeed every country that obtained oil from the Persian Gulf. Had the insurgents defeated the Sultan of Oman, control of the Musandam Peninsula guarding the southern side of the Straits of Hormuz might well have passed into potentially hostile hands, as did the northern shore when the Shah of Iran was overthrown in 1979. Furthermore the security of the United Arab Emirates might have been threatened, with untold consequences.

By 1970 the war was being lost, and the enemy were closing round the port and airfield of Salalah. At this stage the British government, then Labour, and under pressure from the Shah of Persia and other Gulf rulers, decided that the Sultanate must be saved from Marxism. Money and equipment were poured in, which allowed the SAF to buy and acquire helicopters, artillery, SLRs, and other vital weapons. The SAS was sent out to take over the running of the programme of 'turning' the

Dhofari Addu (guerrillas), which was done by such measures as building wells, establishing medical clinics for the tribesmen, and protecting the villages from the Yemenis. Turned Addu were formed into Firquats, commanded by SAS officers and NCOs. Finally, a key move, the old Sultan was overthrown by a British-backed coup, and replaced by his Sandhurst-trained and forward-looking son, Qaboos bin Said al Said. By 1975 the war was won, not only by the SAS, it must be said. Without the SAF it would have had no chance of succeeding.

Most Royal Marine loan-service company commanders who took part in the ten-year Dhofar War were in their mid-twenties, with the local rank of captain, but still substantive lieutenants, and in a Royal Marines unit would have been company seconds-in-command if they were lucky. In the Dhofar, commanding 140 men in action, they grew up very quickly indeed. The soldiering they learned stood them in good stead in the years ahead; Nicholls, Southby-Tailyour, Sheridan, and Gardiner were among those Royal Marines officers whose battle-experience was to prove invaluable in action in the Falklands a decade or more later.

24

Mostly West of Suez, 1967–1999

Since the end of Confrontation in Borneo, and the withdrawal from Aden and its aftermath, the Commandos have not, so far, been employed on operations East of Suez; although both the SBS and Royal Marine Detachments in ships have done so. The 3rd Commando Brigade had completed its redeployment to the United Kingdom by 1972 (45 Commando in November 1967, Brigade HQ and 42 Commando in mid-1971, and 40 Commando in March), and there was a danger, now that the Middle East and Far East roles for Commandos had disappeared, that they too would be axed by the seemingly never-ending round of successive cuts by the Labour government, which resulted in a total manpower reduction in the armed services of 75,000. However, some good staff work and successful lobbying by Royal Marines staffs in Whitehall resulted in the Commando Brigade, with the LPHs and LPDs, being assigned to the North Atlantic Treaty Organization (NATO), to form part of the amphibious force on the Northern and Southern Flanks of the Alliance. In both regions the United States provided by far the greatest proportion of ships and the landing force; the latter furnished by the superbly equipped USMC, which in the early 1970s was twice the size of the British Army, and had the added advantage of possessing a private air force bigger than the RAF. The role of the landing force on both flanks was to arrive in or off the coast of an Alliance country threatened by Warsaw Pact or Soviet forces before fighting began, in the hope of deterring aggression, and if that failed, joining the 'host nation' and other NATO allies to defeat the aggressor.

In another astute move, in the early 1970s the Royal Marines and Netherlands Marine Corps signed a Memorandum of Understanding, the result of which was that the Dutch would provide a battalion to serve in the 3rd Commando Brigade on NATO operations. The formation of the United Kingdom/Netherlands (UKNL) landing force as an officially acknowledged part of the reinforcing formations for Northern European Command was an important political card to be played to Ministers and Navy Board alike when the subject of disbandment or reduction of the two Corps was raised.

First, however, the Brigade HQ and the two Commandos from the Far East had to be retrained from jungle soldiers, and exceedingly good ones, to be able to deal with the very different conditions they would find on the battlefields in Europe, against a first-class, numerically superior enemy, massively equipped with armour. A great number of techniques had to be learned, and much tactical 'baggage' discarded, such as fire bases, and centralized fire control of guns, mortars, and support aircraft (which had been raised to the status of an art form, or tactical nonsense, depending on one's point of view). 45 Commando, which had a head start on the other two, was already engaged in training for a new role by the time its sister Commandos returned, and was for a time not under the command of HQ 3rd Commando Brigade. The successful transformation of the Commando Brigade into its NATO role owed much to Brigadier Ovens, who had brought the formation back from the Far East and commanded it for the first eighteen months West of Suez. His gallant service with 41 Commando in Korea in the Chosin battles with the 1st Marine Division gave him a credibility with the US Marines on the Northern and Southern Flanks which very few Royal Marines serving at the time could match. His perceptive eye and quick brain, disguised by a laid-back manner, identified what practices from Far East days should be axed, and what should be put in their place. Among these, he insisted on restoring 'eyeball' control of supporting artillery and ground-attack aircraft rather than the supposedly intellectually satisfying, but ponderous, Far East practice of fire control by officers grouped round a Supporting Arms Coordination Centre (SACC) table miles away in the Brigade HQ command post.

It had been recognized for some time that the Commando Brigade needed dedicated sapper support. Between 1968 and 1971, 59 Squadron Royal Engineers had worked with the brigade in the Far East, and in April 1971 the squadron was brought back to England and re-formed as a Commando squadron. Like all the other members of the brigade, the sappers were required to pass the Commando course and become fully integrated members of the Commando family. Thanks to some very high quality OCs, officers, warrant officers, NCOs, and sappers, 59 Independent Commando Squadron, Royal Engineers rapidly became one of the élite sapper squadrons in the British Army; the author and the soldiers would say *the* élite, although 9 Parachute Squadron, Royal Engineers might disagree.

In January 1972 the various logistic sub-units attached to the 3rd Commando Brigade were formed into the Commando Logistic Regiment of four squadrons (Transport, Medical, Ordnance, and Workshops) and a headquarters. Among the officers and men in the regiment were Army personnel from the RCT, REME, RAOC, and RAPC, and the Medical Squadron included naval doctors and medical assistants. The only comparable organization in the British forces at the time was the Parachute Logistic Battalion belonging to the 16th Parachute Brigade, which disappeared with the disbandment of that brigade in the late 1970s. The Commando Logistic Regiment, with its 'can do' approach to its tasks, became a byword for efficiency and spirit, and the Royal Marines count themselves fortunate to be supported by their green-bereted Army and Navy comrades.

Eventually, by the mid-1970s, the Commando Brigade's Southern Flank role was discarded, mainly because of lack of shipping and a perception in the UK defence establishment that on the Northern Flank the amphibious force had a more credible task. This concentration on the Northern Flank certainly made arguing the Marine and amphibious case with its masters, the Royal Navy, easier. For the Northern Flank, and in particular denying the Soviets the use of airfields in Norway, could be portrayed as a vital adjunct to the maritime battle to bring convoys carrying reinforcements from the USA across the North Atlantic. This had some appeal to the mainstream of the Navy, who understandably were obsessed with the threat posed by Soviet submarines and maritime air in this battle, and to whom anti-submarine warfare (ASW) was the raison d'être of their service. The ASW warriors were not totally convinced, however, and those in the Navy involved with the nation's deterrent, the Polaris submarines, were not in the least impressed by the arguments for retaining an amphibious capability. So when times were hard, and they increasingly were as the 1970s passed and until early 1982, ditching the Royal Marines and amphibious shipping usually figured high on the list of expedients to keep the Royal Navy afloat in economic hurricanes. In successive years, the LPHs were scrapped or earmarked for disposal, or, in the case of HMS *Hermes*, converted first for ASW, and subsequently for the Sea Harrier (SHAR). The SHAR was not purchased with support of the landing force in mind but in furtherance of the ASW battle, specifically to shoot down enemy aircraft shadowing and passing on information on convoy movements, or attack using stand-off air-to-surface missiles (in the jargon, to 'hack the shad'). By late 1981, the amphibious shipping available to lift the 3rd Commando Brigade was reduced to two LPDs, of which one was in mothballs, and six LSLs. Exercises were occasionally carried out using *Hermes*, or the new carrier, *Invincible*, in the LPH role, but no one, least of all the Royal Marines, believed that if the balloon went up they would be used for anything other than ASW. Plans were afoot to scrap the LPDs when the Secretary of State for Defence visited HMS *Fearless* during an exercise in December 1981. Standing in the tank deck, watching LCUs shuttling to and fro, he turned to the Brigade Commander (the author) and remarked that he was unaware that the Navy had ships that could do what he was seeing. On returning to Whitehall, the LPDs were reprieved, but no plans were made to replace these seventeen-year-old ships.

Relating this sorry tale has taken us to the eve of the Falklands War which forms the subject of the next chapter, and we must fast-rewind to the events of the late 1960s.

Because operations in Norway might be conducted in winter, it was decided that 45 Commando should be based at Arbroath in Scotland, and specialize in winter and mountain warfare. The British had learned the hard way in 1940 that fighting in northern Norway, even as late as April, was made extremely difficult by deep snow and cold. Without skis, movement off the roads was impossible. The Royal Marines had been given a practical demonstration of how fickle the weather could be in Norway north of the Arctic Circle when 43 Commando, in totally unsuitable kit, and without winter training, was caught in blizzards while on exercise in September 1962. Thanks to good leadership by a few winter-warfare trained officers and NCOs, and the innate toughness of the Commandos, no serious cold injuries were sustained, but an unpleasant time was had by all. The Royal Marines were determined that there should be no repeat performances of this fiasco, and 45 Commando began to train comprehensively to master the necessary winter warfare skills, including cross-country skiing. Even more so than in the jungle, merely existing in the harsh environment of the Arctic can pose so many problems that the Marine or soldier can become absorbed with survival to the exclusion of the operation which is the reason for his being there in the first place. The trick is to train him so that he takes the environmental difficulties in his stride and operates at 100 per cent efficiency.

Except for a brief taste of winter warfare in Russia in 1919, the origins of today's Royal Marines expertise in winter training dates back to 1949, when Lieutenant M. E. B. Banks RM was an instructor at the Commando Cliff Assault Centre (CCAC), based at the Commando School at Bickleigh in Devon. The emphasis was on cliff assault, mainly practised at St Ives in Cornwall, and the instruction included snow and ice climbing in Glencoe but not mountain warfare. Banks, who had hopes, later realized, of becoming a polar explorer and Himalayan mountaineer, wanted to make a start in practising the art of living in the snow. After running a course in Glencoe, he sent his students back to Bickleigh, and in his own words, 'went AWOL with Corporal Genge'. They made an entirely unauthorized climb to the top of Ben Macdhui in the Cairngorms, and spent the night there. On his return to the Commando School, he set out his ideas for Commando 'Whiteshod' training in Scotland in a paper to his CO. The first course began in 1950. Soon afterwards, Banks spent two years in the high Arctic, returning to find that the 'Whiteshod' training had been moved to Norway, where he ran the next three courses. From Banks's idea was born the Corps's mastery of winter warfare, the instructors and supreme British military exponents in this art being provided by what, by the 1970s, became the Mountain & Arctic Warfare Cadre (now the Brigade Patrol Troop). Without the ability to train complete Commandos in these skills it is highly unlikely that the Royal Marines would have been assigned the NATO role on the Northern Flank.

Eventually, when the whole brigade became committed to operations in north Norway, everybody underwent winter training. One Royal Marine general put it in a nutshell: the aim was to turn the best jungle soldiers in the world (the Gurkhas might have something to say on that score) into the best Arctic soldiers in the world – not the best skiers, or the best mountaineers, but the best soldiers, rather different. Another Royal Marine general remarked that the training in north Norway was so demanding that troops trained there would be able to cope with war anywhere else. He was to be proved right in 1982, in the Falklands.

NORTHERN IRELAND, 1969–

Meanwhile, the Royal Marines were involved from 1969 in another campaign that at the time of writing is on hold, but is the longest ever fought by the Corps or the British Army in their history; the place, Northern Ireland. There is no doubt that the Catholic minority in the Province between 1922 and the late 1960s were subject to discrimination. This followed 800 years of what Winston Churchill called 'the long sorrowful story of English intervention in Ireland'. In 1169, Richard de Clare, Earl of Pembroke, a French-speaking Anglo-Norman baron leading an army largely of Welshmen, invaded Ireland by permission of the King of England, and the Pope, who also happened to be English (the only one to attain the papacy so far). The cause of the present series of troubles was discrimination against Catholics in jobs, housing, and local government. This led in 1968 to the formation of the Northern Ireland Civil Rights Association (NICRA). We now know that NICRA was the creation of the Irish Republican 'Army' (IRA), in the hope of using the Association as a lever to assist in gaining the IRA's aim, a united Ireland. The IRA's ambitions were greatly assisted by the formation of People's Democracy (PD), an organization of naive student street politicians headed by the far from naive Bernadette Devlin. Although the Northern Ireland government eventually proposed a series of measures that would have granted most of the Catholic demands, they were not good enough for PD, who decided to march in protest from Belfast to Londonderry in January 1969. Their aim was to provoke an incident which would get them the maximum publicity in the world's media.

At their overnight stops, the PD marchers slept in village halls guarded by armed IRA men. The night before they were due to arrive in Londonderry, the reactionary Protestant cleric Ian Paisley held a protest meeting, during the course of which drunken Catholic youths attacked the hall, and burned a car belonging to one of Paisley's supporters. Paisley fell into the trap set for him, and led a furious Protestant mob to confront the PD marchers at Burntollet Bridge. Here violence ensued, in which the RUC reservists joined, and eighty-seven people were seriously injured. The lid was off the pot. Burntollet Bridge was the principal catalyst in the troubles that were to follow.

In the following months serious rioting broke out, first in London-derry and then in Belfast. Protestant mobs invaded the Catholic slums and set fire to houses. When in August 1969 the British Army appeared on the streets to contain the violence, it was greeted as a saviour by the majority of Catholics, and so was 41 Commando when as Spearhead Battalion it moved to Belfast in September 1969.

The only Catholics who did not give the troops a rapturous welcome, including handing out buns and cups of tea, were members of the IRA; although they posed as protectors of the Catholics, they had been so conspicuous by their absence during the 'invasion' by the Protestants that for a while their coreligionists taunted them that the initials IRA stood for 'I Ran Away'. Determined to reassert its authority, the IRA instigated a number of riots, leading, among other things, to searches of property by the Army (in this context including the Royal Marines), in the hope that the honeymoon between the Army and the Catholics would be short. They were not disappointed.

In the ensuing days, disagreement about tactics led to formation of the breakaway Provisional IRA (PIRA), which remains the dominant group to this day. The Official IRA, after a brief attempt at violence, reverted to its policy of gaining its ends by political means alone. At first, and for several years, the PIRA pursued a policy of violence without any serious efforts at including a political component in the campaign. Then some years ago PIRA also entered the political arena, or rather was allowed to do so, under the guise of Sinn Fein, which is one and the same; and it pursued a twin-track strategy of 'bomb and ballot box'. For the moment, the bombs, and weapons, are in the PIRA caches, and at the time of writing no one can predict when they will be brought out again; possibly when PIRA sees that it is not going to achieve its aim by peaceful means. The aim of both the Officials and Provisionals, and other Republican groups, is a united Ireland. It is a goal that is unlikely to be achieved while the majority wish otherwise, unless the British government exerts pressure on the majority Unionists (those who desire to retain union with Britain), something which cannot be discounted in the case of some British politicians. Throughout the years, and to this day, ceasefire notwithstanding, the Provisionals use their armed muscle to intimidate competitors in 'mafia-like' activities totally unconnected with political aims for a united Ireland, including a network of rackets, such as drinking clubs, illegal taxis, smuggling, and drugs. The proceedings from these crimes finance their operations and line the pockets of the 'godfathers'. The Protestant paramilitaries, who sprang up in the wake of PIRA's shooting and bombing of Protestants, follow much the same line of business. The Protestant Paramilitaries leave the British Army alone, but abuse and attack the Royal Ulster Constabulary (RUC) when the police thwart them in their purposes. All paramilitaries of whatever stripe call themselves an 'army', but are a stain on the name 'soldier' – choosing the easy target, shoppers, office blocks, and children, they are totally cynical about causing civilian casualties despite giving warnings with sickening hypocrisy.

However, the PIRA has always been the main threat to security forces (troops and police). Until the present so-called 'ceasefire', it used the classic terror tactics of intimidation, shootings, and bombings, always hoping that the security forces could be provoked into over-reaction. It works to undermine the morale of successive British governments of both political parties and to shock the British public into putting pressure on the politicians to wash their hands of the problem. The beatings and intimidation continue.

41 Commando spent only six weeks in the Province in 1969 and the tour was reasonably quiet. However, they, and all the RM Commandos, would be back many times. 45 Commando, the first Commando to carry out a four-month tour in Northern Ireland, had an altogether busier time. With its affiliated battery, 145 (Maiwand) Commando Light Battery, it arrived in Belfast on 1 June 1970. This was the period of the large riots by both Catholics and Protestants, when crowds of several thousand hurled rocks, bottles, iron piping, broken sheets of glass, and bricks, and catapulted rivets at each other, and at troops in the middle. Troops without riot gear and with rudimentary shields suffered serious injury. Sometimes the confrontations lasted throughout the night. A favourite ploy of the gunmen was to fire on troops trying to keep the mobs apart. The first Marine to die in the present round of troubles was killed by a gunman in the Ardoyne area of Belfast. Fire was returned, which scared off the gunman. In another incident Petty Officer Medical Assistant MacLaughlin was giving first aid to a civilian when, as he was helping his patient into an ambulance, he was hit and wounded. MacLaughlin was awarded the George Medal.

By early 1999 the Commandos had carried out a total of thirty-eight tours of varying length in the Province, totalling some thirteen and a half years in all, in the course of which fourteen Royal Marines had been killed and ninety-four wounded sufficiently seriously to be casevaced to hospital. How many others had been lightly wounded by bricks and bottles, bruised in encounters with violent crowds, or struck with small splinters from bombs and other explosions, and patched up to return to the fray, will never be known. In addition to the Commandos, Royal Marines serve in Northern Ireland in other capacities, ranging from providing small detachments on craft operating in Carlingford Lough and other coastal waters to special duties units: it is impossible to cover all the incidents in which the Marines were involved in this thirty-year campaign. One outcome of the troubles was that earlier efforts by the Army to have the number of Commandos reduced to two were shelved when it realized that without the Royal Marines it would have found the provision of troops to serve in the Province well nigh impossible. As it was, the Army had to send gunners, armoured troops, and sappers there as infantry, to the detriment of training in their proper roles.

When 40 Commando relieved 2 Para in Belfast on 15 June 1972, the PIRA had declared a ceasefire, but the situation soon escalated, and that year saw the worst outbreaks of violence in the Province to date. 40 Commando had responsibility for North Belfast, which included a number of notorious trouble spots – Unity Flats, a Catholic enclave in the city centre, the Catholic New Lodge, and Protestant Tiger Bay districts. Although the Commando, as all other units in the Province, was tasked to assist the Royal Ulster Constabulary with maintaining law and order, this was before the days of 'police primacy', and the overwhelming bulk of operations were military-led, albeit at times responding to Special Branch intelligence and at its request. The Commando maintained a high level of patrolling on the streets, both by vehicle and on foot, as well as OPs, searches, and the provision of troops to quell riots and prevent inter-sectarian violence.

Patrols commanded by corporals, sergeants, and junior officers were carefully coordinated so that each 'brick' of four operated in conjunction with another 'brick' in an adjoining street, or with a vehicle patrol. The rationale was that if a 'brick' in one street came under fire from a gunman, his escape route, typically through back gardens and neighbouring houses out onto another street, might be blocked. Sometimes this worked, but on many more occasions – how often, it is impossible to say – the gunmen, who seldom operated without a comprehensive system of lookouts, would abort the 'shoot' if they discerned, or even suspected, that their escape route was blocked.

One of the keys to avoiding being the target for a shoot was to be overtly professional. A 'brick' moving at times of heightened tension, or along a street in risky areas, which most Belfast 'patches' were, 'hard targeted' themselves, that is made themselves harder to hit by running from cover to cover, covered by one or more of their comrades. Marines on the street learned to keep moving all the time, and even if required to stay in one place for a few moments (while, for example, the patrol commander was running a security check on someone), they would shift position, swaying back and forth, constantly ducking and weaving (known as 'wombling'), and scanning likely fire positions through their SLR sights with the weapon up on aim. Such measures made them marginally more difficult to hit than men who stood rooted to the same spot, and were obviously 'switched off'. PIRA gunmen, who despite all their heroic propaganda treated their own survival as top priority, were less inclined to take on a difficult target who might just be scanning the window from which the shoot was to take place, and ready to fire back. Taking cover in a doorway could be risky, because there might be a booby trap behind it; and for this reason, the doors of derelict houses were best avoided altogether.

Shoots were also carried out by 40 Commando's snipers, from OPs set up to overlook locations that might be used by PIRA gunmen. Some of these were highly successful, killing three PIRA gunmen, and wounding yet more. Shoot-outs were commonplace, and the Commando's first gun fight took place in Unity Flats on 26 June, and was followed by another in Lenadoon Avenue on 9 July.

Although command on the streets was exercised by young junior officers and NCOs in Belfast, the company commander was usually quickly on the scene the minute it looked as if trouble might escalate. The CO spent a great deal of his day driving round the streets with his Rover Group, usually in two vehicles and accompanied by the RSM and escorts, and when he heard of an incident on his radio could be quickly on the scene as well. He might well be followed by the Brigade Commander of 39th Infantry Brigade, and on occasions by the GOC himself. This was a period of intense media interest in Northern Ireland,

and sometimes the TV crews would be at the scene before the troops, especially if, as was not unknown, they had been tipped off by PIRA. All commanders from the CO to junior officers in Commandos and battalions serving in the Province, especially in Belfast and Londonderry, could expect to find themselves being quizzed on camera about their actions. Usually the honesty, directness, and professionalism of those interviewed did much to counter PIRA propaganda. Now, and for many years past, statements to the media are handled by Government Public Relations and it is rarely, if ever, that the troops on the ground find themselves being interviewed.

On 24 March 1972 the British government in Westminster assumed direct responsibility for the government of the Province from the Northern Ireland Parliament at Stormont. Well before 40 Commando's arrival in the Province, PIRA had set up 'no go' areas in Catholic areas such as Andersonstown in Belfast, and the Bogside and Creggan in Londonderry. The Protestant Ulster Defence Association (UDA) attempted to follow suit, without much success. But clearly the PIRA 'no go' areas were a challenge to the government's authority, inviting a 'tit for tat' reaction by the Protestants, so plans were made to remove all barricades, and move into these areas. There was concern that such a move would spark off much bloodshed, especially if PIRA stayed to fight it out. However, any reservations were scotched when on 21 July PIRA detonated twenty bombs simultaneously in Belfast, twelve of them in 40 Commando's area. Overall 10 civilians were killed, and 130 injured, mostly in the main bus station.

This was the catalyst for Operation Motorman, clearing all of the barricades and entering the 'no go' areas in Belfast and Londonderry. Three Commandos were involved, 40, 42, and 45 (41 was in Malta). 42 and 45 Commandos were sent over from Great Britain for the operation, as part of the reinforcement of the Province, bringing the Army presence there up to twenty-seven battalions. The CO of 40 Commando had a total of nine companies under command for Operation Motorman, and joked about 'commanding a brigade'. The Royal Marines landing craft crews were also involved. On the night of 31 July, under the command of Captain S. E. Southby-Tailyour RM, four LCUs from HMS *Fearless* made the forty-kilometre approach up Lough Foyle to Londonderry to land four armoured vehicles Royal Engineers (AVREs – Centurion tanks equipped with dozer blades). The AVREs moved in and swept away the barricades in the Creggan and Bogside without any resistance. The story was the same in Belfast. Tipped off by the British government to minimize bloodshed, the gallant volunteers of the Provisional Irish Republican 'Army' had fled lock, stock, and barrel to safety in the south. The commander of the PIRA North Belfast 'Battalion' even sent the Intelligence Officer of 40 Commando a postcard saying that they had 'gone south'.

They were soon back once the danger of a real battle had receded, and a member of 40 Commando was shot in the back of the head and killed while providing security for an Ulster Defence Regiment (UDR) funeral in Belfast. Shooting incidents resulted in a total of sixteen casualties in 40 Commando, including three dead. As an indication of the intensity of violence in 1972, during 40 Commando's tour in Belfast, 606 shots were fired, and 34 nail or petrol bombs were thrown at the Marines, who replied by firing 602 rounds and 989 baton rounds (so-called 'rubber bullets'). The Commando searched 33,028 cars and 1,292 houses, finding 52 weapons, 4 grenades, 346kg of explosives, and 7,403 rounds of ammunition.[1]

All three UK-based Commandos deployed to the Province again in 1973. In the early 1970s it was commonplace for each Commando to carry out at least one four-month tour per year in Northern Ireland, and sometimes when it was their turn for Spearhead they would be deployed to the Province for a shorter period in addition.

Operations in rural areas, where all the Commandos carried out several tours, were very different from Belfast. One of the most testing, if not the hardest, patch was always South Armagh; 1,000 square kilometres centred around the town of Newry, and including fifty kilometres of border with the Republic of Ireland. The inhabitants in the southern part of the patch were and are overwhelmingly Republican supporters. The PIRA in South Armagh enjoyed a reputation as formidable guerrillas, and to a certain extent still do. The press were quick to dub the place 'bandit country', and in the early days, PIRA in South Armagh liked to depict themselves as being divided into two battalions, and incidents were always claimed by the 1st or 2nd Battalion. In reality, there were about thirty hardcore terrorists who lived over the border in the area of Dundalk, and operated in Northern Ireland, supported willingly or otherwise, actively or passively, by a large majority of the residents of South Armagh.

The terrain is similar to that in Devon on the fringes of Dartmoor: a mixture of rolling countryside covered with small fields, mostly pasture, and rocky hills covered with heather. The thick blackthorn hedges bounding the fields were a considerable impediment to movement. Using the gates too often was an invitation to be blown up by a booby trap – usually an improvised explosive device (IED) consisting of fertilizer and fuel oil, with a commercial explosive primer or booster, detonated by command wire or, as the years passed, by increasingly sophisticated radio-controlled or electronic devices. As the PIRA acquired more commercial explosive, it relied less on the home-made variety. Troops moving in the countryside assume they are under observation all the time. As a good part of the southern and western sections of the patch was easily observed from across the border, monitoring patrols was not too testing for PIRA. Even well north of the border, cover for PIRA OPs was plentiful, in farmhouses, barns, derelicts, hedgerows, and bracken.

The penalty for carelessness, bad fieldcraft, and following a set routine was to be attacked, often with an IED, but sometimes with a shooting, the latter especially near the border. Here PIRA could set up a machine-gun, either just north or south of the border, and engage patrols with impunity, as far as any reaction from the Gardai, the Southern Irish police, were concerned; at least until more recently when the Gardai and Irish Army started taking the threat more seriously. Security forces were not allowed to cross the border into Éire, even in hot pursuit. Patrols engaged from across the border of course replied, and unlike in the cities, gun battles using machine-guns on both sides, firing large quantities of ammunition, were not uncommon. PIRA gunmen engaging patrols from fire positions just north of the border would usually retire rapidly once pinpointed and properly engaged. From positions south of the border, they would sometimes stay longer to fight it out, secure in the knowledge that there was no danger of the security forces cutting in behind them and surrounding them. In the southern part of the South Armagh patch, patrols operated in multiples of at least twelve (three bricks of four). When the threat was at its height in South Armagh, multiples on rural patrols in the 1970s and early 1980s were armed with a mix of SLRs, each with several magazines, 7.62mm Bren LMGs, GPMGs, 79mm grenade launchers, and smoke grenades for marking LZs for helicopters. Patrols were often out for three days or more, and night sights, flares, rations, and warm clothing, added to personal weapon and ammunition, made a substantial load.

Multiples moved tactically at all times, with at least 'one foot on the ground' at all times; the aim, not always achievable, was to deploy so that the ever-watching opposition was not able to pinpoint the complete patrol. This was especially important near the border. PIRA knew perfectly well how the troops operated and how many men were in a multiple. If they could not spot one of the bricks, which they knew must be around somewhere, then there was a possibility that gunmen firing from north of the border would be cut off, and even if the firing point was south of the border, the unaccounted for brick would be in a position to reply immediately and with interest. As the years passed, PIRA received some devastating weapons, of which the .50in Browning heavy machine-gun, and even more so, the .50in Barrett sniper rifle are now rightly regarded by security forces with considerable respect.

To begin with, security forces in South Armagh operated some patrols in vehicles, and resupply of bases was also accomplished by road, but in late 1975 the IED threat became unacceptable. Several large charges were detonated in culverts, and on three occasions Saracen APCs were blown up, killing or badly wounding the crew and passengers. This led to the policy of using helicopters for the movement of troops and all supplies south of Bessbrook, with the exception only of covert cars and vans. For example, during 40 Commando's tour in 1976, the Reconnaissance Troop under Lieutenant Boswell used covert vans to move teams back and forth from OPs, and to counter illegal Vehicle Check Points (VCPs) set up by PIRA.

Manning OPs was an art in itself. They were almost invariably approached at night, and the least obvious place was usually the best. Many were set up within the blackthorn hedges, and for this purpose the team would carry a pair of garden secateurs to snip out room for a hide while disturbing the foliage as little as possible. Camouflage had to be excellent, because the farmers carried out almost daily patrols of their properties and any OPs spotted would be reported to PIRA. A small OP team of around five men was vulnerable to attack if discovered, and PIRA attacked several, so it was usual to split the team, with two men forward, and the remainder back in another location to provide mutual support.

If an OP was abandoned, it was usually unwise to reoccupy it. An OP, albeit not a covert one, on a feature known as the Drummuckavall, overlooking the border, had been occupied by men from 45 Commando for some time, before being withdrawn as a 'come on' for the PIRA. Unfortunately, a Special Forces team watching the OP to catch anyone approaching was withdrawn without telling anyone in the Commando. When it was reoccupied, PIRA initiated from across the border a huge IED that had been cunningly concealed under the OP, killing a corporal and a Marine.

During 40 Commando's 1976 tour, a very successful OP was mounted by the Reconnaissance Troop, initially under Sergeant Moate, in an attic in the Sinn Fein office in Crossmaglen, and maintained for several weeks. Access was achieved by picking the lock on the front door. Changeovers were carried out every five or so nights, through a side window. Food was eaten cold, and the answer to the obvious question is: polythene bags, or cling-film. By removing a tile in the roof, the OP could watch the town square. The Marines could also eavesdrop on some of the conversations in the office two floors below. Unfortunately the cover was blown when a member of the local Sinn Fein branch persuaded his secretary to accompany him to the loft for some horizontal activity. He led the way up the ladder, and on poking his head through the hatch, encountered the muzzle of the OP commander's pistol up his nostrils. The OP was withdrawn, but an attempt was made to conceal the fact that it had been there by threatening the Sinn Fein official that his wife would be told about his extra-marital activity if PIRA came to know of the OPs existence.

It was a pity that the OP was withdrawn, because one of the reasons for it being there in the first place was to command the square, following a mortar attack on the Security Forces base on 23 August 1976, which wounded six members of A Company. In the aftermath, Staff Sergeant Bruce RAOC cleared two of the bombs that had failed to explode, and was subsequently awarded the George Medal. If a further attack was mounted from the square, the OP could give warning, and even engage the terrorists while setting up. This is exactly what happened on 23 October, not long after the OP was withdrawn. This time PIRA launched ten bombs of a new type from a lorry in the square. All exploded, although not all in the base, and virtually destroyed a good deal of the accommodation occupied by A Company around the RUC station. Miraculously no one was killed, but six were wounded, including the

CQMS, Colour Sergeant Jones, for the second time in two months. He was subsequently awarded a bar to his BEM for his tremendous example to the company during and after both mortar attacks. His first BEM had been awarded for excellent under-cover work during 45 Commando's tour in the same patch in 1974.

Another feature of the rural scene was, and is, the clearance of IEDs. Often the IED would have been placed as a 'come on', to catch troops taking part in the clearance, either by gunmen, or more frequently by another IED placed in a likely Incident Control Position (ICP) from which the operation was controlled by the security forces. A good example is provided by an incident on 29 August 1976, which is typical of so many of the sixty such operations carried out by 40 Commando in a four-month South Armagh tour, and by all the other Commandos at one time or another.

At 1000 hours an OP spotted a pig lorry parked and abandoned across a road at Finnegan's Cross, on a road between Jonesborough and Drumintee, near the Belfast to Dublin railway. Part of a troop of C Company, whose responsibility was surveillance of the railway line, moved into OP positions to stake out the area, and keep the Commando HQ in the picture on any PIRA moves. The OPs reported that a barrier had been erected across the road about 600 metres south of Finnegan's Cross, fairly normal PIRA routine to keep locals away. Several questions presented themselves in the CO's mind. What was between the lorry and the barrier? Was this a lead-in to an incident on the railway itself (a frequent occurrence in the past)? Was it a come-on? He ordered that the line be closed to trains. Some local people gave information to patrols that the driver of the lorry had been stopped by three armed masked men who had ordered him to park in that position. An air photographic mission was flown, but the coverage was not sufficient for clearance purposes. By now night was approaching, and there was not enough light for another photographic flight, which would have to be done the following day. In the meanwhile the stake-outs would have to remain and indeed be reinforced to ensure no further devices were placed to catch the clearance party the next day.

After dark more stake-outs provided by the Reconnaissance Troop were flown in using a Scout helicopter with infra-red Nitesun (a large searchlight) and a Puma whose pilot wore Passive Night Goggles. This obviated the use of lights.

At about 0600 hours on 30 August a small explosion occurred in a derelict house bordering the road about halfway between the pig lorry and the barrier. After a second air photographic mission had been flown and the photographs evaluated, the clearance started. A device was found in the house consisting of a beer keg containing 27kg of Frangex (a powerful commercial explosive) and 23kg of scrap metal; a massive anti-personnel mine.

The pig lorry was empty. The position of the device in the derelict house indicated that it was placed to catch a clearance party moving down the road after clearing the pig lorry, which was a come-on. The small explosion which failed to initiate the main charge was caused by the booster charge being blown by radio control. This was an attempt by the terrorists to destroy their own bomb by radio control, possibly from Jonesborough, which was in line of sight of the device. Their trap had failed. Had the photographs the first day been adequate, and the clearance gone ahead, it might have been a different story.

The Belfast–Dublin line was opened as soon as a further search revealed that the area was clear. C Company, based at Forkhill, which had provided most of the stake-outs for this operation, maintained a continuous watch on the railway in a number of different ways, and the men allocated to this task were known as the 'Railway Children'. The railway played a large part in C Company's life right up to the end of this particular tour: on the second last day it was involved in clearing a large car bomb from under a railway bridge on the line.

Clearances were usually under observation from PIRA, to initiate other IEDs, or other action if the opportunity presented itself. As in the urban areas, unwinking alertness, striving to be unpredictable tactically, and good soldiering skills were a deterrent to PIRA action. On one occasion the terrorists placed two milk churns filled with about 120kg of explosives in a culvert under the main road linking Newry and Warren-point. Wires led from the culvert across the Newry River to Éire. An alert patrol spotted the wires, and after staking out the area the bomb was cleared. There was a sequel. Three years later, another bomb was placed under the same culvert: this time it was a radio-controlled device, and there were no wires. It was detonated under a truckload of soldiers from 2 Para, killing fifteen parachute soldiers and two from 1st Battalion the Queen's Own Highlanders (QOH). The CO of the QOH, in whose operational area the explosion had occurred, flew to visit the scene. As he ran from his helicopter past a masonry gatepost, the terrorists initiated another device hidden in it. He was vaporized; all that was found of his body was one of his cloth shoulder rank badges. The watchers three years earlier had noted that the CO of 40 Commando had used the gatepost area as his ICP for the clearance operation.

The way to dominate a rural area was, and is, by good OP work, and highly professional patrolling day and night in all weathers, so the terrorists moving about by car or on foot never know if they were under observation, or are about to bump into a patrol, which has been lying up watching them. By day and night, a snap VCP can be set up before the word gets around that the troops are out on a particular stretch of road, lifted when it has been in place for a while, and reset some distance away on another road, by moving across country. In this way several finds of arms and explosive have been made, and a number of terrorists arrested.

Now technology plays a big part in the surveillance operations in the rural and urban areas. There are fewer temporary OPs, because more permanent installations are now in place, and these coupled with troops on the ground provide a comprehensive coverage of the operational areas. Many more and increasingly sophisticated intelligence methods mean that troops even in the rural areas are mostly concerned with what are called 'framework' operations, providing the framework within which other organizations work, whereas in the earlier days the CO was responsible for all operations in his patch, and his troops carried out most of them. It is impossible to overstate the training value provided by Northern Ireland. Three decades' worth of junior leaders have been tested and their skills kept honed, while higher up, company commanders and Commando COs are also being tested in their own way, as are the strands of command and control throughout the units concerned. So some good comes out of evil. Throughout the present 'troubles', the standard of training and motivation of the RM Commandos has been a notable factor in their almost invariably exceedingly high standard of operating technique, and success.

CYPRUS

The only operational tasks involving the Royal Marines in the 1970s outside Northern Ireland, other than in the Dhofar and Oman, arose in Cyprus, following the Turkish invasion on 20 July 1974. At the time, 40 Commando was Spearhead, and was flown out to Cyprus to help protect the perimeter of the British Sovereign Base Area (SBA), while 41 Commando, based in Malta but embarked in HMS *Albion*, was tasked with evacuating British civilians and other nationals from Kyrenia, now overrun by the Turkish Army. There was no fighting involved, because the Turks were glad to see the back of the residents and other tourists in Kyrenia, and quickly moved in to the various houses and hotels themselves.

In the south of the island, the situation became quiet by 8 August, and 40 Commando was about to return to the UK, indeed the leading elements had already departed, when the Turks mounted a series of thrusts across the plain north of Nicosia. The move of 40 Commando was stopped, and, reinforced by 7 (Sphinx) Commando Light Battery RA and other supporting elements, the Commando reoccupied its old area. Again the British played no part in the fighting, although those who were present in 40 Commando, and others including the CO of the 1st Battalion The Royal Scots, have expressed the view that they could have stopped the Turks dead in their tracks well short of Nicosia had they been allowed to. In the end the threat of using RAF Phantoms and the evident determination of all the British troops prevented the Turks from seizing Nicosia airport, although they captured Famagusta and half of Nicosia city, where they remain to this day. By the end of August the ceasefire lines had been established and by mid-September 40 Commando was flown home, and 41 Commando returned to Malta. Following the Cyprus crisis of 1974, 41 Commando carried out two six-month tours in Cyprus on UN duties, and 40 Commando one.

41 Commando finally left Malta in April 1977, except for an over-strength company group, Salerno Company, which remained until March 1979. When 41 Commando arrived home, it was temporarily

disbanded, but re-formed at Deal in the autumn of 1977. Again it was Northern Ireland that saved the Commando, where it served two tours, one in Belfast and one in South Armagh. But, again, financial pressure on the naval budget in 1981 caused yet another disbandment of 41 Commando in 1981.

THE SBS

Before and after the withdrawal from the Far and Middle East, the SBS was involved in training and reconnaissance tasks in the Gulf, as well as several operations. The reconnaissance consisted of beach reconnaissances, and the training involved instructing the Iranian Special Forces before the abdication of the Shah in 1979. In 1971 the SBS was sent to operate in the Oman, with the SAS, in the Musandam Peninsula. Unfortunately at that time, the higher echelons in the Royal Marines were loath to see the SBS operating with the SAS, and although other opportunities arose for joint operations, they were not taken up, much to the frustration of the former.

An SBS operation that attracted considerable publicity involved the liner *Queen Elizabeth II*. The opening moves in this affair contained an element of farce, and provided an excellent example of how the SAS with its direct lines to the Military Operations branch in the MOD was better placed to get wind of possible operations, and had greater clout when it came to demanding assistance. One morning Lieutenant Clifford was summoned by the OC Special Boat Company, as it was then, and told that two people were required to parachute to a ship out at sea. The OC did not know the name of the ship, or where it was. He did know that an extortion threat had been received by telephone call to Cunard, saying that bombs had been placed on board this ship and demanding ransom money, in return for which the extortioner would reveal where the bombs were located. Clifford and Corporal Jones were selected for the task, and told to get to RAF Lyneham where they would find a C-130 waiting for them. To begin with the RN Air Station at Portland refused to supply a helicopter to fly these two to Lyneham, because there was then no codeword which would authorize the trip – another disadvantage compared with the SAS, which had codewords for many of its possible operations. Eventually Clifford and Jones arrived at Lyneham, and met the Ammunition Technical Officer (ATO), whose job it was to defuse any bombs found on board, and an SAS sergeant, whose role was unclear, and according to Clifford, unnecessary; an SBS sergeant, familiar with ships, would have been far more useful.

The RAF refused to tell the team which ship was involved, except that the ATO was informed that it had seven decks. Not until the team was in the air were they told the name of the ship. The ATO was not parachute trained, and Clifford and the despatcher had to talk him through the drills. As the jump was to be into the sea, and there was a stiff breeze, it was essential that the men did not hit the water still in their parachute harness, because the parachute would catch the wind, and they might be dragged, perhaps for miles, and risked being drowned. The correct drill was: as soon as the canopy deployed, to unclip the reserve on both sides, and let it hang on a short length of line, pull the seat strap well over the buttocks and sit in it as in a child's swing, with the right arm across the chest, grasping the left hand shoulder harness, turn and hit the release box thus allowing the two leg straps to fall away; when your feet touched the water, release the grip on the shoulder straps, raise your arms, and drop out of the harness, while canopy and harness whisked away, but soon collapsed without any weight. All very easy, but not a trick to try for the first time in mid-Atlantic, especially as a wrong move might result in plunging in from several hundred feet and death.

The two NCOs went out on the first pass, each taking a very heavy and oversized container of equipment. Clifford jumped with a small container (which was lost) in order to shepherd the ATO once down in the sea, which was quite rough. The descent went well, and the team was picked up by one of the ship's lifeboats. The ATO and Clifford went to see the ship's captain and gave him the day's newspapers from inside his dry-suit. The Captain said that having had the ship searched, and all the baggage mustered and matched to passengers, only two cases could not be identified. The ATO dealt with these. No bombs were found. The ransom money was delivered but not collected – the hoaxer was never found.

After this operation, some ATOs were parachute trained, and the SBS kept a team on standby for future threats of this type. The next occasion when the SBS was stood to for a similar task was in 1978, and the ship involved was the *Oriana*. In the end the operation was aborted as the team, led by Clifford, were standing in the door, waiting for the 'green' to jump, when a message was received from the *Oriana*'s captain saying that he did not need any assistance.

In the 1970s there were at least two ship operations by the SBS which involved travelling on the ship to provide protection to the passengers. In 1973 a group of American Jews chartered the *Queen Elizabeth II* to take them to Haifa, to participate in the celebration of the twenty-fifth anniversary of the founding of the state of Israel. It was thought that the Palestine terrorist group Black September might somehow infiltrate the ship and attack the passengers. In this, the first covert operation by the SBS, a team was put on board posing as trainee travel agents. They were not very convincing, partly because wearing plain clothes at Poole on duty was frowned on, so operating in such garb was then alien to the SBS, and the men were not allowed to grow their hair to the length fashionable among civilians in the early 1970s, which was long, shaggy, and with generous sideburns. Their cover was blown by the press. A similar operation was mounted on *Queen Elizabeth II* a couple of years later. This time there were two levels of protection: an overt protection team and a covert team, and their cover remained intact.

Throughout the 1970s, 80s, and 90s, the SBS deployed to Norway for winter training each year, as well as carrying out advance force and other reconnaissance tasks for the 3rd Commando Brigade's exercises, both there and elsewhere. It was fortunate that these skills were not allowed to become rusty, for they were vital in 1982.

25

The Falklands, 1982

In the day of battle everything turns, not as in a ship on the captain, but on the individual private.

Arthur Bryant

When other generals make mistakes their armies are beaten: but when I get into a hole, my men pull me out of it.

Wellington

Anyone contemplating the future of the Royal Marines in the New Year of 1982 would have found little from which to take comfort. It was one of the low points in their history since 1945. The main cause for gloom was the refusal of the Government to support the concept of the amphibious force by ordering replacement amphibious ships. The LPH had been taken away for use by the SHARs. The LPDs in service had been saved, for the moment, following the visit of the Secretary of State for Defence to *Fearless* as related in the previous chapter, but no successors were planned, and the future of even the in-service LPDs seemed tenuous. The question was how the LCUs, so vital for the mobility of the Commando Brigade, would be lifted to the operational area without LPDs. All manner of expedients were discussed, including the LCUs making their own passage all the way from Britain, across the North Sea, and up the coast to north Norway. At about the same time, on a visit to the 3rd Commando Brigade, the First Sea Lord, Admiral Sir Henry Leach, informed the Brigade Commander that in the future there would be no more amphibious assaults by the British. Although NATO plans envisaged the brigade arriving in north Norway or Denmark before the start of hostilities, it travelled to its operational area combat loaded, just in case these somewhat optimistic predictions were not fulfilled, and the shooting had started by the time it arrived. Now it appeared that even this elementary military precaution would have to be dispensed with, perhaps in favour of car ferries, or even going by train, as one cynical junior staff officer suggested. Although car ferries formed an important ingredient in the shipping for the brigade, it was never envisaged that they would operate without the back-up of purpose-built amphibious ships and their craft.

Financial stringency imposed by the Navy Department had forced another cut on the Commando Brigade, which boded ill for the future. For the previous three years the whole brigade, less 40 Commando which at that time was not winter trained, deployed to Norway for three months' winter training culminating in a major NATO exercise. In 1982, funds allowed only the deployment of 42 Commando, with some gunner and sapper support, and novice courses to be run for those in the brigade who were not already Arctic Warfare Trained (AWT). HMS *Fearless*, on what might have been her last deployment, had also carried out some valuable training in the northern Norwegian fjords.

Support for the amphibious capability within certain parts of the Navy varied from lukewarm defeatism to downright hostility. In early December 1981, the Director of Naval Operations and Trade protested that the Royal Marines were claiming that the Royal Navy still possessed a substantial amphibious capability, which enabled it to deploy a brigade 'world-wide, without reliance on ports and airfields'. He rushed into print to deny a capacity that did exist (just), saying:

> As the wretched Director of Naval Operations (and of course Trade) who would have to put flesh on such a skeleton, I can't visualise such an operation. Please let the first *victorious* battle of the Falkland Islands remain the only one – otherwise Ministers will be led to believe that we can repulse Argentina et al.

Whether his prescient remark about Argentina was a shot in the dark, or based on knowledge denied to others, is a matter for conjecture, but as the last troops of the 3rd Commando Brigade were returning from Norway in late March 1982 a new crisis loomed which was to change everything for the Royal Marines and the future of British involvement in amphibious operations.

It concerned a group of islands some 400 kilometres off the coast of southern Argentina, the Falklands, a British possession claimed by Argentina, and named by them the Malvinas. The Argentine Junta, headed by General Galtieri, and including Admiral Anaya and Brigadier Lami Dozo (Air Force), had been contemplating seizing the Falklands since coming to power in December 1981. That month Anaya ordered Vice Admiral Lombardo, the Chief of Naval Operations, to prepare a plan to occupy the islands. Anaya had been the Argentine Naval Attaché in London in the early 1970s, a period of perhaps the most spineless government in Britain since the Second World War, and he came away with no high opinion of the British steadfastness in the face of adversity. Firm action to seize the Falklands would, in his estimation, be followed by a period of 'wet henning' about, some squawking and clucking, and climb-down. He had not met Mrs Thatcher. But it must also be remembered that it was members of her cabinet that were allowing the amphibious concept to wither, and ignoring signs of danger to the islands.

No date had been set for the Argentine invasion of the Falklands, but the spark that set off the train of events that followed was the landing of a group of Argentine scrap-metal merchants at Stromness in South Georgia, 1,300 kilometres east of the Falklands, on 16 March 1982. Here they hoisted the Argentine flag. The Governor of the Falklands, Rex Hunt, under whose jurisdiction South Georgia came, ordered them to leave, and the Foreign Office backed this with a threat to remove them using HMS *Endurance*. Seeing this as a golden opportunity to use the crisis to occupy the Falklands, the Argentines countered by sending a ship from their Antarctic Squadron, the *Bahía Paraíso*, accompanied by the corvette *Guerrico*. Meanwhile they polished up their plans to invade the Falklands and South Georgia.

During the last week in March, intelligence received in Whitehall indicated that the Argentines might be contemplating a landing. Among other steps taken at this time, a warning was given to the CO of 40 Commando, Lieutenant Colonel M. P. J. Hunt, that he should be prepared to take his men to the Falklands to pre-empt invasion. How his Commando was to get to Falklands was not stipulated, and clearly had not been thought through by those issuing the 'stand-by' order in Whitehall. The large runway at Mount Pleasant did not exist then. The runway at Stanley airport would take C-130s, but at that time no British C-130s were fitted with refuelling probes to enable them to fly the 6,400 kilometres from Ascension Island, the nearest British base. A journey by sea at full speed would take nearly three weeks.

On 31 March the First Sea Lord, concerned by the conflicting information and suggested courses of action circulating in Whitehall, walked to the House of Commons, where he found the Prime Minister, the Defence Secretary, and the Foreign Secretary in conference.[1] He told the Prime Minister that the United Kingdom would never be the same country again if we did not retake the Falklands should the Argentines invade; this he now judged as inevitable since, at this late stage, there was nothing the British could do to deter them. The Prime Minister authorized him to 'prepare a force which he had advised would be required to retake the islands, without commitment to a final decision as to whether it would sail'. Oddly enough, although the word 'retake' was included in this instruction, and the First Sea Lord had told the Prime Minister that the whole of 3rd Commando Brigade would be required, no one thought to tell the Royal Marines. That very evening the Brigade Commander (Brigadier J. H. A. Thompson) returned from a reconnaissance for an exercise in Denmark, ahead of his staff, and was met by his GSO 3 Training, Major Hector Gullan, seconded from the Parachute Regiment, who told him about the flap earlier in the week, but that everybody who had been alerted had now been stood down, and that the 3rd Commando Brigade was not required.

In the Falklands, a new RM Falkland Islands detachment, Naval Party (NP) 8901, had arrived a few days previously, the relief of the old detachment being due, and not connected in any way with impending invasion. The old NP 8901 was ordered to remain for the time being. Inexplicably, both detachments, totalling some seventy officers, NCOs, and Marines, were placed under command of the incoming Detachment Commander, Major M. Norman, who was a tough and resolute soldier, but did not know the area. However, this did not affect the outcome.

Also on 31 March, a busy day, the *Endurance*'s Royal Marine Detachment, under Lieutenant K. Mills, augmented by nine men from the old NP 8901, a total of twenty-two all ranks, was landed at Grytviken to protect the British Antarctic Survey party, and maintain surveillance over Argentines landed at Leith by the *Bahía Paraíso*.

The following day, Major General J. J. Moore, the MGRM Commando Forces, was in the MOD handing back command of the Corps to the CGRM, Lieutenant General Sir Steuart Pringle, who had returned from convalescence following an IRA bomb attack in which he had lost one leg, and part of the other. No one saw fit to tell either officer, or indeed any other Royal Marine, that the Royal Navy was now preparing a task force which would include 3rd Commando Brigade.

At 0315 hours on Friday 2 April Brigadier Thompson was summoned from bed by a telephone call from General Moore, informing him that the Argentines were about to invade the Falklands (it was still 2315 hours on 1 April in the islands), and that he was to embark his brigade and sail within seventy-two hours. The whole brigade was still at seven days' notice, most of the units were about to go or had gone on Easter leave, except for one of 45 Commando's companies in Hong Kong, on its way home from jungle training in Brunei. Most of the brigade staff were still in Denmark. The Brigade Commander assembled those of his staff remaining in England, including his outgoing DAA&QMG (head logistics staff officer), and got to work to plan the embarkation of his brigade. There were no contingency plans to cater for a British invasion of the Falkland Islands, so the plan for the reinforcement of north Norway under NATO auspices was used as a rough guide. From the outset it was clear that ships taken up from trade (STUFT for short) would be needed in considerable numbers. Get STUFT took on a new meaning.

While the brigade and Commando forces staffs beavered away in Plymouth, 13,000 kilometres away their fellow Marines were engaged on different business. At 2300 hours on 1 April, Falklands time, forty-five minutes before Moore's telephone call, ninety-two Marines of the Argentine Amphibious Commando Company landed at a small beach near Lake Point due south of Port Stanley, as the precursor to the invasion force of two Marine battalions. Incorrectly described in the Argentine press as the Buzo Tacticos, the tactical divers providing a beach reconnaissance party for the main landing (a description picked up and repeated to this day in the world's media, with their unerring talent for perpetuating myth), this Commando company had two tasks: to neutralize NP 8901 in Moody Brook, and to capture the Governor. It failed in both. Moody Brook barracks was empty, and the attempt on Government House ended in the death, wounding, or capture of the entire Argentine snatch party.

The Commando company hardly lived up to its title; some of the Moody Brook party lost their way on a ten-kilometre march, and the leader of the Government House party walked up to the back door intending to demand the Governor's surrender. Unfortunately for him it was the door of another building. A photocopy of the plans of Government House, which earlier that year the Governor had given to an Argentine tourist posing as an architect, were in another ship in the Argentine amphibious force, not the one from which the Commando company had been launched.

The Argentines were not alone in having a less than perfect plan. In the years preceding 1 April 1982, the role of NP 8901 had been changed a number of times. It was recognized that an overgrown platoon would be hard put to defend even Government House, let alone the whole Falkland Islands, against anything stronger than a company. Space precludes detailed discussion of these roles as they changed, suffice it to say that they varied from the fanciful to the impossible. One plan called for the detachment to take to the countryside and conduct guerrilla warfare until a relieving force arrived, weeks later. This could only have been conceived by someone with sparse knowledge of the terrain and conditions in the islands. A case of big hands on little maps. Another, and no less fantastic, mission was to delay the invaders for three weeks to allow time for international negotiations at the UN. This highly unsatisfactory state of affairs was rooted in the lack of any firm British policy towards the Falkland Islands, the lack of contingency plans, and no clear idea of what the Royal Marine Detachment was for, and therefore what equipment was needed. Although the Royal Marines had repeatedly over the years tried to obtain clarification on the role and purpose of NP 8901, this information had never been forthcoming, in part because the views on the future of the islands in British government and official circles were so diverse and contradictory.[2]

In the event the Royal Marine Detachment made preparations to defend the airfield, the road to Port Stanley, and Government House. The main body was sited in Government House, while a small party was sent out into the countryside – in essence a mixture of both roles. Having seen off the snatch squad, the detachment settled down to defend the Governor, and brushed off attacks by small parties of the Commando company sent over from Moody Brook. When it became clear that Government House was about to be attacked by two battalions in armoured tracked amphibians (AMTRACs), supported by artillery, the Governor ordered surrender. Thanks to the Royal Marine Detachment, the Governor was not submitted to the indignity of being taken prisoner by force. Instead, accompanied by two officers, he could walk forward under a flag of truce, to rebuke the Argentine commander, before reluctantly agreeing that, for the time being, superior force had prevailed. Eventually all of NP 8901, including those who had gone into the countryside, were rounded up and flown back to UK via Montevideo. On arrival home, many of them volunteered to go south again with 42 Commando, forming J Company under Major Norman.

Lieutenant Mills's small party at Grytviken took on the *Guerrico*, which had a 3.9in gun and two helicopters, a Puma and an Alouette. As the Puma flew past to land Argentine Marines, Mills's men shot it down, killing the crew and passengers, and forced the Alouette to take evading action and land. *Guerrico* steamed close inshore, past Mills's well-camouflaged positions on the hillside. He engaged her with his 84mm Carl Gustav anti-armour recoilless weapon. He ordered the Marine firing it to aim for *Guerrico*'s bridge, and had it hit there the outcome could have been different, because she might have hauled off permanently. Instead, the projectile hit low, puncturing the hull. The next round punctured her Exocet launcher, and she was hit 1,275 times by GPMG fire. Thereafter she remained out of Carl Gustav and small-arms range, but engaged with her gun, to which Mills's men had no answer. A sailor on the *Guerrico* and two Marines in the Puma were killed, and several men were wounded. Eventually, with one man wounded out of his understrength troop, heavily outgunned, and outnumbered by at least 100 Argentine Marines, Mills surrendered, having downed two helicopters and put a corvette out of action for any serious maritime operations. He was awarded a well-deserved DSC, and his second-in-command, Sergeant Leach, a DSM. He and his men were evacuated to the United Kingdom.

Starting on Tuesday 6 April, the greatly expanded 3rd Commando Brigade sailed south, initially in eleven ships, eventually in fifteen. The final order of battle is shown in Appendix 4, but the major units joining before the brigade sailed consisted of 3rd Battalion The Parachute Regiment (3 Para: Lieutenant Colonel H. W. R. Pike), two troops of the Blues and Royals, another light gun battery, a Rapier air defence battery, the Special Boat Squadron, and D and G Squadrons 22 SAS. Later the brigade was further reinforced by 2nd Battalion The Parachute Regiment (2 Para: Lieutenant Colonel H. Jones), and additional sappers, gunners, and light helicopters. The total strength was about 5,500 men, twenty-four guns, and some twenty-four light helicopters. 3rd Commando

Brigade and the amphibious ships (Commodore M. C. Clapp) each constituted Task Groups in their own right, and came directly under command of Admiral Sir John Fieldhouse, the C-in-C Fleet, based at Northwood outside London, who assumed the title Commander Task Force 317. Contrary to popular perception, neither was under command of the Carrier Battle Task Group Commander, Rear Admiral 'Sandy' Woodward.

On the voyage south the troops concentrated on keeping fit, and on other training, including first aid, mortar and artillery fire procedures so that every Marine and soldier knew how to call for and adjust supporting fire, and familiarization with the terrain in the Falklands. Training aboard some of the smaller, more cramped ships was testing, but all were imbued with the will to overcome such problems and thus avoided the tendency that can master embarked troops, which is to sit back and do nothing on the grounds that it is all too difficult. Troops embarked in the cruise liner *Canberra* had no such problems, one circuit of the boat deck was quarter of a mile. All troops on all ships ran and exercised in boots and equipment daily, and consequently a very high standard of fitness was maintained throughout the seven-week approach to battle period.

While the amphibious ships paused at Ascension Island to restow loads and restore some semblance of order to the chaos on board, much of which resulted from the precipitate departure of the brigade from the United Kingdom, South Georgia was recaptured. South Georgia is a crescent shaped island 170 kilometres long, 29 kilometres across at its widest point, and 1,300 kilometres east-south-east of the Falklands. Much of the island is snow-covered throughout the year, and numerous glaciers run down from the central mountain spine. The weather is violent and unpredictable; a particular feature is the rolling, turbulent wind which blows down the mountainside, rather like a waterfall, or rushing surf. This 'katabatic' wind roars down the fjords, can gust up to 100 knots, and will blow small boats, particularly inflatables, out to sea despite outboard engines being pushed to full power. Violent changes in wind direction follow in quick succession. Ice blown out to sea can suddenly be blown back up the fjord, trapping inflatables and piercing their fabric sides.

The force selected for the operation, codename Paraquet, consisted of M Company 42 Commando, under Captain Nunn, with two 81mm mortars, a section of the Commando Reconnaissance Troop, a section of assault engineers, medics, and logistics, two Naval Gunfire Observer (NGFO) parties, and an SBS section. In overall command of the landing force was Major Sheridan, the second-in-command of 42 Commando. They all flew to Ascension Island on 7 April, where Sheridan found waiting to join, as he had expected, 2 SBS and the Mountain Troop of D Squadron 22 SAS. Sheridan embarked with OC M Company and other elements in HMS *Antrim* on 10 April, while the main body of M Company, less Company HQ, embarked in the oiler RFA *Tidespring*, and the Task Group, under command of Captain Young of *Antrim*, steamed south with HMS *Plymouth*. On 12 April Sheridan was told, somewhat to his surprise, that the whole of D Squadron had been transferred from the RFA *Fort Austin* to shipping heading for South Georgia. Who had authorized this was never made clear to Sheridan, nor was an already confused command set-up improved by the addition of an SAS squadron commander with private satellite communications to Hereford, enabling him to bypass everybody at the scene of the operation. The additions brought the total strength of the landing force up to 230 all ranks.

The Task Group, having rendezvoused with HMS *Endurance* well north of South Georgia, arrived off the island on 21 April. Things started to go wrong almost immediately. The SAS persuaded the Task Group Commander to land reconnaissance patrols on the Fortuna Glacier, contrary to Sheridan's advice, based on considerably greater experience of mountaineering and glaciers. Within twenty-four hours they were asking to be evacuated to avoid cold casualties, having made no headway across the crevasses on the glacier. Eventually, after a gallant and brilliant piece of airmanship by Lieutenant Commander Stanley, flying a Wessex Mk 3 anti-submarine helicopter, they were rescued without casualties. In the process two valuable Wessex Mk 5s crashed on the glacier, fortunately without loss of aircrew, who were also rescued by Stanley. Matters went from bad to worse when subsequent reconnaissance attempts were frustrated by a combination of ice in the fjords and high wind, and in one case incompetence by the SAS Boat Troop.[3] At this point there was a panic reaction to reports of an Argentine submarine in the vicinity, and back-seat driving by Task Force HQ at Northwood, to which it was prone throughout the war, resulted in the bulk of M Company being carted out to sea in *Tidespring*. To quote the captain of *Endurance*, 'in military terms the whole operation had become a monumental cock-up'.[4] Eventually the submarine, the *Santa Fe*, was sighted on the surface and attacked by helicopters dropping depth charges and missiles, damaging her so much she was non-operational, and she limped back into Grytviken.

By now HMS *Brilliant* had been rushed south to join the Task Group, partly to upgrade the ageing anti-submarine capability provided by *Antrim* and *Plymouth*, but also to replace with two Lynx the two Wessex lost on the glacier. Although there were now believed to be some 140 Argentine Marines ashore, and Sheridan had only around 75 men available thanks to the despatch of *Tidespring* out of the area, he pressed Captain Young to attack Grytviken without further attempts at reconnaissance, relying on the shock effect of the attack on *Santa Fe*, and naval gunfire. An ad-hoc company was quickly gathered using the SBS, SAS, M Company HQ, the reconnaissance section, and *Antrim*'s Royal Marine Detachment, and landed in *Brilliant*'s two Lynx and *Antrim*'s one Wessex AS helicopters. *Antrim* and *Plymouth* started a bombardment with their 4.5in guns, the NGFOs 'walking in' the fall of shot from some distance out to within a few hundred yards of the Argentines, who soon hoisted a white flag. Why these tactics, which Sheridan had recommended from the outset, and to which the enemy had absolutely no counter, had not been tried in the first place is a mystery. What is clear is that there were too many 'chiefs' of equal rank on this operation, and too little attention was paid to the officer with the most battle and mountain experience, Major Sheridan, who was in overall command of land operations, but junior to the naval captains, of whom there were no less than three, and equal to the SAS squadron commander. The advice tendered by Captain Barker of HMS *Endurance*, who knew most about local conditions, was also ignored. The Navy's understanding of the command arrangements was further obfuscated by the presence of Lieutenant Colonel Eve RA, the Naval Gunfire Liaison Officer embarked in *Antrim*, who in naval eyes was the senior landing force officer, although he was not there for that purpose, and never once tried to assume that role.

The recapture of South Georgia was only the beginning. The land campaign on the Falkland Islands was the key to winning the war. Only by defeating the Argentine Army and seizing the strategic objective, Port Stanley, could Britain achieve her aim of repossessing the Falkland Islands. Before this could happen, troops had to be landed on the islands. Much time and thought went into deciding where; a joint decision was made by Commodore Clapp and Brigadier Thompson, greatly assisted by Major Southby-Tailyour, whose knowledge of the Falkland Islands proved invaluable, both in the planning and operational phases. The place finally chosen was San Carlos Water, and eventually approved by Fieldhouse back in Northwood. There were many important naval considerations driving this choice, which are not rehearsed here. From 3 Commando Brigade's point of view it was far enough away from Argentine main positions around Port Stanley to enable the build-up to proceed without early interference by enemy ground forces. This was vital, bearing in mind how few helicopters were available, so most ship to shore movement would have to be by slow, vulnerable landing craft. Furthermore, without an LPH, there was no possibility of landing even a rifle company in one wave. HMS *Hermes*, which could have been used as an LPH, was correctly assigned to launching SHAR sorties, mainly in the fighter role. The main disadvantage of landing at San Carlos was the distance to Port Stanley, eighty kilometres in a straight line. However, given that the British no longer had the equipment to make an assault on a well-defended beach such as LVTs, swimming tanks, and gun-armed landing craft to provide intimate support right up the beach, equipment that had been commonplace in Normandy and Walcheren, the brigade had to land where there was no enemy.

In arriving at the choice, considerable effort was put into reconnaissance by the SBS and SAS. From early May, these were forward with Woodward's Carrier Battle Group. In general, Clapp tasked the SBS for reconnaissance connected with the beaches, and Thompson tasked the SAS for reconnaissance inland. Both commanders discussed the missions with Lieutenant Colonel Rose (SAS) and Major Thomson (SBS) before sending tasking signals to Woodward. Amplification of Special Forces tasking could be discussed with Colonel Preston, the landing force adviser on Woodward's staff, on the secure voice telephone link between *Fearless* and *Hermes*. Armed with a tasking signal, and having discussed points of detail on the secure link, Preston could brief patrol commanders on their mission. He was also able to debrief patrols after extraction. The SAS had 'acquired' a satellite communications system which was totally secure and difficult to pinpoint by direction finding. A few SAS patrols could, therefore, transmit reports direct from the Falklands to Hereford, to *Hermes*, and to Rose aboard *Fearless*. The SBS had insecure HF radio sets, which because of the ranges over which they were working could send and receive using Morse only. Messages had to be encoded on a one-time pad, which was time consuming, but more significantly, most messages, such as beach reports packed with information, would take so long to transmit that the Argentines would have had no difficulty in locating the sender. For security reasons it was imperative that the Argentines never had an inkling that the British were interested in San Carlos. Had they done so, they might have deployed more than the company they eventually sent there. For this reason, SAS and SBS patrols were always extracted for debriefing face-to-face with Preston, and were only allowed to send short messages in an extreme emergency.

Patrols, both SBS and SAS, were landed by helicopter, usually at least three nights' march away from their objective in order to avoid compromising their target. For the same reason, extraction by helicopter would usually be from a spot at least one night's march from the objective. Most of the earlier helicopter insertions were launched from a ship about fifty to eighty kilometres off. Insertion of SBS patrols by submarine, which in some cases would have been more satisfactory, was not possible as a suitable boat (diesel-electric) was not made available until near the end of the war. The SSNs deployed down south were far too big and valuable to be risked inshore: although some SBS were sent south in the submarine HMS *Conqueror*, and were the first Marines to deploy, they were cross-decked to another ship before taking part in operations. Later in the war some Special Forces insertions were made by inflatables from destroyers and frigates closing the coast for the purpose.

There were one or two close calls. An SBS patrol on a hillside overlooking San Carlos Water was holed up in a scrape in the peat, covered with chicken wire taken ashore with them, and with peat turfs on top. An enemy helicopter came whirling in right on top of them. The patrol prepared to destroy their codes and fight their way out. Fortunately the hillside was quite steep, and the helicopter was having difficulty in putting down: it hovered with one wheel lightly resting on the roof of their hide before lifting and moving off to land a patrol some distance away. The SBS heaved a sigh of relief, and carried on observing.

Another patrol bumped enemy near Port Stanley, and although no firing took place, in the get-away one man was separated from the others, failing to make the helicopter extraction. He had no radio. There were some tense days wondering if the Marine had been captured. However, he had carried out the correct drill, and went to the emergency

RV, where he was eventually picked up by helicopter. After finishing his emergency rations, he had survived by eating mice he had trapped as they ran through the heather-like 'diddle-dee'.

A key operation was carried out by the SAS to destroy enemy aircraft stationed on Pebble Island, near the mouth of Falkland Sound, down which the amphibious group would transit for the landings. The elimination of these aircraft posing such a potential threat to the Amphibious Operating Area (AOA) was a considerable coup.

There were some lighter moments. Captain McCracken, leading a naval gunfire observer team, was landed before D-Day to spot for naval guns in support of the landings. One night, having been landed by boat near Rookery Point, he saw large numbers of enemy soldiers approaching his hide, and thought the game was up. But he had been deceived by a Falklands phenomenon; the clear unpolluted atmosphere and lack of trees or other features to provide a reference point for scale had tricked him into believing that a flock of penguins was the enemy.

Terrain and climate were an important factor in the land campaign. In East Falkland, where the majority of the action took place, most terrain is peat bog with large areas of hummocky tussock grass in places. Except for a few stunted growths in the settlements, there are no trees at all. In daylight and in good weather, movement on the open hillsides, devoid of cover, can be seen a great distance away in the clear atmosphere. Stone runs are a special feature of the landscape, up to hundreds of metres wide and several kilometres long, like rivers of stone consisting of boulders varying from the size of a car to a human head. Moving across these runs by day was painfully slow, and even more so at night. They were impassable to any vehicle. The mountains are really moorland hills, but almost all were crowned with long rock ridges standing up like the dorsal spine of a vast dinosaur. Few were less than 550 metres long and many were over 2,200. These crenellated bastions, with sudden sheer drops, in places up to 30 metres, with great buttresses, were an obstacle to wheeled and tracked vehicles alike.

In 1982, apart from the immediate area of Port Stanley and the airport, and an unsurfaced track to Fitzroy, there were no roads or tracks. A lightly loaded Land Rover would be lucky to cover six kilometres in the hour, provided it kept off tussock and stone runs, and did not follow the tracks of a predecessor, which had broken through the crust and rendered the going to a black slurry. A wheeled vehicle loaded with ammunition or stores or towing a gun would not move at all. The 3rd Commando Brigade took seventy-six of its BV 202 (Bandwagons), tracked oversnow vehicles, the remainder being stockpiled in Norway. The Bandwagon, with a ground pressure equivalent to a man on skis, would, it was hoped, cope with the peat bog. The only other vehicles with the brigade capable of moving across country were the four Scimitar and four Scorpion Combat Vehicle Reconnaissance Tracked (CVRT), and the light armoured recovery vehicle of the Blues and Royals.

The Falklands lie on the same latitude south as Britain does north, but the great Southern Ocean, with no equivalent of the Gulf Stream to warm it, and the proximity of Cape Horn, the Andes, and the vast frozen continent of Antarctica combine to make the climate significantly different. Icebergs have been known to come within 320 kilometres of the islands. Snow, fog, rain, and brilliant sunshine follow each other with great rapidity, at all times of the year, and the brigade was operating there in the days leading up to midwinter. The wind is constant; the average wind speed in Britain is 4 knots, in the Falklands it is 16 (30 kph).

The harsh terrain, uncompromising weather, lack of roads, and inadequate medium and heavy lift helicopter support shaped the land campaign. The almost total lack of cover and warmth once away from the settlements meant that once a man was wet he usually stayed wet; the best that could be achieved was a state of clammy dampness. Most men's feet never dried: many suffered from trench-foot, and some from frost-bite. Living day and night in peat or rock-walled sangars, where the shallowest scrape filled with water within minutes, was far from pleasant. Ammunition took absolute priority over everything in the competition for helicopters flying forward, as did casualties on return trips. Units were often short of food. Perversely, in this sodden land, water was difficult to find, except in some valley bottoms. Shallow pits in the peat yielded a brackish brew, which Puritabs could sterilize but not remove the sediment causing inflammation of the gut. As the campaign progressed many suffered from 'Galtieri's Revenge', and to avoid delays in disrobing some men dispensed with underpants and cut a slit in the seat of their trousers. On the march and in battle, troops of all arms carried heavy loads. It was a low-tech war; marching, patrolling, freezing days and nights, foot soldiers closing with the enemy, timeless infantry soldiering, primitive and unforgiving.

When Brigadier Thompson gave his orders to his COs for the landing, intelligence indicated that the enemy had some 11,000 troops on the Falklands. Except for detailed locations, especially gun positions, there was a reasonably clear picture of the force around Port Stanley: a reinforced brigade of six infantry regiments (each battalion size), including a Marine unit, a comprehensive gun and surface-to-air (SAM) missile air defence system, and supporting arms and logistic units. The artillery supporting this brigade comprised thirty-eight 105mm pack howitzers with a range of 10,000 metres, and three towed 155mm guns with a range of 24,000 metres. The numerous 35mm and 30mm air defence guns were also used by the Argentines in the ground role on occasions.

Information about enemy strengths at Darwin and Goose Green was less comprehensive. Assessments varied from a reinforced company, the original garrison, to a weak battalion plus Air Force personnel to man the airstrip, and some artillery and air defence. The second estimate was the more accurate. Of the total garrison of 1,500, the Argentines had 544 infantry (a mixed bag made up from three different regiments), three 105mm pack howitzers, and some 30mm air defence guns. Nearly 1,000 of the men were Air Force.

A brigade of two infantry regiments garrisoned West Falkland. Most of the thirty-four airstrips on the islands were assessed as being capable of operating Pucarás, Aermacchis, and other light aircraft. Which were being used, and for what, was never clear right up to the end of the war. One set of clear, up-to-date, air photographs would have helped answer this, and a host of other questions about the enemy, but there were none. If there was friendly satellite coverage of the Falklands, none of the imagery was made available to those who could have used it.

By the start of the land campaign, the force around Stanley alone outnumbered the 3rd Commando Brigade, and had more guns and helicopters, air superiority, and the added bonus of T34C Mentors, Pucarás, Aermacchi M339s, and Augusta Bell 109A attack helicopters deployed in the Islands. The British had declared a maritime and air blockade, but during the day Argentine fighter-bombers were able to penetrate to the islands and attack ships and troops. By night Canberra medium bombers attacked ground targets, not very successfully. The enemy flew C-130s into Stanley airfield with impunity right up to the last night of the war.

The landings at San Carlos, starting just after midnight (local time) on 21 May 1982, took longer than anticipated, for a number of reasons, beginning with the late arrival of some of the ships in Falkland Sound because of a navigational error, and including, among other things, temporary equipment failure in *Fearless*, delaying her docking-down to launch her LCUs, and the embarkation of 2 Para into LCUs from the *Norland* taking longer than planned. With the onset of daylight, the move ashore of follow-up troops and equipment was hampered by Argentine air attacks starting about two hours after first light, and except for a break on D+1 (22 May), persisting for the next six days. The Task Force commander, Admiral Fieldhouse, had stated on more than one occasion that air superiority over the beachhead would be achieved before landings took place. However, it was not achieved, and the landing had to proceed without one of the usual prerequisites for such an operation. On the first day alone, one frigate was sunk, and every destroyer or frigate in the AOA, except one, was hit by bombs or cannon, some being damaged seriously. Other ships were sunk or damaged on the succeeding days of the war, all by air attack.

By midday the brigade had seized all its D-Day objectives and dug in to defend the beachhead while guns, ammunition, and supplies were landed. Two of the brigade's Gazelle helicopters had been shot down by the small Argentine garrison of Port San Carlos. In the first, the pilot, Sergeant Evans, though mortally wounded, managed to land his helicopter in the water. His aircrewman, Sergeant Candlish, swam to the shore, dragging his dying pilot, and survived despite being fired on by Argentine soldiers. Lieutenant Francis and Corporal Giffen were both killed instantly when the bubble in the second Gazelle disintegrated in a hail of machine-gun fire. There were only two other encounters with Argentine ground troops on D-Day. The first was on Fanning Head, where a half company of infantry with a 105mm RCL had posed a threat to shipping entering San Carlos Water. A party of SBS accompanied by an NGFO party had engaged them during the night of D/D+1, and by first light they had run away or been persuaded to surrender by 4.5in shell fire from HMS *Antrim*. Also during the night of D/D+1, a diversionary attack was mounted against Darwin by D Squadron 22 SAS, supported by HMS *Ardent*, to keep the garrison there and at Goose Green occupied and distract them from activity in San Carlos Water.

Without air superiority, the plan to keep most of the brigade's supplies and medical support afloat, ready to move round to support the advance across East Falkland, had to be modified. For the next six days, the helicopters and landing craft were engaged in the logistic offload. The problem now was to move the brigade to the high ground overlooking Port Stanley. Well before landing, the plan had been to fly the bulk of the brigade to Mount Kent and adjacent features, once the five Chinook heavy-lift and six Wessex medium-lift helicopters had arrived in the container ship *Atlantic Conveyor*. These with the eleven Sea King and five Wessex helicopters already in the beachhead would be just sufficient to make the operation feasible. Once established on Mount Kent, LSLs could enter Port Salvador to unload at Teal Inlet, and from here supplies could be flown forward, considerably shorter than the trip from San Carlos Water. An approach from the south and south-west was discarded, because it was assessed that the enemy expected the main assault from that direction.

After a series of discussions with Task Force HQ at Northwood, plans were being made to move the brigade forward to the Mount Kent area using the five heavy-lift Chinook helicopters being brought into the AOA by the *Atlantic Conveyor*, when the news arrived that the ship had been sunk by an air-launched Exocet. All but one Chinook had gone with her, and all the Wessex helicopters on board as well.

Despite this, which left the brigade with the meagre medium-lift helicopter support with which it had landed, augmented by one Chinook without spares, orders were received from Northwood that 3rd Commando Brigade was to start moving out of the beachhead. Furthermore, an attack on Goose Green, originally planned as a raid, and subsequently cancelled by Brigadier Thompson because he judged that it involved too great a diversion of effort, was to be restaged. Accordingly 45 Commando (Lieutenant Colonel A. F. Whitehead RM) and 3 Para were ordered to march to Teal Inlet, where an SBS patrol was already in hiding. 2 Para was told to take the twin settlements of Darwin and Goose Green and hold them.

The Darwin/Goose Green battle has been described elsewhere, and few Royal Marines were involved, although a Scout helicopter on its way to evacuate the dying CO of 2 Para, piloted by Lieutenant R. J. Nunn RM, was shot down by a Pucará, killing him and badly wounding his air gunner, Sergeant Belcher, and at a critical stage of the battle, when the battalion came under attack from Aermacchis, Marine Strange of 3rd Commando Brigade Air Defence Troop shot at one with his Blowpipe, causing it to crash as it took evasive action.

Despite Thompson's reservations about diverting effort to Goose Green and Darwin, which set back the advance on Port Stanley by several days, this battle had a profound effect on the conduct of the land campaign. It signalled to the enemy the absolute determination of the British to succeed. It opened up a southern route to Stanley, and because the Argentines were convinced almost to the end that the main attack would come from the south-west, it served to confirm their perception distracting them from what was actually the main thrust by the 3rd Commando Brigade, from the north and west. The fighting at Goose Green over bare slopes in daylight was costly. From then on the brigade would, if possible, fight at night. Finally, and again unforeseen, the enemy heliborne reserve had been drawn away from the vital area of Mount Kent, to reinforce the Goose Green garrison during the battle, and been taken prisoner. This reserve was, therefore, not able to intervene during the highly risky three days when a light force consisting of part of 42 Commando and an SAS squadron, with minimal support, was pushed forward on to Mount Kent.

While the battle for Goose Green was under way, 45 Commando and 3 Para were marching to Teal Inlet. An attempt made on the night of 29/30 May to fly part of 42 Commando (Lieutenant Colonel N. F. Vaux) to Mount Kent had to be aborted because of a snow blizzard. D Squadron 22 SAS had flown in on successive nights to secure an LZ, starting on the night of 24/25 May. The squadron was finally complete by the night of 28/29 May. Taking five nights to fly in one SAS squadron, about fifty men, is indication enough of the frustrations caused by bad weather at night, woefully few helicopters, and the Goose Green diversion.

On 30 May General Moore, the Divisional Commander, arrived in the beachhead, having been incommunicado for ten days thanks to the radio fit in the liner *Queen Elizabeth II*. After being briefed, he approved all the moves that had been planned. Originally it was decided that 40 Commando, now holding the entire beachhead, would be relieved by a battalion of the 5th Infantry Brigade, which had come south with Moore), and move forward to join its own brigade. So 40 Commando was warned to be prepared to march to Teal Inlet. The 5th Infantry Brigade was ordered to Goose Green, where it would take 2 Para under command.

On the night of 30/31 May, Tac HQ 42 Commando, K Company, the Mortar Troop, and three 105mm light guns of 7 (Sphinx) Commando

Light Battery were flown forward to an LZ below Mount Kent. Lieutenant Colonel Vaux, with K Company, landed on the lower slopes of Mount Kent in darkness to find a battle in progress: D Squadron 22 SAS engaging an enemy patrol. It was fortunate that Brigadier Thompson had resisted pressure from the Task Force Commander at Northwood to dispense with reconnaissance and troops to secure the LZ. In an earlier satellite telephone conversation, the reasons he offered for the time being taken to establish reconnaissance before flying forward a force on Mount Kent had been dismissed by the Task Force commander with an impatient, 'you don't need that [reconnaissance]'. Without D Squadron's presence around the LZ, the enemy special forces would have had a 'turkey shoot' on the vulnerable helicopters and the troops as they jumped out, temporarily disorientated in the darkness; the operation would have been a disaster. As K Company moved off towards the summit, Vaux asked the SAS Squadron commander what enemy they could expect on the top, to which he replied, 'No idea, we've never been up there. Only operated in these valleys around here.' This came as a surprise to Vaux, who had been briefed by Brigade HQ that the summit had been reconnoitred.[5] To his relief, K Company reported that the mountain was free of enemy.

The enemy had sent out strong patrols from 602 Commando Company to cover Mount Kent and other key high ground to report on and harry the British advance, but fortunately they were not very effective. Eventually their operations were almost completely terminated by the attack by the Brigade Reconnaissance Troop (Mountain and Arctic Warfare Cadre) described in the Prologue.

By 4 June most of the 3rd Commando Brigade, less 40 Commando still back at San Carlos, had deployed forward onto the high ground Mount Estancia–Mount Vernet–Mount Kent–Mount Challenger. Despite repeated requests that 40 Commando be released to the 3rd Commando Brigade, Moore decided to keep it back in the beachhead, having been warned by intelligence from Northwood that the enemy were planning an airborne assault on the area. This caused considerable bitterness among all ranks, especially when they saw one of the battalions of the 5th Infantry Brigade failing to march the relatively short distance from San Carlos to Goose Green. First-class leadership by the CO, Lieutenant Colonel Hunt, maintained high morale despite deep resentment among his Commando at not being able to rejoin their own brigade.

By 3 June, 2 Para, the leading element of the 5th Infantry Brigade, was at Fitzroy and Bluff Cove, and the remainder of this brigade moved up over a series of days and nights. Landing craft commanded and crewed by Royal Marines played a key part in these moves, as they had throughout the land campaign. The 2nd Battalion Scots Guards, the first major unit of the 5th Infantry Brigade to move round to Fitzroy/Bluff Cove by sea, had a most unpleasant trip. After a night passage from San Carlos in HMS *Intrepid*, routing south of Lafonia, the intention was to launch the four LCUs, commanded by Major S. E. Southby-Tailyour RM, with the battalion embarked, off Choiseul Sound. This would have entailed a run-in to Bluff Cove of a couple of hours or so; unwelcome enough for even the most experienced troops in lumpy seas, with spray and snow showers in pitch blackness, but no one in this battalion had been in a landing craft before, other than for short trips in sheltered waters, in daylight. Despite protestations by Major Southby-Tailyour, an officer of vast experience in operating landing craft, and with greater knowledge of the waters round the Falkland Islands than anyone in the Task Force, the captain of *Intrepid* launched the LCUs south-west of Lively Island, before steaming off into the darkness. For seven hours, shivering and seasick, the Guardsmen endured. Subsequently, Southby-Tailyour had only the highest praise for their fortitude and morale in these unfamiliar and daunting surroundings. It was fortunate he knew these waters so well, because at one stage the radar on his LCU broke down. At one point the flotilla was fired on by what Southby-Tailyour thought were mortars or artillery, although who fired them is a mystery. This was followed by a heart-stopping moment, when HMS *Cardiff*, on the gun-line bombarding enemy positions round Stanley, challenged and fired star shell. The two ships on the southern gun-line that night were unaware of the move taking place. Disaster was averted when to *Cardiff*'s challenge 'Friend?' by signal lamp, Southby-Tailyour flashed back, 'To which side?'

At least the move of the Scots Guards was not marred by casualties; 1st Battalion Welsh Guards was not so fortunate. A series of unfortunately timed coincidences led to the bombing of LSLs *Sir Galahad* and *Sir Tristram* at Fitzroy on 8 June, with the loss of 43 dead and over 200 wounded, the majority from 1st Welsh Guards. Apart from the other casualties, two companies of 1st Welsh Guards were non-operational, and these were eventually replaced by A and C Companies of 40 Commando.

Lack of space precludes an analysis of what the media persist in calling the Bluff Cove incident, which actually took place at Fitzroy.[6] The story lies within the bailiwick of the Royal Navy and the 5th Infantry Brigade. But it must be said that a major factor was yet more back-seat driving from Task Force HQ at Northwood, forbidding Clapp to send either *Fearless* or *Intrepid* to the south of Fitzroy again. The moral here is that proper command from 13,000 kilometres away is impossible. Among the casualties of this air attack were Colour Sergeant Johnston and his crew of the LCU *Foxtrot Four* (one of *Fearless*'s LCUs). He was on passage in Choiseul Sound, bringing 5th Infantry Brigade HQ communications vehicles from Goose Green to Fitzroy, and was attacked by a Skyhawk with rockets. He was later posthumously awarded the QGM for his bravery when evacuating the crew of HMS *Antelope* as she burned in San Carlos Water earlier in the war: although the ship was about to blow up at any moment, he disobeyed orders to bear off, until he had taken off the last man. He had been ordered by Southby-Tailyour not to sail from Goose Green in daylight. But realizing the imperatives of getting the radio equipment to the 5th Infantry Brigade, for the confusion and total lack of control at Fitzroy was partially due to lack of communications, he disobeyed that order too.

While the 5th Infantry Brigade was concentrating round Fitzroy and Bluff Cove, the 3rd Commando Brigade was patrolling vigorously to obtain information and dominate the enemy. The brigade plan, submitted to Divisional HQ, was to start by seizing three features, Mount Longdon, Two Sisters, and Mount Harriet. Once these were taken, Thompson wanted to exploit forward to Mount Tumbledown, Wireless Ridge, and possibly Mount William. With these in his hands, the way to Stanley would be open. Possession of these features would ensure that he maintained his line of communication by helicopter and Bandwagon following the lower ground along the line of the Estancia House–Moody Brook track dominated by Mount Longdon, Two Sisters, Tumbledown, and Wireless Ridge. Although a track in name only until about 1,500 metres short of Moody Brook, the lower ground, usually mist-free, was the key to ensuring the flow of ammunition forward and casualty evacuation rearward, and could be maintained day and night, in almost all weathers. Mount Harriet would provide a firm anchor to the right flank, and with Two Sisters and Mount Longdon dominate the low ground east of Mount Kent which was needed for gun positions, to enable the artillery to reach subsequent objectives.

By 9 June, Moore had approved the Commando Brigade plan, with the modification that Tumbledown and Mount William were allocated to the 5th Infantry Brigade, to be attacked twenty-four hours after the first phase objectives of Longdon, Two Sisters, and Mount Harriet. 2 Para was returned to 3 Commando Brigade, and 1st Battalion Welsh Guards was given to Thompson as an additional reserve. He allocated the objectives for the first phase as follows: 3 Para, Mount Longdon, and to exploit forward on to Wireless Ridge if possible; 45 Commando, Two Sisters, and to exploit on to Tumbledown (although allocated to 5th Infantry Brigade, it would be foolish not to follow up success if time allowed); 42 Commando, Mount Harriet, and be prepared to follow up 45 Commando through Tumbledown on to Mount William. Each of the assaulting units had a battery of 105mm light guns from 29 Commando Regiment RA, and a frigate or destroyer with 4.5in guns in support. The brigade reserve consisted of 2 Para and 1st Welsh Guards. H-Hour for the attacking units for the night of 11/12 June was between 2001 and 2100 hours. With last light at about 1600 hours, and moonrise at 2000 hours, these timings would allow four to five hours for the approach march in darkness, and about nine hours for fighting through the objectives with the aid of moonlight.

It is now known from the official Argentine report that Mount Longdon was held by B Company 7th Infantry Regiment, reinforced by an engineer platoon in the infantry role, and about eight .50in Browning heavy machine-guns manned by Marines. These heavy machine-guns, which out-ranged any direct-fire weapons in 3rd Commando Brigade, other than those in the CVRT, which could not be used on any of the three features because of the rocky, steep terrain, were deadly in good visibility over the bare moorland slopes; an additional incentive for fighting at night.

Two Sisters was held by B Company of the 6th Infantry Regiment, and a very strong reinforced C Company of the 4th Infantry Regiment. Both company positions included .50in heavy machine-guns. Four 81mm mortars were sited in the centre of the position.

The remainder of the 4th Infantry Regiment, sited on Mount Harriet, consisted of two rifle companies, which with the reconnaissance platoon, two sections of 120mm heavy mortars, regimental headquarters, and other headquarters cooks and bottle-washers, and the ubiquitous heavy machine-guns, were equivalent to a small battalion. There is no reason to doubt the accuracy of the Argentine order of battle in their report, except that, if anything, the loser may play down his strength in order to excuse his failure. Indeed, the maps in the Argentine report frequently show the strengths of attacking British units up to double the actual size.

All the battles fought in the land campaign in the Falklands War, like most others in every war, soon devolved into troop, section, and even individual actions. The Marines' and soldiers' motivation and courage were tested time and again. In an infantry battle, especially at night, there is plenty of scope for those who wish to retire from the contest without actually drawing attention to themselves by running away. Only infantry soldiers or Marines, and representatives from supporting arms on their feet (gunners and sappers), have to make the individual decision to get up and go forward, again and again. Others who fight in crews, or man guns or missile systems, do not experience this. Some, in ships for example, are taken willy-nilly whereso'er the captain orders. They have their horrors peculiar to their calling. But is difficult to overstate the qualifications required of the infantry, and express fully the admiration one has for the young Marines and soldiers on the dark Falklands mountainsides.

Viewed from a distance Two Sisters looks quite insignificant, like a pair of immature breasts. In fact it consists of two peaks and five formidable rock ridges. The north-eastern peak has a spineback about 500 metres long on its crest, and another about the same length directly to the east. The south-western peak, which at 316 metres is slightly the taller of the two, has three rocky spinebacks in line ahead, running east–west, covering about 1,500 metres in all. The whole Two Sisters feature is well guarded by rock runs and the steep 250-metre climb from the valley floor is bare and easily covered by observation and fire. Whitehead opted for a two-phase attack on Two Sisters. In phase one, X Company would attack the south-western peak, which he hoped would divert the enemy's attention from Y and Z Companies' phase two assault from the area of the Murrell Bridge onto the north-eastern peak. X Company was to march due east from Mount Kent, following a route taken a few days earlier by one of their fighting patrols. But their approach, starting at 1700 hours, took nearly six hours instead of the three that Captain Gardiner, the company commander, had calculated. His reconnaissance team did not pick the best route for a company loaded down with not only their own kit, weapons, and ammunition, but also with Milan firing posts and forty Milan missiles, each weighing 13.6kg – for X Company had taken 40 Commando's Milan Troop with them to provide support for their own attack, and if necessary to shoot in the other two companies. 45 Commando's Milan firing posts had all been destroyed when Ajax Bay was bombed on 27 May, and the men had been converted to machine-gunners. With his plan unravelling, Whitehead remained cool, and put no pressure on Gardiner, but encouraged him on the radio. X Company started its assault at 2300 hours.

Whitehead with his Tac HQ, Y, and Z Companies had marched for five hours, covering five kilometres, and lay down in the forming-up position, to wait for X Company. Here he decided not to hang about in an area which was likely to be a target for pre-adjusted enemy artillery defensive fire waiting for X Company, but instead to start the two companies moving forward on to the start line. By now the whole area was well lit, not only by moonlight, but by 3 Para's battle on Longdon, about 3,000 metres to the north-east, and by 42 Commando fighting on Mount Harriet about 5,000 metres to the south. By this time, X Company had started their advance led by Lieutenant Kelly's 1 Troop. They encountered no opposition on their objective. Gardiner sent 3 Troop under Lieutenant Stewart to pass through Kelly's troop. Stewart reported no opposition on his objective, and asked permission to exploit, which Gardiner approved. About halfway up the 1,500-metre-long feature he ran into two machine-guns, one a heavy. Attempts to close with them were met with rifle fire from the flanks. Here, as elsewhere, the Argentines had coordinated the siting of riflemen with night sights and machine-gunners well. Gardiner pulled back 3 Troop and ordered Milan and mortar fire on the position, before ordering in Lieutenant Caroe's 2 Troop. The mortars soon had to stop firing as their baseplates and half the length of the barrels sank into the soggy peat. The artillery was firing on other targets and was not available. The enemy engaged with a 105mm RCL and artillery, but Caroe and his men pitched in among the huge rocks, which made the task rather like fighting among houses. Having gained the objective, they were forced off by enemy defensive artillery fire before returning to secure the objective and kill or drive off the enemy machine-gunners.

At about 0030 hours, while X Company were still fighting through their objective, Y and Z Companies crossed the start line. Just before they moved, an enemy defensive fire mission came crashing down just ahead of them. The going was hard over bog and rock runs, the objective some 1,500 metres ahead clearly skylined. The enemy appeared to be mesmerized by X Company's battle on the south-western peak and took no notice of Y and Z closing in on them, so Whitehead decided to halt and wait for X Company to secure its objective. While Lieutenant Dytor, commanding the right-hand leading troop of Z Company, was scanning the enemy ahead through his IWS, a flare came fizzing out from the position. Dytor shouted to his troop to engage, and almost immediately the Argentines replied with .50in heavy machine-gun fire, GPMGs, and FALs. Luckily Y and Z Companies were lying down, and the fire cracked over their heads. Had Whitehead not ordered them to halt, they would have been badly caught. Captain Cole, commanding Z Company, ordered his FOO to bring down pre-planned artillery fire on the objective, but enemy mortar fire began falling around the company. Dytor, realizing that they must not remain pinned down, jumped up, and started running forward, shouting 'Zulu, Zulu!', the company battle cry. As he ran, he heard his section commanders shout, 'Move now!' and taking up the cry, 'Zulu, Zulu!', the whole troop dashed forward to where the ground was concave, and enemy fire went over their heads. Cole manoeuvred the remainder of his company forward, the MFC with him, bringing down bombs beyond the position and 'walking it back' to thicken up the artillery fire already falling on to the objective. The two leading troops kept up a steady fire with GPMGs and 84mm and 66mm anti-tank weapons to win the firefight.

Y Company on Zulu's right were mortared, wounding two of the troop commanders. Major Davis, Y Company commander, could see battery fire missions coming down on the .50in machine-guns engaging Zulu Company. Their overhead protection was good, because every time the fire lifted, the guns opened up again. Whitehead, on Z Company's right, ordered Y Company up alongside him, and when in position their 84mm MAW gunners engaged the .50in machine-guns holding up Zulu. Cole ordered Dytor forward, supported by 7 Troop, and still shouting, 'Zulu Zulu!' they swept up onto the crest. The remainder of the company came up, turned left, and cleared the ridge. 9 Troop in the rear was down to two sections because of casualties, and remained in reserve. Z Company had secured its objective two and a half hours after crossing the start line. Y Company passed through, and cleared to the end of its objective. By now X Company were firm on the south-western peak, and by 0430 hours 45 Commando had taken all its objectives. As elsewhere, the Argentine 155mm guns engaged the ground they had lost, and the Marines took cover in the deep fissures in the rocks. Sergeant Menghini of 3rd Commando Brigade Air Squadron flew his Scout in to a green torch marking the LZ, from where he picked up the casualties. It was too late to exploit onto Tumbledown, and the Brigade Commander, somewhat to Whitehead's annoyance, told him to go firm on Two Sisters. Had 45 Commando gone forward, daylight would have found it still short of well-prepared and strongly held positions, in the open and exposed to the lash of the .50 Brownings. With few rounds left, the gun positions needed replenishment.

Vaux, to the south of 45 Commando, was faced with either a head-on assault against the most strongly held part of Mount Harriet or a wide right-flanking move. If he tried outflanking to his left, he risked clashing with 45 Commando. Furthermore, the approaches on the north-east side of Mount Harriet are the steepest, in some places consisting of cliffs from fifteen to thirty metres high. Some excellent patrolling by junior officers, and especially by Sergeant Collins of K Company, had found a route through the minefields guarding the western and southern approaches to Mount Harriet to a start line south-east of the position. Most of the minefields were ill-defined, and frequently unmarked: on two successive nights patrols suffered casualties from mines.

Vaux's plan was to feign an attack on the western end of Harriet, using J Company, while K and L Companies marched round to a forming-up place to the south-east of the feature, where a fence provided a convenient start line. He planned a further refinement: as the enemy machine-guns disclosed their positions by firing at the J Company dummy attack, mortars would fire illuminating rounds, enabling the Milan missile aimers sited on the eastern slopes of Wall Mountain to engage (in 1982 the Milan did not have a thermal imaging night sight). Whereas both 45 Commando's and 3 Para's attacks had been 'silent', without preliminary bombardment, Vaux was allowed to use his artillery to distract the enemy's attention from the move of K and L Companies and to lend credibility to J Company's deception.

The long flanking approach march, led by Sergeant Collins, went without incident, although both companies felt very naked against the distinctive bright yellow grass which, even without a moon, allows good visibility. But the peat hags and cuttings provided some shadow and cover. The ground underfoot was more than usually wet, with numerous puddles and the small streams running south off Harriet. At 2200 hours K Company crossed the start line for its 800-metre approach to the objective. The company had covered about 700 metres when enemy were seen and Captain Babbington ordered his men to engage. The battle was on. The whole company was on the same radio frequency, and fought like a well-drilled football team. The first part of the objective contained four 120mm heavy mortars, and being well protected took about three-quarters of an hour to clear. A section commander, Corporal Watts, was killed taking this key position, which would have proved extremely troublesome had it not been eliminated early. Babbington pushed 1 and 3 Troops forward to work on each side of the ridge line. Corporal Ward of 3 Troop reported being held up by machine-gunners and riflemen. Corporal Newland of 1 Troop was in the best position to deal with the problem. Going forward alone, because he reckoned one man would have a better chance of negotiating the steep rocky slabs unseen, he scrambled up one around twenty feet high, peered round a rock, and saw about half of platoon of enemy busily engaged firing at 3 Troop. He pulled back, put a full magazine on his SLR, tossed in two grenades, charged in, and single-handedly killed all the men in the position; or so he thought. Corporal Ward, approaching from another direction, shouted '66' to warn Newland that he was about to fire an LAW. Newland withdrew behind a rock, and immediately after the 66 had slammed into the position went forward again. He was greeted with a burst from an FAL, wounding him in both legs. In Newland's words, 'The Argentine soldier died rather quickly.' Unable to move far thanks to his wounds, he propped himself against a rock, lit a cigarette, and directed 3 Troop towards another machine-gun position he could see further on. His clear directions were of great assistance to Lieutenant Heathcote, commanding 3 Troop, and Corporals Ward and Eccles, in clearing their troop objective.

The handling of the company by Babbington, at night, in the confusion of battle, was a masterpiece. He described it later:

Throughout the early stages, I, with my FOO and MFC, remained out on the open hillside in order to see more clearly what was going on. All my sections were up on the Company radio net which meant I was getting up to date situation reports from my section commanders [by listening to them reporting to their troop commanders], so leaving the troop commanders to get on with directing their own fire fights. It also allowed section commanders to direct mortar and artillery fire through the FOO and MFC by my side. At one stage the FOO was controlling simultaneously 81mm mortar illuminating, a naval gunfire and an artillery fire mission on two targets within 100 metres of us. Enemy fire was fairly heavy, mainly heavy machine guns and automatic rifles. They were using a lot of flares which was to our advantage in indicating their positions.[7]

L Company crossed the start line after K and since surprise had been lost came under immediate and effective fire from heavy machine-guns, taking three casualties at once. Captain Wheen, commanding L Company, called for Milan fire to deal with the machine-guns, which proved effective. The company had to clear six medium machine-gun positions and at least four teams of riflemen equipped with night sights before reaching its first objective, the western end of the Harriet spineback, a fighting advance of about 600 metres, and as each position involved a separate troop or section attack, it took about five hours to cover the distance from the start line. The company kept skirmishing forward throughout, for going to ground for any length of time meant sitting in the middle of enemy artillery defensive fire missions, which inflicted eleven casualties. When L Company arrived on its first objective, it collected large numbers of prisoners. As 5 Troop moved towards L Company's next objective, about 500 metres to the north, it came under heavy fire. Wheen pulled the troop back and hit the enemy with mortar and artillery fire, as well as the GPMGs and LMGs of the other two troops, twelve machine-guns in all that he taken the precaution of concentrating before the troop moved off. 5 Troop dashed forward and winkled the enemy out: some surrendered, and some fled into the morning mist. Vaux ordered L Company to press on to the final objective, Goat Ridge, from which the enemy was fleeing towards Tumbledown, and Wheen's FOO malleted them with artillery fire.

The battle for Mount Harriet is one of the most remarkable of the Falklands War, yet probably the least known – even among the so-called experts. The information gleaned by his patrols enabled Vaux to devise a bold plan, following the great 'Stonewall' Jackson's precept: 'Always mystify, mislead and surprise the enemy . . . strike vigorously and secure all the fruits of victory'. As an example of inflicting the maximum damage on the enemy at least cost to oneself, the battle has few equals.

The commando took in excess of 300 prisoners and much equipment, and inflicted a large number of casualties, for the loss of two dead and twenty wounded.

3 Para had a hard fight on Mount Longdon, but was secure by first light. The daylight brought enemy artillery fire on all the 3rd Commando Brigade objectives, but worst of all on Mount Longdon, which was partially overlooked by Tumbledown. 3 Para lost twenty-two dead and forty-five wounded in the battle and on the subsequent two days. As well as artillery fire, snow fell.

It was now the 5th Infantry Brigade's turn; the objectives were Mounts Tumbledown and William, planned for the following night, 12/13 June. The 3rd Commando Brigade was not to be idle, for Wireless Ridge was to be taken at the same time; 2 Para's task. Brigadier Wilson asked for a twenty-four-hour postponement to restock gun positions, and for his battalion commanders to see the ground. Lieutenant Haddow and Sergeant Wassall of 3 Commando Brigade's M&AW Cadre had some days earlier taken a very successful reconnaissance patrol out to observe Mount Tumbledown, passing right through the enemy lines in the process. Their information was passed to the 2nd Battalion Scots Guards, which was allocated Tumbledown as its objective. It was also suggested to Brigadier Wilson, commanding the 5th Infantry Brigade, that he push his brigade through 42 Commando's positions, instead of his original intention, astride the Fitzroy–Stanley track, the obvious approach; and in addition 42 Commando would secure the Scots Guards' start line. Finally the services of Haddow and Wassall were offered to lead the battalion to its start line. All these ideas were accepted.

The Scots Guards had a very tough time on Tumbledown against a strong position held by the 5th Argentine Marine Regiment, perhaps their best troops on the Falkland Islands. The attack by 2 Para was a model operation. The battalion had the advantage that the rolling slopes were well suited to using CVRT in support, unlike all the other objectives. The CVRT, with its second-generation night sight, and either 30mm automatic cannon or 75mm gun, could bring down a devastating weight of direct fire in support of the battalion. With these, and both their own and 3 Para's mortars, as well as two 105mm batteries and two frigates, the battalion had plenty of support, and the commanding officer, Lieutenant Colonel D. R. Chaundler, made excellent use of it.

Thompson joined Chaundler on Wireless Ridge to learn that the

Argentine army had streamed back into Stanley, although he could see enemy artillery fire still crashing down onto Tumbledown, just across the valley, where the Scots Guards had secured its objectives. As he was issuing orders to follow-up, Moore came on the radio and said that the enemy were asking for a ceasefire, so he gathered up his brigade and ordered everyone to advance. The last shots were fired by 7 Troop C Company 40 Commando, which with A Company was flown forward as part of a two-company lift to secure a forming-up position on Mount William for the Welsh Guards to move onto Sapper Hill. The helicopter pilot carrying 7 Troop misread his map, and deposited the troop on Sapper Hill by mistake. The enemy opened fire, wounding two Marines. In the subsequent battle several Argentines were killed before the remainder surrendered.

Apart from rounding up prisoners, clearing mines, and much sorting out, the war was over. The Falklands War was an example of joint operations par excellence – eventually. Success in the land campaign was due to many units, mainly part of or attached to the 3rd Commando Brigade, including the two splendid parachute battalions, the gunners, sappers, CVRT crews, and logisticians. But it is not an exaggeration to state that without the Royal Marines the Argentine invasion of the Falklands would have ended in humiliation for the United Kingdom. The amphibious expertise that existed in the Corps, and nowhere else apart from among a few naval officers, was absolutely crucial to winning the war. As well as the professionalism of the three Commandos and the SBS, the skill of the Commando Brigade HQ staff, from the Brigade Major, Major J. C. Chester RM, down to the most junior signaller, was a key factor in success, as was that of the mostly Royal Marine Divisional HQ. Royal Marines also filled vital positions on the Commodore's staff and on the amphibious ships. Without the crews of the eight LCUs and eight LCVPs, as well as those of the raiding craft, the amphibious landings, and subsequent crucially important seaborne moves, would never have taken place. Had General Moulton, back in the late 1950s and early 1960s, not fought so skilfully to persuade the MOD to build the LPDs for the Royal Marines' use, it is impossible to imagine how a landing could have been conducted; there would have been no landing craft, and no command and control facilities, therefore no amphibious operations would have been possible, and the Falkland Islands could never have been repossessed.

1982, a year that had started so dismally for the future prospects of the Corps, had by its midpoint seen gloom turned into triumph; vindicating all the hard work by generations of officers, NCOs, and Marines to keep the flame alive despite innumerable vicissitudes over many years.

26

Towards 2000 and Beyond

Standing beside US Marine Lieutenant General Holland M. Smith on the bridge of the command ship *Mt Olympus*, off Iwo Jima on the morning of 23 February 1945, Secretary of the Navy James Forrestal said that the raising of our flag atop Mt Surabachi, 'means there will be a Marine Corps for the next five hundred years.' Moments later, out of Forrestal's hearing, Smith commented, 'When the war is over and money is short they will be after the Marines again, and a dozen Iwo Jimas will make no difference'.[1]

The efforts of the Royal Marines and the amphibious expertise of certain sections of the Royal Navy had played a key part in winning the Falklands War. But the Government whose neck was saved by the exertions of the 'amphibious community' was not disposed to show, by ordering replacement LPDs or a new LPH, its recognition of what a valuable club in the defence bag an amphibious capability was. The battles in Whitehall to obtain these continued for several years, and it was mid-1993 before an order was placed for HMS *Ocean*, the LPH. The decision to order two new LPDs, *Albion* and *Bulwark*, was not finally made until late in the Strategic Defence Review (SDR) of 1998, and hotly contested throughout the discussions leading up to the final decisions in that Review.

Not until the Berlin Wall came down, signalling the end of the Cold War, did prospects for future of the Corps and its amphibious role really start looking bright. The Royal Marines escaped, more or less unscathed, the swingeing cuts of two Conservative Defence Reviews, *Options for Change* and *Front Line First*. While *Options for Change* were still being staffed in Whitehall, the Gulf War was in full swing, and this was followed a year or so later by involvement in the former Yugoslavia. Both these events helped crystallize ministers' minds on the fact that future operations were more likely to be 'expeditionary' in nature than in the two decades since the withdrawal from the Far and Middle East. Amphibious operations were likely to be an important ingredient of many 'expeditions', large or small, and the Royal Marines, with other supporters of the concept within the Royal Navy, were not slow to point this out in Whitehall, and elsewhere.

Meanwhile, following the Falklands War, the Royal Marines continued with their operational tours in Northern Ireland, as well as expanding an existing commitment to anti-terrorist activities offshore. Since the mid-1970s, the Corps had been responsible for Maritime Counter-Terrorist (MCT) operations, providing the armed response, if requested by the police, to any terrorist takeover of offshore oil and gas installations in UK waters. At first this was the responsibility of the Commandos (four, before the disbandment of 41 Commando in 1981), taking it in turn to provide a company on standby for what was known as Operation Oilsafe. The lead element in any operation to regain control of an installation seized by terrorists was provided by the SBS. In the late 1970s, this task was allotted to a specially formed company, named Comacchio Company to keep alive the memory of 43 (RM) Commando and its principal battle honour. Comacchio Company was stationed at Arbroath in Scotland, and as well as the MCT task it provided the guards for the nuclear submarine base at Faslane on the Clyde. Later, 5 SBS was moved up to join them, and the name was changed to Comacchio Group. Still later the company's MCT commitment was expanded to include the response to hijacking by terrorists of any UK-flagged ship, at sea, worldwide, a task which 5 SBS had already had for some years. It was envisaged that this task would probably involve the whole of the SB Squadron. Ships hijacked in harbour were still the responsibility of the SAS.

Until 21 September 1987, the SBS was under command of Headquarters Training Reserves and Special Forces Royal Marines at Portsmouth, although the tasking was likely to come from the highest echelons in the MOD direct. In 1987 it was decided to place the SBS under the operational command of Director Special Forces, along with the SAS. This sensible move was not made without some angst on the part of the SBS, but on the whole it has worked out for the best. The SBS and SAS undergo a common selection, one outcome of which is that more Marines are passing, because the SBS selection was harder.

Marines, as has always been the case, are not allowed to volunteer for the SBS until they have gained their green beret on the demanding Commando Course, and completed at least one tour in a Commando. At the same time the MCT task was removed from Comacchio Group, and all the SBS were concentrated again in one location.

The invasion of Kuwait by Saddam Hussein saw the bulk of UK Special Forces, SBS and SAS, with air support, being sent post-haste to the Gulf. Here they conducted some very useful acclimatization and desert training for a while, because, as related in General Sir Peter de la Billière's book, General Schwarzkopf was averse to employing them behind Iraqi lines.[2] Eventually, at very short notice, operational tasks were found for them. On the whole the SBS was under-employed in the Gulf, mainly because the senior Special Forces commanders were not prepared to let it do what it could do. As is the way of things, the operation that attracted the most publicity, the SAS patrol Bravo Two Zero, was perhaps the least successful carried out by Special Forces in the Gulf War. Only the considerable feats of bravery and endurance by many of the members of the patrol, including one NCO's epic feat of survival and escape into Syria, compensate for what was a cock-up from its conception. Ironically, it was a repetition of the first ever SAS operation in the Western Desert, fifty years before, in 1941, when having dropped by parachute miles from the target the SAS were reduced to the mobility of the boot, and only the presence of the Long Range Desert Group (LRDG) saved the founder, Stirling, and several other key figures, from going into the bag.[3] The Bravo Two Zero patrol was taken in by helicopter, and once down, had only their feet for mobility, in desert, where the enemy had wheels; only this time there was no friendly LRDG patrol to save their bacon.

The first Special Forces operation in the Gulf, mentioned in de la Billière's book, was by the SBS.[4] On 23 January 1991 they flew in Chinooks to a point less than sixty kilometres from Baghdad, where they cut the fibre-optic cable carrying key Iraqi communications traffic from Saddam's HQ. They brought back a length of cable for intelligence purposes, and one of the above-ground markers, which they gave to Schwarzkopf. According to de la Billière, the General

was so delighted and impressed by the success of the mission that he immediately reported it to Colin Powell in Washington. Powell in turn passed the good news to London, so that this first raid made a major contribution to establishing the reputation and capability not only of our Special Force, but of those of America as well.[5]

The cutting of the cable was not a gimmick, because by denying the Iraqi High Command of land line communications they were forced to use radio, which could be monitored, and if needs be jammed, which cable could not.

The Commandos did not deploy to the Gulf; lightly equipped troops would have been out of place in the highly mobile armoured land war. But other Marines deployed to the Gulf, besides the SBS. Naval Sea King helicopters of 845 and 848 Squadrons, normally in support of the Commando Brigade, were sent out to support the British 1st Armoured Division. With them went the mostly Royal Marine Commando Helicopter Operations Support Cell (CHOSC), an organization that was born out of the Falklands War, where the command and control of support helicopters had been less than satisfactory, through no fault of those involved – they simply lacked the manpower and equipment.

Royal Marines were also sent to sea in their old role of ship's detachments, where their duties included boarding suspect ships, manning both the Javelin shoulder-launched surface-to-air missile system (the replacement for the inefficient Blowpipe) and other close-in weapon systems, and providing mine lookouts. The Commander-in-Chief Fleet RM Band was embarked in the RFA *Argus*, a Primary Casualty Receiving Ship, for medical duties. The RFAs were provided with Royal Marine guards, and in almost every HQ, officers, NCOs, and Marines could be found carrying out a variety of tasks. Captain G. S. Mackenzie-Philps described his Gulf experience:

Arriving at Minhad Military Airbase I was met by Captain Simon Pritchard, OCRM Naval Party 1030 (M Coy 42 Cdo). After a short journey we arrived at the Hyatt in Dubai, NP 1030's home. What was most of 42 doing in Dubai? Protecting most of the RN that was also in Dubai, or in their main operating base, Jebel Ali, a few miles along the coast. NP 1030 'Hotel Force' had the vital but monotonous role of protecting the shore facilities and shipping when alongside. Little time was left to enjoy the superb lifestyle that Dubai offers, and even if there was, every man would swap it for a position at the front.

Joining the Task Group Flagship, HMS *London*, I was greeted by more Royals – C/Sgt Kevin Brennan and his 15-man detachment, who over the months previously had built up an awesome reputation first for their skill with the 20mm and 30mm cannons, but more importantly for their professionalism in dealing with sanction-busting shipping. I witnessed one such operation against the Iraqi peace ship, the *Ibn Kaldoon*, which was carrying some 300 peace women and supplies to Umm Qasr. The insertion took place at dawn by Lynx and the RM MIF team took ten seconds from arriving overhead to all-round defence 30 feet below on deck. Commodore Craig, Senior Naval Officer Middle East (SNOME) was justifiably pleased. This professionalism has been shown equally by the boarding teams from *Cardiff*, *Gloucester* and *Brazen*, with the latter doing an outstanding job on *Ain Zalah*.

On the staff of SNOME as MINTO (Military Intelligence Officer) I soon found out I had to be an instant expert on everything vaguely related to land matters. Iraqi orbats [orders of battle], weapons and equipment was straight forward – it was the friendly orbats, logistic resupply, casevac and other procedures that had me. This on top of the RN love of TLAs (three letter abbreviations) that had me thoroughly confused.

A handful of visits to 'Scud City' (Riyadh) to wheedle information out of HQ British Forces Middle East proved extremely valuable in getting a full-blown Land Int/Ops cell up and running. It was on one of these visits that I was pleasantly surprised to meet Majors Ian Corner and Paddy George on the J4 [logistics] desk, and a huddle of RM clerks to whom I owe a debt of gratitude and a few beers.[6]

For lack of space the Royal Marines bands have had scant mention in this story. Their Second World War role of manning the TS in major warships disappeared long ago. Since then these highly intelligent and talented men, and now women as well, have taken on another job in action, support of the medical system – a task undertaken by two bands in the Falklands War, the Band of Commando Forces and C-in-C Fleet's Band. The latter were to be found in the RFA *Argus*, the primary casualty ship, during the Gulf War, as Captain Mackenzie-Philps wrote:

They did an outstanding job, as I discovered during my two week period living on board and commuting daily to the flagship. *Argus* could not function without these multi-talented individuals. I actually discovered they had 37 different jobs, ranging from Argus Airways, ground handling for 846 NAS and organizing the through-put of passengers and freight; casualty handling and decontamination; hospital orderlies, aircraft controllers and even a very swept-up CCTV setup.

Hardly had the dust settled after the successful Allied Coalition land offensive brought hostilities in the Gulf to an end, than Royal Marines were deployed in northern Iraq. On 16 April 1991, the Major General Royal Marines commanding Commando Forces, Major General R. J. Ross, was summoned to the telephone by the MOD to be asked how soon the 3rd Commando Brigade could be deployed to the Turkey–Iraq border, where half a million Kurdish refugees had fled into the mountains as a result of Saddam's brutality to the Kurdish people. Eventually some 23,000 troops from thirteen nations were deployed, under Operation Haven, Ross being in overall charge of the British component, which included 3rd Commando Brigade, less 42 Commando, and a substantial medium- and heavy-lift helicopter and fixed-wing force.

At first relief operations were fairly crude, and the force could do no more than drop urgent requirements – shelter, food, water, and medical supplies – into the refugee settlements from C-130 aircraft. The 3rd Commando Brigade was originally deployed to provide military protection, but it soon became obvious that unless it actually became involved in the running of relief operations, very little progress would be made. The involvement of the Transport and Medical Squadrons of the Commando Logistic Regiment was a turning point. As operations became more refined, the Marines began to get among people on the ground, and to understand the fear that had motivated the Kurds to make their exodus into the mountains. The Iraqi secret police killed and tortured the Kurds, and one of the tasks of the Marines was to protect them. There was always an Iraqi military presence in the Marines area of operations, and it was necessary to make clear to the bestial Iraqi troops that their threats would not be tolerated. Occasionally the Iraqis would fire on the Marines, which was returned with interest, and on the whole they were left alone.

The Marines escorted the Kurds down from the mountains where they had hidden from the Iraqis in terrible squalor and deprivation, and provided them with food, shelter, clean water, and sanitation. In fifty-eight days, the task was done. One of the aspects that struck the Marines, both young and more experienced, was the gratitude and affection expressed so disarmingly by the Kurds – a pleasant contrast from the bitterness and resentment met with in Belfast and Crossmaglen in Northern Ireland. Haven remains the finest example of a limited objective humanitarian operation.

To date no Royal Marines units have deployed to the Balkans, although plenty of officers and NCOs have served there, including Lieutenant Colonel Shadbolt who was Military Assistant to Lieutenant General Sir Michael Rose in Bosnia. The most remarkable contribution by the Royal Marines to the conflict in Bosnia was, however, the provision of a Rapid Reaction Force Operations Staff in 1995.

By mid-1995 the Bosnian Serbs had the upper hand, and increasingly the United Nations Protection Force (UNPROFOR) and the individual nations represented were being humiliated. The troops were of little use as a peace-keeping force. Convoys were being held up for days; UN access to certain areas denied; UN (mainly UK troops) were effectively prisoners in Goražde; hostages were being taken; and the lightly armed peacekeepers were losing minor engagements due to restrictive Rules of Engagement and lack of firepower.

The UN decided to inject an element of peace enforcement into the theatre, and a large part of the UK contingent in Bosnia reorganized into a 'green' task force (green to distinguish it from the blue-hatted peace-keepers, and nothing to do with the Green movement). The French inserted a balanced war-fighting mechanized brigade into the theatre very quickly, and the British deployed the 24th Airmobile Brigade extremely slowly. The British Commander of UNPROFOR, Lieutenant General Smith, who had commanded the British 1st Armoured Division in the Gulf, and is one of the outstanding soldiers of his generation, found himself with a division-size force but without an operational staff beyond a small UN staff designed for peacekeeping. He asked for an operational two-star level headquarters, to be told that there was not one available in the British Army that could be spared. The Royal Marines were asked to provide the commander and main elements of this headquarters, and within ten days Major General Pennefather deployed to Bosnia with about half the staff of Headquarters Royal Marines, supplemented by other Royal Marines and some Army supporting arms representatives. Here they met up with their French counterparts, who formed about one third of the headquarters, and became operational within three days – the first Anglo-French headquarters since Suez nearly forty years before. As well as buckling down to the operational work, including setting up a war-fighting headquarters with communications, Pennefather and his staff had to cope with the commander of the UK contingent in the area, whose nose was severely out of joint. At this stage Srebrenica had just fallen with humiliating results for the Dutch. Bihac and Goražde were under pressure, and the probability of Sarajevo airport being overrun was extremely high. The main effort of the headquarters was however directed to planning the air/ground campaign to pressure the various factions into agreeing a peace settlement.

The day the Air/Ground Operation Order was completed, and Pennefather took it to General Smith for his approval, a mortar bomb was fired which killed some thirty Bosnians. This was the trigger for the execution of the Air/Ground operation, which began that night. For fourteen days Pennefather's headquarters coordinated most of the campaign at the tactical level, as well as providing a 'think tank' for General Smith at the operational level, and occasionally at the strategic level. Following the bombing campaign, the main role of the headquarters was to prepare the ground for the arrival of the International Force and withdrawal of UN troops. During this period Pennefather took over from General Smith for two weeks, on two separate occasions having some seventeen national contingents under command. After five months the largely Royal Marine headquarters returned to Britain, justly proud of what they had achieved. They had accomplished very close cohesion with their French counterparts, standing together against the often less than friendly pressure applied by the UN, NATO, and various national contingent staffs. The campaign planned by Pennefather and his staff had led to the peace accord at Dayton. So Royal Marines played a key part in a defining moment of Balkan history.

*

The 1990s brought an innovation in how Royal Marine Detachments deployed to sea, other than those borne for landing craft and other duties in the amphibious ships. Operations in the Gulf in 1990/1991 saw detachments specially sent to frigates and destroyers, for boarding and other duties. These were not part of the ship's company, and when no longer required were withdrawn. This arrangement has now been formalized by the provision of the Fleet Standby Rifle Troop (FSRT), kept at short notice by each Commando in turn. The FSRT may be sent to join a frigate or destroyer for a number of reasons besides boarding, ranging from provision of an early military presence ashore in (for example) rescue of British nationals from a violent or potentially violent situation, to humanitarian tasks. The FSRT concept is proving to be a great success. Because the troop is surplus to the ship's complement, the age-old issues that have plagued Royal Marine Detachment commanders since the seventeenth century – lack of time to train ashore because of the conflicting demands of ship's husbandry, and reluctance to spare the Marines for sustained operations ashore, because of their commitment to the ship's armament – are no more.

What of the future? The Strategic Defence Review (SDR), carried out under the 'New Labour' Government, has given as clear an indication of an assured future for the Royal Marines and amphibious operations as it is possible to give. The future of the Corps has, perhaps, never looked so promising in its 336-year history. Amphibious operations are firmly top on the Royal Navy's list of priorities – at one time they did not figure on the list at all.

The Corps is fortunate that its intrinsically joint outlook chimes in with a period of British military strategy which places joint operations at the top of its priorities. In our story we have seen how the significance, or otherwise, placed on amphibious, or joint, operations has waxed and waned over the centuries. In a lecture to the Royal United Services Institute on 29 September 1998, the then First Sea Lord, Admiral Sir Jock Slater, reviewed this changing scene, saying that the Royal Navy was the inheritor of two traditions. The first

> is the old fashioned view which contends that the twin principles of the decisive fleet engagement and command of the sea represent the proper application of maritime sea power, particularly British sea power during a period which started with naval pre-eminence [after the Battle of Trafalgar], and still is today characterised by naval prominence.[7]

As we have seen, as the nineteenth century came to a close the Royal Marines had a less and less fulfilling role in this 'tradition', and, although rightly proud of their contribution and the manner in which it was carried out, become in effect surrogate sailors, with secondary roles tacked on.

Admiral Slater continued by outlining the second tradition,

> which sees the application of maritime power as inextricably linked with operations on land. This is a view which is joint rather than navalist and one which sees the coveted fleet engagement as relevant only in so far as its effects can be measured in the prosecution of a land campaign.[8]

Although the Royal Marines had participated in the second tradition, by the late nineteenth century, because of the overriding priority assigned to their shipboard duties, they were perceived as having only a minority role in amphibious operations. Even if landed, the Marines were soon required back on board again, to man guns. It was the Army that Fisher saw as being a projectile to be fired by the Navy, not the Royal Marines, who, unlike today, were in no sense the custodians of the amphibious art. Furthermore, as Admiral Slater went on to say:

> These two traditions I have described cohabited for most of the nineteenth century but became perilously close to divorce in the early twentieth century.[9]

This 'divorce' nearly had as one of its outcomes putting the lid on any Royal Marine aspirations in the realm of amphibious operations. Faint glimmers of hope were seen after the efforts at Gallipoli and Zeebrugge in the First World War, extinguished in the inter-war period, and lost in the muddle of jobs given to the Corps in the early years of the Second World War. Only with the conversion to Commandos and landing craft halfway through that war did Royal Marine ambitions become reality. The phasing out of large ships after the Second World War, forcing the Corps to redefine its role, and the period of almost continuous active service since 1945, in which the Royal Marines were to the fore so often, saved them from extinction. Despite this gallant and distinguished performance, their very existence was called into question on a number of occasions.

The road in Whitehall trod by those putting the amphibious case to the SDR was rocky, uphill, and beset with thorns. The amphibious capability received longer and harder scrutiny than any other comparable area, as civil servants exercised the prejudices accumulated over a generation. But, in the event, the strength of the operational arguments would not be denied. The amphibious capability lies at the heart of the maritime contribution to joint operations; the Royal Navy's 'flagship' concept for the twenty-first century. In a sense our story has come full circle, because the Royal Marines are now firmly part of that Royal Navy 'flagship'; but among the lead players, rather than as part of the supporting cast, as in earlier days.

Today the standard of officers joining has never been higher: the pass mark for Royal Marines on the Admiralty Interview Board, and the intellectual quality of the candidates, well exceeds that of their naval counterparts – a far cry from the Fisher era at the start of the twentieth century, and even further than the impoverished Marine officer of the mid-eighteenth century, denied membership of the wardroom. All is rosy, it would seem. Therein may lie the danger. For the first time in the history of the Royal Marines, the axe no longer seems poised. The threat of that axe has kept many generations of Marines on their toes, ever mindful of the need to strive to be the best. It has also, among some officers, been counter-productive, inducing a defensive attitude in their dealings with other services. Perhaps the time has come to be more arrogant, to define clearly the Royal Marines' role in the wider scheme of things, and in doing so to take their place at the top table.

In late 1998 a decision was made by the Navy Board to align RM officer ranks with the Army, to take effect on 1 July 1999. With increasingly joint Armed Forces that had been reducing in size significantly over the last few years, it was inevitable that the anomalous RM officer rank structure would have to be rationalized. Hitherto RM officers carried a higher rank when serving afloat than when ashore; so at sea a major was equivalent to a commander RN (Army lieutenant colonel), while ashore he was equivalent to a lieutenant commander RN (Army major). There was enthusiasm in some quarters for officers to change to Naval badges and rank, forgetting, or conveniently ignoring, the fact that Marines, back to the days of their redcoat forebears, are soldiers who go to sea, not sailors who go ashore. Fortunately common sense prevailed and military titles and rank remain, thus reflecting the primary purpose of the Corps, which is to fight the land battle, albeit deployed from the sea, and perhaps more to the point avoiding the bizarre situation where officers with the badges and titles of sailors are commanding NCOs and Marines with the badges and titles of soldiers.

What is certain is that despite the high probability of most future operations being international peacekeeping, the day will come when, either with allies or alone, there will again be a need for Marine Bootneck to grasp whatever weapon he his equipped with at that moment, and advance towards an enemy who is doing his best to kill him. Marine Bootneck may have arrived by battlefield helicopter, armoured oversnow vehicle, or hovercraft, and may indeed go into battle in one of these, but the outcome will depend upon his courage, motivation, will to win, and above all training. Some things never change, and one of them is that the unexpected always happens.

APPENDICES

Appendix 1

Regiments of the Line who have been Marines

Marine Title – Short History

Seymour's – Raised in 1680 during reign of Charles II as 2nd Tangier Regiment. Became The Queens Marines (Seymour's) in 1702. Royal Regiment of Marines 1710–1715 before returning to the line to take up title The King's Own Regiment and reassume its proper place in the Line as 4th of Foot.[1] Now part of The King's Own Royal Border Regiment by amalgamation with the Border Regiment.

Saunderson's – Raised in 1702 as Saunderson's Marines. Disbanded after Treaty of Utrecht. Re-formed 1751 as 30th of Foot. Subsequently The East Lancashire Regiment, and now part of The Queen's Lancashire Regiment.

Villiers's – Raised in 1702 as Villiers's Marines. Disbanded after Treaty of Utrecht. Reformed in 1715 as 31st of Foot. Subsequently The East Surrey Regiment. Amalgamated with The Queen's Royal Regiment (West Surrey) in 1959 to form The Queen's Royal Surrey Regiment. In 1966 became part of The Queen's Regiment along with The Queen's Own Buffs, The Royal Sussex Regiment, and The Middlesex Regiment. Now part of The Princess of Wales's Royal Regiment, following the amalgamation of The Queen's Regiment with The Royal Hampshire Regiment.

Fox's – Raised in 1702 as Fox's Marines. Disbanded after the Treaty of Utrecht. Reformed in 1715 as 32nd of Foot. Subsequently the Duke of Cornwall's Light Infantry, and now part of The Light Infantry.

Appendix 2

Army regiments who served at sea: the Wars of the French Revolution, 1793–1802

Title at the time	Title now and some previous titles
2nd Foot	1661 the Tangier Regiment of Foot, Mordaunt's 1881 The Queen's (Royal West Surrey Regiment) 1921 The Queen's Royal Regiment (West Surrey) 1966 The Queen's Regiment Now part of The Princess of Wales's Royal Regiment *Nicknames as 2nd Foot: The Tangerines, Kirke's Lambs,* *The Mutton Lancers*
10th Foot	1685 Earl of Bath's Regiment of Foot 1747 10th Regiment of Foot 1881 The Lincolnshire Regiment Now part of The Royal Anglian Regiment *Nickname as The Lincolnshire Regiment: The Poachers,* *The Springers*
11th Foot	1685 The Duke of Beaufort's Musketeers 1881 The Devonshire Regiment Now part of The Devonshire and Dorset Regiment *Nicknames as 11th Foot: The Bloody Eleventh*
25th Foot	1689 The Earl of Leven's Regiment of Foot 1887 The King's Own Scottish Borderers One of the few regiments never to have been amalgamated *Nicknames: The KOSBs, The Botherers, Kokky-Olly-Birds*
29th Foot	1694 Colonel Farrington's Regiment of Foot 1881 The Worcestershire Regiment

Now part of The Worcestershire and Sherwood
   Foresters Regiment
Nicknames as 29th Foot: The Old and Bold

30th Foot   1702 Thomas Saunderson's Regiment of Marines
                     30th (Cambridgeshire) Regiment of Foot
                     1881 amalgamated with the 59th (2nd
                        Nottinghamshire) Regiment of Foot to form The
                        West Lancashire Regiment then The East Lancashire
                        Regiment
                     Now part of The Queen's Lancashire Regiment
                     *Nicknames as 30th Foot: The Three Tens, The Yellow
                        Bellies (after their facings)*

49th Foot   1743 Colonel Trelawny's Regiment of Foot
                     1881 Amalgamated with the 66th (Berkshire) Regiment
                        of Foot to form Princess Charlotte of Wales's
                        (Berkshire Regiment)
                     Now part of The Royal Gloucestershire, Berkshire and
                        Wiltshire Regiment

69th Foot   1756 2nd Battalion 14th Regiment of Foot
                     1881 amalgamated with 41st (the Welsh) Regiment of
                        Foot to become The Welsh Regiment (redesignated
                        1921 as The Welch Regiment)
                     Now part of The Royal Regiment of Wales
                     *Nicknames as 69th Foot: The Ups and Downs, The Old
                        Agamemnons*

86th Foot   1793 86th (Royal County Down) Regiment of Foot
                     1881 amalgamated with 83rd (County of Dublin)
                        Regiment of Foot to form The Royal Irish Rifles
                     1921 The Royal Ulster Rifles
                     1968 Part of The Royal Irish Rangers
                     Now part of The Royal Irish Regiment
                     Nicknames as 86th Foot: The Irish Giants

2/90th Foot   1794 raised as 90th Regiment of Foot (Perthshire
                        Volunteers) (Light Infantry)
                     1881 amalgamated with 26th (Cameronian) Regiment

of Foot to form The Cameronians (Scotch Rifles),
redesignated The Cameronians (Scottish Rifles)
Disbanded 1968
Nickname as 90th Foot: The Perthshire Greybreeks

95th or Rifle   1800 Experimental Corps of Riflemen or Rifle Corps
Regiment   1803 95th or Rifle Regiment
                      1816 Rifle Brigade
                      1966 Amalgamated as 3rd Battalion The Royal Green
                          Jackets
                      Disbanded after Options for Change in 1992
                      Nicknames as Rifle Brigade: Green Jackets, The Sweeps

Appendix 3

Royal Marine deployment, early 1945

A Royal Marine Office paper (RM 465/13/44 G(SD), dated 5 December 1944) to the First Lord of the Admiralty, quoted in the diary of Brigadier C. F. Phillips, showed the deployment and strengths of the Corps at the time of raising the two RM Brigades, as follows:

Employed afloat	7,838
Employed on active operations	14,117[1]
Combined operations personnel	17,341[2]
In RM establishments	
Home	2,409
Abroad	2,909
In RN Air Establishments	1,762
Miscellaneous units	2,326
RM HQ and training establishments	17,833[3]

By late 1944, even with nine Commandos and two brigade headquarters engaged, as well as men in minor landing and support craft, engaged for some of the time, and ship's detachments, a great deal of the Corps (some 40 per cent) was either misemployed, or not on operations, or not engaged in activities in direct support of operations. Hence the scope for raising two infantry brigades.

Appendix 4

Units in 3rd Commando Brigade Royal Marines, Falklands War 1982

Brigade Headquarters

Two troops of B Squadron RHG/D The Blues and Royals

29 Commando Regiment Royal Artillery
       7 (Sphinx) Commando Battery
       8 (Alma) Commando Battery
       79 (Kirkee) Commando Battery
       148 (Meiktila) Commando Battery[1]

  and: 29 (Corunna) Field Battery, 4 Regiment Royal Artillery
       Battery commander and OP parties 41 Regiment Royal Artillery
       T (Shah Shujah's Troop) Air Defence Battery[2]

59 Commando Squadron Royal Engineers

  and: 2 Troop, 9 Parachute Squadron Royal Engineers
       One team 49 Explosives Ordnance Disposal Squadron, 33 Engineer
         Regiment
       One Explosives Ordnance Team RAF

40 Commando Royal Marines

42 Commando Royal Marines less M Company, but plus J Company[3]

45 Commando Royal Marines

2nd Battalion The Parachute Regiment

3rd Battalion The Parachute Regiment

Special Boat Squadron Royal Marines

D and G Squadrons 22 Special Air Service Regiment

Mountain and Arctic Warfare Cadre (M&AW) Royal Marines[4]

3 Commando Brigade Air Squadron

   and: One flight 656 Squadron Army Air Corps

3 Commando Brigade Air Defence Troop Royal Marines

   and: Two sections 43 Battery, 32 Guided Weapons Regiment Royal
               Artillery

605, 611, and 612 Tactical Air Control Parties Royal Marines[5]
613 Tactical Air Control Party

3rd Commando Brigade Headquarters and Signal Squadron Royal Marines

   and: Satellite Communications Detachment Royal Signals
               1 Raiding Squadron Royal Marines
               Commando Forces News Team

Commando Logistic Regiment Royal Marines
   Postal and Courier Communications Unit Royal Engineers
   Elements Transport Squadron
   Medical Squadron
      and: Surgical Support Team
                  Parachute Clearing Troop
                  Commando Forces Band
   Ordnance Squadron
   Elements Workshop Squadron
   Force Reinforcement Holding Unit
   Field Records Office

Maps

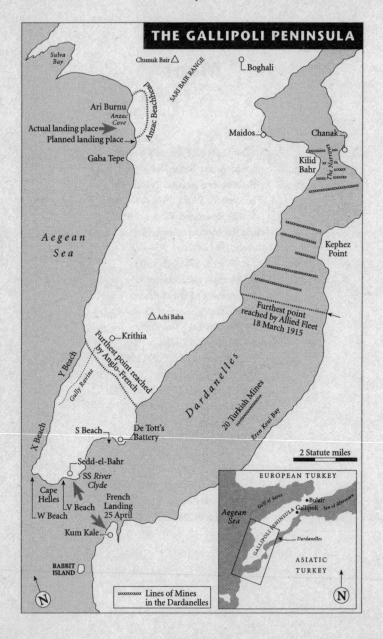

THE GALLIPOLI PENINSULA

Sulva Bay

Chunuk Bair △

SARI BAIR RANGE

Boghali

Ari Burnu
Anzac Cove

Anzac Beachhead

Actual landing place
Planned landing place

Gaba Tepe

Maidos

Chanak

Kilid Bahr

The Narrows

Aegean Sea

Kephez Point

△ Achi Baba

Furthest point reached by Allied Fleet 18 March 1915

● Krithia

Furthest point reached by Anglo-French

Y Beach

Gully Ravine

Dardanelles

20 Turkish Mines

Eren Keui Bay

X Beach

S Beach

De Tott's Battery

Sedd-el-Bahr

SS *River Clyde*

Cape Helles

French Landing 25 April

V Beach

W Beach

Kum Kale

RABBIT ISLAND

N

Lines of Mines in the Dardanelles

2 Statute miles

EUROPEAN TURKEY

Aegean Sea

Gulf of Saros

● Bulair

Gallipoli

Sea of Marmara

GALLIPOLI PENINSULA

Dardanelles

ASIATIC TURKEY

N

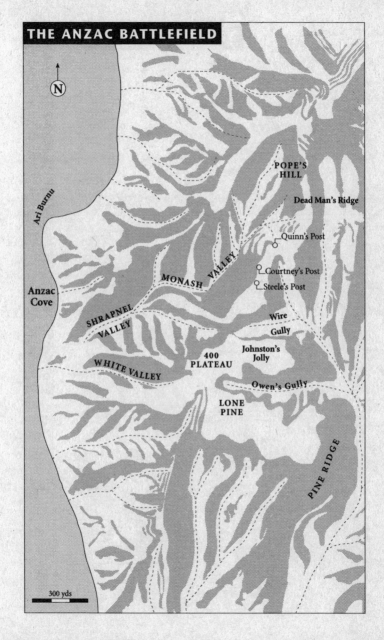

THE ANZAC BATTLEFIELD

N

POPE'S HILL

Dead Man's Ridge

Quinn's Post

Courtney's Post

Steele's Post

Ari Burnu

MONASH VALLEY

Anzac Cove

SHRAPNEL VALLEY

Wire Gully

Johnston's Jolly

400 PLATEAU

WHITE VALLEY

Owen's Gully

LONE PINE

PINE RIDGE

300 yds

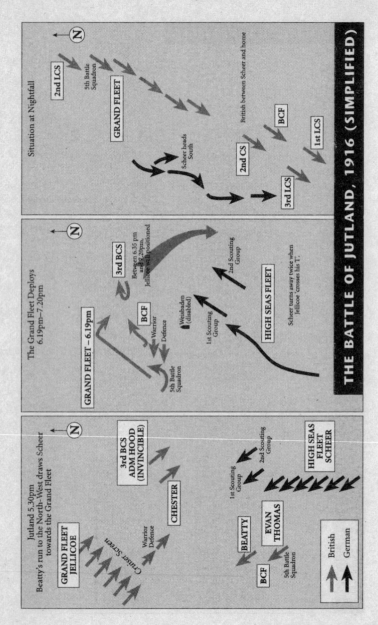

Jutland 5.30pm
Beatty's run to the North-West draws Scheer towards the Grand Fleet

GRAND FLEET JELLICOE

Cruiser Screen

3rd BCS ADM HOOD (INVINCIBLE)

Warrior
Defence

CHESTER

BCF

5th Battle Squadron

BEATTY

EVAN THOMAS

1st Scouting Group

2nd Scouting Group

HIGH SEAS FLEET SCHEER

British
German

The Grand Fleet Deploys
6.19pm–7.20pm

GRAND FLEET – 6.19pm

5th Battle Squadron

Defence

Warrior

BCF

3rd BCS

Between 6.35 pm and 7.20pm, Jellicoe well positioned

Wiesbaden (disabled)

1st Scouting Group

2nd Scouting Group

HIGH SEAS FLEET

Scheer turns away twice when Jellicoe 'crosses his T'.

Situation at Nightfall

2nd LCS

5th Battle Squadron

GRAND FLEET

Scheer heads South

British between Scheer and home

2nd CS

BCF

1st LCS

3rd LCS

THE BATTLE OF JUTLAND, 1916 (SIMPLIFIED)

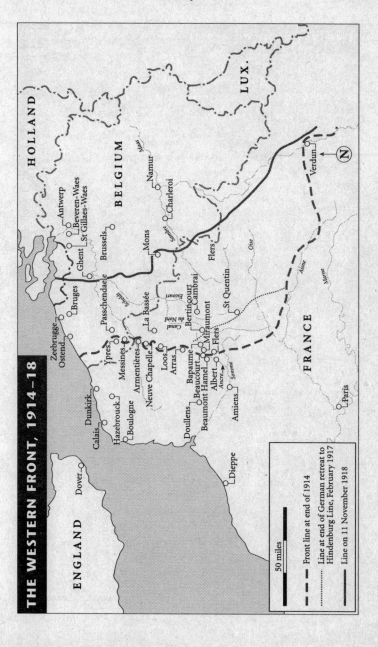

THE WESTERN FRONT, 1914–18

ENGLAND

HOLLAND

BELGIUM

LUX.

FRANCE

Dover

Calais
Dunkirk
Zeebrugge
Ostend
Hazebrouck
Boulogne
Bruges
Ghent
Antwerp
Beveren-Waes
St Gillaes-Waes
Brussels
Passchendaele
Ypres
Messines
Armentières
Neuve Chapelle
La Bassée
Mons
Namur
Charleroi
Flers
Loos
Arras
Bapaume
Beaucourt
Beaumont Hamel
Albert
Flers
Mirfaumont
Bertincourt
Cambrai
St Quentin
Doullens
Amiens
Dieppe
Paris
Verdun

Schelat
Escaut
Canal du Nord
Ancre
Somme
Sambre
Maas
Oise
Aisne
Marne

50 miles

- - - Front line at end of 1914
······· Line at end of German retreat to
        Hindenburg Line, February 1917
——— Line on 11 November 1918

N

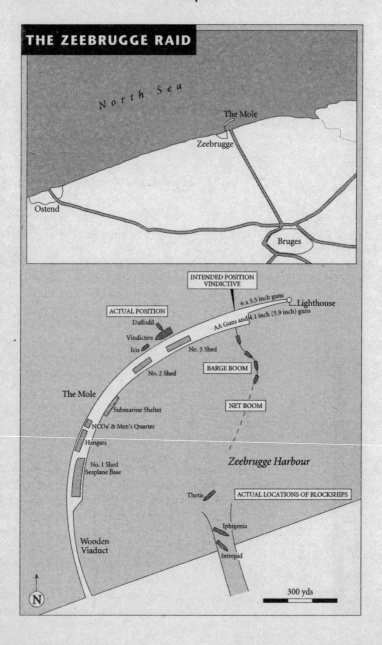

THE ZEEBRUGGE RAID

North Sea

The Mole

Zeebrugge

Ostend

Bruges

INTENDED POSITION
VINDICTIVE

6 x 3.5 inch guns   Lighthouse

ACTUAL POSITION

AA Guns and 4.1 inch (5.9 inch) guns

Daffodil

Vindictive

Iris

No. 3 Shed

BARGE BOOM

No. 2 Shed

The Mole

NET BOOM

Submarine Shelter

NCOs' & Men's Quarter

Zeebrugge Harbour

Hangars

No. 1 Shed
Seaplane Base

Thetis   ACTUAL LOCATIONS OF BLOCKSHIPS

Iphigenia

Wooden
Viaduct

Intrepid

N

300 yds

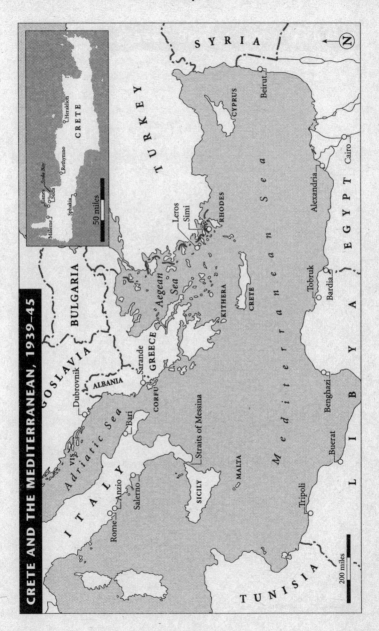

CRETE AND THE MEDITERRANEAN, 1939–45

MALAYA, 1941–42 AND 1950–52

N

Gulf of Thailand

SIAM
(THAILAND)

Kota Bahru

Penang
Grik
Lenggong
Kuala Kangsar
Taiping
Ipoh
PERAK
Tapah
STATE

MALAYA

Kuala Lipis
Kuantan

*Repulse
Prince of Wales*
} sunk 10 Dec 42

Port Swettenham
Kuala Lumpur

Strait of Malacca

SINGAPORE

Johore Bahru

SUMATRA

100 miles

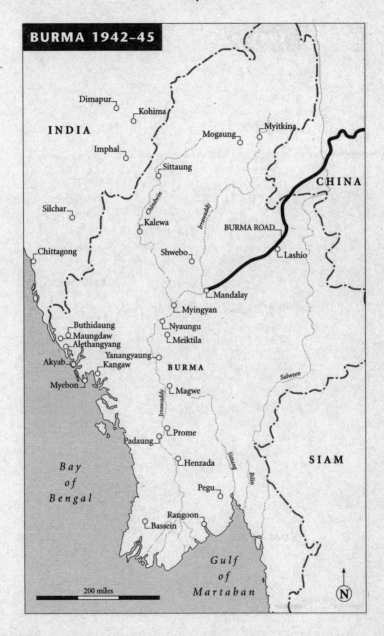

BURMA 1942–45

INDIA

Dimapur

Kohima

Imphal

Mogaung

Myitkina

Sittaung

CHINA

Silchar

Chindwin

Irrawaddy

BURMA ROAD

Kalewa

Shwebo

Lashio

Chittagong

Mandalay

Myingyan

Nyaungu

Buthidaung

Maungdaw

Meiktila

Alethangyang

Yanangyaung

Akyab

Kangaw

BURMA

Salween

Myebon

Irrawaddy

Magwe

Prome

Sittang

SIAM

Padaung

Henzada

Bilin

Bay
of
Bengal

Pegu

Rangoon

Bassein

Gulf
of
Martaban

200 miles

N

OPERATIONS BY ROYAL MARINES DETACHMENT 385 FEB–SEP 1945 (refer to numbers on map opposite)

Op no	Month	Type of op	Result	Op no	Month	Type of op	Result
①	February	Snatch locals	Unsuccessful	⑪	April	Intelligence	Successful
②	February	Snatch locals	Unsuccessful	⑫	April	Intelligence/ deception	Successful
③	February	Snatch locals	Successful				
④	March	Intelligence	Unsuccessful	⑬	April	Recce & fighting patrol	Partial Success
⑤	March	Deception & recce	Successful				
⑥	March	Deception	Unsuccessful	⑭	April	Recce	Aborted
⑦	March	Pick up operators	Successful	⑮	May	Land arms Recover 12 men	Successful
⑧	March	Rescue operators lost in No. 6	Unsuccessful	⑯	June	Land agent & stores Ship attack on coastal craft	Partial Success (Agent landed, no ship attack opportunity)
⑨	March	Deception	Partial Success				
⑩	April	Pick up Fleet Air Arm pilots	Pilots did not keep RV	⑰	June	Establish stores dump	Successful
				⑱	July	Establish stores dump	Successful
				⑲	August	Occupation of Penang with Marines of Far East Fleet	Successful

THE STORMING OF DIÉGO-SUAREZ

COMMANDOS UNABLE TO OBTAIN CRAFT AFTER TAKING D.S.

Anthony lands 50 Marines for attack in rear

Destroyer *Anthony* embarks Marines for attack on Antsirane

5 COMMANDO 1 COY. E. LANCS
□ WINDSOR CASTLE

POSITION OF   SHIPPING FOR ASSAULT

Courrier Bay

Ramillies

Orangea

Diego-Suarez   Antsirane

R.W. E. & S. LANCS FUS.

Ft. Caimans   Ft. Bellevue

R.S. FUS.

Ambararata

AIRFIELD □

MAIN ATTACK

10 miles

To Mahagaga   To Ambodivahibe

N

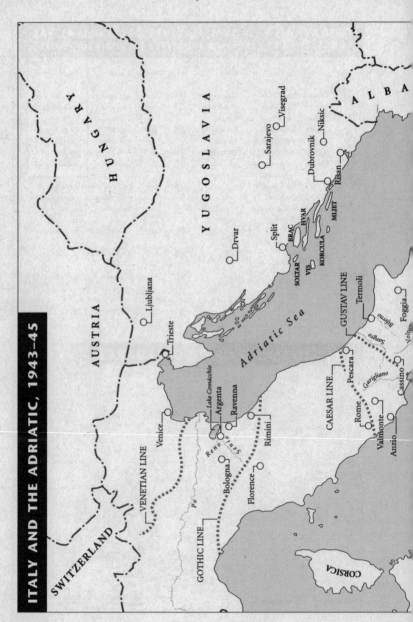

ITALY AND THE ADRIATIC, 1943–45

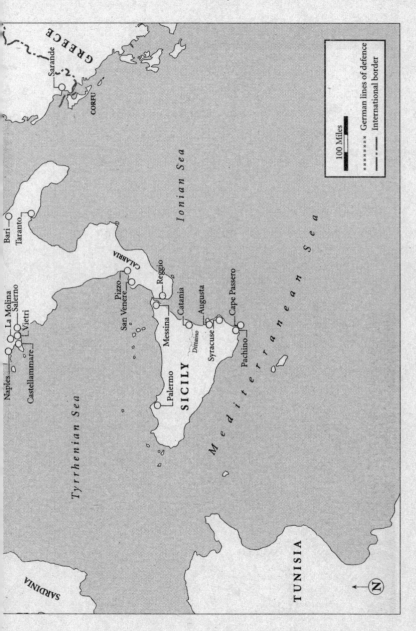

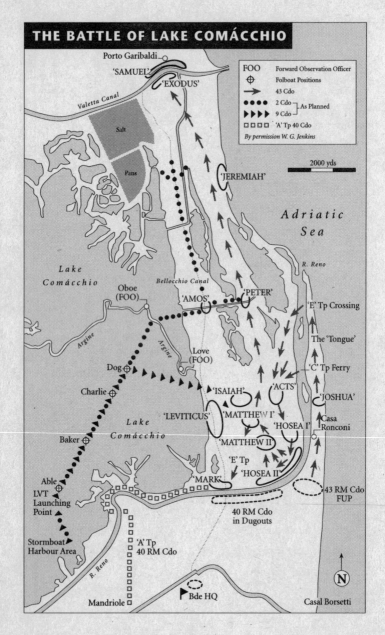

THE BATTLE OF LAKE COMÁCCHIO

Porto Garibaldi

'SAMUEL'

'EXODUS'

Valetta Canal

Salt

Pans

FOO	Forward Observation Officer
⊕	Folboat Positions
→	43 Cdo
●●●●	2 Cdo — As Planned
▶▶▶▶	9 Cdo
☐☐☐☐	'A' Tp 40 Cdo

By permission W. G. Jenkins

2000 yds

'JEREMIAH'

Adriatic Sea

Lake Comácchio

Oboe (FOO)

Bellocchio Canal

'AMOS'   'PETER'

R. Reno

'E' Tp Crossing

Argine

Argine

Love (FOO)

The 'Tongue'

'C' Tp Ferry

Dog ⊕

'ISAIAH'   'ACTS'

'JOSHUA'

Charlie ⊕

'LEVITICUS'   'MATTHEW I'

Casa Ronconi

Lake Comácchio

'HOSEA I'

Baker ⊕

'MATTHEW II'

Able ⊕

'E' Tp   'HOSEA II'

LVT Launching Point

'MARK'

43 RM Cdo FUP

Stormboat Harbour Area

40 RM Cdo in Dugouts

R. Reno

'A' Tp 40 RM Cdo

▶ Bde HQ

Mandriole

N

Casal Borsetti

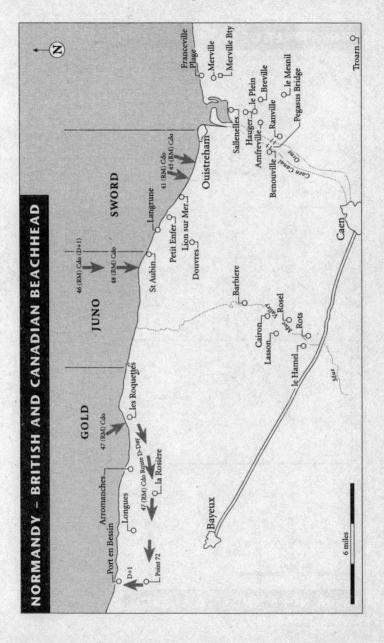

NORMANDY – BRITISH AND CANADIAN BEACHHEAD

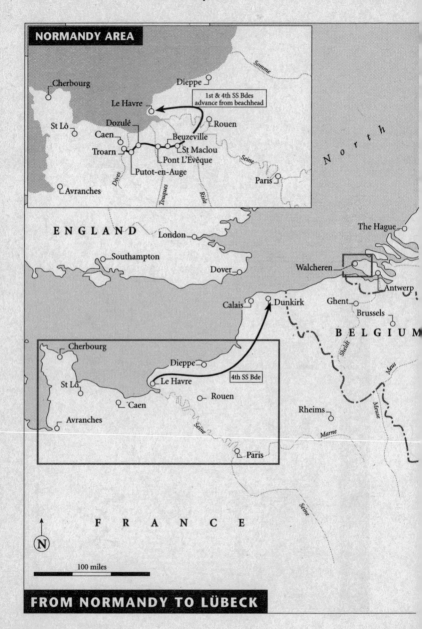

NORMANDY AREA

Cherbourg

Dieppe

Somme

Le Havre

1st & 4th SS Bdes
advance from beachhead

St Lô

Dozulé

Rouen

Caen

Beuzeville

Troarn

St Maclou

Pont L'Evêque

Putot-en-Auge

Seine

Dives

Avranches

Touques

Risle

Paris

N o r t h

ENGLAND

London

The Hague

Southampton

Dover

Walcheren

Antwerp

Calais

Dunkirk

Ghent

Brussels

BELGIUM

Cherbourg

Dieppe

Scheldt

St Lô

Le Havre

4th SS Bde

Caen

Rouen

Meuse

Avranches

Seine

Rheims

Meuse

Paris

Marne

FRANCE

Seine

N

100 miles

FROM NORMANDY TO LÜBECK

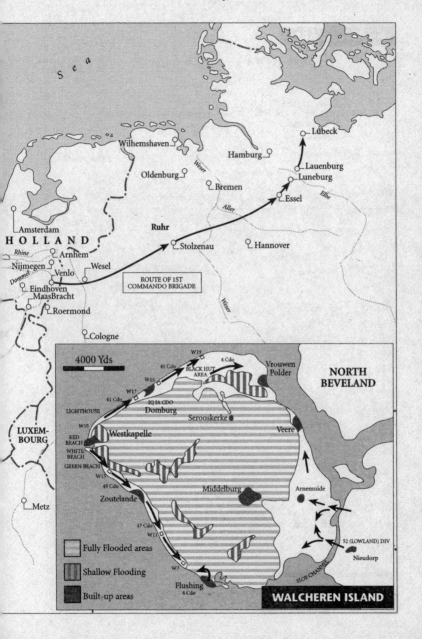

Sea

Wilhemshaven

Hamburg

○ Lübeck

Oldenburg

Weser

○ Bremen

○ Lauenburg
○ Luneburg

Essel

Aller

Elbe

Amsterdam

Ruhr

HOLLAND

Rhine

○ Arnhem

○ Stolzenau

○ Hannover

Nijmegen

Venlo
○ Wesel

Eindhoven

Dommel

MaasBracht

ROUTE OF 1ST
COMMANDO BRIGADE

Roermond

Weser

○ Cologne

4000 Yds

W19

41 Cdo

4 Cdo

Vrouwen
Polder

**NORTH
BEVELAND**

BLACK HUT
AREA

W18

41 Cdo

W17

LIGHTHOUSE

IQ IA CDO

Domburg

Serooskerke

Veere

W15

Westkapelle

RED
BEACH

WHITE
BEACH

GREEN BEACH

48 Cdo

Middelburg

Arnemuide

W13

Zoutelande

47 Cdo
W11

52 (LOWLAND) DIV

Nieudorp

W7

Flushing
4 Cdo

SLOE CHANNEL

Fully Flooded areas

Shallow Flooding

Built-up areas

WALCHEREN ISLAND

LUXEM-
BOURG

○ Metz

KOREA

CHINA

USSR

Ch'ongjin

Kyongsong-man

Songjin

Yalu

Chongchon

Hungnam

Sorye Dong

Sea
of
Japan

Taedong

Pyongyang

Wonsan

Imjin

CEASEFIRE LINE 1953

38°

Panmunjom

Seoul

Inchon

Han

38°

Pyongtaek

SOUTH KOREA

Yellow
Sea

100 miles

Naktong

Nam

Masan

Pusan

USSR

CHINA

KOREA

JAPAN

Korea Strait

QUELPART

N

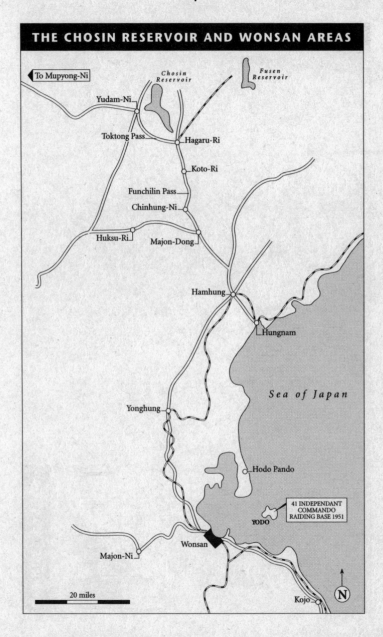

THE CHOSIN RESERVOIR AND WONSAN AREAS

To Mupyong-Ni

Chosin Reservoir

Fusen Reservoir

Yudam-Ni

Toktong Pass

Hagaru-Ri

Koto-Ri

Funchilin Pass

Chinhung-Ni

Huksu-Ri

Majon-Dong

Hamhung

Hungnam

Sea of Japan

Yonghung

Hodo Pando

41 INDEPENDANT
COMMANDO
RAIDING BASE 1951

YODO

Majon-Ni

Wonsan

20 miles

Kojo

N

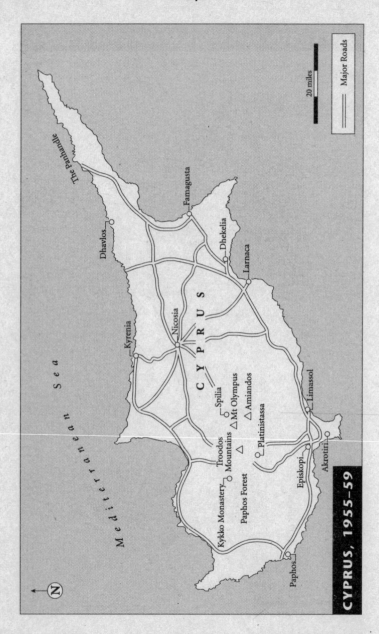

Major Roads

20 miles

The Panhandle

Dhavlos

Famagusta

Dhekelia

Larnaca

Kyrenia

Nicosia

C Y P R U S

Spilia

Mt Olympus

Amiandos

Limassol

Platinistassa

Troodos
Mountains

Paphos Forest

Episkopi

Akrotiri

Kykko Monastery

Paphos

M e d i t e r r a n e a n   S e a

N

CYPRUS, 1955–59

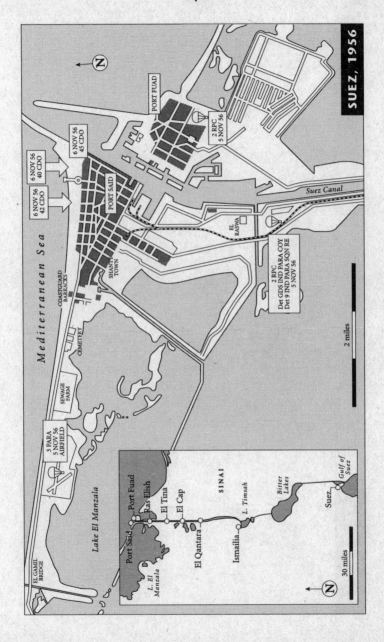

SUEZ, 1956

N

PORT FUAD

2 RPC
5 NOV 56

6 NOV 56
45 CDO

6 NOV 56
40 CDO

6 NOV 56
42 CDO

PORT SAID

Suez Canal

EL
RASWA

COASTGUARD
BARRACKS

SHANTY
TOWN

2 RPC
Det GDS IND PARA COY
Det 9 IND PARA SQN RE
5 NOV 56

Mediterranean Sea

CEMETERY

SEWAGE
FARM

3 PARA
5 NOV 56
AIRFIELD

2 miles

EL GAMIL
BRIDGE

Lake El Manzala

L. El
Manzala

Port Said

Port Fuad

Ras Elish

El Tina

El Cap

El Qantara

Ismailia

L. Timsah

SINAI

Bitter
Lakes

Suez

Gulf of
Suez

N

30 miles

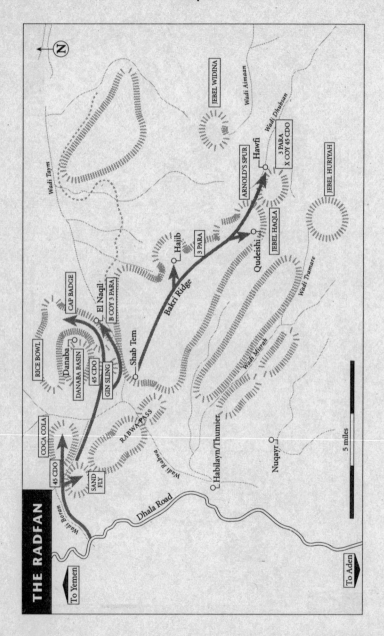

THE RADFAN

JEBEL WIDINA

Wadi Aimaan

Wadi Dhubsan

Wadi Taym

ARNOLD'S SPUR

Hawfi

3 PARA X COY 45 CDO

3 PARA

Hajib

JEBEL HAQLA

Qudeishi

JEBEL HURTYAH

RICE BOWL

CAP BADGE

El Naqil

Bakri Ridge

Danaba

B COY 3 PARA

DANABA BASIN

45 CDO

Shab Tem

Wadi Misrah

GIN SLING

Wadi Tramare

COCA COLA

RABWA PASS

45 CDO

Wadi Rabwa

Habilayn/Thumier

SAND FLY

Nuqayl

5 miles

Dhala Road

Wadi Beran

To Yemen

To Aden

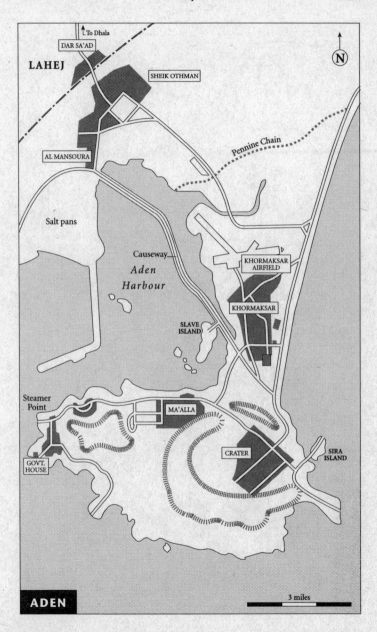

To Dhala

DAR SA'AD

LAHEJ

SHEIK OTHMAN

AL MANSOURA

Pennine Chain

Salt pans

Causeway

Aden Harbour

KHORMAKSAR AIRFIELD

KHORMAKSAR

SLAVE ISLAND

Steamer Point

MA'ALLA

CRATER

SIRA ISLAND

GOVT. HOUSE

N

ADEN

3 miles

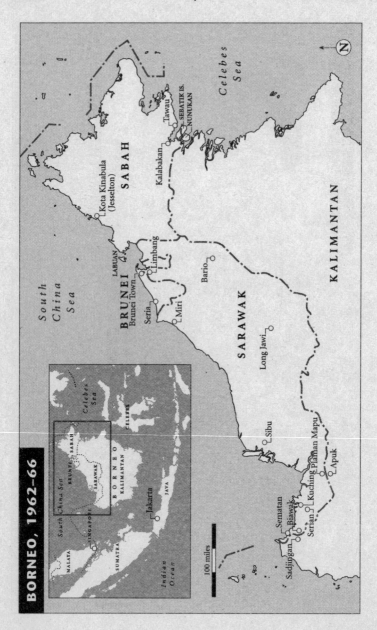

BORNEO, 1962–66

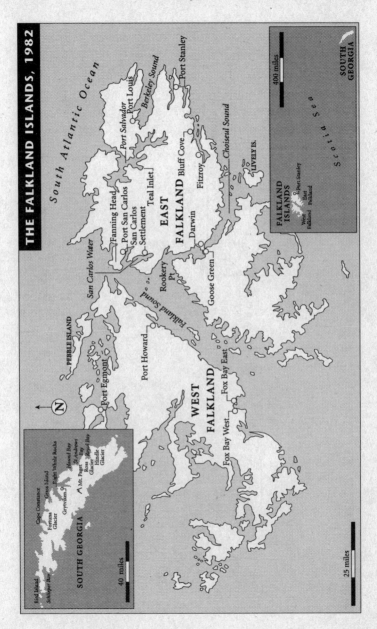

THE FALKLAND ISLANDS, 1982

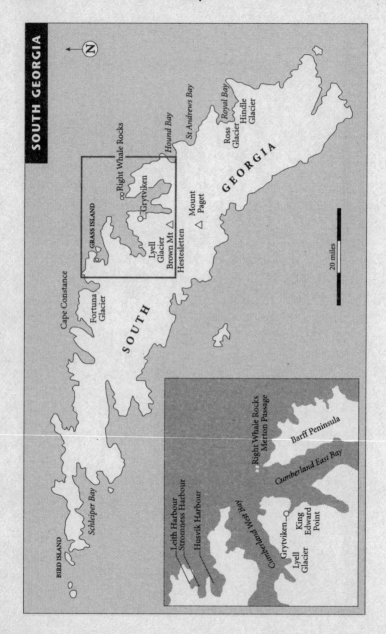

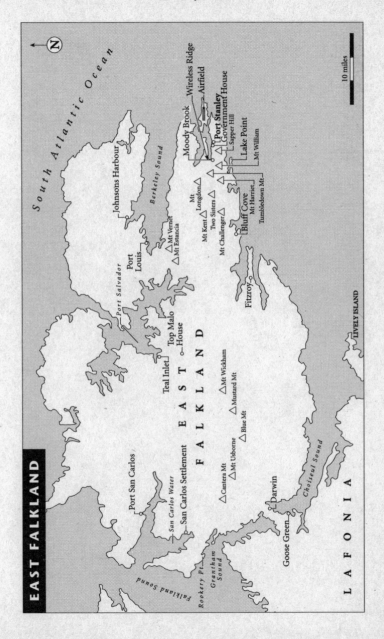

EAST FALKLAND

N

10 miles

South Atlantic Ocean

Johnsons Harbour

Berkeley Sound

Port Salvador

Port Louis

Moody Brook

Wireless Ridge

Airfield

Port Stanley

Government House

Sapper Hill

Lake Point

Mt William

△ Mt Vernet

△ Mt Estancia

Mt
Kent △ △ Longdon

Two Sisters △

Mt Challenger △

Bluff Cove

Mt Harriet

Tumbledown Mt

Fitzroy

Top Malo
House

Teal Inlet

E A S T

F A L K L A N D

△ Mt Wickham

△ Mustard Mt

△ Blue Mt

△ Mt Usborne

Port San Carlos

San Carlos Water

San Carlos Settlement

△ Cantera Mt

Rookery Pt

Grantham Sound

Falkland Sound

Darwin

Goose Green

Choiseul Sound

L A F O N I A

LIVELY ISLAND

Glossary

ALC – Assault Landing Craft, later changed to Landing Craft Assault (see LCA).

APC – Armoured Personnel Carrier, an armoured tracked or wheeled vehicle designed to carry infantry into battle. Less heavily armoured than a tank.

APD – The US Navy converted thirty-two destroyers during the Second World War for raiding operations, described as Fast Light Transports (APD). They carried about 140–200 troops, depending on the length of passage, and four LCP(L) or LCP(R) and inflatable rubber boats. (What APD stands for is not clear: suggestions range from Assault Platform Destroyer escort to Auxiliary Platform Destroyer escort.)

Bandwagon BV 202 – Tracked, articulated, oversnow vehicle, consisting of a towing vehicle and articulated trailer, built by Volvo. Highly successful on peat bog in the Falklands War. Now replaced by the tracked All Terrain Vehicle (ATV), of which there is shortly to be an armoured version.

Bangalore Torpedo – A length of piping filled with explosive, used for blowing a gap in barbed-wire entanglements.

BAT – Literally Battalion Anti Tank(gun). A 120mm recoilless anti-tank gun, firing a High Explosive Squash Head (HESH) shell, which replaced the 17-pounder anti-tank gun in British infantry battalions in the late 1950s.

Besa – Machine-gun used in British armoured cars and tanks. Originally the Czech ZB vz/53 (7.92mm) and ZB vz/60 (15mm) bought by Britain and manufactured by the Birmingham Small Arms (BSA) Ltd as a tank co-axial gun (i.e., mounted in the turret alongside the main armament, and pointing where the main armament pointed). There were several marks produced during the Second World War.

Bolo – British slang for Bolshevik, hence a Bolo machine-gun was a machine-gun manned by Bolsheviks.

Bren – The British light machine-gun of the Second World War and until the late 1950s. Fired a standard .303in round from a 28-round magazine. Modified to fire 7.62mm ammunition with the introduction of the SLR in the late 1950s. Replaced in Commandos by the GPMG in the mid-1960s.

Brigade Major (BM) – The senior operations officer of a brigade, de facto chief of staff.

Buffalo – American Landing Vehicle Tracked, an amphibian with a water speed of 5 knots and land speed of 25 mph. Propulsion in the water was by grousers on the tracks. The later version had a stern ramp and could lift a jeep or a 25-pounder field gun. The earlier model had no ramp, and could carry twenty-five men.

Cadre – A group of men usually under training for a specific skill. In the case of the Mountain & Arctic Warfare Cadre, training instructors in mountain warfare. Their wartime role was as the 3rd Commando Brigade Recce Troop.

CGM – Conspicuous Gallantry Medal, instituted 1855, and awarded to ratings of the Royal Navy (and Royal Marines NCOs and Marines when under naval command) for gallantry in action. Now discontinued. See DSC.

Champ – British attempt in the 1950s at producing a successor to the Jeep. Poorly designed, expensive to maintain, and a failure. Nothing like as popular as the Land-Rover.

Chaung – Burmese for watercourse or minor river; they could be as narrow as a ditch, or wide enough for small craft, particularly near the coast.

Chinook – Large, twin-rotor helicopter with a payload of ten tons.

Churchill tank – A heavy, but undergunned, British tank designed in 1940.

Commando – Either the individual commando soldier or Marine (as 'commando'), or the unit (as 'Commando'). Originally it was the name given to fighting units raised by the Boers in South Africa from a particular district, for example the Jacobsdal Commando. Eventually, Commandos came to be called after their leaders, e.g. Smuts's Commando. The name was given by Lieutenant Colonel Dudley Clark to the Army special service units raised on Churchill's orders in 1940. Dudley Clark had been brought up in South Africa and read Denys Reitz's book *Commando*, describing his service under Jan Smuts against the British in the Second Boer War. The name is retained by the Royal Marines and the British Army to this day.

Corps – (1) A formation of at least two divisions commanded by a lieutenant general.
(2) The collective way of referring to Royal Marines, and for that matter Royal Engineers and other 'corps' in the British Army.

CSM – Company Sergeant Major

CVRT – Combat Vehicle Reconnaissance Tracked – Scorpion or Scimitar. Built by Alvis with same hull, chassis, and drive, Scorpion has a 76mm gun and Scimitar a 30mm automatic cannon.

DCM – Distinguished Conduct Medal, instituted in 1854, the equivalent of the DSO for Warrant Officers, NCOs, and soldiers of the Army (and Royal Marines when under Army command). Awarded for gallantry in action. Now discontinued.

DF – Defensive Fire – mortar, artillery, or machine-gun fire by troops in defensive positions against attacking troops or patrols.

Direct Fire – Weapons that have to be aimed directly at the target, as opposed to indirect fire weapons such as mortars and artillery.

DSC – Distinguished Service Cross, instituted in 1914, and awarded to officers of the Royal Navy (and Royal Marines when serving under naval command), for gallantry in action. Now all ranks are eligible.

DSM – Distinguished Service Medal, instituted in 1914, the naval equivalent of the DSO for ratings of the Royal Navy (and Royal Marines NCOs and Marines when under naval command). Awarded for gallantry in action. Now discontinued.

DSO – Distinguished Service Order, instituted in 1886, and until the awards system was changed in 1994, a dual-role decoration, recognizing gallantry at a level below that qualifying for the VC by junior officers, and generally exceptional leadership by senior officers. Officers of all three services were and are eligible. Now it is awarded for highly successful command and leadership in operational circumstances.

DUKW – American six-wheeled amphibious truck. Initials from maker's code, pronounced 'duck'.

DZ – Dropping Zone, the area chosen for landing by parachute troops.

FAL – Semi-automatic 7.63mm rifle designed in Belgium by the Fabrique Nationale (FN) in 1949. Various marks produced, including the automatic versions. The Argentines had the FAL model 50–64 which fired semi- and fully automatic and had a folding butt. The British Self-Loading Rifle (SLR) was made under licence based on the FN design but it was semi-automatic only.

FDLs – Forward Defended Localities – the forward part of a defensive position. Now Forward Edge of the Battle Area (FEBA).

Flag Captain – The captain of the flagship.

Flak – German slang for anti-aircraft fire, from the German for anti-aircraft gun, *fliegerabwehrkanone.*

FOB – Forward Observer Bombardment – a Royal Artillery officer who spotted for naval guns bombarding shore targets in Second World War. His party consisted of Royal Naval telegraphists (the RN name for a radio operator), to communicate with the supporting ships. See NGFO.

Folboat – The Mark I was a two-man collapsible canoe built for sporting purposes by the Folboat company. It had a wooden frame and rubberized canvas cover. It was fragile, easily punctured, and totally unsuitable for operations, as the cockpit was not covered, and there were no buoyancy or stability aids. Some eight marks of canoe were designed and built by the British during the Second World War. Improvements and modifications to different marks of canoe included (the list is not exhaustive): cockpit covers; buoyancy aids; plywood decks and hulls; outriggers; a lateen sail; an engine; and a rudder. No mark incorporated every single one of these, and many other, features; each mark had characteristics suited to a particular role or roles. There was even a Motor Submersible Canoe (MSC), the 'Sleeping Beauty'. A good summary of the plethora of canoes, boats, and other equipment used by the British in minor waterborne operations in the Second World War and after is given in Appendix III to James Ladd's book, *The Invisible Raiders* (Fontana, 1984).

FOO – Forward Observation Officer, an artillery officer who directs artillery fire. From Second World War onwards, normally one with each forward rifle company and provided by artillery battery supporting the Commando or battalion.

Force 136 – The Far East branch of the Special Operations Executive (a British

Second World War secret service intended to promote subversive warfare in enemy-occupied territories). Force 136 operated extensively in Burma, and also in Thailand, French Indo-China, and Malaya.

47/32 anti-tank gun – Italian anti-tank gun.

GOC – General Officer Commanding.

GSO – General Staff Officer, a staff officer who dealt with General (G) Staff matters (operations, intelligence, planning, and staff duties), as opposed to personnel (A, short for Adjutant General's Staff), or logistic matters (Q, short for Quartermaster General's Staff). The grades were GSO 1 (Lieutenant Colonel), GSO 2 (Major), and GSO 3 (Captain).

HE – High Explosive.

Heinkel III – A German medium bomber that saw service throughout the Second World War. Top speed 258 mph.

H-Hour – The time that the first wave of craft touch down in an amphibious operation, or the leading troops cross the start line in a land battle.

IWS – Individual Weapon Sight: a night sight using image-intensification technology which could be fixed on top of an SLR (see SLR). In a Royal Marines Commando and British Infantry battalion there were about 90 of these, allowing about 25 per rifle company and the remaining 15 to reconnaissance troops/platoons and other specialists such as snipers.

JU 88 – A German medium bomber that saw service throughout the Second World War. Top speed 292 mph.

LAW – Light Anti-armour Weapon.

LCA – Landing Craft Assault, maximum load an infantry platoon (thirty men). Designed to be carried at a ship's lifeboat davits, and to land infantry in a beach assault. Armoured to give its passengers some protection against small-arms fire and shrapnel, but not air-burst.

LCG – Landing Craft Gun. A number of versions were produced, based on the LCT hull (see below). Their purpose was to provide close support for troops landing on a defended beach. Some had two 4.7in naval guns, and other lighter weapons. Others had two 17-pounder anti-tank guns.

LCI(L) – Landing Craft Infantry (Large), designed as a large raiding craft, of 387 tons for long-range raids, capable of carrying 9 officers and 196 troops. Troops landed down two 36-foot bow gangways.

LCI(S) – Landing Craft Infantry (Small), adapted from coastal forces craft. Landed infantry down gangplanks launched over rollers on the bow. Originally designed for raids, these craft proved too vulnerable for assault against defended beaches. They had unarmoured, high-octane petrol tanks.

LCM – Landing Craft Mechanised, for landing armoured vehicles. There were a number of marks of this craft produced during the Second World War. Superseded by the LCU (see below).

LCP(L) – Fast landing craft (20 knots) of American design and originally bought by the British for Commando raids. They had no ramp, and a spoon bow over which troops landed either by gangplank or jumped straight into the sea, the latter producing a very wet landing. Although some had light armour, they were unsuitable for assaulting a defended beach.

LCP(R) – The same design as LCP(L) but fitted with a bow ramp.

LCT – Landing Craft Tank – a landing craft capable of taking six Churchill or nine Sherman tanks, or a mix of trucks, armoured vehicles, and stores and landing them over a bow ramp on shallow beaches.

LCU – Landing Craft Utility – a landing craft capable of carrying 200 men or 22 tons of stores, or four large trucks. Four LCUs are carried by each of the two British LPDs in their docks.

LCVP – Landing Craft Vehicle and Personnel – the modern version of the LCA, and capable of carrying an infantry platoon (thirty men), or, unlike its Second World War predecessor, a Land Rover and trailer.

LPD – Landing Platform Dock – assault ship. Britain still has two, *Fearless* and *Intrepid*, although the latter has now been so cannibalized for spares that the chance of her being operational again is remote. Two replacements were confirmed in the 1998 Strategic Defence Review, *Albion* and *Bulwark*, due to come into service in 2002 and 2003.

LPH – Landing Platform Helicopter – originally an aircraft carrier converted to carry RM commandos and helicopters to fly them ashore. The US Navy has had purpose-built LPHs for years. The first British purpose-built LPH is HMS *Ocean*.

LSL – Landing Ship Logistic – roll-on, roll-off ships manned by the Royal Fleet Auxiliary.

LST – Landing Ship Tank, for follow-up armour and vehicles. Had a bow door and ramp, the ancestor of modern ro-ro car ferries. Could beach if required. Some carried LCAs at davits.

Lewis gun – First World War vintage, air-cooled light machine-gun, firing .303in ammunition loaded in a circular pan on top of the gun. Superseded by the Bren before the war, but still around in some theatres for the first few years of the Second World War.

LVT – Landing Vehicle Tracked: Buffalo.

LZ – Landing Zone, originally an area chosen for glider landings. (Modern usage is Zone for Helicopter Landings.)

MC – Military Cross. Instituted in 1914, and awarded to Army officers (and Royal Marines when under Army command) of the rank of major and below, and Warrant Officers, for gallantry in action. Now all ranks are eligible.

ME 109 – Messerschmitt 109. The classic German fighter of the Second World War. Several marks. The 1939 model had a top speed of 354 mph, and was armed with two 20mm cannon, and two machine-guns, all forward firing.

Milan – Wire-guided anti-tank missile, also very useful for bunker-busting.

Minenwerfers – A generic name for German mortars of various calibres.

ML – Mountain Leader, an instructor in mountain and arctic warfare (see Cadre).

MLC – Mechanised Landing Craft, for landing armoured vehicles, later changed to Landing Craft Mechanised (see LCM).

MM – Military Medal, instituted in 1916, and awarded to Army NCOs and soldiers (and Royal Marines when under Army command) for gallantry in action. Now discontinued, see MC.

MO – Medical Officer.

MPAJA – Malayan People's Anti-Japanese Army, formed by the Chinese members of the Malayan Communist Party (MCP), the nucleus of which had been trained by SOE in Singapore before the island fell to the Japanese.

MTB – Motor Torpedo Boat, a small, fast vessel mainly armed with torpedoes.

NCO – Non-commissioned officer; from lance-corporal to colour-sergeant.

NGFO – Naval Gunfire Forward Observer – the modern term for the FOB.

OC – Officer Commanding.

'O' group – Short for Orders Group, the group to which orders are given at any level of command from platoon to army group, e.g. at troop/platoon level the platoon commander briefing his section commanders, and at brigade level, the brigade commander briefing his Commando/battalion and supporting arms COs, and other people who need to know the plan.

OP – Observation post.

Pack Howitzer – A small gun which can be taken to pieces, and the parts carried on several mules or horses, or for short distances by people. It can be quickly assembled to bring it into action. A howitzer is a short-barrelled light gun designed to fire at a high angle in order that its shells can more easily hit targets behind cover.

Pangyi – A sharpened stake usually made out of bamboo. Sometimes the point is hardened by scorching in a fire. These are excellent for use in booby traps, or obstacle belts, and can be concealed in pits, covered with twigs and grass or leaves, or planted in undergrowth. Once impaled on a bamboo stake, it is difficult to pull oneself off, because the bamboo fibres act like a barb.

PIAT – Projector Infantry Anti-Tank, the hand-held anti-tank weapon of the British Second World War infantryman from about mid-1942 on. Consisted of a powerful spring, mounted in a tube which threw a hollow-charge projectile. Effective up to 100 yards.

Pom-pom – A 2-pounder quick-firing gun originally of Boer War vintage. Given its name because of the 'pom-pom' sound it made when fired. A multi-barrelled version was fitted in warships for close-in anti-aircraft protection before the Second World War.

PT – Physical Training.

QGM – Queen's Gallantry Medal. Awarded to all ranks for acts of bravery, usually for those which do not qualify for awards such as the Military Cross.

RAMC – Royal Army Medical Corps.

RAP – Regimental Aid Post, the place where the Medical Officer (MO) of a battalion, or equivalent size unit, set up his aid post. Usually the requirement here was to administer 'sophisticated first aid' to stabilize the casualty sufficiently to enable him to survive the next stage of evacuation; in 'conventional' warfare, usually within hours.

RCL – Acronym for recoilless. That is, a weapon that has no recoil because the gases, instead of being contained by a closed breech, are allowed to escape to the rear through a venturi (a cone-shaped orifice), thus dispensing with the need for a buffer system to take up the recoil and thereby saving weight.

Regiment – Originally of horse, dragoons, or foot. Raised by command of King, and later Parliament, and named after its colonel, originally a royal appointee.[1] The regiment has become the basic unit of organization of the British Army for armour, artillery, engineers, signals, Army Air Corps, and logistic units equivalent to battalions of those arms in other armies. In the case of the infantry, the British Army battalion belongs to a regiment, of which there may be one or more battalions.

RFA – Royal Field Artillery. Throughout the First World War, there were three branches of the Royal Artillery: Royal Horse Artillery (RHA), originally formed to accompany cavalry; Royal Field Artillery (RFA), who manned field guns (the majority); and Royal Garrison Artillery (RGA), who manned guns in fortresses, but also the heavy guns in the field.

RV – Rendezvous.

Sangar – A protective wall built of stone, or in the Falklands, peat blocks, constructed in ground too hard to dig, or when trenches are flooded.

Sapper – The equivalent of private in the Royal Engineers, or a name for all engineers.

sausages – The heaviest bomb fired by the largest German mortar in the First World War. It was a most unpleasant weapon, because it contained far more explosive than a heavy shell and could collapse trenches and dugouts, burying the occupants.

SBS – There were two organizations with the acronym SBS in the Second World War. The first one was founded by Lt Courtney of the KRRC when in number 8 Commando in 1940 as a Folbot Section, and it became known as the Special Boat Section. It operated throughout the Second World War as the SBS in the

Middle East, the Mediterranean, North-West Europe, and the Far East. This was entirely separate from the Special Boat Squadron formed by Jellicoe in 1943 as part of, and one of the squadrons of, the SAS (except that by then some SB Section people, left in the Middle East when Courtney went home, had to their chagrin been 'hijacked' by the SAS). Jellicoe's Special Boat Squadron, also known as SBS, changed its name by early 1945 to the Special Boat Service, because by then they were in fact no longer under SAS command, although they continued to wear the SAS sand-coloured beret and winged dagger.

schu-mines – German Second World War wooden anti-personnel mines, difficult to detect because only the detonator was made of metal.

Sea King – A medium-lift helicopter built by Westlands. The Mark IV designed for troop lift can carry about twenty men, depending on the equipment with which they are loaded. The anti-submarine version can carry about ten men.

SEAC – South East Asia Command. The Supreme Allied Commander SEAC, Admiral Mountbatten, was responsible direct to the British Chiefs of Staff in London, and through them to the Combined British and US Chiefs of Staff for all operations by land, sea, and air in Burma, Malaya, and Sumatra, and for clandestine operations in Thailand and French Indo-China.

Schmeisser – German sub-machine-gun, fires a 9mm round.

serials – In the context of a fire support programme (artillery, mortar, or machine-gun), each target is given a serial number, and number of rounds fire for effect. If one has a radio to the supporting guns, to ask for more fire on a target which has not been dealt with to one's satisfaction, it is necessary merely to say something on the lines of, 'Tango 123 repeat.'

SHAR – Sea Harrier.

SLR – Self-Loading Rifle – adapted from the Belgian FN design. The British version did not fire automatic.

Sixty-six – 66 – a shoulder-held light anti-armour weapon (LAW) in a one-use throw-away launcher.

SP – Self-propelled gun, an armoured artillery piece on tracks.

Spandau – Allied name for the German MG34 and MG42 machine-guns.

Start Line – A line in the ground, usually a natural feature (stream, bank, or fence), preferably at ninety degrees to the axis of advance, which marks the start line for the attack and is crossed at H-Hour in attack formation. Can be marked by tape if there is no natural feature which lends itself to being used as a start line. (The American term is Line of Departure (LOD), which has now been copied by the British.)

Sten gun – A cheap, mass-produced sub-machine-gun of British design. It fired 9mm ammunition, and had a 32-round magazine. Ineffective except at close quarters; it was inaccurate and the round had poor penetrating power. Because of its propensity to fire by mistake, it was sometimes more dangerous to its owner and those standing around than to the enemy.

Stick – An aircraft load of parachute troops due to drop on one DZ in one run over it, or the troops travelling in one helicopter, usually destined for one LZ.

Skua – A Fleet Air Arm fighter/dive-bomber, top speed 225 mph.

Tac HQ – Tactical Headquarters, a small group including the CO, or brigade commander forward of the main HQ.

Tellermine – A German mine initiated by a trip wire which jumped into the air before exploding at about knee-level.

Terrapin – Inferior British version of DUKW.

Troop – In a Commando context during the Second World War and until 1961, each Commando had five or six rifle troops, each commanded by a lieutenant or captain; each troop was sixty strong, and divided into either two sections or platoons, each commanded by a lieutenant or second lieutenant. After 1961, Commandos had three rifle companies each, divided into three rifle troops of around thirty men, commanded by lieutenants or second lieutenants. Each troop consisted of a headquarters and three sections each commanded by a corporal. The troop sergeant is the second-in-command.

TSM – Troop Sergeant Major.

USMC – United States Marine Corps.

Verey Pistol – A smooth-bore pistol for firing green, red, or white signal cartridges.

Vickers Medium Machine-gun – First World War vintage belt-fed water-cooled machine-gun, rate of fire 500 rounds per minute. Maximum range with Mark VIIIZ ammunition, 4,500 yards.

VC – Victoria Cross, the highest British award for bravery in the face of the enemy. To date, in the 145 years since its inception by Queen Victoria after the Crimean War of 1854–6 (it was made retrospective, to apply to the war) only 1,354 VCs have been awarded, including three double VCs, and the one presented to the American Unknown Warrior at Arlington National Cemetery. This figure includes the many awarded to Imperial, Commonwealth, and Dominion servicemen.

The statute of the VC allows for the decoration to be awarded by ballot. However, if two are to be awarded in this way, there should be a ballot of the officers and a separate one of the NCOs and privates (or their equivalent).

VHF – Very High Frequency radio.

Whizz-bangs – The German 77mm field gun of the First World War, named from the sound it made: a whizz followed by a bang.

Bibliography

Many books in addition to those listed below were consulted; however, the following were especially valuable.

Charles **Allen**, *The Savage Wars of Peace: Soldiers' Voices 1945–1989* (Futura, 1991).

Nick **Barker**, *Beyond Endurance, An Epic of Whitehall and the South Atlantic Conflict* (Leo Cooper, 1997).

Correlli **Barnett**, *Engage the Enemy More Closely, The Royal Navy in the Second World War* (Hodder & Stoughton, 1991).

J. C. **Beadle**, *The Light Blue Lanyard: 50 Years With 40 Commando Royal Marines* (Square One Publications, 1992).

Antony **Beevor**, *Crete the Battle and the Resistance* (John Murray, 1991).

Eversley **Belfield** and Hubert **Essame**, *The Battle for Normandy* (Severn House, 1975).

Patrick **Bishop** and Eamonn **Mallie**, *The Provisional IRA* (Heinemann, 1987).

Donald F. **Bittner**, *Royal Marines spies of World War One era*, Part One: *Royal Marine Spy 1910–1913, Captain Bernard Frederick Trench RMLI* (Royal Marines Historical Society, 1993).

H. E. **Blumberg**, *Britain's Sea Soldiers*, Vol III (Swiss & Co., 1927).

British Official Histories, all published by Her Majesty's Stationery Office:

— L. F. **Ellis**, *Victory in the West: The Defeat of Germany*, Vol. I, 1962; Vol. II, 1968.

— I. S. O. **Playfair**, *The Mediterranean and the Middle East*, Vol. I, 1954; Vol. II, 1956; Vol. III, 1960; I. S. O. **Playfair** and C. J. C. **Molony**, Vol. IV, 1966; C. J. C. **Molony**, Vol. V, 1973; Vol. VI part I, 1984; W. J. **Jackson**, Vol. VI part II, 1987; Vol. VI part III, 1988.

— S. Woodburn **Kirby**, *The War Against Japan*, Vol. II, 1958; Vol. III, 1961; Vol. V, 1969.

— Anthony **Farrar-Hockley**, *The British Part in the Korean War, Vol I: A Distant Obligation*, 1990; *Vol II, An Honourable Discharge*, 1995

Robert Bruce **Lockhart**, *The Marines Were There: The Story of the Royal Marines in the Second World War* (Putnam, 1950)

Field Marshal Lord **Carver**, *Britain's Army in the Twentieth Century* (Macmillan, 1998)

Winston S. **Churchill**, *The World Crisis*, Vols 1–4 (Odhams Press, 1938)

— *The Second World War*, Vols I–VI (Cassell & Co., 1948–54)

Kenneth J. **Clifford**, *Amphibious Warfare Development in Britain and America from 1920–1940* (Edgewood Inc.: New York, 1983)

Anthony **Crockett**, *Green Beret, Red Star* (Eyre & Spottiswoode, 1954)

John **Day**, *A Plain Russet-Coated Captain* (Day, 1993)

Michael **Dewar**, *Brush Fire Wars: Campaigns of the British Army since 1945* (Robert Hale, 1984)

Peter **Elphick**, *Singapore, The Pregnable Fortress* (Hodder & Stoughton, 1995)

C. **Field**, *Britain's Sea Soldiers*, Vols I and II (Lyceum Press, 1924)

Orlando **Figes**, *A People's Tragedy: The Russian Revolution 1891–1924* (Pimlico, 1996)

Tony **Geraghty**, *The Irish War: The Military History of a Domestic Conflict* (Harper Collins, 1998)

Andrew **Gordon**, *The Rules of the Game: Jutland and British Naval Command* (John Murray, 1996)

Max **Hastings**, *The Korean War* (Michael Joseph, 1987)

Christopher **Hibbert**, *Redcoats and Rebels: The War for America 1770–1781* (Grafton, 1990)

Michael **Hickey**, *Gallipoli* (John Murray, 1995)

L. **Hollis**, *One Marine's Tale* (André Deutsch, 1956)

Robin **Hunter**, *True Stories of the SBS* (Virgin, 1998)

W. G. **Jenkins**, *Commando Subaltern at War: Royal Marine Operations in Yugoslavia and Italy, 1944–1945* (Greenhill Books, 1996)

D. **Jerrold**, *Royal Naval Division* (Hutchinson, 1923)

P. K. W. **Johnson**, *The Story of 46 Commando Royal Marines* (Gale & Polden, 1946)

Robert **Kershaw**, *D-Day: Piercing the Atlantic Wall* (Ian Allan, 1983)

Frank **Kitson**, *Low Intensity Operations, Subversion, Insurgency & Peacekeeping* (Faber & Faber, 1971)

James **Ladd**, *Commandos and Rangers of World War II* (Macdonald, 1978)

— *SBS: The Invisible Raiders* (Fontana, 1984)

— *The Royal Marines, 1919–1980* (Jane's, 1980)

Brian **Lavery** (ed.), *Shipboard Life and Organisation, 1731–1815* (Navy Records Society, 1998)

Charles **Messenger**, *The Commandos: 1940–1946* (William Kimber, 1985)

Ministry of Information, *Combined Operations, 1940–1942* (HMSO, 1943)

Raymond **Mitchell**, *They Did What Was Asked of Them, 41 (Royal Marines) Commando, 1942–1946* (Firebird Books, 1996)

Thomas R. **Mockaitis**, *British counterinsurgency in the post-imperial era* (Manchester University Press, 1995)

John **Moffatt**, *The Plymouth Argylls*, Royal Marines Historical Society publication, Sheet Anchor, Vol. XXI, No. 2

J. L. **Moulton**, *Haste to the Battle, A Royal Marine Commando at War* (Cassell, 1963)

—*Battle for Antwerp: The Liberation of the City and the Opening of the Scheldt, 1944* (Ian Allan, 1978)

—*Defence in a Changing World* (Eyre & Spottiswoode, 1964)

Robin **Neillands**, *By Sea and Land: The Royal Marine Commandos, A History 1942–1982* (Weidenfeld & Nicolson, 1987)

—*A Fighting Retreat: The British Empire 1947–97* (Hodder & Stoughton, 1996)

Derek **Oakley**, *Behind Japanese Lines*, Royal Marines Historical Society Special Publication Number 18

Tom **Pocock**, *East and West of Suez: The Retreat from Empire* (The Bodley Head, 1986)

—*A Thirst for Glory: The Life of Admiral Sir Sydney Smith* (Aurum Press, 1996)

Michael **Reynolds**, *Steel Inferno, 1st SS Panzer Corps in Normandy: the story of the 1st and 12th SS Panzer Divisions in the 1944 Normandy campaign* (Spellmount, 1997)

Robert **Rhodes-James**, *Gallipoli* (Batsford, 1965)

Nicholas **Rodger**, *The Wooden World: An Anatomy of the Georgian Navy* (Fontana, 1988)

Hilary St George **Saunders**, *The Green Beret, The Story of the Commandos: 1940–1945* (Michael Joseph, 1952)

Field Marshal The Viscount **Slim**, *Defeat Into Victory* (Corgi 1971)

G. **Sparrow** and J. MacBean **Ross**, *On Four Fronts with the Royal Naval Division* (Hodder & Stoughton, 1918)

Ewen **Southby-Tailyour**, *Reasons in Writing, A Commando's View of the Falklands War* (Leo Cooper, 1993)

Ewen **Southby-Tailyour** and Michael **Clapp**, *Amphibious Assault Falklands: The Battle of San Carlos Water* (Leo Cooper, 1996)

Nigel **Steel** and Peter **Hart**, *Defeat at Gallipoli* (Macmillan, 1994)

John **Terraine**, *To Win a War: 1918 The Year of Victory* (Sidgwick & Jackson, 1978)

Peter **Thomas**, *41 Independent Commando Royal Marines Korea 1950–1952* (Royal Marines Historical Society, 1990)

Sir Robert **Thompson**, *Defeating Communist Insurgency, Experiences from Malaya and Vietnam* (Chatto & Windus, 1974)

David **Young**, *Four Five: the Story of 45 Commando Royal Marines 1943–1971* (Leo Cooper, 1972)

40 Commando RM in Haifa, January to June, 1948, compiled by the Intelligence Section, 40 Commando RM, Giovanni Muscat (Malta, 1948)

Notes

For sources of quotations from the Department of Documents or Sound Archives in the Imperial War Museum, and documents in the Royal Marines Mueseum Archives, see Index of Contributors. Where there are no notes in the text, the chapter is omitted below.

1. Sea Soldiers

1. Winston Churchill, *History of the English Speaking Peoples*, Purnell, Vol. 5, Chapter II, p. 2104.
2. Despite the imposition of a tariff on the price of commissions imposed by George I, who disapproved of purchase, there was a wide variation in the price of commissions. See Alan J. Guy, *Colonel Samuel Bagshawe and the Army of George II* (Army Records Society, 1990), pp. 13–14 and 38 for an excellent resumé of the system.
3. Guy, p. 2.
4. N. A. M. Rodger, *The Wooden World: An Anatomy of the Georgian Navy* (Fontana, 1988), p. 28.
5. Rodger, p. 28.
6. Rodger, p. 67.
7. Rodger, p. 257.
8. Lawrence James, *Raj: The Making and Unmaking of British India* (Little, Brown and Company, 1987), p. 130.
9. See Orders for the Officers of Marines on Board HMS *Mars*, 31 May 1799, in Brian Lavery (ed.), *Shipboard Life and Organisation, 1731–1815* (Navy Records Society), pp. 227–223.
10. The official figures are the figures that Parliament voted for each year. They are larger than the number actually borne – in 1765, for example, this was 15,863 – but these figures are not always known accurately, and the official figures were used in planning and in histories.
11. 4th Regiment of Foot, now part of The King's Own Royal Border Regiment;

23rd Regiment of Foot, now The Royal Welch Fusiliers; 47th Regiment of Foot, now part of The Queen's Lancashire Regiment.

12. Christopher Hibbert, *Redcoats and Rebels: The War for America 1770–1781* (Grafton, 1990), p. 35.

13. See Appendix 2, page 596.

14. J. L. Moulton, *The Royal Marines* (Leo Cooper, 1972), pp. 18–19.

15. Lavery, p. 219.

16. The Hon. E. C. G. Howard, *The Memoirs of Sir Sydney Smith* (London, 1839), vol. I, p. 157. Quoted in Tom Pocock, *Thirst For Glory, the Life of Admiral Sir Sydney Smith* (Aurum Press, 1996), pp. 98–9.

17. Now part of The Royal Gloucestershire, Berkshire and Wiltshire Regiment. The companies of the 49th Foot and the Riflemen were not a ship's detachment in the true meaning of the word, but were in modern terminology the Landing Force, i.e. embarked specifically for landing at Copenhagen, and not, as Marine detachments were, carried at that time for duties on board ships with landing as a secondary duty on an ad hoc basis. Although they were not landed, some officers served with the guns of the fleet.

18. Later the 95th or Rifle Regiment, the Rifle Brigade, and now part of The Royal Green Jackets.

19. Later 2nd Battalion King's Shropshire Light Infantry, and now part of The Light Infantry.

2. Victoria's Jollies

1. Nicholas Rodger in correspondence with the author.

2. Albeit they were at a disadvantage because Marine commissions were less valuable in financial terms – see Chapter 1.

3. C. Field, *Britain's Sea Soldiers* (Lyceum Press, 1924), Vol. 2, p. 132.

4. Field, vol. 2, pp. 132–3.

5. C. S. Forester, *Captain Hornblower* (Michael Joseph, 1942), p. 632.

6. Later the Seaforth Highlanders, subsequently the Queen's Own Highlanders, and now The Highlanders.

7. Andrew Gordon, *The Rules of the Game: Jutland and British Naval Command* (John Murray, 1996).

8. Gordon, p. 168. The Admiralty paid for three coats of paint a year, but a ship might need as many as eight, and the other five were paid for out of

her officers' pockets. Admiral Sir Percy Scott, a gunnery enthusiast, tells of one case when gunpowder was sold and paint bought with the proceeds.

9. Maurice Hankey, *Supreme Command* (Allen & Unwin, 1961), Vol. 1, pp. 79–80.

10. W. G. F. Jackson and Lord Bramall, *The Chiefs : The Story of the United Kingdom Chiefs of Staff* (Brassey's, 1992), p. 46.

11. A. J. Marder, *Fear God and Dread Nought; The Correspondence of Admiral of the Fleet Lord Fisher of Kilverstone* (Jonathan Cape, 1952–59), Vol. 1, *The Making of an Admiral*, p. 241.

12. Fisher Papers 1, Navy Records Society, Vol. 1, pp. 405–6.

13. J. L. Moulton, *Defence in a Changing World* (Eyre & Spottiswoode, 1964), pp. 113–14.

14. General Sir Leslie Hollis, *One Marine's Tale* (Andre Deutsch, 1956), p. 23.

15. To this day Marines refer to 'going ashore' when proceeding on leave, short or long, whether from a ship, barracks, camp, or bivouac site.

3. The Outbreak of the First World War – The First Months

1. Martin Gilbert, *Churchill: A Life* (William Heinemann, 1992), p. 267.

2. Winston S. Churchill, *The World Crisis* (Odhams, 1938 edition), pp. 171–2.

3. Now called the Commandant General Royal Marines, the professional head of the Corps.

4. The whole ship's company of every warship, including all officers other than the captain, always took part in coaling ship. Coal dust coated everybody from head to foot, and permeated everywhere.

5. Martin Gilbert, *Winston S. Churchill*, vol. III, *1914–1916* (Heinemann, 1971), p. 104.

6. In the Royal Marines until the early 1970s, when the rank of Warrant Officer Class One and Two was introduced into the Corps, the Company Sergeant Major was always a Quartermaster Sergeant Instructor, QMSI, or QMS for short, which is why Baker refers to this character who was ripping off the recruits as the Quartermaster Sergeant. He was not the Company Quartermaster Sergeant in charge of stores.

7. H. E. Blumberg, *Britain's Sea Soldiers: A Record of the Royal Marines During the War 1914–1919* (Swiss & Co., 1927), p. 134.

4. The Dardanelles – The Naval Assault

1. Lord Hankey, *The Supreme Command* (Allen & Unwin, 1961), Vol. I, pp. 265–6.
2. J. L. Moulton, *Haste to the Battle* (Cassell, 1963), p. 194. This attitude persisted until after the Second World War.

5. The Dardanelles – The Landings, 25 April 1915

1. H. E. Blumberg, *Britain's Sea Soldiers: A Record of the Royal Marines During the War 1914–1919* (Swiss & Co., 1927), p. 127.

6. The Dardanelles: The Royal Marines at Anzac and Cape Helles

1. Douglas Jerrold, *The Royal Naval Division* (Hutchinson & Co., 1923), pp. 116–17.
2. H. E. Blumberg, *Britain's Sea Soldiers: A Record of the Royal Marines During the War 1914–1919* (Swiss & Co., 1927), p. 136.
3. Blumberg, p. 139.
4. Jerrold, p. 116.
5. Blumberg, p. 141.
6. Blumberg, p. 141 .
7. Michael Hickey, *Gallipoli* (John Murray, 1995), p. 168.
8. Blumberg, p. 163.

7. The Battle of Jutland

1. L. Hollis, *One Marine's Tale* (André Deutsch, 1956), p. 24.
2. Hollis, pp. 21–2.
3. Hollis, p. 22.

8. The Royal Marines on the Western Front, 1915–1917

1. Now part of The Royal Anglian Regiment.
2. The HAC formed two infantry battalions for the First World War, and likewise in the Second.
3. Known as bubbly in the Navy because when water is added to rum the

froth bubbles. In this case it was being poured neat into the cocoa, Army fashion.

4. Douglas Jerrold, *The Royal Naval Division* (Hutchinson & Co., 1923), p. 241.

5. It could be argued that out of a total strength of around 55,000 in 1917/ 1918, the Corps could have found sufficient men to man the units doing most of the fighting. However, as part of the Naval Service, the Royal Marines had commitments imposed on them which were considered more important. With the introduction of conscription, the Corps continued to enlist for long and short service, for which the Navy had priority, so a proportion of recruits for the RMLI battalions in France were obtained from the Army pool at Reading. They were given six weeks' training at Deal, followed by another six weeks at the RND training establishment at Blandford before being drafted to France.

6. Jerrold, pp. 250–51.

7. H. E. Blumberg, *Britain's Sea Soldiers: A Record of the Royal Marines During the War 1914–1919* (Swiss & Co., 1927), p. 336.

9. Zeebrugge, 23 April 1918 (St George's Day)

1. This remark by Chater reveals the relationship between the Navy and Royal Marines at the time. Now no captain of an amphibious ship would dream of issuing an order which affected matters entirely within the business of the CO of the landing force without consulting him. If he did, he would quickly have the error of his ways pointed out to him.

2. See Glossary for VC balloting procedure.

10. The Western Front, 1918

1. Later the Royal Northumberland Fusiliers, now part of The Royal Regiment of Fusiliers.

2. In early 1918 every division was given a fourth Machine Gun (MG) Company, and all MG companies in each division were grouped into an MG battalion. An MG battalion had sixty-four Vickers machine-guns. Each gun was crewed by six men. Two such gun detachments formed a sub-section under a sergeant and a corporal, two sub-sections a section, and four sections a company. An MG battalion required thirty-two four-horse limbers to haul its sixty-four guns and equipment, which included pack

saddlery so that the guns could be 'packed' (on the horses' backs) over terrain impassable to the wheeled limbers.

3. Disbanded in 1922.

4. A favourite Army betting game, officially illegal.

5. Later part of The Queen's Royal Surrey Regiment, then The Queen's Regiment, now part of The Princess of Wales's Royal Regiment (Queen's and Royal Hampshires).

6. J. L. Moulton, *The Royal Marines* (Leo Cooper, 1972), p. 60.

7. John Terraine, *To Win a War: 1918 The Year of Victory* (Sidgwick & Jackson, 1978), p. 231, n. 26.

11. Russia, 1918–1919

1. Orlando Figes, *A People's Tragedy: The Russian Revolution 1891–1924* (Pimlico 1996), p. 574.

2. Figes, p. 560.

3. Now part of The Royal Green Jackets.

4. Cmd 818, HMSO 1920, p. 11.

5. Shore leave refers to any kind of leave in the Royal Marines. This battalion was not in a ship at this time. (See Chapter 2.)

6. From an account written by Captain Jameson and made available to the author by his grandson Alastair Grant.

7. Not to be confused with present day Warrant Officer. The WO in the RN at the time was senior in status to the WO of today.

12. The Twenty-Year Truce

1. Originally formed as a sub-committee of the CID in 1922, and on the demise of the CID on the outbreak of War in 1939, became a committee in its own right, but reporting to the War Cabinet.

2. A hangover from the days when Egypt was part of the Ottoman Empire, before being 'annexed' by Britain. The ranks in the Egyptian Army were Turkish. Chater at this time was a Bimbashi. Anglo-Egyptian Sudan was benevolently administered by the British, and consequently the inhabitants, Arab and Black Sudanese, were rather better off then than they are at the time this is being written – however politically incorrect it may be to say so.

3. The cynical version, favoured by junior officers, was 'time spent in

reconnaissance is *always* wasted', the implication being that the officer carrying out the reconnaissance in question was useless.

4. The Army and RAF were much less seriously affected by the pay cuts than the Navy. Whereas 72.1 per cent of its Chief and Petty Officers (and Royal Marines SNCOs) were on the 1919 rates, only 31 per cent of the Army and 40 per cent of the RAF were similarly affected.

5. The Admiralty paid a marriage allowance direct to wives. Most men allotted an additional allowance to their wives, which was also paid direct. This practice continued long after the Second World War; it was better for the wives because in the days before telebanking, if their husbands were away, it was difficult to send money from say Rosyth to Plymouth, let alone from China.

13. 1939–1940

1. Julian Thompson, *The Imperial War Museum Book of The War at Sea: The Royal Navy in the Second World War* (Sidgwick & Jackson, 1996), pp. 3–4.
2. See Glossary, page 00.
3. James Ladd, *The Royal Marines 1919–1980* (Jane's, 1980), p. 81.

14. The Mediterranean and Atlantic, 1941–1942

1. Forester, *The Ship* (Penguin Books, 1949), pp. 123–4.
2. W. S. Churchill, *The Second World War*, Vol. III (Cassell & Co., 1950), p. 239.
3. Julian Thompson, *The Imperial War Museum Book of War Behind Enemy Lines* (Sidgwick & Jackson, 1998), pp. 45, 48, and 49.
4. Antony Beevor, *Crete the Battle and the Resistance* (John Murray, 1991), p. 219.
5. Julian Thompson, *Ready for Anything, The Parachute Regiment at War 1940–1982* (Fontana, p. 51).
6. J. C. Beadle, *The Light Blue Lanyard: 50 Years with 40 Commando Royal Marines* (Square One Publications, 1992), p. 29.
7. See Thompson, *The Imperial War Museum Book of War Behind Enemy Lines*, for details of the raising of the SBS by Army Commandos.

15. The Far East, Burma, and the Indian Ocean, 1941–1942

1. John Moffatt, The Plymouth Argylls, Royal Marines Historical Society publication, Sheet Anchor, Vol. XXI, No 2, p. 23.
2. See Peter Elphick, Singapore, The Pregnable Fortress (Hodder & Stoughton, 1995), p. 283.
3. Elphick, p. 338.
4. Moffat, p. 28.
5. Moffat, p. 30.
6. Readers might be tempted to compare this with the 1982 operation to regain the Falklands, in which the distance was 8,000 miles from Britain, and the time between the decision to sail a task force and the first landings about the same. However, for Madagascar, the British had the use of the well-equipped Simonstown base at the Cape about 2,000 miles from Diégo-Suarez, and from Durban considerably less, whereas the only staging post available to the British for the Falklands War was Ascension Island, 4,000 miles from the Falklands, with an airfield, but no port.
7. W. S. Churchill, The Second World War, Vol. IV (Cassell & Co., 1954), p. 212.

16. The Great Reorganization and Marines in the Mediterranean – Sicily to Anzio

1. W. S. Churchill, The Second World War, vol. IV (Cassell & Co., 1951), pp. 776–7.
2. J. L. Moulton, The Royal Marines (Leo Cooper, 1972), p. 77.
3. Later to command 1st Airborne Division at Arnhem.
4. Later The Royal Hampshires, now part of The Princess of Wales's Royal Regiment (Queen's and Royal Hampshires).
5. Later 4th Battalion The Royal Regiment of Fusiliers, disbanded 1969.
6. Later part of 2nd Battalion The Queen's Regiment, now part of The Princess of Wales's Royal Regiment (Queen's and Royal Hampshires).
7. Later part of 1st Battalion The Queen's Regiment, now part of The Princess of Wales's Royal Regiment (Queen's and Royal Hampshires).

17. North-West Europe, 1944–1945

1. Winston Churchill, *The Second World War*, Vol. VI (Cassell & Co., 1954), p. 177.
2. J. L. Moulton, *The Royal Marines* (Leo Cooper, 1962), p. 79.
3. 'Eddy' (*nom de plume* for John Day), '45 RM Cdo at Merville-Franceville Plage', *Globe & Laurel*, Sep/Oct 1997, pp. 314–15.
4. Ibid.
5. 'Eddy', 'Baptism of Fire', *Globe & Laurel*, Nov/Dec 1997, pp. 378–380.
6. Ibid.
7. Ibid.
8. Ibid.
9. Ibid.
10. Ibid.
11. Ibid.
12. Ibid.
13. Later the Royal Lincolnshire Regiment, now part of 2nd Battalion The Royal Anglian Regiment.
14. Robert Kershaw, *D-Day: Piercing the Atlantic Wall* (Ian Allan, 1983), pp. 171–2 and 185.
15. P. K. W. Johnson, *The Story of 46 Commando Royal Marines* (Gale & Polden, 1946), p. 5.
16. Michael Reynolds, *Steel Inferno, 1st SS Panzer Corps in Normandy* (Spellmount, 1997), pp. 87–8.
17. Johnson, p. 51.
18. Hilary St George Saunders, *The Green Beret: The Story of the Commandos 1940–1945* (Michael Joseph, 1952), p. 280.
19. Johnson, p. 11.
20. Johnson, p. 14.
21. Moulton, *Haste to The Battle* (Cassell, 1963), p. 116.
22. Moulton, *Haste to The Battle*, p. 117.
23. Moulton, *Haste to the Battle*, p. 147.
24. Number 10 InterAllied Commando (10 IA Commando) was formed from troops of various Allied nationalities whose countries were under German occupation, French, Dutch, Norwegian, Czechs, Poles etc., including some German Jews. The Commando never operated as a unit, instead troops and individuals were attached to other Commandos for specific operations.
25. Moulton, *Haste to The Battle*, p. 153.

26. Moulton, *Haste to The Battle*, p. 155.

27. Moulton, *Battle for Antwerp: The Liberation of the City and the Opening of the Scheldt, 1944* (Ian Allan, 1978), p. 168.

28. Moulton, *Haste to the Battle*, p. 160.

29. Moulton, *Battle for Antwerp*, p. 177.

30. 'Eddy', '45 RM Commando's Action at the Montfortebeek Dyke', *Globe & Laurel*, Jan/Feb 1995, pp. 32–3.

31. *Hansard*, Vol. 409, p. 195.

32. John Day, *A Plain Russet-Coated Captain*, privately printed, p. 70.

33. Day, p. 79.

34. Day, pp. 85–6.

35. Day, p. 86.

36. Johnson, p. 31.

37. Johnson, p. 34.

38. Day, p. 93.

39. The Seabees were units formed by the US Navy in 1941 for naval base construction and repair. The name was derived from the acronym CB (Construction Battalions).

40. See Appendix 3 for breakdown of RM deployment in late 1944.

18. The Aegean, Adriatic, and Italy, mid-1944 to May 1945

1. J. C. Beadle, *The Light Blue Lanyard: 50 Years with 40 Commando Royal Marines* (Square One Publications, 1992), p. 108.

2. Quoted in Charles Messenger's *The Commandos* (William Kimber, 1985), p. 347.

3. Beadle, p. 115.

4. Later part of The Queen's Royal Irish Hussars, now part of The Queen's Royal Hussars (The Queen's Own and Royal Irish).

5. Beadle, p. 144.

19. South-East Asia and the Pacific

1. Julian Thompson, *The Imperial War Museum Book of War Behind Enemy Lines* (Sidgwick & Jackson, 1998), p. 168.

2. Correlli Barnett, *Engage the Enemy More Closely, The Royal Navy in the Second World War* (Hodder & Stoughton, 1991), p. 885.

3. Extra pay for 'hard lying' conditions, paid to submariners and coastal forces.

4. Derek Oakley, *Behind Japanese Lines*, Royal Marines Historical Society Special Publication Number 18, p. 45.

5. Thompson, pp. 391–402.

6. Oakley, p. 80.

7. Maj Gen J. I. H. Owen, 'Burma and the Battle of Kangaw', *Globe & Laurel*, Jan/Feb 1995, pp. 34–7.

8. Letter to author.

9. 19th King George's Own Lancers.

10. Owen.

11. Owen.

12. Owen.

13. Letter to author.

14. Owen.

15. Letter to author.

16. Letter to author.

17. Letter to author.

18. Owen.

19. Ibid.

20. Letter to author.

21. J. L. Moulton, *The Royal Marines* (Leo Cooper, 1962), p. 83.

Introduction to Part Five

1. Robin Hunter, *True Stories of the SBS* (Virgin, 1998), p. 222.

20. Counter-Insurgency before 1960

1. Royal Marines Historical Society Publication, *Sheet Anchor*, Vol XXIII, No 1, p. 5. See also *40 Commando RM in Haifa, January to June, 1948*, compiled by the Intelligence Section, 40 Commando RM, Giovanni Muscat (Malta, 1948), pp. 7 and 8.

2. *40 Commando RM in Haifa*, p. 19, and *Sheet Anchor*, p. 6.

3. *Sheet Anchor*, p. 8.

4. Ibid., pp. 7–8.

5. Lieutenant Colonel Thomas in letter to author.

6. *Sheet Anchor*, p. 8.

7. *40 Commando RM in Haifa*, p. 37.

8. Letter to author.

9. The 1st and 2nd SAS Regiments were disbanded at the end of the Second World War, and only the TA Regiments, 21 and 23 SAS, survived. Michael Calvert, ex-Chindit and last commander of the SAS Brigade in the Second World War, raised the Malayan Scouts, which became the present-day 22nd SAS.

10. Robin Neillands, *A Fighting Retreat: The British Empire 1947–97* (Hodder & Stoughton, 1997), p. 239.

11. Now part of The Royal Anglian Regiment.

21. Korea

1. Later part of The Queen's Regiment, now part of The Princess of Wales's Royal Regiment (Queen's and Royal Hampshires).

2. Now part of The Royal Anglian Regiment.

3. Thompson, *Lifeblood of War: Logistics in Armed Conflict* (Brassey's, 1991), p. 108, quoting Victory, *The Commonwealth Artillery in the Korean War 1950–53* (Tactical Doctrine Retrieval Cell No. 8137), p. 1.

4. Lieutenant Colonel P. R. Thomas RM, *41 Independent Commando RM, Korea 1950–1952* (Royal Marines Historical Society, 1990), p. 11.

5. Letter to author.

6. Anthony Farrar-Hockley, *The British Part in the Korean War*, Vol. I, *A Distant Obligation* (HMSO, 1990), p. 328.

7. Thomas, p. 14.

8. Thomas, p. 16.

9. Thomas, p. 16.

10. Max Hastings, *The Korean War* (Michael Joseph, 1987), p. 186.

11. To this day, the USMC jealously guards its air wings from misappropriation, or misemployment, by the Air Force. Marines have too many memories of battle when only the intervention of Marines flying in support of Marines have saved the day. Their attitude can be summed up by a remark made by a US Marine in the presence of the author, at a NATO conference when the RAF and USAF were trying to prise USMC aircraft away from them, 'we regard airplanes as just Goddam rifles with wings'.

12. Thomas, p. 21.

13. Thomas, p. 17.

14. Thomas, p. 21.

15. Thomas, p. 22.
16. Farrar-Hockley, p. 341.
17. Farrar-Hockley, p. 22.
18. Farrar-Hockley, p. 28.
19. Farrar-Hockley, *The British Part in the Korean War*, Vol. II, *An Honourable Discharge* (HMSO, 1995), p. 310.
20. Lieutenant Colonel Thomas in letter to author.
21. See Julian Thompson, *The Imperial War Museum Book of War Behind Enemy Lines*.
22. Farrar-Hockley, Vol. II, p. 310.
23. Ibid., p. 302.
24. Ibid., p. 266.
25. Ibid., p. 266.
26. Ibid., p. 277.
27. Ibid, p. 411.

22. Suez, 1956

1. Royal Marines Historical Society publication, *Sheet Anchor*, Vol. XXI, No. 2, p. 6. The FN rifle, which was just coming in to service as the SLR, was withdrawn because it was feared that it would jam in sandy conditions, having failed its desert conditions test.
2. Ibid., p. 4–5.
3. Ibid., pp. 6–7.
4. Ibid., p. 12.
5. Ibid., p. 7.
6. Later part of The Duke of Edinburgh's Royal Regiment (Berkshire and Wiltshire), now part of The Royal Gloucestershire, Berkshire and Wiltshire Regiment.
7. *Sheet Anchor*, p. 8.
8. Ibid., pp. 13–14.
9. Ibid., pp. 17–18.
10. Ibid., p. 5.
11. Ibid., p. 8.
12. Ibid., p. 9.

23. Somewhere East of Suez, 1960–1968

1. Poett had commanded the 5th Parachute Brigade in the 6th Airborne Division in Normandy, the Rhine Crossing, and advance to the Baltic.
2. And continued to do so until the end of the Cold War in 1989.
3. Letter to author.
4. Letter to author.
5. Letter to author.
6. Letter to author.
7. Among the honourable exceptions were seasoned war reporters such as Tom Pocock of the *Daily Express*.
8. Now part of The Highlanders (Seaforth, Gordons and Camerons).
9. Not Royal until January 1966.
10. Letter to author.
11. Letter to author.
12. Robin Neillands, *Fighting Retreat: The British Empire 1947–1997* (Hodder & Stoughton, 1996), p. 385.
13. Letter to author.
14. Neillands, p. 387.
15. Letter to author.
16. Night sights were not issued until several years later.
17. Leading scouts were the best shots, the best soldiers and the most observant men in the troop, and were usually sent on a tracking course at the Jungle Warfare School.
18. Letter to author.
19. Letter to author.
20. Raffi Gregorian, *The Black Cat Strikes Back: Claret Operations during Confrontation 1964–1966*, Department of War Studies, King's College London, Extended Essay 1989.
21. Michael Dewar, *Brush Fire Wars: Campaigns of the British Army since 1945* (Robert Hale, 1984), p. 112.
22. The Northern Frontier Regiment, the Desert Regiment, the Muscat Regiment, and the Gendarmerie.

24. Mostly West of Suez, 1967–1999

From this point in the narrative forward metric units are used; the Royal Marines adopted metric in conformity with NATO practice.

1. J. C. Beadle, *The Light Blue Lanyard: 50 Years with 40 Commando Royal Marines* (Square One Publications, 1992), p. 289.

25. The Falklands, 1982

1. The conflicting information included the joint views of his Army and Air Force colleagues that nothing could or should be done.
2. See Ewen Southby-Tailyour, *Reasons in Writing* (Leo Cooper, 1993), for the only authoritative published discussion of this unhappy saga.
3. Nick Barker, *Beyond Endurance: An Epic of Whitehall and the South Atlantic Conflict* (Leo Cooper, 1997), p. 183.
4. Barker, pp. 184–5.
5. Nick Vaux, *March to the South Atlantic* (Buchan & Enright, 1986), p. 113.
6. The only full and accurate accounts are in two books: Ewen Southby-Tailyour, *Reasons in Writing*, Chapter XVIII, and Michael Clapp and Ewen Southby-Tailyour, *Amphibious Assault Falklands: The Battle of San Carlos Water* (Leo Cooper, 1996), Chapter 8.
7. Extract for an interview for a training film.

26. Towards 2000 and Beyond

1. Victor H. Krulak, *First to Fight: an Inside View of the US Marine Corps* (United States Naval Institute, Annapolis, Maryland USA, 1984), p. 15.
2. General Sir Peter de la Billière, *Storm Command: A Personal Account of the Gulf War* (HarperCollins, 1992), p. 191.
3. Julian Thompson, *The Imperial War Museum Book of War Behind Enemy Lines* (Sidgwick & Jackson, 1998), p. 55.
4. De la Billière, pp. 222–223.
5. De la Billière, p. 223.
6. *Globe & Laurel*, Mar/Apr 1991, p. 89.
7. *RUSI Journal*, December 1998, p. 20.
8. Ibid., p. 21.
9. Ibid., p. 21.

Appendix 1

1. The order of precedence of the Line is determined by the seniority of the regiment, based on the date of its forming.

Appendix 3

1. Including 4,023 in Allied Naval Command Expeditionary Force in NW Europe.
2. Including 13,875 in minor landing craft and support craft, and 1,896 in 27 and 28 Battalions RM.
3. Including 1,058 in the RM School of Signals alone! [Exclamation mark inserted by Phillips.]

Appendix 4

1. Provides Observer Parties to control Naval Gun Fire Support and liaison teams aboard firing ships.
2. Rapier Battery.
3. M Company in South Georgia force, and J Company formed from NP 8901 and Headquarters Company.
4. As Brigade Reconnaissance Troop.
5. To control air strikes.

Glossary

1. See Field Marshal Lord Carver, *The Seven Ages of the British Army* (Weidenfeld and Nicolson, 1984), pp. 60–61.

Index of Contributors

IMPERIAL WAR MUSEUM

This index from collections of papers and recorded interviews serves two purposes: it lists those whose writings or recordings are here quoted and gives due acknowledgement to the copyright holders who have kindly allowed the publication of material held in the Imperial War Museum's collections. If the copyright owner is not the contributor, their name appears in round brackets after the contributor with whom they are associated. Where the papers quoted are not contained in a collection under the contributor's name, but form part of another collection, this is indicated in round brackets. Every effort has been made to trace copyright owners; the Imperial War Museum would be grateful for any information which might help trace those whose identities or addresses are not known. The number in square brackets is the accession number in the collection.

Ranks are as they were at the time of the experiences described; if subsequently promoted, that rank is not given unless the person concerned is mentioned in the text in that rank. Decorations are not shown. The page numbers on which the quotation appears are shown after the accession details.

Department of Documents

Private T. H. **Baker** RMLI [84/52/1] (Mr Alan F S Baker): 124–125.

Lieutenant C. N. C. **Carryer** RM [66/202/1]: 413.

Second Lieutenant (later Captain) A. R. **Chater**, RMLI [74/101/1]: 51–52, 59, 66, 68, 69–70, 72, 109, 113, 114, 115, 116, 119, 120, 120–121, 122, 123, 168–169, 170, 171, 173, 174, 175, 177, 177–178, 230.

First Lord of the Admiralty, Winston S. **Churchill** [special misc. N6]: 67.

Major Paddy **Donnell** RM [94/34/1] (Mrs Donnell): 333, 334.

A. C. **Hampshire** collection, including Force Viper Reports [83/34/5]: 284, 285, 286, 287, 288, 290, 291, 293.

Sound Archive

ROYAL MARINES MUSEUM

The following index lists pages on which quotations appear taken from papers in the Royal Marines Museum, which owns the copyright. The collection number is in square brackets, and the same rules on rank apply as in the case of the Imperial War Museum listed above.

KING'S COLLEGE LONDON

Index